Lovecraftian Voyages

BOOKS BY KENNETH W. FAIG, JR.

FICTION

Tales of the Lovecraft Collectors (1995)
Lovecraft's Pillow and Other Strange Stories (2013)

NONFICTION

H. P. Lovecraft: His Life, His Work (1979)
The Parents of H. P. Lovecraft (1990)
Some of the Descendants of Asaph Phillips and Esther Whipple (1993)
Devonshire Ancestry of Howard Phillips Lovecraft
    (2003; with Chris J. Docherty and A. Langley Searles)
The Unknown Lovecraft (2009)

AS EDITOR/PUBLISHER OF WORKS BY EDITH MINITER

Going Home and Other Amateur Writings (1995)
The Coast of Bohemia and Other Writings (2000)
Dead Houses and Other Works (2008; with Sean Donnelly)
The Village Green and Other Pieces (2013; with Sean Donnelly)

Lovecraftian Voyages

Kenneth W. Faig, Jr.

Hippocampus Press
New York

Copyright © 1973, 2013, 2017 by Kenneth W. Faig, Jr.
Foreword copyright © 2013, 2017 by S. T. Joshi.
Preface, additional notes and other editorial matter
copyright © 2013, 2017 by Christopher M. O'Brien and J.-M. Rajala.

Published by Hippocampus Press
P.O. Box 641, New York, NY 10156.
http://www.hippocampuspress.com

All rights reserved.
No part of this work may be reproduced in any form or by any means
without the written permission of the publisher.

An earlier version of this book was issued privately in 2013 by Ultratelluric Press
on the occasion of the 65th birthday of Kenneth W. Faig, Jr. ("who only wrote it").

Cover photograph of H. P. Lovecraft taken by
Lucius B. Truesdell, June 16, 1934.
Cover design by J.-M. Rajala. Cover production by Barbara Briggs Silbert.
Hippocampus Press logo designed by Anastasia Damianakos.

First Hippocampus Press Edition 2017
1 3 5 7 9 8 6 4 2

ISBN 978-1-61498-205-0

Contents

Foreword .... *vii*

Preface .... *ix*

Lovecraftian Voyages *1*

1. Lovecraft's family and childhood 3
2. Grandfather Whipple and the collapse of the Phillips household 17
3. Lovecraft's literary executor and the John Hay Library collection 26
4. Some Lovecraftiana; bibliographical research and amateur press work 36
5. The ultra-collectables; planned edition of the *Fungi from Yuggoth* 48
6. *The Shunned House* book 56
7. The rarest Lovecraft editions 70
8. Some additions to the Lovecraft bibliography 73
9. The "Lost Lovecrafts" 84
10. Lovecraft in Rhode Island newspapers 92
11. Lovecraft's destroyed and abandoned fiction 105
12. Lovecraft's use of dreams and newspaper clippings in his fiction 115
13. Lovecraft's planned novels 123
14. Lovecraft's revisory work; a few miscellaneous observations 129
15. Lovecraft's financial affairs 134
16. Notes on the education of Lovecraft's family 143
17. Lovecraft's travelogues; the Arkham country 146
18. Real New England locales in Lovecraft's fiction 154
19. Who Ate Roger Williams? 157
20. Searching for the Dark Swamp 164
21. Lovecraft's pseudonyms 169
22. The Kalem Club; Lovecraft's correspondence with his wife 175
23. About the pronunciation of Cthulhu 178
24. Of the Commonplace Book 179
25. Lovecraft's Providence 195

Appendix: Calculations of Lovecraft's earnings *219*

Notes *227*

Bibliography *277*

Index *319*

Foreword

Kenneth W. Faig, Jr., is a legend in the world of Lovecraft scholarship. He preceded even the great Dirk W. Mosig in undertaking the detailed study of Lovecraft and his milieu in the early 1970s; but his focus, unlike Mosig's, was Lovecraft's life. The remnants of that life—ranging from astronomy articles buried in obscure local newspapers to traces of Lovecraft's footsteps all around his native city—still lay in abundance in Providence, R.I., when Ken came there as a graduate student in 1970. His untiring work over the next few years laid the groundwork for the serious study of Lovecraft the man and writer—and that is a legacy that makes him a kind of benevolent uncle to all who followed in his wake.

Ken's findings during those incredibly productive years in Providence were embodied in a lengthy manuscript entitled *Lovecraftian Voyages*—the book that you now, at long last, hold in your hands. It is rare that a work that never achieved print could have exercised such a wide-ranging influence, but such is the case. There is no question that L. Sprague de Camp mined the book for his *Lovecraft: A Biography* (1975); and I myself have drawn upon Ken's research time and again in my own biographical and critical work. Ken, of course, published segments of *Lovecraftian Voyages* as separate articles, ranging from the groundbreaking "Howard Phillips Lovecraft: The Early Years, 1890–1914" (a two-part piece that ran in *Nyctalops* in April 1973 and July 1974) to "Lovecraft's Providence" (*Tamlacht,* 1973), a description of Lovecraft's favourite sites in the city of his birth.

But Ken did much more than follow Lovecraft's peregrinations in Providence. *Lovecraftian Voyages* ranges far and wide, covering such things as Lovecraft's Kalem Club during his New York years (1924–26), the New England sources for some of the fictitious places in his "Arkham country," and a detailed discussion of Lovecraft's stillborn book, *The Shunned House* (1928). What Ken showed, in this treatise and in his later works, is that the study of Lovecraft's work—fiction, poetry, essays, letters—cannot be separated from the study of his life and thought. This holistic approach has been immensely influential among such later scholars as Donald R. Burleson, David E. Schultz, and Steven J. Mariconda.

But Ken has not stopped there. *Lovecraftian Voyages* was only the stepping-stone to a succession of landmark works that shed light on all things Lovecraftian. From his treatise on R. H. Barlow to *The Parents of Howard Phillips Lovecraft* (1990) to his searching studies of Lovecraft's ancestry (now gathered in the essay collection *The Unknown Lovecraft* [2009]), Ken has continued to be a pathfinder in Lovecraft studies, not merely exploring obscure or insignificant corners of Lovecraftiana but fundamental issues such as Lovecraft's relations with his parents and the influence of his wide-ranging travels on his life and work.

Kenneth W. Faig, Jr., at the age of sixty-five, is hardly finished as a Lovecraft scholar. He could easily rest on his laurels and preen himself for the pioneering work he has already done; but, humble as he is gracious and generous, he continues to probe the complex nexus of Lovecraft's life, work, and thought in ways that few others have the foresight or expertise to do; and I daresay that the coming years will see further revelations from his skilled pen.

S. T. JOSHI
Seattle, Washington
August 2013

Preface

While a work now over forty years old, we feel that Kenneth W. Faig's *Lovecraftian Voyages* is a book that very much deserves to be published and finally given a wider audience. In the four decades following its original composition the field of Lovecraft studies has undergone a thorough transformation, maturing from a fledgling field that was largely dominated by fan or semi-professional magazines into one of considerable scholarly rigor; and with the passage of time the number of publications both by and about H. P. Lovecraft has grown immense. While a number of questions still remain to be answered—if indeed they ever can be conclusively explained—a vast array of data has been unearthed, and our understanding of Lovecraft and his writings now rests on a much more secure foundation than it did at the beginning of the 1970s. In this effort Faig has remained a prime mover, even if he has been content to toil largely outside the limelight, disseminating his variegated and penetrating research mainly through amateur press organizations and the publications of his own Moshassuck Press.

If it then appears, as a consequence of the critical as well as the biographical and bibliographical work that followed, that in many regards *Voyages* has now been superseded, it can only be because it has remained in manuscript, seen in complete form only by the few, inaccessible to most modern scholars and other readers. It is certainly true that portions of the book have been fashioned into separate essays—although even some of these appearances are now a little difficult to come by—and that Faig himself has drawn upon the fruits of his original research in later articles focusing on the various topics here explored. But the illusory nature of such a perspective is revealed if we look at the treatise from the position of what the understanding of Lovecraft the man and writer was at the turn of the 1970s. It then becomes apparent how singular an undertaking it was for its time, how probing and prescient its execution. Only few others were at the time involved in this kind of painstaking, disciplined inquiry; and most of them either largely limited their attention to some particular avenue of investigation—such as George T. Wetzel to bibliographical questions—or were involved with the field in only limited capacity, or ultimately drifted away.

Reading the work in light of the scholarship that did ensue, it is notable how accurate Faig was in some of his more tentative conjectures. At that time the Lovecraft collection of the John Hay Library of Brown University in

Providence, built upon the donations made by R. H. Barlow and H. Douglass Dana, was just being reorganized, and Faig was among the first to make good use of its holdings, already bountiful at that date, while also casting his net on such other primary sources as the files of different Rhode Island newspapers—an aspect of the Lovecraft bibliography that has still not been completely exhausted for research. In many of these endeavors Faig, like Wetzel and also R. Alain Everts before him, was something of a pioneer; and although many other scholars have since then taken heed of his example—for instance, the bibliographical points having been, by and large, resolved by the 1981 publication of S. T. Joshi's *H. P. Lovecraft and Lovecraft Criticism: An Annotated Bibliography*—certain queries raised here by Faig still remain to be followed up on and thoroughly examined.

In addition to its marshalling of an impressive range of information, *Lovecraftian Voyages* also contains many perceptive observations, the more remarkable given the relatively young age at which it was written. With the advent, in particular, of Joshi's sympathetic and copiously documented biography in 1996, we may now take many of these views as granted, but it has to be remembered that forty years ago Lovecraft was still a much misunderstood writer, a fact that the long-awaited publication of *Selected Letters* (beginning in 1965) and such revealing portraits as Willis Conover's *Lovecraft at Last* (1975) were then only starting to change. In these particulars it also pointed for way to what would come after.

One interesting feature of the book that can be here noted is that it is almost as much concerned with R. H. Barlow, Lovecraft's youthful "literary executive," as it is with Lovecraft himself; a fact that reflects Faig's parallel and extensive research into Barlow which culminated in the pioneering monograph already mentioned in the foreword. And as S. T. Joshi there remarks, it is indeed evident that L. Sprague de Camp utilized *Voyages* in his 1975 Lovecraft biography and in places relied heavily upon its findings; along with Faig's further work, it has provided valuable primary research to other scholars as well. It may be that the publication of de Camp's book—and the planned biographies of James D. Merritt and Robb Baker, even if in the end neither ever appeared—in part dissuaded him from seeking a publisher for a work cast in a less straightforward narrative format. Be that as it may, what matters at this point, however, is that Kenneth W. Faig's monograph is still of interest and its renewed circulation is amply justified.

—CHRISTOPHER M. O'BRIEN
J.-M. RAJALA

A Note on the Text

Since the writing of the manuscript published in this book, a number of further correspondence files have surfaced and made their way to Brown University, including those to F. Lee Baldwin and Clark Ashton Smith. The publication of *Selected Letters* was completed in five volumes by Arkham House in 1976, but perhaps more notably, several unabridged cycles of letters to individual correspondents have seen print during the last two decades. Of the letters read in holograph by Faig at the John Hay Library and cited by him, principally those to E. Hoffmann Price have yet to be fully published, superseding the extracts given in *Selected Letters*, while those to Elizabeth Toldridge, J. Vernon Shea and Duane W. Rimel have only recently been issued. With these necessary omissions in mind, additional references have been duly supplied in this edition, for both the majority of the citations of Lovecraft's letters that at the time of writing in 1973 were still unpublished—whether wholly so or having been printed only in condensed form in *Selected Letters*—and also for other writings that have since then been issued in better or more accessible editions. (Occasional references to particular letters being unpublished have thus been accordingly removed.)

The works most often cited can be found in the list of abbreviations that follows, with full information given in the bibliography of works cited. For the Arkham House trilogy of Lovecraft's fiction, the pagination of the original 1960s edition has been retained, complemented by citations of the recently published Hippocampus Press variorum edition, *Collected Fiction*.

In presenting this book for publication, some consideration must also be given to the more than four decades of subsequent scholarly work on Lovecraft's life and writings. While the text itself—aside from correcting a few very minor errors and inaccuracies now revealed—has largely been left to stand as it is, the editors have augmented it with a number of additional annotations which, it is hoped, will be of use to the reader in providing further information. These can be distinguished from the author's notes by being placed in brackets, either directly following them (usually as separate paragraphs) or as their own endnotes, elucidating other points in the text where that has become possible. Faig's detailed calculations, forming the basis of his discussion of Lovecraft's estimated revenue from his original fiction and poetry in chapter 15 and appended to the manuscript, are given in an appendix preceding the notes.

We have also taken the liberty of adding editorial chapter divisions to the original manuscript, in order to assist the reader in locating a particular topic. In this manner of presentation, *Lovecraftian Voyages* can be read as a connected sequence of essays that explore various Lovecraftian facets, as the overall title itself implies. The book is additionally supplemented by what is—while certainly not exhaustive—to date the most complete listing of works by and about Faig that has been assembled, celebrating his unstinting and continuing devotion to the study of the Providence writer.

Finally, in bringing this book into print, the editors would like to acknowledge the kind assistance and encouragement of John D. Haefele, Derrick Hussey, S. T. Joshi, Marcos Legaria, Graeme Phillips, David E. Schultz, and the late Ned Brooks.

Abbreviations and Short Titles

AG	*Letters to Alfred Galpin* (2003)
AT	*The Ancient Track* (2001; rev. 2013)
BWS	*Beyond the Wall of Sleep* (1943)
CE	*Collected Essays* (2004–06; 5 vols.)
CF	*Collected Fiction* (2015–17; 4 vols.)
DH	*The Dunwich Horror and Others* (1963)
ES	*Essential Solitude: The Letters of H. P. Lovecraft and August Derleth* (2008; 2 vols.)
ET	*Letters to Elizabeth Toldridge & Anne Tillery Renshaw* (2014)
FLB	*Letters to F. Lee Baldwin, Duane W. Rimel, and Nils Frome* (2016)
IAP	Joshi, *I Am Providence* (2010; 2 vols.)
JFM	*Letters to James F. Morton* (2011)
JVS	*Letters to J. Vernon Shea, Carl F. Strauch, and Lee McBride White* (2016)
LCL	Wetzel, *The Lovecraft Collector's Library* (1952–55; 7 vols.)
LR	Cannon, *Lovecraft Remembered* (1999)
LVW	*Lord of a Visible World: An Autobiography in Letters* (2000)
MF	*A Means to Freedom: The Letters of H. P. Lovecraft and Robert E. Howard* (2009; 2 vols.)
MM	*At the Mountains of Madness and Other Novels* (1964)
MTS	*Mysteries of Time and Spirit: The Letters of H. P. Lovecraft and Donald Wandrei* (2003)
MW	*Miscellaneous Writings* (1995)
Notes	Derleth, *Some Notes on H. P. Lovecraft* (1959)
NY	*Letters from New York* (2005)
OFF	*O Fortunate Floridian: H. P. Lovecraft's Letters to R. H. Barlow* (2007)
RB	*Letters to Robert Bloch and Others* (2015)
RFS	*Letters to Richard F. Searight* (1992)
RK	*Letters to Rheinhart Kleiner* (2005)
SL	*Selected Letters: 1911–1937* (1965–76; 5 vols.)
SR	*The Shuttered Room and Other Pieces* (1959)
UL	Faig, *The Unknown Lovecraft* (2009)
WT	*Weird Tales* (magazine)
WW	Joshi, *A Weird Writer in Our Midst* (2010)
CAS	Clark Ashton Smith
HPL	H. P. Lovecraft
JHL	John Hay Library of Brown University, Providence
NAPA	National Amateur Press Association
RHB	R. H. Barlow
UAPA	United Amateur Press Association

Lovecraftian Voyages

Apology

These "voyages" are the random reliquiae of two years of intermittent research on H. P. Lovecraft and his circle which I undertook while I was in Providence in 1970–1972. For encouragement and substantial help during this period, I am indebted to all the following individuals and institutions: Everett Wayne and Sarah Barlow; Claire Beck; Henry L. P. Beckwith, Jr.; Eric Carlson; Thomas G. L. Cockcroft; L. Sprague de Camp; R. Alain Everts; Larry B. Farsaci; the John Hay Library; John J. Koblas; Glenn Lord; Harry O. Morris, Jr.; the New York Public Library; the Providence Public Library; the Rhode Island Historical Society; Barton Levi St. Armand; George T. Smisor; Roy A. Squires; Richard L. Tierney; George T. Wetzel; and many others whose help and encouragement was no less valuable. Especial thanks are due Mr. Everts for an invaluable critical reading of the manuscript.

I also wish to make grateful acknowledgement to Arkham House: Publishers and the Estate of August Derleth for permission to quote from unpublished letters of H. P. Lovecraft and from miscellaneous material from Arkham House books; to Everett Wayne Barlow, for permission to quote from unpublished letters of Robert Hayward Barlow; and to Eric Carlson and Glenn Lord, for permission to make brief quotation from their letters.

Finally, these "voyages" are dedicated to Harry O. Morris, Jr., fellow Lovecraftian and friend.

Kenneth W. Faig, Jr.
Joliet, Illinois
January 5, 1973

1. *Lovecraft's family and childhood*

The evidence regarding the residence of Lovecraft's parents during the first years of his life, before the commitment of his father to Butler Hospital in Providence as an "insane person" in April 1893 permanently returned the family to Providence, seems to be rather confusing.[1] While Providence city records definitely establish that Lovecraft was born in Providence on August 20, 1890, Lovecraft himself wrote to Rheinhart Kleiner on November 16, 1916 (*SL* 1.31; *RK* 64):

> I was born on the 20th of August, 1890, at No. 454 (then numbered 194) Angell Street, in the city of Providence. This was the home of my mother's family; my parents' actual residence at the time being in Dorchester, Mass.

Of course, it is not difficult to summon up a rationale for Lovecraft's birth in Providence—for it would have been the most natural thing in the world for Sarah Susan (Phillips) Lovecraft to return to her father Whipple V. Phillips's house on Angell Street in Providence for the delivery of her baby—but it is still a little difficult to think of Lovecraft, whose Providence childhood was so pivotal in his later writing, as a resident of Massachusetts (Dorchester was a southern suburb of Boston, annexed in 1870) for part of his early life. The careful reader of Lovecraft's *Selected Letters* will know that Lovecraft's first conscious memories were of Auburndale, Massachusetts (a far western suburb of Boston), where his parents shared the house of the poetess Louise Imogen Guiney (1861–1920) during the winter of 1892–1893 (see for instance *SL* 1.31–33, 2.107, 3.184), but in Lovecraft's letter to Kleiner there seems to be indication of an even earlier residence in Massachusetts. (The time of the Lovecrafts' residence with Miss Guiney in Auburndale is somewhat confused, although Lovecraft's own reference to "the winter of 1892–93" in his letter of March 3, 1927, to Bernard Austin Dwyer [*SL* 2.107] seems to be the most definitive statement now available. In his letter to Kleiner of November 16, 1916 [*SL* 1.31; *RK* 65], Lovecraft says that he was one and a half years old at the time his parents moved to Auburndale, placing the beginning of his residence there ca. February 1892; in the same letter [*SL* 1.32] he speaks of recalling "the quiet, shady suburb as I saw it in 1892." In his letter of October 4, 1930, to Robert E. Howard [*SL* 3.184; *MF* 1.74], however, he states that he was "three years old when we spent a whole winter at the Guiney home in Auburndale, Mass.") Indeed, we do know that Lovecraft had at least touched Massachusetts soil in the year of his birth; for writing to J. Vernon Shea on July 19, 1931 (*SL* 3.383; *JVS* 27–28), Lovecraft gave a chronology of states which he had entered up to that time, in which both Rhode Island and Massachusetts were listed for 1890. (I believe Lovecraft's 1932 travels took him to at least Louisiana, Alabama, Mississippi, and Tennessee, in addition to the states mentioned in his 1931 letter to Shea.) So what are we to make of Lovecraft's statement to Kleiner that his parents were actually residents of Massachusetts at the time of his birth?

I doubt that anything definitive can be said on the subject, barring a further revelation in Lovecraft's own letters. However, there are several clues which we can adduce as evidence. As August Derleth remarked in his introduction to *The Dunwich Horror*, Lovecraft was customarily quite reticent about his father; and beyond the assertions that Winfield Scott Lovecraft was born in Rochester, New York, in 1853 (his tombstone in the Phillips lot in Swan Point Cemetery in Providence gives the exact date as October 26, 1853), the third-born child and only son of George and Helen (Allgood) Lovecraft (*SL* 1.5); that he was "constantly warned not to fall into Americanisms of speech and provincial vulgarities of dress and mannerisms—so much so that he was generally regarded as an Englishman despite his birth in Rochester, N.Y." (*SL* 3.362); that he received his formal education "both privately, and at a military school, making modern languages his specialty" (*SL* 1.5); and that in April 1893 he was stricken with "a complete paralysis resulting from a brain overtaxed with study & business cares," was never thereafter "able to move hand or foot, or to utter a sound," and died in 1898 after five years in Butler Hospital (*SL* 1.33; *RK* 66); there are virtually no references to him in Lovecraft's published letters. Indeed, Lovecraft himself could "just recall" (*SL* 3.362) his Anglophile father, so that in fact he may never have known the more sordid facts concerning his father's life.

The facts, of course, are far less glamorous than Lovecraft would have had them. Nowhere in Lovecraft's as-yet published letters, insofar as I know, is there a reference to his father's occupation. (The ellipsis in the last paragraph of *SL* 3.366, in Lovecraft's letter of April 5, 1931, to Maurice W. Moe, however, is indication that something may be discovered when the full transcripts or the originals of Lovecraft's published letters are made available to scholars, as August Derleth stated several times in print they would be.) However, this information became available as early as 1944, when Winfield Townley Scott's research in Providence (described in his lengthy essay "His Own Most Fantastic Creation" in *Marginalia*) revealed that Winfield had been a travelling salesmen for the Gorham Company, a famous Rhode Island firm of silversmiths, now part of Textron, Incorporated. He further quoted a friend of the Lovecraft family that Winfield had been a "pompous Englishman,"[2] but his major discovery was that Winfield had died at Butler Hospital on July 19, 1898, in an advanced stage of general paresis, as attested to by his death certificate at City Hall in Providence.[3]

Scott's conclusion from his research was that Mrs. Lovecraft had been a "touch-me-not" and that her husband had been forced to take his sexual pleasures elsewhere; although, of course, it is probably very likely that his promiscuous sexual habits (and his syphilis) considerably antedated his marriage. The record of this marriage Scott was unable to find in Providence, although the date, June 12, was given in Sarah Susan Lovecraft's commonplace book at the John Hay Library.[4] Acting upon Lovecraft's statement to Kleiner that his parents had been residents of Dorchester, Massachusetts, at the time of his birth, the present author checked the Registry of Marriages in Boston (which annexed the Dorchester records in 1870) in April 1972 and succeeded in finding the record of Winfield and Sarah Susan's marriage there. According to the record in Boston, they were married on June 12, 1889, by the Reverend William J. Harris in St. Paul's Church (Episcopal; now St. Paul's Cathedral Church) on Tremont Street in Boston, with Edward G. Barrett (the sexton of the church) and John L. Taylor as witnesses.[5] (John L. Taylor, who is listed in Boston Directories of the time as on employee of the Boston Dash Stitching Works at 28 Sudbury, may well have been a friend of Winfield's; however, all of significance that I have been able to find about him is that he removed to Plymouth, Massachusetts, in 1904.) The registry entry lists the age, parents, and place of birth of both Winfield and Sarah Susan, and also lists Winfield's occupation as "salesman," but most importantly for our purposes it gives the residence of Winfield at the time of his marriage as New York, New York, and that of Sarah Susan as Providence, Rhode Island. Thus, neither Winfield nor Sarah Susan was a resident of Boston at the time of their marriage—June 12, 1889. Nor was either a member of St. Paul's Church (where I also consulted the records relating to the marriage), since officials told me that the record would otherwise have contained notice of this fact.

Of course, Winfield and Sarah Susan could have set up housekeeping in Dorchester shortly after their marriage. Lovecraft's letter to Kleiner of November 16, 1916 (*SL* 1.33; *RK* 66) seems to indicate that Winfield and Sarah Susan had acquired property for their first home in Auburndale during the winter of 1892–1893, before Winfield's illness forced a permanent return to Providence, but they could well have taken a flat or other rented accommodation in Dorchester in 1889–1890. Moreover, Boston as the hub of the

Northeast would have furnished a natural territory for a salesman such as Winfield; in his letter to Dwyer (*SL* 2.107), Lovecraft says specifically that his father's business affairs in Boston were the cause of the Lovecrafts' residency in the Guiney house in Auburndale in 1892–1893. The same business affairs could well have dictated a Dorchester residency in 1889–1890. (Insofar as I was able to determine from Boston City Directories of the period, the Gorham Company, for whom Winfield worked, had no offices in Boston during this period; home offices were at Steeple and Main Streets in Providence.)[6] Unfortunately, however, when I checked Boston City Directories for the entire period 1889–1894, I was able to find no listing whatever under the name Lovecraft. I must admit that I am not perfectly sure that these directories included listings for Dorchester—although they did cover Roxbury and other nearby south Boston communities. (I did find several Dorchester "bluebooks" listed in the catalogue of the Boston Public Library, but unfortunately none of them were for appropriate years.) The only further recourse that I can think of would be a consultation of the Providence City Directories (a complete file is at the Rhode Island Historical Society) to see for which years Sarah Susan Lovecraft is missing from the list of residents at her father Whipple Phillips home at 194 Angell Street (changed to 454 Angell Street between 1894 and 1899)—the listings in Providence City Directories did in general include all the adults permanently residing in a given house. However, I was unable to do this—because of geographical separation from Providence—and of course any answer would not render any definitive information about the supposed residency of Lovecraft's parents in Dorchester.

I do not think there is any good reason to doubt Lovecraft's assertion that his parents were actually residing in Dorchester at the time of his birth; indeed, there is the fact that his parents were married in Boston to bespeak some connection with the city. (St. John's Cathedral in Providence—whose churchyard was the site of many midnight visits by Lovecraft and his friends—is Episcopal and was founded in 1723.) Indeed, it seems natural to suppose that Winfield and Sarah Susan were married at the same time at which they acquired independent lodgings in Boston (Dorchester). How ephemeral this initial residence in Dorchester was, is difficult to say. The elided passage in Lovecraft's letter to Moe of April 5, 1931, might well furnish a clue, since it seemingly discusses the financial difficulties of his father. It is of course certain that the Dorchester residency had ended by the winter of 1892–1893, since we then have the Lovecrafts at Miss Guiney's in Auburndale. I have myself found nothing in the as-yet published letters of Lovecraft and those of his unpublished letters which I read at the John Hay Library to indicate definitely that the Lovecrafts had returned to Providence as permanent residents inter 1889–1892. (One might here again make a check of the Providence City Directories.) It is certain, of course, that there were numerous visits by Mr. and Mrs. Lovecraft to Providence; both to visit Mrs. Lovecraft's parents and sisters (who were still both unmarried at this period) and to consult the home office of the Gorham Company, for which Winfield worked. If—as seems likely—the abnormality induced by Winfield's paresis had begun to manifest itself before his final collapse in Auburndale in April 1893 then it is also perfectly possible that Sarah Susan and her son returned to Providence to live in her father's house without her husband some time during the 1889–1892 period. This in itself would explain the birth of Howard in Providence on August 20, 1890. However, I think we are ultimately likely to get a good answer to our question of whether Rhode Island or Massachusetts had its claim on H. P. Lovecraft between 1890 and 1892 only in the event that Lovecraft told the story himself.

For the Lovecrafts' residence in the Guiney home in Auburndale, Massachusetts, during the winter of 1892–1893 there is of course considerably more evidence than we have for any earlier residences in Massachusetts. In the first instance, we have Lovecraft's own dim recollections of the Auburndale period; in Auburndale, he writes (*SL* 1.32), "consciousness first came to my infant mind." In his letters of November 16, 1916 to Rheinhart Kleiner (*SL* 1.31–33) and of February 4, 1934 to J. Vernon Shea (*SL* 4.354–55; *JVS* 219) he gave detailed accounts of his own memories of the Auburndale period: the railway bridge of the Boston and Albany railroad which stuck most clearly in his mind, the poetess Miss Louise Imogen Guiney and her St. Bernard dogs, the recitations of poetry before assembled adults, the dim recollection of his "immaculately" dressed father, his nicknaming as "Little Sunshine" by Miss Guiney's mother. The visits of Dr. Oliver Wendell Holmes, Sr., to the Guiney household, during which the famed poet allegedly held the young Lovecraft in his lap, Lovecraft admitted in his letter to Shea of February 4, 1934, were the memories of his mother alone, he himself having no independent recollection of them. Sarah Susan Lovecraft had originally come to know Miss Guiney, according to Lovecraft's letter of November 16, 1916 to Kleiner (*SL* 1.32; *RK* 65), during Miss Guiney's much earlier education in Providence.

Now, all of this seems perfectly well and good—and certainly the connection of the Lovecraft family with a poetess of mild repute such as Miss Guiney and the several visits of Dr. Holmes were precisely the kind of thing

Lovecraft liked to recall in his background; after all, for him the really best days were those spent in the Victorian mansion of his grandfather Whipple Phillips on the corner of Angell Street and Elmgrove Avenue in Providence. (A modern apartment building rises there today.)

Yet, we might ask if the memory of this connection with Miss Guiney is perhaps not a little too fortunate. After all, Lovecraft conceded that his own memories of the Auburndale period were quite dim, and admitted that he had no recollection of Dr. Holmes at all. Might then Mrs. Lovecraft not have embroidered upon her casual acquaintance with Miss Guiney to make it into a bona-fide coresidence with the Guiney family in Auburndale? It would have been the perfect kind of thing to compensate for the deterioration of her marriage which was taking place during this period. Perhaps to a certain degree Lovecraft may have accepted his mother's accounts of the period as his own. Certainly, he was customarily frank and accurate in his letters; yet there are certain statements concerning particularly his early life and ancestry, occurring in his letters, which seem to bear a definite mark of embellishment. For instance, when he writes of his "nervous collapse" of 1908 to Bernard Dwyer on March 3, 1927 (*SL* 2.110), he states that the collapse occurred "immediately after graduating" from high school; in fact, if one takes the time to survey the yearbooks of the Hope Street High School in Providence for the years 1904–1910, Lovecraft's name does not occur among any of the lists of graduates. (His name is present only in the 1907 yearbook, for which see my own "A Lovecraftian Note," *The Dark Brotherhood Journal* 1, No. 1 [June 1971]. Mr. R. Alain Everts has obtained Lovecraft's actual high school record and found that he did not attend at all after 1907, in which year he was a sophomore.)[7]

His purported paternal ancestry as given in his letters of November 1927 to Frank Belknap Long (*SL* 2.179–85), and of April 5, 1931 to Maurice W. Moe (*SL* 3.359–62), smacks strongly of some embellishment; whether on Lovecraft's own part, or on the part of his mother and other relatives, it is difficult to say. (In his letter to Long, Lovecraft speaks of copying much of the paternal data from the chart of his great aunt Sarah Allgood—the sister of Helen Allgood, the wife of his Lovecraft grandfather George—which is also a hint for anyone who would like to try to establish further information about Lovecraft's line.) Both Henry L. P. Beckwith, a genealogist, professor at the Rhode Island School of Design, and distant relative of Lovecraft's, and R. Alain Everts, one of the most gifted Lovecraftian researchers, told me that their researches left little reason to believe in the actuality of the purported gentlemanly past of the Lovecraft family at "Minster Hall" in south

Devonshire in England—or in the existence of any "Minster Hall" for that matter.[8] This is a shame in a way, for I myself vastly enjoyed Lovecraft's account of the doings of the profligate Tom Lovecraft (1745–1826), who squandered the family fortune and lost Minster Hall in 1823, sending his sixth child Joseph Lovecraft—HPL's great-grandfather—scurrying across the Atlantic to seek his fortune in 1827 (*SL* 3.360–61). (Note that Lovecraft's letter to Kleiner of November 16, 1916 [*SL* 1.31; *RK* 64] says that his grandfather George Lovecraft came to New York from Devonshire in *1847*; however, the letter to Moe of April 5, 1931, makes clear that Joseph Lovecraft brought "himself, wife [daughter of the Vicar of Dunsford] and offspring," including George Lovecraft, across the Atlantic with him in *1827*; and the same information is given in his letter to Long of November 1927 [*SL* 2.182]. Mr. R. Alain Everts has done thorough genealogical work on both the American and the English branches of the Lovecraft family, and it is to be hoped that he will one day present his findings in print.)

Further, according to the as-yet unpublished research of Mr. Everts, the Lovecraft family in America (residing principally in Rochester and Mount Vernon, New York) were of decidedly lower middle-class origins and only gradually worked themselves up to a comfortable middle-class status—hardly the kind of family to produce a really desirable husband for Sarah Susan Phillips, the daughter of Whipple and Robie Phillips of Angell Street in Providence.[9] (Lovecraft does remark in his letter to Moe that the Lovecrafts' fortunes were improved by several advantageous marriages, perhaps including the one of Winfield's sister Emma Lovecraft to Mr. Isaac Hill of Pelham, New York.) There is a hint of financial difficulty in Winfield's past in the elision in Lovecraft's letter to Maurice W. Moe of April 5, 1931 (*SL* 3.366); and although Lovecraft says in the same place that his father eventually regained a "modest property" and left "ten thousand dollars," a consultation of the published tax lists of Providence County for the years 1893–1898 shows that Albert A. Baker, Winfield's guardian, was paying taxes on only $4000 personal property during those years. (At the same time, Whipple was paying taxes on about $20,000 valuation of real property.)

Altogether, Sarah Susan's marriage to Winfield Lovecraft would hardly seem to have been an advantageous alliance for the Phillips family, although one must remember that at the time of the marriage in June 1889 neither of Sarah Susan's surviving sisters had married and Whipple was undoubtedly concerned that all three of his daughters would remain old maids. (All of them did eventually marry: Annie married Edward F. Gamwell in 1897 and Lillian, Dr. Franklin C. Clark in 1902. Annie's marriage produced two children,

Phillips [1898–1916] and Marion Rhoby [1900–1900] Gamwell, neither of whom survived to majority, but was not happy; she and her husband were separated by the early years of the century, and Edward F. Gamwell is hardly ever thereafter mentioned in Lovecraft letters, although he did not die until 1936. Although the marriage of Lillian and Dr. Clark appears to have been happy, it did not produce any children—Lillian being nearly forty-six and Dr. Clark nearly fifty-five at the time of the marriage. Lillian was left a widow with the death of Dr. Clark in 1915. Whipple and Robie Phillips's third daughter, Emeline Phillips, had died in Greene in 1865 at the age of six years and nine months, and only the first, second, and fourth daughters—Lillian, Sarah Susan, and Annie, respectively—survived to maturity.)

Additionally, of course, Sarah Susan may simply have been swept off her feet by the immaculately dressed and mannered Englishman whom we see in the family portrait in the frontispiece of the Arkham House collection *The Shuttered Room and Other Pieces*. (This photograph and several others in the volume were from the collection of Philip Jack Grill, who had obtained them from one of Annie Gamwell's surviving cousins following her death on January 29, 1941.)[10] In any case, it is really not Winfield's precarious financial status which makes the story of the Auburndale residency difficult to believe, but rather the low social esteem in which his occupation was held at the time and even more importantly the growing abnormality which certainly preceded his final collapse in April 1893. The mere fact of his illness alone makes difficult to credit the story of his residence amidst genteel poet-folk immediately before his final commitment as "an insane person" (so the probate court record in Providence reads). One can only speculate upon the extent to which his promiscuity and infidelity became known to his wife and her family; but there is certainly little doubt that they—and those of "polite" society who came to know—were scandalized by his final paralysis and insanity. All of those reasons, then, make us wonder whether there was in fact some embellishment on Lovecraft's part in his account of what must have been this most difficult time for his family.

Lovecraft's account of the relationship of his family with the poetess Miss Guiney is not without a thread of verifiable accuracy, however, for Miss Guiney was a poetess of considerable if moderate reputation in her day and there is a considerable literature concerning her life and work. (Her poems, collected in *Happy Ending*, except those of them which strive I think artificially to glorify ultrapatriotism, have a spiritual beauty which deserves attention even today.) Even standard reference works like the *Dictionary of American Biography* have entries for Miss Guiney from which we can verify many of the facts given in Lovecraft's principal account of her in his letter to Kleiner of November 16, 1916 (*SL* 1.31–33; *RK* 1.64–65).

Louise Imogen Guiney was born on January 7, 1861, in the Roxbury section of Boston, the only child of Patrick Robert and Janet Margaret (Doyle) Guiney. Her father, born in Parkstown, County Tipperary, Ireland, on January 15, 1835 served with heroism as an officer of the Ninth Massachusetts Infantry during the Civil War, and was mustered out as a brevet brigadier general after being gravely wounded at the Wilderness. Just as Lovecraft recounts in his letter to Kleiner, he survived, a respected and admired civic figure, until he finally collapsed and died on the streets of Boston in March 1877. One gets the impression from reading the biographies of Miss Guiney by E. M. Tenison (*Louise Imogen Guiney: Her Life and Works*) and others that the death of Patrick Robert Guiney left his wife and child in what could hardly be called rosy financial shape. Nevertheless, Miss Guiney's education was pursued, and most importantly for us, we find that her secondary education was secured at Elmhurst, the convent school of the order of the Sacred Heart in none other than Providence, Rhode Island, where she was graduated in 1879.

Here clearly, is the link with Lovecraft's mother which Lovecraft wrote of in his letter to Kleiner. Born on October 17, 1857, Sarah Susan Phillips was an approximate contemporary of Miss Guiney, and although she herself secured her education at the Wheaton Seminary (now Wheaton College) in Norton, Massachusetts (cf. Lovecraft to Moe, January 1, 1915, *SL* 1.6), her commonplace book, preserved at the John Hay Library, contains long listings of English and American poets and authors—made on an early age—which confirm her interest in literature.[11] Although of course they did not share the same religion,[12] I think it is perfectly plausible that Sarah Susan and Louise Guiney became acquaintances through some connection in the polite society of Providence's old East Side—just then first beginning to be built up—and continued their friendship after Miss Guiney's graduation in 1879 took her back to Boston. There, Miss Guiney published her first book of poems, *Songs at the Start*, in 1884, followed in one year by a book of essays, *Goose Quill Papers*—works which established her literary reputation and earned her many friends in Boston literary circles. Yet, the dogs of financial trouble seem to have continued to follow Miss Guiney and her mother, and at some time around 1890 (I did not find the exact date) she and her mother moved to the suburb of Auburndale. *The Letters of Louise Imogen Guiney* (2 vols., 1926), edited by her niece Grace Guiney, contain a photograph of her as an intense young woman (ca. 1894) and a photograph of her study in the Auburndale home, where HPL may have stood on the table and recited nursery rhymes for Miss Guiney and the other adults.

Nowhere, unfortunately, could I find any reference to either Winfield Lovecraft or Sarah Susan Lovecraft in these published letters; nor any in the biographies of Miss Guiney—but of course this does not prove anything, since everyday visitors may well not even have merited mention in Miss Guiney's letters to her friends, let alone the published extracts. The hope of finding a reference to the Lovecrafts even in the unpublished letters of miss Guiney does not seem especially bright; when I wrote the Curator of Manuscripts of the College of the Holy Cross in Worcester, Massachusetts, where Grace Guiney deposited perhaps the largest extant collection of her aunt's papers, the Curator, the Reverend Eugene J. Harrington, S.J., replied in part:

> There are 48 letters of Miss Guiney that date to the years 1892–93. I have read through these and I fail to find any reference to a Mr. and Mrs. Lovecraft. There is no indication of anybody living with them [the Guineys], strange as it may seem. Our card catalogue shows no letter from Lovecraft to Miss Guiney.

The letters of Miss Guiney to Anne Whitney, held at Wellesley College according to the Union Catalog of Manuscripts, extend only from 1894 to 1914, according to the librarian there—outside of the period when the Lovecrafts supposedly shared the Guineys' house. Finally, perhaps more hopefully, the Library of Congress wrote to me that there are 104 letters of Miss Guiney to Frederick Holland Day and five transcripts of letters of Miss Guiney to Louise Chandler Moulton assignable to the years 1892–1893 in the collection there. Of all the answers which I obtained, this seems the most promising, and I hope that I or others will eventually be able to consult the Guiney letters there to see whether the story of the Lovecrafts' residency with the Guineys in 1892–1893 can be confirmed. (There are several other collections of Guiney letters listed in the Union Catalog of Manuscripts, but I did not write more than these three.) Of course, it would also be of value for the support of Lovecraft's recounting of this period to make a wider survey of the Guiney letters, in order to trace any evidence of Miss Guiney's friendship with Sarah Susan Phillips, which presumably began in the 1870s.

What are we left to say about the probability of Lovecraft's recounting of this period? Lovecraft's customary frankness and accuracy and the facts of Miss Guiney's education are the principal supporting evidence for his recounting of events. The social status and probable reputation of Winfield Lovecraft, along with the abnormality which must have preceded his commitment in April 1893 are the principal arguments against Lovecraft's account. The fact that Lovecraft had no recollection of his own of Dr. Holmes bespeaks the dimness of his own memories of this period; even his father he could only "just recall"—so that he may well have been susceptible—and if he suspected the true nature of the illness of his father, eager to accept—a romanticized recounting of events as given by his mother.[13]

Although Lovecraft's usual characterization of the Auburndale episode was as "a long visit" to the home of Miss Guiney and her mother during the winter of 1892–1893 (see for instance his letter to Kleiner of February 2, 1916, *SL* 1.20; *RK* 30), other references make clear that as he understood it the plan of his parents was to establish a residence of their own in Auburndale (see his letter to Kleiner of November 16, 1916, *SL* 1.33; *RK* 66); so that as he wrote to Robert E. Howard on October 4, 1930 (*SL* 3.184; *MF* 1.74), residence with the Guineys in Auburndale was for "a whole winter." Somewhere among the preserved letters and papers of Miss Guiney, it would seem, there ought to be a reference to house guests of such duration, but perhaps the attrition which time wreaks even on the possessions of the semi-great has made this impossible of determination. That some elements of Sarah Susan's recollection (or fabrication) were present in Lovecraft's own accounting may perhaps be indicated by a note from R. H. Barlow's 1934 diary, published in *Some Notes on H. P. Lovecraft* (p. xxx; *OFF* 407; *LR* 354):

> Mrs. Gamwell told of how H.P.L., when young, for a while insisted "I'm a little girl"—and of how he would be set up on the table to spout Tennyson's *Maud*—"Come into the garden, Maud, for the black bat Night has flown . . ." She recalled, too, that as a baby, he had visited Oliver Wendell Holmes, and as a boy visited Imogen Guiney, a friend of his mother's.

Here the accounting does not seem to be of any prolonged coresidency, but merely of the calls of one friend upon another. However, whatever the actual facts of the 1892–1893 Auburndale episode were (and it is perhaps likely that we never know), there does seem to be little reason to question the fact that Miss Guiney and Sarah Susan Phillips were friends from their schooldays and that they did exchange visits occasionally. Certainly, the Phillipses would have been as fortunate a connection for Miss Guiney as Winfield Lovecraft was unfortunate. At the end of all these of discussions of Massachusetts, then, we had better put Lovecraft back exactly where he belongs as a boy, in the mansion of his grandfather Phillips on Angell Street in Providence, where he was born on August 20, 1890, and where we surely have him from April 1893 onwards.[14]

Of Miss Guiney? Financial need tied her to demanding jobs as postmistress of Auburndale from 1894 until 1897 (during which period she was nearly driven out by vicious agitation against the appointment of a Catholic to this office) and as a cataloguer in the Boston Public Library from 1897 until 1901. During this period, literature continued to be her consolation, and she produced several memorable volumes. Finally, after the death of her mother, she was free to pursue her real interests, and she spent the last twenty years of her life working in Oxford upon two greet projects, a study of Henry Vaughn and an anthology of Catholic poets from Sir Thomas More to Alexander Pope. She died on November 2, 1920, in Chipping Campden, Gloucestershire, and was buried in Wolvercote Cemetery near Oxford.

Louise Imogen Guiney (1893)

(*F. Holland Day, Library of Congress*)

***

The question of whether Lovecraft knew the true nature of his father's illness is probably one which will never be settled from references in his letters—since, as we have seen, he was customarily reticent about his father, and when he did discuss him described his illness as "complete paralysis resulting from a brain overtaxed with study & business cares," Anything definitive on the subject would likely have had to come from the reminiscences of a close friend or confidant of the Phillips family, and there seems little likelihood of anything of this nature turning up at this late date. Certainly, there is no question that Lovecraft's mother made her son the object of all the shame and shock which she experienced as a result of her husband's condition; the physicians' records which Winfield T. Scott consulted at Butler Hospital—supposedly destroyed in the 1955 fire—and the reminiscence of Miss Clara L. Hess that Mrs. Lovecraft customarily described her son as a "hideous" creature who had to hide from public view—related in her letter reproduced in Derleth's memoir "Lovecraft's Sensitivity" (*LR* 34)—make clear this part of their relationship.

However, I think there are at least a few further indications that Lovecraft may indeed have been aware of the true nature of his father's illness. His reminiscence of his father's immaculate dress and precise English customs of speech and mannerisms are infinitely suggestive. "I have myself worn some of his old ascots and wing collars, left all too immaculate by his early illness and death," writes Lovecraft to Moe on April 5, 1931 (*SL* 3.362). What he also specifically remembers of his father is his delight when his infant son would walk on his unsteady legs across the sitting room at the Guineys' and slap his hands on his father's knees, exclaiming, "Papa, you look just like a young man!" (Lovecraft to Shea, February 4, 1934, *SL* 4.355; *JVS* 219)[15]— just as if he were painfully aware in retrospect that his father had already spent all his vigor. Finally, there are his vague statements regarding his father's formal education—which he would appear to wish us to believe was considerable, involving the special study of foreign languages and the accumulation of a considerable personal library, despite the fact that he himself writes to Moe that none of the Lovecrafts were university men. And also his vague statements regarding his father's success in business—which he would appear to wish us to believe was considerable, despite the fact that he never reveals in the published letters that his father's occupation was, as Colin Wilson, puts it, that of a "commercial traveller."

Perhaps even stronger indication that Lovecraft knew, or at least suspected, the true nature of his father's illness is the consistent theme of hereditary degeneracy in his stories—ranging from the inbred degeneracy of the Martense family in his early "shilling shocker" "The Lurking Fear;" to the taint of bestial strains in "Arthur Jermyn;" and the cannibalistic degeneracy of the Delapore family in his classic "The Rats in the Walls." Many further examples might be adduced. There are even several entries in the Commonplace Book which show how strongly the image of his father—the tainted line—was replaced by that of his grandfather Whipple Phillips:

> (167) Boy rear'd in atmosphere of considerable mystery. Believes father dead. Suddenly told that father is about to return, Strange preparations—consequences.
>
> (162) Ultimate horror—grandfather returns from strange trip—mystery in house—wind & darkness—granf. & mother engulfed—questions forbidden—somnolence—investigation—cataclysm—screams overheard.

In another entry we see that the dislike which Lovecraft customarily expressed regarding all things Victorian may indeed have had at least some of its origin with the illness and death of his all-too-Victorian father:

> (159) Certain kinds of deep-toned stately music of the style of the 1870s and 1880s recalls certain visions of that period—gas-litten parlours of the dead, moonlight on old floors, decaying business streets with gas lamps &c—under terrible circumstances.

(It might be recalled that funerals at the time were often held in private homes; the notice of Winfield Lovecraft's death on July 19, 1898, appeared in the *Providence Journal* for July 21, 1898, with the notation that the funeral would be private.)[16] Altogether, there is probably more than enough evidence to draw an ample portrait of Lovecraft's psyche from his fiction and his letters; only let us hope he will be spared another Marie Bonaparte!

2. Grandfather Whipple and the collapse of the Phillips household

Lovecraft's early transfer of his allegiance and attention to his grandfather Whipple Van Buren Phillips may be reflected in his later tendency to make his protagonists wise, grandfatherly scholars of means and maturity. Certainly, however, his attention points to the importance of the study of Whipple Phillips's own life for the understanding of Lovecraft's life and work. Although, of course, Lovecraft's central recollection of this period was the security and fascination of his grandfather's great manse on Angell Street and the surrounding fields and woods (Elmgrove and Angell was quite on the outer limits of Providence's East Side—at least the built-up part—when Lovecraft was born), it also becomes readily apparent from his letters that there was after a certain age also an acute awareness of the gradual falling-off of his grandfather's prosperity and a sense of the vicissitudes and trials through which the family had passed. For, to say the least, although Whipple Phillips had always been a respected man in business, fraternal, and public affairs, his rise to financial security in Providence in the 1880s and 1890s was certainly not without its difficulties, nor in fact was it to be maintained at the same level in the remaining years before his death in 1904—which spelled financial disaster for the Phillips family.

Whipple Van Buren Phillips was born on November 22, 1833 in the town of Foster, Rhode Island, presumably in his grandfather Asaph Phillips's house on Howard Hill, the fourth of five children of Jeremiah and Robie (Rathbone) Phillips.[17] He received his primary education in the schools of the town of Foster and his secondary education at the East Greenwich Academy (called the Providence Conference Seminary at the time according to Lovecraft's letter to Moe of January 1, 1915, *SL* 1.6). Tragedy, however, was not long in striking, for by the age of fourteen Whipple was left an orphan, the final blow coming when his father Jeremiah Phillips was crushed to death after being caught in the gearing of his grist mill on the Moosup River on November 20, 1848, aged only forty-eight. His sister Susan S. Phillips died in her early twenties in 1850, yet further reducing the family.

Consequently, with the completion of his studies at the East Greenwich Academy, about 1852, Whipple went to the home of his uncle James Phillips, the brother of Jeremiah Phillips, in Illinois to live. There, his obituary in the *Providence Journal* for March 31, 1904, remarks, he was stricken ill because of the climate, and he returned to Foster after about a year. Lovecraft mentions in his letter to Moe that his grandfather thereafter tried teaching in the country schools in Foster for a brief while, but soon, in 1855, he married Robie Alzada Place, and took charge of the country store in Moosup Valley in Foster, which Robie's cousin Casey B. Tyler had previously managed from 1844 until 1853. After about two years in business in Moosup Valley, Whipple closed the Tyler store (which then remained vacant until 1867) and moved about three and one third miles south to the hamlet of Coffin's Corners in the town of Coventry,[18] where he acquired extensive real estate holdings, to the extent that he himself renamed the hamlet Greene, Rhode Island. According to Squire Wood in his *History of Greene and Vicinity* (p. 12), Whipple's "very comfortable home, with a large barn carriage house," was the second in the hamlet, after that of his own father. (Coffin's Corners had originally developed as a refueling stop on the railroad to Providence.)

Until his removal to Providence in 1874, Whipple was to be crucially involved in the civic and economic development of the village which he had virtually founded, of which considerable details are given by Squire Wood in his history. The first resident doctor in the village, Dr. Frank B. Smith of Moosup, Connecticut, made his office originally in Whipple's home; and from 1860 until 1863 Whipple himself conducted the first country store in the village in the basement of the home of Squire G. Wood, the father of the author. From 1860 until 1866 Whipple was in addition postmaster of the village, and in the early 1860s he made the first attempt to organize a lodge in the village, affiliated with the Independent Order of Good Templars, a temperance organization. Although the lodge of the Independent Order of Good Templars promptly disappeared, Whipple finally succeeded in organizing in 1870 along with fifteen others Ionic Lodge 28 of the Fraternal and Ancient Order of Masons in the village. The lodge at first held its meetings in the small assembly hall which Whipple had earlier built as a meeting place and social center for the village, although it afterwards moved its lodge rooms to the Rice City Church. Whipple was the first master.

While attending to these civic affairs, of course, Whipple was in addition busy with the economic affairs of the village. In 1866, according to Squire Wood's history (p. 35), Whipple organized with Leonard Tillinghast and Stephen H. Brown a company "to erect a building and equip it for carrying on the wood and grain business in Greene." According to Squire Wood, "the mill was erected in 1867 and stood where the house owned by Mrs. Arthur

Dexter now stands. It was built with a high basement capable of holding one or more steam railroad cars to be loaded with kindling and short wood." A railroad spur was eventually built to the mill, which Wood narrates continued in operation for some twenty years, during which time, according to Whipple's obituary, Whipple V. Phillips & Company "furnished thousands of cords of wood for the locomotives of the old Hartford, Providence, and Fishkill Railroad." During this time, Whipple also continued his extensive acquisitions of real estate in the town of Coventry (in which Greene lay) and also entered the grain and coal businesses, acquiring in particular a large coal business in the city of Providence.

However, steady prosperity and growth were not to continue for long. In the year 1869, according to the typed transcript of an old scrap book of "Historical Reminiscences of Foster, R.I." owned by Mrs. Alvero Kennedy[19] which is held by the Rhode Island Historical Society Library (RI Towns, F–2–15, sec. XV), Robie Place's cousin Casey B. Tyler, who had operated a country store in nearby Clayville after his departure from Foster, "lost about $10,000 through a pretended friend named Hugog." In 1870 a similar disaster befell Whipple, when in the words of the old scrapbook, he "at last fell a prey to the demon Hugog and lost much." Apparently this fellow Hugog had a note which he insisted that Whipple honor at an inconvenient moment; for according to Lovecraft in his letter to Moe of April 5, 1931 (*SL* 3.363), Whipple's sudden financial collapse in 1870 could have been averted "by disavowing responsibility for a single note," which his grandfather as a gentleman refused to evade.[20]

After this disaster, Whipple seems to have turned his principal attention to his businesses in Providence, although he remained in the village of Greene for several more years thereafter and undoubtedly retained at least some of his real estate holdings in Coventry. From May 1870 until May 1872 he served in the Rhode Island House of Representatives, and during the same period he was active on the State Board of Valuation, where his knowledge of real estate values held him in considerable stead. In 1874 (1873 according to Lovecraft's letter to Moe of January 1, 1915, *SL* 1.6), Whipple finally moved his family to Providence to conduct his real estate and mercantile businesses and established his offices in the Wilcox Building on Custom House Street, where he remained until shortly before his death when he transferred to the Banigan Building. (Squire Wood disagrees with Lovecraft and with Whipple's *Providence Journal* obituary in fixing the date of Whipple's removal to Providence as "about 1880" [p. 12]. Further, although Lovecraft says that Whipple "disposed of his estate and interests at

Greene" in 1873, Squire Wood asserts that the final failure of Whipple V. Phillips & Company did not come until 1879. He writes [p. 36]:

> The failure of W. V. Phillips & Company in 1879 brought to an end the industries in Greene and was a hardship to many, some losing heavily—and the depression has lasted until the present time.

However, it may be that the Company retained its original name even after Whipple had sold all his interests to his partners or others. Because of the greater authority of the other two sources, Squire Wood is almost certainly in error with regard to the date of Whipple's removal to Providence.)

Whipple's first home in Providence was not on Angell Street but rather on Broadway—then a fashionable West Side address—but by 1876 he and his family were firmly established in the Angell Street manse on the corner of Elmgrove Avenue. Here in Providence, Lovecraft writes in his letter to Moe of April 5, 1931 (*SL* 3.363, 367), a "happy financial recovery took place," so that Whipple was again "fully on his feet" when Lovecraft was born at the Phillips manse on August 20, 1890. Although Whipple's principal business was his real estate brokership (so Winfield T. Scott's essay in *Marginalia* [*LR* 10], at least, would lead us to believe), his other business interests over the thirty years of his residence in Providence were many and varied. His obituary records:

> He acquired extensive interests in real estate, and was interested in mining and irrigation properties in the West and in various mechanical inventions. In the advancement of the latter, he spent considerable time in travel, going to the Paris Exposition in 1878 and spending about a year on the continent at the time. Two years later he made another protracted business visit to London and Liverpool.

(Note that Lovecraft himself writes to Moe on April 5, 1931 [*SL* 3.361] that his grandfather tried unsuccessfully for a Rathbone family fortune in 1878. If the records of the Lovecraft chancery case which Lovecraft saw advertised ca. 1911 still exist in London, we might be able to learn a great deal more about the Lovecraft family from them.)

Two autograph letters of Whipple Phillips addressed to his young grandson (dated 1894 and 1899) which are in the Lovecraft Collection at the John Hay Library—presented to the Library by Mr. Robb Baker—confirm Whipple's wide travels in pursuit of his business interests.[21] The 1899 letter was written from the Snake River Valley in Idaho, where Whipple had extensive interest in land and irrigation properties as a result of his office as President and Treasurer of the Owyhee Land & Irrigation Company, an Idaho corporation with offices in Providence. (Lovecraft's letter to Moe of April 5 1931 [*SL* 3.367] indicates that Whipple had assumed the presidency of this corporation by the time of Lovecraft's own birth in 1890.)

Unfortunately, the road to success was not always smooth for the Company, and Lovecraft recorded in his letter of November 16, 1916 to Rheinhart Kleiner (*SL* 1.40) that his grandfather led the Company through many calamities, including the bursting of a dam on the Snake River.[22] For some time the disasters seem to have outweighed any progress which was made, so that, as Lovecraft wrote to Moe on April 5, 1931, "actual decline did set in when I was about ten years old; so that I saw a steady dropping of servants, horses, and other adjuncts of domestick management." "Even before my grandfather's death," he continues, "a sense of peril and falling-off was strong within me, so that I felt a kinship of Poe's gloomy heroes with their broken fortunes. Of the "frightful crash" which followed upon the death of his grandfather in 1904 and the subsequent break-up of "all his recuperative plans" (Lovecraft to Moe, April 5, 1931, *SL* 3.367), Lovecraft wrote to Kleiner on November 16, 1916 (*SL* 1.40; *RK* 75–76):

> But my progress had received its severest blow in the spring of 1904. On March 28th of that year my beloved grandfather passed away as the result of an apoplectic stroke, & I was deprived of my closest companion. I was never afterward the same. His death brought financial disaster besides its more serious grief. As President of the Owyhee Land & Irrigation Co., an Idaho corporation with Providence offices, he had struggled hard to achieve vast success in the reclamation of Western land. He had weathered many calamities such as the bursting of a dam on the Snake River; but now that he was gone, the company was without its brains. He had been a more vital & important figure than even he himself had realized; & with his passing, the rest of the board lost their initiative & courage. The corporation was unwisely dissolved at a time when my grandfather would have *persevered*—with the result that others reaped the wealth which should have gone to its stockholders.

The death of his grandfather and the subsequent forced removal of Lovecraft and his mother to humbler quarters at 598 Angell Street—and more particularly the collapse of the fortunes of his once proud and well-to-do family—haunted Lovecraft for the rest of his life; as Winfield Scott writes in his brilliant essay in *Marginalia* (reprinted in his book *Exiles and Fabrications*), Lovecraft throughout his life clung desperately to the shabby fringes of gentility on Providence's old East Side and more than once wrote to friends that he would finally make an end of his life if finances eventually made gentlemanly quarters impossible for him. (Fortunately, he ended his life in a house which he dearly loved, the Samuel Mumford House which stood at 66 College Street until it was removed in 1959 to 65 Prospect Street, a few blocks away.) His stories—perhaps *The Case of Charles Dexter Ward* is the prime example—are full of weak, introverted sons of distinguished families of pragmatists and businessmen, who pursue their bookish interests too far or are otherwise led unresistingly into disaster. (T. G. L. Cockcroft has remarked upon the terribly compromising situation—in practical terms—in which the protagonist of "The Shunned House" finds himself at the end of the story; and upon the general lack of initiative and stupidity of most of Lovecraft's protagonists. See his letter in *Nyctalops* No. 6, pp. 40–42.)

In fact the shock of his grandfather's death and the removal from 454 Angell Street were in 1904 so strong that Lovecraft more or less seriously, according to his own account (which can be found in his letter to Moe of April 5, 1931 [*SL* 3.367–68] and in his letter to Shea of February 4, 1934 [*SL* 4.357–61; *JVS* 221–22]), contemplated suicide in that year. He wrote Shea of riding his bicycle across the Seekonk to East Providence and down to the Barrington River, where for hours he contemplated drowning himself in the quiet waters. (This detail was elided in the letter of April 5, 1931, to Moe, as published, accounting for the mysterious reference to his bicycle and the Barrington River in *SL* 3.368. This bicycle trip of five miles and more was actually a short one for Lovecraft. He wrote of being a veritable "bicycle centaur" between 1900 and 1913 [in which latter year he finally abandoned bicycling because of the incongruousness of that mode of transportation for a grown man in his eye], and his explorations often extended far into the Rhode Island and Massachusetts country-sides. This indeed was how he acquired some of his love for the country towns and steeples which he so deeply admired. In fact, Mr. R. Alain Everts told me that Lovecraft was such an adept bicyclist that he would even travel by bicycle to visit his cousins the Thomases in East Greenwich, Rhode Island, making a round trip of over twenty-five miles in one day.)

Eventually, however, his interest in the things around him predominated and he recovered from the deep melancholy which followed his grandfather's death. The haunting vision of financial collapse, which played such a central role in the illness of Sarah Susan Lovecraft according to the authentic testimony gathered by Winfield Scott, however, never did leave him. Almost certainly, the economic uselessness of Howard was the subject of many sharp words between Mrs. Lovecraft and her son which we shall of course never know. Writing to Moe on April 5, 1931 (*SL* 3.367), he continued:

And economic decline continued steadily—without a break to this day, and with several sharp jogs downward, as when an uncle lost a lot of dough for my mother and me in 1911, and (of course) when my poor health and jazzed-up nerves made it clear that I was not going to be any wow at sestertius-scraping myself.

The uncle to whom Lovecraft refers was probably, in my judgment, Edwin E. Phillips (1864–1918), the only son of Whipple and Robie. I do not think Lovecraft knew Mr. Isaac Hill, the husband of his paternal aunt Emma Lovecraft, at all well, and of the husbands of his maternal aunts, Dr. Clark was certainly too exemplary a figure in Lovecraft's mind ever to be given such a reference in one of his letters and Edward F. Gamwell had probably already by 1911 left the family circle as the result of his separation from his wife Annie Gamwell. (Annie and Edward were never divorced, at least not in Cambridge between the time of their marriage in 1897 and Edward's death in 1936. In addition, her tombstone bears the legend "wife of Edward F. Gamwell.") According to Whipple's obituary in the *Providence Journal*, Edwin Phillips had been associated with his father in business; however, according to Mr. Everts, Edwin was a failure as a businessman and had little if any real association in his father's real estate brokerage and other ventures. Although he married Martha H. Mathews (1868–1916) in 1894, Edwin had no children. Edwin is listed as a "manager" at 63 East Manning Street on the East Side in the 1911 Providence City Directory; however, economic decline sent him shortly thereafter to the less prestigious West Side, where he is listed at 233 Webster Avenue in 1915 and as an "agent" at 874 Chalkstone Avenue in 1917, the last year of his appearance in the Directories.[23]

Unfortunately, I never did attempt to consult all the records which might yield a full picture of the economic decline of the Phillipses, but I think the way is open for an interested investigator to do so. The published Providence County taxbooks could yield some kind of barometer of Whipple's varying fortunes over his years of business activity. In addition, whatever official records may be retained in Rhode Island of Whipple V. Phillips & Company (formed in 1866) and in Idaho of the Owyhee Land and Irrigation Company, Inc., could yield some further picture of his business dealings. In addition, Whipple's own will, dated July 2, 1903, can be found in the office of the probate court in Providence, along with all the relevant documents pertaining to the inventory and disposition of his estate. I saw only the will (1904, 8639) myself, but from the recordbook entries concerning the other documents pertaining to the estate, I would judge that there was considerable difficulty in settling the estate, perhaps necessitating the sale of the majority of Whipple's real estate holdings. Ultimately, someone with sufficient financial know-how should examine all these documents so that we can have a true picture of the Phillips estate as of 1904.

By the terms of the will, Whipple's three daughters—Lillian, Sarah Susan, and Annie—were left $5000 each and his two grandsons—HPL and Phillips Gamwell—$2500 each. The remainder of the estate was to be divided equally between Lillian, Sarah Susan, Annie, *and* his son Edwin. These figures are actually rather coincidental, since the total amount specifically bequeathed—$20,000—is precisely the amount at which Sonia H. Davis in her memoir (*LR* 255) said the Phillips estate stood at in 1922 or thereabouts. (She says that the aunts regularly paid Lovecraft $15 a week from this amount, although this was reduced to $5 a week—and that not always regular—during the time of his residence in New York, when she largely supported him.)

Of course, the Phillips estate must have amounted to considerably more than the $20,000 specifically bequeathed in 1904, or it must have been considerably increased by the estates of Winfield Lovecraft, Dr. Clark, and other relatives in order for $20,000 to remain ca. 1922. Lovecraft says in his letter to Moe of April 5, 1931 (*SL* 3.366–67) that his own father left an estate of $10,000—although the Providence taxbooks for 1893–1898 show Winfield's guardian paying taxes on only $4000 of personal property. (To the best of my memory, Whipple was taxed on about $20,000 of real property in these years, but I do not have the exact figures.) Dr. Clark's will (1915, 16763) is present in the probate court in Providence, but there may not be an inventory of his estate since it was left in its entirety to his widow Lillian (Phillips) Clark. Edwin Phillips, who died November 14, 1918, apparently left no will; and although, since he left no widow or children, his estate would have naturally settled upon his sisters, one imagines there was very little to bequeath. During this time, of course, Edward F. Gamwell was undoubtedly supporting Annie and her son Phillips (who died December 31, 1916), but he himself did not die until May 10, 1936, in Boston, which pretty well eliminates him as a part of the financial picture of the Phillips estate except for the support of his estranged wife Annie and her son while he lived. (According to the inventory [1917. Mar. 9. 866264] of Phillips Gamwell's estate in Cambridge, of which Annie was appointed Administratrix, Phillips left $2875.66 in personal property, only slightly greater than the amount left him by Whipple Phillips.)

If any more distant relatives and in-laws augmented the estate, it is difficult to judge who they might be. According to Lovecraft's letter to Moe of January 1, 1915 (*SL* 1.6), Lillian Clark worked for some time as a schoolteacher, but I doubt if she continued to do so after her marriage in 1902; and in addition to his biographical notes on Lovecraft in *HPL* (Meade and Penny Frierson, Birmingham, 1972), George T. Wetzel says that Annie Gamwell worked for some time for the Shepley Museum on Benefit Street—however, this would seem to be the extent of the income created by Whipple Phillips's daughters. Lovecraft himself, I would judge, was probably very lucky to derive $1000 a year from his professional writing and revision—and that only in a good year. (The largest single payment he ever received for any work was undoubtedly the $595 check he received from Street & Smith for *At the Mountains of Madness* and "The Shadow out of Time," published in 1936 in *Astounding Stories*.)

Nevertheless, through economy and their own efforts, Lovecraft and his aunts seem to have been at least adequately provided for until their deaths. The inventory of Lovecraft's own estate was virtually nil—including only the mortgage which he held on the quarry operated by Mariano de Magistris at Cortez and Manton Streets in Providence, whose fair value was estimated at $500. (Today, of course, the appraised value of the personal papers he left would be several millions.) Despite her financial worries in her last years, even Mrs. Gamwell would appear to have been adequately provided for by the remainder of the Phillips estate; the inventory of her own estate shows $11,000, nearly all in cash and securities, which was ultimately divided between her two assigns, Mrs. Ethel Phillips Morrish, a cousin, and Miss Edna W. Lewis, a close friend.[24]

3. Lovecraft's literary executor and the John Hay Library collection

The disposition of Lovecraft's own personal effects is a sad-happy story which probably deserves some development. In mid-March 1937 Lovecraft's close friend Harry Brobst of Providence, Rhode Island, wrote Robert H. Barlow of Lovecraft's grave illness—he had been hospitalized on March 10 and shortly thereafter diagnosed as suffering from terminal cancer of the intestine. As soon as he received Brobst's letter—which may or may not have been after HPL's death early in the morning of March 15, 1937[25]— Barlow left by bus from Kansas City for Providence to give what small aid he could. He arrived in Providence shortly after Lovecraft's burial on March 18, lodged at the YMCA, and began the sorting of Lovecraft's papers during the succeeding days. Mrs. Gamwell showed him a manuscript memorandum entitled "Instructions in Case of Decease" which she had been startled to find on Lovecraft's desk in the fall of 1936, sometime before his death, a memorandum whose first sentence was: "All files of weird magazines, scrapbooks not wanted by AEPG, all original mss. to R. H. Barlow, my literary executive. [sic]" The second sentence bequeathed Lovecraft's copy of Cotton Mather's *Magnalia Christi Americana* to his good friend James Ferdinand Morton, Jr. The third sentence left all of his publications connected with amateur journalism to Edwin Hadley Smith.[26] Then: "Of all other articles first choice to be had by AEP Gamwell." The next sentence left Lovecraft's file of the *Old Farmer's Almanac*—which had been one of his principal interests as a collector—to his friend W. Paul Cook.[27] Then: "Books of general English literature, after the preceding choices—poetry, essays, 18th century memoirs &c., to be chosen by Rheinhart Kleiner." Finally: "After the preceding, first choice of all books, pictures, curios & other articles to be had by R. H. Barlow." Second choice: Clark Ashton Smith. Finally, there was appended a long list of friends to be consulted in the disposition of the remainder of the estate.

Since Mrs. Gamwell wished to retain the original of her nephew's "Instructions in Case of Decease" she made a copy in her own handwriting for Barlow to retain and in addition gave him the original covering envelope of the memorandum, both of which documents Barlow ultimately deposited with the John Hay Library, where they are today. Wishing to give legal confirmation to Lovecraft's wishes as expressed in his "Instructions in Case of Decease," which were of course not part of his formal will, Barlow and Mrs. Gamwell had drawn up in legal phraseology and signed on March 26, 1937 an agreement whereby, for her part, Mrs. Gamwell agreed to transfer to Barlow title to Lovecraft's manuscripts and notebooks, as soon as she should receive it, and Barlow, for his part, agreed to arrange for the publication and republication of Lovecraft's works, for the consideration of a three percent agent's commission.[28]

Even before Barlow left Providence in the early days of April 1937 he made the decision to deposit most of the Lovecraft papers which he had sorted in the John Hay Library of Brown University, Lovecraft's next door neighbor, for safekeeping. With the cooperation of Samuel Foster Damon, then curator of the Harris Collection, Barlow accomplished these transfers in the last days of March, after he had given a rough organization to the papers. (It is grossly untrue to state, as Lin Carter does on p. 139 of his otherwise accurate and well-researched book *Lovecraft: A Look Behind the Cthulhu Mythos*, that "Barlow never catalogued the manuscripts, never seems to have even gone through them, and had no idea what was there." This is refuted by August Derleth himself on p. viii of his *Some Notes on H. P. Lovecraft*: "Certainly no Lovecraft manuscript was lost, for R. H. Barlow soon took possession of all the writings and gave a careful account of them, within a fortnight after Lovecraft's untimely death." In fact, the basic organization which Barlow gave the Lovecraft papers which he deposited in the John Hay Library—a rough although minimally adequate one—persisted until 1970–1971, when the Library gave the Lovecraft papers a complete cataloguing. Contrary to what Mr. Carter writes, Barlow had an intimate knowledge of Lovecraft's literary affairs—else he would hardly have been named "literary executor" by Lovecraft himself.) Some typescripts which he felt might be of textual value for the anthology of Lovecraft stories which was even then being planned by August Derleth and Donald Wandrei and in addition some of Lovecraft's juvenilia and fragments which had not yet been transcribed Barlow did ship back to Kansas City with him; but all of these materials eventually returned to the John Hay Library, either directly from Barlow or through Arkham House.

In addition, after his return to Kansas City, Barlow began the shipment to the John Hay Library of all the manuscripts which Lovecraft had presented to him before his death—constituting of course the bulk of the important story manuscripts which were preserved. Indeed, by October 1942 Barlow could write Professor Damon of the Library that he was completely cleaned out of Lovecraft manuscripts, except for the notebook in which Lovecraft had written out "The Shadow out of Time" in longhand, which he wished to retain as a keepsake of his friend. (The whereabouts of this manuscript is apparently still unknown today. It was not found among Barlow's papers in Mexico at the time of his death in 1951, as were his letters from Lovecraft, which were presented to the John Hay Library after Arkham House had copied the passages it wanted for the envisaged *Selected Letters*.)[29]

It was not, however, Barlow's handling of Lovecraft's manuscripts which was ultimately to bring him to grief and finally drive him nearly completely from the Lovecraft Circle. For it was his choice of several cartons of books of weird fiction—about 150 in all—from Lovecraft's library that cost him the friendship of a whole group of Lovecraft's friends, including Clark Ashton Smith, Samuel Loveman, Donald and Howard Wandrei, and Farnsworth Wright, who charged that the books and magazines—these latter including Lovecraft's 1923–1937 file of *Weird Tales*—which Barlow had selected from Lovecraft's library might have brought needed revenue to Mrs. Gamwell. This at least was the stated reason for the unhappiness of these friends with Barlow. Some of them, however, may have resented the fact that a youth such as Barlow had been named Lovecraft's "literary executive." The charge that Barlow did not cooperate fully with the issuance of Lovecraft's work by Arkham House, which Mr. Carter makes in his book, however, remains to be substantiated.[30] After Robert Lowndes's fanzine *Le Vombiteur* had in early 1939 published an item regarding the dispute over Lovecraft's library which left open the interpretation that there had been a falling out between Barlow and Arkham House, involving the conflict of two parties trying to exercise "literary executorship" at the same time, August Derleth wrote Lowndes, in a letter which was printed in the April 1, 1939, issue: "I cannot understand where such an item could have come to birth, for Bobby Barlow has cooperated uncomplainingly and continues to do so; he and I have no disagreements; and yet the offending paragraph would make it seem as if we had."[31]

If anything, the credit given to Barlow for his part in the posthumous publication of Lovecraft's work was inadequate. While August Derleth and Donald Wandrei by all accounts contributed the great majority of the hard work which preceded the publication of *The Outsider and Others* in 1939, even this surely did not justify all the publicity which was launched in *Weird Tales* regarding their "discovery" of the novels *The Case of Charles Dexter Ward* and *The Dream-Quest of Unknown Kadath*. Lovecraft had given the holograph manuscripts of these works to Barlow in 1934 or 1935 for transcription—a task which was still incomplete at the time of Lovecraft's death.[32] In 1938, Barlow began travels which were to take him to California and Mexico, so that before he left Kansas City, he made film copies of the manuscripts of the two novels and then shipped the original manuscripts to the John Hay Library for safekeeping. Donald Wandrei had seen these novels during his 1927 visit to Lovecraft in Providence, and when Arkham House enquired of them at his suggestion, Barlow apparently found his film copies inaccessible in Kansas City—and much of his material there may have eventually been thrown out if it was not shipped back to his Florida home—and had only the partial transcripts to send Arkham House. Some delay may have been incurred—perhaps in the attempt to get a hold of the film copies—but it was eventually Barlow who in 1940–1941 temporarily removed the original manuscripts from the John Hay Library—as is verifiable from documents there—for transcription at Arkham House. As the original manuscripts of the novels were the only complete copies (aside from the putative film copy), it is impossible that Arkham House secured the text from any other source.[33] It is difficult to believe that the manuscripts of the novels were "misplaced for a time," as Derleth wrote on p. viii of *Some Notes on H. P. Lovecraft*, unless Barlow forgot that he had deposited them in the John Hay Library—which seems little likely.

In any case, the acrimony over the books and magazines which Barlow had removed from Lovecraft's library rose to such a point that in October 1938 Albert A. Baker, Lovecraft's executor, wrote Barlow a letter demanding that he return all the manuscripts, books, and magazines which he had removed from the library.[34] Barlow's reply, dated October 12, 1938, is the fullest statement concerning his actions in March 1937 and deserves to be reproduced in full:

℅ Claire P. Beck
BOX 27
Lakeport, Calif.
October 12, 1938

Mr. Albert A. Baker,
Baker & Spicer,
1502 New Industrial Trust Bldg.,
Providence, R.I.

Dear Sir:

Your letter of October 7th has reached me here in carbon copy. I am recuperating from a long and dangerous illness, but will endeavor to answer it, beginning with a recapitulation of certain events. When Howard Lovecraft died, he left a manuscript memorandum (prepared in the autumn of 1936)—doubtless still in the possession of Mrs. Gamwell—regarding the disposition of his library and literary works; which he did not consider of sufficient importance to incorporate in the formal will. This specified "all my manuscripts to go to R. H. Barlow, my literary executive," and, further, "first choice of weird books and magazines to R. H. Barlow." I have a copy of this which Mrs. Gamwell wrote out for me, but wishing also to have her legal confirmation, had the contract of March 26, 1937, drawn up. Now as to matters covered by this contract:

(1.) Manuscripts (holograph): were involved only in the case of two or three weird fragments of a few pages each, written ca. 1922; and also in the case of non-weird productions done on commission or as ghost-writing. Of the extant weird holograph Ms. from his pen, all but four had been given me during his lifetime, accompanied by letters of presentation. (These four are in the possession of Messrs. Samuel Loveman, Duane Rimel, and a party unknown to me.)[35] I have deposited the majority of those I have in a public collection for preservation, but since they are personal gifts of a date previous to his death, they do not concern us here. The typescripts and carbon copies I took charge of in March 1937 are only of textual value, rather than bibliophilic.

(2.) Books from his library: I selected two cartons of these with the permission of Mrs. Gamwell, and added them to my private library which is now temporarily in storage. You will recall it was his wish I have these, as he had said in life and recorded in his *Instructions in Case of Decease*. There was also a file of Weird Tales and a few issues of another magazine I had bound and given him . . . all of which returned to me under these sad circumstances. Other books which I had given to him I did not take, though Mrs. Gamwell offered me them; though I did take two small still-life paintings which she gave to me. As recently as a month ago she authorized the sending of these magazines (previously stored for me in her home) to me; an operation performed by Claire Beck.

(3.) My position as agent for the Ms.: In March of 1937 there appeared no other person to act in this capacity. With Mr. Derleth's later offer to do so I have cooperated fully, at no time invoking the contract despite labour and expense which I have incidentally contributed. This has been explained to Mrs. Gamwell. I would not, however, as you assume, be unable to accomplish publication myself if such action were desirable. It is merely that I stand aside voluntarily in favour of Mr. Derleth's superior opportunities. As for delay in publication, if Mr. Derleth has accomplished the sale of a collection or of anything aside from pulp publication, he has not troubled to inform me. The Commonplace Book [published by the Futile Press with Barlow's authorization in the summer of 1938] was taken from a manuscript given me in 1934, as you may observe from the text, and the payment sent her [Mrs. Gamwell] was less obligatory than a token of sincerity.

I am sorry Mrs. Gamwell believes—as you state—that I "rushed her" in fulfilling Howard's instructions. It had been my hope to reach Providence before his death—when I could not, I went to give what small aid I could. As she will tell you, I knew his literary affairs better than anyone else, and it is not without significance that he wished me, and not Mr. Derleth, or Mr. Wandrei, or some other person, to take care of them.

A copy of this letter will reach Mrs. Gamwell—I am moved by the keenest desire to cooperate with her; but in view of the above-mentioned circumstances, not, perhaps, fully known to you, cannot feel obliged to comply with your demands. It is immeasurably depressing to be confronted with such an attitude over the gifts and will of my dead friend.

Most sincerely yours,
R. H. Barlow

(For the record, Claire Beck states that he was not allowed to remove Lovecraft's file of *Weird Tales* as Barlow had asked him to do on his trip East in 1938; Mr. Beck feels that Barlow wrote this letter before he knew of his own failure to remove the magazines. However, Lovecraft's *Weird Tales* file did eventually reach Barlow, and between 1942 and 1946 he sent the John Hay Library the complete 1923–1937 file, supplementing some missing issues from his own Florida collection.)

After receiving Barlow's letter, Mr. Baker, on behalf of Lovecraft's estate, withdrew his demands with the understanding that Barlow would continue to cooperate with Arkham House in the publication of Lovecraft's work.[36] In view of the later statements of both Barlow and Derleth that this was indeed the case, there seems to be little which can be added to the story of Barlow's handling of Lovecraft's effects. Barlow offered his entire collections of manuscripts, books, and magazines of weird fiction for sale or trade to the John Hay Library in 1946, but unfortunately adequate arrangements could not be made at the time. His library of weird fiction in Mexico—which included approximately one-half of the books he removed from Lovecraft's library—was sold to a New Orleans bookseller on behalf of Barlow's estate in 1951. Most of the manuscripts (all non-Lovecraftian), books, and magazines in his Florida collection—which included the other half of the removals from Lovecraft's library—were sold to the collector Walter Coslet of Helena, Montana, by Barlow's mother in 1952.[37] (The story in Harry Warner's *All Our Yesterdays* that Dr. C. L. Barrett bought most of Barlow's Florida collection is incorrect.)

Fortunately, sales lists were kept of all the most important books and magazines sold from the Barlow collections, so that it is even today possible to specify the majority of the books which he chose from Lovecraft's library. Nor indeed—extremely fortuitously—are we lacking in knowledge of the general contents of Lovecraft's library, which form an invaluable tool for the man and the writer. For, in 1940, when Mrs. Gamwell's health was declining—she died January 29, 1941—and the expenses of her stay in a sanatorium in Newport were beginning to concern her, her downstairs neighbor at 66 College Street, Miss Mary Spink, who had moved in after the time of Lovecraft's death, made for her a complete listing of Lovecraft's library as it then stood. This list eventually came into the hands of Miss Dorothy C. Walter of the *Providence Journal*, an acquaintance of both Lovecraft and Paul Cook, and she shortly sent it off to Paul Cook for publication in his magnificent magazine *The Ghost*. Unfortunately, Cook died before Miss Spink's listing could be published, and the listing, along with a partial preface which had been begun by Cook, returned to Miss Walter, who eventually donated it to the John Hay Library in 1958. Today, it is certainly one of the most valuable Lovecraft "documents" remaining unpublished, and I sincerely hope that Arkham House or some other publisher will one day present it to the public. The reassembling of Lovecraft's library—not the actual books which he himself owned but the same titles—would be a diversion to keep even such a Lovecraft collector as the late Jack Grill happy for a lifetime.[38]

The most remarkable story concerning the disposition of Lovecraft's effects following the death of Mrs. Gamwell does not concern his books at all, but rather a whole group of important Lovecraft manuscripts which Mr. Dana rescued just as they were about to be relegated to the furnace by the people who were cleaning out the rooms which Mrs. Gamwell and her nephew had occupied at 66 College Street. This cache of manuscripts included such remarkable things as an entire file of typescripts and clippings of Lovecraft's poetry (Barlow had definitely given Brown the holograph poetry manuscripts); numerous typescripts of his tales; the holograph—and presumably only—manuscript of the prose-poem "What the Moon Brings" (printed before Lovecraft's death in *The National Amateur*);[39] several dozen manuscripts of travelogues and other essays, including the 138-page holograph manuscript of his unpublished historical travelogue of Quebec; sixteen letters to Lovecraft; drawings of Lovecraftian monsters presented to Lovecraft by Robert Bloch, R. H. Barlow, and Harry Fischer;[40] several heads of his monsters, sculpted, I presume, by Clark Ashton Smith or Barlow; and, in addition to the manuscript material, a large file of amateur and fan magazines in which Lovecraft had been published. Because Mr. Dana was an admirer and student of Lovecraft's work in addition to being a bookseller, he did not sell these unexpectedly recovered items for the collectors' prices which they might have commanded, but let the John Hay Library purchase them for a nominal price for permanent preservation in their file of Lovecraftiana.[41]

Why were these manuscripts and associational items neglected by Barlow when he went through HPL's papers in March 1937? It's difficult to say. The majority of the typescripts of stories which Barlow neglected or missed were indeed of stories which had already been published in some form before Lovecraft's death, so that he may have considered their textual value small. (Although, naturally, one would expect any manuscript of the author to be a better text than any printed version of the same.) Moreover, some of the stories represented—"Beyond the Wall of Sleep," "The Nameless City," and "The Tree" among them—had appeared only in small amateur and fan magazines prior to Lovecraft's death, magazines whose availability has always been difficult and whose standards of typographical and textual accuracy were to say the least uneven. (Lovecraft's friend Rimel found some fifty-eight errors in the short tale "The Nameless City" as printed by Wilson Shepherd in 1936.)[42]

But it is the presence of the considerable number of holograph manuscripts of travelogues and essays in the cache of material recovered by Dana which is the most disturbing—for unless Barlow felt that such things as Lovecraft's historical travelogue of Quebec were utterly worthless—which I think is highly doubtful—there is no other explanation than the presumption that one or more files of material in Lovecraft's jammed study simply eluded him during the fortnight or so he was in Providence in March 1937. Certainly, he would hardly have left behind the holograph manuscript of "What the Moon Brings" had he seen it. Barlow unfortunately fell out of correspondence with Mrs. Gamwell about 1940; that he was concerned that he had missed some important Lovecraft material is indicated by a letter of his to Albert Baker of 1942, inquiring of the fate of Lovecraft's remaining effects after the death of Mrs. Gamwell. (Baker could not recall.) Fortunately for us, Dana did manage to save at least some of the material which was still in HPL's study; the future editor of Lovecraft's collected travelogues—and I have every reason to believe that there will ultimately be such a volume—ought certainly to be very grateful.[43]

Yet, there were certainly some things lost to students of Lovecraft in this disposition of his effects after the death of Mrs. Gamwell. Certainly, Mrs. Gamwell had kept all the family photographs and scrapbooks which Lovecraft had; and these seemingly perished in the flames. (The collector Philip Jack

Grill did succeed in locating several photographs of Lovecraft's family—some of them reproduced in *Fantasy Commentator*, *The Shuttered Room*, and other places—in the hands of cousins of Mrs. Gamwell after her death, but these photographs may well have been simply their possessions and not removed from 66 College Street. The researcher R. Alain Everts has succeeded in locating a number of additional photographs in the hands of other members of the Phillips and Lovecraft families—his particular quest being for photographs of members of the Lovecraft family, of whom only a photograph of Winfield [with his wife and child, from the Grill collection; see the frontispiece of *SR*] has to date been published.[44] However, it is probably unlikely that we will ever be able to gather together anything like the accumulation of family photographs and genealogical material which Lovecraft himself possessed. Some lines in his letter of February 12, 1935 to Elizabeth Toldridge [*ET* 294] give some indication of the size of his collection: "I have three or four family albums (& drawers & boxes full of daguerreotypes and other ancestral pictures); though I don't keep them on the table in Victorian fashion for the delectation of the common visitor.")[45]

How one wishes it had been possible to preserve Lovecraft's papers and furnishings exactly as they had been left at his death, as Clark Ashton Smith proposed on behalf of himself and Lovecraft's friends Helen Sully and her mother in a letter to Barlow of April 8, 1937—some years before the Smith rupture between Smith and Barlow over the disposition of Lovecraft' effects occurred—but of course, as Lovecraft was still a virtual unknown as a literary figure and Mrs. Gamwell's finances were dwindling as it was, this did not prove to be a practical suggestion. Even had Lovecraft's quarters been preserved as they were left at his death—by some miracle of philanthropy—his most ardent students would have been disappointed: for Lovecraft himself did not customarily retain complete files of the letters and other material he received.[46] Those which he did not immediately discard or cannibalize for his own writing he seems to have cleared out in the pruning of files he was compelled to institute every few years for reasons of space—there was such a pruning in connection with his move from 10 Barnes Street to 66 College Street in 1933 and yet another in the year before his death—so that there are some surprising gaps in the files of letters to Lovecraft which are held at the John Hay Library. (One file which was virtually complete was the file of Robert Ervin Howard letters to Lovecraft, which were removed from the John Hay Library in 1937 at the request of Dr. Isaac Howard [1871–1944], who wanted them for the Robert Ervin Howard memorial collection which he was trying to establish for Howard Payne College. Unfortunately, this collection was stillborn, but the Howard letters to Lovecraft have survived and are now the property of Mr. Glenn Lord, the agent for the Howard estate, who hopes to see a collection of selections from the file published eventually. Lovecraft's letters to Howard, unfortunately, are still missing and presumed destroyed—although August Derleth and Donald Wandrei did manage to borrow at least some of the Lovecraft letters from Dr. Howard about 1937 to copy passages for the *Selected Letters*, where they have begun to appear with the third volume.)[47] Some of Lovecraft's household furnishings—for instance the paintings by his mother and his aunt Lillian Clark which he had owned—were given away by Mrs. Gamwell following HPL's death; and of course everything remaining was sold by Mrs. Gamwell's executor (Ralph Greenlaw) after her death.[48] As for the stored bulk of the effects from grandfather Phillips's Angell street manse, one might wonder whether they are still rotting in storage somewhere. Lovecraft wrote Barlow on April 20, 1935 (*OFF* 242): "Our stored stuff is all in the attic of a friend's stable—in chaotic shape—& we haven't a key. It's a hell of a mess to get at anything."

Considering the chaos the passage of time generally wreaks in human affairs, however, we probably could have done very much worse in the preservation of Howard Lovecraft's effects. After the volumes of transcripts of letters which August Derleth wrote of reach the Lovecraft Collection in the John Hay Library, there should be an admirably complete range of material for the study of the man and the writer there.

4. Some Lovecraftiana; bibliographical research and amateur press work

In moments of bibliophilic madness I have sometimes wondered precisely what constituted Lovecraft's smallest printing, that ultimate *rara avis* which would constitute the Lovecraft collector's supreme prize. Of course, one must immediately clarify the problem by asking whether one wishes to speak of the rarity of extant copies or of the quantity of the original issue. Copies of the October 1923 issue of *Weird Tales*, which printed Lovecraft's story "Dagon" (along with some snappy comments of his regarding Vincent Starrett and George Sterling which he had intended for editor Baird alone—and not for "The Eyrie," cf. Lovecraft to Long, October 7, 1923, *SL* 1.253–54), or of the issues of George Julian Houtain's semi-professional magazine *Home Brew* which contained "Herbert West—Reanimator" were certainly worth less than nothing to the hundreds of newsstand dealers who probably had to return many unsold copies; today, of course, the sale of a single copy, ragged and browned, of either of these magazines would likely see a financial transaction in two figures.[49]

As early as December 31, 1941, in a letter to Professor Damon of the John Hay Library, Barlow estimated that there were probably no more than a dozen complete sets of the rare 1923–1924 issues of *Weird Tales* still extant. (I think he may have slightly underestimated the number of devoted readers who began to read and collect *Weird Tales* from the beginning or close to the beginning. Nevertheless, I recall reading somewhere that one dealer, who purportedly knew what the market would bear, had offered a bound set of the early 1923–1924 issues for $1000.) In any case, Lovecraft's early appearances in *Weird Tales*—which are of course the true first printings of many of his tales, except for those which were given earlier amateur publication—are certainly among the rarest Lovecraft items in terms of copies still surviving. And interestingly enough, several dealers have told me that these very rarest of the early pulp magazines (the first years of *Weird Tales*, the first year of *Astounding* and *Amazing*, etc.) are generally among the most difficult to sell, not only because of the high prices which they command, but also because magazine collectors usually like to try to collect complete runs or runs over considerable periods, and the collection of complete years of the earliest pulp magazines is financially impossible for all but the very-well-to-do, those who started early and cheaply, or the occasional lucky person who may come into a windfall. However, a Lovecraft collector looking for appearances in *Weird Tales* alone might well still be able, over the course of a number of years, to assemble a complete file of the issues which contained Lovecraft material. As the first professional printings of most of his tales, these issues of *Weird Tales*—particularly in reasonably good condition—would certainly make eminently fine additions to any Lovecraft collection.[50]

Another conceit would be to try to collect all the printings of favorite Lovecraft stories: from the first appearance perhaps in an obscure amateur magazine, through the reprinting in a thirties fanzine, the first professional printing in *Weird Tales*, the first paperback anthologization, all the Arkham House editions, and the numerous later anthologizations, translations, and other editions. (Harry Morris's recasting of the Chalker bibliography in *Nyctalops* Nos. 2–4 is in the form which would be most useful to such a collector.)[51] Of course, the ultimate in such a conceit would be to try obtain all the extant manuscripts and proofs of the particular story involved; and here the best the eager collector can probably hope for would be a typescript of his story—if one ever turned up and could be demonstrated to be authentic. Holograph manuscripts of Lovecraft stories are probably nearly impossible for the private collector—and perhaps luckily so—but then again there is of course still that notebook containing "The Shadow out of Time" floating around somewhere. I believe that Lovecraft may have believed he gave the holograph manuscript of "The Rats in the Walls" to his friend A. Merritt; but when Barlow inquired after Lovecraft's death, Merritt stated that he believed only a printed copy of the story had been involved. Lovecraft also thought that he might have given the holograph manuscript of "Imprisoned with the Pharaohs"—from which he and Sonia Davis hurriedly made a new typescript after the loss of the original in Union Station in Providence on the eve of Lovecraft's marriage—to Samuel Loveman, to whom he did definitely give "The Shunned House" and possibly also gave "The Horror at Red Hook," now in the New York Public Library.[52] The destruction of the holograph manuscript of "The Colour out of Space" Barlow is sure of in his article "The Wind that is in the Grass" in *Marginalia* (*LR* 361); but I believe that in at least one letter to either Rimel or Barlow Lovecraft himself was unsure of the survival of this.

Issues of amateur magazines containing contributions by Lovecraft have undoubtedly suffered much the same kind of attrition as the popular magazines which originally published his stories—although their survival rate must necessarily have been somewhat higher, otherwise there would be hardly any copies of any of them left. (Both the UAPA and NAPA of Lovecraft's day apparently had several hundred members; his own *Conservative* had 210 copies printed of its first number—by a commercial printer in Providence who left them riddled with errors, hardly a happy experience for a literary purist like Lovecraft.[53] Naturally, however, amateur journalists would have had more inclination to save and collect the magazines which after all constituted the heart of their hobby than would casual readers have had the inclination to preserve issues of *Weird Tales* and the like.)

Altogether, I would guess that there are probably extant not more than a dozen copies of any of the issues of most of the amateur magazines in which Lovecraft had material printed; although one might make exceptions for eminently collectible items like Bradofsky's *Californian* and Cook's *Ghost* issued in the thirties and forties when Lovecraft's general literary reputation was beginning to grow.[54] Cook made a point of sending his publications concerned with weird fiction only to those whom he thought would appreciate them—thus, one does not doubt that most of the copies of *The Recluse*, *The Ghost*, and other similar items which were sent out by him all still have their good homes. (By the way, Cook also invoked a curse in the colophon of *The Ghost* against anyone who should ever presume to *sell* a copy, which was all part of his fanatical devotion to amateurdom; for which he did so much at-cost or below-cost printing over the years. After Lovecraft's meeting with Cook in Providence in 1917—for which see Kleiner's "By Post from Providence" [*RK* 118]—I believe Lovecraft had most of the remaining issues of *The Conservative* printed by him.)[55]

One might also accept certain earlier amateur magazines, like Walter Coates's magazine of regional poetry *Driftwind* (1926–1948), which had a considerable circulation outside of amateurdom and was continued by W. Paul Cook (1881–1948)[56] following the death of Coates in 1941. After the collapse of Cook's venture in East Saint Louis, Illinois, in the early thirties, he had become associated with Coates in the Driftwind Press in North Montpelier, Vermont. The bread and butter of Coates's press was apparently vanity publishing, although of course he did issue a number of other items intended specifically to please his own friends. (Lovecraft, by the way, was a member of the editorial board of *Driftwind* from June 1935 until his death; the magazine printed two of his essays, "The Materialist Today" [October 1926] and "Vermont: A First Impression" [March 1928] and later ten of his "Fungi from Yuggoth" between 1930 and 1937. The April 1937 issue contained a brief obituary.)[57]

But where is one to look for small amateur papers containing Lovecraft's work which were circulated before he gained any reputation whatever outside the amateur press associations: *The United Amateur* for November 1916 which contained Lovecraft's early story "The Alchemist" (1908) and which was presumably the first printing whatsoever of any Lovecraft fiction; *The Vagrant* for June 1918 wherein Paul Cook published Lovecraft's first substantial story, "The Beast in the Cave" (1905); *The Vagrant* for November 1919 and for March 1922 wherein Cook printed, respectively, "Dagon" and "The Tomb," stories which he had encouraged Lovecraft to write in 1917; or *The Blarney-Stone* for July–August 1914 wherein was printed Lovecraft's poem "On a Modern Lothario," presumably his first contribution to an amateur press association magazine—but not his first published poem, which was "Providence in 2000 A.D.," printed in the Providence newspaper the *Evening Bulletin* for March 4, 1912. In that poem Lovecraft took the then-current idea of the Italians on Federal Hill in Providence to rename their principal thoroughfare, Atwells Avenue, as Columbus Avenue and satirized it with the vision of a Providence completely turned into a foreign colony by 2000 A.D. According to Lovecraft (cf. letter to Kleiner, November 16, 1916, *SL* 1.41; *RK* 76), the poem sparked much discussion locally at the time of its publication—and, needless to say, Atwells Avenue still remains Atwells Avenue. "Providence in 2000 A.D.," in addition to its importance as Lovecraft's first published poem, deserves reprinting today for its testimony that a healthy satiric humor could break through some of Lovecraft's darker manifestations of racial prejudice. (Then again, there is another early poem, "On the Creation of Niggers," preserved on what is apparently a hectographed slip of paper at the John Hay Library, which would undoubtedly have been considered as tasteless in its day as it is today—despite the fact that it reflects the common view of the "old gentry" of Lovecraft's time. Mr. Everts dates this poem 1910–1911.)

Fortunately, however, for the student of Lovecraft, he needn't try the near-impossible task of collecting these ephemeral publications of Lovecraft's work in order to see them. Edwin Hadley Smith, one of the pioneer amateur printers and editors, began before the turn of the century a collection of amateur papers which he intended as a central record of amateurdom's output. This collection, augmented by Mr. Smith and others over the years, found a permanent home at the Franklin Institute in Philadelphia in the 1930s and was transferred to the Special Collections of the New York University Library in the 1960s. As the reader will recall, Lovecraft's own collection of amateur publications—at least most of it—was sent by Barlow to

Smith in 1937 to be incorporated into the general collection founded by Smith. This makes the collection, which is officially known as the Library of Amateur Journalism although it has also been called the Fossil Library and the Edwin Hadley Smith Memorial Collection, doubly valuable as a source for Lovecraft material.

Insofar as I know, George Wetzel was the first to consult this collection with the aim of compiling a bibliography of Lovecraft's amateur press works. According to Wetzel's article "The Research of a Biblio" (published in *HPL: Memoirs, Critiques, and Bibliographies*, pp. 41–46), he made his first trip for research to the Franklin Institute in Philadelphia in the early summer of 1946, after seeing in December 1945 a short little note by R. H. Barlow in the summer 1943 issue of Laney's *The Acolyte* (1, No. 4) entitled "Pseudonyms of H. P. Lovecraft," wherein Barlow suggested that the "diligent" might seek out work by Lovecraft published in the amateur magazines which he had sent for incorporation into the Library of Amateur Journalism. (This information was also contained in the Laney–Evans bibliography published for FAPA in 1943, but according to Mr. Wetzel's essay [p. 43], he did not see this work until 1952, when Bill Evans sent him a copy, after the publication of Wetzel's first bibliography of Lovecraft's amateur press works in *Destiny* for summer–fall 1951. This fact will become important in one of our later discussions.)

Encouraged by the printing of his first bibliography in *Destiny* after a long struggle over publication, Wetzel made several more trips to the Library of Amateur Journalism at the Franklin Institute to collect more listings. At about the same time, Wetzel came into correspondence with Leon Stone, an Australian ajay and the happy possessor of a collection of some 15,000 amateur papers, who had published his own bibliography of Lovecraft's amateur press works in his amateur press association magazine *Koolinda*, issues five (April, 1948) through nine (December 1952). While Wetzel's research of 1946 and 1951–53 had provided him with far more listings than had been compiled by Stone, the Stone research did contain a number of items which he had been unable to find in the Library of Amateur Journalism, which he incorporated into his listings. A chronological listing of Lovecraft's amateur press works which embodied part of Wetzel's research appeared shortly thereafter in the first and second issues of John Murdock's fanzine *Vagabond*; but his definitive compilation was to come in the seventh volume of *The Lovecraft Collector's Library*, which Wetzel edited for SSR Publications from 1952 until 1955. (Robert E. Briney compiled the "professional" section of this bibliography, which was the fullest to date although Laney–Evans and Joseph Payne Brennan [*H. P. Lovecraft: A Bibliography*, 1952] had earlier covered some of the same ground. The Wetzel–Briney bibliography was also published in *HPL: Memoirs, Critiques, and Bibliographies* in 1955.)

The later bibliography by Jack L. Chalker (Chalker & Associates, Baltimore, 1962; reprinted in *The Dark Brotherhood*) relied heavily upon these earlier compilations, although according to Thomas S. Dilley (*Nyctalops* No. 6, Supplement) "the Wetzel listings were checked, wherever possible, against the actual appearances & corrected where necessary." Chalker's Mirage Press has in addition announced for future publication a revision and updating of his bibliography by the talented young bibliographer Mark Owings, whose own work in the cataloguing for sale of the monumental collection of Philip Jack Grill and research with other original source materials ought to provide a valuable confirmation and augmentation of earlier listings.[58] Indeed, particularly with Lovecraft's amateur press works, the bibliographer's task will probably never be completely accomplished to his own satisfaction—since even the holdings of the Library of Amateur Journalism itself are incomplete in this field. (The discovery by Leon Stone of Lovecraft contributions in magazines not found in the Library of Amateur Journalism by Wetzel in his 1946 and 1951–53 research is proof positive of this fact; and Mr. R. Alain Everts, another Lovecraft researcher, has written to me of seeing numerous publications in the homes of various old amateurs which were unrepresented in the Library of Amateur Journalism. This phenomenon may be explainable by the fact that some amateurs—like Paul Cook with his *Recluse*, *Ghost*, and memorial to Lovecraft[59]—only sent certain of their publications to those who they felt would be truly interested in them.)

Thus, one hopes that the good work which has been begun with Lovecraft's amateur press contributions by Wetzel and other pioneers will continue to attract the attention and efforts of future bibliographers of his work in order that they be motivated to pursue the research with collections of amateur press publications which will almost certainly yield at least a small budget of additional material of value from Lovecraft's pen.[60] Insofar as I know, the Library of Amateur Journalism has been the principal archive of amateur publications to which Lovecraft bibliographers have resorted in the past, and although of course its collections are also being augmented through the gifts of amateur journalists and the dedicated efforts of amateurs like Sheldon Wesson (who has for some years been curator of the Library of Amateur Journalism), the Stone discoveries and the statements of other investigators like Everts—who has centered his principal attention on Lovecraft's life rather than the bibliography and criticism of his works—is certainly a strong indication that an investigation of other public and private collections of amateur journals is called for by future Lovecraft bibliographers. For instance, the John Hay Library has a large file of amateur magazines—the collection of W. Paul Cook—which certainly deserves going-over to double check (and possibly augment) the listings of previous researchers based upon the holdings of the library of Amateur Journalism.[61] I do not personally know of any other public collections of amateur journals, but I feel certain that the interested investigator could track down at least several more.

(Interested amateur journalists apparently encountered some frustration throughout the years in securing proper preservation of their philanthropic gifts of materials relating to amateur journalism in public collections, until the efforts of Edwin Hadley Smith secured at least one secure and permanent home for such material in the Library of Amateur Journalism.[62] George Wetzel's "Biblio Notes" in *Vagabond* No. 2 record a reference in Bradofsky's *Californian* for spring 1938 [5, No. 4] to the plans of certain local amateurs to deposit a collection of amateur journals in the Los Angeles Public Library; and I believe I have myself read somewhere of collections—or at least of attempts to start collections—at the Cleveland Public Library and the Library of Congress.[63] Since most amateur journals were published without copyright, the Library of Congress did not receive copies at the time of publication. Truman's Spencer's *History of Amateur Journalism*, the files of *The Fossil* (*The Official Publication of the Fossils, Inc., Historians of Amateur Journalism*) itself and of Edwin Hadley Smith's papers pertaining to the Library of Amateur Journalism, and presently active members of the amateur press associations all ought to be good sources for information on other collections of amateur journals which interested bibliographers could consult.)

Another useful tact would of course be to try to locate former amateurs active during the period of Lovecraft's activity (1914–1937) to seek permission to consult their personal libraries of amateur journals for Lovecraft material. Many of the amateurs of Lovecraft's day are of course long dead, but surprisingly enough, many are still alive, since the hobby always attracted a considerable number of young people. The bibliographic consultation of such collections for Lovecraft material in the near future has an added importance, since many fine collections of amateur journals have undoubtedly already been lost through the ignorance of the importance of these papers on the part of those who inherited them. In the 1950s George Wetzel wrote a number of former amateurs who had been active in Lovecraft's day in the quest for bibliographical and other information, but received only a small number of replies by mail. (See his essay "The Research of a Biblio" in *HPL: Memoirs, Critiques, and Bibliographies*, p. 43.) In more recent times, beginning in 1965, Lovecraft researcher R. Alain Everts has been considerably more successful in obtaining information for his own biographical research on Lovecraft from former amateurs; and it would certainly be highly worthwhile for Lovecraft bibliographers to follow up at least some of the unique collections of amateur material which he uncovered in the course of his research. The importance of such consultations is made evident by the fate of Leon Stone's own magnificent collection, which supplemented Wetzel's research—according to Everts, it was some years ago destroyed by fire.[64] Then there is the story in Harry Warner's *All Our Yesterdays* (p. 21) of how Howard Davison's trunk of amateur materials—including a Lovecraft manuscript and many letters of his—came to reside anonymously in a second-hand store—until, fortunately, someone discovered the nature of the contents and, hopefully, secured their preservation.

Bibliographical research on Lovecraft's amateur press works has in fact produced far more than simple listings of his amateur press contributions.[65] However, many gems of far more immediate appeal to the ordinary Lovecraftian have been recovered for us by research into HPL's amateur appearances; for in the case of many of the early stories and prose poems which he had printed in amateur magazines, Lovecraft himself did not retain anything more than the printed copy which he received—insofar as we can tell from those of his papers which ultimately came to the John Hay Library through R. H. Barlow and H. Douglass Dana. The bulk of Lovecraft's own collection of amateur journals, as we have earlier remarked, was sent by Barlow to Edwin Hadley Smith for incorporation into the general files of the Library of Amateur Journalism—so that, indeed, this collection, and other similar collections of amateur journals, became the *only* sources for a number of Lovecraft's early stories and prose poems after his death. In fact, I think we can safely make the general presumption that those of Lovecraft's literary works—including poems and essays—which cannot be found in the collection of his papers at the John Hay Library were either recovered for us by research into the files of the Library of Amateur Journalism or other similar collections or in fact found in the possession of one of his friends or correspondents following his death.

(Some posthumously published Lovecraftian stories and essays were in fact actually extracts from letters to friends. Thus, "The Wicked Clergyman" was taken from one of his letters from Lovecraft by Bernard Austin Dwyer. The piece published as "The Very Old Folk" in *Marginalia* is evidently taken from a letter of Lovecraft's describing his famous Roman dream.[66] The essay "Poetry and the Artistic Ideal" published in Laney's *Acolyte* for spring 1943 [1, No. 3] was actually an extract from a Lovecraft letter to Miss Elizabeth Toldridge dated September 3, 1929 [*ET* 99–103]. Wilfred B. Talman wrote me that the essay "Some Backgrounds of Fairyland," as published in *Marginalia* [pp. 174–83; *CE* 3.323–27], was actually an extract from a Lovecraft letter to him. As "Some Causes of Self-Immolation," also first printed in *Marginalia* [pp. 184–98; *MW* 179–89; *CE* 5.77–84], is also uncredited in all of the bibliographies of Lovecraft's amateur press works, I suspect that it, too, was an extract from a Lovecraft letter.)[67]

Of the fugitive Lovecraft pieces which *were* actually printed in the amateur press during his lifetime, the early stories "The Alchemist," "Poetry and the Gods," and "The Street" were all recovered by George Wetzel's research in the Library of Amateur Journalism and first republished in his *Lovecraft Collector's Library*. Letters in the papers of R. H. Barlow establish that the prose-poem "Nyarlathotep," for which there is seemingly no manuscript in Lovecraft's papers at the John Hay Library, was retrieved for him by an old amateur journalist ("ajay") with access to one of the magazines in which it was originally printed. The prose poems "Memory," and "Ex Oblivione," for which there are also seemingly no manuscripts at the John Hay Library, were probably recovered in a similar manner.[68] The manuscript of "What the Moon Brings," of course, just made its way into the John Hay collection by the skin of its teeth, among the materials which Dana salvaged from the flames; although it, too, might have been recovered from its original printing in the *National Amateur* for May 1923.

An extremely curious case is that of the short story "The Thing in the Moonlight." Lovecraft describes the dream upon which this story was based in his letter to Donald Wandrei of November 24, 1927 (*SL* 2.199–200; *MTS* 186–87; also, *Dreams and Fancies*, pp. 14–26). Yet the narration of the story in a formal first person manner and Derleth's dating of it as 1934 would seem to indicate that "The Thing in the Moonlight" is not simply a letter extract but a formal manuscript left by Lovecraft. Unless I am wrong and the manuscript of this tale is in the Lovecraft Collection at the John Hay Library, however, it is difficult to understand how "The Thing in the Moonlight" came to be printed for the first time nearly four years after Lovecraft's death in a fanzine entitled *Bizarre*, edited by Walter Earl Marconette and J. Chapman Miske. During this period (1941), Arkham House did much to discourage the publication of

Lovecraft's work in the amateur press; so that there is little likelihood that Arkham House was the source for "The Thing in the Moonlight" for editors Marconette and Chapman. One is left to conclude that "The Thing in the Moonlight" was probably obtained from the papers of one of Lovecraft's friends and correspondents; it may be significant that *Scienti-Snaps*, the predecessor of *Bizarre*, printed "The Very Old Folk," presumably a Lovecraft letter extract, for the first time in its summer 1940 issue.[69]

Nor is it completely impossible that additional material by Lovecraft—even prose poems and short stories—may yet be recovered from collections of amateur journals and the correspondence files of Lovecraft's former friends in amateur journalism.[70] Somewhat later on, in connection with "lost" stories by Lovecraft, I want to discuss two titles recalled by George Wetzel as possible prose poems: "Life and Death" and "A Singer of Ethereal Moods and Fancies." In a more general sense, however, Rheinhart Kleiner, who ought to have known, wrote in his memoir of Lovecraft in *Californian* for summer 1937 (p. 7):

> Many amateurs will remember him as a prolific letter-writer. The exact number of his correspondents may never be known, but, from the evidence already at hand, it would seem that no one is yet justified in regarding his own collection of Lovecraft epistles as exceptional either for quality or for bulk. There are at least four or five such treasuries in Greater New York,[71] and the existence of others in various parts of the country is known or surmised. The present writer has a collection dating from 1915, which, in addition to letters of staggering length, includes humorous, satirical and serious poetry in large quantities, as well as carefully drawn caricatures and portraits of well-known amateurs, to say nothing of documents, booklets and folders, all patiently printed and colored by hand. [Presumably, some of Lovecraft's hectographed juvenile publications.] More valuable collections may contain the manuscripts of stories not yet printed, for Lovecraft cast his largesse abroad with a prodigality quite unsurpassed in modern amateur history.

And again:

> Regret has been expressed that he did not concentrate more fully upon his production of short-stories, but an examination of his papers may prove him to have been much more persistent in these labors than some suppose.

Presumably, of course, all of the Lovecraft papers at the John Hay Library have been thoroughly examined for significant reliquiae of Lovecraft's literary endeavors. However, Kleiner's remark concerning Lovecraft's largesse with his manuscripts is provocative. Many of the manuscripts which he submitted to amateur editors for publication seemingly went on their way in the form of the holograph originals, with no copies made, since Lovecraft detested the typewriter. (His typewriter, a used model which he purchased in 1906, held up until 1937, which ought to be some indication of the infrequency with which he employed it.)

Proof that Lovecraft did send holograph manuscripts through the mails is seemingly given in the file of materials pertaining to "The Transatlantic Circulator" at the John Hay Library. Here, along with commentaries on his stories by various members of the "Circulator," are Lovecraft's three long essays in defense of his story "Dagon"—"In Defence of Dagon," "The Defence Reopens," and "The Defence Remains Open," as I undoubtedly inexactly recall the titles—which by all indications he circulated in their original form among members of the "Circulator," after he had previously circulated his story "Dagon" and received much unfavorable commentary upon it. There is no indication in the file of material at the John Hay Library that the "Circulator" was in fact anything more than a correspondence circle or chain or that the members thereof—some of whom were Lovecraft, Leilah A. Ashley, John Munday, Elsye Tash Sater, Elizabeth A. Taylor, A. H. Brown, John Ravenor Bullen, and Franc Pelion—ever published anything resembling a joint magazine. Thus, the listing of Lovecraft's story "The Nameless City" as having been published in "The Transatlantic Circular" [sic] at some unspecified date in the twenties which has occurred in every bibliography of Lovecraft's amateur press contributions from Laney–Evans on was probably based upon the misinterpretation of one of Lovecraft's remarks in a letter to a friend who was among those who helped with the original Laney–Evans compilation—Derleth, Cook, Barlow, Baldwin, Rimel or others.[72]

(I do not think the remark occurred in Lovecraft's letters to Barlow or to Rimel, since I have read those in the original at the John Hay Library and did not find any such reference. My own best guess would be that the reference to the "Circulator" occurred in a letter to F. Lee Baldwin, who contributed a separate section of material regarding Lovecraft's newspaper and amateur press appearances to the bibliography evidently based upon his letters from Lovecraft; but George Wetzel has suggested that the reference might also have come from a former ajay. When I inquired of Mr. Baldwin of the matter, he replied regretfully that his letters from Lovecraft were in storage but that he hoped for their publication someday. Perhaps the mystery of this reference will then be resolved.)

Since there is no indication in fact that the "Circulator" ever published anything, future Lovecraft bibliographers would probably be well advised to remove the "Nameless City" as having been published in "The Transatlantic

Circular," in the absence of additional evidence, unless they wish to regard mere circulation among a circle of correspondents publication. If they wish to do this, "Dagon" and "The Doom that Came to Sarnath" should probably also be listed, as certainly the first and I believe also the second (based upon my recollection of the letters of criticism in the file at the John Hay) were also circulated within the circle. (Lovecraft was active therein 1920–1921.) The three essays by Lovecraft in defense of his work, by the way, are most important and substantial of his works remaining unpublished; only a small sampling of the first essay, "In Defence of Dagon," has been published, and that in the consummately rare second issue of R. H. Barlow's fanzine *Leaves*, issued from Lakeport, California, in a minuscule edition in December 1938. One hopes very much that these essays, at least in edited form, will have a place in the announced *Miscellaneous Writings* or some other future volume of Lovecraftiana.[73]

Another indication that Lovecraft did send material out for publication in holograph form is given in the anonymous listing of Lovecraft's manuscripts in *Nyctalops* No. 3, in which the author notes from the Person catalogue of 1970 a typescript of "Psychopompos" bearing the annotation: "This is the earliest surviving ms of the lines in question. H. P. Lovecraft (original used in VAGRANT.)" This seems to indicate that Paul Cook read from Lovecraft's holograph manuscript when he set "Psychopompos" into type for the October 1919 *Vagrant*; perhaps Lovecraft only later made the typescript advertised by Person for his own files. In any case, it seems perfectly reasonable that Lovecraft's flowing pen and his notorious dislike of the typewriter—coupled of course with the lack of importance which he attached to his own work—caused him to send out to amateur publishers many manuscripts in their original holograph form, making no copies. Now, knowing something of the sometimes unpredictable habits of amateur publishers—past and present—have we not a right to ask with Mr. Kleiner: May there not still be unpublished Lovecraft stories, poems, and essays lurking out there somewhere in the wilderness of Lovecraft letter files?[74]

5. The ultra-collectables; planned edition of the Fungi from Yuggoth

But the discussion of Lovecraft's amateur appearances—certainly all but impossible for the collector today—has taken us far from our original purpose of discussing some aspects of the collecting of Lovecraft's work. (In connection with the difficulty of amateur items, however, one might note that Philip Jack Grill is reputed to have purchased numerous copies of *Tryout* for his collection for a humble nickel apiece.) As Stuart Schiff remarked in his essay on Lovecraft collecting in *HPL*, the classic *collectanea* for the Lovecraft devotee are certainly HPL's books and *separatea*, which have long had an honored place in the bibliographies of his work. Certainly, there can be little argument with Mr. Schiff's selection of a basic quadrivium of highly collectible Lovecraftiana—*Shunned House* (1928), *The Shadow Over Innsmouth* (1936), *The Outsider and Others* (1939), and *Beyond the Wall of Sleep* (1943). (Mr. Schiff leaves the inclusion of the last title as a matter of choice.) Achieving all four volumes of that quadrivium in decent condition might well cost considerably more than $500 today—but in a happy mood we can take that more as an indication of the growth of Lovecraft's literary reputation than as a woeful indication of inflation.

Certainly, Lovecraft's current literary reputation makes his early editions eminently collectable items—particularly in fine condition—but the collector interested in his hobby only as a hedge against inflation might well give some thought to the matter before investing heavily in the work of an author of such a *specialized* reputation as Lovecraft. Tastes are fickle, and despite the fact that Lovecraft's place in literature as a master of the weird tale and an eminent epistolarian seems assured, the current fashionability of his work in academic and literary circles could well evaporate into a trickle of indifference. After all, Lovecraft's books commanded fancy prices in the auction rooms and literary salons of the cataclysmic forties and then fell to such a state in the bee-bop fifties that even *The Outsider and Others* declined in worth to $17.50 and Arkham House hardly published any books at all during the entire decade. What is most sobering to reflect, however, is that had either Cook or Barlow succeeded in publishing *The Shunned House*, the collector present at the time of the publication of Mr. Schiff's basic quadrivium could likely have obtained them all for just a little over ten dollars—I believe that Barlow intended to charge $1.00 apiece for his bound copies of *The Shunned House* (Cook would have undoubtedly charged a bit more because of his prestigious Recluse Press imprint), and the later volumes, as I understand it, were available at $1.00, $3.50, and $5.00, respectively, to the earliest comers. That's $10.50 in all.

Mr. Schiff's choices of three "ultra" Lovecraftian collector's items—*The Cats of Ulthar* (The Dragon-Fly Press [Robert H. Barlow], Christmas 1935), *HPL* (Corwin Stickney, 1937), and *The Notes and Commonplace Book, Etc.* (The Futile Press, May–June 1938)—is equally hard to fault. However, because of the importance which Mr. Schiff and other astute collectors of Lovecraft's have attached to prehumous publications of Lovecraft's work—particularly of his fiction and poetry—I would like to argue for the inclusion of yet a fourth item in Mr. Schiff's second list, namely, the edition of Lovecraft's *Fungi from Yuggoth* which Robert H. Barlow was preparing for the Dragon-Fly Press in Cassia, Florida, in 1936, until the domestic blow-up in his household forced the removal of Bob and his mother to live with their relatives in Kansas City, Missouri, in the summer of that year. I hope to argue later on that the famed *Shunned House* was not published in any acceptable sense of the word until Arkham House bound up approximately one hundred copies for sale (at $17.50) in 1962; so that surely we cannot apply a doctrinaire criterion of publication for the "ultra" quadrivium, lest *The Shunned House*—at least in its most desirable states—be eliminated from our "basic" list. And indeed Barlow progressed surprisingly far in the printing of the *Fungi from Yuggoth* before the domestic disruption in his household in the summer of 1936 ended his efforts, as two sets of the sheets for his edition of the "Fungi" which are at the John Hay Library amply attest.[75] The first set of sheets—let us call these variant A—has Lovecraft's corrections in pencil and was presented to the Library by Barlow himself. The second set—variant B—was presented to the Library in 1961 by August Derleth, who eventually came to acquire the entire uncompleted edition of Barlow's "Fungi," and presumably is typical of the majority of sets of the uncompleted edition. Variant A, with Lovecraft's penciled corrections and annotations, consists of twelve double sheets, folded, as follows:

1. covering sheet (no printing) with list of misprints in pencil in Lovecraft's hand and a list of poems by Elizabeth Toldridge in pencil in Barlow's hand [Barlow had planned to issue a collection of her verse from the Dragon-Fly Press]; note stapled to this sheet in Barlow's hand reads: "This is a dummy of the book I was printing. I have these sheets stored in Leavenworth; it seems too bad for them to rot. Please return."; 2. title page (illustration by Clark Ashton Smith), with a penciled annotation in Barlow's hand; 3. HPL's poem "To A Dreamer" [HPL noted in his list of misprints on sheet one (1) that this poem was not among the "Fungi"]; 4. sonnet II; 5. sonnet IV; 6. sonnet VI; 7. sonnet VIII; 8. sonnet X, with a correction by Lovecraft in pencil; 9. sonnet XI, with a correction by Lovecraft in pencil; 10. sonnet XIV; 11. sonnet XVI and sonnet XXII (verso); and 12. sonnet XVIII.

Properly, variant A might be regarded as a set of proof sheets for the edition; evidently, it is the earliest surviving state of the sheets. The thematic appropriateness of "To a Dreamer" as an introduction to the "Fungi" is of course evident, but Lovecraft swiftly noted in his corrections that it was not to be printed as part of the series. (Barlow also had in mind for ultimate publication two additional slim volumes of Lovecraft's verse—one of his best macabre poems apart from the "Fungi" to be entitled *The Ancient Track* and another comprising a selection of his eighteenth-century verse. Needless to say, Barlow never began work on either project, but it might be noted that the organization of the ultimate *Collected Poems* published by Arkham House parallels precisely Barlow's plans for the three volumes from his press. The typescript text for *The Ancient Track* was among the papers from his literary files microfilmed by George T. Smisor in Mexico following Barlow's suicide in January 1951.) Variant B, donated by Derleth and without annotation, evidently represents the final state of the sheets as left by Barlow and consists of "thirteen double sheets, folded, as follows:

1. title page (illustration by Clark Ashton Smith); 2. sonnet I and sonnet II (verso); 3. sonnet II; 4. sonnet IV; 5. sonnet VI; 6, sonnet VIII; 7. sonnet X; 8. sonnet XII; 9. sonnet XIV; 10. sonnet XVI and sonnet XXII (verso); 11. sonnet XVI and sonnet XXII (verso) [precisely the same as sheet ten (10)]; 12. sonnet XVIII; 13. sonnet XVIII [precisely the same as sheet twelve (12)].

(All of the sets of sheets ultimately acquired by Derleth may not be completely uniform with variant B—the inclusion of both sheets 12 and 13— identical—in the same set is probably a fluke, although sheets 2 and 3 do represent two distinct variants which may represent different states of the uncompleted sheets.)

In addition, there were found among Barlow's effects in Mexico at the time of his death four double sheets, folded, of the "Fungi," as follows: 1. sonnet XIV; 2, sonnet XVI; 3. sonnet XVIII; 4. sonnet XXII. These sheets were ultimately offered for sale by Roy Squires in his Catalog II, 1969. If we call them variant C, at least the following distinct printed sheets of Barlow's edition are identifiable: A.3, B.1–B.10, B.12, C.2, and C.4.[76] (Note that A.4 = B.3, B.9 = C.1, and B.12 = C.3.) Altogether, Barlow printed at least eleven distinct "Fungi" (I, II, IV, VI, VIII, X, XII, XIV, XVI, XVIII, and XXII), "To a Dreamer" (A.3), and the title page (A.2 = B.1).

The later history of the printed sheets of Barlow's edition of the "Fungi" is not too difficult to trace. During the summer of 1937, when he was living with relatives in Leavenworth, Kansas, Barlow received from Clark Ashton Smith a copy of his slim collection *Nero and Other Poems* printed by the Futile Press of Lakeport, California. (Brothers Claire and Groo Beck were partners in the Futile Press; a third brother, Clyde F. Beck, assisted but was not officially a partner.) Impressed by this handsome edition of Smith's poems—in which he saw a reflection of his own thwarted plans for private press editions of fantasy authors and poets—Barlow enthusiastically wrote the Futile Press to commend the partners on *Nero and Other Poems* and to suggest that they consider doing an illustrated edition of Smith's long poem "The Hashish-Eater," of which Barlow then possessed the original manuscript. (This manuscript was offered for sale in Roy A. Squires's Catalog II in 1969; a microfilm copy of it is in the Lovecraft Collection at the John Hay Library.) Unfortunately, Barlow was ultimately unable to obtain satisfactory reproductions of Smith's illustrations for the poem by lithography, so that the idea of an illustrated edition of "The Hashish-Eater" had to be abandoned, but in the course of his correspondence with the Futile Press, he had already suggested many other possibilities for private press editions of fantasy material—one of which ultimately came to fruition in the summer of 1938 as the Futile Press edition of Lovecraft's Commonplace Book, which even today remains the only reasonably faithful rendering of Lovecraft's original manuscript.[77]

(Other projects which Barlow suggested to the brothers Beck included a collection of Clark Ashton Smith's poems entitled *Incantations* [which ultimately saw print in Smith's *Selected Poems*] and a collection of Lovecraft's eighteenth-century verse—both of which he had had in mind for the Dragon-Fly Press before the domestic upheaval in his family in 1936 had separated him from his press. He also suggested that the Becks consider reprinting Smith's *Sandalwood*, the most notoriously rare of his early poetry collections, and encouraged them in their plans for a collection of Robert

Ervin Howard's poems, to be entitled *Echoes from an Iron Harp*. The Becks themselves proposed a reprinting of Lovecraft's essay *Supernatural Horror in Literature* [originally published in Cook's *Recluse* in 1927 and serialized—but not completed—in Hornig's *Fantasy Fan* in 1933–35], but were encouraged by Barlow to concentrate upon unpublished material like *Incantations* first. Unfortunately, none of these other projects ever developed to fruition—and a proof page of the poem "Semblance" from the intended collection *Incantations* is all that survives today.)[78]

What concerns us here, however, was first mentioned by Barlow in his letter to the Becks of February 14, 1938, written from Kansas City, Missouri:

> The doctors here confirm what I have long expected—my eyesight will give out unless I stop all literary & artistic work. (This means being a farmer or a mountain climber, I fear!) As a consequence, our current job [the proposed edition of Smith's "The Hashish-Eater"] will probably remain my swan-song. When it is done I'm going to leave this environment for a more physical one—what, I've not yet decided, though I'm considering attending Commonwealth Labour College in Arkansas. I want to leave my house in order—no use letting these publications of my erstwhile self decay. I have also the partly printed Lovecraft sonnets, together with paper for completing an edition of 100 copies. This is in 12 pt Caslon & ought not to be hard to match typographically. If Derleth raised no objections, what would you say to taking the job over? About 25 sonnets to print. If I seem to be slinging this stuff out at random it is because I know that I shall never be able to do it myself & that a phase of my life is being shoved into the past. And I see in your activities & interests a parallel to mine.

At the same time or shortly thereafter, Barlow may well have sent the set of sheets which I have called variant A to the Becks for inspection, indicating in his note that the bulk of the edition was in storage in Leavenworth. By the time he wrote the Becks on July 2, 1938, again from Kansas City, Missouri, Barlow had apparently already shipped at least part of the incomplete edition in bulk:

> As to the Fungi, I believe you have the whole stock of printed sheets— however unimpressive it looks. There don't seem to be any more here. I'll give you a little data, for current & later use, & you can check the material I sent you. *36* sonnets comprise the whole series. I was printing every other one, & intended to go back & fill in—this seemed the best plan when I did it—though now I admit its logic is obscure. At any rate, the book was to be served with cord, in one signature opening at the middle—in the same style as the *Dragon-Fly* [an amateur magazine of which Barlow had produced two issues under the Dragon-Fly imprint in 1935 and 1936] & bound in heavy paper of some greenish cast. I have an idea there were two kinds of text

> paper, one of rag, for a special edition . . . you can easily tell if this is so, & segregate accordingly. The title-page (did any copies survive? I forget, having destroyed many after the frustration of my plans, but I have one "dummy" which I can send if you need it) featured the CAS cut I mailed to you last spring, & this might well be retained. When you are ready—perhaps after the CAS book—to work on the job, I'll prod Derleth into withdrawing his objection. WT ought to have bought what it wants by then.[79] Other jobs should come first, however, in your calendar. The edition was 100 or 125, & you can tell me in your next letter if all are present. These small-scale publishing jobs look pretty slight in spite of the sweat & swearing they occasion!

Only a few days later, Claire Beck, one of the partners in the Futile Press, visited Barlow in Kansas City on his way East; Barlow, about to depart for a visit to Mexico himself, wrote back to Groo Beck in Lakeport on July 15, 1938:

> Claire pulled in here one morning before I was up, & spent several days with me. (He left yesterday, the 10th) We went over the ground of book & magazine plans pretty thoroughly, & did up a bundle of stuff—since augmented by me including the last Fungi sheets discovered by accident . . . I have assembled—during the chaos of general packing for storage—a regular bale of stuff addressed to #27 [the box number of the Futile Press in Lakeport] . . . a shipment which will probably come by freight when shipped, but am *not* sending it as yet. This is an expansion of the material Claire & I put together, & of which he doubtless spoke to you—parts of Leaves II [the last issue of Barlow's mimeographed fanzine, finally issued from Lakeport in December 1937], with unprinted stencils, sheets finishing the Fungi fragment, & God knows what—a really massive stack all told. However, I believe there is no immediate reason to ship it: you are likely to be busy until fall with material already at hand, such as the INCANTATIONS job; & Claire indicated his own return wouldn't be until around October. Having this in mind, & hoping to come up your way myself at the end of the year, for a shorter or longer period, I am leaving this stuff all ready to ship, in storage, & shall have it sent at a more felicitous date. It's really too much to hassle in my present state of dementia—an inevitable accompaniment to migration in our household!

Unfortunately, there is no direct evidence in the file of Barlow letters at the Futile Press (which were made available to me through the courtesy of Claire Beck) to indicate that this final shipment of the remainder of the edition of the "Fungi" to Lakeport was actually made. Barlow did spend the fall of 1938 with the Becks in Lakeport—after having been delayed by typhoid in Mexico—and it seems reasonable to guess that this last bundle of material in Kansas City was shipped to him by his mother before she herself left for the west coast sometime later.

However, there does seem to be a possibility that some Barlow material was lost in Kansas City, i.e., left behind after Barlow's mother left for the west coast to join him. Writing to the John Hay Library on October 4, 1942, from Berkeley, California, where he was then pursuing graduate studies in anthropology, Barlow stated that he was completely cleaned out of manuscript material by Lovecraft unless perchance some remained inaccessible in Kansas City—so that there seems to have been the feeling in Barlow's mind at the time that he might have left some material there. (Barlow had stayed in Kansas City with his Langworthy aunt.[80] When Lovecraft researcher R. Alain Everts interviewed the daughter of this aunt, she stated that everything had either been checked out or left behind in Kansas City at the time her mother died and that she presently had nothing relating to Barlow. Certainly, nothing was lost from either Barlow's Mexico collection or his Florida collection. George Smisor carefully microfilmed all of Barlow's literary papers in Mexico in 1951 and made a catalogue of his library of weird fiction there; and both August Derleth and Walter A. Coslet bought from Barlow's mother what one imagines was all the important material remaining in his Florida library at the time of his death. As for Leavenworth, Kansas—Barlow apparently spent only the summer of 1937 there and even the "Fungi" sheets undoubtedly accompanied his and his mother to the Langworthys' home in Kansas City.)

In any case, there seems to be good evidence that at least part of the incomplete edition of the *Fungi from Yuggoth* reached Barlow on the west coast and was probably thereafter stored by him in various places in San Francisco and Berkeley after the idea of completing the edition was abandoned. (This may well have been in deference to Derleth's hoped-for sale of some of the "Fungi" to *Weird Tales*—which did indeed occur—although Barlow had left Lakeport by the early months of 1939 to live in San Francisco.) The *Fungi from Yuggoth*—rather thirty-three of the thirty-six sonnets—were first published in collected form by William H. Evans for FAPA in June 1943, whether by leave of Barlow or of Derleth or of both, I do not know. The entire series appeared in *Beyond the Wall Sleep* some six months later.[81]

In 1957, August Derleth wrote to Glenn Lord that Barlow had sent to Arkham House before his death "some printed pages of his projected edition of the FUNGI FROM YUGGOTH"—presumably, as much of the incomplete edition as Barlow found accessible on the west coast. (Only the four proof sheets offered for sale by Squires in his Catalog II were found among Barlow's effects in Mexico after his death; and the earlier statements we have quoted seen to make clear that the "Fungi" sheets did get as far as Kansas City.) At the time of his writing to Lord, it was Derleth's impression that none of the sets of sheets he had were complete, and, presumably, the set which he presented to the John Hay Library in 1961—which I have called variant B—is as complete a set as any which he found among those which he obtained. Whether any of these incomplete sets of sheets were ever offered for sale to collectors by Arkham House, as were about fifty sets of sheets of *The Shunned House*, according to Roy A. Squires, I do not know; diehard collectors might inquire. Perhaps Arkham House will one day bind up the incomplete sheets of Barlow's edition of the *Fungi from Yuggoth*, as was done with one hundred remaining copies of *The Shunned House* in 1961; as an unpublished pre-humous printing of Lovecraft's work, these sheets would certainly enjoy an eminent status as collector's items. If anything like the original total of 100–125 sets of sheets came to Arkham House from Barlow, a completion of the *Fungi from Yuggoth*—as Barlow himself intended for the Futile Press—night even be considered; for myself, I'd nominate for the task private pressman Roy Squires, who has already enthroned several of Lovecraft's works in fine, limited editions.

6. *The Shunned House* book

Of course, no discussion of collector's editions of Lovecraft's work would be complete without some kind of rambling discussion of *The Shunned House*. Roy Squires gives in his Catalog VI (*Modern Literature*) a detailed discussion of the history of *The Shunned House* based primarily upon Lovecraft's letters to Clark Ashton Smith, which he owns; now I add what few bits of information I have found among the Lovecraft letters at the John Hay Library of Brown University. Squires finds evidence of Cook's intention to print the book in Lovecraft's letter of March 15, 1927 to Smith; of Lovecraft's presence during the actual printing of some of the pages in his letter of July 28, 1928 to Zealia Brown Reed (*SL* 2.245); and of the sending of the sheets to a Boston bindery (despite Cook's own ill health) in his letter of June 23, 1930 to Smith.[82] In his letter of April 29, 1931, to Elizabeth Toldridge, Lovecraft gave some further word of the difficulties into which his book had fallen (*ET* 183):[83]

> By the way—Cook's failure (financial as well as physical) probably means the total loss of my small 60-page book "The Shunned House," which was to have appeared long ago. The loose sheets of the whole edition are tied up in a Boston bindery, & nobody seems to know how to finance their extrication—or, for that matter, what to do with them if they were extricated.

Judging from the letters which I saw at the John Hay Library, little word on the fate of *The Shunned House* seems to have filtered out to Lovecraft's correspondents for several years after the writing of this letter to Elizabeth Toldridge; however, on January 28, 1933 (*OFF* 50), Lovecraft informed Barlow that the unbound edition of his book—which he estimated at 250 copies—had not been lost but was at the home of Cook's sister in Sunapee, New Hampshire.[84] Lovecraft's letter to Barlow of February 18, 1933 (*OFF* 53–54) indicates that Barlow had made an inquiry about the possibility of taking over the edition on behalf of Lovecraft; in his subsequent letter of March 14, 1933 (*OFF* 56) Lovecraft commented further on Barlow's ideas for what was to become in the end the Dragon-Fly Press. Finally, word seems to have come from Cook regarding Barlow's proposal; writing to Smith in a letter postmarked May 31, 1933, Lovecraft stated that Cook had found the unbound sheets and that they would be bound by his friend Walter J. Coates. Writing to

Barlow on April 9, 1933 (*OFF* 60), Lovecraft explained with regrets that Cook had earlier made an agreement with Walter J. Coates that he should take over the edition, so that Barlow could not have the job of binding and selling *The Shunned House*. Whether the unbound sheets now went to the bindery a second time—as legend seems to have it—remains to be determined from further evidence. (Perhaps Coates bound his own books.) In any case, Coates was unable to undertake the binding and selling of the book because of his own financial struggle during the period.

On January 31, 1934 Lovecraft wrote to Barlow that the Coates issue of *The Shunned House* had fallen through and that Cook, recalling Barlow's interest in taking over the edition, wondered if he still wanted it (*OFF* 103). Barlow's plans for a private press were still in their infancy during this period; but a book by Lovecraft, already printed and lacking only a binding, would by any accounts have been an egregious start for such a press, so that Barlow responded enthusiastically in the affirmative to Cook's inquiry. Lovecraft's February 1934 letter to Barlow (*OFF* 110) indicates that Cook and Barlow were in touch regarding the edition. Lovecraft's own prolonged visit to the home of Barlow's parents in Cassia, Florida, intervened, and from there on May 13, 1934 he wrote his young friend Duane W. Rimel (*FLB* 172):

> Another event since my arrival is the coming—at last—of the loose sheets of "The Shunned House" from Cook. There are only about 115 copies left (some being lost or spoiled), but Barlow plans to bind & issue them eventually.

In another letter of May 30, 1934 to E. Hoffmann Price, he wrote: "About half of the edition of my 'Shunned House' has come from Cook, & Barlow intends to bind & issue it." In Lovecraft's subsequent letter of June 1, 1934 to Rimel, there was more good news (*FLB* 178):

> About "The Shunned House"—it appears that the other half of the edition is *not* lost after all, but merely sidetracked in the cellar of Cook's sister. Therefore there are about 225 copies instead of 115. I doubt if the sale will be rapid. Naturally, you'll get one . . . though probably there will be nothing done toward distribution till autumn.

A Similar report regarding the discovery of the remainder of the edition of *The Shunned House* undoubtedly went out about the same time to Lovecraft's other young friend from Asotin, Washington, F. Lee Baldwin; for in Baldwin's column "Within the Circle" in the September 1934 issue of Hornig's *Fantasy Fan* (p. 7; *FLB* 358) is a note that Barlow would issue a 225-copy edition of *The Shunned House* in the fall. At this point, however, another of the misfortunes which so bedeviled the fate of Lovecraft's book occurred; for Barlow's mother, having been told that her young son would lose his sight shortly without treatment, sent him packing off to Washington, D.C., for treatment by an army specialist there. (Barlow's father, Everett Darius Barlow, Jr. [1881–1952], was a career military officer, so that his family was afforded free medical care.) Naturally, nothing could be accomplished toward the issuance of *The Shunned House* during the period of this treatment in Washington, D.C., which lasted until the late spring of 1935. Finally, apparently growing somewhat anxious about Barlow's inability to do anything about the book, Lovecraft wrote on May 24, 1935 (*OFF* 273):

> He [Cook] speaks of sending 150 more copies (lately discovered) of "The Shunned House" down to Cassia—but are you sure you want to bother with this proposition, now that you have so many others? I wouldn't mind taking it off your hands for the sake of freedom in distributing copies to those who have requested them—I'd reimburse you for the express-collect charges on the first 115.

Lovecraft went on to say that another 150 copies would undoubtedly constitute a formidable inundation and that although Kenneth Sterling, another young friend, had proposed the idea of a cheap paper edition, he personally preferred to take over the edition himself and to distribute the sheets *gratis*—provided Barlow could not accomplish the issuance of the edition. Shortly thereafter, however—on June 9, 1935—Lovecraft arrived for his second lengthy visit in the Barlow home, and young RHB promptly made amends by presenting HPL with a copy of his book beautifully bound in full leather and inscribed: "For HPL—who only wrote it—with the compliments of the binder. R.H.B. June 9, 1935. On the occasion of his second visit." (This copy was discovered among HPL's effects by Mrs. Gamwell in 1938 or so and returned by her to Barlow. It was subsequently found among Barlow's effects in Mexico and offered for sale in Roy A. Squires's Catalog I [1968].)

About this time, Barlow was finally beginning to get his printing and binding equipment set up; and on July 9, 1935, with HPL's help, the separate cabin near the Barlow home in which RHB intended to conduct the Dragon-Fly Press was finished. By the time he wrote E. Hoffmann Price on July 25, 1935, HPL was busy setting type for Frank Belknap Long's collection of poems, *The Goblin Tower*. (In fact, Lovecraft revealed in his letter to Duane W. Rimel of December 15, 1935 (*FLB* 307), "that book of Long's verse—'The Goblin Tower'—was printed during my sojourn in De Land [the nearest city to the Barlow home; Cassia was only a tiny hilltop hamlet]—in fact, I set up most of the type myself." The printing of the book was completed by Barlow and Lovecraft in August 1935 but issuance in a one hundred-copy edition was held up until December 1935 by the binding process (see Lovecraft's letter of December 5, 1935, to J. Vernon Shea; *JVS* 276),[85] making the first issue of Barlow's amateur magazine the *Dragon-Fly*, dated October 15, 1935, the first publication of the Dragon-Fly Press. The third publication of Barlow's press was the Christmas booklet *The Cats of Ulthar*; the fourth and last was the second issue of the *Dragon-Fly*, dated May 15, 1936. The incomplete edition of Lovecraft's *Fungi from Yuggoth* and several (at least two) proof sheets of *Caneviniana* are seemingly the only other physical reliquiae of the Dragon-Fly Press. Barlow's remaining stock of *The Goblin Tower* (31 copies) and of the *Dragon-Fly* (seven copies of the first issue with covers and six of the second with covers; eleven copies of each issue without covers) was ultimately taken over by the Futile Press for sale, along with the remaining copies of the first issue of his mimeographed magazine *Leaves*, which he had published in a one hundred-copy edition from Leavenworth in August 1937 with the financial assistance of his fellow amateur Ernest A. Edkins. (The second issue of *Leaves*, dated December 1938, was prepared by Barlow in Kansas City, Mexico City, and Lakeport; the sixty copies designated for commercial sale were advertised by postal card by the Futile Press.)

On August 4, 1935 (*FLB* 282), Lovecraft wrote to Rimel that Barlow had shelved his plans for *Caneviniana*—a 35-copy edition of which had been announced in F. Lee Baldwin's column "Side Glances" in the April 1934 issue of *The Fantasy Fan* (1, No. 8, p. 116; *FLB* 355)—but that he was still hoping to issue *The Shunned House* eventually. Unfortunately, I was able to find no direct evidence in the files of Lovecraft letters at the John Hay Library that the remaining 150 copies which Cook had discovered in his sister's cellar in Sunapee were shipped at this time. Certainly, it would have been the logical moment—while Lovecraft himself was still visiting with Barlow, On this score, however, we do at least have the evidence of Barlow's later letter, dated October 29, 1942, to Larry B. Farsaci (published in the tenth issue of Farsaci's fanzine *Golden Atom*, winter 1943), to which he appended the information:

> Lovecraft sent me the whole edition of the SHUNNED HOUSE about 1934 or 5; it had been lying in storage in Vermont, and the idea was to rescue and circulate it. A few were circulated; but the OUTSIDER volume made it no longer appropriate

In a somewhat later letter to Farsaci, undated but also published in part in the tenth *Golden Atom*, Barlow provided some further information:[86]

> Loveman, by the way, has the longhand mss. of THE SHUNNED HOUSE; the proof-sheets survived until about 1933 or 34 when they were lost en route to (I think) Rimel; and the printed edition, unbound, except for a half-dozen copies which were distributed, is somewhere in storage among my things—in Florida or Kansas City I suppose. There is no point, other than a bibliographic quaintness, in circulating them now that the whole thing is available in THE OUTSIDER.

Now, of course, we can see here that Barlow's memory was not wholly accurate; he stated that the sheets were discovered in Vermont, whereas they were actually found in the home of Cook's sister in Sunapee, New Hampshire; and, moreover, he could not recall the exact place in which his own copies were stored. However, since Barlow knew from Lovecraft's letters of the 150 additional copies discovered by Cook in the cellar of his sister's hone, it hardly seems likely that he could have stated—even seven years after to Farsaci—that he had the *entire* edition if he had in fact only received Cook's original shipment, which is accurately fixed at 115 copies. Indeed, *if* Arkham House received all of its copies from Barlow, then we know that Barlow received more copies than the original shipment of 115—for in addition to the one hundred copies which were bound by Arkham House in 1961, some fifty sets of the loose sheets were also sold by August Derleth. (See "The Mystery of *The Shunned House*" in Roy Squires's Catalog VI [*Modern Literature*].) Writing to George T. Smisor, who had taken charge of Barlow's literary effects in Mexico, on March 19, 1951, Derleth stated that Barlow had "sent *all* the unbound sheets to us" [my italics] before his death. Later, upon the occasion of Glenn Lord's ordering one of the sets of unbound sheets (with Arkham House copyright sticker) which had been offered for sale by Arkham House, Derleth wrote to Lord on November 4, 1957:

> These unbound sheets [of *The Shunned House*] were in part destroyed, but some time before his death . . . Barlow shipped the remaining sets to us here, together with some printed pages of his projected edition of the FUNGI FROM YUGGOTH.

The clear indication, coupled with Barlow's statement to Farsaci that he had received the "whole edition" of *The Shunned House*, seems to be that all of the Arkham House copies were from Barlow and that Barlow shipped to Arkham House all the unbound copies which he had. Some further evidence is given in Derleth's letter to Barlow of June 4, 1949 (in the Robert H. Barlow Papers microfilmed by George T. Smisor),[87] wherein Derleth acknowledged the receipt of thirteen sets of *The Shunned House* sheets and asked Barlow how many more were in his possession. Unfortunately, the file of Derleth letters in the Barlow Papers does not appear to be complete, and there is no further mention of *The Shunned House* in the Derleth letters which are there, but perhaps it is a reasonable assumption that Barlow shortly afterward arranged for the shipment of the remaining sets of unbound sheets in his possession to Derleth. (The question might be settled definitively by consultation of the Barlow letter file in the August Derleth Papers at the Wisconsin State Historical Society Library.)

What peregrinations saw the remaining sheets of *The Shunned House* shipped to Arkham House in 1949 or thereabouts? Here we should return briefly to 1935. Lovecraft had no great confidence in the ability of Barlow—still a young lad of seventeen at the time, if brilliantly precocious—to carry through to completion all the ambitious plans he was making for the Dragon-Fly Press, and urged him in letters subsequent to his summer visit to concentrate his energies upon one project at a time. The printing of the first issue of the *Dragon-Fly* and the binding of Long's *The Goblin Tower* were occupying Barlow at the time, but Lovecraft suggested the printing of Clark Ashton Smith's *Incantations* as his next project.

On September 5, 1935, apparently concerned that *The Shunned House* would never be bound up among the welter of Barlow's other projects, Lovecraft wrote Barlow to ask if he would be amenable to a suggestion of Samuel Loveman's to advertise *The Shunned House* in the catalogues issued by Loveman's book business (*OFF* 291). This would involve, wrote Lovecraft, six to twelve bound copies initially and a commitment to bind up additional copies as more orders came in. Barlow, however, apparently did not wish to make the binding of *The Shunned House* his next project; in the last weeks of 1935, he was busy printing the small booklet *The Cats of Ulthar* as a surprise Christmas present for HPL, and by December 20, 1935, according to Lovecraft's letter to Elizabeth Toldridge of that date (*ET* 319), he had begun printing Lovecraft's *Fungi from Yuggoth*, setting aside for the moment Smith's *Incantations*, which Lovecraft had suggested as the second book from the Dragon-Fly Press. By February 1936, according to Lovecraft's letter to Barlow of that date (*OFF* 319), Loveman had still not received an answer to his proposal regarding *The Shunned House*; Barlow, it appeared was still preoccupying himself with the printing of HPL's own "Fungi" and perhaps beginning work on the second issue of the *Dragon-Fly*, which in fact turned out to be the fourth and last completed publication from his press.

By June 13, 1936 Lovecraft was once again urging Barlow to concentrate all his energies on one project and suggesting that one be Smith's *Incantations*, and not his own *Fungi from Yuggoth* (*OFF* 343). By this time, however, the life of the Dragon-Fly Press was nearly over, The domestic upheaval in the Barlow family sent Barlow himself scurrying northward for a visit with Lovecraft in Providence which lasted from July 28, 1936 until September 1, 1936, at which date Barlow left not for Florida, but for Kansas City, Missouri, to join his mother there at the home of her relatives. (It was during this long visit in Providence—on August 8, 1936, to be exact—that Lovecraft, Barlow, and Adolphe de Castro composed their famous acrostic sonnets on Edgar Allan Poe in St. John's Churchyard, at Barlow's suggestion.) During this visit, Lovecraft had little success in arguing Barlow out of his overambitious plans for the Dragon-Fly Press; now, with the recent death of Robert Ervin Howard, who had been a correspondent of his, Barlow wanted to produce a memorial collection of his poems, and he was still talking about the collections of verse by Elizabeth Toldridge and of weird stories by C. L. Moore which he had in mind. (Ultimately, verse by Elizabeth Toldridge appeared in the first issue of *Leaves*; C. L. Moore's story "Werewoman," in the second.)

Unfortunately, however, when Barlow arrived in Kansas City—where he studied for a time under Thomas Hart Benton at the Kansas City Art Institute—he found his printing and binding equipment inaccessible in Cassia; and he was forced to concentrate his plans and energies on the mimeographed literary fanzine *Leaves* which he had planned with Lovecraft in Providence. (Among the file of notes and miscellaneous papers in the Lovecraft Collection at the John Hay Library is a sheet with the tentative contents of the first three issues—in Lovecraft's handwriting, as I recall.) The situation *vis-à-vis The Shunned House* remained doubtful. On November 30, 1936 Lovecraft wrote Barlow to ask whether he had any accessible sets of sheets of the book, as Donald Wandrei had recently discovered that the set which he had obtained—probably from Cook far earlier—was defective and he wanted to have the book done up in a collector's binding. He commented (*OFF* 373):

> Gawd, the luck that poor book has had! I wish I could get ahold of the edition before something else happens to it & pay off my donative promises with sets of the sheets.

Unfortunately, the word soon came back from Barlow that the sheets of *The Shunned House* were stored among his things in Florida and temporarily inaccessible. The sheets of *The Shunned House*, Lovecraft wrote to Elizabeth

Toldridge on December 12, 1936 (*SL* 5.373; *ET* 349), were now "stranded in storage in De Land." (This is another indication that Barlow did receive the second "half" of the edition from Cook in 1935; otherwise, Lovecraft might have resorted to Cook in order to satisfy requests for the unbound sheets.)[88]

There would be no good reason to suppose anything other than that the edition of *The Shunned House* remained in storage at Barlow's Florida home until it was shipped to Arkham House around 1949, were it not for the fact that Arkham House seems to have acquired at most 150 copies—"slightly fewer" than fifty sold as unbound sheets and precisely one hundred in bound form, according to Roy Squires in his Catalog VI. Now, if Barlow was the sole source for the Arkham House sheets—as seems to be indicated—then he must necessarily have received more than the original shipment of 115 copies. His own statement to Farsaci indicates that he received the "whole edition."

In the letters at the John Hay Library, we find essentially two estimates for the quantity of the edition: that of 225 copies given in Lovecraft's letter of June 1, 1934 to Rimel (*FLB* 178), and that of 265 copies which is obtained by adding the number of copies which arrived in Cassia in May 1934 (115; see Lovecraft to Rimel, May 13, 1934, quoted above; *FLB* 172) and the number of copies which Cook subsequently discovered in the cellar on his sister's home (150; see Lovecraft to Barlow, May 24, 1935, quoted above; *OFF* 273). These copies were evidently the same ones whose discovery Lovecraft announced to Rimel on June 1, 1934 while he was staying at Barlow's home; evidently, he was simply reminding Barlow of their existence when he wrote again on May 24, 1935, although the estimate of the number of copies remaining at Cook's sister's had risen from ca. 110 (225 – 115) to ca. 150 in the interim. (Perhaps Lovecraft based the information given Rimel and Baldwin upon an earlier understanding of the total quantity of the edition.) R. Alain Everts wrote me that Cook's own records indicate that he printed some 300 copies of *The Shunned House*—which actually tallies rather well with either the 225 of 265-copy figure, since Cook often—according to Mr. Everts—had to print many more copies than the planned quantity of an edition to allow for spoilage. Working from the 225-copy figure printed in *The Fantasy Fan*, Roy Squires, an experienced printer himself, "guesstimates" the original edition at ca. 250 copies, allowing for some few copies which may have been distributed by Cook or Coates in the form of unbound sheets. (In his Catalog II [1969], Squires catalogued what is evidently one such set of the sheets, inscribed by Lovecraft to his bibliophile friend Samuel Loveman. The defective set of sheets which Donald Wandrei had in 1935 [see above] may be yet another such set.) I think Squires intends the ca. 250-copy figure as the total number of sheets printed which were deemed suitable for publication, not the total originally printed, allowing for spoilage, which was presumably 300, according to the records consulted by Everts. I hope I am not misinterpreting here—if I am, and the 300-figure is that of the total edition deemed suitable for publication, there may yet be "publishable" copies lurking around somewhere up in New Hampshire or Vermont—presumably, up to 75 (300 – 225) of them. Even under my assumption, there might still be inferior copies among Cook's things.

Whether the number of copies obtained by Barlow was 225 of 265, however, we are left with the mystery of how he came to have only 150 copies or less to transmit to Arkham House. As we have seen, Barlow stated to Farsaci that the publication of *The Outsider and Others* (1939), which contained "The Shunned House," made the circulation of Cook's original edition inappropriate; and there is little if any reason to believe that Barlow circulated as many as 75 or 115 (225 – 150 or 265 – 150) copies in the form of unbound sheets between 1934, when he first acquired part of the edition, and 1939, when *The Outsider* was published. We are in fact entitled to deduct only the half dozen or so copies which Barlow did bind up and "circulate from this total, leaving either 69 or 109 copies (approximately) unaccounted for, presuming that Barlow did receive the entire edition. Derleth's own statement to Glenn Lord (November 4 1957, quoted above) that the unbound sheets of *The Shunned House* "were in part destroyed" would seem to refer to these copies, especially in light of his statement that Barlow sent him "all the unbound sheets" (see above) and Barlow's own statement that he received the "whole edition" (see above). The alternative, of course, is that these 75 or 115 sets of sheets never reached Barlow—which would leave the entire history of Cook's edition of *The Shunned House* open. Proceeding under our basic assumption that Barlow did receive the entire edition, less a very few given away as loose sheets by Cook or Coates, and that Derleth received all that Barlow could find ca. 1949, we are left with the question of how 69 or 109 of the 225 or 265 copies shipped to Barlow in 1934–1935 came to be "destroyed," as we must assume from Derleth's letter.

The last reference to the sheets in Lovecraft letters at Brown is seemingly to their inaccessibility in Florida in December 1936 (see Lovecraft to Toldridge, December 12, 1936; *SL* 5.373; *ET* 349). Barlow himself had returned to Kansas City, Missouri, in September 1936 and remained there until Lovecraft's death summoned him to Providence in March 1937. After completing the sorting of Lovecraft's papers, Barlow headed back for Kansas City, presumably to complete his semester at the Kansas City Art Institute. Most of the summer of 1937 he spent with relatives in Leavenworth, Kansas (during which period he prepared *Leaves* I, issued in August 1937 from Leavenworth); however, I believe that he also made at least a short visit to Florida that summer during which he could have exhumed some of the sheets of *The Shunned House*. In the fall of 1937, Barlow was back in Kansas City, Missouri (attending another semester at the Kansas City Art Institute?), having apparently brought whatever he had had in Leavenworth with him. Now, it is passing strange that in all his extant correspondence with the Futile Press Barlow made no reference to *The Shunned House*—if he had at least some of the sheets with him. He suggested so many of his former projects to the partners in the Futile Press, that one would naturally have expected him to mention *The Shunned House* had he had the sheets available to him, even in part.

However, in this regard it might be noted that in the fall of 1937 Derleth had just been able to land "The Shunned House" with Farnsworth Wright of *Weird Tales*—constituting one of the first and most substantial posthumous sales of Lovecraft material which Derleth, with the help of Donald Wandrei, was able to make on behalf of Mrs. Gamwell. (Aside from the novels *The Case of Charles Dexter Ward* and *The Dream-Quest of Unknown Kadath*, "The Shunned House" was surely the most substantial Lovecraftian fiction published after his death.) The novelette received its first true publication in *Weird Tales* for October 1937, from which copyright was released to Derleth and Wandrei for future Arkham House publications. (More on the chimerical Barlow "edition" of *The Shunned House* in a little while.) Thus, with "The Shunned House" freshly published in *Weird Tales*, Barlow may have considered the time inappropriate to propose a completion of the original Cook edition, even if he did have at least some of the sheets in Kansas City with him. Indeed, it is in Kansas City that I suspect the 69 or 109 missing sets of sheets for *The Shunned House* may have been lost or destroyed, for as we have seen, Barlow departed from there in the summer of 1938, never to return again, insofar as I know. His mother remained there until 1939 or 1940, when she joined him in California; in 1942, after Barlow's graduation from Berkeley in remarkable time, she returned, not to Kansas City, but to Cassia, where she spent the rest of her life. Barlow was in touch with his Langworthy uncle in Kansas City[89] as late as 1942, but in October 1942 he wrote the John Hay Library that his Florida and California collections were cleaned out of manuscript material by Lovecraft and that if anything remained it would have to be in Kansas City. This seems to indicate that he did have difficulty learning precisely what had been left in Kansas City following the shipments to the Becks in the summer of 1938; as I have remarked before, I think that his difficulty in getting a hold of his own copies of the two posthumously published Lovecraft novels may have been explainable by the fact that they were stored in Kansas City.

Now, when Barlow died in January 1951 there followed a thorough going-over of his Mexico and Florida collections; in neither were any unbound sheets of *The Shunned House* found. Presumably, Barlow had sent to Derleth all of the sheets which he found accessible in Mexico and all of those which his mother found accessible in Florida, constituting the slightly less than 150 copies which Arkham House ultimately disposed of. However, I do not know that Barlow was ever able to have made a survey of whatever material he had stored in Kansas City for remaining sheets of *The Shunned House*. Of course, Mrs. Barlow may well have shipped whatever her son had had stored in Kansas City back to Florida upon her own departure for the west coast in 1939–1940; but the fact that at least some sheets of the edition were evidently lost leads one to believe that the removals were not complete. (Of course, she might have also shipped Kansas City material out to the west coast; to be fair, Barlow did lose a few issues of Lovecraft's file of *Weird Tales* somewhere in San Francisco, which he later replaced with copies from his own Florida collection. It is possible, therefore, that he also lost sheets of *The Shunned House* in San Francisco.) According to Mr. Everts, the Langworthy daughter[90] now knows nothing of any Barlow material which may have been stored in Kansas City; thus there seems to be at least some reason for supposing that whatever loss of sheets may have occurred during the storage of *The Shunned House* with Barlow may well have occurred there. Derleth's own statement that part of the edition was "destroyed" indicates that he himself had some further definite information in the matter; and future investigators of "The Mystery of *The Shunned House*" would probably do very well to look to the Derleth Papers at the State Historical Society of Wisconsin in Madison—and particularly to the files of letters from Barlow and Cook which are presumably there—for further elucidation.[91]

To have one last fling at *The Shunned House* before leaving it to future and more exacting investigators, let us consider the matter of Barlow's own "edition." Barlow's statement in the tenth *Golden Atom* that he distributed "a half-dozen copies" is of course an early source straight from the horse's mouth for the long bibliographic tradition that Barlow bound and distributed some "six or seven copies." The next reference in print to this "edition" of *The Shunned House* seemingly occurs in Joseph Payne Brennan's 1952 bibliography of Lovecraft's professional appearances; and although I think it is likely that Brennan obtained his information from August Derleth (who in turn would have had his information from a Barlow letter), he may have also seen the *Golden Atom* correspondence. In any case, the Barlow letter clearly establishes the basis for the bibliographic tradition. Such a small "edition" evidently establishes the need for a census of copies; so let us briefly consider how many copies were distributed to whom and how many are findable today.

In the first instance, there is the ultimately desirable copy bound in full leather for presentation to Lovecraft himself on the occasion of his arrival in Cassia for his second visit in 1935. As we have already related, this copy was returned to Barlow after Mrs. Gamwell found it among HPL's effects in 1938 or so. (It was not one of Barlow's 1937 choices from HPL's library.) It was found by George T. Smisor among Barlow's effects in Mexico and afterwards offered for sale by Roy Squires in his Catalog I (1968) and sold to a private collector.

In the second place, there are three other bound copies which were found—two at first and one a little later—among Barlow's effects in Mexico after his death by George T. Smisor. The first two of these copies, according to Smisor's letter to August Derleth of April 25, 1951, were bound with "cloth back and paper sides;" the third copy, discovered a little later, was presumably similarly bound. Of these copies, the first two were sold to Derleth by Smisor on behalf of the Barlow Estate; the third was included in the sale of Barlow's general collection of weird fiction (Mexican portion only) which was sold to Cecil Davis of the Coronet Bookshop in New Orleans, who had requested its inclusion in the sale for his own personal collection. Yet another copy, presumably bound in this manner, was found by Mrs. Barlow in Cassia and also sold to Derleth. (I do not know the fate of the three Barlow-bound copies which were sold to August Derleth, other than that the Arkham copyright sticker was inserted in them after purchase. They might still reside in Derleth's private collection; have been sold as is; or rebound to form a part of the one hundred-copy Arkham "edition" of 1961.)

In any case, none of these Barlow-bound copies, save perhaps the presentation copy which belonged to Lovecraft, really concerns us here, since none of them save that one could be said to have been "distributed." Of copies which were "distributed," I can only specify two extant copies today. The first occurs in Squires's Catalogs I (item 32) and II (item 53), where it was advertised for sale for $325; I do not know whether it has yet been sold. (Well-heeled collectors might inquire!) This copy is "case-bound ... in boards and half cloth with stamping on front cover and spine," "rather crudely," according to Squires's Catalog I. Further, the original copyright notice ("Copyright 1928 by W. Paul Cook") "has been changed by pen and ink to '... 1936 ... R.H. Barlow.'" (Was this Clark Ashton Smith's copy? Squires [Catalog VI] cites Lovecraft's letter postmarked October 23, 1935, to Smith, which indicates that Smith did receive a copy bound by Barlow.)

The second extant copy which I can specify was the one sent to Frank Belknap Long by Barlow. I believe this copy is now in the Philip Jack Grill collection; interested bibliophiles please wait for Mark Owings's catalogue of this collection for a full bibliographic description of this book.[92] Presumably, however, the binding of Long's copy would have been similar to that of the copy catalogued by Squires, particularly if this latter was indeed Clark Ashton Smith's copy. Then, there are two putative copies of the Barlow-bound "edition" whose existence I presume from references in Lovecraft letters at the John Hay Library but whose present whereabouts I know nothing of. Writing to Duane W. Rimel on August 27, 1936 (*FLB* 330), Lovecraft stated that Barlow had bound up a special copy of his book *The Shunned House* for presentation to the Robert Ervin Howard Memorial Collection then being organized by Dr. Isaac Howard for Howard Payne College in Brownwood, Texas. Presumably, this copy was duly sent to Dr. Howard for the Collection. (As, indeed, were Howard's letters to Lovecraft, originally deposited at Brown University by Barlow in March 1937.) Of this collection, Glenn Lord wrote me on March 11, 1971:

> The memorial collection at Howard Payne College was withdrawn early in 1937, with the exception, I believe, of the books in REH's library. A few years ago I came across a copy of C. A. Smith's EBONY AND CRYSTAL in the library, with the bookplate of the REH Memorial Library and an inscription from CAS to REH.

Presumably, Barlow's bound copy of *The Shunned House*, presented to Dr. Howard for the Collection after REH's death, would not qualify as a book of REH's library; however, it may well still be found someday among the materials which old Dr. Howard once had, some of which have evidently been scattered or lost.[93] Finally, Lovecraft's letter of December 12, 1936, to Miss Elizabeth Toldridge (*SL* 5.374; *ET* 349) indicates that Miss Toldridge had also received a copy of *The Shunned House*, presumably Barlow-bound. Of what became of her copy, I have no idea. (R. Alain Everts wrote me that Miss Toldridge [1861–1940] worked for the government in Washington, D.C., before her retirement and left no close relatives at her death. Barlow secured her letters from Lovecraft for presentation to the John Hay Library—to which they came after Derleth and Wandrei had gone over them for *Selected Letters*—sometime after Lovecraft's death.)

Here then are at least five putative copies bound and distributed by Barlow: the Lovecraft, Smith, Long, Howard Memorial Collection, and Toldridge copies. The additional copies needed for Barlow's "half-dozen" undoubtedly also went to Barlow's friends and correspondents; in the thirties, he also corresponded quite closely with E. Hoffmann Price and C. L. Moore and intermittently with various members of Lovecraft's circle of young "fan" correspondents—Rimel, Baldwin, Wollheim, Sterling, Lowndes, Conover, Blish, and many others. And, of course, if Squires's case-bound copy was not Clark Ashton Smith's copy, it is presumably yet a sixth presumably extant copy.

(Even though the Squires case-bound copy would seem to indicate that Barlow bound two additional copies to file for copyright in 1936, the *Catalog of Copyright Deposits* and the main card catalogue of the Library of Congress contain no record of any such work filed for copyright. In any case, it is clear that Barlow's distribution of a "half-dozen" copies—all to close friends of his own and Lovecraft's—could hardly be held to constitute "dedication to the public," but rather merely "private circulation." Even if Cook did obtain copyright in 1928—and this is hardly likely, since a book can be copyrighted only in published form—this would not necessarily be fatal to the protection of the work, since courts have held that only a published date of copyright posterior to the time of actual publication is fatal to protection. If the date of copyright indicated in the notice is prior to the time of publication, the period of protection is merely shortened. It seems clear that "The Shunned House" was first published in any legally acceptable sense in the October 1937 issue of *Weird Tales*.)

Well, enough for *The Shunned House*. May it continue to delight and enchant Lovecraft collectors for years to come![94]

7. The rarest Lovecraft editions

Before closing our discussion of basic quadriviums and ultra-quadriviums of Lovecraft *collectanea*, we ought probably to consider what was in fact the smallest quantity of any of the editions of his books and "separates," which of course have always seemed to be foremost in the eyes of collectors. (For myself, I think I'd be more than willing to trade some of them for things like a file of *The Conservative* or early issues of *Weird Tales* and *Home Brew*, though.) Now, no fair counting the Barlow-bound edition of *The Shunned House*. (Let's see, in addition to the "half-dozen" distributed copies of this, we have four "undistributed" copies found among Barlow's effects in Mexico and Florida. Here we are counting the Lovecraft presentation copy—also found in Mexico—as "distributed.") And no fair counting a variant of a published edition—like the two (or three: see Squires's Catalog II) copies of *The Cats of Ulthar* on Red Lion Text. So what's the answer? Even so, *The Cats of Ulthar*, with 42 copies in all, you say? Wrong. I propose the brochure *The Materialist Today*, first in the Chalker listing of "Books and Pamphlets" as the "rarity" champion until further evidence enthrones another.[95] This "brochure" was published by Walter John Coates of the Driftwind Press; and in the thirties issue of *Driftwind* containing the bibliography of Driftwind Press publications to which I have already referred in connection with the "Fungi from Yuggoth," there is the following entry for it:

> *The Materialist Today*, Howard P. Lovecraft, n.d., n.p. [May 1926] Not for sale. 12mo, pa, 8pp. Only 15 copies printed.

Presumably, then, *The Materialist Today* was in the nature of an offprint produced for the private use of Lovecraft and his publisher (The essay "The Materialist Today" appeared in *Driftwind* itself only in October 1926; presumably, however, the printer had printed the sheets by May or had kept the type set up until used for *Driftwind*. One can hardly imagine a separate edition of fifteen copies!) Moe's hectographed edition of *Four Acrostic Sonnets on Edgar Allan Poe* (1936)—containing the three sonnets composed by Lovecraft, Barlow, and de Castro on August 8, 1936, in St. John's Churchyard in Providence and an additional one of Moe's own composition—might come close to rivaling *The Materialist Today* in paucity of original issue—it was produced primarily for the instruction of Moe's English classes—but, technically, it is an *anthological appearance* anyway. Herman C. Koenig's mimeographed edition of *Charleston*, issued in the spring of 1936, likely also appeared in a minuscule edition—although likely nothing rivaling *The Materialist Today*, the hectographed *Four Acrostic Sonnets on Edgar Allan Poe*, or even *The Cats of Ulthar* (which appeared in an edition nearly three times as large as that of *The Materialist Today*). Both Chalker and Wetzel list this in their "Amateur Press Essays" section as a brochure printed by Herman C. Koenig. Roy Squires gave the first full bibliographic description of the booklet in his Catalog III (*H. P. Lovecraft: A Basic Collection, etc.*), which was distributed principally to academic libraries. Because of this limited circulation, his entry probably deserves reprinting here:

> II.1. CHARLESTON by H. P. Lovecraft. N.p., n.d. Various references attribute publication to H. C. Koenig; probably issued through one of the amateur journalism societies. Consists of 20 numbered pages of text plus two of itinerary, mimeographed; one page of architectural sketches by HPL with many notes in his hand and two pages of maps drawn and heavily annotated by HPL, all photo-lithed. In stiff paper covers with typewritten label, as issued. Laid in are two pages of Errata in HPL's hand, photo-lithed. This copy has glued into the front cover a 3½ × 5 inch reproduction of the oft-reprinted Finlay portrait of Lovecraft, added by a former owner. $135
>
> All of the bibliographies of Lovecraft give this as "A Guide to Charleston, S.C." and none of them date it. Lovecraft's Errata establish it as ante-mortem. The essay appears in *Marginalia* (1944) as "A Guide to Charleston, South Carolina," with the major portion of one of the pages of illustration. The only other copy known to me lacks the Errata pages. A rare item of exceptional interest.

My own dating of *Charleston* I establish from Lovecraft's letter to Barlow of March 11, 1936 (*OFF* 326), wherein he announced that Herman C. Koenig had produced his essay on Charleston in the form of a mimeographed booklet with reproductions of Lovecraft's own drawings. (The original holograph manuscript of the essay, a typescript presented to R. H. Barlow, and a copy of the published mimeographed booklet were all among the material salvaged at the last moment from the furnace at 66 College Street in January 1941 by H. Douglass Dana, subsequently transferred to the John Hay Library, where all three items are today, for Lovecraft researchers who wish to consult them.) Certainly, however, the information given by Mr. Squires establishes *Charleston* as a legitimate, ante-mortem "separate" edition of Lovecraft's work—if such lesser publications as *Looking Backward* (1920), *The Materialist Today* (1926), *Further Criticism of Poetry* (1932), *The Cats of Ulthar* (1935), and *Some Current Motives and Practices* (1936)[96] are to be so considered, anyway. It deserves inclusion in the "Books and Separates" sections of future Lovecraft bibliographies.

Koenig's *Charleston* is also important for its published reproductions of Lovecraft's own drawings.[97] Insofar as I know, if one discounts his hectographed juvenile astronomical publications (which included star-maps and other astronomical drawings), drawings by Lovecraft were published in only two other places during his lifetime. Star-maps and other astronomical drawings made by Lovecraft appeared occasionally along with his monthly astronomical articles in the *Providence Evening Tribune* between 1906 and 1908 (my own bibliography of these articles—doubtless incomplete—is presently scheduled to appear in *Nyctalops* No. 11).[98] The other ante-mortem appearance of drawings by Lovecraft was reported by George Wetzel in his "Biblio Notes" attached to the second part of his chronological bibliography of Lovecraft's amateur press works which appeared in the second issue of *Vagabond*: for here Wetzel reported that "'Ward Phillips' (HPL) illustrated a story by Frank Belknap Long in a 1921 issue of UNITED AMATEUR." The first posthumously published illustrations by Lovecraft seemingly appeared in the summer 1943 issue of *The Acolyte* (1, No. 4), where drawings of "Pickman's Model" and "Cthulhu" were reproduced (i.e., traced onto stencil) from F. Lee Baldwin's letters from Lovecraft. A third illustration from the Baldwin file, of the "Blasted Heath" (presumably from "The Colour out of Space") was not reproduced in *The Acolyte* because the text on the back of the drawing made tracing impossible. Since 1943, numerous illustrations in Lovecraft's hand have been reproduced from his papers and letters, particularly in the *Selected Letters* but also in other Arkham House volumes and other publications.[99]

8. Some additions to the *Lovecraft bibliography*

I have personally delved very little into the field of Lovecraft bibliography which has been so ably pioneered by Francis T. Laney, William H. Evans, Joseph Payne Brennan, Leon Stone, George T. Wetzel, Jack L. Chalker, Robert Weinberg, Eddy C. Bertin, Mark S. Owings, and all their collaborators, virtually my only original contribution being a listing of Lovecraft's astronomical articles in the Providence newspapers which is scheduled for appearance in *Nyctalops* No. 11, but I do have a very few general bibliographical notes on Lovecraft's published work which may be of interest to persons active in the field.

While I was doing research at the John Hay Library, I found among the file of printed sheets and cuttings of Lovecraft's poetry (which, by the way, was another of Dana's recoveries) a printed sheet on coated stock which included Lovecraft's poem "The Marshes at Ipswich (entitled "On Receiving a Picture of the Marshes at Ipswich" in its printing in the amateur magazine *Merry Minutes* in March 1917). The heading on the sheet indicated that it was taken from a publication entitled the *National Magazine*, but despite the obvious suggestion that it was issued by the members of the National Amateur Press Association (which Lovecraft finally broke down and joined in November 1917—see his letter to Rheinhart Kleiner of November 8, 1917; *RK* 120), none of the contents of the tearsheet of the *National Magazine* in the John Hay Library seemed to indicate any connection with amateur journalism. I finally found confirmation of my suspicion that the *National Magazine* was not in fact connected with amateur journalism in the second of the lengthy defenses of his story "Dagon" and of fantasy literature in general which Lovecraft circulated among the members of the "Transatlantic Circulator;" for in "The Defence Reopens" (dated January 1921), Lovecraft states on sheet III (*MW* 151; *CE* 5.50):

> Some day I will copy for the Circulator my various verses on America & England, as published in amateur journals on both sides of the water. One of them appeared in the (professional) *National Magazine* in Boston, & brought me an offer (albeit an impractical one) from the book-publishing house of Sherman, French, & Co.

So here in fact is confirmation for a new listing which should go into the "Professionally Published Magazine Poetry" sections of future Lovecraft bibliographies; I regret, however, to say that I do not myself have the exact reference. The tearsheet from the *National Magazine* which is in the John Hay Library, may well be dated—I simply don't recall—but even if it is not, it certainly bears a page number which should assist future Lovecraft bibliographers in the search for this reference. Because of the already-noted appearance of the poem—or rather, what I presume is the same poem under a slightly different title—in *Merry Minutes* for March 1917, I would recommend to researchers a first search in the volumes of the *National Magazine* from 1917 until 1921, and then backtracking if necessary. Certainly, the printing of "The Marshes at Ipswich" in the *National Magazine* is an important early professional appearance of Lovecraft's work and eminently deserves listing in future bibliographies.

Indeed, if we do not consider work embodied in letters published in magazines or contributed to newspapers as "professional appearances, the printing of "On Receiving a Picture of the Marshes at Ipswich" in the *National Magazine* might well be considered Lovecraft's first professional appearance.[100] According to Lovecraft's own statement (to Kleiner, November 16, 1916, *SL* 1.41; *RK* 76) the first printing of one of his verses was that of "Providence in 2000 A.D." in the Providence newspaper the *Evening Bulletin* for March 4, 1912; I wonder whether the poem which Robert H. Davis printed under the title of "Lovecraft Comes Back: Ad Criticos" in the January 1914 issue of *The Argosy* (which Sam Moskowitz uncovered and printed in part on p. 377 of the chapter "H. P. Lovecraft and the Munsey Magazines" in his history-anthology *Under the Moons of Mars*) was the first appearance of one of his poems in the letter column of a professional magazine.

The first appearance of any Lovecraft letter in print—and indeed of any material whatsoever by Lovecraft in print—was by his own statement (*SL* 1.40; *RK* 75) in the "letters" column of the *Providence Sunday Journal* (a newspaper) for June 3, 1906;[101] I do not know when one of his letters first appeared in a professional magazine. The earliest Lovecraft letter printed in the Munsey Magazines which is directly cited by Sam Moskowitz (*op. cit.*) is evidently that which appeared in *The Argosy* for September 1913. However, Lovecraft's own statement in his letter printed in the *All-Story Weekly* for March 7, 1919 (quoted by Moskowitz, pp. 373–74) that he had read every number of the *All-Story Magazine* from its inception in January 1905 probably makes it possible that Lovecraft letters predating that in the September 1913 issue of the *Argosy* might be found in the files of the *All-Story Magazine* or other Munsey publications—using Lovecraft's dating of June 3, 1906, as his first appearance in print whatsoever as a starting point. (Both the Wetzel and Chalker bibliographies list "letter excerpts from *Argosy* as appearing in *Golden Atom* for December 1940 but Barlow's letter to Farsaci commenting upon that issue of *Golden Atom*, itself published in part in the winter 1943 issue, states:

> Your *Cavalier* letters in the G.A. (for which thanks), incidentally, do look like HPL, though in an unusually high & moralistic & Puritan mood—which was not uncommon with him in his early days especially. I wonder if he might have partly revised the letter of some friend, instead of being the author alone?

Now, who is correct in his reference, Barlow or Wetzel–Chalker? According to Moskowitz' definitive history of the Munsey "pulps," *Cavalier* had its own run from 1908 until 1914, when it was merged into the *All-Story Weekly*, whose title thereupon became the *All-Story Cavalier Weekly* [changed back to the *All-Story Weekly* with the issue of May 15, 1915]; the *All-Story Weekly* and the *Argosy* did not combine into the *Argosy All-Story Weekly* until 1920. If the December 1940 *Golden Atom* did indeed print letters from the *Cavalier*, they would seemingly be distinct from any of the letters quoted by Moskowitz from the *All-Story Weekly*, the *All-Story Cavalier Weekly*, and the *Argosy*. Curiously enough, Lovecraft wrote Barlow on July 28, 1932 [*OFF* 34], that he had read every number of the *Cavalier*; however, his statement in the letter published in the *All-Story Cavalier Weekly* for August 15, 1914 [quoted by Moskowitz, *op. cit.*, pp. 374–75] that he ultimately ceased reading the *Cavalier* because of the stories of Fred Jackson printed in its pages would seem to be more definitive, as a far earlier statement.)[102]

Indeed, there are undoubtedly many unknown Lovecraft letters in periodicals and newspapers from 1906 onward. Many of these he evidently bought or subscribed to himself—cf. his often-quoted statement that he was innocent of any idea of personal economy until 1910–1915 when the declining fortunes of his family finally brought home the necessity for frugality—although he also made far greater use of the Providence Public Library in these early years than he did later in life. (The list of periodicals taken by the Library between 1905–1920 would probably be a very good indication of the range of his reading. I wonder where he may have seen the advertisement of a Lovecraft estate tied up in chancery in London, which he mentions having seen ca. 1911 in his letter to Maurice W. Moe of April 5, 1931 [*SL* 3.361–62].) A file of his cuttings from scientific journals (dating principally 1903–1905) which is in the Lovecraft Collection at the John Hay

Library indicates that his family indulged his interests even to the point of subscribing to these relatively expensive publications.[103]

Of course, the first professional appearance of Lovecraft's fiction seems firmly established as having been that of the serial "Herbert West—Reanimator" in six parts in George Julian Houtain's *Home Brew* in 1922, but nevertheless, as Mr. Moskowitz comments, these early appearances of Lovecraft's letters and verse in the general media warrant considerable attention. His own suggestion that the letters of both Lovecraft and his principal opponents on the Fred Jackson controversy be reprinted from the Munsey pulps of 1913–1914 is an especially happy one; and, certainly, no one would be a better editor for such a specialist booklet than Mr. Moskowitz himself, if a willing publisher could be found.[104] The search for all of the "professional" material which Lovecraft published during the first decades of the century is likely to occupy Lovecraft researchers for generations, however.[105] Certainly, the individual letters which appeared in the Munsey magazines which have been discovered by Moskowitz and other researchers deserve listing in future Lovecraft bibliographies.

The most important published letters by Lovecraft, however, were undoubtedly those which he contributed to the "Eyrie" of *Weird Tales*. Thomas G. L. Cockcroft of Lower Hutt, New Zealand, has indexed the "Eyrie" and the reader's columns of the other weird fiction magazines; and of course his research includes all of the letters by Lovecraft which appeared in those pages. I hope at least a portion of his research—perhaps the citations for letters by professional authors alone—will ultimately be published (his data on letters by Clark Ashton Smith in these magazines was published in *CAS: Nyctalops*);[106] some of the interest of the Lovecraft letters alone is indicated by Lovecraft's statement to Frank Belknap Long (October 7, 1923, *SL* 1.253–54) that editor Baird had printed "a whole page about your Grandpa in *The Eyrie*, including some very indiscreet extracts from letters with unflattering allusions to Messrs. Vincent Starrett and George Sterling" in the same issue of *Weird Tales* (October 1923) which printed his "Dagon." ("If Starrett and Sterling don't start out after their Grandpa Theobald with stilettos and automatics," Lovecraft added characteristically, "it'll be merely because they don't believe in bothering to swat small skeeters . . ." Actually, these references did not prevent at least Vincent Starrett—if indeed he ever saw the October 1923 issue of *Weird Tales*—from entering into an interesting correspondence with Lovecraft; witness letters 310 and 316 of *Selected Letters* [2.209–211, 218–222]. To judge from the first letter, Starrett wrote Lovecraft after reading his essay on *Supernatural Horror in Literature* in Cook's *Recluse*.¹⁰⁷ Starrett was a contributor to the detective pulps in the 1920s, as well as being a distinguished poet and bookman.)

I can, however, make one small addition to the list of published letters by Lovecraft, again based upon a magazine tearsheet in the Lovecraft Collection in the John Hay Library. Lovecraft's letter of June 14, 1922 to Mrs. Anne Tillery Renshaw (*SL* 1.185–89; *ET* 370–72) mentions that his persistent revision client David V. Bush, then operating as an itinerant lecturer and author in the field of "popular psychology" and "success," had recently begun his own magazine, *Mind Power Plus*, as another money-making operation. In the John Hay Library is a tearsheet from this magazine, with a letter of Lovecraft's, dated June 20, 1922, commenting upon the fact that Dr. Bush's dynamic ideas might well take firm root among New England conservatives after an initial struggle for acceptance. Lovecraft evidently wished to retain the favor of his once-voluminous revision client, for in private correspondence he was considerably more skeptical of the validity of Bush's ideas and indeed his motives in propagating them. In any case, his letter in *Mind Power Plus* is an interesting reflection of his association with Bush, and might possibly be just one of a number of Lovecraft contributions to the magazine.¹⁰⁸ Certainly, if any Lovecraft researcher ever finds himself confronted with a file of this obscure item—apparently a mere droplet in the huge sea of Bush's publications—there would be more than a little justification for a search of the files to locate the exact reference for Lovecraft's June 20, 1922 letter, and other possible Lovecraft items.¹⁰⁹

Another obscure item which has seemingly not yet appeared in Lovecraft bibliographies is the essay "Some Dutch Footprints in New England," which Lovecraft wrote at the suggestion of Wilfred B. Talman for *De Halve Maen*, a small journal which Talman was at the time editing for the Holland Society of New York. Lovecraft's letters indicate that his essay appeared in *De Halve Maen* in 1933 or thereabouts.¹¹⁰ There is certainly no doubt that a Lovecraft enthusiast with access to a file of this magazine—and there certainly ought to be several in New York libraries—could make a definite contribution to the bibliography of Lovecraft's work. (Indeed, one might wonder whether an entirely new subdivision of "professionally published essays" might have to be opened in Lovecraft bibliographies to accommodate this listing. Lovecraft's astronomical articles in the Providence newspapers could be fitted neatly into the same category; and his two *Driftwind* essays could also justifiably be included—since that magazine was truly "semi-professional.")

The final offering I have for Lovecraft bibliographers concerns the listing of the poem "Edith Miniter" in the amateur poetry sections of both the Wetzel–Briney and Chalker bibliographies as having been published in a "booklet" or "chapbook" entitled *In Memory of Edith Miniter*, which is undated. (A poem entitled "Edith Miniter," dated September 10, 1934, appeared on pp. 68–69 of the summer 1968 issue of the *Arkham Collector*, and is presumably the same poem.) My reason for questioning this listing is as follows: after the death of Mrs. Miniter in 1934, Paul Cook resolved to publish a memorial to her including her own best work and tributes from her friends. Lovecraft himself had become the trustee of a considerable number of Mrs. Miniter's literary manuscripts following her death and held these in trust for Cook's memorial. Unfortunately, however, the economics of the depression intervened, and Cook was unable to undertake his ambitious memorial during Lovecraft's lifetime. Upon Lovecraft's death, as we have seen, Robert H. Barlow took charge of his papers—among which were the Miniter manuscripts and Lovecraft's own essay "Mrs. Miniter—Estimates and Recollections." Longtime amateur Ernest A. Edkins had given Lovecraft twenty-five dollars to hold in trust to help to finance the Miniter memorial, but when Lovecraft and Barlow hit upon the idea of the literary "fanzine" *Leaves* during Barlow's own 1936 visit to Providence, Edkins agreed to reassign his donation to finance the production of *Leaves*, since hopes for the publication of the Miniter memorial had by then grown very dim. Following Lovecraft's death, Edkins reaffirmed his decision to assign the donation which he had left with Lovecraft to help with the production of *Leaves*, and the first issue accordingly emerged in August 1937 from Leavenworth, Kansas, with a printed acknowledgement of Edkins's help.

From among the Miniter manuscripts which he had inherited from Lovecraft, Barlow printed the essay "Dead Houses" in this first issue of *Leaves*. Then the trouble began. Cook, always temperamental, exploded. He had expressly given Lovecraft instructions, he said, that Barlow was not even to see "Dead Houses," which he had planned to use as the crowning jewel of the Miniter memorial. Now, Cook charged in a later letter to Edward H. Cole (in the Lovecraft Collection in the John Hay Library), Barlow had effectively "preempted" the Miniter memorial by rushing "Dead Houses" into print in *Leaves*. The fairness of this charge seems dubious. Barlow may indeed have known nothing of Cook's injunctions regarding the Miniter manuscripts when he inherited them from Lovecraft in March 1937. If, on the other hand the plan of the first three issues of *Leaves* which is in the Lovecraft Collection in the John Hay Library does include Mrs.

Miniter's "Dead Houses" for the first issue and furthermore if that plan is in Lovecraft's hand, then we seemingly must assume that Lovecraft had either forgotten Cook's injunctions against the use of "Dead Houses" or that he undertook to convince Cook to allow Barlow to use the essay for *Leaves* in view of the dim prospects for the publication of the Miniter memorial at the time. In any case, it is difficult to imagine that Barlow, a thoroughly honorable and devoted young man, would have deliberately violated Cook's injunctions against the publication of "Dead Houses" had he known that Cook still considered them to be in effect following Lovecraft's death.

In any case, from this moment onward, Cook seems to have considered the question of the Miniter Memorial dead; certainly, by the time he wrote Cole in 1941, he had still not published it. Hyman Bradofsky, one of the most dedicated and talented young amateurs of the period, decided shortly after Lovecraft's death that Mrs. Miniter—whose work was by and large unknown to the young amateurs of the era—should not go without some remembrance in lieu of Cook's ambitious memorial. He solicited several of the Miniter manuscripts from Barlow, who had himself been a frequent contributor to Bradofsky's *Californian*, and published them along with Lovecraft's essay "Mrs. Miniter—Estimates and Recollections" in the spring 1938 issue of the *Californian*. Even this did not end Barlow's troubles in *re* the Miniter manuscripts, however. One of the manuscripts which Barlow certified as an original, unpublished manuscript from the Lovecraft bequest turned out to have been published—unknown to Barlow—nearly twenty years previously in the *Random Amateur*, another amateur press association magazine, and Bradofsky became quite angry with him. Barlow finally ended his travails over the Miniter manuscripts by sending the remainder of what he had to the John Hay Library as an associational item for the Lovecraft Collection on July 10, 1943; there they still are today.

All of this history of frustrated plans and controversy in *re* the Miniter memorial, however, leads us to ask where the "booklet" or "chapbook" entitled *In Memory of Edith Miniter* fits into the picture. Have Lovecraft's bibliographers simply followed up a misleading reference in one of Lovecraft's letters and assumed the memorial which was planned by Cook was ultimately issued? I do not have accessible at the present time a copy of the Laney–Evans bibliography to determine whether this "booklet" is listed therein; but both Wetzel–Briney and Chalker both have it listed as the place of publication of the poem "Edith Miniter," without any further bibliographical information. Did then one of these bibliographers actually see a copy of this publication in one of the various collections of amateur journals? If so, it is difficult to believe that the booklet would have been so anonymous as to lack any publication information and a further bibliographic description is certainly warranted. Just as an offhand guess—if this "booklet" has in fact been actually seen by Lovecraft bibliographers and if it in fact lacks publication information—I would hazard the suggestion that it might have been an early, provisional tribute issued by the Driftwind Press in anticipation of the later memorial. In this case, it would surely be listed in the bibliography of the Driftwind Press which appears, as we have noted, in one of the issues of *Driftwind* itself from the thirties.[111]

* * *

Professor Barton L. St. Armand of Brown University told me a fascinating anecdote about Lovecraft's 1923–1937 file of *Weird Tales* (deposited in the John Hay Library by Barlow between 1942 and 1946), which he read in preparation for writing his own master's thesis on Lovecraft and his work ("H. P. Lovecraft: The Outsider in Legend and Myth," Brown University M.A. thesis, 1966). When Professor St. Armand was reading in one of the browned and fragile copies of Lovecraft's file—I doubt that he remembers precisely which issue—he discovered, laid in between two of the pages, a sheet of paper with notes in Lovecraft's handwriting for what he described to me as an entirely new pantheon of gods which Lovecraft was evidently considering to replace or augment his original Cthulhuian pantheon. Unfortunately, I think, that page of notes by Lovecraft is still there between the pages of an anonymous issue of *Weird Tales* in the John Hay Lovecraft Collection; hopefully, however, it will someday be rediscovered by another researcher using the Collection and brought to the attention of the authorities of the Library so that it may be properly catalogued among Lovecraft's surviving notes. What with the detailed scholarship which has been developed around Lovecraft's "Mythos," these notes would evidently be of the greatest interest to fans and students alike.

With regard to *Weird Tales*, by the way, it gives me great pleasure to say that the few copies which now reside in public collections will not simply be allowed to crumble into dust. An official of the Library of Congress assured me that *Weird Tales* is high on the list of popular fiction magazines slated for preservation on microfilm. Unfortunately, the Library of Congress did not begin saving the copies of *Weird Tales* which were deposited for copyright until the 1950s, making the task of the present librarians in trying to preserve the magazine on microfilm somewhat more difficult, but with a little cooperation from public collections and individual collectors, the task ought ultimately to be accomplished. In addition to the 1923–1937 file of

Weird Tales—mostly Lovecraft's own copies—whose deposit at Brown University Barlow recorded in his essay "The Wind that is in the Grass" in *Marginalia* in 1944 (*LR* 362; *OFF* xxxiii), I have myself read of a near-complete collection at the University of Kansas and a collection lacking only the very first years at Eastern New Mexico University. Can anyone add to this census of copies in institutional collections for the benefit of future researchers?[112] (I nearly omitted one rather important collection: the British Museum, unlike our Library of Congress, wisely saved all of its issues of *Weird Tales*; from 1925 until 1954.)

* * *

Occasionally the editing of Lovecraft's letters in *Selected Letters* makes for a little confusion. I myself observed what I believe is one such incidence in Lovecraft's long autobiographical letter to Rheinhart Kleiner of November 16, 1916. On p. 36 of *Selected Letters* I, a portion of this letter evidently pertaining to Lovecraft's first public school experience at the Slater Avenue School in Providence is elided. Then, on p. 39, describing his further education at Hope Street High School in Providence, Lovecraft writes:

> Slater Avenue School is public, but it is rather a neighbourhood affair, with most of its pupils drawn from the old families. But Hope Street is near enough to the "North End" to have a considerable *Jewish* attendance . . . Knowing of my ungovernable temperament, & of my lawless conduct at Slater Avenue, most of my friends (if friends they may be called) predicted disaster for me, when my will should conflict with the authority of Hope Street's masculine teachers. But a disappointment of the happiest sort occurred. The Hope Street preceptors quickly *understood* my disposition as "Abbie" had never understood it; & by *removing all restraint*, made me apparently their comrade & equal; so that I ceased to think of discipline, but merely comported myself as a gentleman among gentlemen.

Aside from the fact that Lovecraft certainly cast himself as much more of a "bad boy" in the primary grades than he likely ever was and that he certainly also romanticized the liberality of his high school experience (free schools in those days?), his reference to "Abbie" appears to be completely unexplained. For quite a long time, I took "Abbie" to be a generic reference to fellow students who were Jewish, and made the inference that Lovecraft had had problems with such students because of his early prejudices—which he later overcame to the extent that his wife and several of his closest friends and correspondents were Jewish. But then, one would have expected Lovecraft to spell this "Abie," and not "Abbie," which was a fairly common women's name of the day. Finally, I hit upon what I think is the solution to this dilemma; for in examining the Providence school directories which were published every other year or so during the period, I found that the principal of the Slate Avenue School during the period of Lovecraft's attendance there (1898–1903, with some interruptions) was none other than one Abbie A. Hathaway. I do not know whether consultation of the full text of Lovecraft's letter to Kleiner—when that becomes available to researchers—will bear me out, but I suspect that referring to his troubles with "Abbie," Lovecraft was referring to his doubtless somewhat exaggerated career as a "bad boy" under the tutelage of none other than Abbie A. Hathaway (1852–1917) of the Slater Avenue School.[113]

In another letter—I believe the letter to Helen Sully of December 4, 1935—Lovecraft speaks of having a photograph of the Slater Avenue graduating class of 1903 in his possession. This is interesting, since in my own work with Lovecraft's astronomical articles in the Providence newspapers, I found that these newspapers—especially the *Providence Evening Tribune*—would about May or June of each year begin to print photographs of the graduating classes of even the grammar schools in Providence. Since so many of the photographs which Lovecraft possessed were evidently lost following Mrs. Gamwell's death, I think it would be well worth the time of a future researcher interested particularly in Lovecraft's life to search the newspapers of May and June of 1903 for a possible Slater Avenue graduation photograph. Aside from the various family photographs obtained from relatives of Lovecraft's by Philip Jack Grill and R. Alain Everts, this photograph—if extant in published form in one of the Providence newspapers of May or June 1903—might be one of the very earliest photographs of Lovecraft in existence.[114] Since Lovecraft did not graduate from Hope Street High School, he is of course not depicted in the photographs of the graduating class or any of the yearbooks of that institution between 1904 and 1910. There is one individual in the photograph of the graduating class of 1908 who looks quite a bit like Lovecraft—but since Lovecraft's name is not among the names of the graduating seniors for that year and in addition official records—this according to Mr. Everts—establish that he did not graduate, it is evidently not he. His name occurs only in the 1907 yearbook, in which he is listed as a member of the sophomore class; and Mr. Everts tells me that this was indeed the last year he attended high school. (He also appears—as H.P.L.—as a character in the "class play" of that year—where he is caricatured as an overly erudite scientific *wunderkind*. In my own article on this subject in the first issue of the *Dark Brother-*

hood Journal [June 1971], however, I regret to say that the reproduction of the portion of the "class play" in which HPL occurs is marred by several [obvious] misprints and that I carelessly put down the name of the English teacher who questioned the authorship of one of his astronomical essays [until he presented it to her in printed form under his own byline] as Mrs. Baker, when, according to his long autobiographical letter to Kleiner [*SL* 1.39; *RK* 75], it was Mrs. Blake.)

9. The "Lost Lovecrafts"

In our discussion of the provenance of Lovecraft's literary manuscripts, we quoted Rheinhart Kleiner to the effect that he expected that a great body of unpublished fiction would be found among the effects of his late friend; and that these discoveries would increase significantly Lovecraft's literary reputation. If we ignore for the moment Lovecraft's magnificent letters, however, it is evident that what Kleiner envisioned did not happen at all. True enough, the great bulk of Lovecraft's papers came to be deposited and preserved at Brown University; but the number of really major Lovecraftian works which came to light posthumously in this collection and in others was actually very small. *The Case of Charles Dexter Ward*, *The Dream-Quest of Unknown Kadath*, "The Shunned House"—this is about the totality of major fiction from Lovecraft's pen which saw its first publication only posthumously. (Most of the lesser stories published in *Weird Tales* following Lovecraft's death had been published years before in amateur magazines.) Aside from the three major works which received first publication posthumously, only a very few extremely minor fictional pieces were found among Lovecraft's papers to be published for the first time following his death—the fragments "The Book," "The Descendant," and "Azathoth," discovered by Barlow in March 1937 and first published in the second issue of his *Leaves*; the notes for *At the Mountains of Madness* and "The Shadow out of Time;" the discarded draught of "The Shadow over Innsmouth;" the outline of the story which Derleth wrote as "The Survivor;" the notes for "The Round Tower" and the supplementary "Other Notes" (first published in *Golden Atom*, winter 1943) which Derleth also used in part in writing *The Lurker at the Threshold* (1945); the very early fictional juvenilia published for the first time in *The Shuttered Room* (1959); the seemingly difficult-to-account-for short story "The Thing in the Moonlight" (first published in *Bizarre*, January 1941);[115] and that is about all. Perhaps the Commonplace Book, first published by the Futile Press in 1938, should also be included.

Admittedly, many Lovecraft stories and prose poems—some of which he considered to be repudiated—were rescued only from the most obscure amateur journals to be republished after Lovecraft's death—like "Nyarlathotep," "Ex Oblivione," "The Street," "Poetry and the Gods," "The Alchemist," and others—but they had in fact been *published* during Lovecraft's lifetime and were by-and-large recovered in printed form in collections of amateur journals. A few Lovecraft "stories"—like "The Wicked Clergyman" and, evidently, "The Very Old Folk"—were trumped up from his letters to correspondents and presented as posthumously published fiction following Lovecraft's death;[116] but the list of posthumous fiction never did receive the augmentation from Lovecraft's letter files that Kleiner predicted in 1937. The essential Lovecraft output remained what he had published—however obscurely—during his own lifetime. Various essays and minor poems discovered among his papers in the John Hay Library were the bulk and essence of the material which received its true first publication following Lovecraft's death, in the Arkham House volumes of his work and in other places.

What then, one is tempted to ask, were the "lost Lovecrafts"—the stories and prose poems which he himself destroyed in dissatisfaction with his writing; the stories and prose poems which were actually printed in obscure amateur journals and remain still to be brought to light; the stories and prose poems which withered unpublished in the files of old amateur journalists until they perished of neglect. Of the third class, of course, we can say very little, except to remark Kleiner's statement that Lovecraft was customarily prodigally generous with his manuscripts, and that he may have sent many of these out in their original handwritten form, without making a copy for retention in his own files. For instance, we find in Lovecraft's letter to Kleiner of January 20, 1916 (*SL* 1.19; *RK* 29) that Lovecraft's amateur credential "The Alchemist" was to have appeared in a paper issued by George Schilling, but did not, and finally saw print only in the *United Amateur* for November 1915; when it is further remarked that the text of this story was evidently recovered for posthumous republication only from a printed copy of that issue of the *United Amateur* and that there is apparently no manuscript of "The Alchemist" in the principal collection of Lovecraft's papers in the John Hay Library, the precariousness of his amateur submissions becomes readily evident. One hardly suspects that a great many of Lovecraft's literary productions were so lost, for courtesy would have surely demanded the return of material left unpublished; but if as great a bulk of material as one imagines was sent out for submission in the form of one-of-a-kind holograph manuscripts, there must inevitably have been some loss.

One need only observe that the number of Lovecraft poems which have been found in amateur journals far exceeds the number of Lovecraft poems which are in manuscript in the John Hay Library, to conclude that Lovecraft sent out a great many of his amateur contributions in the form of one-of-a-kind holograph manuscripts. The alternative—that he kept typescript carbon copies and then destroyed them following amateur publication—does not make good sense. Lovecraft evidently destroyed the holograph manuscripts of most of his professionally published fiction upon publication simply because he deemed the holograph originals useless for the purpose of private circulation. To my knowledge, he did not destroy typescripts of his professionally published fiction upon publication. Convenience inevitably dictated that a great many of his amateur contributions flowed directly from his facile pen onto paper and into the mails in their original form.

Whether this presumptive loss of material involved any works which might properly be called "stories" is probably impossible to say; Lovecraft's amateur press essays and poems far outnumber his amateur press stories, and one presumes the same approximate ratio held for his contributions. Of course, with all of the steady work of Arkham House and of private researchers there will still never be found all of the countless files of letters Lovecraft sent out in twenty-five years of amateur activity. To judge from the published *Selected Letters*, the loss of very early letters—from 1914 until 1923—has evidently been the greatest and this, after all, represented the peak years of Lovecraft's amateur activity and correspondence. One surely can be confident that he did not allow to be lost without some effort at recovery any material which he himself then esteemed; but amidst such a prodigal outpouring of time and effort, some things, surely, we must presume, were lost. Thus, in effect, there will always be the possibility that an old trunk somewhere will be opened to find a thick file of Lovecraft letters containing unpublished or undiscovered literary works, albeit, we can probably be assured, of a very minor importance; that the story of the effects of Howard Davison which Harry Warner narrates in *All Our Yesterdays* will happen again in the future.[117] The game will evidently ever be afoot; and if the hopes for the discovery of something significant are uniformly dim, they will evidently yet be always present.[118]

Our second subdivision of material which was actually printed during Lovecraft's lifetime but is still unrecovered from the original (and presumably obscure) place of publication is nearly as difficult to discuss, Here at least we can afford to be somewhat more specific, however. Certainly, the testified incompleteness of all the amateur journalism collections consulted by Lovecraft bibliographers to date is some testimony itself in favor of the presumption that there may be at least some amateur press contributions by Lovecraft lurking in yet-undiscovered amateur journals. What with the high mortality one imagines such materials suffer in transference from one generation to the next, further bibliographical work on Lovecraft's amateur appearances assumes even greater importance for the coming decades. (George Wetzel, for instance, wrote me that some of his listings came from the review columns of the *United Amateur* and the *National Amateur*, and not from actual consultation of the amateur magazines cited, which were then not among the holdings of the Library of Amateur Journalism. Of course, Wetzel, like all good bibliographers, did make a concerted effort to "see" as many of the items which he listed as possible, and some of his listings were in addition confirmed by the research of the Australian ajay Leon Stone; but the scarcity of the rare issues of amateur magazines containing Lovecraft's contributions in publicly accessible collections again points out the need for a future Lovecraft bibliography coding its listings of Lovecraft's amateur appearances to the collections in which they were observed or to the review columns in which they were cited.)

As we have remarked earlier, Wetzel's research with the Library of Amateur Journalism in 1946 and 1951–1953 was crucial in recovering the text of a number of Lovecraft's stories of which he had apparently kept no manuscripts copies himself—"The Alchemist," "The Street," and "Poetry and the Gods" among them. Writing in his "The Research of a Biblio" (*HPL: Memoirs, Critiques, and Bibliographies*, 1955), Wetzel remarked upon his fortune in "stumbling across" Lovecraft's "Poetry and the Gods," written in collaboration with Anna Helen Crofts and under the pseudonym Henry Paget-Lowe"[119] and first published in the *United Amateur* for September 1920, and speculated that Lovecraft might simply have forgotten about the story when he composed the 1935 story list (evidently part of a letter to F. Lee Baldwin) which was used in compiling the Laney–Evans bibliography.

I would merely add to this, that it is also possible that Lovecraft had "repudiated" "Poetry and the Gods" at the time of the composition of his 1935 story-list and did not include it by his own choice. His letters were always full of his dissatisfaction with his earlier work; and I have myself seen several in which he referred to "Memory" and "Nyarlathotep" as repudiated and to "From Beyond" and "The Tree" as near-repudiated. Significantly, neither of the two chronologies of Lovecraft's fiction (in his own hand) which are catalogued in the Lovecraft Collection in the John Hay Library[120] contain any of his early, minor tales—"The Beast in the Cave," "The Alchemist," "Poetry and the Gods," "The Street," "Memory," "Nyarlathotep," "Ex Oblivione," "What the Moon Brings," "The Transition of Juan Romero." Lovecraft certainly did not "forget" the existence of all of these stories; evidently, he either considered them too minor for inclusion in a listing of his literary production or wished to renounce then as part of this production. "The Transition of Juan

Romero," at least, he considered firmly repudiated; and although he presented Barlow with the original manuscript in return for a typed copy, he did not permit the publication of the story during his own lifetime. (It was first published in *Marginalia*.) The fact that Lovecraft evidently retained only the published copies of most of these early, minor stories—indeed, as we have remarked, he may very well have submitted the only extant manuscripts to their publisher—and that he did not later prepare typescript copies for circulation among his friends is further evidence that he in fact wished to renounce the bulk of these stories. Nevertheless, it is hardly an act of literary grave-robbing to strive to recover as many as possible of the words Howard Lovecraft ever set down in print; as Max Brod remarked with regard to Kafka's injunction that his novels—*The Trial, The Castle,* and *Amerika*—be destroyed without publication, the author is not always the best judge of his own work. Winfield Townley Scott took this observation a step further by remarking in his essay "A Parenthesis on Lovecraft as a Poet" that, in fact, *everything* written by an author as unique and important within his own genre as Lovecraft is worth attention.

Indeed, it was Wetzel's fate to see at least one, and possibly more, early stories by Lovecraft in his research with the Library of Amateur Journalism, which are seemingly still unreprinted today. The most famous of these was "Life and Death," which Wetzel still recalls as a "prose poem" evidently based upon the entry in Lovecraft's Commonplace Book:

> (27) *Life and Death*. Death—its desolation & horror—bleak spaces—sea bottom—dead cities. But Life—the greater horror! Vast unheard-of reptiles & leviathans—hideous beasts of prehistoric jungle—rank slimy vegetation—evil instincts of primal man—Life is more horrible than death.

According to his essay "The Research of a Biblio," Wetzel found and recorded this prose poem in his original research with the Library of Amateur Journalism in Philadelphia in 1946; then through misadventure or malice—perhaps it is better not to revive the subject at this late date—he lost the sheet of his research containing his reference for "Life and Death." He feels that the loss of some of his listings for 1920–1921, most of which he recovered in his later visits to the Franklin Institute in 1951–1953, is made evident by the paucity of listings for those years in his chronological listing of Lovecraft's amateur press works which was published in the first and second issues of John Murdock's fanzine *Vagabond*.[121] Nevertheless, despite his purposeful and thorough searching during his return visits to the Library of Amateur Journalism in 1951–1953, Wetzel was never able to recover the prose poem "Life and Death."[122] It is listed as "written 1920" in his *Vagabond* bibliography; with a query as to its place of publication; and is listed in virtually the same manner in his 1955 bibliography. The Chalker bibliography and later compilations omit the listing.

Now, all of these assertions regarding the existence of "Life and Death" would be simply assertions of Mr. Wetzel were it not for a very singular fact, and that is, that in the general alphabetical listing of the Laney–Evans bibliography (1943) there occurs a listing of "Life and Death" which dates the story as ca. 1920 and further suggests that it may have been both "repudiated" and "unpublished." What makes this listing singularly important is that it is demonstrably completely unrelated to Wetzel's first listing of "Life and Death" in his 1951 bibliography in *Destiny*; for, writing in the introduction to his chronological bibliography in *Vagabond* I, Wetzel stated (p. 42):

> Sometime in 1951 or 1952 I heard that Bill Evans and Francis Laney had compiled a Lovecraft biblio in 1943. Copies of it were not to be bought or found. A letter to Laney requesting some information on it and also a statement of my own efforts in producing a Lovecraft biblio went unanswered. Laney had similarly ignored my first Lovecraft biblio when I suggested it as an item to run in ACOLYTE. In fact, I never have received any sort of a letter from him regarding any of my Lovecraft research that I wrote and told him about.[123]
>
> However, his collaborator on their 1943 biblio, Bill Evans, turned out to be very friendly and generous once I located him. Prior to that I was able to buy a copy of their biblio, (a few items of which appear in this one) though the most of their biblio I had to uncover myself in Philadelphia. The Laney–Evans biblio is strong on professionally published stories and only gives a scattering of his poetry and essays in the amateur press. My own work, then, fills this gap.

What is important in these remarks of Wetzel's is of course the establishment of the fact that Wetzel had had no access to the bibliography compiled by Laney and Evans when he first found "Life and Death" in the Library of Amateur Journalism in 1946; and, moreover, that he had likely still not seen the Laney–Evans bibliography at the time of the first publication of his bibliography, containing the listing of "Life and Death" without place of publication, in *Destiny* in 1951. (Even if his purchase of the Laney–Evans bibliography preceded the first publication of his research in *Destiny* in 1951, his first manuscript bibliography of Lovecraft's amateur press works—including "Life and Death"—had been circulating in fandom in search of a publisher for years. Indeed, even under the fantastic assumption that a proven researcher like

Wetzel had fabricated a listing for a Lovecraft story which did not exist, he could hardly have made a worse choice, according to the Laney–Evans bibliography, for there it was speculated that "Life and Death" was both unpublished and repudiated—so that the only logical place to have searched for it would have been in Lovecraft's papers in the John Hay Library in Providence. Wetzel's listing of "Life and Death" in an unknown amateur magazine of 1920 runs against the suggestions of the Laney–Evans bibliography regarding the story.)[124]

Nor are these two independent listings—Laney–Evans and Wetzel—all the evidence we can adduce for the existence of "Life and Death," although most of the rest of what I have been able to accumulate is purely circumstantial. One might first note Lovecraft's great burst of weird fiction-writing in 1919–1921, which he never thereafter equaled, at least in published stories. It is perfectly reasonable that among this large number of stories—many of which he later chose to withdraw from circulation and renounce—there were some which have yet eluded detection in collections of amateur journals. (Indeed, what is probably most likely is that there are some in amateur journals which are not in any of the collections yet consulted by Lovecraft bibliographers.) Moreover, the theme of "Life and Death," as given in the entry in Lovecraft's Commonplace Book—which seems to me very reminiscent of Gustav Aschenbach's Dionysian dream of the jungle in Thomas Mann's *Death in Venice*—a work which Lovecraft probably would have condemned yet felt some sympathy for—is very similar in its misanthropy to other Lovecraft stories of the period—the horror of the discovery of tainted (jungle) ancestry in "Arthur Jermyn," the senseless cruelty of the cat-killer in "The Cats of Ulthar," the terrible instincts of the aged recluses in "The Picture in the House" and "The Terrible Old Man," the horror of murdered idealism and purity in "Celephaïs" and "The Tree," and perhaps, most particularly, the stylized vision in "Memory" (1919) of the primal "jungle" world after the demise of man in his own folly:

> And within the depths of the valley, where the light reaches not, move forms not meant to be beheld. Rank is the herbage on each slope, where evil vines and creeping plants crawl amidst the stones of ruined palaces, twining tightly about broken columns and strange monoliths, and heaving up marble pavements laid by forgotten hands. And in trees that grow gigantic in crumbling courtyards leap little apes, while in and out of deep treasure-vaults writhe poison serpents and scaly things without a name.

Indeed, the primal vision here is virtually the same as that of the "Life and Death" entry: transferred from the depths of the ocean to the primal jungle. One might see further reflections of the theme in the eerie underwater netherworld in "The Temple" (1920). The final piece of circumstantial evidence for Wetzel's discovery, however, is the dating of the "Life and Death" entry in Lovecraft's Commonplace Book—1919. (Lovecraft evidently dated the entries in his Commonplace Book when he presented the original manuscript to Barlow in 1934. This original manuscript, now in the Lovecraft Collection in the John Hay Library, contains Lovecraft's datings.) Thus, Lovecraft set down his basic idea for "Life and Death" at a time well agreeable with his presumptive writing of Wetzel's fugitive prose poem in time for publication in an amateur magazine of 1920. Considering all of the evidence—the early listing of "Life and Death" in Laney–Evans in 1943, Wetzel's statement of his discovery in 1946, and the circumstantial evidence relating to the "Life and Death" theme—it is quite evident that further search for "Life and Death" itself and for evidence relating to it will be a worthy task for Lovecraftian researchers until the question is finally definitively resolved. As Wetzel remarked in his "The Research of a Biblio," such searching could well lead to the discovery of additional material—including minor stories and prose poems—still buried in obscure amateur magazines. If collections of amateur magazines other than the already-researched Library of Amateur Journalism are brought into play, one feels particularly confident of this eventuality. Lovecraftian scholarship and research could not help but be significantly enriched by such discoveries.[125]

10. Lovecraft in Rhode Island newspapers

The range of material by Lovecraft which remains unrecovered from its original place of publication—unrecovered in the sense of being unnoted by bibliographers as well as being un-reprinted—is certainly not limited to the material which he had published in amateur press association magazines, however. In connection with the appearance of the poem "The Marshes at Ipswich" in the *National Magazine* of Boston, we discussed at some length the possibilities for the discovery of further early contributions by Lovecraft to professional magazines—principally, published letters of comment. The remaining significant source for further discoveries of printed material by Lovecraft is I think the newspaper press. I hope myself to have made a small contribution to this endeavor with a listing of those astronomical articles by Lovecraft which I found in the *Pawtuxet Valley Gleaner* for 1906, the Providence *Evening Tribune* from 1906 until 1908, and the *Providence Evening News* from 1914 until 1918—scheduled for ultimate publication in *Nyctalops*—but this research is demonstrably incomplete even for Lovecraft's astronomical *articles alone*. (Although these astronomical articles are admittedly among the least interesting aspects of Lovecraft's work, they contain reflections of his early attitudes and interests which are valuable for the completist. Indeed, by the time his column concluded in the *Evening News* in 1918, Lovecraft was customarily utilizing two or three full columns of newspaper type and bringing to bear all kinds of poetical and mythological allusions for his principal subject material—the astronomical ephemera for the month.)

For instance, in researching Lovecraft's astronomical articles in the *Evening Tribune*, I found far more of these articles missing from the period around the end or the beginning of the month—the period when a column of monthly ephemera would naturally appear—than it seems reasonable to assume considerations of space forced out. This in spite of Lovecraft's statement to Kleiner in his letter of November 16, 1916 (*SL* 1.40; *RK* 75), that he ultimately transferred his articles to the *Evening News* because the editors there allowed him all the space he desired. In some of these instances, the absence of an article may be explained by the fact that the first of the month fell on a Sunday; and I am still not sure whether the *Evening Tribune* published a Sunday edition. The thought also occurs to me that for at least part of this period (1906–1908) there was also published a *Morning Tribune*, which I did not consult in my work; perhaps some of the articles which I did not find appeared only in those pages.[126] In addition, Lovecraft customarily stated to correspondents that his astronomical articles appeared in the *Tribune* and the *Evening News* between 1906 and 1918; however, my own searching failed to reveal any articles in the *Evening Tribune*, at least, after June 1, 1908, or any articles in the *Evening News* before January 1, 1914. This of course does not contradict Lovecraft's statement; indeed, as we have seen, he was wont to cast his childhood and youth in the most favorable possible light in order—one imagines—to compensate for their sorely felt disappointments. His statement regarding his astronomical columns, which would seem to imply a steady stream between 1906 and 1916 and yet does not specifically state so, is to my way of thinking characteristic of this frame of mind.

In addition, from a biographical point of view, the years 1908–1916, during which Lovecraft's astronomical articles seemingly disappear, were undoubtedly among the darkest in his life. He had suffered a nervous collapse which prevented him from finishing high school or matriculating at Brown University, as he had desired; he had failed to make a go of correspondence courses or to make any visible progress toward a career; and, in addition, his uncle Edwin, we presume, had lost a good deal of his mother's remaining money in a financial speculation in 1911. Lovecraft's sense of failure and disappointment during this period must have been immense. In addition, researcher R. Alain Everts once wrote me that Sarah Susan Lovecraft had imparted to friends unfavorable comments about her son considerably stronger than her remarks to Clara Hess (see "Lovecraft's Sensitivity," *LR* 32, 34–35) concerning his appearance, and considering her later preoccupation with her financial worries ("His Own Most Fantastic Creation," *LR* 15–16), one can hardly doubt that at least some of these unfavorable comments concerned her son's economic uselessness. Her remark to the psychiatrist at Butler Hospital concerning her sacrifices on behalf of "a poet of the very highest order," as recorded by Scott in his admirable "His Own Host Fantastic Creation," bespeak a relationship alternating between overwhelmingly possessive adoration and bitter condemnation and rejection.)

Nevertheless, unless a clearer statement by Lovecraft regarding his articles in the *Tribune* and the *Evening News* can be discovered, it may well behoove future researchers to do more searching in the *Tribune* (including the *Morning Tribune*) and the *Evening News* for the missing years 1908–1914.[127] That Lovecraft was not totally dormant as a newspaper contributor during this period is indicated by the appearance of his poem "Providence in 2000 A.D." in the *Evening Bulletin* for March 4, 1912. (Yes, Providence and its environs had many newspapers in those days; in fact, according to a recent survey, Providentians are still among the most diligent newspaper readers in the nation, although the surviving dailies have shrunk to two, the *Journal* and *the Evening Bulletin*.[128] The best collection of all the relevant newspapers—on microfilm—resides with the Rhode Island Historical Society.)

In contrast to the articles in the *Evening Tribune*, however, the articles in the *Evening News* appeared with clockwork regularity near the end of the month, so that I believe I have in my listings all the regular articles which appeared between January 1, 1914, and May 2, 1918. However, clearly, I did not get all of the astronomical material which Lovecraft had published in the *Evening News*—in fact, I omitted what are probably the most entertaining articles. While I was working with the Lovecraft Collection in the John Hay Library, I found a letter from Lovecraft to E. Hoffmann Price, dated February 15, 1933, which spoke of a heavy newspaper campaign which he had undertaken against a local defender of astrology in 1914 (*SL* 4.153). Now this statement confused me, since none of Lovecraft's regular astronomical articles for the *Evening News* for 1914 seemed to have the character of an antiastrological campaign. Embarrassingly enough, I eventually found the answer to my confusion in Lovecraft's letter to Moe of December 8, 1914, the second letter in the *Selected Letters*:

> Recently a quack named Hartmann, a devotee of the pseudo-science of Astrology, commenced to disseminate the usual pernicious fallacies of that occult art through the columns of *The News*, so that in the interest of true Astronomy I was forced into a campaign of invective and satire. I began seriously, with *Science versus Charlatanry*, which I followed up with *The Falsity of Astrology*, but eventually the stupid persistence of the modern Nostradamus forced me to adopt ridicule as my weapon. I thereupon went back to my beloved age of Queen Anne for a precedent, and decided to emulate Dean Swift's famous attacks on the astrologer Partridge, conducted under the non de plume of Isaac Bickerstaffe (or Bickerstaff—I have seen it spelled both ways). Accordingly I published a satirical article wherein I gave with an air of solemn gravity the most nonsensical collection of wild prophecies that my brain could conceive; the whole entitled *Astrology and the Future*, and signed Isaac Bickerstaffe, Jr." I there "predicted" the end of the world by an explosion of internal gases in the year 4954. Hartmann scarce

knew whether or not to take me seriously, and kept up his mountebank performances, so I prepared another Bickerstaffe paper whose ridicule should become more open toward the end. In this final effort, *Delavan's Comet and Astrology*, I explained how the human race shall be preserved after the destruction of the earth, by transportation to the planet Venus! Even the obtuse intellect of the charlatan must have discovered the sarcastic nature of this ponderous prophecy, for he has now quietly ceased to inflict his false notions on a gullible public.

I hope some future Lovecraft bibliographer will dig out the exact references for this series of articles for us—they certainly sound to be Lovecraft's most amusing astronomical writing and might make a fine specialist booklet of the same kind which Sam Moskowitz suggested for Lovecraft's *Argosy–All Story* letters. (Perhaps one would want to include the responses of Lovecraft's opponent Hartmann, just as Moskowitz suggested that the responses of Lovecraft's opponents John Russell & Co. be included in the booklet which he suggested. These exchanges might also make good material for the announced *Miscellaneous Writings* from Arkham House.)[129]

In addition, of course, Lovecraft's letter to Moe yields us yet another published pseudonym of Lovecraft—that of "Isaac Bickerstaffe, Jr.," used on at least two published articles, "Astrology and the Future" and "Delavan's Comet and Astrology," published in the *Providence Evening News* circa October 1914.[130] Even this is not the end of the possible confusion concerning Lovecraft's astronomical articles, however. With regard to his contributions to the *Pawtuxet Valley Gleaner* (a rural, Phenix, West Warwick, Rhode Island weekly newspaper which began in the 1870s), Lovecraft wrote to Moe on January 1, 1915 (*SL* 1.9):

> In August, 1906, I commenced a series of monthly astronomical articles in *The Providence Tribune*, and began to contribute miscellany to *The Pawtuxet Valley Gleaner*, a country paper which my mother's family had taken years before when they lived in Greene. Later I changed my monthly articles from *The Tribune* to *The News* (where I obtained more favourable space) and was deprived of my other medium through its failure and discontinuance.

Later, on November 16, 1916, he wrote to Kleiner (*SL* 1.40; *RK* 75):

> During 1906, 1907, & 1908 I flooded the *Pawtuxet Valley Gleaner* with my prose articles. This rural paper was the oracle of that section of the country from which my mother's family had originally come, & was taken for old times' sake in our household. The name "Phillips" is a magic word in Western Rhode Island, & the *Gleaner* was more than willing to print & feature anything from Whipple V. Phillips's grandson. Only the failure of the *Gleaner* put an end to my activity in its columns.

Now, working from the microfilm in the Rhode Island Historical Society Library, I found astronomical articles by Lovecraft in nearly every weekly issue of the *Gleaner* from July 27, 1906 until December 28, 1906. His first six articles were featured on the first page, just as Lovecraft said in writing to Kleiner. However, the mystery is that the microfilm file of the *Gleaner* at the Historical Society stopped with the end of 1906 and that a telegraphic inquiry to all Rhode Island libraries and a consultation of all appropriate reference books failed to uncover any issues for 1907, 1908. The Reference Department of the Providence Public Library, which assisted me in my inquiry, wrote that it was probably likely that Lovecraft was mistaken in his memory of the dates for which his articles had appeared in the *Gleaner* and that the paper had indeed ceased publication in 1906; but I was never able personally to ascertain that this was so. I feel, however, that this information is very probably still ascertainable—perhaps from the files of another rural paper like the *Pawtuxet Valley Times* if not from the files of the *Gleaner* itself—and I hope that Lovecraftian researchers will eventually investigate the matter to settle the question of whether the record of Lovecraft's articles in the *Gleaner* is complete. For myself, I lean heavily toward the opinion that Lovecraft was mistaken in his citation of dates to Kleiner. The Champlin Memorial Library in West Warwick, Rhode Island, which possesses the principal file of original copies of the *Gleaner* in existence, has all the issues from the inception of the paper until the end of 1906, and it seems little likely to me that the Library would have then ceased to take the paper if it had continued.

However, there is the opposing evidence of F. Lee Baldwin's small section of the Laney–Evans bibliography, which indicates that Lovecraft had astronomical articles in the rural press in 1906–1907. If this dating is in fact correct, however, I myself would lean toward the view that Lovecraft's astronomical articles continued in some other rural weekly after the presumptive failure of the *Gleaner* at the end of 1906—this despite the seeming indication in Lovecraft's letter to Moe of January 1, 1915 (*SL* 1.9) that the Gleaner was his only "other medium" during the period his astronomical articles appeared in the *Providence Tribune* (1906–1908). Certainly, Lovecraft's statement in two places—in his letter to Kleiner and in the presumptive letter to Baldwin upon which his section of the Laney–Evans bibliography was based—that his astronomical articles in the rural press persisted beyond the end of 1906 is sufficient ground for at least some further bibliographical search in 1907, 1908. Only another, more definitive reference in a Lovecraft letter will probably resolve the matter for sure, but in the meantime bibliographers might have a go at the *Pawtuxet Valley Times* and other rural papers for 1907, 1908. (While bibliographical search is certainly no pleasantry, the rural press of the day as typified by the *Gleaner* is delightful to read today, and I am sure that any prospective bibliographer would rapidly find himself enthralled by far more than the search for unknown Lovecraftiana.)

To carry our discussion of Lovecraft's astronomical articles to a conclusion, however, we ought also to mention the frequent reference which has been made to the appearance of these articles in the *Providence Journal*. For instance, on pp. 91–92 of *HPL: A Memoir*—which Eric Carlson kindly copied for me—August Derleth attributes the piece "Does Vulcan Exist?" to the *Journal* for 1906, despite his earlier statement on p. 12 that Lovecraft contributed his astronomical articles to the *Tribune* during that period.[131] Even the prestigious Wetzel–Briney bibliography (*LCL* 7.42) attributes one of Lovecraft's astronomical series to the *Providence Evening Journal* beginning January 1, 1914, when the bibliographers surely mean the *Providence Evening News*. Might, however, Lovecraft have contributed astronomical articles to the *Journal* in addition to the series and individual articles in the *Tribune* and the *Evening News* mentioned in his letters? Certainly, I cannot claim to recognize the piece "Does Vulcan Exist?" as an extract from any of the columns which I saw in those places; however, my memory does not allow me to say with any confidence at all that such a discussion did not occur in one of those columns. (The piece reprinted in *HPL: A Memoir* is certainly too short to constitute the full text of any of the columns which I found.)

The evidence for the possibility of such articles, indeed, seems to be quite slim and circumstantial—barring the discovery of a definitive statement in Lovecraft's own letters, Now, Lovecraft's mentor in his youthful dedication to astronomy was Professor Winslow Upton (1860–1914) of Brown University, who introduced young HPL to Percival Lowell following a lecture in Sayles Hall of Brown University in 1907 (see Lovecraft to Kleiner, February 19, 1916, *SL* 1.21–22; *RK* 32). The connection between Lovecraft and Professor Upton is further verified in Lovecraft's astronomical juvenilia, preserved in the Lovecraft Collection in the John Hay Library, which mention his visits to Brown's Ladd Observatory, and in later letters. After Lovecraft failed to matriculate at Brown University in 1908–1909, however, he ceased to visit the facilities at Brown. As he wrote to Kleiner on December 4, 1918 (*SL* 1.78; *RK* 152):

> I no more visit the Ladd Observatory or various other attractions at Brown University. Once I expected to utilise them as a regularly entered student, and some day perhaps control some of them as a faculty member. But having known them with this "inside" attitude, I am today unwilling to visit them as a casual outsider and non-university barbarian and alien.

Presumably, he met Professor Upton seldom after this date. Near the end of his life, Lovecraft did relent to some degree and began to attend lectures at Brown University once more; a letter to E. Hoffmann Price of October 31, 1936, speaks of his attendance at a session of an amateur astronomy club at Brown.[132] The same letter also mentions the recent death of Frank Seagrave (1860–1934), a longtime Rhode Island amateur astronomer who had had his own observatory and who is also mentioned once in Lovecraft's astronomical juvenilia. Thus, Seagrave may also have had some personal role in encouraging Lovecraft's early interest in astronomy. Of course, the antique astronomy books which Lovecraft's maternal grandmother Rhoby Alzada (Place) Phillips (1827–1896) had used at the Lapham Seminary in North Scituate, Rhode Island, in the 1840s were his first inspiration.

Professor Upton, who had directed the Ladd Observatory from its foundation in 1891 and served as Chairman of the Astronomy Department at Brown from 1884, died suddenly on January 8, 1914, and his obituary in the *Providence Journal* for the following day gives a generous outline of his career. Among other information, the obituary reveals that Professor Upton conducted a monthly astronomical column for the *Providence Journal* from 1893 until his death—information enough, certainly, to make us suspect that Professor Upton may have had a considerable role in arranging for Lovecraft's similar articles in the *Tribune* (1906–1908). Whether he may have encouraged Lovecraft in addition to contribute any articles to the *Journal* is a question which will likely wait some time for a definitive answer. Certainly, Lovecraft would have had no regular astronomical series in the *Journal* between 1906 and 1914, since Professor Upton was then himself conducting the monthly astronomical column there. Nor do I think it very likely that Lovecraft could have succeeded Professor Upton in the conduct of the column following the latter's death in January 1914, since Lovecraft had by then already begun his monthly column for the *Journal's* competitor, the *Evening News*. (I searched for astronomical columns in the *Journal* following professor Upton's death, and the first one I found was "Planets and Stars for May" by C. H. Currier in the May 1, 1914 issue.)

There is nothing in all of this to say that Lovecraft made no contributions as astronomical material to the *Journal*, however. Unfortunately, Lovecraft does not seem to have saved a complete file of his astronomical articles—or if he did, there is no such file today in the John Hay Library. Thus, we must rely principally upon Lovecraft's statements in his letters to lead us to his astronomical articles; and perhaps a letter will ultimately be found which will completely clarify the matter of these articles. With specific reference to August Derleth's attribution of "Does Vulcan Exist?" to the *Journal*, a future bibliographer might well seek clues in the Derleth Papers at the Wisconsin State Historical Society to the origin of this piece. It seems likely to me that if "Does Vulcan Exist?" is not represented in the Lovecraft Collection in the John Hay Library, then it was likely sent to Derleth by Lovecraft himself or some correspondent of Lovecraft's.[133]

There is ample indication, however, that Lovecraft's astronomical articles—perhaps the least interesting facet of his work for the general reader—are not the only material which remains yet uncovered in Providence newspapers. We have remarked already several times upon the publication of "Providence in 2000 A.D." in the *Evening Bulletin* for March 4, 1912; and there is little doubt that Lovecraft followed this initial appearance of one of his poems in print with many others in the pages of local newspapers. Lovecraft bibliographers have already noted "An Elegy on Franklin Chase Clark, M.D." in the *Evening News* for April 29, 1915; "The Beauties of Peace" in the same newspaper for June 17, 1916; "An Elegy on Phillips Gamwell, Esq." in the same newspaper for January 5, 1917; and "The Volunteer" in the same newspaper for February 1, 1918. In addition, as we have already noted, "The Messenger," "East India Brick Row," and five of the "Fungi" were printed in the *Providence Journal* in 1929–1930.

However, this is hardly the full bulk of Lovecraft's newspaper verse. In connection with my own bibliographical research on Lovecraft's astronomical articles, I uncovered at least five additional poems by Lovecraft in the pages of the *Evening News*: "Ode for July Fourth, 1917" (July 3, 1917); "Autumn" (November 5, 1917); "A Winter Wish" (January 2, 1918); "March" (March 1, 1918);" and "Ver Rusticum" (April 1, 1918). Now all of these poems were also printed in the amateur press, as one can readily ascertain from the Chalker bibliography; but the really important observation to make is that all five turned up completely by chance in my search for Lovecraft's regular astronomical articles. (In addition, I found at least four Lovecraft poems embodied in the text of his astronomical articles; one of these, published within his "August Skies" in the *Evening News* for August 1, 1916, I can identify as "On Receiving a Picture of Swans," also printed in *The Conservative* for January 1916; the others, however, I shall have to leave for other researchers to identify if they were published elsewhere. In addition, there is a cutting of the poem "Quinsnicket Park" in the Lovecraft vertical file at the Providence Public Library and a cutting of the poem "Brumalia" in the Lovecraft Collection in the John Hay Library—both of which seem to come from the *Evening News*, but for neither of which I have an exact date.)[134] Now, these five poems I discovered because they were printed on the same pages as various ones of Lovecraft's astronomical columns, which, because of their regularity, were fairly easy to find. Since so many poems appeared by chance in conjunction with Lovecraft's astronomical articles in the *Evening News*, however, one is compelled to ask how many more appeared elsewhere in the files of the *Evening News*—and other Providence newspapers—from 1912 on. The Wetzel–Briney bibliography (1955), to my knowledge, is the only one containing a statement regarding Lovecraft's newspaper verse (*LCL* 7.22):

> This index does not include poems published in newspapers, of which there were a considerable number, especially in Lovecraft's earlier years. The majority of these were patriotic poems, or elegies on the deaths of friends, and appeared in *The Providence News*, and other local papers, ca. 1916–19.

The bibliographical search for further newspaper verse from Lovecraft's pen will undoubtedly be difficult, however, for the files of large dailies like the *Evening News* and the *Journal* are an entirely different matter than the files of a rural weekly like the *Gleaner*. Indeed, perhaps a general search for Lovecraft's newspaper verse—if is ever to be undertaken—should await the day when more files of Lovecraft's early letters—to friends like Maurice W. Moe, Rheinhart Kleiner, James F. Morton, and George Macauley—are available to researchers for the culling of references to such appearances.[135]

In view of the termination of Lovecraft's astronomical series in the *Evening News* in 1918, Wetzel–Briney's date of 1919 is probably a good termination date for intensive searching of the files of the *Evening News*. By the twenties, Lovecraft seems to have narrowed his reading of the local papers to the *Providence Journal*, insofar as one can judge from occasional reference in his letters. (Although Sam Moskowitz speculates that Lovecraft may have continued to read the Munsey fiction magazines after 1920, I do not believe that he did so for long. By the thirties, he would buy only *Weird Tales* from the stands. Robert E. Howard and other writers of his circle sometimes sent him copies of other magazines in which their work had appeared for his reading.) So that the *Providence Journal* is probably the likeliest place to search for Lovecraft contributions in the 1920s and beyond.[136] Although Winfield Townley Scott believed his list of Lovecraft contributions to *Journal* in the fall 1944 issue of the *Acolyte* (2, No. 4) to be complete, as we have already seen, it omitted at least Lovecraft's first appearance in print of June 3, 1906, and his letter to the editor of October 10, 1926. Now, of course, Bertrand K. Hart's column "The Sideshow" (1929–1941) is the best place to look for Lovecraft contributions in the thirties, but I believe there is also good reason to suspect that the previous two decades of the *Journal* contained at least a small budget of material by Lovecraft.

One such incidence may well be Lovecraft's parody of T. S. Eliot's poem "The Waste Land," whose revision by the late Ezra Pound has—recently been in the limelight. Winfield Scott properly remarked in "His Own Most Fantastic Creation" that Lovecraft actually had much in common intellectually with Eliot, but, of course, being a traditionalist in verse, Lovecraft did not approve of "The Waste Land" as art. Writing to his friend Frank Belknap Long on May 26, 1923 (*SL* 1.230), Lovecraft gave his quick reactions to the poem as it had appeared in *Dial*. However, there has long been kicking around the story that Lovecraft went further than merely panning "The Waste Land" in his letters and in fact composed a parody of his own. I found the existence of this parody confirmed in Lovecraft's letter to J. Vernon Shea of March 24, 1933 (*SL* 4.159; *JVS* 126), wherein he simply stated that he had published a parody of "The Waste Land" in a newspaper. Now that is very little to go on, but if the matter ultimately comes down to a search of newspaper files, I would suggest that a start be made with the *Journal* for 1923. Useful preliminaries to launching such a search, however, would be a survey of the poetry file in the John Hay Library (where HPL's parody may well be in manuscript) and a search of Lovecraft's letters of the period for more direct references. (Indeed, since Lovecraft's letter to Long of May 26, 1923, was edited for inclusion in *Selected Letters*, the original letter may well contain the parody itself!) Certainly, the transcriptions of the Long file which were evidently made by Arkham House would be a vital place to start searching for references to HPL's parody.[137]

One last curiosity might be noted with regard to Lovecraft's undetected newspaper contributions. As we have seen above, Lovecraft described his contributions to the *Pawtuxet Valley Gleaner* as "miscellany" in his letter to Moe of January 1, 1915 (*SL* 1.9); in his later letter to Kleiner of November 16, 1916 (*SL* 1.40; *RK* 75), he spoke of flooding the *Gleaner* with his "prose articles." Furthermore, in "Some Notes on a Nonentity" (*MW* 560; *CE* 5.209), Lovecraft wrote that he had at last—when sixteen—broken into actual newspaper print with astronomical matter, contributing monthly articles on current phenomena to a local daily, and flooding the weekly rural press with more expansive miscellany.

Now there may seem to be some indication in Lovecraft's choice of words in these three instances that his contributions to the rural press (in which of course he included the *Gleaner*) extended beyond astronomical treatises. The idea that more general essays from Lovecraft's pen—or even perhaps examples of his early fiction, all of which he destroyed in 1908 with the exception of "The Beast in the Cave" and "The Alchemist" and a few of his very earliest productions[138]—might survive undetected in the files of obscure rural papers of 1906–1907–1908 is certainly an attractive one; but I do not consider it myself very likely. With regard to his early fiction, there is the dogmatism of his statement that only "The Beast in the Cave" and "The Alchemist" remained of his reasonably literate early work; certainly, one feels, had he had anything fictional published early on in the rural press he would certainly have recalled it in later letters when it had become apparent that fiction was to be his true creative vocation. After all, amateurs did manage to coax both "The Beast in the Cave" and "The Alchemist" out of Lovecraft for early publication. The possibility that Lovecraft published more general essays in the rural press seems at least a little more likely; but again I think the majority of the evidence is against this possibility. His clear intention in the statement in "Some Notes on a Nonentity," it seems to me, is to place his "more expansive miscellany" in the rural press under the general heading he starts out with—"astronomical matter." And, indeed, in the *Pawtuxet Valley Gleaner*, the only rural paper which has to date been mentioned as a source of Lovecraft material in his published letters, all of the material which I found was astronomical. (Of course, this does not necessarily represent all of the material by Lovecraft which appeared in the *Gleaner*.)

However, as Lovecraft remarks in "Some Notes on a Nonentity," the range of the *Gleaner* articles is indeed considerably wider than the range of the monthly columns dealing with astronomical ephemera which Lovecraft wrote for the *Tribune* and the *Evening News*; for along with articles descriptive of the monthly astronomical ephemera, Lovecraft also wrote for the *Gleaner* a number of articles of a more expository and general nature (albeit still astronomical): "Is Mars an Inhabited World?: Startling Theory of Prof. Lowell on the Subject" (September 7, 1906); "Are There Undiscovered Planets: Boundaries of our Solar System still Shrouded in Obscurity" (October 5, 1906—might this be the column from which the discussion which Derleth entitled "Does Vulcan Exist?" and attributed to the *Journal* was drawn?); "Can the Moon be Reached by Man?: Showing That the Trip to

Our Satellite, Heretofore Attempted Only in Fiction, May Be a Scientific Possibility" (October 12, 1906); and several other articles dealing with the moon, the sun, comets, the fixed stars, and clusters and nebulae with less attention-grabbing titles. These articles are all characteristic of the type of general astronomical exposition on elementary topics which Lovecraft also undertook in his hectographed *Rhode Island Journal of Astronomy*, and it is my belief that he intended the term "miscellany" to apply to them. Certainly, his attention in these years was singularly fixed upon astronomy—to the extent that even the school composition on which he was challenged (see Lovecraft to Kleiner, November 16, 1916, SL 1.39; *RK* 75) was on the subject of astronomy—on the planet Mars or the moon, according to his recollection to Kleiner. (The article which he handed in, only to be accused of plagiarism by Mrs. Blake until he presented her with the same article printed under his own byline, was thus probably one of the following four Gleaner articles: "Is Mars an Inhabited World" [September 7, 1906]; "Is There Life on the Moon?: Strange Revelations of Modern Science" [September 14, 1906]; "Can the Moon be Reached by Man" [October 12, 1906]; or "The Moon: A Brief Description of Our Satellite" [October 19, 1906].[139] Certainly, along with the astrological exchange which occurred in the *Evening News* in late 1914, these expository articles in the *Gleaner* would be among the most reprintable of Lovecraft's astronomical writings.)

In addition, of course, we have the statement in Baldwin's section of the Laney–Evans bibliography that Lovecraft contributed "astronomical articles" to the rural press in 1906–1907. Thus, the majority of the available evidence would seem to weigh in favor of the supposition that all of Lovecraft's 1906–1908 printed output dealt with astronomical subjects. Certainly there was no poem published until 1912 and almost as certainly no fiction until 1916.[140] The only remaining possibility would seem to be essays or editorial letters ranging beyond the field of astronomy. Whether any published essays of this more general character will ever be found, however, seems at the moment indeterminable to me. Certainly, Lovecraft's dating of his *Gleaner* articles as 1906, 1907, and 1908 in his letter to Kleiner and the statement regarding astronomical contributions to the local press in 1906–1907 in the Laney–Evans bibliography would seem to indicate that Lovecraft's astronomical articles in the rural press extended beyond his appearances in 1906 in the *Gleaner*. Although Lovecraft was most certainly in error when he stated to Kleiner that he had flooded the *Gleaner* with his prose articles in 1906, 1907, and 1906 (since the *Gleaner* almost certainly discontinued publication at the end of 1906), his references to the "weekly rural press" in "Some Notes on a Nonentity" and the reference to astronomical articles in the rural press in 1906–1907 in the Laney–Evans bibliography would seem to indicate at least some possibility that other rural papers did print some of Lovecraft's material (probably astronomical) in 1906–1908.

To argue the opposite side of the question, there is Lovecraft's statement in the aforementioned letter to Kleiner that the *Gleaner* was his "other medium" in 1906–1908 in addition to the *Tribune*—this would seem to indicate that the *Gleaner* was the sole rural paper in which he appeared during the period. Also there is Lovecraft's customary statement that his astronomical columns in the Providence newspapers extended from 1906 until 1918, whereas there appears to be a long gap from 1906 until 1914, to indicate that he may have been trying to embellish his production for the rural paper(s), both with respect to the number of rural newspapers in which he appeared and to the duration of his appearances. Certainly, in view of Lovecraft's own phenomenal memory, his 1906–1907–1908 dating of his *Gleaner* appearances is suspect in this manner. Ultimately, however, the question of whether a further bibliographical search would be justified seems to be indeterminable in lieu of further direct evidence.[141] Perhaps this will one day be forthcoming.

11. Lovecraft's destroyed and abandoned fiction

The last category of "lost" Lovecraft work which we set about to consider was the material which he himself destroyed in dissatisfaction or failed to develop. In general, it is very difficult to judge how many weird stories he may have destroyed in dissatisfaction, for in general, there seem to be very few references to abandoned work in the as-yet published Lovecraft letters and the Lovecraft letters available in the Lovecraft Collection in the John Hay Library. In the 1929 autobiographical memoir published under the title *E'ch-Pi-El Speaks* by Gerry de la Ree in December 1972, however, Lovecraft stated that he had retained roughly seven-eighths of his fictional output from his resumption of fiction-writing in June–July 1917 until the time of his writing in 1929 (p. 10). (In this memoir, Lovecraft dates "The Tomb" as June 1917 and "Dagon" as July 1917 [p. 9]; his later more formal autobiography "Some Notes on a Nonentity" [1933; *MW* 561; *CE* 5.209] dates both stories as July 1917.)

What with Lovecraft's grave dissatisfaction with his writing in later years, we can only presume that the proportion of destroyed stories rose in the years following the writing of his 1929 memoir. For instance, we know that Lovecraft destroyed one or two short versions of "The Shadow out of Time" before writing it out at the length which he felt the story deserved; and even at that, Barlow barely managed to coax the notebook in which he had written his final draught out of him for transcription. (In his *Marginalia* essay, Barlow stated that he had kept this notebook alone of all his Lovecraft manuscripts, as a keepsake of his friend [*LR* 362]. However, the notebook was not among Barlow's effects in Mexico at the time of his death [as it probably was at the time of his writing in 1944], and it is still among the few major Lovecraft literary manuscripts missing from the collection of Lovecraft's papers in the John Hay Library.)[142] The Barlow typescript was circulated among Lovecraft's friends for comment; Donald Wandrei (see "Lovecraft in Providence" in *SR*; *LR* 315) retyped the story and submitted it to *Astounding Stories* without Lovecraft's knowledge, and so it came to be published. (Wandrei's account of his submission of *At the Mountains of Madness* to *Astounding* at the same time, however, is contradicted by Lovecraft letters which state that agent Julius Schwartz submitted this story in Lovecraft's behalf.)

We know that at least several Lovecraft stories were nearly withdrawn from circulation and destroyed after adverse comment from some members of Lovecraft's circle of friends; among these were "The Dreams in the Witch House" (1932) and "The Haunter of the Dark." (1935). Thus, it is quite reasonable to assume that there were some Lovecraft stories which were repudiated and destroyed during this period. The majority of these he may have discarded as unsuccessful experiments without permitting them any circulation at all. One doubts that any of Lovecraft's correspondents would admit to seeing any stories which were subsequently destroyed, for fear that their own friendly criticism might be misinterpreted, but one rather imagines the category of stories repudiated and destroyed after circulation was very slim. Lovecraft hated typing with a passion and would hardly have gone to the trouble of typing anything with which he himself was sorely dissatisfied. (He did not allow his unpublished manuscripts to circulate in holograph form and several times stated to his correspondents that certain stories were unavailable for private circulation because of his lack of any typescript of them.) After all, he did submit and allow to be printed both "The Dreams in the Witch House" and "The Haunter of the Dark," despite the adverse criticism from members of his circle.[143]

Of course, any treatment of the subject of stories destroyed by Lovecraft without circulation must necessarily rely almost exclusively upon his letters and the reminiscences of friends, and, unfortunately, the references which appear in the as-yet published letters and the letters at the John Hay Library are few and far between. There seem to be virtually no references to approximate the one-eighth of his production which Lovecraft destroyed between 1917 and 1929 in the as-yet published letters and the letters at the John Hay Library—which is hardly an indication that we can expect many revelations in forthcoming volumes of *Selected Letters*.[144] If, however, I had to recommend one letter file to the particular attention of students of Lovecraft's work with regard to this subject, it would certainly be Lovecraft's letters to Clark Ashton Smith. Despite the fact that they never met personally, Smith was certainly Lovecraft's closest friend and confidant among professional writers, and those of his own letters to Lovecraft which survive in the files of the John Hay Library bespeak a lively interchange of information pertaining to planned and actual writing projects. Regrettably, the file of Smith's letters to Lovecraft at the John Hay Library seems to be woefully incomplete—for Lovecraft did not by custom save many letters—but, more importantly for our own considerations, the Lovecraft letters to Smith are still complete in the hands of bookseller and printer Roy A. Squires, who has stated in his catalogues that copies will be made of any letters sold separately so that the letter file itself will be kept complete. Hopefully, this file will someday be available to students of Lovecraft's work for the investigation of this question and many others.[145]

However, even with the available materials incomplete as they are, we can make the beginnings of a discussion of Lovecraft stories in our last category. In the first instance, we have Lovecraft's early stories (1896–1908), all of which—with the exception of "The Beast in the Cave," "The Alchemist," and "a few grotesque infantile experiments" (*E'ch-Pi-El Speaks*, p. 9)—perished by fire in 1908. Indeed, the very first story Lovecraft could remember is no longer extant. Writing to J. Vernon Shea on July 19, 1931, Lovecraft stated (*JVS* 25):

> As for my early stuff—the first story I can recall writing was called "The Noble Eavesdropper," & concerned a boy who overheard some horrible conclave of subterraneous beings in a cave. I no longer have it.

Yet, at least at a period somewhat earlier, Lovecraft seems to have had a considerable number of his "grotesque infant experiments" (say, those stories dating from 1896, the year of "The Noble Eavesdropper" and "The Little Glass Bottle," to 1902, the year of "The Mysterious Ship") still in his possession; witness his letter of August 27, 1917 to Rheinhart Kleiner ("By Post from Providence," *The Californian* 5, No. 1 [Summer 1937], p. 12; *RK* 114):

> I had wholly forgotten about the story "The Secret Cave," which you returned. I was a persistent fiction-writer in youth, and turned out rubbish of that sort by the bushel. A large proportion is still in my possession, hence one tale was scarcely to be missed. The next time I visit the attic I will bring down two or three "thrillers" of the vintage of 1899 or 1900—which I will send you for your amusement. I revelled in tragedy and sudden death, and had a marked partiality for graveyards and ghosts.

Now, at this point we are likely to puzzle sometime over the apparent contradiction between the "large proportion" of a "persistent" output which survived in Lovecraft's attic in 1917 and his statement in 1929 that all but a "few" of his earliest stories had perished in the general destruction of 1908. Yet, it is important to note that in all the other as-yet published discussions of his earliest output (Lovecraft's letter to Bernard Austin Dwyer of March 3, 1927 is another), Lovecraft never mentions any titles beyond the four which reside today with the John Hay Library and which were published in *The Shuttered Room*: "The Little Glass Bottle," "The Mysterious Ship," "The Mystery of the Grave-Yard," and "The Secret Cave." Indeed, these are the only four stories included in the transcript of his juvenilia (including poems)[146] which Lovecraft made in 1936 or thereabouts, today also at the John Hay Library. Thus by 1936, and probably by the time of his writing in 1929 also, Lovecraft evidently had no more than these four stories left of his earliest productions. Indeed, "The Noble Eavesdropper" is the only story in addition to these four which is specifically mentioned in the as-yet published *Selected Letters* volumes; and there may thus be some ground to cast doubt upon the accuracy of Lovecraft's 1917 statement to Kleiner. If, however, Lovecraft did indeed still have a considerable parcel—certainly, more than four—of his earliest stories in his attic at 598 Angell Street (where he shared a half-house with his mother), the best possible assumption—barring a further revelation from his letters—is probably that the stories were finally discarded in the expediency of one of his later moves. When his aunt Mrs. Clark moved from the half-house at 598 Angell Street to an apartment on Waterman Street in 1924, the disposition of a large bulk of accumulated effects was probably necessary. (Mrs. Clark, widowed in 1915, kept house for her nephew at 598 Angell Street from 1919 until his removal to New York in March 1924; indeed, she had been very much in and out of the house before then, although I believe she kept rooms elsewhere until at least 1920. She and her nephew were reunited at 10 Barnes Street in 1926, where Lovecraft had a large ground floor room and Mrs. Clark a large room on the floor immediately above.)

Indeed, even though Lovecraft's later removal to 66 College Street in May 1933 provided him with more spacious quarters than he had had at 10 Barnes Street, he still used the occasion to dispose of a large body of accumulated papers and unwanted books, perhaps in part to make room for some of the artifacts from Grandpa Phillips's 454 Angell Street house which he and Mrs. Gamwell rescued from a long repose in storage to decorate their new quarters. (Unhappily for students of Lovecraft, he undertook another such massive file-cleaning in 1936.) To state, as he did in his 1929 memoir, that all but a few of his "grotesque infant experiments" had perished in the 1906 holocaust may simply have been far easier than to go into all of the losses occasioned by his changing domestic fortunes. Although he certainly counted his early stories for little, Lovecraft did distinctly regret some of the other losses which he and his family incurred following the death of Whipple Phillips and was probably naturally reticent about them. His longing to recapture his grandfather's Angell Street house was probably more whimsy than anything else, but in Paul Cook's recounting of Lovecraft's resentment at finding some of the books which had formerly belonged to his personal library displayed for sale in a Providence bookshop there is a genuine note of bitterness (*LR* 108).

In any case, unless some of Lovecraft's correspondents were more neglectful about returning samples of his juvenile fiction than Kleiner was in 1917 (which instance might place some of Lovecraft's juvenile fiction in our first category), we probably have today all of his earliest work that we shall ever have.[147] In addition to the four stories in *The Shuttered Room*, the only titles we seem to have are those given under "fiction" in a listing of works offered for sale which Lovecraft appended to his small manuscript book *Poemata Minora*, vol. II (copied in his 1936 transcript of his juvenilia): "The Noble Eavesdropper," "Haunted House," "The Secret of the Grave" (= "The Mystery of the Grave-Yard"?), and "John, the Detective" (= "The Secret Cave or John Lees Adventure"?). Actually, of course, our richest source of information regarding Lovecraft's early intellectual interests are his own letters and autobiographical memoirs, written as an adult; however, even those slight juvenile stories which survive have their role in confirmation and elucidation of his later statements. One particularly wishes that "The Noble Eavesdropper" had survived, what with its importance as Lovecraft's very first fictional effort and its obvious parallel "The Beast in the Cave" and other, later Lovecraft stories dealing with hideous subterranean doings; perhaps also "The Haunted House," with its obvious parallel with the principal themes of Lovecraft's mature work. What we have of this earliest work is a small sample indeed—and probably unrepresentative—but at least it is Lovecraft and as such a significant tool in understanding the later development of the man and his work.[148]

Lovecraft's preoccupation with science as a teenager reduced the amount of time which he devoted to fiction-writing. He relates the circumstances succinctly in "Some Notes on a Nonentity" (*MW* 560; *CE* 5.209):

> It was while in high school—which I was able to attend with some regularity—that I first produced weird stories of any degree of coherence and seriousness. They were largely trash, and I destroyed the bulk of them when eighteen; but one or two probably came up to the average pulp level. Of them all I have kept only "The Beast in the Cave" (1905) and "The Alchemist" (1908). At this stage, most of my incessant, voluminous writing was scientific and classical, weird material taking a relatively minor place. Science had removed my belief in the supernatural, and truth for the moment captivated me more than dreams.

Indeed, the first burst of Lovecraft's juvenile scientific publications (including principally *The Rhode Island Journal of Astronomy* and *The Scientific Gazette*) in 1903–1904 could hardly have left him much time for fiction-writing. According to Lovecraft's more detailed letter to Bernard Dwyer of March 3, 1927 (*SL* 2.105–113), his teenage interests were dominated by scientific and classical subjects, just as he suggests in "Some Notes on a Nonentity." After pondering over the illustrations of "Philosophical and Scientific Instruments" in the back of *Webster's Unabridged Dictionary* at the age of eight, he first fixed his attentions upon chemistry in March 1899, setting up a laboratory in the basement of his grandfather's Angell Street home and producing the first number of *The Scientific Gazette* at that time. Then, in 1902, geography—and particularly the geography of the mysterious Antarctic region which was later mirrored in his novel *At the Mountains of Madness*—captured his principal interest, followed closely in 1903 by astronomy, which became his most enduring scientific love. The death of his grandfather on March 28, 1904, and the subsequent shock of the forced removal from 454 Angell Street wrought a brief depression during the summer of 1904; but in the fall, Lovecraft began high school, and the study of the Latin language revived the strong identification with classical antiquity which he had first experienced with his introduction to Greek and Roman mythology in 1895. Then, in 1905–1907, high school courses in physics and chemistry once again revived his interests in science; by April 1905, he had revived the dormant *Rhode Island Journal of Astronomy,* and by July 1906 he had made his debut with astronomical material in the newspaper press.

All of this certainly left only a small budget of time for fiction-writing. After, however, Lovecraft failed to proceed with high school, and thereafter there entered his life a dark depression and feeling of general worthlessness which was not fully dispelled until he found his first role in life as a member of the amateur journalism societies.[149] Certainly, one imagines, the holocaust which devoured the bulk of his teenage fiction in 1908 was one of the first manifestations of this long spell of depression; the apparent end of his astronomical articles in the *Tribune* in June 1908 was undoubtedly another. Both the *Rhode Island Journal of Astronomy* and *The Scientific Gazette* breathed their last in 1909; and Lovecraft's slim astronomical notebook for 1909–1915, described by David Keller in the third issue of the *Lovecraft Collector* (October 1949), bespeaks the diminution of his interest in the following years. One correspondence course in chemistry was apparently the extent of his efforts to pursue his formal education in those years. (R. Alain Everts wrote me that several early friends of Lovecraft recall his having attended either night school or extension courses at Brown University; but unfortunately no records were maintained for course work which did not lead to a degree.) Finally, however, literature began to reassert its place among Lovecraft's interests around 1911; but now his principal attention settled upon developing his skill as a poet. In this endeavor he was encouraged by his learned uncle Dr. Franklin Chase Clark (1847–

1915); and, as we have seen, first publication followed in the *Evening Bulletin* for March 4, 1912. Then finally, in 1913–1914, his role as one of the principals in a controversy in the letter departments of *Argosy* and *All-Story* brought him to the attention of Edward Francis Daas (1879–1962), a recruiter for the United Amateur Press Association, and on April 6, 1914, with his application for membership in UAPA, a completely new phase of Lovecraft's life ensued. However, during his first two and a half years in amateurdom, he remained solely a poet and essayist; even his credential, the story "The Alchemist" remained unpublished until November 1916. (The circumstances of how this came about are related in Lovecraft's letter to Kleiner of January 20, 1916, *SL* 1.19; *RK* 29.) This work drew the attention of W. Paul Cook, and at Cook's urging, Lovecraft at last found his true *métier* in the weird tale with the writing of "The Tomb" and "Dagon" in quick succession in June and July 1917. However, as August Derleth has remarked, the entire decade 1908–1917 produced no new fiction from Lovecraft's pen.[150] Thus, we must necessarily look back to Lovecraft's high school years (1904–1908) to find any evidence of his development as a fictioneer between the poles of his very earliest experiments (1896–1902) and the beginning of his mature work (1917).

There is really very little we can say about Lovecraft's teenage fictional production, beyond bringing forth the surviving examples, "The Beast in the Cave" (1905) and "The Alchemist" (1908). The creative growth evidenced by the differences between these two tales, however, makes clear that Lovecraft was hardly dormant as a fiction-writer during his high school years, even if scientific subjects occupied his principal attention. First and foremost, of course, we know that the popular fiction magazines of the era—the *Argosy*, *All-Story*, *Cavalier*, the *Black Cat*, *Golden Book*, and others—played a large role in Lovecraft's early reading, and that he inevitably imitated the tales of fantasy and scientific romance which he found in those pages in his early writing. Of course, his primary interest in the spectral and macabre had begun with his discovery of Edgar Allan Poe in 1898 or thereabouts (see Lovecraft to Dwyer, March 3, 1927, *SL* 2.109); and as the anthological and historical delvings of Sam Moskowitz have revealed, the popular fiction magazines were hardly devoid of tales in the Poesque vein. (See particularly his anthologies, *Science Fiction by Gaslight*, *Under the Moons of Mars*, and *Ghostly by Gaslight*.)

In particular vein of the horror story, Lovecraft recalled as late as 1932 (see Lovecraft to Barlow, July 28, 1932, *OFF* 34), the effect which Don Mark Lemon's atmospheric horror story "The Gorilla," in *All-Story Weekly* for October 1905, had had upon him. In the same vein, Lovecraft's letter published in *All-Story Weekly* for March 7, 1914, cited by Sam Moskowitz in the *Under the Moons of Mars*, praised the spectral achievements of Lee Robinet in "The Second Man" and of Perley Poore Sheehan in "His Ancestor's Head." In the domain of general fantasy and scientific romance, the work of Garrett P. Serviss, George Allan England, Edgar Rice Burroughs, and Albert Payson Terhune is mentioned in the same letter, adding the name of Frances Stevens in a pair of 1919–1920 letters also cited by Moskowitz. In his 1932 letter to Barlow (see above), Lovecraft reaffirmed these early choices, citing Terhune's "The Barge of Haunted Lives," Lemon's "The Gorilla," and Serviss's *Columbus of Space* and *The Second Deluge* as among his favorites from his early reading in the pulp fiction magazines.

Of Lovecraft's own early writing, which he undertook during the period of his greatest influence by these magazines, there is very little discoverable, however. He did recall to Rheinhart Kleiner in his letter of January 20, 1916 (*SL* 1.19; *RK* 29) one early scientific romance which he had written under the influence of Verne and his successors:

> When I was about twelve I became greatly interested in science, specialising in geography, (later to be displaced by astronomy), and being a Verne enthusiast, in those days I used to write fiction, and many of my tales showed the literary influence of the immortal Jules. I wrote one story about that side of the Moon which is forever turned away from us—using, for fictional purposes—the Hansen theory that air and water still exist there as the result of an abnormal centre of gravity in the moon. I hardly need add that the theory is really exploded—I even was aware of that fact at the time—but I desired to compose a "thriller."

Some of the titles which Lovecraft chose for his expository articles in the *Gleaner* also reveal his interest in the scientific romance during this period— "Is Mars an Inhabited World?: Startling Theory of Prof. Lowell on the Subject;" "Is there Life on the Moon?: Strange Revelations of Modern Science;" "Are there Undiscovered Planets? Boundaries of our Solar System still Shrouded in Obscurity;" and "Can the Moon be Reached by Man?: Showing that the Trip to our Satellite, Heretofore Attempted only in Fiction, May be a Scientific Possibility." (A concurrent discussion regarding the possibility of life on Mars which Lovecraft conducted in his own *Rhode Island Journal Astronomy* confirms his familiarity with the work of H. G. Wells— and in particular with *The War of the Worlds*.)[151]

In the domain of the more orthodox horror story, we have from this period "The Beast in the Cave" and "The Alchemist," and in addition one tantalizing reference in Lovecraft' Commonplace Book:

(19) Revise 1907 tale—painting of ultimate horror.

This entry, the nineteenth in the original holograph manuscript of the Commonplace Book, is undated there; since, however, the twenty-fifth entry (comprising his famous dream of the bas-relief of Cthulhu) is the first dated there, and is dated 1919, we may assume that this entry belongs to 1919 or earlier.[152] The cover which Barlow designed for the manuscript, presented to him on May 7, 1934 in return for a typed copy (whose alterations of the original text, unfortunately, wreaked havoc with the later Arkham House editions of the Commonplace Book), indicates that the manuscript contained entries dating from 1918 to 1934, so that entries one through twenty-four presumably date to 1918. Lovecraft's statement to Kleiner of January 23, 1920 (*RK* 178) that he had recently begun keeping a Commonplace Book for the first time in his life is in opposition to the earliest datings in the manuscript of his Commonplace Book (which datings he apparently inserted when the manuscript was presented to R. H. Barlow in 1934); perhaps, however, if he did indeed first begin his Commonplace Book in 1920, he first set down a block of ideas and dreams which had occurred to him earlier.

Whatever our dating of this entry, however, it seems tantalizingly clear from Lovecraft's injunction to *revise* his early 1907 tale that at least one other early horror story survived the 1903 holocaust, at least for a time. He, of course, ultimately used the same theme of an horrific painting in his novel *The Case of Charles Dexter Ward*;[153] however, the number of such stories, including such masterpieces as Whitehead's "Seven Turns in a Hangman's Rope," is undoubtedly too great to speculate very usefully about Lovecraft's intentions for his 1907 tale. In view of his strong remembrance of Don Mark Lemon's "The Gorilla" in *All-Story* for October 1905, however, I wonder whether the following story by Lemon (cited by William H. Evans in his "Thumbing the Munsey Files" in *Fantasy Commentator* for fall 1948 [2, No. 8]) may have had some role in the inspiration of Lovecraft's 1907 tale:

> *All-Story.* August, 1906. "?" by Don Mark Lemon (5pp.): An artist paints a picture of an imaginary man. Later he is amazed to sight the man himself in the street. Returning to his studio, he finds that the picture has disappeared from the canvas. Several horrible murders are committed, and the description of the perpetrator fits that of the mysterious subject. When the latter suddenly reappears on the canvas, the artist attempts to burn it. Then the figure steps from the flames and kills the artist. Quite good.[154]

(In the same listing, Evans describes "The Gorilla" [7pp.] as a "superb atmospheric horror story.")

This is all very little to go by on in discussing Lovecraft's early weird fiction; however, the anthologist of Lovecraft's favorite stories from *Weird Tales* (discussed by Thomas G. L. Cockcroft in a letter in *Nyctalops* No. 6) might well give thought to including Lemon's "The Gorilla," Robinet's "The Second Man," and Stephen's "His Ancestor's Head" as examples of his favorites among the earlier magazine work in the weird fiction field.[155] However, we ought not to imagine that all of Lovecraft's teenage fiction fell into the domains of the weird tale and the scientific romance. A paragraph in his letter to Rheinhart Kleiner of February 2, 1916 (*SL* 1.20–21; *RK* 30) makes clear that his early reading and activity in the Providence Detective Agency during his Slater Avenue days carried over to the writing of detective "thrillers":

> I used to write detective stories very often, the works of A. Conan Doyle being my model so far as plot was concerned.
>
> But Poe was my God of Fiction. I used to love the horrible and the grotesque—much more than I do now—and can recall tales of murderers, spirits, reincarnations, metempsychoses, and every shudder-producing device known to literature! One long-destroyed tale was of twin brothers—one murders the other, but conceals the body, and tries to live the life of both—appearing in one place as himself, and elsewhere as his victim. (Resemblance had been remarkable.) He meets sudden death (lightning) when posing as the dead man—is identified by a seer, and the secret finally revealed by his diary. This, I think, antedates my 11th year . . . .

That final ellipsis, which precedes a discussion of "The Beast in the Cave," certainly indicates a place where future researchers might well seek for further discussion of Lovecraft's teenaged production; but, after all, despite the destruction of most of the relevant material in 1908, we probably have a rather accurate picture of Lovecraft's early writing. It were well to have more—but here Lovecraft again exercised his right to determine to some degree his own literary posterity.[156]

12. Lovecraft's use of dreams and newspaper clippings in his fiction

There is much less to say about destroyed stories from Lovecraft's period of mature literary production, beginning in 1917, save for the general considerations which we have already made.

Perhaps the forthcoming volumes of *Selected Letters* and some of the original files of Lovecraft's letters will eventually yield more information. We can, however, give some discussion of a number of literary works which he envisioned and then seemingly failed to carry to completion or destroyed in dissatisfaction. Certainly, in the first instance, his Commonplace Book is a gold mine of undeveloped ideas, images, and dreams, many of which, one feels, he would have ultimately utilized in his writing and some of which he clearly did utilize in surviving stories. (Others may possibly have been the basis for stories destroyed in dissatisfaction.) Lovecraft makes clear the nature of his entries in his presentation of the original manuscript of the Commonplace Book to Barlow:

> This book consists of ideas, images, & quotations hastily jotted down for possible future use in weird fiction. Very few are actually developed plots—for the most part they are merely suggestions or random impressions designed to set the memory or imagination working. Their sources are various—dreams, things read, casual incidents, idle conceptions, & so on.
>
> H. P. Lovecraft
>
> Presented to R. H. Barlow, Esq. on May 7, 1934—in exchange for an admirably neat typed copy from his skilled hand.

The annotations which August Derleth and Donald Wandrei provided for the Commonplace Book in *The Shuttered Room* (which in following Barlow's "admirably neat typed copy" of 1934, departs regrettably from the text of the original manuscript, which the Futile Press followed for its 1938 editions of the Commonplace Book) serve admirably to point to the development which Lovecraft gave some of the entries in his finished work.[157]

Lovecraft's dreams, as recorded in his letters, are another rich source for ideas which did not receive full development in his preserved fiction. Here the admirable Arkham House volume *Dreams and Fancies* and the *Selected Letters* are invaluable sources, although the Commonplace Book also contains the outlines of some of Lovecraft's dreams. (For instance, of the dreams which

Lovecraft related to Rheinhart Kleiner in his letter of May 21, 1920 [*SL* 1.113–17; *Dreams and Fancies*, pp. 9–12], both the dream of the bas-relief of Cthulhu and the dream of the headless warriors are recorded in the Commonplace Book—they are respectively the twenty-fifth and the twenty-sixth entries, both dated 1919 by Lovecraft in 1934.) The very last entry in Lovecraft's Commonplace Book is also manifestly one of his dreams, as the quotation from Lovecraft's letter to Barlow of May 11, 1935 (*OFF* 261), which has been printed along with it in the Futile Press and *The Shuttered Room* editions of the Commonplace Book, amply demonstrates.

Then, of course, there is also Lovecraft's famous dream of a lost Roman legion, recounted at length in his letter to Bernard Dwyer of November 1927 (*SL* 2.188–97; *Dreams and Fancies,* pp. 14–26), which was ultimately incorporated in Frank Belknap Long's novel *The Horror from the Hills* (*Weird Tales*, January and February–March 1931) with Lovecraft's permission. The Roman dream, however, was also printed under the title "The Very Old Folk" in the amateur magazine *Scienti-Snaps* for summer 1940, and reprinted under the same title in the Arkham collection *Marginalia*. If the text of "The Very Old Folk" as printed in these places is the same as that of Lovecraft's November 1927 letter to Dwyer—I myself lack a copy of *Marginalia* to check—there is probably a good chance that Dwyer was editor Marconette's source for Lovecraft material—recall that Marconette printed Lovecraft's "The Thing in the Moonlight" for the first time in the first and only issue of *Bizarre* in January 1941.[158] Dwyer did excerpt from one of his letters from Lovecraft the "story" "The Evil Clergyman" and send it in for publication in *Weird Tales* (where it appeared in April 1939 under the title "The Wicked Clergyman");[159] and Sam Moskowitz' history *The Immortal Storm* establishes that Dwyer contributed material of his own to the amateur magazine *Fantasmagoria* produced by John J. Weir (1922–1977) of Perth Amboy, New Jersey, in the thirties.[160]

"The Thing in the Moonlight" may in fact be simply another excerpted passage from a letter to Dwyer—although, as we have earlier remarked, the original occurrence of the dream in 1927 (see Lovecraft to Wandrei, November 25, 1927, *SL* 2.199–201; *MTS* 186–88; *Dreams and Fancies*, pp. 26–28) and the formal narration of the story and Derleth's dating of it as 1937 argue against this presumption.[161] Lovecraft's imagination was always strongly stimulated by the electrical trolley cars, which were the principal mode of public transportation in Providence in his day. His letter to Kleiner of May 21, 1920, cited above, mentions another fascinating dream related to the subject:

> Did I tell you in my last letter about my dreams . . . (3) of the street car that went by night over a route that had been dismantled for six years, and that lost five hours in climbing College Hill, finally plunging off the earth into a star-strewn abyss and ending up in the sand-heaped streets of a ruined city which had been under the sea? Those were *some* dreams, believe your Grandpa Theobald!![162]

As a boy, he had constructed his own "railroad" from packing crates, making the carriage house at 454 Angell Street his principal depot and the paved walkways in the yard his tracks; in December 1901 he even produced a single number of *The Railroad Review: Published by the Little Fourke* (still preserved at the John Hay Library), which was apparently meant to be the official organ of his line. Also in 1901, in celebration of a trip on one of the electrical interurban cars of the day, Lovecraft wrote his amusing poem "An Account in Verse of the Marvelous Adventures of H. Lovecraft, Esq., Whilst Traveling on the W&B Branch NY, NH & H RR in Jany. 1901 in One of Those Most Modern Devices, to Wit: An Electric Train of Prov. R.I.," which still resides—unpublished despite the fact it is among the finest specimens of Lovecraft's juvenile writing—in the John Hay Library.[163] (NY, NH & H = New York, New Haven, and Hartford; W & B Branch = Warren & Bristol Branch.) As late as 1911, his fascination with trolley cars was still so great that he spent the entire day of his twenty-first birthday—August 20, 1911—riding trolley cars all over Providence. During his New York "exile," he wrote to Mrs. Clark of the contrast between the bizarre foreign fashions of "Babylon" and the traditionalism of dress on the Butler Avenue streetcars. Although in later years he was principally a walker, he would often use the trolley cars to return from his longest walks—such as the long hike he took out the Plainfield Pike to Neutaconkanut Hill in 1936.[164] Some of the idyllic description which he gave of the region which he found there was incorporated by August Derleth in his posthumous "collaboration" with Lovecraft, "The Lamp of Alhazred."

Another Roman idea which Lovecraft never carried to completion (at least in any of his preserved stories) is outlined in his letter of September 16, 1929, to Elizabeth Toldridge (*SL* 3.27; *ET* 106):[165]

> . . . . . The cuttings you enclosed are all interesting. That Roman coin in the Indian grave could be used fictionally to sustain a notion on which I have been ruminating for years—a forgotten colony of Rome on American soil, including a city of Roman architecture with temple-crowned citadel, columned forum, & marble arenas & baths. I would have it come in conflict with the representatives of some native civilisation—Maya, Aztec, &c.—& perhaps suffer extirpation in a desperate battle, or sink amidst an earthquake.

> The Malaysian temple item also has fictional possibilities—for a story could connect it with the unknown & primordial Pacific-island culture whose Cyclopean masonry & colossi are found in places like Ponape, in the Carolines, or Easter Island . . .

In general, Lovecraft's imagination was strongly stimulated by the nineteenth- and twentieth-century archaeological discoveries which brought a whole new era of human "prehistory" to the attention of scholars. He himself kept a file of newspaper clippings relating to the discoveries which most fascinated him—included in which were "weird" items of a more traditional nature—but unfortunately this file does not seem to have survived. Dana recovered several files of clippings (now in the John Hay Library) from 66 College Street in 1941, but most of these clippings—if not all—concern themselves with the eighteenth-century American antiquities in which Lovecraft was so deeply interested. The files would certainly bear close examination for references which occur in Lovecraft's fiction, however. (Miss Toldridge was one of the most persistent contributors of clippings for Lovecraft's files. One curious item in the list of material recovered by Dana is *A Catechism of Mayan Doctrine*, a 72-page booklet published by the "Mayan Temple" and presented with a letter to HPL. Perhaps this was given him by Stuart Morton Boland, a young archaeological enthusiast who met Lovecraft personally [cf. his "Interlude with Lovecraft" in the *Acolyte* for summer 1945] and presented him with several Indian relics from his own travels in Mexico.[166] Boland's file of Lovecraft letters—if still extant—would undoubtedly be quite valuable for the references which the letters would inevitably contain to Lovecraft's fascination with archaeology. Because of the clippings which she habitually sent, the Toldridge file [in the John Hay Library] is also valuable for its reflection of Lovecraft's varied interests, in addition to his dicta about poetry. I recall one letter—although, unfortunately, I do not have the precise reference—which discussed a particularly fascinating blighted region in the west.)

Nevertheless, this one quotation shows that Lovecraft's antiquarianism reached much further back than the eighteenth century alone for fictional inspiration. Certainly, one cannot doubt that he was fascinated by the archaeological discoveries which were made in Rhodesia and other parts of Africa during his lifetime—and one can hardly doubt that his poem "The Outpost" presaged a whole cycle of stories of the role of the Ancient Race in these antique African civilizations. (In addition to the poem "The Outpost," we also have the poem "Beyond Zimbabwe"—still unpublished but present in typescript text in the John Hay Library—which, along with "The White Elephant,"

Lovecraft and Barlow wrote as part of a rhyming game during Lovecraft's visit to Florida in 1934.)[167] It remained, of course, for Brian Lumley, a gifted young British writer, to develop this locale for the purposes of the Cthulhu Mythos in his stories in *Tales of the Cthulhu Mythos*.[168] Lovecraft's fascination with the mammoth statutes on Easter Island finally found its expression in the Mythos in Donald Wandrei's novel *The Web of Easter Island*;[169] and Stonehenge, which undoubtedly also fascinated Lovecraft, came in for its own in Colin Wilson's *The Philosopher's Stone*. Yet another Lovecraft letter— probably one of the letters to Miss Toldridge although again I do not have an exact reference—spoke of his plans to utilize the ancient Khmer ruins in Cambodia for the purposes of his fiction. I do not know whether this locale has yet been exploited for the purposes of the Mythos; although Derleth's story "The Lair of the Star-Spawn," written in collaboration with Mark Schorer and first published in *Weird Tales* for August 1932, comes close.[170] Yet another archaeological site of great antiquity—the Inca City of Machu Picchu—was used as the setting for a Mythos story by August Derleth in "The Gorge Beyond Salapunco," first published in *Weird Tales* for March 1949. The cyclopean masonry which A. Merritt wrote of in his story "The Moon Pool," which Lovecraft read in its original magazine appearance in 1918, certainly influenced to some degree at least his conception of sunken R'lyeh; and August Derleth seems to have adopted Merritt's setting of his story on Ponape in the Carolines in his story "The Black Island" (*Weird Tales*, January 1952), despite the fact that Lovecraft's own location of R'lyeh in "The Call of Cthulhu" placed it far away from the Carolines or indeed any other known island group. Perhaps this choice was also related to Lovecraft's setting of the evil Kanaky race in the South Pacific in "The Shadow over Innsmouth." Speaking of the islands in which the Marshes traded, old Zadok Allen related:

> Matt Eliot, his fust mate, talked lot too, only he was agin' folks's doin' any heathen things. Told abaout an island east of Otaheité whar they was a lot o' stone ruins older'n anybody knew anything abaout, kind o' like them on Ponape, in the Carolines, but with carvin's of faces that looked like the big statues on Easter Island. Thar was a little volcanic island near thar, too, whar they was other ruins with different carvin's—ruins all wore away like they'd ben under the see onct, an' with picters of awful monsters all over 'em.

The atlas which I have here does not list any "Otaheité;" however, the Marshes would have had to have sailed far, far from the ordinary shipping channels to come upon the volcanic rock which rose as R'lyeh in 1925.[171] According to Lovecraft's location (S. Lat. 47° 9', W. Long. 126° 43') of the lair of Cthulhu in "The Call of Cthulhu" itself (cf. *DH* 154; *CF* 2.50), now-sunken R'lyeh lies in a vast open space in the South Pacific about halfway between New Zealand and Chile. The nearest known islands are apparently Pitcairn, Henderson, and Ducie (all British), more than one thousand miles to the north, with Easter Island and Sela-y-Gomez (Chilean) not much further off to the northeast; the nearest appreciable island group is apparently the Iles Gambier of the Tuamoto Archipelago. Richard L. Tierney has done some remarkable work concerning the chronology of the rising of R'lyeh in 1925 (scheduled for publication in *Etchings and Odysseys* No. 1);[172] one might, however, also approach the question from the viewpoint of its geological likelihood. A Rand McNally map which I have shows the site of R'lyeh lying in the Southwestern Pacific Basin some hundreds of miles west of the Pacific–Antarctic Ridge. Perhaps someone can someday research the history of volcanic activity and sunken islands in the area; but I suspect it is sparse.[173] In general, however, the entire history of archaeological and geological discovery during Lovecraft's lifetime inevitably provides a rich field for research on the backgrounds of his fiction.

We have remarked upon Lovecraft's (apparently lost) file of newspaper and magazine clippings of "weird" items, which undoubtedly included a healthy budget of archaeological and geological items. Of especial interest in connection with "The Shadow over Innsmouth," Lovecraft also kept a file of notes on Polynesian folklore, which specifically bequeathed in his "Instructions in Case of Decease" to his friend Edward Lloyd Sechrist, then living in Papeete, Tahiti. Barlow's "The Wind that is in the Grass" confirms that these notes were indeed sent to Sechrist, who thereafter returned to the western United States. If they could still be recovered at this late date, they might add a great deal to our knowledge of Lovecraft's sources for Pacific lore. Even so, however, we need hardly stretch our imaginations very far to imagine the fascination which Lovecraft felt regarding the archaeological and geological discoveries which so broadened our knowledge of man and his ancestors during this century and the preceding one. Entire realms of discovery still remain to be exploited for the purposes of the Mythos—only consider the potential of Roy Chapman Andrews's discoveries in the Gobi for the writing about that central Asian wasteland Plateau of Leng; of the Leakey discoveries in Olduvai Gorge for a further development of the African branch of the Mythos; of all the great discoveries of mysterious ancient civilizations around the world for writing in the Mythos in general. Lin Carter recently dissected the whole fascination of "prehistory" in his article "The Real Hyborian Age" in *Amra* for June 1972 (2, No. 56); and, indeed, the filling-in of the story before the facts begin has always been, and will always be, a preoccupying subject for writers of romances of all ages. (Even the authors in favor during the Nazi period in Germany drew upon the fascinating subject of prehistory to glorify the Nazi ideas of race-time continuum and the mystic unity of the folk-nation. Hans Friedrich Blunck, one of the prominent authors of the period, drew upon folklore and mythology for his prehistoric *Urvätersaga*, a trilogy which sought to give artistic expression to these values.) Certainly, the mystery of the past—the days of his own brief life enigmatically passed beyond his own experience; the recent past of New England and other parts of colonial America passed beyond even memory but close enough to recover a mental image of the period; the less recoverable historical past; and the mythical period of prehistory and the aeons before—was always a prominent creative preoccupation for Lovecraft. One reading of his Commonplace Book alone ("talking Rock of Africa—immemorially ancient oracle in desolate jungle ruins that *speaks* with a voice out of the aeons" and other such entries) is enough to confirm a lasting belief in this preoccupation. Certainly, it is hardly imaginable that such fascinations will not continue to inspire writers in Lovecraft's Mythos for many years to come.[174]

Indeed, the backgrounds which Lovecraft envisioned for his work went quite beyond the mysteries of our own earth. As early as March 25, 1923, Lovecraft is writing Smith (*SL* 1.214) of his plans for a series of tales "involving other planets—both of this system & of other stars." "I want the things to be the fruit of a mind stored with all the primordial, colourful, morbid, & grotesque lore of literature—& hitherto my reading has had some lamentable lacunae." Again he writes to Clark Ashton Smith on December 3, 1929 (*SL* 3.88):

> I shall sooner or later get around to the interplanetary field myself—& you may depend upon it that I shall not choose Edmond Hamilton, Ray Cummings, or Edgar Rice Burroughs as my model! I doubt if I shall have any *living* race upon the orb whereto I shall—either spiritually or corporeally—precipitate my hero. But there will be Cyclopean *ruins*—god! what ruins!—& certain *presences* that haunt the ruin nether Vaults.

In 1930 and 1934–1935, of course, he carried at least some of these ambitious plans into reality with "The Whisperer in Darkness" and "The Shadow out of Time." (His 1936 collaboration with Kenneth Sterling, "In the Walls of Eryx," might also be included.) One feels that Lovecraft was not completely comfortable in the genre of the interplanetary tale; and certainly critical opinion varies widely about the worth of his later science fictional stories. His essay "Some Notes on Interplanetary Fiction" (*Marginalia*; *MW* 117–22; *CE* 2.178–82) contains strictures that few science fiction writers themselves would admit. Nevertheless, commentators have correctly emphasized the cosmic nature of Lovecraft's work; for nearly all his work looks toward the frontiers of knowledge and exploration rather than into the ordinary course of life. (The ordinary of yesterday and tomorrow, however, were of course the extraordinary of the present. Lovecraft, as an antiquarian, certainly slanted his work toward the fascination of yesterday; whereas, of course, science fiction is slanted toward the fascination of the future.) His streetcars plunge off into abysses of wonder; a world of faery drifts in over Kingsport; and cosmic horrors stalk his crabbed, Puritan New England.

13. Lovecraft's planned novels

It would serve little purpose to try to give a complete enumeration of the dreams and images mentioned in Lovecraft's letters, dreams and images which he might have eventually woven into stories. *Dreams and Fancies* gives an admirable selection (for instance, Lovecraft's letter to Smith of November 29, 1933, printed therein, surely contains background for Derleth's "The Dark Brotherhood"); *Selected Letters* contains more; and the 1934 Barlow journal printed in *Some Notes on H. P. Lovecraft* and *The Dark Brotherhood*[175] an additional couple (the dream of the monster-thing pursued by a band of medieval soldiers and the dream of the strange magician with his remarkable wooden spheres). In addition, of course, the fragments which Lovecraft left in manuscript—"Azathoth," "The Book," "The Descendant," "Of Evil Sorceries," "The Round Tower," and the outline for "The Survivor"—have all been given publication by Arkham House. (The last three in the section "The Unfinished Manuscripts" in *Some Notes on H. P. Lovecraft*; reprinted in *The Dark Brotherhood*.) Only the notes upon which August Derleth planned to base *The Watchers Out of Time*—relating to an ancient house in Kingsport and the mysterious lure of a glass "eye" in one of its carved walls—remain unpublished by Arkham House at the time of this writing; although perhaps they may be published along with the portion of *The Watchers Out of Time* which Derleth completed before his death when an omnibus volume of his posthumous "collaborations" with Lovecraft is published by Arkham.[176] (The notes have, however, already appeared in print. They appeared under the title of "Other Notes" in the winter 1943 issue of Larry Farsaci's *Golden Atom*, by leave of Barlow. For information on these notes, see *Some Notes on H. P. Lovecraft*, p. xvii. All of the above-mentioned notes and fragments—and Lovecraft's notes for "The Shadow out of Time" and *At the Mountains of Madness*—are present in the Lovecraft Collection of the John Hay Library in the form of the original manuscripts. When I last visited the Library, some were contained in the "miscellaneous" file.)[177]

Information regarding stories abandoned and destroyed by Lovecraft will probably have to await revelation in further published letters or in files of original letters—if such information ever does some to light in any amount. However, as a final consideration regarding the "lost" or "unfinished" Lovecrafts, we might consider the small parcel of novel-length plans which he brought up in his letters at irregular intervals over the years. As early as

March 7, 1920, Lovecraft wrote to Rheinhart Kleiner (*SL* 1.110; *RK* 183): "I am at present full of various ideas, including a hideous novel to be entitled *The Club of the Seven Dreamers*." That, seemingly, is the last reference to this projected novel in the as-yet published letters—unless the provisional title changed later.[178] The title hints of a connection with the famous legend of the Seven Sleepers of Ephesus. Dreams and dreamers played a prominent part in Lovecraft's fiction from this period; witness the thirty-fourth entry in his Commonplace Book (dated 1919):

> Moving away from earth more swiftly than light—past gradually unfolded—horrible revelation.

The next mention of a novel-length project in the published letters occurs in Lovecraft's letter to Frank Belknap Long of June 9, 1922 (*SL* 1.185):

> *Imagination* is the great refuge. That is the theme of the weird Vathek-like novel *Azathoth*, on whose opening pages I have been experimenting. I planned it long ago, but only began work—or play—on it a few days ago. Probably I'll never finish it—possibly I never get even a chapter written—but it amuses me just now to pretend to myself that I'm going to write it . . . .

(Note that at the time of his writing to Long, Lovecraft had just recently read *Vathek* for the first time. "I never got ahold of *Vathek* till 1921, & all of Hoffmann is still ahead of me" writes Lovecraft to Clark Ashton Smith on March 25, 1923 [*SL* 1.214].)

Unfortunately, Lovecraft never did get beyond the first few pages of *Azathoth* (two manuscript pages are all that are preserved in the John Hay Library), although the plan for the novel remained active for some time longer. From what survives, about all we can say is that Lovecraft intended a highly stylized and bizarre document of escape from the mundane, dreary world, much after the fashion of Clark Ashton Smith's writing. Whether he might ultimately have taken his readers through his own vision of a sinister underground netherworld like Eblis, is difficult to say. (Certainly, he accomplished something of this aim in his fantastic picaresque *The Dream-Quest of Unknown Kadath*—which he wrote, admittedly, to get the dreamland motif once and for all out of his blood. In this light, the fantastic adventures and travels of Carter in *The Dream-Quest* might well be seen as a partial carrying-out of Lovecraft's plans—insofar as we can judge anything of them—for *Azathoth*.) The next-published reference to *Azathoth*, however, also betokens the much more concrete beginning of yet another novel length project. Lovecraft writes to editor Edwin Baird on February 3, 1924 (*SL* 1.295):

> The only part of his [Henneberger's] letter that brought me in was a request for a novel of 25,000 words or over, which I shall be happy to send when I finish it. I've nothing of that length complete, but after trying serial stuff for *Home Brew* I experimented a bit with the novel form, and an idea partly shaped which will probably suit Mr. Henneberger's requirements. It is a hideous thing whose provisional title (subject to change) is *The House of the Worm*. All this part from my big novel idea—*Azathoth*—which will be exotic and highbrow, and wholly unsuited to *Weird Tales*.

A few days later (February 7, 1924), he writes to Frank Belknap Long (*SL* 1.304):

> .... But one thing interests me—Henneberger wants a novel or a novelette from me—something unspeakably terrible, and over 25,000 words in length. I think I shell comply with his request, developing a monstrous and noxious idea which has for some time been simmering unwholesomely in my consciousness—a ghastly thing to be intitul'd *The House of the Worm*....

It is difficult to say what Lovecraft intended for *The House of the Worm*; it is not mentioned again in the as-yet published letters. Perhaps the ravenous "blood-red thing" which devours the mimes in the tragedy "Man" in Poe's poem "The Conqueror Worm" gives some indication of Lovecraft's intentions; certainly, such an idea would qualify as "monstrous," "ghastly," and "noxious." Alternatively, perhaps, he may have intended a development along the more traditional lines of the English legends of "warts" or "dragons." Lovecraft's letter to Frank Belknap Long of October 7, 1925 (*SL* 1.255) indicates that he had just read (on loan from Cook) Bram Stoker's last book, *The Lair of the White Worm*—a novel which drew much of its inspiration from these same legends. (The novel was reprinted in the United States a few years back by Paperback Library under the title *The Garden of Evil*; it is still in print in both hardcover and paperback in England and has been a consistently steady seller over the years—second only to Stoker's masterpiece *Dracula*.) Lovecraft later wrote of Stoker's conception for the novel (*Supernatural Horror in Literature*; *CE* 2.112):

> Better known than Shiel is the ingenious Bram Stoker, who created many starkly horrific conceptions in a series of novels whose poor technique sadly impairs their net effect. *The Lair of the White Worm*, dealing with a gigantic primitive entity that lurks in a vault beneath an ancient castle [the soul or life force of which is shared with a beautiful woman], utterly ruins a magnificent idea by a development almost infantile.

Setting aside Lovecraft's critical judgment, which I believe to be unjustifiably harsh, there nevertheless appears the possibility that Lovecraft may have decided to remedy Stoker's deficiencies and to give the "worm" theme a treatment of his own. Certainly, Lovecraft would have had a vast body of reading to draw upon in developing this theme; indeed, despite his oft-expressed dislike for things medieval, his early stories, dreams, and Commonplace Book entries literally reek with strange medieval castles. Stoker's theme of the sharing or takeover of human beings by alien entities was also a common one with Lovecraft; witness his outlining of a story of possession to Rheinhart Kleiner in his letter of December 27, 1919 (*SL* 1.98–99; *RK* 175–76); the horrible thing which flaps down from a medieval rooftop to occupy the body of a soldier in the dream related to Barlow (*Notes* xxv–xxvi; *OFF* 402); the strange things in "The Thing on the Doorstep;" and the dream of insect invasion of human intelligence which became the last entry in Lovecraft's Commonplace Book and was ultimately adopted by Colin Wilson for use in his first Cthulhu Mythos novel *The Mind Parasites*.[179] In any case, however, despite the indication in Lovecraft's letter to Baird that he had already begun work on *The House of the Worm*, we hear no more of it in the as-yet published letters. While it seems doubtful that Lovecraft could have equaled the power of the later stories along this theme by David Keller and Robert E. Howard ("The Worm," *Amazing Stories*, March 1929; "The Valley of the Worm," *Weird Tales*, February 1934—both reprinted in first Arkham collections of the work of their respective authors), his development" of the "worm" idea—if indeed he intended a development along traditional lines—would have been immensely interesting. Nothing suggestive of any reliquiae of Lovecraft's efforts seems to exist in the John Hay Collection, however, so that we are left to wonder about Lovecraft's plans.

There follows a long dearth in the published letters of references to plans for projected novel-length works; indeed, I do not believe that another such reference occurs in either *SL* II or *SL* III. However, at least one additional reference to a novel-length work planned by Lovecraft has appeared in print, in Ernest A. Edkins's essay "Idiosyncrasies of H.P.L." in *HPL: Memoirs, Critiques and Bibliographies*, which also appeared in the sixth volume of Lovecraft Collectors' Library. Thomas L. Cockcroft kindly transcribed Mr. Edkins remarks for me (*LR* 94–95):

> Just before his death Lovecraft spoke to me of an ambitious project reserved for some period of greater leisure, a sort of dynastic chronicle in fictional form, dealing with the hereditary mysteries and destinies of an ancient New

England family, tainted and cursed down the diminishing generations with some gruesome variant of lycanthropy. It was to be his *magnum opus*, embodying the results of his profound researches in the occult legends of that grim and secret country which he knew so well but apparently the outline was just beginning to crystallize in his mind, and I doubt if he left even a rough draft of his plan.

Writing of Lovecraft's plans for the story which became "The Survivor" in posthumous "collaboration" with August Derleth, Barlow suggested that these plans were the "last" which Lovecraft ever formulated for a story; he and Lovecraft discussed them during Lovecraft's visit to Florida in 1934. The precise date of Lovecraft's setting-down of his ideas for "The Survivor" might possibly be dated by the newspaper cartoon on which he penciled his outline, still present in the Hay Collection. However—despite the fact that Barlow would have been intimately knowledgeable about Lovecraft's literary plans in 1935–1936—Lovecraft spent most of the summer of 1935 in Florida with Barlow and his family, and Barlow in return spent the month of August 1936 with Lovecraft in Providence—Edkins's reference to Lovecraft's communication of his plans "just before his death" seems to indicate strongly that these novel-length plans were in fact later than those for "The Survivor."[180] Lovecraft did virtually no creative writing after 1935. In the early part of 1936, his schedule was disrupted by the serious illness of his aunt Mrs. Gamwell, which involved a long hospital and sanatorium stay and subsequent nursing at home; and then, in mid-year, Lovecraft was occupied with the demanding job of revising (or virtually rewriting) Anne Renshaw's *Well Bred Speech* and with Barlow's month-long visit; finally, by the end of the year, he was a dying man. Certainly, any plans for creative fiction which occurred to him after the writing of "The Haunter of the Dark" in 1935 remained undeveloped.

Lovecraft's plans for his New England familial chronicle of horror, as related by Edkins, follow in the clear line of Lovecraft's greatest chronicles of hereditary decay and horror, from "The Rats in the Walls" to "The Shadow over Innsmouth," from "Arthur Jermyn" and "The Picture in the House" to "The Dunwich Horror." Perhaps the closest thing to Edkins's outline is Lovecraft's shoddy serial of the Martense family, "The Lurking Fear"—although, of course, in that case the family hardly suffered from "diminishing generations"—below-ground. Perhaps Lovecraft saw the powerfulness of the concept of ancestral horror and decay which he had developed so crudely in "The Lurking Fear" and so brilliantly in other stories—and intended to go back and give the theme the novel-length treatment which he felt it deserved.

In the eyes of many critics, such a return to his original powerful vein of horror from the science fictional constructions of his later years would been a highly welcome development; of such a return, however, "The Haunter of the Dark" is seemingly the only survivor. There we have it then: the "lost" Lovecrafts. A minor part of the consideration of his work, surely, but a highly interesting one.[181]

14. Lovecraft's revisory work; a few miscellaneous observations

We will probably never know the exact extent of Lovecraft's revisionary work, since, as Paul Cook remarked in his memoir *H. P. Lovecraft: A Portrait* (pp. 50–52; *LR* 144–46), Lovecraft did not consider it ethically proper to reveal his often large role in such work. (He did sometimes discuss his revisions in the domain of the macabre in private letters to close friends like Clark Ashton Smith and Frank Belknap Long.)[182] From his letters we do know that he revised such things as a history of Dartmouth College and Anne Renshaw's *Well Bred Speech* (1936);[183] and doubtless during his twenty-five years of activity as a revisionist, he had a role in many other such works outside the domain of the macabre. In his memoir, Cook remarks that Lovecraft's revisionary work secured at least three genuine, if evanescent, poetical reputations—and he does not seem to indicate that these were merely amateur reputations. (Lovecraft did, however, devote a great deal of time to the revision of poems by fellow amateurs—Elizabeth Toldridge, Eugene B. Kuntz, Roy M. Ivens, and doubtless many others—undoubtedly contributing his work gratis in the majority of cases.[184] He also played a considerable role in preparing the poetry of his friends John Ravenor Bullen, Jonathan E. Hoag, and Arthur Goodenough for publication.) Of course, Lovecraft's most consistent revision customer was lecturer David V. Bush—but it is difficult to believe that his poetry, even as revised by Lovecraft, could have won any kind of genuine reputation, even of the evanescent kind which Cook suggests.[185] Cook's description of a woman, "very earnest, very soulful, writing by the yard but unable to achieve anything printable," for whom Lovecraft secured a brief poetical reputation by his revision, seems to mirror Lovecraft's own announcement to James F. Morton on May 23, 1927 (*SL* 2.129; *JFM* 138) that he was then suffering under "the most deodamnate piece of unending Bush-work I've ever tackled since the apogee of the immortal Davidius himself—the sappy, half-baked *Woman's Home Companion* stuff of a female whose pencil has hopelessly outdistanc'd her imagination."

Because of the appearance of Zealia Bishop among Lovecraft's correspondents in the *Selected Letters* shortly after the writing of his letter to Morton and because of Mrs. Bishop's principal devotion to the women's magazines, I had always assumed that Lovecraft was referring to her in the passage of his letter to Morton; but perhaps not so. In the first instance

Lovecraft's use of the phrase "Bushwork" would seem to indicate that he was revising poetry for his new client; whereas Mrs. Bishop's output seems to have been principally stories and articles. Moreover, if Lovecraft in his letter to Morton was referring to the same woman whom Cook mentions, Cook's reference to the ultimate refusal of this woman to pay her revision bills would seem to make it further unlikely that Lovecraft was referring to Mrs. Bishop— for he later remarked that although she was sometimes late in her payments, she always paid dutifully in the end. Some clue to the identity of Cook's mystery poetess, however, may be given in the listing of material which H. Douglass Dana recovered from 66 College Street in 1941. Among the miscellaneous books and magazines in his listing of material recovered from 66 College Streets are listed four issues of the *Chicago Tribune* poetry annual the *Livebook*—for 1926, 1927, 1928, 1929. Now why would Lovecraft have had these issues of the *Livebook* among his papers? There seem to be only three logical explanations: (1) he himself contributed material still undetected by Lovecraft bibliographers, and received the issues as contributor's copies; (2) he was sent them by a friend who had contributed work; or (3) he was sent them by a client whose work had appeared in them with his help. Certainly, appearances in the *Livebook* would indicate the kind of genuine—if perhaps only evanescent—reputation of which Cook spoke; so that perhaps our third alternative is worthy of further investigation. Indeed, Chicago is a very likely place for a Lovecraft revision client to have lived; for among his friends there were people in editorial work like Vincent Starrett and Farnsworth Wright who could very well have directed welcome work to him. (Indeed, Starrett was the longtime book reviewer for the *Chicago Tribune*; and from the *Selected Letters* [Lovecraft to Morton, September 26, 1930, *SL* 3.170–71; *JFM* 232–34], we know that Farnsworth Wright did indeed refer at least one revision client to Lovecraft—one who, unfortunately, later refused to pay.)[186]

* * *

The several references which have appeared in print regarding essays on Shakespeare allegedly published by Lovecraft within the amateur press associations are troubling—for the very compelling reason that persons who have examined the files of amateur magazines in the Library of Amateur Journalism have found nothing of the sort. Lovecraft's biographer L. Sprague de Camp, who looked over these files, told me that he found only occasional casual references to Shakespeare in Lovecraft's contributions and criticism. Contrast these findings, however, with this item in "The Eyrie" in *Weird Tales* for October 1933 (p. 517; *WW* 76):

Alexander Ostrow, of New York City, writes us a side light on H. P. Lovecraft. "I have just finished reading your August number," he writes to the Eyrie. "All the stories were so equally excellent that I hesitate to cast my favorite stories ballot. In all the time that I have been reading *Weird Tales* I have never cast a ballot for the reason, although when Howard Philip [sic] Lovecraft appears in any issue, there is no question as to which story is *the* best. Your readers might be interested in knowing that not only is Lovecraft a master of weird fiction, but that he is also an authority on Shakespeare. I have in my possession and have seen elsewhere a variety of essays on the works of Shakespeare written by Lovecraft when he was active in the affairs of the National Amateur Press Association.[187]

The second reference in print to these alleged essays occurs in F. Lee Baldwin's brief contribution to the Laney–Evans bibliography; therein—perhaps following the 1933 Ostrow letters—he states that Lovecraft wrote essays on the work of Shakespeare while he was active in the National Amateur Press Association. Now what are we to make of these statements in view of the failure of researchers—insofar as I know of—to find any of these essays? A reference which I found in a 1933 letter of Clark Ashton Smith to Lovecraft in the John Hay Library may provide something of a clue. Smith remarked upon Ostrow's reference to Shakespearean essays by Lovecraft—a facet of Lovecraft's work which he had not seen in the eleven prior years of their correspondence—asked Lovecraft in his letter whether Ostrow might have been confusing his name with that of his friend Sam Loveman, who had contributed essays on Shakespeare to the pages of amateur press association magazines. Perhaps the fourth volume of the *Selected Letters* will contain Lovecraft's answer; in any case the question would be worthy of further pursuit by Lovecraft researchers.[188]

Lovecraft's letter to Alfred Galpin of November 1918 (*SL* 1.76–77; *AG* 48–50) discussing *Hamlet*, is ample evidence of the interest which any further discussions of Shakespeare's work from his pen would bear. Late in life, Lovecraft was called upon once again to expostulate informally upon his views on Shakespeare in a letter: for very late in 1936 young correspondent then in high school, Thomas Kemp Bordley, then of Chestertown, Maryland, came to Lovecraft with a request for character sketches of the major characters in *Hamlet* and *Macbeth*, which he needed for a writing assignment. With his customary generosity, Lovecraft sent Bordley his observations upon the major characters of those plays, and Bordley later wrote back of the good stead in which they had served him in his assignment. Perhaps Lovecraft's letter to Bordley embracing his character sketches is already among those scheduled for the *Selected Letters*, perhaps not.[189] Willis Conover, once a correspondent of Lovecraft himself, wrote me that he had last seen Bordley in a Washington restaurant in 1954, at which time Bordley told him he had abandoned his interest is science fiction and fantasy for an interest in the occult. Mr. Conover knew nothing more of Thomas Kemp Bordley; but Lovecraft researcher R. Alain Everts recently wrote me that he had at last tracked him down—alas, only to find that he had died in 1968. Whether the Lovecraft letter in which we are interested perished with his death; whether it had perished years before; whether in fact it still survives and merits publication—these would be questions for future researchers to consider.

* * *

A large body of criticism has developed around Poe's mysterious novel *The Narrative of A. Gordon Pym*, and it is probably only a matter of time before an equally large body of comparative scholarship develops around *Pym*'s literary posterity—Jules Verne's *The Sphinx of the Ice Fields* (*Le sphinx des glaces*) and Lovecraft's own *At the Mountains of Madness*. One such article, "Tekeli-Li. La Postérité littéraire d'Arthur Gordon Pym" by Demètre Iokimidis and Pierre Strinati, has already appeared in print in the Swiss journal *Cahiers d'Etudes d'Ailleurs* for January 1959 (No. 3), reprinted in *Fiction* for January 1960 (No. 74). However, one note which ought to be brought to the attention of future comparative scholars occurs is Lovecraft's letter to Richard Ely Morse of November 20, 1936 (held at the New York Public Library): "I never could get ahold of the Arthur Gordon Pym sequel, & would gobble it up today if it ever crossed my path." Since Lovecraft had not seen *The Sphinx of the Ice Fields* by November 1936, it seems likely that he never saw it. (Had he chosen to make use of the Brown University Library—whose principal collections were lodged in the John Hay Library during Lovecraft's lifetime—he could have seen the novel in the American edition of *The Works of Jules Verne* published by V. Parke in New York in 1911. Bleiler [1948] lists no separate American edition of *The Sphinx of the Ice Fields*; note that it is not the same as *The Field of Ice*. The more recent Fitzroy edition of Verne's work prints *The Sphinx* together with *Pym* but is a textual horror to the extent that it is difficult to tell who was writing what. Verne's novel, of course, is available in French.) Certainly, we may conclude that Verne's conceptions played no role in the writing of *At the Mountains of Madness* in 1931.

* * *

J. Vernon Shea and Darrell Schweitzer have recently written interestingly about the potentialities of Lovecraft's work for adaptation by the visual media.[190] Although Lovecraft was actually a mildly enthusiastic devotee of the cinema (*Berkeley Square* [1933] with Leslie Howard was his favorite film— and a Lovecraftian film buff could undoubtedly do a fascinating article on this subject),[191] however, he did not deem his own work especially suitable for cinematic adaptation. Writing to his aunt Mrs. Clark of meeting Loveman's friend Leonard Gaynor, then with Paramount, in a letter of July 10, 1931, Lovecraft stated: "However, in cold fact nothing of mine could ever be suitable for his purposes [cinematic adaption]. Cinemas want action—whereas my own specialty is atmosphere." Perhaps, however, Lovecraft underestimated the atmospheric effects which could be achieved by modern film makers—certainly, the much-debunked *The Dunwich Horror* (1970) showed a certain amount of ingenuity in portraying Wilbur Whateley's twin brother and *The Haunted Palace* (1963) was full of interesting effects. In the hands of more sophisticated directors, Lovecraft's works might be impressive on film indeed. Only imagine *The Case of Charles Dexter Ward* filmed in Providence! Speaking at the 1972 Boston Science Fiction Convention ("Boskone"), Professor Barton L. St. Armand of Brown University announced that the French director Alain Resnais (*Last Year at Marienbad*, etc.) was contemplating filming several of Lovecraft's works in Providence—possibly along with a cinematic biography of Lovecraft himself. So perhaps the future will hold interesting things for Lovecraftian film fans indeed.[192]

* * *

The editors of *Selected Letters* dated the photograph of Frank Belknap Long, HPL, and James F. Morton in front of the Poe Cottage in upper Manhattan as ca. 1920 when they published it opposite p. 70 in the third volume. They need hardly have been so inexact. Lovecraft's first visit to New York City lasted from April 6 until April 12, 1922 during which period he and Samuel Loveman shared Sonia Greene's apartment at 259 Parkside in Brooklyn. Lovecraft's letter of May 3, 1922, to Anne Tillery Renshaw (*SL* 1.174; *ET* 369–70) establishes that he, Long, and possibly several other amateurs made the trek to the Poe Cottage during this visit. The photograph establishes that Morton was along; perhaps Sam Loveman, Rheinhart Kleiner, or Sonia Greene took the photograph.[193]

15. Lovecraft's financial affairs

Lovecraft was customarily reticent about his financial affairs, and very little has appeared in print concerning the remuneration he received for his professional stories.[194] His letter to Anne Tillery Renshaw of October 3, 1921 (*SL* 1.154–55; *ET* 367) indicates that he received—or rather, was promised—$5.00 for each of the installments of "Herbert West—Reanimator" which appeared in George Julian Houtain's magazine *Home Brew*. (One imagines that Lovecraft was paid his $30—otherwise, he would hardly have written "The Lurking Fear" later on.) His letter to Farnsworth Wright of July 16, 1927 (*SL* 2.154–55) shows that he received $165.00 for "The Call of Cthulhu"—a story which Wright had long hesitated over because of its innovations and also—one suspects—because of its length. (The length at which Lovecraft wrote his stories in later years greatly impaired his sales to *Weird Tales*, which did not have much money to spend. Lovecraft wrote to Barlow on January 29, 1932 [*OFF* 22], that he received 1½¢ per word, the highest *Weird Tales* rate—making Lovecraft's longest stories very costly for low-budgeted Farnsworth Wright.) Indeed, perhaps the largest sum Lovecraft ever received from *Weird Tales* for a single story was the $350.00 he received for "The Whisperer in Darkness" in 1930 (see Lovecraft to Smith, October 17, 1930, *SL* 3.193).[195]

Lovecraft's letter to Barlow of January 29, 1932, reveals the price which Lovecraft received for two additional famous tales: $55.50 for "The Strange High House in the Mist" and $240.00 for "The Dunwich Horror."[196] In selling stories to *Weird Tales*, Lovecraft seems to have sold all serial rights (with options for anthologies); at least, his letter to J. Vernon Shea of June 19, 1931, indicates that he received nothing whenever one of his stories was reprinted in *Weird Tales,* but that he received a small sum whenever one of his stories was selected for an anthology.

There seems to have been some controversy about the unpaid reprint policy of *Weird Tales*—when E. Hoffmann Price asked Lovecraft to join a protest against this policy, however, Lovecraft replied in his letter of October 1932 that he thought he owed it to his reading public to allow Wright to reprint his stories from unavailable early issues of *Weird Tales*. A long letter of Otis Adelbert Kline to Dr. Isaac M. Howard which was published in the first issue of the amateur magazine *OAK Leaves* (David A. Kraft, 1970) indicates that it was standard *Weird Tales* practice in the first decade of its existence to buy all serial rights from the best authors. Later on, Kline, insisted that *Weird Tales* buy only first North American serial rights on the stories which he offered through his agency; and Lovecraft, one of the magazine's best-established authors, may have been able to insist upon such purchases, too, although, of course, he sold very little to *Weird Tales* in the 1930s. Writing to Barlow on March 4, 1932 (*OFF* 25), regarding Carl Swanson's proposed weird fiction magazine *Galaxy* (never published), Lovecraft stated that he had been forced to offer Swanson his inferior, non-professionally published stories because Wright "resented" the sale of reprint rights—which gives some credence on the other hand to the assumption that Lovecraft sold only first North American serial rights all along and that he allowed Wright to reprint his earlier stories gratis because of the dire financial straits of *Weird Tales*, the desire of the readership to see these tales republished, and his own hopes to foster further sales to Wright. The records which would establish the actual terms of sale have probably long perished; indeed, Kline warned Dr. Howard in 1941 that even at that time *Weird Tales* might not have retained a full record of the terms of all of its purchases and that the publishers could probably decline to render such information anyway and be protected by the law of laches.[197]

It is clear, however, that Lovecraft sold only options for anthologies to *Weird Tales* and that he sold no book rights—so that these rights resided with his Estate following his death on March 15, 1937, which is to say that *Weird Tales*, as proprietor of copyright on most of the individual stories, would have been obliged under the original contract for publication to license such uses of these stories, if not to assign copyright. For instance, Lovecraft's letter to Helen Sully of March 5, 1935 indicates that he submitted collections of his tales to at least four publishers other than *Weird Tales* during his lifetime: Putnam's (1931), Vanguard (1932), Knopf (1933), and Loring & Mussey (1935).[198] The small amount of money which Lovecraft received from resale of his stories to anthologies can be seen from his letter to E. Hoffmann Price of October 1932 wherein he discusses the publishing history of his story "The Music of Erich Zann," first published in *Weird Tales* for May 1925. (It was eventually reprinted in the same magazine—undoubtedly without fee—in November 1934.) This story was first resold to Dashiell Hammett for $25.00 for his anthology *Creeps by Night* (1931). Lovecraft then received $10.00 for the use of the story in the British edition of the same anthology. (I believe the British edition was entitled *Modern Tales of Horror*, published by Victor Gollancz, Ltd., in London in 1932. I do not, however, have a copy of *Creeps by Night* to compare the contents. Lovecraft says in his letter to Price that "Curtis Brown" paid him the fee for the British edition; perhaps "Curtis Brown" was a literary agency which handled such matters for Gollancz.

According to the bibliography of Jack L. Chalker, "The Music of Erich Zann" also appeared in the *London Evening Standard* for October 24, 1932. This, however, was clearly not the anthological appearance Lovecraft mentioned to Price.) Finally, Lovecraft mentioned to Price that he expected to sell the story one more time (for $30–$35) to Christine Campbell Thomson for the "Not at Night" series.[199]

In spite of these few sales to anthologies[200], however, it is clear that Lovecraft earned only a very few thousand dollars from his own writing (excluding his professional revisions—which were often very nearly his own writing) during his lifetime. In fact, if we count an Arkham page (*The Dunwich Horror and Others*, 1963; *At the Mountains of Madness and Other Novels*, 1964; and *Dagon and Other Macabre Tales*, 1965) as approximately 400 words and apply Lovecraft's customary *Weird Tales* rate of 1½¢ per word (see Lovecraft to Barlow, January 29, 1932, *OFF* 22)—i.e., approximately $6.00 per Arkham page—except where other facts are known,[201] we can even attempt to make a rough estimate of Lovecraft's total earnings from his fiction during his lifetime:

Key in price figures:

- * based upon $6.00 per Arkham page (1½¢ per word)
- ** price stated in Lovecraft's letters
- † based upon Lovecraft's estimation (Lovecraft to Price, October 1932) that he would receive $30–$35 from Selwyn & Blount for the use of "The Music of Erich Zann" (9 Arkham pp.)—i.e., $4.00 per Arkham page
- ‡ extrapolation based upon the $5.00 per installment rate for "Herbert West—Reanimator"
- (n) special note, see below
- # a guess

Story (Arkham Pages)	Paid Appearances During Lovecraft's Lifetime	Estimated Price
***The Dunwich Horror and Others*, Arkham House, 1963**		
In the Vault (9)	*WT*, April 1932	$54 *
Pickman's Model (14)	*WT*, October 1927	$84 *
	By Daylight Only, Selwyn & Blount, 1929	$56 †
	Not At Night Omnibus, Selwyn & Blount, 1937?	$56 †
The Rats in the Walls (20)	*WT*, March 1924	$120 *
	Switch on the Light, Selwyn & Blount, 1931	$80 †

The Outsider (7)		
	WT, April 1926	$42 *
The Colour out of Space (29)		
	Amazing Stories, September 1927	$25 (1)
The Music of Erich Zann (9)		
	WT, May 1925	$54 *
	Creeps at Night, John Day, 1931	$25 **
	Modern Tales of Horror, Gollancz, 1932	$10 **
	The London Evening Standard, Oct. 24, 1932	$10 #
The Haunter of the Dark (23)		
	WT, December 1936	$138 *
The Picture in the House (9)		
	WT, January 1924	$54 *
The Call of Cthulhu (30)		
	WT, February 1928	$165 **
	Beware After Dark!, Macauley, 1929	$120 #
The Dunwich Horror (43)		
	WT, April 1929	$240 **
Cool Air (9)		
	Tales of Magic and Mystery, March 1928	$54 #
The Whisperer in Darkness (66)		
	WT, August 1931	$350 **
The Terrible Old Man (3)		
	WT, August 1926	$18 *
The Thing on the Doorstep (27)		
	WT, January 1937	$162 *
The Shadow over Innsmouth (62)		
	Visionary Press (book), December 1936	$00 #
The Shadow out of Time (62)		
	Astounding Stories, June 1936	$595 (2)

At the Mountains of Madness, Arkham House, 1964

At the Mountains of Madness (100)		
	Astounding Stories, February–March–April, 1936	$— (2)
The Case of Charles Dexter Ward (121)		
	posthumous	—
The Shunned House (26)		
	Recluse Press (unbound book), 1928	$00
The Dreams in the Witch House (36)		
	WT, July 1933	$216 *
The Statement of Randolph Carter (6)		
	WT, February 1925	$36 *
The Dream-Quest of Unknown Kadath (96)		
	posthumous	—
The Silver Key (12)		
	WT, January 1929	$72 *
Through the Gates of the Silver Key (34)		
	WT, July 1934	$102 (3)

***Dagon and Other Macabre Tales*, Arkham House, 1965**

Story	Publication	Price
Dagon (6)	*WT*, October 1923	$36 *
The Tomb (10)	*WT*, January 1926	$60 *
Polaris (4)	amateur publication only	—
Beyond the Wall of Sleep (11)	amateur publication only	—
The Doom that Came to Sarnath (7)	amateur publication only	— (4)
The White Ship (6)	*WT*, March 1927	$36 *
Arthur Jermyn (9)	*WT*, April 1924 (as "The White Ape")	$54 *
The Cats of Ulthar (4)	*WT*, February 1926	$24 *
Celephaïs (6)	amateur publication only	— (4)
From Beyond (7)	amateur publication only	—
The Temple (13)	*WT*, September 1925	$78 *
The Tree (5)	amateur publication only	—
The Moon-Bog (8)	*WT*, June 1926	$48 *
The Nameless City (12)	amateur publication only	—
The Other Gods (5)	amateur publication only	—
The Quest of Iranon (7)	amateur publication only	—
Herbert West—Reanimator (29)	*Home Brew* (six parts), 1922	$30 **
The Hound (8)	*WT*, February 1924	$48 *
Hypnos (7)	*WT*, May–June–July 1925	$42 *
The Lurking Fear (20)	*Home Brew* (four parts), 1923	$20 ‡
	WT, June 1928	$78 **
The Festival (9)	*WT*, January 1925	$54 *
The Unnamable (8)	*WT*, July 1925	$48 *
Imprisoned with the Pharaohs (26)	*WT*, May–June–July 1924 (as by Houdini)	— (5)
He (10)	*WT*, September 1926	$60 *

The Horror at Red Hook (20)		
	WT, January 1927	$120 *
	You'll Need a Night Light, Selwyn & Blount, 1927	$80 †
	Not at Night!, Macy-Masius, 1928	$00 (6)
The Strange High House in the Mist (9)		
	WT, October 1931	$55 **
In the Walls of Eryx (28)		
	posthumous	—
The Evil Clergyman (5)		
	posthumous	—
Early Tales (33)		
	amateur publication only, with the exception of "The Transition of Juan Romero," posthumous	—
Fragments (12)		
	posthumous	—
Supernatural Horror in Literature		
	The Recluse, 1927	$00 (7)
	Total	**$3909**

NOTES:

(1) In a letter published in *Nyctalops* 6 (pp. 40–41), T. G. L. Cockcroft states: "I have been told that in a letter published in recent years (though not in *Selected Letters*) Lovecraft mentioned being paid $25.00 for The Colour out of Space—and apparently he had to wait a long time to be paid this, too." Where was this letter published?[202]

(2) This was the sum received from Street & Smith for both "The Shadow out of Time" and *At the Mountains of Madness*. One of Lovecraft's 1936 letters at the John Hay Library breaks this down; but I did not take a note on it. HPL probably got about 1¢ per word for these stories; if my estimate of 400 words per Arkham page is correct—and it is probably somewhat high—then the two stories together amounted to about 64,800 words—40,000 for *At the Mountains of Madness* and 24,800 for "The Shadow out of Time," The prices paid for the stories were undoubtedly in the some ratio as the word counts.[203]

(3) Lovecraft's ordinary *WT* rate would have made the price of this story $204; but Lovecraft split the price with his collaborator E. Hoffmann Price. In fact, I have lately discovered, in Lovecraft's letter to Barlow of November 29, 1933 (*OFF* 88), that Lovecraft and Price were paid only $140.00 altogether for "Through the Gates of the Silver Key" (somewhat less than 1¢ per word by my estimates); thus, assuming an even split, my totals should be reduced by $32.[204]

(4) Chalker lists the appearances of "The Doom that Came to Sarnath" and of "Celephaïs" in William L. Crawford's *Marvel Tales* as professional appearances. I doubt seriously whether Lovecraft was paid anything for these stories, however. Most of the early fanzines of the thirties pretended to professional status in that they were available only by subscription or contribution; few if any, however, paid anything for contributions. Crawford did envision *Marvel Tales* as a semi-professional publication, however, and he may possibly have paid some minuscule fees to his authors.

(5) I do not believe the as-yet published letters contain information regarding the fee which Lovecraft received for the ghostwriting of "Imprisoned with the Pharaohs;" had he submitted the tale to *Weird Tales* himself he would have received about $156 at the maximum 1½¢ per word rate. Indeed, "Imprisoned with the Pharaohs" is not really properly part of Lovecraft's own fictional output but is better considered to be one of his revisions—since one of these, "The Mound," was developed from a single paragraph of plot outline and many others amounted to virtual rewritings. Some gauge of the low rates which Lovecraft charged for his painstaking revisionary work can be derived from the fact that he charged Zealia Bishop only $17.50 for the revision and preparation of final typed manuscript of her story "The Curse of Yig" (*Weird Tales*, November 1929); see his letter to her of March 9, 1929 (SL 2.232–33).[205]

"The Curse of Yig" occupies 16 Arkham pages in *The Horror in the Museum and Other Revisions* and so by our estimate is approximately 6400 words long. In the last months of 1927, Lovecraft quoted to Adolphe de Castro his rates for a published book which de Castro wanted rewritten: normal rates, $1.00 per page untyped and $1.50 per page typed; "best" rates, 50¢ per page untyped and 65¢ per page typed. Presuming that do Castro's book *In the Confessional and The Following* (Western Authors' Publishing Association, New York and San Francisco, 1893) also had ca. 400 words per page, this would make "The Curse of Yig"—prepared in final typescript—cost ca. $24.00 at normal rates and ca. $10.40 at "best" rates—in fair agreement with the price Lovecraft actually charged. This seems to put Lovecraft's usual rate for revision and preparation final manuscript at about ¼¢ per word during this period, with "best" rate about a third lower. L. Sprague de Camp wrote in *Fantastic* (August 1971, p. 105): "His charges [for revision] rose slowly from an eighth to a quarter of a cent a word, although in 1933 he was still rewriting an 80,000-word novel for a mere $100.00." In 1936 he revised Mrs. Renshaw's entire *Well Bred Speech* (writing "Suggestions for a Reading Guide" from scratch as part of his task—although this did not appear in the published book) for $100.00, also, although he had written correspondents that he ought to have asked for at least $200 for the task. In general, of course, one feels that Lovecraft varied his rates considerably according to the ability of his customers to pay; Houdini undoubtedly paid far more generously for "Imprisoned with the Pharaohs" than did Zealia Bishop, Adolphe Castro, and Hazel Heald for the work which Lovecraft did for them. At the ¼¢ per word revision rate cited above, Lovecraft probably wrote "The Mound" for Mrs. Bishop for about $68; had he written the story under his own name and submitted it to *Weird Tales* he would have received about $400—six times as much—at his best rate. ("The Mound" is 68 Arkham pages in *The Horror in the Museum and Other Revisions* or ca. 27,200 words by our estimation.) Judging from several letters of David V. Bush to Lovecraft in the John Hay Library, Lovecraft's rate for the revision of poetry was approximately 2¢ per line in 1919–1920, with extra charges for Bush's frequent "rush orders." What with his painstaking methods and cheap rates, Lovecraft was probably very lucky to earn $500 a year in his professional revisionary work.[206]

(6) Even if the suit against Macy-Masius which Lovecraft spoke of in his letter to Wright of February 15, 1929 (*SL* 2.260–61) was actually filed by *Weird Tales*, it seems doubtful that Lovecraft ever received any benefits.

(7) *The Recluse* seems to have been more or less the equivalent of a sophisticated literary journal like the late *Kenyon Review*, etc. Lovecraft certainly received nothing more than contributor's copies for his long article; however, he did derive some auxiliary benefits, such as his subsequent correspondence with Vincent Starrett.

* * *

Indeed, our estimate of $3909 from his professional fiction from 1922 until his death in 1937 is probably quite high. We have no verified instances of Lovecraft's receiving *Weird Tales* best 1½¢ per word rate until the publication of "The Call of Cthulhu" in 1928. (Otis Kline's letter to Dr. Howard seems to indicate that the 1½¢ per word best rate did not take hold until the late 1920s.) In addition, in estimating the sum he would have received from Selwyn & Blount for "The Music of Erich Zann" at $30–$35 Lovecraft may have been citing a flat rate rather than a per word rate. If we assume that Lovecraft received only ½¢ per word from *Weird Tales* from 1923 until the break in 1924 and only 1¢ per word from 1924 until the publication of "The Call of Cthulhu" in February 1928 and that the Selwyn & Blount payments were a flat $35, our estimate becomes considerably lower—$3202. (I have allowed only

$35 for the appearance of "The Call of Cthulhu" in *Beware After Dark!* in making this estimate. It is well to remember that even in 1923–1924 owner Henneberger esteemed Lovecraft's stories—particularly "The Rats in the Walls"—as the best which had appeared in *Weird Tales*—so that he would certainly have been receiving the highest rate of payment available at the time. Editor Edwin Baird even requested him to send his manuscripts directly to Baird's home in Evanston, Illinois, for personal attention.) Averaging things out, perhaps $3500 is a good round estimate of Lovecraft's total lifetime earnings from his professional fiction. Certainly, this was no mean accomplishment for a writer who refused to conform to the "action" standards of all his principal outlets; indeed, the amount compares very favorably with the grand total of 635 pounds which Lovecraft's literary idol, Arthur Machen, received from his eighteen volumes of fiction and essays over twenty-two years (see Aidan Reynolds and William Charlton, *Arthur Machen: A Short Account of His Life and Work*, p. 160). Indeed, one cannot resist quoting a few sentences from Machen's 1937 speech (wherein he revealed his total earnings) which demonstrate in an utterly convincing way the great aesthetic motivations which he and Lovecraft had in common:

> What first set me on writing was the sight of the long range of mountain from Twyn Barlwm to Mynydd Maen, with the white-washed farms shining in the sunlight on a clear, frosty November morning . . . . Let me speak for myself. Other and happier writers may have found the job an easy one; I have found it beyond expression difficult, severe, abounding in disappointments and despairs. (Reynolds and Charlton, *op. cit.*, pp. 159–60)[207]

16. Notes on the education of Lovecraft's family

Writing to Maurice Moe on January 1, 1915 (*SL* 1.6), Lovecraft stated that his mother and his aunt Lillian had been educated at the Wheaton Seminary in Norton, Massachusetts. Recently, I wrote the Wheaton College Library in the attempt to confirm Lovecraft's information, and Mrs. Ruth A. Fletcher, the Reference Librarian there, provided me with a helpful answer which I cannot do better than to quote:

> In the Thirty-Seventh Annual Catalogue of Wheaton Female Seminary, Norton, Mass. for the year ending July 1872 (Norton: 1872), p. 11, Lillie D. Phillips and Sarah S. Phillips, both of Greene, R.I., are listed as members of the Preparatory Course. They are also listed on p. 13 as among the pupils in instrumental music. On p. 17 the course of study for the Preparatory Class is given as:
>
> Arithmetic, to ratio and Proportion
> English or Latin Grammar
> Geography
>
> In the Thirty-Eighth Annual Catalogue of Wheaton Female Seminary, Norton, Mass. for the year ending July 1873 (Norton: 1873), p. 9. Lillie D. Phillips of Green [*sic*] R.I., is listed as a member of the Junior Class; on p. 11, she is included in the pupils in Latin.
>   P. 18 lists the course of study for the Junior Class as:
>
> First Term:
>   Arithmetic completed
>   English Analysis, or Caesar
>   United States History
>
> Second Term:
>   Algebra
>   English Analysis completed or Quintus Curtius
>   United States History completed
>
> Third Term:
>   Algebra completed
>   Physiology
>   Natural History, or Sallu[s]t

I find no mention of Anna E. Phillips in any of the catalogues. As far as we know, there is no photographic material.

This answer has several interesting consequences. Once again, Lovecraft appears to have embellished slightly upon his family's fortunes when he wrote to Frank Belknap Long on June 4, 1921 (*SL* 1.135), following the death of his mother: "My mother was a person of unusual charm and force of character; accomplished in literature and fine arts—a French scholar, musician, and painter in oils. She was a *graduate* [my emphasis] of Wheaton College." As we have seen, Sarah Susan Phillips certainly did not graduate from anything more than the preparatory course at the Wheaton Female Seminary. (Of course, there is no reason to doubt Lovecraft's remarks about the skill of his mother and his aunt Lillian as artists. Most of his adult life Lovecraft kept on his wall the crayon drawing which his mother had done of her birthplace, the Stephen Place house in Foster, Rhode Island. When Lovecraft and his aunt Annie Gamwell moved into larger quarters at 66 College Street in May 1933 a large oil painting of the seacoast by his aunt Lillian [1855–1932] joined them. Presumably, this had previously been in storage among the other effects from the ancestral mansion at 454 Angell Street. I wonder whether any of the paintings and drawings of Sarah Susan and Lillian might still be extant today; they would certainly be an interesting gauge of the sincerity of Lovecraft's comments. In one letter to Winfield Townley Scott which is in the John Hay Library, Muriel Eddy stated that she knew of the disposition of several of Sarah Susan's paintings.)

The lack of photographic material at Wheaton College is also interesting in that it tells us that the early family photographs of the Phillips sisters which Philip Jack Grill and R. Alain Everts obtained from members of the Phillips family are probably all that we shall ever have. (One might make one last stab by trying to locate the records of the Rhode Island State Normal School, which, according to Lovecraft's letter to Moe cited above, Lillian attended for some time following her attendance at the Wheaton Female Seminary. The Brown University Archives, by the way, has youthful photographs of Dr. Franklin Chase Clark [1857–1915] and Edward Francis Gamwell [1869–1936], both of when received their bachelor's degrees from Brown, in 1869 and 1894, respectively. Gamwell continued for his master's degree from Brown in 1895, serving as an instructor of English in 1894–1895; he thereafter engaged in editorial and advertising work in Providence, Cambridge, and Boston. He was a member at Phi Beta Kappa and secretary of his graduating class; the Archives still has the original draught of his commencement address. Dr. Clark, if anything, was a more gifted student than Gamwell. After graduating from Brown in 1869, he spent a year in graduate studies under Oliver Wendell Holmes, Sr. He secured his medical degree from the College of Physicians and Surgeons of Columbia University in New York City, and then returned to Providence for internship at Rhode Island Hospital and a long private practice on the East Side. Despite his other preoccupations, however, he was quite active as a general and medical writer. According to Lovecraft, his papers were deposited with the Rhode Island Historical Society Library following his death is 1915; today these papers are in the Brown University Archives—perhaps transferred there because Dr. Clark was a Brown graduate. [The Historical Society still has three volumes of historical newspaper clippings gathered by Dr. Clark.] Dr. Clark's poetry—including his translation of Virgil's *Aeneid*—is among these papers; and some day a Lovecraftian student especially interested in Lovecraft's poetry ought surely to go over this work to determine its influence on Lovecraft's own early work.)[208]

17. Lovecraft's travelogues; the Arkham country

It should by no means be thought that Providence and its immediate environs are the only source for Lovecraftiana. Lovecraft's antiquarian travels ranged up and down the eastern seaboard, from Quebec to Key West (in 1931 he was deterred only by lack of money from extending his travels southward to Cuba), and as far west as New Orleans (where he met his friend E. Hoffmann Price for the first time in 1932). He left detailed accounts of these travels in his letters and his more formal travelogues—of which only a small minority have to date been published. In this line, Arkham has printed principally his account of Charleston (first published by Herman C. Koenig in 1936), an account of his visit to the Endless Caverns, and a number of brief letter extracts pertaining to his travels. Much more remains, however. Lovecraft's letters to Mrs. Clark from the spring of 1931 contain a marvelous account of St. Augustine and the other parts of Florida which he visited at that time—an account which was only minimally published in *Selected Letters* III. In addition, there remain unpublished a number of more formal travelogues including the lengthy historic-travelogue of Quebec mentioned in *Selected Letters* III.[209] Indeed, I think that an ambitious Lovecraftian might eventually make a very fine volume indeed by combining Lovecraft's travelogues with photographs and illustrations of the most prominent places he visited. The hordes of postcards which he sent to his correspondents during his travels could serve as illustrations in those instances in which the original sites which Lovecraft visited have been substantially altered.

The Massachusetts shoreline north of Boston, of course, was the principal setting for his most famous stories of the "Cthulhu Mythos"—although he would occasionally take his characters farther north—to Maine in "The Thing on the Doorstep" and to Vermont in "The Whisperer in Darkness." That Salem was the prototype of his Arkham and Marblehead the prototype of his Kingsport is well established from his own statements in published letters.[210] From brief visits to both of these places, I can say that they will undoubtedly continue to provide a rich inspiration to future Lovecraftians. Marblehead in particular is still the virtually unchanged eighteenth-century town with narrow colonial lanes and clapboard buildings which virtually transported Lovecraft into a fit of ecstasy—at finding himself in what amounted to a physical remnant of his beloved eighteenth-century—when he first discovered it on a snowy day in December 1922. (This experience inspired his story "The Festival.") Salem—as the prototype of Arkham—is also full of beautiful colonial buildings which amply evoke the atmosphere of the principal "metropolis" of Lovecraft's Mythos, although unfortunately it is far more commercialized and altered than Marblehead and other New England towns. Certainly, an ambitious Lovecraftian ought someday to set about comparing Lovecraft's plan of the town of Arkham (reproduced in *Marginalia*) with the actual plan of Salem—some interesting associations might result. The "Witch House" is a prominent feature both in Lovecraft's map and in Salem today—so that could well serve as a starting point to researchers seeking to compare Lovecraft's plan of Arkham with the actual city which served as its inspiration. Of course, one would hardly expect to find exact parallels; but dominant features shared by Salem and Lovecraft's fictional Arkham might rapidly become apparent.[211]

Indeed, there is at least one place in Salem which played a directly verifiable role as the inspiration for a Lovecraft story. (Although, of course, the actual "Witch House" must have had some relation to the "witch house" in "The Dreams in the Witch House.") Writing to Bernard Austin Dwyer in June 1927 (*SL* 2.138) about his use of a passage from Cotton Mather's *Magnalia Christi Americana* in the development of his story "The Unnamable," Lovecraft further stated: "There is actually an ancient slab half engulfed by a giant willow in the middle of the Charles St. Burying Ground in Salem." This setting for "The Unnamable" is in addition confirmed in Lovecraft's letter to Duane W. Rimel of February 14, 1934, held in the Lovecraft Collection in the John Hay Library (*SL* 4.386; *FLB* 140)—although, in copying from that letter, I copied "Charter Street," rather than "Charles Street." Anyone familiar with Salem can probably say immediately which version is correct.[212]

There is also a hillside tomb—not a slab such as Lovecraft describes in "The Unnamable"—in St. John's Churchyard in Providence which impressed George Wetzel as a possible setting for Lovecraft's story because of the large tree which rises immediately above the tomb on the hillside. Wetzel's photograph of the tomb appeared facing p. 226 of *The Shuttered Room*, with the notation that it had served as the setting of "The Unnamable." I think the two Lovecraft letters cited above, however, make it clear that this tale had a Salem setting. St. John's Churchyard was of course the site of many a midnight visit by Lovecraft and his friends; in fact, in his memoir of Lovecraft, W. Paul Cook indicates that H. Warner Munn—whom he mysteriously refused to refer to by name—became so disturbed during one vigil in the Churchyard that he never thereafter recaptured the graveyard morbidity of his earlier weird tales (see *LR* 124–25). The Churchyard was also the site of the writing of the three famous acrostic sonnets on the name of Edgar Allan Poe by Lovecraft,

Barlow, and Adolphe de Castro in August 1936—Poe himself having wandered in the churchyard during his courtship with the Providence poetess Sarah Helen Whitman, whose home abutted on the Churchyard.[213]

Of course, Salem and Marblehead are hardly the whole of the Lovecraft territory in Massachusetts. In June 1928, as we learn from his letter to Zealia Bishop of July 28, 1928 (*SL* 2.244–46), Lovecraft visited his friend Edith Miniter (1867–1934) and her cousin Evanore Beebe at their rambling colonial home in North Wilbraham, Massachusetts. Describing the region to Mrs. Bishop, he wrote:

> Far to the west, across marshy meadows where at evening the fire-flies dance in incredibly fantastic profusion, the benign bulk of Wilbraham Mountain rises purple and mystical. The region, being very old and remote, is full of the most extraordinary folklore; some of which will certainly find lodgment in my future stories if I ever live to write any more. The scenery thereabouts is magnificent—as I can testify after a walk around the mountain and almost over its crest.

According to Paul Cook's memoir *H. P. Lovecraft: A Portrait* (p. 36; *LR* 133–34), Lovecraft wrote a memoir of his fortnight's visit in north Wilbraham for the memorial which was planned for Mrs. Miniter; as I have stated in an earlier note,[214] I do not believe this memorial was ever published by Cook, but the Lovecraft memoir to which he referred is probably the same as "Mrs. Miniter—Estimates and Recollections," published in the *Californian* for spring 1938. Unfortunately, I have not myself ever seen this article of Lovecraft's; but from Cook's remarks in his own memoir (pp. 36–38) we cannot doubt that Lovecraft soaked up as much of the lore and legendry of the Wilbraham region as he could during his visit. Writes Cook (p. 37): "In Miss Beebe and Mrs. Miniter Howard had hosts, guides, and teachers who knew literally all there was to know on the subjects in which he was interested. Either was the best in New England on the history, antiques, folklore, myth, legendry, superstition and scandal of the region."[215] I have been told that Lovecraft's own article on Mrs. Miniter specifically acknowledges his debt to Mrs. Miniter and Miss Beebe for much of the local legendry which he used in the writing of his famous story "The Dunwich Horror" in June and July 1928, shortly after his visit to North Wilbraham—local legendry which included in particular the calling of whippoorwills for the souls of the deed which he used so prominently in his story. Writing to August Derleth on November 6, 1931 (*SL* 3.432–33; *ES* 1.405) regarding the settings of his famous New England tales, Lovecraft conceded that Arkham and Kingsport were vague equivalents of Salem and Marblehead, respectively, and continued with respect to the Dunwich country:

> Similarly, there is no "Dunwich"—the place being a vague echo of the decadent Massachusetts countryside around Springfield—say Wilbraham, Monson, and Hampden. It would be impossible to make any real place the scene of such bizarre happenings as those which beset my hypothetical towns. At the same time, I take pains to make these places wholly and realistically characteristic of genuine New England seaports—always being authentic concerning architecture, atmosphere, dialect, manners and customs, &c.[216]

The vague identification of the Dunwich region with the Wilbraham–Monson–Hampden area seems to have become fairly canonical on the basis of this letter to Derleth. However, this identification has not gone without some dissent. Arguing principally on the basis of local legendry and stone formations, Andrew E. Rothovius suggested an alternative in his essay "Lovecraft and the New England Megaliths" in *The Dark Brotherhood and Other Pieces* (p. 184):

> The identification Lovecraft himself gave out of the Dunwich country, was that it corresponded to the Wilbraham–Hampden–Monson area, southeast of Springfield and south of Quabbin. This section has not yet been extensively searched for specimens of the megaliths, but so far none are known to exist there. To the writer it would seem that in making this identification, Lovecraft may have sought for some reason to draw attention away from his true locale, which I believe to have been more to the north—i.e., in the towns of Leverett, Shutesbury, Pelham, and Wendell, and the now drowned villages of Prescott, Enfield, and Dana, sleeping forever beneath the waters of Quabbin Reservoir . . .

Certainly, there is nothing I can do to add to or to detract from Mr. Rothovius's marshalling of legendry, topography, and archaeological discoveries to argue his case. I feel that he is wrong in suggesting that Lovecraft may have wished to divert attention from the true locale of his story—that as Lovecraft himself stated in his letter to Derleth, there were no exact equivalences between the settings of his fantastic stories and actually existing regions. In light Lovecraft's own statements (particularly in "Mrs. Miniter—Estimates and Recollections") and the coincidence of his visit to North Wilbraham in June 1928 with the writing or "The Dunwich Horror" in June and July 1928, there can be little reasonable doubt that some of the lore and legendry he absorbed from Mrs. Miniter and Miss Beebe went into "The Dunwich Horror"— and perhaps some of the local scenery, too. However, there are several statements in Paul Cook's memoir of Lovecraft, not cited by Mr. Rothovius, which seem to support his contention that some of the inspiration for the terrain described in "The Dunwich Horror" derived from the Quabbin Valley to the north of the Wilbraham–Monson–Hampden region. According to Lovecraft's letter to Mrs. Bishop of July 28, 1928 (*SL* 2.245), Lovecraft spent a week at the home of Paul Cook in Athol, Massachusetts, just north of the Quabbin Valley, just prior to his invitation to North Wilbraham for a fortnight's stay with Mrs. Miniter and Miss Beebe. Cook writes of Lovecraft's trip from Athol to North Wilbraham in his memoir (*op. cit.*, pp. 36–37; *LR* 134):

> Starting from the dreary town in northern Massachusetts [Athol] where I was immured, he went towards Springfield on what was known as the "Rabbit" train, either because it hopped from town to town or because if a passenger spied a rabbit the train would halt for him to go out and chase it. The trip was especially interesting to H.P.L., because it ran through a valley [the Quabbin Valley—as is clear from a map] that was to be flooded and the railroad abandoned. We had been through the valley by road, and now Howard could see the line of the railroad before the rails were torn up. He reported most favorably on the impression the line made on him. The train would stop at a cute little station, deserted. The trainman would descend, unlock the doors, put mail bags in, take mail bags out, take what express there was and sign for it, lock up the station and hop along. Occasionally a lone traveler would be waiting, who seldom had a ticket, but paid his fare on the train. The valley was already dying, but the train must make its daily trips as long as an inhabitant remained. Acting on instructions, Howard got off the train at a dinky, deserted station before arriving in Springfield, and struck out by the compass in his head over back roads, following one side of an equiangular triangle to the station of North Wilbraham on the Boston to Springfield division. From there he easily located the Beebe place, which was known far and wide.

Whether the motor tour through the Quabbin Valley of which Cook writes took place during Lovecraft's visit to Athol in June 1928 or earlier, I do not know. The *Selected Letters* establish that Cook and Munn visited Lovecraft in Providence in July 1927, while Donald Wandrei was also visiting (Lovecraft to Moe, July 30, 1927, *SL* 2.157–58); later, in October and November 1927 Cook visited Providence once again (Lovecraft to Long, November 1927, *SL* 2.185). However, Lovecraft's visit to Arthur Goodenough in Vermont in August 1927—his first sight of that state—may possibly have included a visit with Cook in Athol, during which time the motor tour of the Quabbin Valley might have been made; see Lovecraft to Long, August 1927, *SL* 2.158–59.[217] When Lovecraft visited Cook in Athol in May 1929 (Lovecraft to Toldridge, May 29, 1929, *SL* 2.358; *ET* 72), Cook and Munn did take him on a number of motor trips—one of them to visit Goodenough in Vermont.[218] "Finally I decided to conclude my two months of varied wandering, & had Cook bring me down to Providence in his car—traversing the territory described in my 'Dunwich Horror'."

Now, none of these details of Lovecraft's travels would be particularly important, were it not for several earlier paragraphs of Cook's memoir. Writing of Athol, where he spent many of his adult years, Cook bemoaned the fact that even Lovecraft was able to find little of interest within its dismal precincts. However, Cook does give one extremely interesting little piece of information about an Athol place name which Lovecraft adopted for his fiction: "The only thing he carried away from the town itself for literary use was the name 'Sentinel Hill,' but he had to move that hill several miles down into the doomed valley in order to get it into a romantic environment." (*LR* 129) Now, "Sentinel Hill" is the name of the hill where the Whateley family performs its rites in "The Dunwich Horror;" and Cook states quite clearly here that Lovecraft adopted the name from an Athol feature and then applied it to what could only have been Quabbin Valley scenery for the purposes of his fiction. (On the basis of Lovecraft's description of "Sentinel Hill" in "The Dunwich Horror," Rothovius [*op. cit.*, p. 184] identifies it with "Mineral Mountain in the northeastern corner of Shutesbury." The entire Quabbin Valley, by the way, was not submerged when the reservoir was built; and Shutesbury is one of the towns still above water.)

Clearly, then, we do have some evidence that some Quabbin Valley features went into the writing of "The Dunwich Horror," in addition to Wilbraham–Monson–Hampden lore and legendry. Indeed, the further remarks of Cook in his memoir would make it seem as if the Quabbin Valley was the principal setting for Lovecraft's story (p. 31; *LR* 129–30):

> From that entire section Howard carried the color for only one story. The valley stretching for thirty miles south of the town [Athol] was in the first stages of preparation for being flooded for an immense reservoir for metropolitan Boston. Characteristic of the valley were low hills, their tops rounded off by glacial action in a curiously regular manner. These became the "domed hills" of his story. And on some of these hills were indeed boulders left by the same glaciers, and these became the rings and squares and pentagons and strange designs in stone laid out by an ancient people. The whole layout was made to order for the writer of weird fiction. A half a dozen towns were to be wiped off the map, homesteads occupied by generations were to be covered with fifty feet of water, and, most fascinating of all, the graveyards were all to be dug up and their contents transferred—when there were contents. We speculated as to what longchained forces of evil might be released by this wholesale opening of crypts, vaults, and impregnated earth.

Howard never exhausted (in fact he hardly touched) the possibilities of the subject, although he frequently referred to it. In this valley doomed to destruction there were several examples of the best period of colonial church architecture and contemporary farmhouse construction, which Howard of course lamented.

Compare this with Lovecraft's descriptive passages at the beginning of "The Dunwich Horror" (*DH* 160–61; *CF* 2.418):

> When a rise in the road brings the mountains in view above the deep woods, the feeling of strange uneasiness is increased. The summits are too rounded and symmetrical to give a sense of comfort and naturalness, and sometimes the sky silhouettes with especial clearness the queer circles of tall stone pillars with which most of them are crowned.

Cook's Quabbin Valley, it seems clear, did play quite a significant role in Lovecraft's topographical conception of the Dunwich country.[219] Perhaps it was principally lore and legendry which Mrs. Miniter and Miss Beebe contributed from the Wilbraham–Monson–Hampden region—although of course Mr. Rothovius brings forward a healthy body of Quabbin Valley lore and legendry which also might have gone into the writing of "The Dunwich Horror." (Perhaps Mrs. Miniter and Miss Beebe were authorities on the lore and legendry of this region, too.) Indeed, it is characteristic of Lovecraft to have amalgamated bits and pieces of New England scenery and legends from various places in order to form his fictional setting—atmospherically if not factually veracious. For instance, one might consider his famous story "The Strange High House in the Mist," whose setting was fictional Kingsport, the rough equivalent of Marblehead. However, in the same letter in which Lovecraft communicated this rough identification to August Derleth (Lovecraft to Derleth, November 6, 1931, *SL* 3.432–33; *ES* 1.405), Lovecraft added the rejoinder:

> As for that rocky promontory—the coast north of Boston *is* composed of high rocky cliffs, which in several places rise to considerable altitudes as bold headlands. Of course, though, there is nothing as dizzy as the fabled seat or the Strange High House. If I had any promontory specifically in mind when writing that tale, it was the headland near Gloucester called "Mother Ann"—though that has no relation to the city as my mysterious cliff has to "Kingsport." Marblehead has rocky cliffs—though of no great height—along the neck to the south of the ancient town . . . .

Writing of his summer travels in Maine and Massachusetts in his letter to Frank Belknap Long of September 6, 1927 (*SL* 2.164), however, Lovecraft gave yet another identification of the promontory in "The Strange High House in the Mist," this time with "the titan cliffs of Magnolia—memories of which prompted 'The Strange High House the Mist'." (Lovecraft had visited Magnolia with his wife-to-be Sonia H. Greene in 1922.)

The setting of Lovecraft's "Innsmouth" is another difficult problem. Lovecraft was thoroughly familiar with the Massachusetts shoreline north of Boston; witness, among many others, his letter to Zealia Bishop of September 8, 1927 (*SL* 2.166–67). Andrew Rothovius (*op. cit.*, p. 182) expressed his opinion that Ipswich was the actual setting for "The Shadow over Innsmouth." Eric Carlson, who designed the fine map of Innsmouth which appeared in *Nyctalops* No. 6 following Lovecraft's original plan published in *Something about Cats and Other Pieces* (p. 174; *CE* 5.252)—and adding considerable detail based upon his own readings of "The Shadow over Innsmouth"—took another tack in discussing the setting of Innsmouth in a letter to me:

> Yes, my friend, Innsmouth is a sticky wicket . . . . Colin Wilson (*Tales of the Cthulhu Mythos*, p. 387) attempted to place it at "Cohasset, a rundown fishing village between Quonochontaug and Weekapaug in Southern Rhode Island." . . . Cook said it could "easily" be identified (*HPL: A Portrait*, p. 43; *LR* 139), then promptly wandered off without having done so. Ipswich has been suggested (*Dark Brotherhood*, p. 182), and even Derleth (*Selected Letters* II p. xxiii) states Marblehead "gave him the locale" for Innsmouth, in spite of the fact that HPL stated that "'Kingsport' corresponds to Marblehead." (*Selected Letters* III p. 432).
>
> But the only obvious answer that I could find is his [HPL's] letter to Klarkash-Ton in *Selected Letters* III p. 435), which projects Newburyport as the setting, quite positively, I think.

18. Real New England locales in Lovecraft's fiction

Of course, Lovecraft's fictional settings were not limited to the decaying seaports and countryside of Massachusetts. Many times he used his own native Providence as the setting for his stories—"The Shunned House," *The Case of Charles Dexter Ward*, and "The Haunter of the Dark" come immediately to mind. Even metropolitan Boston came in for treatment in Lovecraft's setting of Richard Upton Pickman's residence in a decaying section of the North End in "Pickman's Model." Lovecraft gives only vague directions in the text of his story (he does fix the site of the Pickman residence firmly in the North End with his statement that the Copp's Hill Burying Ground "could not be many blocks away"); but, unfortunately, we do know that the actual site of his inspiration has perished. Witness Lovecraft's letter of September 22, 1927, to Zealia Bishop (*SL* 2.170):

> Incidentally, the setting of that tale ["Pickman's Model"] was very close to fact up to this year, and I was tremendously mortified last July when I tried to show the district to one of my guests (the Donald Wandrei whose "Red Brain" appears in the current *Weird Tales*) and found the whole scene torn down for two blocks around! I imagine the building inspectors must have found those ancient houses as sinister as I did, albeit with a different sort of perception. That is the perennial grief of an architectural antiquarian—in a city as large as Providence or Boston something quaint is always being demolished in the interest of alleged progress . . . .

(This same anecdote is repeated in Lovecraft's letter of February 14, 1934, to Duane W. Rimel [*SL* 4.386; *FLB* 140].)[220]

Surprisingly, even New York City, Lovecraft's hated "Babylon," provided a number of settings for his stories. I can recall reading a lengthy letter from Lovecraft to Frank Belknap Long in manuscript at the John Hay Library—a letter which gave an exhaustive tour of colonial survivals in lower Manhattan—details certainly reflected in Lovecraft's later story "He." (Lovecraft's letter to Moe of May 18, 1922 [*SL* 1.175–83] refers to a tour which Kleiner gave Lovecraft and Loveman of the lower East Side; but my memory insistently tells me I saw a much fuller account in a letter to Long at the John Hay Library. Neither the Long nor the Moe files of letters were at the John Hay Library when I was there, but there were typescript carbons of several long "travelogue" letters which Lovecraft sent to Long.) Lovecraft's letter to Mrs.

Clark of September 29, 1922 (*SL* 1.198; *NY* 28–29) relating his discovery of the ancient churchyard of the old Dutch Reformed Church—which I believe the original unedited letter in the Lovecraft Collection at the John Hay Library establishes was in Brooklyn near Sonia's apartment at 259 Parkside—also bears a manifest relationship to his story "The Hound," also written in that year. While he lived with Sonia in her Brooklyn apartment, Lovecraft took much of his writing to nearby Prospect Park, and, as I believe I have mentioned before, he called at least one section of the Park "the vale of Pnath" in a letter to his aunt Mrs. Clark. (I lack the precise reference. In general, Lovecraft loved the effect of natural grottos and ravines. In his memoir of Lovecraft, Winfield Townley Scott relates that Lovecraft and his mother would most often meet at the "grotto" on the Butler Hospital Grounds during her confinement there in 1919–1921. In addition, Lovecraft loved the effect of the steep hillside ravines descending to the river in Blackstone Park in Providence.) Another Brooklyn site connected with Lovecraft is of course the hideous "Red Hook" section, on whose edges he lived at 169 Clinton Street in 1925 and 1926. In November 1971 Robb Baker, a gifted young writer who was then working on a biography of Lovecraft which I hope he will someday resume, guided me to this "mouldering brownstone mansion" of which Lovecraft gave such a colorful description himself in his letter to Bernard Austin Dwyer of March 26, 1927 (*SL* 2.114–20). (Lovecraft indicates at the beginning of this letter his intention to write a story around this residence, but I do not believe he ever did so.)[221]

As for Red Hook in general, it may yet today exist much as it did at the time of the writing of Lovecraft's story "The Horror at Red Hook" in August 1925; Lovecraft wrote to Rimel on February 14, 1934 (*SL* 4.386; *FLB* 140), that he suspected that Red Hook was then still much the same as it had been at the time of his writing. A final and rather obscure Lovecraftian site in Brooklyn is revealed in Lovecraft's letter to Mrs. Clark of July 10, 1931:

> After dinner Loveman & I took McGrath [Pat McGrath] out to see Union Place—that ancient & spectral courtyard which inspired my "Fungi from Yuggoth". [Probably, most notably the individual sonnet "The Courtyard."] It is just the same as ever—though we were there just too early to catch the most ghoulish note in its sequester'd & mouldering personality. It is, as I have told you, wholly hidden from the street proper—reached by an archway & long passage.

That evening, Lovecraft and his friends had dined at the Bristol Dining Room on Willoughby Street (near Fulton) in Brooklyn, so that Union Place is probably somewhere nearby.[222] In the same letter to Mrs. Clark, Lovecraft spoke of revisiting the old Dutch Reformed Church whose graveyard had so impressed him in 1922: "... the ancient Church Ave. steeple still rears its Georgian height above the Dutch-inscribed gravestones of the rambling cemetery." The address which he gives—which is almost certainly one in Brooklyn—ought to help Lovecraftian researchers in digging out the principal inspiration for "He," too.[223] Even nearby Elizabeth, New Jersey is not without an important Lovecraftian place, witness Lovecraft's letter to Mrs. Clark of November 4–5, 1924 (*SL* 1.357; *NY* 82) describing a particular house found in that city:

> And on the northeast corner of Bridge Street and Elizabeth Avenue is a terrible old house—a hellish place where night-black deeds must have been done in the early seventeen-hundreds—with a blackish unpainted surface, unnaturally steep roof, and an outside flight of steps leading to the second story, suffocatingly embowered in a tangle of ivy so dense that one cannot but imagine it accursed or corpse-fed. It reminded me of the Babbitt house in Benefit Street [135 Benefit Street], which as you recall made me write those lines entitled "The House" in 1920. Later its image came up again with renewed vividness, finally causing me to write a new horror story with its scene in Providence and with the Babbitt house as its basis. It is called "The Shunned House", and I finished it last Sunday night.

Thus, the famous structure at 135 Benefit Street in Providence is not the sole dwelling with which we may rightfully associate his famed story "The Shunned House"—for in Elizabeth, New Jersey, on the corner of Bridge Street and Elizabeth Avenue, there is—or at least was in 1924—another avatar of Lovecraft's fictional creation. (George Wetzel wrote me that Jack Grill visited the house in Elizabeth, New Jersey, but I do not know whether he photographed it.)[224] The description which Lovecraft gives of the "Shunned House" is clearly a description of the house on Benefit Street in Providence; however, at least some echo of the Elizabeth structure might be seen in the fact that Lovecraft makes William Harris, Jr., the son of the original builder of his fictional "Shunned House,"[225] marry Phebe Hetfield of Elizabethtown, New Jersey ("The Shunned House," *MM* 229; *CF* 1.459). Elizabethtown was the name of Elizabeth in colonial times. So we see that even hated New York and its environs are not devoid of singularly Lovecraftian horrors—and, as Lovecraft himself once warned his friend Sam Loveman when they walked past the "Shunned House" in Providence, it may well be true that—even amidst the bustle and activity of New York—*the end is not yet.*

19. Who Ate Roger Williams?

During the winter of 1955–1956, there appeared in the third issue of John Murdock's fanzine *Vagabond* what purported to be a note from the pen of H. P. Lovecraft—given the title "Who Ate Roger Williams?" by the owner of the original manuscript—accompanied by an explanatory note by Lovecraft scholar George Wetzel. We cannot do better to begin our discussion of this purported piece of Lovecraft's than to quote this appearance in full:

WHO ATE ROGER WILLIAMS?
A Note by H. P. Lovecraft

Roger Williams died in March, 1684 and was buried in his home lot on the steep hill back of his house, which lay on the north side of the present Bowen St. hill. Grave site is now in the yard of Sullivan Dorr Mansion, built in 1809.

In 187– Betsey Williams, a lineal descendant of Roger, died and left her estate (in the S. part of Providence) to the city for use as Roger Williams Park. On this estate was an old graveyard in which many of the Williams family were interred, and the city decided to remove the remains of Roger and his wife to this spot—erecting a suitable monument over them.

When the old hillside graves were opened, no trace of the actual bodies remained—the outlines of the coffins being barely discernable as deposits of disintegrated wood. In Roger's grave, however, there was a slender root from a neighboring apple tree; which had a curious contour resembling that of a human body or skeleton—or rather, as if it had followed the lines formed by a body or skeleton. This was thought by many to have been exactly what it seemed—a rootlet which had entered the grave before the dissolution of the body, and which had consequently been bent as it traversed the mouldering remains. The theory is by no means universally accepted, but the root is still preserved in the museum of the R.I. Hist. Society. In Steele's "14 Weeks in Chemistry", published in the 1880s, this fact that roots draw nourishment from the soil and transmit it to their branches and fruits, and that the edible fruit may contain actual chemical atoms and molecules once a part of that nourishing soil, Steele whimsically pictures some one as eating an apple containing matter from Roger's bones, and asks the somewhat flippant question "Who Ate Roger Williams?". [The last sentence is reproduced as it stands in *Vagabond*.]

NOTES ON THE ABOVE

Jack Grill, collector of Lovecraftiana, discovered this unpublished article of Lovecraft's—"Who Ate Roger Williams?"—along with another unpublished Lovecraft ms—a travel letter about Washington, D.C. Grill had bought from Wilfred Talman, an old friend of Lovecraft's, a number of items and among them was the above, which was typed with a pencilled correction on it by Lovecraft, on a letter-size sheet, without a title (Grill gave it the present and apt one). Talman used the facts in this ms. of Lovecraft's for a story he wrote for an undertaker's mag which Seabury Quinn edited at one time. The ms. is interesting in the fact that its idea forms part of the story in Lovecraft's THE SHUNNED HOUSE; where he mentions the queer contours assumed by certain of the sinuous tree roots that thrust their way into the cellar of the "shunned house". Curiously enough, I once ran across a datum similar to that mentioned of Roger Williams' grave and the human-shaped root. It was in the "Boonsboro Odd Fellow" (a Maryland paper) for July 10, 1879: In Hagerstown, Md., while some bodies were being removed from a graveyard, there was found the roots of an apple tree had completely filled a skeleton, in such a manner that if removed intact the roots would have closely resembled the human form.

Now, this grim little narrative concerning the exhumation of Roger Williams's remains would seem to be precisely the kind of thing which would attract Lovecraft's attention. Indeed, the essential veracity of the account of the matter given in "Who Ate Roger Williams?" is verified in "The Book Notes" for March 15, 1890, by Sidney Rider, one of the most eminent authorities on Rhode Island, which I reproduce here entire:[226]

> It is thirty years ago, (March 22nd, 1860,) that a party of gentlemen opened the graves of the family of Roger Williams, which were supposed to be upon the land of Mr. Sullivan Dorr, on Benefit street, the same land now owned by Mr. Samuel Ames. Nothing was found which would afford positive proof that the graves opened were actually those of Roger Williams and of his immediate family. This was assumed. But certain curious facts were described to which Mr. Zachariah Allen made some allusion in a memorial written by him at the time. But one result follows, which was little thought of by those engaged in the investigation. This was that their work would be used as an illustration in chemistry in the school books of the time, and even to this time. Mr. J. D. Steele, the author of an elementary treatise on chemistry, made use of the circumstance to illustrate the circulation of matter. Here is his note: "The truth that matter passes from the animal back to the vegetable, and from the vegetable to the animal kingdom again, received a curious illustration not long since, as stated in the *Hartford Press*. [Rider here omits a note which Steele appended to his discussion on p. 259 of the edition cited: 'The author has in his possession a letter, from a gentleman who was present at the opening of this grave, attesting the truth of this singular statement.'] For the purpose of erecting a suitable monument in memory of Roger Williams, the founder of Rhode Island, his private burying-ground was searched for the graves of himself and wife. It was found that everything had passed into oblivion. The shape of the coffins could only be traced by a black line of carbonaceous matter. The rusted hinges and nails, and a round wooden knot,

alone remained in one grave; while a single lock of braided hair was found in the other. Near the graves stood an apple-tree. This had sent down two main roots into the very presence of the coffined dead. The larger root, pushing its way to the precise spot occupied by the skull of Roger Williams, had made a turn as if passing around it, and followed the direction of the backbone to the hips. Here it divided into two branches, sending one along each leg to the heel [the edition of the Steele book which I saw has here the obvious misprint 'head'], when both turned upward to the toes. One of these roots formed a slight crook at the knee, which made the whole bear a striking resemblance to the human form. There were the graves, but their occupants had disappeared; the bones even had vanished. There stood the thief—the guilty apple-tree— caught in the very act of robbery. The spoliation was complete. The organic matter—the flesh, the bones, of Roger Williams—had passed into an apple tree. The elements had been absorbed by the roots, transmuted into woody fibre, which could now be burned as fuel, or carved into ornaments; had bloomed into fragrant blossoms, which had delighted the eye of passers-by, and scattered the sweetest perfume of spring; more than that—had been converted into luscious fruit, which, from year to year, had been gathered and eaten. How pertinent, then, is the question, 'Who Ate Roger Williams?'"

(Steele's *Fourteen Weeks in Chemistry*, p. 259). (1867).

" But the jolly old apple tree rooting around
   Seeking for phosphates under the ground;
   Followed his back bone all the way down,
      And old Mother William's, too.

What's bred in the bone, the flesh will show,
What's bred in the root, the fruit will know,
For two hundred years, this fruit did grow,
   Till posterity ate him up."

These two comical verses are taken from Mr. Charles Miller's facetious poem, "The Settlement of Rhode Island," (1874). To him who reads the memorial of Mr. Zachariah Allen (1860) will be discovered the fact, that all the chemical ideas set forth by Mr. Steele had been previously stated by Mr. Allen, whose very language had in part been employed.

The Rhode Island Index in the Reference Department of the Providence Public Library contains an exhaustive listing of treatments of the story of Roger Williams and the apple tree, in historical, literary, and scientific works.[227] The definitive treatment of the entire matter, however, is undoubtedly Howard Miller Chapin's[228] *Report on the Burial Place of Roger Williams* (Providence, 1918, 30pp.), which even has as its frontispiece a photograph of the famed root itself. (The root is still the property of the Rhode Island Historical Society, although it is now in storage and no longer on display in the museum of the

Society [John Brown House, 52 Power Street].) Chapin gives a complete discussion of all the anecdotal evidence that the graves in the backyard of the Sullivan Dorr Mansion were those of Williams and his family and reproduces entire the memorial of Zachariah Allen, along with a number of detailed maps and sketches. For the later history of such "dust" as was found in the grave which was reputedly Roger Williams's, the fourth volume of the *Old Stone Bank History of Rhode Island* (pp. 57–60) is a good source. (Many newspaper articles relating to the subject of the Roger Williams gravesite and the later transfers of his "dust" are also indexed by the Rhode Island Index in the Reference Department of the Providence Public Library.) As I recall, the "dust" was not transferred to the property of Betsey Williams in south Providence but rather to the Randall tomb in the Old North Burial Ground for interment. It was finally transferred to the base of the statue of Roger Williams which overlooks Providence from Prospect Terrace in the late thirties, where it remains today. (And hopefully will remain for some time hence—barring desecration by some latter-day Charles Dexter Ward!) The site of the presumed Williams graves (sans apple tree) can still be seen today in the backyard of the beautiful Sullivan Dorr Mansion (on the hill above the mansion—the same hill the leering tenements of Lovecraft's Commonplace Book entry climb on the opposite side of Bowen Street) and is marked by a broken base which was originally intended to support one of the columns of the Arcade in downtown Providence.

The attribution of the short note "Who Ate Roger Williams?" to Lovecraft was not to stand for long, however. In 1958 Wilfred Talman wrote George Wetzel that what he had certified to Grill as an unpublished Lovecraft manuscript was in fact probably only "a copy in his handwriting" of one of Talman's own articles.[229] To support his conclusion, Talman made brief quotation from Lovecraft's letter to him of December 12, 1931, which offered comment upon a discussion of Roger Williams and the apple tree which had then but recently taken place in Bertrand K. Hart's column "The Sideshow" in the *Providence Journal*:

> Enclosed are a couple of articles from my favourite "Sideshow" which you can add to your morgue if you like. The one on "Who Ate Roger Williams" is the one I spoke of before. As I now see upon a full reading, (I had only a glance before) the anecdotal text is indeed properly traced to Joel Dorman Steele as an original source—so that *your Quinn article* [my italics] remains as veracious in fact as it always was in intent. And to think poor Joel is forgotten by all you young fellows![230]

Although the second page of Talman's 1958 letter was lost by George Wetzel, it seems clear from this passage that it was his intention to indicate that he himself had written the "Who Ate Roger Williams?" manuscript in some stage of preparation for an article for Seabury Quinn's *Casket and Sunnyside*, an undertaker's trade magazine. In 1972, Mr. Talman kindly elaborated on this point at some length for me. The subject of Roger Williams and the apple tree first arose on one of Talman's visits to Lovecraft at 10 Barnes Street during the 1920s.[231] Lovecraft related to Talman the traditions concerning Roger Williams and the apple tree, and Talman in turn related to Lovecraft a similar story which had been published about Major John Andre (1751–1780), the British officer who served as intermediary between Sir Henry Clinton and the traitor Benedict Arnold. Andre was hanged as a spy after he fell into the hands of the Americans while trying to pass through their lines in civilian dress with Arnold's plans for the American fort at West Point in his boots. According to the published story, when Andre's remains were exhumed some forty years later, the roots of a nearby peach tree were found to have enmeshed his skull. Nearby in Tappan—almost within sight of Andre's grave—there was a tavern where the favorite drink in those days was peach brandy—some of it made, perhaps, from peaches from the very tree whose roots had invaded Major Andre's skull. Thus, Talman suggested to Lovecraft, "Who Drank Major Andre?" could well be a companion story to "Who Ate Roger Williams?" "To this," writes Talman, "he agreed with his customary cacophonous chuckle." The discussion of "Who Ate Roger Williams?" in Hart's "Sideshow" column for November 27, 1931, naturally brought the subject up between them again.

In the meantime, however, Talman had met Seabury Quinn of *Casket and Sunnyside* and agreed to do a story on the parallel legends for his magazine.[232] Talman still remembers well researching the Roger Williams story at the New York Public Library—perhaps he consulted the Allen memoir, the Steele book, or both—and he duly wrote the story under the title "The Fruit of the Vine." It appeared in *Casket and Sunnyside* and was evidently the article Lovecraft was referring to in his letter to Talman of December 12, 1931.

What are we to make, then, of "Who Ate Roger Williams?" as it appeared in *Vagabond*? Certainly, it would be quite helpful to know whether a page of holograph manuscript in Lovecraft's hand or a typescript with a single penciled correction in his hand was the source of the piece published in it. Wetzel's notes and Talman's own statement (made some years after he had given the manuscript to Grill) differ on this point. Perhaps the catalogue of the Grill Collection which Mr. Binkin plans to publish will ultimately make the point clear. Under either assumption, however, I think Mr. Talman's own suggestion regarding the origin of "Who Ate Roger Williams?" is the best: "Perhaps I sent Lovecraft a copy of an early version of 'The Fruit of the Tree.' [sic] I sometimes did this." Certainly, the text of "Who Ate Roger Williams?" as published in *Vagabond* is not that of a finished article or note: to cite only two evidences, abbreviations are used throughout and the date of the death of Betsey Williams is left uncertain. As to authorship, if we are willing to take the risk of trusting the text in *Vagabond*, we can certainly say that Lovecraft himself would not have written "neighboring" in the third paragraph, but rather "neighbouring," since he consistently used British spellings in his writing. (Only to find his preferred spellings altered by some of his editors! At least one amateur editor, however, consistently honored Lovecraft's preferences. Of all the people who wrote for the *Vagrant*, Paul Cook allowed only Lovecraft the British "u" in his spellings and sometimes sent proof back over and over again to his compositors until they got Lovecraft's spellings right.) Even if "Who Ate Roger Williams?" is a genuine holograph manuscript in Lovecraft's hand, it is not totally unfeasible that Lovecraft was merely copying Talman's preliminary notes for "The Fruit of the Vine." He would sometimes, for instance, write out revised stories in his own hand; in fact, he quoted lower rates to clients who would accept work in this form.

But the alternative which we originally set out to decide—notes by Lovecraft or notes by Talman corrected and/or copied by Lovecraft—will have to remain, for the moment, without a definite answer. Lovecraft's letters to Talman might provide an answer—but at the present time, according to Mr. Talman, they are being held by a researcher who had promised to present them to the John Hay Library on behalf of Talman.[233] After all, however, the authorship of this small note is really of small importance. The fact that Lovecraft knew and undoubtedly enjoyed the stories which we have here told—that is of importance.[234]

Who Ate Roger Williams? 163

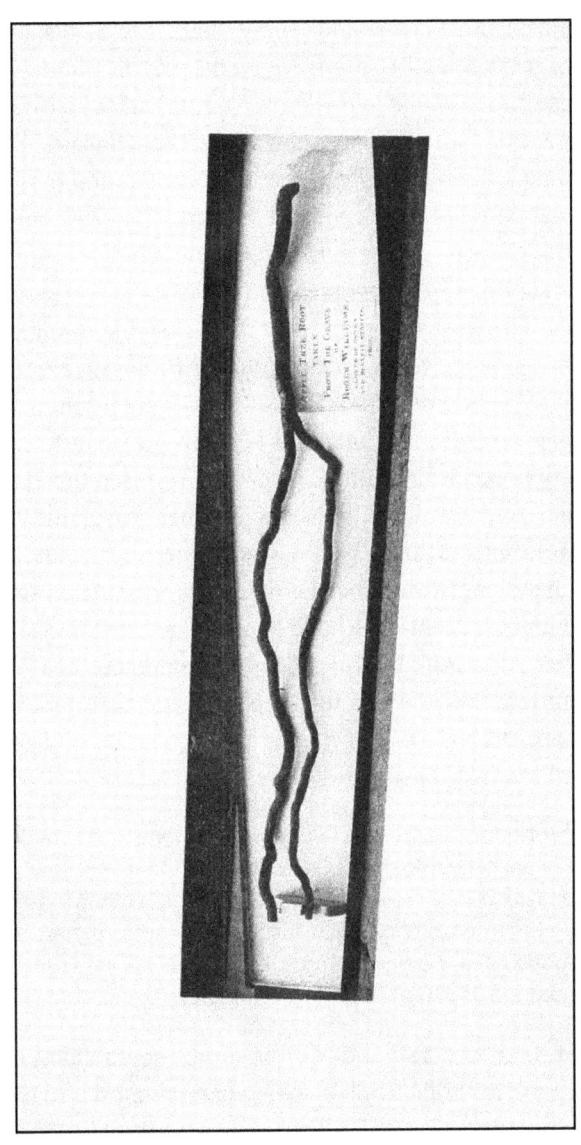

the Roger Williams root

(*Report on the Burial Place of Roger Williams*)

20. Searching for the Dark Swamp

One of Lovecraft's most interesting rural rambles was his journey out the Putnam Pike with his friend Clifford M. Eddy, Jr., on Sunday, November 4, 1923, in the search of the hideous "Dark Swamp" of which Eddy had heard evil rumors from the rustics around Chepachet, Rhode Island.[235] Lovecraft and his friend Eddy took the bus to Chepachet and there inquired of the town clerk about the whereabouts of the ill-rumored swamp. The clerk confessed to little knowledge of the swamp beyond its evil reputation and directed Lovecraft and Eddy to the home of one Mr. Sprague, who he believed had guided "a party of gentlemen from Brown-University thro parts of the swamp in quest of botanick specimens, some twelve years gone." Mr. Sprague, it developed, had not led the party of gentlemen from Brown University through the swamp, but he knew that one Fred Barnes had, and he drew Lovecraft and Eddy a map whereby they might reach Fred Barnes's house. To reach this house, Lovecraft says that he and Eddy walked for some distance "over the same highroad travers'd by Mortonius and me"—obviously referring to his earlier journey west of Chepachet along with James Ferdinand Morton, Jr. in search of Durfee Hill, one of the highest points in Rhode Island. Lovecraft described this earlier journey in his letter to Frank Belknap Long of September 21, 1923 (*SL* 1.250–52). He and Morton took the bus to Chepachet and then "tramped westward along the Putnam Pike (U.S. 44), through a region as wild and desolate as anything in rural Maine." Then:

> Guided by Mortonius' map, we turned south along a by-road some three miles from Chepachet, striking a hilly, wooded section, and finally coming to a junction for which the chart had not prepared us. Here Mortonius chose a central path which my geographical instinct led me to demur at—and sure enough, it landed us in a brambly forest beside a pond, far from all access to Durfee Hill, and too late to permit of a second hillward effort!

I would suggest that Lovecraft and Morton turned south along the Durfee Hill Road and then took a wrong branch somewhere along the road, necessitating the abandonment of their quest for Durfee Hill itself. This is in good accord with Lovecraft's description of his November 4, 1923, journey in search of the Dark Swamp, for after Fred Barnes directed Lovecraft and Eddy "to find 'Squire James Reynolds, who dwells at the fork of the back road beyond the great reservoir, south of the turnpike [Putnam Pike]," they did not stop again until they came to "Cody's Tavern, built in 1683," where they stopped for lunch.

At this point an 1895 atlas of Providence County which I found in the map room at the Brown University Library provides a good deal of help. (This same atlas is undoubtedly available at the Rhode Island Historical Society Library; the librarians there believe that they have every published map of Rhode Island.) In particular, the plate for the town of Glocester[236], which shows many individual buildings and residences, is very helpful. For, just east of the large Bowdish Reservoir and west of the point at which Durfee Hill Road branches southward, there is marked on the Putnam Pike none other than Cady's Tavern. ("Cody's Tavern" in *SL* 1.265–66 undoubtedly represents a mistranscription of Lovecraft's script.) Moreover, Reynolds Road is shown to branch southward from the Putnam Pike just beyond the Bowdish Reservoir, and at the point at which the first gravel road forks from Reynolds Road (eventually to join the Willie Woodhead Road) there is shown the residence of none other than James Reynolds! Surely; this information alone is enough to establish that Lovecraft and Eddy walked past the Bowdish Reservoir and turned south on the Reynolds Road in their search for the Dark Swamp. But to return to Lovecraft's description of his search:

> ... passing the reservoir we turn'd south into the backwoods, coming in proper season to Squire Reynolds' estate. We found the gentleman in his yard; a man well on in years, and having a very markt rural speech which we had thought extinct save in stage plays. He told us, we had better take the right fork of the road, over the hills to Ernest Law's farm; declaring, that Mr. Law owns Dark Swamp, and that it was his son who had cut wood at the edge of it. Following the Squire's directions, we ascended a narrow rutted road betwixt picturesque woods and stone walls; coming at last to a crest that stood mysteriously limned against the fire and gold of a late afternoon day. Another moment and we had spy'd what stretcht beyond it: to the right the antient farmhouse of Mr. Law, and to the left the most gorgeous and spectacular agrestic panorama that either of us had been beheld or indeed conceiv'd to exist .... We found Mr. Law, whose venerable farmhouse is very curious and engaging, to be of the small country gentry; an handsome blue-eyed man of the middle size, about sixty years old, and having a quaint rustic speech. He inform'd us, that Dark Swamp lyes in the distant bowl betwixt two of the hills we saw; and that 'tis two miles from his house to the nearest part of it, by a winding road and a cart-path.

Here the plate of Glocester in the 1895 atlas is once again useful, for along the Sheldon Hill Road, which Reynolds Road runs into less than two miles from Squire Reynolds's home, the atlas shows three Law farms—one of them, that of "E. F. Law," just about at the spot where the second small lake is shown to the east of Sheldon Hill Road on the modern official Rhode Island highway map. Moreover, Reynolds Road (leading into Sheldon Hill Road) is clearly the right fork of the road at the Reynolds home—the left fork being the gravel road leading into the Willie Woodhead Road. Of course, the location of Ernest Law's farm still leaves us far from finding the Dark Swamp—for according to Lovecraft, the Dark Swamp lay in a bowl between two distant hills and was at its nearest point two miles distant from the Law farm. Indeed, the Army Map Service maps cited above show a number of swampy areas within two miles of the site of the law farm which might qualify as the Dark Swamp. Here, however, a typescript *Gazetteer of Rhode Island* (1927) by Howard Miller Chapin —whom we have mentioned before in connection with Roger Williams and the apple tree—which I found on the shelves of the Rhode Island Historical Society Library—came to the rescue with a listing:

> Dark Swamp. In Glocester, now n. end of Ponaganset Reservoir.

A penciled notation on the typescript gave Walling's 1863 map of Rhode Island as a reference. Looking at this map, I found Lovecraft's account confirmed: for, roughly two miles southeast of the site of the Ernest Law farm, between the Willie Woodhead Road and the Durfee Hill Road and just north of the then-Ponaganset Pond, there was shown none other than the Dark Swamp. Ominously, the swampland to the south of the Ponaganset Pond was marked "proposed reservoir."[237] And the 1863 Walling map contained more confirmation of Lovecraft's account. At the juncture of Reynolds Road with the subsidiary road where the home of James Reynolds is shown in the 1895 atlas, the home of "O. Reynolds" is shown on Walling's map. Further south along the Reynolds Road is the home of H. Law, and on the Sheldon Hill Road—seemingly at the site of the E. F. Law home in the 1895 atlas—is the home of N. Law. All of this seems to confirm quite clearly Lovecraft's account of his 1923 exploration with Clifford M. Eddy, Jr. A troubling point remains, however. According to Chapin's *Gazetteer*, the Dark Swamp had been inundated to form the north end of the present Ponaganset Reservoir by 1927. The entirety of the Ponaganset Reservoir, however, is of no such modern date. Indeed, even the plate of Glocester in the 1895 Providence County atlas shows not the Ponaganset Pond and surrounding swamps shown by Walling's 1863 map, but rather the Ponaganset Reservoir. I wish I now had a copy of that plate to compare the then-outlines of the Ponaganset Reservoir with the present outlines of the Ponaganset Reservoir, but I do not. Until a more thorough geographical investigation is made, however, I think the indication on Walling's 1863 map that the swampland to the south of the then-Ponaganset Pond was to constitute the "proposed reservoir" may provide some hint of the proper solution to this problem. Perhaps only the swampland to the south and west of the 1863 Ponaganset Pond was at first inundated; and then, between Lovecraft's 1923 visit to Ernest Law and 1927, the Dark Swamp was at last inundated to form the northern end of the Reservoir. This presumption can undoubtedly be proven or disproven by research with Rhode Island maps dating from 1923 until 1927, and I hope someone will someday undertake the investigation. It is indeed a shame that the Dark Swamp is now seemingly lost—but only the assumption that it was inundated to form the northern end of the present Ponaganset Reservoir between 1923 and 1926 would seem to be consistent with the statements of both Lovecraft and Chapin. (I wonder whether the ca. 1912 Brown University botanical expedition which Fred Barnes guided through the outskirts of the Dark Swamp might have taken any photographs of the Swamp to accompany their specimens.) Lovecraft in his letter to Long probably gives most of the folklore which was connected with the Swamp, although a diligent investigator in the Chepachet area might still uncover more stories. And, of course, we all still have Clifford M. Eddy's novelette based upon the Dark Swamp lore, which I believe is entitled "Black Noon," to wait for. In his obituary of Mr. Eddy in the *Arkham Collector* for summer 1968 (No. 3, p. 80), August Derleth announced "Black Noon" for publication in the coming Arkham anthology *Dark Things*; but when this book appeared in 1971, "Black Noon" was not included. Perhaps it will ultimately appear in some other Arkham volume; all those who have been enchanted by Lovecraft's account of the lore of the Dark Swamp as given in his letter to Long would certainly be glad to see it.[238]

* * *

Another famous excursion of Lovecraft's was his visit of August 8, 1921, along with his boyhood friend Harold Bateman Munroe (1891–1966), to the site of their onetime clubhouse on Great Meadow Hill near Rehoboth, Massachusetts—where, to their vast surprise, they found the entire tar-papered edifice which they had last seen about 1913 still intact. Lovecraft discussed this excursion in three letters published in *Selected Letters*: to Kleiner, August 11, 1921 (*SL* 1.143–44; *RK* 211–12); to Annie E. Phillips Gamwell, August 19, 1921 (*SL* 1.144–47)—the fullest published account; and to the Gallomo, August 31, 1921 (*SL* 1.150–51; *AG* 96–98).[239] According to the directions given in Lovecraft's letter to Mrs. Gamwell, Lovecraft and Munroe drove along the Taunton Pike (the same U.S. 41 which is called the Putnam Pike to the west of Providence), through Rehoboth, to Taunton, where Munroe had several commercial missions to attend to before the pair sought out the site of the old Great Meadow Hill Clubhouse. "But finally we left trade & Taunton behind, & rattled along the pike toward the greatest adventure of all—a pious pilgrimage to the tomb of our dead youth—Great Meadow Hill & the old clubhouse!" wrote Lovecraft to Mrs. Gamwell. Now there is given here no direction, but I believe that Lovecraft and Munroe actually headed back toward Rehoboth and Providence along the Taunton Pike. In his letter to Mrs. Gamwell, Lovecraft indicates that he and Munroe turned off the pike at Wheeler's Corners, a place which I do not find on modern maps of Massachusetts, to join the rutted road which took them to the still-standing Greet Meadow Country Clubhouse. A few sentences later, however, he seems to indicate that the clubhouse and Great Meadow Hill were near "drowsy Rehoboth," where "even relentless Time sometimes nods & lets a few years slip away undevastatingly." This is still all rather vague in terms of directions, but in fact Great Meadow Hill is still easily findable on detailed maps of the Rehoboth region. The following maps of the U.S. Army Map Service series V814—produced in the 1940s, I believe—clearly show Great Meadow Hill just northeast of Rehoboth:

Norton: AMS V814 6767 1 NW
Somerset: AMS V814 6767 1 SW

These Army Map Service maps of the 1940s show Great Meadow Hill still unoccupied as of that period, except for a fire tower near the top. Indeed, perhaps it is still preserved in this state. Perhaps even the Great Meadow Country Clubhouse—or at least the "chimney" built by old James Kay—still stands. (Mr. R. Alain Everts has in his collection of Lovecraft material an early photograph of Lovecraft standing in front of the clubhouse in his Dutch sailor's cap.) If someone has the initiative to go out looking for it, I hope he will take along a camera and properly record for posterity anything that remains.[240] On modern highway maps of Massachusetts, the site of Great Meadow Hill is very near the intersection of U.S. 44 and Massachusetts 118 just northeast of Rehoboth. It lies in the northeast quadrant determined by the intersection of the two highways. Happy hunting!

21. Lovecraft's pseudonyms

As the reader of these notes will doubtless recall, it was R. H. Barlow's short note "Pseudonyms of H. P. Lovecraft" in the *Acolyte* for summer 1943 (1, No. 4) which first set George Wetzel to his bibliographical work on Lovecraft's amateur appearances. In his article "The Research of a Biblio" in *HPL: Memoirs, Critiques, and Bibliographies*, Wetzel combined the list of Lovecraft pseudonyms compiled by Barlow and another such list compiled by August Derleth with his own research to form the most comprehensive listing of Lovecraft pseudonyms which has ever—to the best of my knowledge—appeared in print:

> Humphrey Littlewit
> Ward Phillips
> Richard Raleigh
> Edward Softly
> John J. Jones
> Augustus T. Swift
> Albert Frederick Willie
> Lewis Theobald
> Henry Paget-Lowe
> Lawrence Appleton
> Ames Dorrance Rersley (Rowley)[241]
> Archibald (Maynwaring)

Of these pseudonyms, the last, Archibald (Maynwaring), was Wetzel's own discovery. The listing "Archibald xxx, surname forgotten by HPL" had appeared in Barlow's compilation of Lovecraft pseudonyms in the *Acolyte* (which derived from a listing of pseudonyms which Lovecraft himself had given Barlow); in his subsequent research at the Franklin Institute in 1946 and 1951–1953, Wetzel discovered only one byline containing the name "Archibald," that of Archibald Maynwaring. Because of internal evidence in the two poems which he found under the byline of Archibald Maynwaring, Wetzel concluded that this name had indeed been Lovecraft's "lost pseudonym." He printed the two poems—"To the Eighth of November" and "The Pensive Swain"—as the last selections in the third volume of *The Lovecraft Collector's Library, Selected Poetry I* (1953), along with his full case for their attribution to Lovecraft. Unfortunately, Mr. Wetzel did not included these two poems by Archibald Maynwaring in the 1955 bibliography which he undertook in collaboration with Robert E. Briney, and the poems have not been restored to any later Lovecraft bibliography that I know of. Certainly, they very much deserve listing in such bibliographies, with an explanatory note as to the case for their attribution to Lovecraft.[242]

A rather interesting fact comes to light when one actually goes through the Wetzel–Briney and the Chalker bibliographies to look for pseudonyms, however. Jacques Van Herp undertook this task for the bibliography which he compiled for the L'Herne *Lovecraft* (1969) following principally Chalker and came up with the following classified list of pseudonyms:

As an essayist:
   L. Theobald
   L. Theobald Jr.
   Zoilus

As a poet:
   Lawrence Appleton
   John J. Jones
   H. Paget-Lowe
   Henry Paget-Lowe
   Ward Phillips
   Ames Dorrance Rowley
   Edward Softly
   L. Theobald
   L. Theobald Jr.
   Lewis Theobald
   Albert Frederick Willie

As a story-writer:
   Houdini
   Henry Paget-Lowe
   Ward Phillips
   Theobald Jr.
   Lewis Theobald
   Lewis Theobald Jr.

As I verified for myself, this is a complete listing of all the pseudonyms given in the actual listings of the Wetzel–Briney and Chalker bibliographies. Even if we ignore minor variations of the "Lewis Theobald" and "Henry Paget-Lowe" pseudonyms, however, some striking differences rapidly become evident if we compare the Van Herp listing—based upon the *listings* of the Chalker bibliography—with the Wetzel listing in "The Research of a Biblio"—based principally upon the compilations of R. H. Barlow and August Derleth. In the first instance, the Van Herp listing adds two pseudonyms which do not occur in the Wetzel listing—"Zoilus" and "Houdini." Of these two additional listings, only that of "Zoilus" is really a legitimate addition to the catalogue of Lovecraft pseudonyms, since the name of "Houdini" is obviously included by virtue of Lovecraft's having ghostwritten "Imprisoned with the Pharaohs" for Harry Houdini; if we were to choose to include the names of persons for whom Lovecraft did ghostwriting (or what amounted to ghostwriting) as among his pseudonyms, we should have to add the names of Zealia Bishop, Hazel Heald, and undoubtedly several others to that of Houdini. Van Herp's listing of the pseudonym "Zoilus" evidently derives from Chalker's listing of "'The Vivisector' (as by Zoilus)" in the *Wolverine* for June 1921 as among Lovecraft's amateur press essays, a listing which does not occur in Wetzel's bibliography of Lovecraft's amateur press contributions. The case for the attribution of this essay (and therefore the pseudonym) to Lovecraft is not given in the Chalker bibliography as printed in *The Dark Brotherhood*; but one imagines that there were ample grounds for its listing—either textual or bibliographical.[243] If Lovecraft could forget the surname of one of his pseudonyms, then surely he could have forgotten another pseudonym completely when he imparted his listing to Barlow in 1934 or 1935.[244]

The most striking difference between the Van Herp and Wetzel listings, however, is the total absence in the Van Herp listing of four pseudonyms listed by Wetzel: Humphrey Littlewit, Richard Raleigh, Augustus T. Swift, and Archibald (Maynwaring). The absence of the last of these we have already explained; but as for the others—all of which, I believe, occur in Barlow's original 1943 listing in the *Acolyte*—they simply do not seem to be used on any Lovecraft works yet discovered or listed by his bibliographers, notably, Wetzel, Briney, and Chalker. Perhaps Lovecraft restricted his use of the Littlewit, Raleigh, and Swift pseudonyms to his letters (his letter to Rheinhart Kleiner of November 9, 1919 (*SL* 1.91–93; *RK* 171–73), for instance, is signed "Humphrey Littlewit, Gent."); but had he intended to include all the appellations with which he signed his letters in the listing he imparted to Barlow, he would have had to include many, many more—"Ech-Pi-El," "Grandpa," "L. P. Drawoh," "Tibaldus" and all the other Latinized versions of "Theobald," "L. Metadivs Caelo," "Jonathan Swift," "Timon Coriolanus, Esqr.," "H. Lollivs," "Horace Walpole," "H. von Liebkraft," and many others. Indeed, Sam Moskowitz, in his research with the Munsey magazines (see *Under the Moons of Mars*, pp. 378–79), found two published letters in the *Argosy Weekly* under the "Augustus T. Swift" byline—in the issues for November 15, 1919, and for May 22, 1920. Perhaps this is some indication that the pseudonyms "Humphrey Littlewit" and "Richard Raleigh" were also used on published letters—which would distinguish them from all the other appellations which Lovecraft used to sign his correspondence.[245] Indeed, the wide-open area of bibliographical research on Lovecraft's newspaper poetry and magazine and newspaper letters leads one to believe that "Humphrey Littlewit" and "Richard Raleigh" may well eventually turn up among Lovecraft's published pseudonyms.

Certainly, Lovecraft bibliographers would be well to be on the lookout for all the pseudonyms listed by Wetzel in 1955. Indeed, Lovecraft's letter to Maurice Moe of December 8, 1914 (*SL* 1.3–5) gives us one additional pseudonym unlisted by Wetzel in 1955—that of "Isaac Bickerstaffe, Jr.," which Lovecraft signed to two articles—"Astrology and the Future" and "Delavan's Comet and Astrology"—which he published in the *Providence Evening News* ca. December 1914 in refutation of the astrologer Hartmann. For what it is worth, I counted the number of uses of each of Lovecraft's pseudonyms[246] using the Wetzel–Briney and Chalker bibliographies (along with the other sources noted above) and came up with the following results:[247]

		Number of recorded use on:		
Pseudonym	**Poems**	**Essays**	**Stories**	**Published Letters #**
Lawrence Appleton	2	—	—	—
Isaac Bickerstaffe, Jr.	—	2	—	—
John J. Jones	1	—	—	—
Humphrey Littlewit	—	—	—	—
Archibald Maynwaring	2	—	—	—
Henry Paget-Lowe	3	—	1 †	—
Ward Phillips	9	—	1	—
Richard Raleigh	—	—	—	—
Ames Dorrance Rowley	1	—	—	—
Edward Softly	6	—	—	—
Augustus T. Swift	—	—	—	2
Lewis Theobald	21	2	3 ‡	—
Albert Frederick Willie	1	—	—	—
Zoilus	—	1	—	—

\# ante-mortem only
† including collaboration with Anna Helen Crofts
‡ two of these in collaboration with "Elizabeth Neville Berkeley"
   = Winifred Virginia Jackson

* * *

One curious circumstance which I happened upon in paging through the Chalker bibliography of Lovecraft's work is the following: although Lovecraft's prose poem "Nyarlathotep" is listed therein (and in Wetzel–Briney) as having appeared in the *United Amateur* for November 1920, Lovecraft's letter to Rheinhart Kleiner of December 14, 1920 (*SL* 1.160–62; *RK* 200–201) would seem to indicate that Lovecraft had but recently written "Nyarlathotep"—"of late" in his own words. There are two possible explanations for this apparent contradiction. The first and I think the best is that the letter to Kleiner is misdated in *Selected Letters* and ought to be December 14, 1920, rather than December 14, 1921. Witness the following passage from the letter (p. 162):

> The other piece—"Celephaïs"—weaves together a large number of my recent dreams on a thread of pathos. It is the first non-horror story I have written since "The White Ship". The remaining three are not of the fantastic but of the realistically gruesome type—the last, which I finished day before yesterday [December 12], being rather unique .... The title is "The Picture in the House" ....

Now if the chronology of Lovecraft's stories published in *Dagon and Other Macabre Tales* can be relied upon (and I suspect it was taken literally from one of Lovecraft's own chronologies which lacked only *The Dream-Quest of Unknown Kadath* and *The Case of Charles Dexter Ward*[248]—which Lovecraft sometimes omitted from chronologies of his work sent to correspondents because he had no copies other than the original manuscripts to circulate). "Celephaïs" is properly dated 1920, and by the end of 1921 Lovecraft had written the additional Dunsanian stories "The Other Gods" and "The Quest of Iranon." In addition, Paul Cook writes in his *H. P. Lovecraft: A Portrait* (p. 56; *LR* 148) that "The Picture in the House" "should not be dated before the very last of 1920 or the first of 1921."[249] In the same passage in his memoir, Cook offers the second possible explanation for our apparent contradiction. For, "The Picture in the House," despite Cook's own statement and the evidence of Lovecraft's letter to Kleiner (whether that letter is properly dated 1920 or 1921), appeared in the *National Amateur* for July 1919. The explanation: In 1919, Cook was unable to secure the official reports for the July 1919 issue of the *National Amateur*, the last for which he was official editor. So he simply set the already-printed sheets and already-composed galleys away and gradually, over 1920 and 1921, printed more material—including Lovecraft's "The Picture in the House"—in anticipation of eventually circulating the issue as a limited edition to friends. By 1921, the issue was nearly ready to bind, and under pressure to add to the activity record of the new administration which took over that year, Cook at last bound it and mailed it out—the July 1919 issue, in 1921. This suggests that a similar fate might have befallen the *United Amateur* for November 1920—which is my second possible explanation for the apparent contradiction. However, because of the internal difficulties involved in dating Lovecraft's December 14 letter to Kleiner as 1921, I believe that letter is properly dated 1920.[250]

22. The Kalem Club; Lovecraft's correspondence with his wife

In his essay "H. P. Lovecraft and His Work" in *The Dunwich Horror and Others* (p. xi) August Derleth gave what must be a near-complete listing of the members of the Kalem Club, the informal group of New York litterateurs which derived its name from the fact that nearly all the members had surnames beginning with the letter "K," "L," or "M." Indeed, in Derleth's listing of the members of the Kalem Club in addition to Lovecraft there are only two exceptions: James F. Morton, Samuel Loveman, Frank Belknap Long, Everett McNeil, *Vrest Orton*, *Wilfred B. Talman*, Arthur Leeds, Herman C. Koenig, Rheinhart Kleiner, and George Kirk. Of course, many other persons attended at least a few of the informal meetings of the Kalem Club, so that it is probably a futile exercise to try to compile a definitive listing of members. However, James F. Morton's letter to Lovecraft of January 12, 1930 (in the Lovecraft Collection in the John Hay Library) does specifically mention the bookseller Martin Kamin as a "marginal member" of the Kalem Club. Another name which is often enough mentioned in Lovecraft's letters in connection with informal club gatherings to merit inclusion as a "member" is that of Loveman's friend Pat McGrath. Recall that it was McGrath who accompanied Lovecraft and Loveman on their visit to Union Place in Brooklyn in 1931; and, according to Samuel Loveman in his article "Lovecraft as a Conversationalist" in *Fresco* for spring 1958 (8, No. 3), it was McGrath who was responsible for the famous incident of the spiking of Lovecraft's punch. In addition, the attendance of the New York amateur Blue Pencil Club and the Kalem Club may have occasionally overlapped. At least Lovecraft, Kleiner, and Morton were solid members of each. In a letter to Lovecraft of November 30, 1923 (in the Lovecraft Collection in the John Hay Library), James F. Morton mentioned some additional members of the Blue Pencil Club: Pearl Merritt, Ernest Dench, Ernest Adams, Otto Knack, A. M. Adams, and Miss Voelchert. Lovecraft, I believe, regularly attended the meetings of both the Kalem Club and the Blue Pencil Club while he was in New York in 1925–1926; and, of course, he made an effort to see as many of his old friends as possible on the eight or ten brief visits he later made to New York in connection, mostly, with his antiquarian travels along the eastern seaboard.

* * *

Lovecraft was so prolific as an epistolarian, that many of his readers are probably surprised to learn that he did not leave behind volumes and volumes of personal diaries—another eighteenth-century preoccupation. The fact is, of course, that Lovecraft considered his own daily affairs so unimportant and prosaic that he did not customarily bother to keep a diary. Whenever he was away from Providence for any length of time, however, he would see that his aunts Mrs. Clark and Mrs. Gamwell received a day-by-day account of his activities—either through long travel letters covering a week or more or minutely written postcards covering a single day. (He would in fact often title these postcards "Diary for —," giving the date concerned.) In addition, when Mrs. Gamwell was confined in a hospital and then a sanatorium for eight weeks or so in early 1936 as the result of a serious illness, Lovecraft kept for her a day-by-day account of daily happenings at 66 College Street which he mailed to her in letters covering several days at a time. Certainly, this series of letters—which, like all of Lovecraft's letters to his aunts, is preserved in the Lovecraft Collection in the John Hay Library—is the closest thing we have to a day-by-day diary of Lovecraft's life in Providence in his later years—although, of course, it is somewhat atypical because Mrs. Gamwell was away from 66 College Street for the period during which Lovecraft set down his day-by-day accounts.

Actually, however, at least one formal Lovecraft "diary" exists in the files of the John Hay Library. This journal covers the year 1925, spent at 169 Clinton Street in Brooklyn. I never examined this diary myself, but Mrs. Deborah Niswonger, who catalogued the Lovecraft Collection for the John Hay Library in 1970–1971, told me that it consisted nearly entirely of prosaic entries relating to time of awakening and retirement, diet, and the like. Nevertheless, this diary might prove to be of some use in establishing particular details of Lovecraft's daily life during 1925. Certainly, any light the diary might shed upon Lovecraft's psychological state during that year—of which different writers have given widely varying interpretations—would be immensely valuable for Lovecraft students. Of course, we lost the most detailed record Lovecraft left of his daily life in the twenties when his wife, Sonia H. Davis, some years later burned all of the letters she had received from Lovecraft with the exception of a portion of one which was published in the *Arkham Collector* for winter 1971 (No. 8).[251] According to Mrs. Davis's memoir "Lovecraft as I Knew Him" in (*LR* 252–63), her correspondence with Lovecraft was steady from the time of their first meeting in 1921 until their holiday in Magnolia, Massachusetts, in 1922; nearly daily, from that time until their marriage in March 1924; and once more nearly daily from the time Lovecraft was installed at 169 Clinton Street in January 1925 until Lovecraft informed his wife that he had obtained a divorce in March 1929.[252] (In fact, it has been confirmed by several researchers that, although judgment in favor of divorce was granted by Judge J. Pouliot in Providence in March 1929, on the grounds of "willful desertion" [Lovecraft was the plaintiff], Lovecraft in fact failed to sign the final decree of divorce, leaving him Mrs. Davis's lawful husband in the eyes of Rhode Island law.)[253] In all, there were supposed to have been more than two thousand letters, amounting to nearly a trunkful. In fact, according to Sonia's memoir, Lovecraft wished to continue their marriage through correspondence. Certainly, there will never be any adequate replacement for the vast outpouring of Lovecraft's life and thought which posterity lost in his letters to Mrs. Davis.

* * *

One does not usually think of Howard P. Lovecraft as a step-father. But, of course, such he was, to Sonia Greene's child by her earlier marriage, Florence Greene. According to R. Alain Everts, Florence Greene broke with her mother over her marriage to Lovecraft and never thereafter saw her again; but even before the marriage of Lovecraft and Sonia in 1924, one can see evidence of Lovecraft's disapproving look across the generation gap. Witness his letter of May 18, 1922, to Maurice Moe (*SL* 1.180; *NY* 11; *LVW* 99):

> At dinner—about one-thirty—were Loveman, Theobald, Long, Mme, Greene, and the latter's flapper offspring, yclept Florence—pert, spoiled, and ultra-independent infant rather more hard-boiled of visage than her benignant mater.

According to Sonia Davis's memoir (*LR* 256), her daughter later became Paris correspondent for various American newspapers.[254]

23. About the pronunciation of Cthulhu

Lovecraft's own preferred pronunciation for the name of the Lord of R'lyeh always intrigued his friends and readers. Several of his friends recorded what they themselves managed to worm out of Lovecraft in the matter. Writes Paul Cook in his memoir of Lovecraft (*op. cit.*, p. 63; *LR* 154):

> Writing "Cthulhu" above has reminded me that Lovecraft denied any derivative of phonetic source or system for the combination of letters making up that word and others. The reader must pronounce to suit himself. In that especial case, however, he suggested "Clutu," both "u"'s long. Some of them are less easy.

On the other hand, Donald Wandrei recorded in his memoir "Lovecraft in Providence" (*SR* 131–35; *LR* 313):

> Another of these dreams he had used as a basis for Pickman's Model, while still another formed the nucleus for The Call of Cthulhu. I referred to this story one day, pronouncing the strange word as though it were spelled K-Thool-Hoo. Lovecraft looked blank for an instant, then corrected me firmly, informing me that the word was pronounced, as nearly as I can put it down in print, K-Lütl-Lütl. I was surprised and asked why he didn't spell it that way if such was the pronunciation. He replied in all seriousness that the word was originated by the denizens of his story and that he had only recorded their own way of spelling it. Lovecraft's own invention had assumed an actual reality in his mind.

Finally, we find in R. H. Barlow's diary of Lovecraft's 1934 visit to his home in *The Dark Brotherhood and Other Pieces* (p. 318; *LR* 353):

> Lovecraft pronounced Cthulhu as *Koot-u-lew*—representing sounds never meant for human vocal organs . . . .

And there is undoubtedly more on this subject in Lovecraft's letters and in memoirs which I have neglected.[255] Of all the pronunciations recorded above, I think I like that recorded by Donald Wandrei the best—pronounced quickly, it sounds chitinous and insectlike, and, gutturally, almost frighteningly alien. In the vein of readers' settling upon their own pronunciation, however, the pronunciation I once heard from one of Lovecraft's Providence readers is remarkable for its delightful illogicality—Kloo-Thoo. (Scholars should attribute it to Mark Asquino in their record books.)

24. Of the Commonplace Book

Differences between the version of Lovecraft's Commonplace Book published by the Futile Press in 1938 and the version published by Arkham House in *Beyond the Wall of Sleep* in 1943 attracted the attention of Lovecraft students early on. First of all, the entries were in an entirely different order in the two different editions. Secondly, the entries in the Futile Press version were dated, whereas the entries in the Arkham version, arranged differently, were not. Thirdly, two entries in the Futile Press version were merged into one in the Arkham version; two entries in the Arkham version were merged into one in the Futile Press version; and two entries in the Futile Press version were scrambled into two distinct entries in the Arkham version. Finally, and perhaps most importantly, at least thirty-two entries in the Futile Press version were wholly omitted in the Arkham version. George Wetzel was one of the first persons to make a partial collation of the two different versions of the Commonplace Book, and in his article "The Research of a Biblio," he published two tentative explanations of the differences which August Derleth had made in separate letters to him:

> To the best of my knowledge there were two separate "Commonplace Book" manuscripts. The Futile Press book appears to have been a selection from both. I do believe we have all the Lovecraft manuscript of this work in our *Beyond the Wall of Sleep*. We followed HPL's form and they did not. I do not know why the Futile Press people did as they did; we always sought to follow Lovecraft's manuscripts without alteration . . . .
>
> Differences between the published texts of HPL's "Commonplace Book" may be due to various factors—l) an incomplete text sent to us by Barlow; 2) the interpolation of some of Barlow's own notes into the . . . text . . . ; 3) secretarial errors in copying.

Later on, in anticipation of an annotated reprinting of the Commonplace Book in *The Shuttered Room and Other Pieces*, Derleth wrote Claire Beck of the Futile Press for an explanation of the differences between the two editions; but, unfortunately, by that time, Beck no longer had the Barlow typescript which the Futile Press had followed for their edition and could offer no explanation. In the edition published in *The Shuttered Room and Other Pieces*, then, Derleth and Wandrei sought essentially to combine and annotate the two earlier, varying editions. Derleth's preface to this edition of the Commonplace Book probably represents his most definitive statement regarding the differences in the earlier editions:

> The Commonplace Book was first printed by the Futile Press of Lakeport, California, in 1938, as prepared by the late R. H. Barlow, who was in possession of the original, of which he had made a typescript copy, whereupon Lovecraft returned the original to him with this inscription: "Presented to R. H. Barlow, Esq., on May 7, 1934, in exchange for an admirably neat typed copy from his skilled hand. H. P. Lovecraft." Curiously enough, such an "admirably neat typed copy" came to hand here at Arkham House, but there are marked differences between it and the version published by the Futile Press. It is possible either that Barlow unearthed other notes, or that he added some of his own to the manuscript, which ultimately saw print in *Beyond the Wall of Sleep*. The Futile Press version also included Lovecraft's *Suggestions for Writing Story, Elements of a Weird Story & Types*, which are not reproduced here, and *A List of Certain Basic Underlying Horrors Effectively Used in Weird Fiction* and *A List of Primary Ideas Motivating Possible Weird Tales*, which are added to the notes of the Commonplace Book here.
>
> Since Lovecraft acknowledged the typescript copy from Barlow, one can assume that he approved and recognized it as his work; he did not see the Futile Press version, which in some part may have been a rearrangement of his notes, with additions from his letters to Barlow. The present version represents an attempt to combine the two, but is essentially an annotated version, attempting to show how Lovecraft made use of the notes in his own work, or how they were used in posthumous collaborations. Annotations appear here in italics, within parentheses.

In combining the two earlier editions (FP = Futile Press; *BWS* = *Beyond the Wall of Sleep*) of the Commonplace Book for their annotated edition in *The Shuttered Room and Other Pieces* (*SR*), Derleth and Wandrei preserved as their basic text that of the *BWS* edition. Six early entries from the FP edition (the second, fourth, seventh, tenth, eleventh, and twelfth) were incorporated into the basic *BWS* text near the beginning. At the end of the basic *BWS* text, twenty-one additional entries from the FP edition not included in the *BWS* edition were listed in the order of their appearance in the FP edition, except that the first entry listed in this section was actually the last such omitted entry in the FP edition. (Actually, this section added only twenty new entries to the *BWS* text. The twentieth entry in this separate listing—"Horrible boarding house. Closed door never opened."—may be found as part of one of the entries in the *BWS* edition on p. 106 of the *SR* edition.) Finally, six entries from the FP edition not included in the *BWS* edition were not restored in any form in the *SR* edition.

How did the differences between the FP and *BWS* editions originate? Through a little study of the manuscripts of the Commonplace Book which reside with the Lovecraft Collection in the John Hay Library, I believe that I can offer at least a partial answer. The following four manuscripts of the Commonplace Book reside in that collection:

a—A.Ms., small bound volume, 57pp. used—has all the lists which preceded the Commonplace Book itself in the FP edition; some unpublished plot summaries of famous weird stories; and the "remembrancer" entry published at the end of the Commonplace Book and subsidiary lists in the *BWS* edition;

b—A.Ms., 1919–1934, 35pp.—Lovecraft's holograph original, mostly in pencil, with inserted presentation sheet explaining the character of the entries and acknowledging the receipt of an "admirably neat typed copy" (c) from R. H. Barlow in return for the original manuscript; this original manuscript, which has a decorative cover handmade by Barlow, is unbound, but would make a small chapbook if stitched or stapled along the central fold of the sheets; it is read in proper order in this manner;

c—A.&T.Ms., small loose leaf notebook, 40pp. used—Barlow's "admirably neat typed copy" of 1934 and the model for the *BWS* edition; the first section of this notebook consists of loose leaf sheets with Barlow's typed copies of some of the entries from (b), in rearranged order; the second section, of loose leaf sheets with Lovecraft's holograph entries for 1934 and after; this latter section consists of the entries printed under the heading "from a later notebook" in the FP edition;

d—T.Ms., 12pp.—a typescript made by Barlow ca. 1937–1938; follows (b) for pre-1934 entries; (c) for post-1934 entries; and (a) for subsidiary lists; i.e., follows Lovecraft's original holograph entries in their proper order; the Becks followed a carbon copy of this typescript for their edition of the Commonplace Book.

Several facts become quickly apparent from the study of these manuscripts. First of all, the *BWS* edition of the Commonplace Book follows our manuscript (c) for the text of the Commonplace Book itself and our manuscript (a) for the subsidiary lists which have traditionally been printed with the Commonplace Book. The *BWS* edition, therefore, reflects the rearrangement and omission of entries from Lovecraft's 1919–1934 holograph manuscript (b) which was embodied in Barlow's "admirably neat typed copy" (c) of 1934. It is wholly reliable only for Lovecraft's post-1934 entries—contained in holograph original at the end of Barlow's "admirably neat typed copy" (c)—and for the subsidiary lists—for which Arkham House evidently followed our manuscript (a). (That Arkham House did have access to our manuscript (a) is shown by the inclusion of the "remembrancer" entries from that manuscript at the end of the Commonplace Book itself and the subsidiary lists in the *BWS* edition; these "remembrancer" entries are not contained in our manuscript (d) or in the FP edition.)

Indeed, it seems quite clear that the "two separate 'Commonplace Book'" manuscripts of which Derleth wrote to Wetzel were our manuscripts (a) and (c)—both little black notebooks, one bound and the other loose leaf. The title page of our manuscript (d) contains notes ("Commonplace Book—(printed version is inaccurate);" and, in the upper, right-hand corner, "Simply keep this—don't bother to copy") which indicate that Arkham House did at one time see this typescript (the notes are in Barlow's handwriting; the "printed version" he refers to is the FP edition, which contained many typographical errors, acknowledged and unacknowledged); but the decision of the Arkham House editors was apparently to follow manuscripts (a) and (c), which, after all, as little black notebooks, looked as if they would render a more accurate version of Lovecraft's original than Barlow's typescript. At some point, of course, Barlow deposited the original holograph manuscript (b) of the Commonplace Book with the John Hay Library; but the mystification of the Arkham editors as late as 1959 regarding the reason for differences between the FP and *BWS* editions of the Commonplace Book indicates that they had still not seen this manuscript, containing Lovecraft's holograph entries for 1934 and earlier in their proper order. That is, the principal text of the annotated *SR* edition of the Commonplace Book—which follows the text of the *BWS* edition—still reflects all the vagaries of Barlow's "admirably neat typed copy" (c) of 1934.

The obvious question, of course, is why Barlow's "admirably neat typed copy" (c) did not follow Lovecraft's holograph original (b)—in return for the presentation of which, of course, the "admirably neat typed copy" of 1934 was made. With regard to the omission of some thirty-two entries contained in the original holograph manuscript, we are not without some answer. Eight of these omitted entries were crossed out in the original manuscript; indeed, all but one of them have alongside annotation as to the stories in which they were used. The one deleted entry which does not bear such annotation in the original manuscript is:

> Monsters—born living—burrow underground & multiply, forming race of unsuspected daemons.

This entry was dated 1919 upon presentation of the original manuscript to Barlow in 1933; perhaps it was used for "The Lurking Fear."

Somewhat more mysteriously, the remaining twenty-four omitted entries have marked alongside of them in the original manuscript an "x" mark in ink. In the same ink, all the entries in the original manuscript are given the rough dating which was reproduced in typescript (d) and the FP edition. The only logical assumption seems to be that Lovecraft marked these twenty-four entries for omission when Barlow set out to make a typed copy of the original manuscript in 1934. At the same time, it seems, he made the rough dating of the entries in the original manuscript. As a bibliophile, albeit a young one, Barlow would hardly have made these marks on the original manuscript himself. Why did Lovecraft mark these twenty-four entries for omission from Barlow's typed copy of 1934? To this question, I can really offer no good answer. Let us look at these twenty-four entries (the numbering which I give is of the order of appearance in the original holograph manuscript (b)):

(2) x Inhabitants of *Zinge*, over whom the star Canopus rises every night, are always gay & without sorrow.

(3) x The shores of Attica respond in song to the waves of the Aegean.

(4) x Horror Story—man dreams of falling—found on floor mangled as tho' falling from a vast height.

(6) x In L^d. Dunsany's "Idle Days on the Yann" The inhabitants of the antient Astahahn, on the Yann, do all things according to antient ceremony. Nothing new is found. "Here we have fetter'd & manacled Time, who wou'd otherwise slay the Gods."

(7) x *Horror Story* The sculptured hand—or other artificial hand—which strangles its creator.

(9) x Dr. Eben Spencer plot.

(11) x Odd nocturnal [midnight (*deleted*)] ritual. Beasts dance & march to musick.

(12) x Happenings in interval between preliminary sound & striking of clock—ending—"it was the tones of the clock striking three."

(16) x The walking dead—seemingly alive, but—

(32) x As dinosaurs were once surpassed by mammals, so will man-mammal be surpassed by insect or bird—fall of man before the new race.

(33) x Determinism & prophecy.

(41) x The Italians call *Fear* La figlia della Morte—the daughter of death.

(49) x AZATHOTH—hideous name.

(50) x Phleg'e-thon—a river of liquid fire in Hades.

(63) x Sinister names [. . . . . . . Kaman-Thah . . . . . (*erased*)]

(64) x Identity—reconstruction of personality—man makes duplicate of himself.

(70)   x *Tone of extreme phantasy* Man transformed to island or mountain.
(81)   x Marblehead—dream—burying hill—evening—unreality Festival?
(101) x Hideous secret society—widespread—horrible rites in caverns under familiar scenes—one's own neighbour may belong.
(103) x Sealed room—or at least no lamp allowed there. Shadow on wall.
(107) x Wall paper cracks off in sinister shape—men dies of fright. Rats in Walls.
(138) x Someone or something cries in fright at sight of the rising moon, as if it were something strange.
(158) x Thing on Doorstep Man has terrible wizard friend who gains influence over him. Kills him in defense of his soul—walls body up in ancient cellar—BUT—the dead wizard (who has said strange things about soul lingering in body) *changes bodies with him* . . . leaving him a conscious corpse in cellar.
(183) x Reference in Egyptian papyrus to a secret of secrets under tomb of high priest Ka-Nefer. Tomb finally found & identified—trap door in stone floor—staircase, & the illimitable black abyss.

Now, some of these entries were manifestly used in Lovecraft's fiction, and their marking for omission by him is therefore readily understood. All that I can hazard about the remaining entries is that Lovecraft may have considered them sufficiently inferior to be unusable by 1934, and therefore have marked them for omission in Barlow's typed copy. Indeed, the first eighteen 4 entries so marked with an "x" were dated as 1919 or earlier by Lovecraft in 1934—and it was during this early period, when Lovecraft was just beginning his Commonplace Book, that he set down the most entries, many of which he undoubtedly later considered inferior. Certainly, few of the entries so marked for deletion are among the most provocative entries of the notebook. (I would myself here except 12, which seems to me to be one of the most fascinating entries in it.)

But the omission of these eight deleted and twenty-four marked entries from Barlow's 1934 typescript is not its most serious fault as a basic text for the Commonplace Book. The really serious fault of Barlow's 1934 typescript (our manuscript (c)) is the havoc which it wreaks with the ordering of Lovecraft's entries. His 1934 datings of the entries in his original holograph manuscript have obvious and considerable scholarly value—to cite a single instance, the date of an entry clearly marks the date of the earliest stories which it might have influenced. Why Barlow—even the very young Barlow of 1934—saw fit to alter the basic chronological order of Lovecraft's original manuscript in making his "admirably neat typed copy" in 1934, I do not know.

His later, ca. 1937–1938 typescript (d), used by the Futile Press for its edition of the Commonplace Book, closely follows Lovecraft's original manuscript—preserving the original order of the entries and including those which Lovecraft had earlier crossed out or marked with an "x." Perhaps some later investigator can determine the rationale for the arrangement of Barlow's "admirably neat typed copy" (c) of 1934; I could not.

The essential point to be made, however, is that Lovecraft's original manuscript (b) ought to be the source for the pre-1934 entries in any future edition of the Commonplace Book. His datings in this original manuscript should also be preserved. The holograph post-1934 entries in the rear of Barlow's "admirably neat typed copy" (c) of 1934 are of course the definitive source for the last entries in the Commonplace Book; and our manuscript (a) —all in Lovecraft's own hand—is the definitive source for the supplementary lists which have traditionally been printed with the book itself. A new edition of the Commonplace Book following these principles would be a considerable addition to the body of material available for Lovecraft scholarship. The FP edition is minimally adequate, but is full of misprints which considerably diminish its scholarly value. Moreover, it is today essentially unobtainable—the original edition having amounted to only seventy-five copies. None of this, of course, is intended to diminish the importance of annotative and other scholarly work which has already been done with the Commonplace Book—it is merely to say that a *really good* edition would make that scholarship all the richer and more precise.[256]

* * *

A discussion of the seminal influence which the entries in the Commonplace Book had upon Lovecraft's own writing and upon the writing of later writers in the Mythos would go far beyond the bounds of a set of random notes like these. August Derleth and Donald Wandrei have already made a good beginning in this direction with their annotation of the Commonplace Book in *The Shuttered Room and Other Pieces*; and there is undoubtedly still a great deal more information regarding Lovecraft's aesthetic sensitivities and creative processes which future researchers will draw from the notebook. I can offer a few additional technical comments, however. Of the six entries in Lovecraft's original manuscript of the Commonplace Book which were not restored in some fashion to the text of the *SR* edition are the following (numbering is the order of entries in the original manuscript):

(9)   x Dr. Eben Spencer plot.
(70) x *Tone of extreme phantasy* Man transformed to island or mountain.
(81) x Marblehead—dream—burying hill—evening—unreality Festival?
(103) x Sealed room—or at least no lamp allowed there. Shadow on wall.
(107) x Wall paper cracks off in sinister shape—men dies of fright. Rats in Walls.
(132) x [Mad artist in ancient sinister house draws *things*. What were his models? Glimpse. Pickman's Model (*deleted*)]

These entries are dated 1919 or before, 1919, 1919, 1923, 1923, and 1925, respectively, in Lovecraft's original manuscript. Lovecraft's first dating of an entry in his Commonplace Book is that of entry 25 of the original manuscript—his dream of the bas-relief of Cthulhu—as 1919; thus, entries 1–24 are presumably 1919 or earlier; I believe the FP edition takes entries 1–24 as 1918. We have already remarked upon the question which Lovecraft's letter of January 23, 1920, to Rheinhart Kleiner (*SL* 1.106–107; *RK* 178)—indicating that he had "lately" begun keeping a Commonplace Book "for the first time in my life"—throws upon Lovecraft's earliest datings in the original manuscript. In addition, his letter to Kleiner of May 21, 1920 (*SL* 1.113–17; *RK* 188) describes his dream of the ebbing Seekonk—entry 29 in the original manuscript of his Commonplace Book, dated 1919 in 1934—as having occurred on the night of May 20–21, 1920. This same letter describes the visit of the feline friend who inspired the story "The Cats of Ulthar"—and the basic passage of description which Lovecraft records in his letter is also entry 28 of the Commonplace Book, dated 1919 in 1934—as having occurred "the other night."

In the same letter, Lovecraft describes two dreams which are also clearly recorded in the Commonplace Book—that of the headless warriors on an English plain (entry 26; dated 1919) and that of the bas-relief of Cthulhu (entry 25; dated 1919)—in these cases, however, there is no indication of how recently the dreams had occurred. Lovecraft's letter to the Gallomo of 1920 (*SL* 1.100–102; *AG* 71–73) contains a detailed account of his Dr. Eben Spencer dream (entry 9; dated 1919 or earlier); but Lovecraft only indicates in his letter that the dream had occurred "lately." (Perhaps his reason for marking this entry for omission in 1934 was that he had forgotten the substance of his dream by then.) The evidence does seem clear, however, that, Lovecraft did date some of the first entries in his Commonplace Book too early in 1934. His letter to Kleiner of January 23, 1920 indicates that the Commonplace Book was not begun until very late 1919 or early 1920; and, moreover, the definite reference to his dream of the ebbing Seekonk in his letter to Kleiner of May 21, 1920 clearly dates entry 29 as 1920. Entry 83 was the first entry which Lovecraft dated as 1920 in 1934; presumably, at least entries 29–82 also date from that year.)

The six entries omitted from the *BWS* edition which were restored to the body of the text in the *SR* edition were:

(2) x Inhabitants of *Zinge*, over whom the star Canopus rises every night, are always gay & without sorrow.

(4) x Horror Story—man dreams of falling—found on floor mangled as tho' falling from a vast height.

(7) x *Horror Story* The sculptured hand—or other artificial hand—which strangles its creator.

(10) x Celephaïs [Dream of flying over city (*deleted*)]

(11) x Odd nocturnal [midnight (*deleted*)] ritual. Beasts dance & march to musick.

(12) x Happenings in interval between preliminary sound & striking of clock—ending—"it was the tones of the clock striking three."

All of these entries are in the section dated 1919 or earlier by Lovecraft in 1934. In his letter to the Gallomo of 1920 (*SL* 1.100–102; *AG* 71–73; *LVW* 76–78), Lovecraft remarked upon the influence of a rereading of Mary Shelley's *Frankenstein* upon his Dr. Eben Spencer dream (entry 9); this rereading undoubtedly also influenced entry 7 above. Entry 7 in the original manuscript (b) is also interesting for another reason; for under it, there is an erased entry which is just barely decipherable in part:[257]

Man climbs mountain toward some goal. Cloud passes over—man . . . .
[*indecipherable*] . . . . men.

I do not believe this erased entry has been included in any of the published editions of the Commonplace Book. One partially erased entry "(63) x Sinister names [. . . . . . Kaman-Thah . . . . . (*erased*)] was included in the FP edition of the Commonplace Book; it was restored in the segregated section of the *SR* edition. Under the preceding entry (62) in the original manuscript there was also erased material, but I could not decipher it. There is apparently another erased entry under the eighty-fifth entry in the original manuscript; but again I could decipher nothing.

Of course, the manuscripts in the Lovecraft Collection in the John Hay Library establish that Barlow did not add entries of his own to Lovecraft's Commonplace Book when he made his typescript (d) for the Futile Press edition. He followed only the holograph material by Lovecraft in manuscripts (a), (b), and (c), discarding his earlier rearrangement of the pre-1934 entries in (c). However, I believe that the last two entries in the original holograph manuscript of the Commonplace Book (b) may be in Barlow's hand:

> (200) Invisible Thing felt—or seen to make prints—on mountain top or other high, inaccessible place.
> (201) Planets form'd of invisible matter.

Since Barlow added no further notes to the original holograph manuscript (b), I suspect that he may have set these two entries down during Lovecraft's visit to his home in May–June 1934. However, Barlow early on cultivated a hand which was quite similar to Lovecraft's, so that these last entries in manuscript (b) may in fact be in Lovecraft's hand. Of course, Barlow did add to the FP edition of the Commonplace Book the passage from Lovecraft's letter to him of May 11, 1935, which discussed the dream from which the very last entry in Lovecraft's hand in manuscript (c)—which recall contains Lovecraft's post-1934 entries in holograph—developed. This passage was also printed as an annotation in the *SR* edition.

At least five entries in the original manuscript of the Commonplace Book were internally altered in the "admirably neat typed copy" (c) of 1934 and therefore in the *BWS* edition. The separate entries

> (205) person gazes out window & finds city & world dark & dead (or oddly changed) outside,
> (206) Trying to identify & visit the distant scenes dimly seen from one's window—bizarre consequences

are merged into a single entry in the *BWS* and *SR* editions. (The bars which Lovecraft drew between the individual entries in his original manuscript clearly establish the separateness of these entries.) Both occur among the post-1934 entries in manuscript (c).[258] In addition, the following two entries in Lovecraft's original manuscript (b), dated 1923 and 1926, respectively, therein:

> (104) Old sea tavern non far inland from made land. Strange occurrences—sound of lapping waves.
> (145) horrible boarding house—closed door never opened.

were jumbled into the following entries in Barlow's "admirably neat typed copy" (c) of 1934 and therefore in the *BWS* (xviii) and *SR* (106) editions:

> Old sea tavern now far inland from made land. (Deleted).

Horrible boarding house—closed door never opened. (Ref. to immediate above.) Strange occurrences—sound of lapping of waves.

The *SR* edition omits the annotation "deleted" from the first entry. Why this entry was marked "deleted" in Barlow's "admirably neat typed copy" (c) as 1934, I have no idea; it does not seem to be deleted in the original manuscript (b). If I recall correctly, the annotation "ref. to immediate above" was inserted in manuscript (c) in Lovecraft's hand and undoubtedly means that "strange occurrences—sound of lapping of waves" belongs to the foregoing entry in Barlow's rearranged manuscript (c). A curious result of this jumbling of two entries in the original manuscript in Barlow's "admirably neat typed copy" (c) of 1934 was the inclusion of entry 145 of the original manuscript both in the body of the *SR* edition (in the jumbled form of the *BWS* edition) and in the section of restored entries in the same edition (*SR* 118). Thus, there are really not twenty-one separately restored entries in that edition, but only twenty. Together with six entries restored in the body of the *SR* edition and six not restored at all, that makes thirty-two entries present in the FP edition but not in the *BWS* edition. According to the enumeration of the original manuscript, the separately restored entries of the *SR* edition (in order of their appearance in the book) are: 183, 3, 6, 16, 25, 28, 32, 33, 41, 43, 49, 50, 63, 61, 87, 95, 101, 138, 139, 145 (already included in jumbled form), and 158. Of these, 25, 28, 43, 87, 95, and 139 are crossed out in Lovecraft's original manuscript; the rest, with the exception of 145, are marked with an "x" in the original manuscript.

Two items from the back of Lovecraft's original manuscript (b) of the Commonplace Book did make Barlow's "admirably neat typed copy" (c) of 1934 (and thus the *BWS* and *SR* editions) and not his 1937–1938 typescript (d) (and thus not the FP edition). The first item was an entry or annotation in the back of the original Commonplace Book manuscript (b) which Barlow inserted among the other entries of the body of the Commonplace Book in his "admirably neat typed copy" (c):

> Quoted as motto by John Buchan. "The effect of night, of any flowing water, of the peep of day, of ships, of the open ocean, calls up in the mind an army of anonymous desires and pleasures. Something, we feel, should happen; we know not what, yet we proceed in quest of it." R. L. Stevenson.

Certainly, this entry is a happy addition to the Commonplace Book and should be retained as an appendage to a critical edition; it has a manifestly important relationship to Lovecraft's own lifelong sense of "adventurous expectancy" concerning landscapes and buildings. (Can anyone say where in Stevenson—

or Buchan for that matter—this quotation comes from? Sometimes such things are quite difficult to find. Barton St. Armand once asked me where the quotation from Blackwood which prefaces "The Call of Cthulhu" comes from; evidently, it is not from any of Blackwood's best-known stories.)[259]

The original holograph manuscript of the Commonplace Book (b) also has at the end the listing of "books to mention in new edition [serialization in the *Fantasy Fan*] of weird article," i.e., *Supernatural Horror in Literature*. This list appeared on p. xxiii of the *BWS* edition but did not appear in the FP or *SR* editions. Nor does the appearance of this list in the *BWS* edition contradict our assumption regarding the use by Arkham House of only manuscripts (a) and (c)—for in the back of the loose-leaf notebook which constitutes (c), Barlow in 1934 inserted several typed pages which reproduce Lovecraft's "books to mention in new edition of weird article." Lovecraft himself made a few additions in holograph to these typed pages, reproduced in the printing of the list in *BWS*. (Still unpublished is a long section of plot summaries of famous weird tales in manuscript (a), which otherwise contains the subsidiary lists of "certain basic underlying horrors, etc." which have traditionally been printed with the Commonplace Book itself.)[260]

* * *

Lovecraft was not the only writer to make use of his Commonplace Book. He wrote to Robert E. Howard on January 30, 1931 (*SL* 3.284; *MF* 1.144):

> I have a whole book full of idea-jottings which I could never write up if I lived to be a thousand—indeed, I sometimes lend it to other writers and invite them to borrow from it. That's where, for instance, Long got the idea of his "Black Orchid". Just now I'm lending it to Whitehead. If you ever want to see it, let me know . . . .

Moreover, according to a biographical note on Frank Belknap Long (probably written by Donald Wandrei) which appears on the back flap of the dust jacket of his recent Arkham House collection *The Rim of the Unknown* (1972) "Long has the honor of being one of the six individuals designated by Lovecraft at his death to make use of his Cthulhu Mythos and his idea-book for literary purposes, a privilege that Long has used only sparingly." (This provision is recorded neither in Lovecraft's 1912 will nor in the copy of "Instructions in Case of Decease" which Mrs. Gamwell made for R. H. Barlow. However, that copy of "Instructions in Case of Decease" bears the notation that it is only a partial copy of Lovecraft's original, and this additional may be included in the original if it still survives or indeed in some other document. In 1971, amateur editor E. Paul Berglund received from one of the personal representatives of the August Derleth Estate—which has claimed control of Lovecraft's writings—a letter conceding the free use of the background of Lovecraft's Cthulhu Mythos for literary purposes.)[261]

The richest posthumous use of Lovecraft's Commonplace Book was undoubtedly made by August Derleth, who wove some of his most masterful Mythos stories out of Lovecraft's scattered entries. Someone familiar with these stories and with Lovecraft's Commonplace Book could undoubtedly do a highly interesting article on the way in which Derleth adapted a large number of the Commonplace Book entries for his stories, some of which, indeed, he wrote in "posthumous collaboration" with Lovecraft.[262] Probably the clearest-cut instance of the use of Lovecraft's Commonplace Book by one of his fellow writers before his death stemmed from the look which Henry S. Whitehead took at the Commonplace book in 1931. Witness entry 133 in the original holograph manuscript of Lovecraft's Commonplace Book, dated there as 1925:

> (133) Man has miniature shapeless Siamese twin—exhib. in circus—twin surgically detached—disappears—does hideous things with malign life of its own. HSW—Cassius.

Of course, "HSW" refers to Whitehead, and "Cassius" to his story of that title, written from the basic idea suggested by Lovecraft in his entry 133. (Of course, the annotation "HSW—Cassius" was added later than 1925, probably in 1931 after Whitehead had made use of the entry. His story "Cassius" was first published in *Strange Tales* for November 1931.)

Then, there is also Lovecraft's reference in his letter to Howard of January 30, 1931 (*SL* 3.284) to the use of one of the entries in his Commonplace Book by Frank Belknap Long for his "Black Orchid." Unfortunately, there is no such story by Long listed in either Cockcroft's *Index to the Weird Fiction Magazines* or Day's *Index to the Science Fiction Magazines 1926–1950*; the only two story titles beginning with the word "black" are "The Black Druid" in *Weird Tales* for July 1930 and "The Black Vortex" in *Thrilling Wonder* for June 1937. Unless "The Black Orchid" was an unpublished story by Long—in which case it is dubious that Howard would have been familiar with it—"The Black Orchid" should probably be "The Black Druid."[263] This story of Long's concerns a man who went to the library to consult a strange passage concerning Druidism, which intimated that the Druids infected with evil everything which they merely even touched, and who, upon picking up the wrong coat in leaving the library, found himself in a ghastly primal battle with some hideous Druid horror, for the possession of his body. In the course of this struggle, which he won, the protagonist was urged on by ancestral memories of the battles successfully fought against the Druid (Celtic) menace by his Anglo-Saxon forbears. Now, granted that "The Black Druid" was the story to which Lovecraft refers in his letter to Howard, which of the entries of Lovecraft's Commonplace Book served as its model? There are many entries which deal with forbidden books—but forbidden books are really not the principal theme of Long's story. Moreover, none of the "forbidden books" entries seem to suggest any outline of Long's plot. The only good guess which I can hazard is the following 1923 entry:

> (113) Biological-hereditary memories of other worlds & universes. Butler—God Known & Unk. p 59

Even this entry, however, is not terribly suggestive of Long's story. Three other instances of attribution of entries to other writers occur within the original holograph manuscript of Lovecraft's Commonplace Book itself. Two of these instances involve entries with subsequently crossed-out annotations as to their use by other writers:

> (74) Italian revenge—killing self in cell with enemy—under castle [used by FBL Jr. (*deleted*)]
>
> (153) [Old Calif. kittie (*deleted*)]—Black cat on hill near dark gulf of ancient inn yard. Mews hoarsely—invites artist to nighted mysteries beyond. Finally dies at advanced age. Haunts dreams of artist—lures him to follow—strange outcome (never wakes up? or makes bizarre discovery of an elder world outside 3-dimensioned space?) [used by Dwyer (*deleted*)]

These entries are dated 1919 and 1928, respectively, in the in the original manuscript of the Commonplace Book.

Evidently, both Long and Dwyer eventually decided against the use of Lovecraft's entries, and Lovecraft subsequently removed the annotations of their use by these writers. Entry 153 is clearly about Lovecraft's long-lived feline friend "Old Man" (b. 1906 d. 1928), who belonged to the proprietor of a grocery store which once stood at the bottom of hilly Thomas Street and whom Lovecraft would often meet lurking in the dark recess of a colonial archway (leading to an interior "inn yard") on the hill above. As late as the mid-thirties, Lovecraft wrote to Duane Rimel of his intention to write the story about "Old Man" which he outlined in entry 153 (cf. *SL* 5.81–82; *FLB* 243–45); in fact, he promised Rimel the original manuscript in case he ever did write the story. Unfortunately, he never did, which is indeed a loss—since Lovecraft esteemed his earlier "cat" story "The Cats of Ulthar" as the best of all his early Dunsanian and folkloric pieces and would have undoubtedly written a masterful story about "Old Man." As it is, we are left with the cat-lore in "The Cats of Ulthar," *The Dream-Quest of Unknown Kadath*, and a singularly charming series of letters which Lovecraft wrote to Marian F. Bonner on behalf of the Kappa Alpha Tau fraternity (in reality, the group of cats which met on the top of a shed adjoining the boarding house which lay across the back garden at 66 College Street)—letters which now reside in the Lovecraft Collection in the John Hay Library. Perhaps the deleted portion of the beginning of Lovecraft's entry 153 was a reference to Clark Ashton Smith's old black cat—a female named "Simaetha" I believe.[264] Indeed, the other attribution in Lovecraft's Commonplace Book involves Lovecraft's friend Smith, with whom he so often exchanged story ideas:

> (181) Inhabitant of another world—face masked perhaps with human skin or surgically alter'd to human shape, but body alien beneath robes. Having reached earth, tries to mix with mankind, Hideous revelation. suggested by CAS

This entry is dated 1930 in Lovecraft's original manuscript.[265] Its theme, of course, is manifestly important in such later Lovecraft stories as "The Whisperer in Darkness" and "The Shadow out of Time." Of course, all of this technical analysis still leaves the more important work of research into Lovecraft's sources, based upon the Commonplace Book, to be carried forward—on the firm foundation laid by Derleth and Wandrei in their annotated version in *The Shuttered Room and Other Pieces*. I cannot, however, resist pointing to one entry for which a very concrete source is given in Lovecraft's published letters, to wit:

> (175) Little green Celtic figures dug up in an ancient Irish bog.

This entry is dated 1930 in Lovecraft's original manuscript of the Commonplace Book. Now witness his remarks in his letter to Robert E. Howard of October 4, 1930 (*SL* 3.184; *MF* 1.75):

> Another Celtic sidelight of my youth was still nearer home—my next-door neighbours and best playmates being three brothers whose relation to the Irish stream might be said to be your own, reversed—that is, they were descended from a line of Irishmen given to marrying Rhode Island Yankees, so that although they were about 80% Anglo-Saxon, they considered themselves heirs to the Irish tradition through descent in the male line and the possession of the

name Banigan. Their family always made it a point to travel to Ireland as often as possible, and were great collectors of Celtic antiquities. Their grandfather had a veritable museum of prehistoric Irish artifacts—indeed, I wish I knew what has become of that collection now that the family has left Providence and the brothers are all dispersed! Observing my admiration for these reliques of unknown yesterdays, they gave me two little greenish figures of a sort quite numerously represented in their collection; figures which they held to be of vest antiquity, but concerning which they admitted very little was known. Some seem to be metallic, whilst others are clearly carved of some light sort of stone. Their average length or height is only an inch and a half, and they are all overlaid with a greenish patina. They are grotesque human figures, sometimes in conventional poses and with curious costume and headdress. Their vast age is held to be indicated by the prodigious depth at which they are found in ancient peat-bogs. My two—one stone and one metal—have always appealed prodigiously to my imagination, and have formed high spots of my own assortment of curiosities.[266]

25. Lovecraft's Providence

When I think of Lovecraft, I should have to say that I think more of Providence—of what is the city today and what can be summoned up in the mind's eye of the city of the past—than of anything else. I agree completely with Winfield Townley Scott that all of the best of Lovecraft's writing is in the dark New England atmosphere—scenery, legends, history—which he creates in many of his stories; and that all of the worst of his writing is in the all too-concrete monsters which he summoned up in some of his tales. These monsters have been the object of innumerable critical attacks over the years—perhaps the most famous having been Edmund Wilson's remark that such monsters looked very well on the covers of pulp magazines but hardly belonged in shelves of serious literature. These critics, however, fail to give Lovecraft adequate credit as a writer simply because they fail to consider adequately other aspects of his writing than the outer happenings of his stories, which, granted, are sometimes melodramatic and sometimes even a little ridiculous upon logical analysis. (This seldom depreciates their entertainment value as well-told tales, however.)

Of course, all of the real merit of Lovecraft's writing lies in its sustained expression of his philosophical proclivities—his outlook on life, if you will. Confronted by the scientific and technical revolutions which left man a meaningless cog in a depersonalized universe, Lovecraft did not withdraw to fight a savage attack on reality as Colin Wilson supposed in his book *The Strength to Dream*, but rather he sought for himself in his mental life those elements which might render his life meaningful and purposeful. His antiquarianism was one expression of his search for meaningfulness in a depersonalized and mechanized society. The adumbrations of things beyond the scope of our everyday lives in his weird fiction were another. (And of course his bizarre and outré creatures are meant only as symbols of this line of outsideness. Moreover, Lovecraft's descriptions of them are far better than most of his critics and illustrators have given him credit for; although, for my part, I much prefer his meticulously scientific description of his Antarctic race to that of the "rugose cones" of his Great Race. Certainly, also, Wilbur Whateley's twin brother is far more provocatively described than Wilbur himself.)

However, Lovecraft's principal mental preoccupation was always the enigmatic philosophical problem of time—which no more creates for us a moment of cognition and being ("I think, therefore I am") than it takes away the world in which that act of being took place forever. For after all, what is the special aspect of the present? If the universe is in reality four-dimensioned, we each of us represent a curve in that four-dimensioned space, and no one point on that curve is any more real than any other. Of course, the riddle of those curves are the endpoints, representing the bounds of each individual's life (period of consciousness?) in the four-dimensioned space. Thus, indeed, are the life-lines of the past only very dimly known to us through what has been set down in books or handed down by oral tradition. Even our own life-lines fade before us through the ravages of forgetfulness. We become so absorbed in whatever our consciousness is—and perhaps it is only a spark of energy running along a fixed and immutable curve in four-dimensioned space—that we rarely even think of our life-line apart from a very small interval about our "position." Modern science and technology have snuffed out whatever small subjective pleasure we could once take in our *being* in that small interval; and I think it was one of Lovecraft's central achievements and merits that he stepped back to look at space-time in the stasis in which it really exists; that he sought to assay the meaning of the quick jumps of our consciousness of physical reality along these curves. For in the ability of our minds to survey more than the narrow interval around our present point of observation of the physical universe is our ability to gauge for ourselves—logically and emotionally—the meaning of the observations we make of the physical universe—the brief illumination for our minds of each of our life-curves by the spark of energy or life which traverses its length. In the intangibility of this mental life—and surely our mental life is as distinct from the chemical activity of our neurons as is the thought on a printed page distinct from the printed page itself—is our renewed ability to take a meaningful outlook on life. This Lovecraft did with his constant fascination with the entire problem of time. He would doubtless not have agreed with some of the statements I have made above—certainly he would say that our life-curves represent only a certain pattern in the space-time curves of the individual atoms of physical matter of the universe. But he would still not have thereby explained the illumining spark, and he knew this himself.

His fascination with the problem of time was by no means unique among writers; but it nevertheless gave his work the permanent quality which will insure its endurance. Of course, Providence was the principal laboratory upon which he fixed his own mental life—and more specifically, the course of his own life-line through that general region of four-dimensional space which one might call "Providence." He perceived of course quite clearly the artificiality of any coordinate system one might try to impose upon such a space, but nevertheless there was only for him—as for each of us—what could be illumined for the mental life by an ephemeral spark in the physical world. This was indeed the central philosophical problem which he always treated; witness him writing to his aunt Mrs. Gamwell on August 19, 1921 (*SL* 1.147), following his jaunt to the Great Meadow Country Clubhouse with Harold Munroe:

> It is now past midnight—and officially the 20th according to civil time. (By astronomical time it is still the 19th until the following noon.) At 9 A.M. I will be one more milepost nearer the welcome sepulchre which yawns for my gray head. 31! How I wish those numbers read backward, giving me the youth & the optimism of 13! I yet recall the happiness of Aug. 20, 1903, when I attained that age—the balmy evening in the yard at 454 under the trees with my telescope, seemingly secure in a prosperous environment, & fresh with the wonder of gazing up through space to other worlds. And my old nigger-man was leaping in & out of the shadowy bushes, occasionally deigning to let his Grandpa Theobald pick him up, put his green shining eye to the telescope, & show him the cryptical surfaces of remote planets—where for all we know the dominant denizens may be lithe, quadrupedal, sable-furred gentlemen exactly like Nigger-Man himself! . . .

Thus, I am hoping—admittedly in rather flighty language—that a few more Providence observations will not be unwarranted. After searching all the dream worlds for the city of ultimate loveliness which he has seen in his dreams, Randolph Carter learns that the shining visions which he had seen were simply his memories of his native city of Boston. Similarly, Iranon learns after a lifetime of search that the marvelous city of Aira was his own personal world of dream. Thus, Lovecraft ever returns to Providence. In his article "Facts in the Case of H. P. Lovecraft" in *Rhode Island History* for winter 1972, Barton St. Armand specifically delineates much of the rich historical and antiquarian background which went into the writing of Lovecraft's Providence masterpiece *The Case of Charles Dexter Ward*—the parallel between the expurgation of Joseph Curwen's den of horror overlooking the Pawtuxet and the burning of the Gaspée by the colonists in 1772 and the use by Lovecraft in his fictional narrative of many of the same historical personages involved in the burning of the Gaspée. Indeed, it is only surprising that Lovecraft had his colonists meet in "the great room of Thurston's Tavern at the Sign of the Golden Lion on Weybosset Point across the bridge," whereas the actual meeting of the colonists who burned the Gaspée occurred at Sabin's Tavern at the corner of South Main (Town) and Planet Streets on Weybosset Neck. (This ancient tavern stood until about 1899; and the paneling of the room in which the colonists met is still preserved intact in a house on the East

Side. I do not know anything about Thurston's Tavern; the Rhode Island Historical Society Library, however, has someone's typescript article on old Providence taverns and other public places which would undoubtedly have all the relevant information.) Here again, of course, Lovecraft was subtly melding fact and fiction—just as he teases us in "The Shunned House" with actual factual data concerning the original home lots along Town Street and the straightening of Benefit (Back) Street, only to inject the doubtless (I hope!) fanciful element of the lease granted to Etienne Roulet in 1697. Note that he also has the climactic raid on Curwen's Pawtuxet premises take place in April 1771—whereas, of course, the burning of the Gaspée occurred in June 1772. Another matter of large interest is the location of the decaying Curwen house in Providence wherein young Charles Ward found the evil portrait of Curwen himself. Writes Lovecraft on pp. 110–111 of the Arkham text (*MM*, 1964; *CF* 2.227):

> He fled from Salem to Providence . . . at the beginning of the great witchcraft panic . . . and was seen found qualified to become a freeman of Providence; thereafter buying a home lot just north of Gregory Dexter's at about the foot of Olney Street. His house was built on Stampers' Hill west of the Town Street, in what later became Olney Court; and in 1761 he replaced this with a larger one, on the same site, which is still standing.

We find even more precise directions in the letter from Joseph Curwen to Jedediah Orne which Charles Ward discovers in Salem (p. 143; *CF* 2.270):

> Turne into Prou. by Patucket ffalls, and ye Rd. past Mr. Sayles's Tavern. My House opp. Mr. Epenetus Olney's Tavern off ye Towne Street, 1st on ye N. side of Olney's Court. Distance from Boston Stone abt. XLIV Miles.

Now all of this information ought to enable anyone skilled in antiquarian investigations to locate the site of Curwen's house fairly easily. Indeed, Olney Street (which was called Olney Lane in colonial times) still exists, and Lovecraft's location of the Curwen house "at about the feet of Olney Street . . . on Stampers' Hill west of the Town Street" fixes the site fairly well. I did not myself locate "Stampers' Hill" or "Olney Court" on any of the old maps which I saw while I was in Providence but I rather imagine that a more sustained investigation would eventually succeed in locating these places names on same ancient map of the city. Indeed, Lovecraft writes that Ward himself knew the Curwen house well from his "antiquarian rambles over Stampers' Hill." He writes further of his return to Providence after his discovery in Salem (*CF* 2.271):

Young ward came home in a state of pleasant excitement, and spent the following Saturday in a long and exhaustive study of the house in Olney Court. The place, now crumbling with age, had never been a mansion; but was a modest two-and-a-half story wooden town house of the familiar Providence colonial type, with plain peaked roof, large central chimney, and artistically carved doorway with rayed fanlight, triangular pediment, and trim Doric pilasters. It had suffered but little alteration externally, and Ward felt he was gazing on something very close to the sinister matters of his quest.

Of course, the obvious question is whether the Curwen house had as its model an actual house which Lovecraft knew on "Stampers' Hill." The information that the house was crumbling when Ward made his discovery in 1919, however is not hopeful; even less so is the information that the town (and "Stampers' Hill") were west of the Town Street (now North Main Street). For if this is so and the house was indeed on the Weybosset Neck (i.e., east of the Moshassuck), it is almost certainly gone today—for the entire area (apart from a few commercial buildings which will also go soon in the renovation of North Main Street) has long been leveled. Yet, the investigation of the site of the Curwen house and of the question of whether Lovecraft's presumptive model still stood when he wrote in 1926–1927 ought to be a fascinating task for a Lovecraftian with an antiquarian bent. All apart from the task of locating "Stampers' Hill" and "Olney Court," such a researcher might in addition derive some clue from the typescript article on Providence taverns which we have mentioned above—for Lovecraft clearly indicates that the Curwen house was opposite the tavern of Epenetus Olney.[267]

Of course, only a true Providence antiquarian can probably appreciate all the richness of Lovecraft's great Providence novel. (A fine book to start out with in a quest for such a background is Cady's *Civic and Architectural Development of Providence* published by The Book Shop in Providence in 1957, I believe. After that, the early official records of the city are only a beginning to the vast richness of material which is available at the Rhode Island Historical Society and the Providence Preservation Society.) But there are many places mentioned in the novel which one can still see without much trouble. The Charles Dexter Ward house itself is of course the beautiful Halsey Mansion on Prospect Street, which Lovecraft could see from his own windows at 10 Barnes Street.[268] Then there is the Old North Burial Ground, where Ward and Curwen before him conducted their ghoulish exhumations, which is north of Olney Street on North Main. The vast, hilly sprawl of the Old North Burial Ground contains graves from all periods and of all varieties—from entire sections of ancient colonial tombstones of slate to entirely modern sections of flat slabs, from the magnificent sepulchre of the Browns atop one of the loftiest hills, to a neglected potter's field overgrown with weeds which the fast-moving stream of traffic on Interstate 95 unfeelingly ignores. Here are also large fields of war veterans, firemen, lodge members, even an entire section devoted to the remains of generations of widowed old ladies who died in a single home for aged women. Here also is the Randall tomb where old Roger's dust—if it was old Roger's dust—resided for so long and . . . well, one could go on endlessly. Indeed, there may even be somewhere in the cemetery the grave of poor Ezra Weeden (1740–1824), who was not left in peace by his enemy Curwen even after his death. His remains, one hopes, *are* still in the cemetery. Altogether, the Old North Burial ground is as fine a reflection of all the variegated phases of Providence life from colonial to modern as is Swan Point Cemetery, on the Seekonk, of the stately Victorian neighborhood with its open fields and wild river bank into which Lovecraft was born.

From Lovecraft's text (*MM* 115; *CF* 2.233) we also learn that Curwen had his warehouse in ancient Doubloon Street in the upper harbor on the Providence River northwest of the present Fox Point Hurricane Barrier. Here also Charles Ward himself found fascination two hundred years later:

> Then came the exquisite First Baptist Church of 1775, luxurious with its matchless Gibbs steeple, and the Georgian roofs and cupolas hovering by. Here and to the southward the neighbourhood became better, flowering at last into a marvellous group of early mansions [including the John Brown House, the present headquarters of the Rhode Island Historical Society and a must see on any tour of Providence, and the Joseph Nightingale House, the largest frame mansion on the North American continent]; but still the little ancient lanes led off down the precipice to the west, spectral in their many-gabled archaism, and dipping to a riot of iridescent decay where the wicked old waterfront still recalls its proud East India days amidst polyglot vice and squalor, rotting wharves, and blear-eyed ship-chandleries and such surviving alley names as Packet, Bullion, Gold, Silver, Coin, Doubloon, Sovereign, Guilder, Dollar, Dime and Cent. (*MM* 108; *CF* 2.223–24)

Indeed, all of these quaint alleys still remained when I came to Providence in 1970, although the warehouses which had lined there western ends along South Water Street were long gone. Several leering rows of early nineteenth-century warehouses still guarded their eastern portals along South Main Street, however. Finally, in the summer of 1972, alas, the majority of these old buildings fell to the wrecker's axe to make way (so I heard) for new "garden apartments." To the developer's credit, however, several of the best buildings along the stretch—including the largest remaining warehouse (ca. 1840)—were restored and will be preserved as commercial buildings. Most of the old alleys whose names were so reminiscent of the old East India trade were officially disestablished as public thoroughfares at that time—whether any of the names will be remaining for future visitors to Providence to see I do not know. Indeed, Lovecraft's listing of the names of these narrow harborside byways in *The Case of Charles Dexter Ward* was hardly complete. My 1911 Providence House Directory shows the following hillside lanes and harborside alleys branching from South Main at that time:

LEFT	RIGHT	
	1	Market Square
4	3	College
	3	Leonard
	47	Wyeth
52		Hopkins
	61	Hutchinson
	81	Mark Lane
	103	Crawford
	131	Custom Ave.
	155	Ward
	175	Packet
198	199	Planet
	213	Bullion
250	233	Power
	257	Gold
268		Harding's Alley
	277	Silver
	295	Coin
302		Pioneer Lane
	313	Patriot
332		Williams
	349	Sovereign
	371	Guilder
398	395	James
436	435	Transit
	opp. 441	Wickenden
	455	Dollar
	467	Dime
480	477	Gregory
484	485	Cent
516	515	Bridge
580		Link
562	561	Pike
600	599	Tockwotton
636	0	India

The streets to the left are the hillside streets; those to the right the harborside alleys, running from South Main to South Water. Indeed, from Market Square to Hopkins Street along South Water was the famous "Brick Row" of 1816 warehouses whose passing in 1929 Lovecraft mourned so deeply (cf. his poem "Brick Row," dated December 7, 1929, which appeared as "East India Brick Row" in the *Providence Journal* for January 8, 1930). A set of aerial photographs made of Providence in 1924 (a copy of which I saw on the shelves of Brown's Rockefeller Library) only hints of the vast charm which these ancient buildings bore. Perhaps there are better photographs available at the Providence Preservation Society or the Rhode Island Historical Society. The Brick Row came down in 1929 to clear an open space in front of the then-new Providence County Courthouse, which had just replaced the previous Victorian edifice which had stood at Benefit and College Streets; today the site is devoted to a small park honoring Verrazzano for his early voyage up Narragansett Bay. In Lovecraft's time, the decaying upper harbor—amply shown by the 1924 aerial photographs—lay to the southward; today the harbor is virtually gone and only the small Rhode Island Fish Company operates from docks north of the Fox Point Hurricane Barrier, installed after disastrous floods in 1938 and 1954. (I am giving these two dates from memory. Several downtown Providence buildings have placards indicating the height to which the waters rose. The most disastrous flood in Providence history, however, was caused by the hurricane of 1815; Lovecraft refers to this disaster in "The Shunned House.")

Indeed, looking at the present-day Providence River—which divides into the Moshassuck and the Woonasquatucket just under the post office annex downtown and is so industrially fouled that sometimes it barely flows—it is difficult to imagine that it once opened up into a large salt cove just about where the Moshassuck and the Woonasquatucket now make their juncture and that the India schooners once sailed north as far as the "falls" on the Moshassuck. Of this same river, William Hazlitt's older sister recorded in her diary in 1784, that it was "the most beautiful river that ever was seen!" (quoted by Scott in his "His Own Most Fantastic Creation"); and one can only imagine the beautiful sight which greeted the first settlers in 1636. (The original 1636 dwellings, all destroyed long before this century, lay along North Main [Town] Street. The spring from which the original settlers drew their fresh water is still preserved as a small park on the west side of North Main; a plaque on a decaying building just opposite [that was still standing in 1972] marks the site of Roger Williams's first home. Of course, he was buried straight up the hill on the grounds of the present Sullivan Dorr Mansion—as we have mentioned before in connection with "Who Ate Roger Williams?")

Such were the idyllic scenes which Lovecraft's vivid antiquarianism created for his inner vision. The cove basin was restored as an ornamental circular lake in the 1890s but rapidly fell prey to the demands of commerce and industry and was reclaimed and bridged over. The area is now occupied principally by large parking lots used by Rhode Island State employees. The beautiful 1898 Capitol, which Lovecraft admired, overlooks the erstwhile basin from the northwest. As for the sinister decay of the old upper harbor to the south, we need only recall how Professor George Gammell Angell of Brown University met his death in "The Call of Cthulhu" (*DH* 131; *CF* 2.22):

> The professor had been stricken whilst returning from the Newport boat [which docked on India Street near Fox Point]; falling suddenly, as witnesses said, after having been jostled by a nautical-looking negro who had come from one of the queer dark courts on the precipitous hillside which formed a short cut from the waterfront to the deceased's home in Williams Street. Physicians were unable to find any visible disorder, but concluded after perplexed debate that some obscure lesion of the heart, induced by the brisk ascent of so steep a hill by so elderly a man, was responsible for the end. At the time I saw no reason to dissent from this dictum, but latterly I am inclined to wonder—and more than wonder.

Indeed, somewhere in the Lovecraft Collection in the John Hay Library is a letter which describes the sinister character which decaying South Main Street impressed upon him and his aunt Mrs. Gamwell on one late-night return from the Newport boat. In fact, when James F. Morton was visiting in Providence on December 27, 1923, he and Lovecraft extended their explorations from the grim expanse of South Main and Water Streets to the abandoned India Point docks where the Browns had plied their trade (Lovecraft to Loveman, January 5, 1924, *SL* 1.280):

> ... [we] set out to walk to the New York packet along the frightful deserted length of horrible South Water Street, where murther lurks in the alleys, and one stumbles over corpses in the gutters. Reaching the ship without stumbling, but carrying a confus'd blur of pallid lamps and Hogarth vistas in our eyes, we dispos'd of Mortonius' valise and set out to kill the few moments before sailing time.
>
> We edg'd thro' ghastly channels between black silent freight cars on the India wharf at the northern tip of Providence's eastern peninsula, a region I had never penetrated, tho' I had for twenty years and more wonder'd about it. It was an eldritch wriggle, like that of Alciphron in the tortuous crypts under Egypt, and at last we came out where pale phosphorescence effus'd from century'd rotting piles, and the distant harbour lights bobb'd and twinkled away to the south, the far south, the south of dreams and templed isles, and

curious ports, and pagodas of gold with savour of spice and incense around them. Then we edg'd back to the *Concord* frigate, said farewell, and ended the travelogue. Mortonius sail'd into the starry sea—I went to a cinema.

Whether Lovecraft and Morton walked all the way northeast to India Point from Morton's boat near Fox Point I do not know; but when I visited the same region in 1971 the rotting piles were still there, although all the railroad spurs had long vanished. A few commercial concerns—shipbuilders, junk dealers, shippers, and others—still plied their trade along the lower reaches of the Seekonk, cut off from the rest of the Neck by Interstate 195, but the decaying pilings along the waterline were soon to be swept away in the construction of what promises to be a very lovely park along the lower banks of the Seekonk. A footbridge over the Interstate will make this park accessible to the residents of the nearby Fox Point neighborhood; the only access by car is from South Water and Gano Streets.

This neighborhood north of the old India docks Lovecraft undoubtedly knew quite well. The western half of the lower Neck—particularly the east-west streets intersecting Benefit below Power—is full of colonial houses which he undoubtedly admired. In one letter, he recorded his delight at discovering a whole row of small colonial houses along Dove Street—transverse to these major east-west thoroughfares—on a walking tour with his aunt Mrs. Gamwell. In the same area, one finds picturesquely-named alleyways like Copley Lane, Broome Lane, Mohawk Lane, and Neighbors Lane. The eastern half of the lower Neck was once dominated by a grim slum which clung to the then-Fox's Hill, but the improvement-conscious city administration of the late nineteenth century (which built the present City Hall which Lovecraft considered anathema) leveled the slum and Fox's Hill. Today, the region is mainly a Portuguese ethnic neighborhood consisting of plain late nineteenth-century buildings, although there are several great churches of interest. (Once, when several friends and I were touring Fox Point, we encountered a large religious procession slowly winding its way through the streets on the way to the cathedral for speeches and celebrations—a sight which would have undoubtedly delighted Lovecraft.) The higher rents which the presence of nearby Brown University stimulated in the area have had some deleterious effects on the neighborhood; but, hopefully, this situation is changing. In fact, Brown University now officially discourages students from seeking homing in the area. I think Lovecraft gradually came to appreciate the essential uniqueness of even Providence's ethnic neighborhoods, and he undoubtedly would have approved of this action—even though, of course, he liked himself to picture the region as it was in Georgian days—unsettled, with a brook running down the present course of Brook Street, and Fox's Hill to the east. (What later became the best residential district, to the north of Fox Point, was at the time merely the site of several swamps.)

As Lovecraft remarked in the letter to Rimel which we have cited in connection with the Shunned House, the solidly-built portion of the town did not attain the top of College Hill until around 1800 (see *FLB* 148). From an earlier period, the marker at Gano and Williams Streets marks the spot where Roger Williams first touched land in 1636 and received the greeting "What Cheer, Netop" from the local Indians—a greeting which later provided the name of innumerable Providence firms. Of course, the first settlers ultimately built along North Main Street, and from there the settlement climbed College Hill and spread across the Great Salt River (now the Providence River) to the site of Providence's present downtown district.

Of course, Lovecraft was far less familiar with Providence apart from College Hill. Writing to Maurice Moe on November 24, 1923 (*SL* 1.268–72), Lovecraft described his first visit to the Italian district on Federal Hill, made on November 22, 1923 with his friend Clifford M. Eddy, Jr., as his tour guide. Federal Hill, still a heavily Italian neighborhood with Atwells Avenue as its principal thoroughfare, still rises to the northwest of the principal downtown area, although it is today separated from it by Interstate 95. Here one can still see along Atwells Avenue the profusion of open-air markets and restaurants which Lovecraft described; and in the side streets, the profusion of plain nineteenth-century dwellings which the Irish first built on the Hill. Of course, Lovecraft immediately sought for remaining colonial buildings on the Hill, but here the pickings were sparse since, as Lovecraft recorded in his letter to Moe, "Federal Hill was sparsely settled in the Colonial period, a church and a few houses being shewn in Avery's 1777 view." "Only on the north slope, in the dark winding alleys by the railway," he continued, "will one find any of the remaining Colonial houses." Unfortunately, the north brow of the hill, overlooking the railway and the Woonasquatucket River to the southwest of the 1898 Capitol, is today completely demolished—having evidently been the most decayed section of the Hill in Lovecraft's day, it probably became the first section to fall before the wrecker's axe. However, the dark alleys and decayed colonial dwellings which Lovecraft discovered on the north brow of the Hill in 1923 undoubtedly continued to have a strong influence upon his imagination—even if they perished before his own death. Witness his letter to Clark Ashton Smith of November 29, 1933 (*Dreams and Fancies*, pp. 37–42;

SL 4.325) relating the dream which later became the framework for August Derleth's story "The Dark Brotherhood":

> Last week I had a very vivid dream of forming the acquaintance of a group of quiet, well-bred, and apparently wholesome young men, all of whom lived in quasi-bohemian apartments in ancient houses along a hill street in Providence which I had never before discovered (and which doesn't exist except as a wide variant of certain far less ancient streets in the Federal Hill Italian Quarter).

Of course, the most famous building which Lovecraftians have sought on Federal Hill has been the church which presumably inspired Lovecraft's dark Starry Wisdom Church in "The Haunter of the Dark"—the church whose evil spire young Robert Blake would spend hours studying from his windows at 66 College Street. Wrote Lovecraft of Blake's discovery of the Church (*DH* 102–103; *CF* 3.456–57):

> Then suddenly a black spire stood out against the cloudy sky on his left, above the tiers of brown roofs lining the tangled southerly alleys. Blake knew at once what it was, and plunged toward it through the squalid, unpaved lanes that climbed from the avenue. Twice he lost his way, but he somehow dared not ask any of the patriarchs or housewives who sat on their doorsteps, or any of the children who shouted and played in the mud of the shadowy lanes.
> At last he saw the tower plain against the southwest, and a huge stone bulk rose darkly at the end of an alley. Presently he stood in a windswept open square, quaintly cobblestoned, with a high bank wall on the farther side. This was the end of his quest; for upon the wide, iron-railed, weed-grown plateau which the wall supported—a separate, lesser world raised fully six feet above the surrounding streets—there stood a grim, titan bulk whose identity, despite Blake's new perspective, was beyond dispute.
> The vacant church was in a state of great decrepitude. Some of the high stone buttresses had fallen, and several delicate finials lay half lost among the brown, neglected weeds and grasses. The sooty Gothic windows were largely unbroken, though many of the stone mullions were missing. [. . .] The massive doors were intact and tightly closed. Around the top of the bank wall, fully enclosing the grounds, was a rusty iron fence whose gate—at the head of a flight of steps from the square—was visibly padlocked. The path from the gate to the building was completely overgrown. Desolation and decay hung like a pall above the place, and in the birdless eaves and black, ivyless walls Blake felt a touch of the dimly sinister beyond his power to define.

Earlier, he had gazed for hours at the grim Church from his study windows (*DH* 100–101; *CF* 3.454–55):

Of all the distant objects on Federal Hill, a certain huge, dark church most fascinated Blake. It stood out with especial distinctness at certain hours of the day, and at sunset the great tower and tapering steeple loomed blackly against the flaming sky. It seemed to rest on especially high ground; for the grimy facade, and the obliquely seen north side with sloping roof and the tops of great pointed windows, rose boldly above the tangle of surrounding ridge-poles and chimney-pots. Peculiarly grim and austere, it appeared to be built of stone, stained and weathered with the smoke and storms of a century and more. The style, so far as the glass could shew, was that earliest experimental form of Gothic revival which preceded the stately Upjohn period and held over some of the outlines and proportions of the Georgian age. Perhaps it was reared around 1810 or 1815.

Now, as anyone who has ever looked out from the new Albert and Vera List Art Building of Brown University (which stands on the site of Lovecraft's College Street house, moved to 65 Prospect Street in 1959) will know, there is no such church of equivalent prominence on Federal Hill. In fact, writing to Duane W. Rimel on November 12, 1935 (*FLB* 299), Lovecraft stated specifically that the Starry Wisdom Church had *no* actual equivalent on Federal Hill and that at the very most his fictional creation represented a "wide variant" of a church there which had lost its steeple in a storm the previous summer. Now, certainly, Lovecraft was familiar with the large churches on Federal Hill; witness his letter to Wilfred B. Talman of June 25, 1926 (*SL* 2.59): "Last Saturday I 'did' Mount Pleasant, Davis Park, and Federal Hill—and was astonished by the great Italian Churches."

The only question is which Federal Hill church he had in mind as the "wide variant" of his fictional creation. In May 1972 Bill Wallace, Larry Shaw, and I spent some time driving over Federal Hill, and I think we concluded that only the great church which rises on the south side of Atwells Avenue just before that thoroughfare descends to cross the Woonasquatucket bore any real similarity to Lovecraft's description. Certainly, it is not located in any maze of alleys—and perhaps there is a church located in a square reached only by such alleys which we missed—but as I recall, it *was* slightly raised above the pavement level by a retaining wall. All of this, however, is only from my memory, and certainly the definitive search for Lovecraft's "wide variant" still remains to be made. (I do not even have the name of the church on Atwells Avenue, although I believe Bill Wallace took notes.) One avenue of investigation would certainly be Lovecraft's remark that his "wide variant" had lost its steeple in a storm in the summer of 1935. This is striking, since the denouement of Lovecraft's "The Haunter of the Dark" takes place during an electrical storm on the night of August 8–9, 1935. Now, anyone who has read Richard L. Tierney's article regarding the chronology of Great Cthulhu's rising from R'lyeh in 1925 (*Etchings and Odysseys* No. 1) will not think it too wide a speculation that Lovecraft here once again adapted the date of an actual event—the loss of a church steeple on Federal Hill—for the fictional happenings in his story. I did make a brief check of the *Providence Journal* for August 9, 1935, myself; but my failure to find anything relating to a storm or lost church steeple is certainly not any compelling evidence that there was not something relating to these subjects in that edition somewhere. In addition, of course, Lovecraft may have altered his dates. In this case, the only solution that I can think of would be to compile a list of prospective candidates on Federal Hill and then to check the Rhode Island Index for possible references to lost steeples in summer 1935. This may be going too far in the search for what was only a "wide variant," however; certainly a visit to Federal Hill yields an ample measure of all the atmosphere which Lovecraft adapted for his fictional purposes in "The Haunter of the Dark." Indeed; it seems quite appropriate that his last story—for he did no writing of fiction in 1936–1937 that has been preserved—should have once again returned to his native Providence for inspiration.[269]

One description in "The Haunter of the Dark" which is not a wide variant of reality is Lovecraft's description of his own residence on College Street; here he had young Robert Blake take his lodgings (*DH* 99; *CF* 3.453):

> Young Blake returned to Providence in the winter of 1934–35, taking the upper floor of a venerable dwelling in a grassy court off College Street—on the crest of the great eastward hill near the Brown University campus and behind the marble John Hay Library [where Lovecraft's papers reside today; on the northwest corner of College and Prospect Streets]. It was a cozy and fascinating place, in a little garden oasis of Village-like antiquity where huge, friendly cats sunned themselves atop a convenient shed. The square Georgian house had a monitor roof, classic doorway with fan carving, small-paned windows, and all the other earmarks of early nineteenth-century workmanship. Inside were six-paneled doors, wide floor-boards, a curving colonial staircase, white Adam-period mantels, and a rear set of rooms three steps below the general level.

This indeed is a perfect description of Lovecraft's last home at 66 College Street in its original setting—where he and his aunt Mrs. Gamwell kept joint housekeeping on the second floor from May 1933 until Lovecraft's death in March 1937. (Mrs. Gamwell kept her residence there until her death in January 1941, although the last few months of her life were spent in a sanatorium in Newport.) The shed which Lovecraft mentions adjoined the boarding house which stood on Waterman Street across the rear garden of the "Garden House" at 66 College; and here Lovecraft's beloved Kappa Alpha Tau fraternity would hold its meetings on the roof. According to the placard which now marks the house at its new site at 65 Prospect Street, Lovecraft's "Garden House" was built by Captain Samuel Mumford around 1825; however, I believe Lovecraft claimed to be able to discern the house in somewhat earlier views of Providence—probably either the famous theater curtain now in the Rhode Island School of Design Museum (which is either 1809 or 1819—I cannot recall) or one of the early eighteenth century paintings of the city now in the Rhode Island Historical Society Museum in the John Brown House. (There was also there a portrait of one of Lovecraft's ancestors—I cannot recall precisely whom—which friends of the family said was Lovecraft's own spitting image.)[270]

Finally, the photograph of Lovecraft's 66 College Street house on its original site which has appeared in various ones of the Arkham House volumes of his work (most recently in *Selected Letters* III, opposite p. 390) deserves a little comment. For, very clearly, the photographer could not have been looking up from lower College Street; otherwise, the marble bulk of the John Hay Library, which stood directly above the "Garden House" on the hill, must needs have appeared in the background of the picture—which it does not. In fact, 66 College Street stood, not directly on College Street itself, but in a small "grassy court" just off the street behind the John Hay Library. This court was known as "Ely Court" in colonial times; in fact, it is still listed as from 64 College Street in my copy of the 1911 Providence House Directory, although no houses are shown on it. By that time, apparently, the "Garden House" had been assigned a number on College Street. Curiously, however, my 1911 House Directory lists no number 66 on College Street. Only the following numbers above 60 are listed:

- 62   Sherrer Arnold E. electrician h
- 64   Vacant
- 65   Delta Kappa Epsilon Fraternity
- 69   Burleigh S R h
        Wilkinson Sarah S Mrs h
        cor Prospect, John Hay Library

Since "Ely Court" is listed as from 64 College, however, I rather imagine that number 66 was then the "Garden House." A slight renumbering may have occurred later.

Now, the photograph in *Selected Letters* III does not look directly into our "grassy court," but into a service driveway directly behind the John Hay Library—a driveway which, in fact, still exists today. Thus, looking into this driveway from College Street, we see a high wall in the foreground, on the other side of which is apparently a house on College Street itself. Then, there is the actual subject of the photograph, the "Garden House," standing in the "grassy court" off College Street. (It seems clear from the photograph that access to "Ely Court" was from below the house shown in the foreground and not from the service driveway behind the John Hay Library.) Then, in the background, is probably the rear of the boarding house on Waterman Street (now demolished) where so many of Lovecraft's visitors at 66 College Street stayed. On the top of the shed adjoining the rear of this building, the Kappa Alpha Tau fraternity held its meetings.

Of course, this is all a hypothetical interpretation of the photograph and deserves confirmation by a more thorough investigation; but I do believe that it is certain from the configuration of the doors and windows of the "Garden House" on its new site, that we do see the front of that house in the photograph in *Selected Letters* III and that the photograph is not a mirror image of the real configuration. The high wall in the foreground seems a little mysterious; but perhaps it was merely meant to shield the service driveway or the John Hay Library. Indeed, recall that "students in the Psi Delta house, whose upper *rear* windows [my emphasis] leaked into Blake's study, noticed the blurred white face at the westward window on the morning of the ninth" in Lovecraft's "The Haunter of the Dark." The location of the Psi Delta house in a 1935 City Directory might provide a significant clue as to the configuration at 66 College Street. I suspect that this fraternity house was on Waterman Street, slightly below the "Garden House," whose western windows look down the hill. The windows of the "Garden House" which show in the *Selected Letters* photograph are the south windows; Lovecraft's study had windows to the south and to the west. However, the building shown behind the wall in the *Selected Letters* photograph might also just be the Psi Delta house—although I do not think that the rear windows would have provided a very good view of the "westward" windows of the "Garden House." Lovecraft's study windows [on the second floor] now face north and west at 65 Prospect Street.) The principal question concerning the *Selected Letters* photograph, then, is simply this: what is shown in the foreground?" I will be severely confounded if anyone can prove to me that it is actually part of the John Hay Library.[271]

Lovecraft's other residences in Providence are equally well-known. The large half-house at 10 Barnes Street in which Lovecraft had a ground floor room from 1926 until 1933 still stands—a Victorian monstrosity *par excellence* if the truth be known. The half-house at 598 Angell Street which he shared with his mother and off and on with his aunts from 1904 until 1924 also remains. Grandpa Phillips's manse at 454 Angell Street (the northwest corner of Angell and Elmgrove), alas, fell to the wrecker's axe around 1961; but at least we have the fine photograph of it which has appeared in *Selected Letters* III and other Arkham volumes. (The caption which has been printed with this photograph lists Annie Phillips Gamwell, Mrs. Winfield Lovecraft Sr., Winfield Lovecraft Sr., and Sarah Phillips Lovecraft in the foreground; I believe that this should be Annie Phillips Gamwell, Robie Alzada [Place] Phillips [1827–1896], Whipple Van Buren Phillips [1833–1904] and Sarah Susan Phillips Lovecraft. Winfield Lovecraft [1853–1898] was neither senior nor junior. Lovecraft stated in letters that he never saw his Lovecraft grandfather George Lovecraft [1815–1895] and that his Lovecraft grandmother Helen [Allgood] Lovecraft died before his birth. Since Robie Alzada [Place] Phillips died in January 1896, the photograph undoubtedly precedes that date. The Phillips manse was originally numbered 194 Angell Street, but as the East Side was built up, a renumbering became necessary, and in 1895 the Phillips manse was assigned the new number 454.)

A not very commonly noted fact, however, is that the house on Angell Street was not the first Phillips residence in Providence after Whipple's removal from Greene in 1873 or 1874. Lovecraft wrote to Barlow on April 20, 1935 (*OFF* 241), that Whipple's first residence in Providence had actually been at 276 Broadway on the West Side, then quite a fashionable address, vide Lovecraft's letter to Miss Elizabeth Toldridge of March 10, 1930 (*SL* 3.120; *ET* 133):

> Our *Broadway* was once a splendid residential street, a mile long & lined with mansions, but is now sunk to a slum & is rapidly being engulfed by the vast Federal Hill Italian colony. Two or three of the ancient families, however, still cling to their old homes—odd cases amidst a desert of Sicilian squalor & Neapolitan noisomeness!

When he wrote to Barlow in 1935, Lovecraft speculated that Whipple's house at 276 Broadway might still exist on some back street or alley; but frankly I doubt whether the course of the street was changed between 1873–74 and 1935. Indeed, unless the street was renumbered, I believe that the site of Whipple's original Providence home is now the site of a theater specializing in *risqué* movies; and, indeed, may have been so even during Lovecraft's lifetime.[272] In general, however, Lovecraft was quite correct in writing Miss Toldridge that most of the fine residential districts of the West Side have long perished. What there is, of course, is a huge conglomeration of plain, nineteenth-century working class houses and tenements on Federal and Smith Hills.

In warm weather, of course, Lovecraft was a great walker, and probably few sections of Providence escaped his survey, if not his detailed investigation. For him, a walk five miles north to his favorite Quinsnicket Woods and back was nothing; sometimes, he would range much farther into the countryside and then return by bus from the nearest available town. Within Providence itself, although College Hill and the bank of the Seekonk were his principal stamping grounds, we find him taking many longer walks. In his letter to Wilfred B. Talman of June 25, 1926 (*SL* 2.58–59), for instance, he wrote of hiking all the way to the Pawtuxet River—where, as readers of *The Case of Charles Dexter Ward* will recall, Joseph Curwen had his hideous laboratory. Even as late as October 28, 1936 (see Lovecraft to Derleth, November 18, 1936, *Notes* xxxix–xlii; *ES* 2.756–57), we find him hiking as far west as Neutaconkanut Hill to discover an utterly intriguing rural vista (still there?) from the western brow of the hill. And, although of course Blackstone Park was his favorite in Providence itself, he would sometimes walk south to Roger Williams Park to do his writing in good weather.

Clifford M. Eddy, Jr., recorded many of his memorable walks with Lovecraft in his article "Walks with H. P. Lovecraft" in *The Dark Brotherhood and Other Pieces* (*LR* 65–68); of these, we have already discussed their famous jaunt in search of the Dark Swamp at some length. Another jaunt was along the length of Poe Street, which parallels Allen's Avenue along the Providence Harbor. When they visited Poe Street late one evening about 1923 or 1924, Eddy and Lovecraft found a desolate, unpaved stretch of some fourteen blocks with only three or four decayed houses—and for the rest only overgrown weeds—along the sides. Alas, time has not been kind even to Poe Street, for the construction of Interstate 95, cutting it off from the other residential sections of south Providence, seems to have ended its already dubious viability as a residential street. Today, as the traffic on the Interstate rushes past, there is only a large parking lot used by employees of firms on Allen's Avenue to see along most of the length of the western side of Poe Street. On the eastern side of the street are mainly the backlots of firms on Allen's Avenue; there are a few weedgrown patches on which houses apparently once rose—but nothing there now. For the last third of its length, the street becomes somewhat narrower and there are a few ordinary-looking commercial buildings nearby; but very soon thereafter a high retaining wall rises up (protecting the embankment of the Interstate) and Poe Street turns off onto Lehigh Street toward the harbor. Indeed, there appears to have been little but desolation along Poe Street for most of its existence. It first pops up in Providence City Directories for the very first years of this century, in which a few boarding houses occupied by laborers and working men are listed. Throughout all of its history, no more than four or five separate residential addresses appear and by 1950 the total was down to one. Even this listing finally disappeared from the Directories in 1963. Thus, Poe Street seems to have proceeded further into desolation than even Eddy and Lovecraft ever supposed it would; but such is Providence's memorial to the famous poet who visited, Edgar Allan Poe. (There is also a Helen Street commemorating his fiancée Sarah Helen Whitman, who is buried in the Old North Burial Ground.)

One other famous exploration took Lovecraft and his friend Eddy to the hideous "Ghoul's Court." Wrote Lovecraft to his friend Maurice W. Moe on November 24, 1923 (*SL* 1.269–71):

> Animated by these reflections, I joyn'd my adopted son Eddy on the following day (22nd November—my grandfather's birthday) for a tour of exploration of certain parts of Colonial Providence which I had never before seen or more than vaguely heard of. I refer to the southerly, section west of the Great Bridge, around Richmond and Chestnut Streets; new sunk to slums and on that account avoided by me, but prov'd by the 1777 view to be genuinely Colonial. Here indeed I found a world of wonder that for 33 years I had ignor'd! Not a stone's throw from the travell'd business section, tuckt quietly in behind Broad and Weybosset Streets, lurk the beginnings of a squalid Colonial labyrinth in which I mov'd as an utter stranger, each moment wondering whether I were in truth in my native town or in some leprous distorted witch-Salem of fever or nightmare. I had not thought my own city to be so large and vary'd—so London-like in containing separate worlds unsuspected one by another. This antient and pestilential reticulation of crumbling cottages and decaying doorways was like nothing I had ever beheld save in dream—it was the 18th century of Goya, not of the Georges; of Hogarth, not of Horace Walpole. Eddy knew it, and was my guide. Led by him, I wander'd up hills where rotting Dorick columns rested on worn stone steps out of which rusted footscrapers rose like malignant fungi. Dirty smallpan'd windows leer'd malevolently on all sides, and sometimes glasslessly, from gouged sockets. There was a fog, and out of it and into it again mov'd dark monstrous diseas'd shapes. They may have been people, or what once were, or might have been, people. Only the gods know who can inhabit this morbid maze—On thro' the fog we went, threading our way thro' narrow extinct streets and unbelievable courts and alleys, sometimes having the antient houses almost meet above our heads, but often emerging into unwholesome little squares or grassless parks at crossings or junctions where five or six of the tangled streets or lanes meet and open out into expanses as loathsome as Victor Hugo's *Cour des Miracles*. Eddy inform'd me, that these little squares are characteristick of the old west side of Providence, but I had

never heard of them. Then, when we wou'd reach the crest of some eminence in this uneven ground, we wou'd see on every hand the strange streets stretching down silent and sinister to the unknown elder mysteries that gave them birth ... grotesque lines of gambrel roofs with drunken eaves and idiotick tottering chimneys, and rows of Georgian doorways with shatter'd pillars and worm-eaten pediments ... streets, lines, rows; bent and broken, twisted and mysterious, wan and wither'd ... claws of gargoyles obscurely beckoning to witch-sabbaths of cannibal horror in shadow'd alleys that are black at noon ... long, long hills up which daemon winds sweep and demon riders clatter over cobblestones ... and toward the southeast, a stark silhouette of hoary, unhallow'd black chimneys and bleak ridgepoles against a mist that is white and blank and saline—the venerable, the immemorial sea; the ancient harbour where pirate barques once rode unquietly at anchor. Many of these places—especially a "Gould's Court" of black, gnawing hideousness which I call'd "Ghoul's Court" upon seeing it in the lone pallid lamplight after the sun had set—Eddy tells me are famous in the annals of crime—but I do not read police reports. There must be crime where so many dead things are ... the mass'd dead of Colonial decay ... the dead that draw shapes out of the night to feed and feast and fatten ... No, I had not thought that Providence held such places as this. We came out silently.

Lovecraft's fascination with such slums—which he shared in common with writers like Eugène Sue and Lafcadio Hearn—would make the subject for a dissertation too long for us to undertake here. Just think of Richard Upton Pickman's wards in "Pickman's Model" (*DH* 22; *CF* 2.60):

> The place for an artist to live is the North End. If any aesthete were sincere, he'd put up with the slums for the sake of the massed traditions. God, man! Don't you realise that places like that weren't merely *made*, but actually *grew*?

Or the following entry dated 1919 (probably incorrectly) in Lovecraft's Commonplace Book:

> (78) Wandering thro' labyrinth of narrow slum streets—come on distant light—unheard-of rites of swarming beggars—like Court of Miracles in Notre Dame de Paris

As for "Gould's Court" and the surrounding area of colonial decay which Lovecraft and Eddy explored in 1923, however, I am sorry to say that they are all gone. In general, I fancy the area which Lovecraft and Eddy explored was that bounded by Weybosset and Broad Streets to the north and west and by Dudley Street and the harbor to the south and east. Today, the area is cut nearly in two by Interstate 95; and while to the south there remains a decayed residential area mostly of late nineteenth-century and early twentieth-century visage, to the north there is only a flattened and utterly commercialized district—where once were Lovecraft's leering colonial survivals. (There were a few decaying nineteenth-century houses still standing on Pine Street just north of the Interstate when I was last in Providence, but as for the area around Richmond and Chestnut Streets, it consists entirely of ugly, twentieth-century commercial buildings. Several of these commercial streets, like Pine, however, betray their ancientness by their aged brick pavements. Indeed, my favorite bookshop in Providence—and perhaps one known by Lovecraft—was a leering hole-in-the-wall on Richmond Street, whose aged proprietor presided over tottering stacks of dusty tomes.)

Perhaps the survival most characteristic of Lovecraft's descriptions in his letter to Moe are the strange open squares to the south of the Interstate where as many as four or five of the decaying streets come together at once—but that Lovecraft would still find colonial survivals here, I very much doubt. (When a friend of mine who was working on a biography of Lovecraft took an apartment on decaying West Clifford Street in this area to the south of the Interstate, I told him that he was chasing a very Lovecraftian spot.) As for the terrible "Gould's Court" itself, it has been literally wiped from the map. Its site is very readily determined from old plat maps of the city. It lay amazingly to the principal commercial thoroughfare of Broad Street—in the block bounded by Broad, Claverick, Pine, and Chestnut Streets. In the earliest nineteenth-century City Directories which survive, Gould's Street is listed; and the information in the Directories and the plat maps show that it bisected the block, running parallel to Broad and Pine from Claverick to Chestnut. Two more entities, Gould's Court and Gould's Place, are shown on the maps as follows:

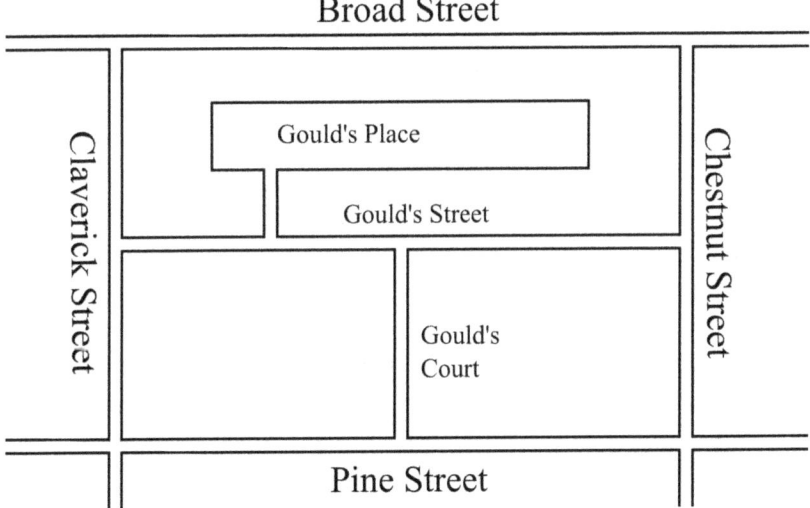

Here, the hideous Gould's Court is an alleyway running from 235 Pine to 12 Gould's Street. Gould's Place is an interior courtyard adjoining on 3 Gould's Street. So close to the everyday commercial affairs of Providence was this realm of colonial decay which Lovecraft discovered with Eddy's help in 1923—literally a "stone's throw," as Lovecraft remarked, to the principal business district.

Now, in all of the Providence Directories, there are never any residences listed on the hideous Gould's Court—but in the late nineteenth and early twentieth centuries, Gould's Street, Pine Street, and the interior Gould's Place were teeming with boarding houses and cheap eating places. Undoubtedly, many of the backs of these ancient tenements and buildings abutted on Lovecraft's Gould's Court. At least, such is the sight which we must imagine he and Eddy saw. By the 1930s, the entire block seems to have begun its ultimate decline, although as late as 1960, one Charles E. Titus maintained a lodging house at 20 Gould's Street. By 1963 and 1964, only one Theodore J. Dumas, a painting contractor, is listed for the entire block—at 17 Gould's Street. Then in 1965 and 1966, Gould's Street, Gould's Place, and Gould's Court are listed, but without a single resident for any of them. In 1967, all three are dropped—forever—from the Providence Directory; and on the block there now rises a large modern apartment building with a statue of Providence's late nineteenth-century Mayor Doyle, a major renovator, on the lawn. (The address is 100 Broad Street.) The only other remaining building on the block, the beautiful Arnold–Palmer house (1826), designed by Providence's master architect John Holden Greene, is not in fact an original denizen of the block. It was originally located at 577 Westminster Street—part of the fine nineteenth-century residential neighborhood which stretched along Weybosset, Westminster, and Broadway until it was utterly destroyed by the spread of commercial establishments from the original downtown area (of which the Round Top Beneficent Congregational Church [1810] was the historic center) and cheap private dwellings from Federal Hill. Probably moved from its original site after the leveling of the Gould block in 1967 or thereabouts, the Arnold–Palmer house is today the *only* existing example of the fine architecture once found on the West Side. So much for the "Ghoul's Court"—I suppose we will have only Lovecraft's description of it unless someone unexpectedly manages to come up with some photographs.

But it is hardly fitting to end a rambling discussion of Lovecraft's lifelong fascination with his native city on such a depressing note. Rather let us quote from his letter written to August Derleth from the "open fields near the River" in mid-to-late September, 1930 (*SL* 3.171–72; *ES* 1.278–79):

> . . . I am sitting in the glow of a warm autumnal sunset amidst the ancient and unchanging weeds and fields which I have known and loved and wandered through since infancy. I surely thank heaven for the fortuitous circumstances which have preserved such a generous and glamorous slice of the primal countryside so close to the thickest part of residential Providence. Beginning on the south is a long stretch of metropolitan park land. Then, contiguous with this (or just across a reedy salt creek) is the parklike domain of a sanatorium which admits the public except on Sunday. Then, piecing out still farther northward is the scenic expanse of Swan Point Cemetery—the borders of which are sheer countryside without graves, kept thus for aesthetic embellishment. Farther north still—over the city line in Pawtucket—is still another river-bank cemetery; but this is not so beautiful. The net result of all this is the preservation of a splendidly rural series of river-bluffs, wooded ravines, and meadows for a space of at least two miles along the shore, and extending considerably inland. Its ownership and conditions are fixed, hence it has been the same throughout my life and is always likely to stay so. I can shed the years uncannily by getting into some of my favourite childhood haunts here. In spots where nothing has changed, there is little to remind me that the date is not still 1900 or 1901, and that I am not still a boy of 10 or 11. Images and ideas and perspectives of that period flood up from subconsciousness with amazing vigour and volume, and do much to prove the relativity and subjectivity of time. Sometimes I feel that if I went home to my birthplace and up the steps, I would still find my mother and grandfather alive, and my old room and things in accustomed 1900 order.
>
> At this moment the setting sun is throwing the long shadows of great ancient elms across a broad, level stretch of silent greensward. At the far side is an old New England stone well covered with ivy, and beyond it a line of trees marks the course of a venerable curving road—half deserted now that newer trunk roads have cut it off as a line of through traffic. In suggestions of a magic annihilative of natural laws and material, spatial and temporal restrictions, this scene and hour would be hard to beat . . .

This part of Lovecraft's Providence, at least, is still as it once was and is likely to remain so for as long as Lovecraft himself predicted.

* * *

How does one properly make an end of even so diffuse a work as this—when the subject is as fascinating as Howard Phillips Lovecraft and his work? I do not think I could write a fitting conclusion myself. However, some lines of Lovecraft's might serve. During his 1931 visit with Henry S. Whitehead in Dunedin, Florida, Lovecraft made the acquaintance of a young poet who was a friend of Whitehead's, Allan Brownell Grayson, then of 701 West 178th Street in New York City. Lovecraft wrote for Grayson a short poem which he included in his letter to his aunt Mrs. Clark of May 30, 1931:

To a Young Poet in Dunedin

You haunt the lonely sand where herons hide,
And palm-framed sunsets open gates of flame;
Where marble moonbeams bridge the lapping tide
To westward shores of dream without a name.

Here, in a haze of half-remembering,
You catch faint sounds from that far, fabled beach.
The world is changed—your task henceforth to sing
Dim, beckoning wonders you could never reach.

—H. P. Lovecraft

Appendix: Calculations of Lovecraft's earnings

PAID APPEARANCES OF FICTION YEAR-BY-YEAR	HIGH	LOW
"Herbert West—Reanimator" (six parts)	$30	$30
Home Brew, Feb., Mar., Apr., May, June, and July 1922		
Total—1922	**$30**	**$30**
"The Lurking Fear" (four parts)	$20	$20
Home Brew, Jan., Feb., Mar., and Apr. 1923		
"Dagon"	$36	$12
WT, October 1923		
Total—1923	**$56**	**$32**
"The Picture in the House"	$54	$18
WT, January 1924		
"The Hound"	$48	$16
WT, February 1924		
"The Rats in the Walls"	$120	$40
WT, March 1924		
"Arthur Jermyn" (as "The White Ape")	$54	$18
WT, April 1924		
"Hypnos"	$42	$14
WT, May–June–July 1924		
"Imprisoned with the Pharaohs"	—	—
WT, May–June–July 1924		
Total—1924	**$318**	**$106**
"The Festival"	$54	$36
WT, January 1925		
"The Statement of Randolph Carter"	$36	$24
WT, February 1925		
"The Music of Erich Zann"	$54	$36
WT, May 1925		
"The Unnamable"	$48	$32
WT, July 1925		
"The Temple"	$78	$52
WT, September 1925		
Total—1925	**$270**	**$180**

"The Tomb"		$60	$40
	WT, January 1926		
"The Cats of Ulthar"		$24	$16
	WT, February 1926		
"The Outsider"		$42	$28
	WT, April 1926		
"The Moon-Bog"		$48	$32
	WT, June 1926		
"The Terrible Old Man"		$18	$12
	WT, August 1926		
"He"		$60	$40
	WT, September 1926		
Total—1926		**$252**	**$168**
"The Horror at Red Hook"		$120	$80
	WT, January 1927		
"The White Ship"		$36	$24
	WT, March 1927		
"The Colour out of Space"		$25	$25
	Amazing Stories, September 1927		
"Pickman's Model"		$84	$56
	WT, October 1927		
"The Horror at Red Hook"		$80	$35
	You'll Need a Night Light, Selwyn & Blount, 1927		
Total—1927		**$345**	**$220**
"The Call of Cthulhu"		$165	$165
	WT, February 1928		
"Cool Air"		$54	$54
	Tales of Magic and Mystery, March 1928		
"The Lurking Fear"		$78	$78
	WT, June 1928		
"The Horror at Red Hook"		$00	$00
	Not at Night!, Macy-Masius, 1928		
"The Shunned House"		$00	$00
	Recluse Press (unbound book), 1928		
Total—1928		**$297**	**$297**
"The Silver Key"		$72	$72
	WT, January 1929		
"The Dunwich Horror"		$240	$240
	WT, April 1929		
"Pickman's Model"		$56	$35
	By Daylight Only, Selwyn & Blount, 1929		
"The Call of Cthulhu"		$120	$35
	Beware After Dark!, Macauley, 1929		
Total—1929		**$488**	**$382**

Appendix: Calculations of Lovecraft's earnings 221

Total—1930	**$00**	**$00**
"The Whisperer in Darkness"	$350	$350
WT, August 1931		
"The Strange High House in the Mist"	$55	$55
WT, October 1931		
"The Rats in the Walls"	$80	$35
Switch on the Light, Selwyn & Blount, 1931		
"The Music of Erich Zann"	$25	$25
Creeps by Night, John Day, 1931		
Total—1931	**$510**	**$465**
"In The Vault"	$54	$54
WT, April 1932		
"The Music of Erich Zann"	$10	$10
London Evening Standard, October 24, 1932		
"The Music of Erich Zann"	$10	$10
Modern Tales of Horror, Gollancz, 1932		
Total—1932	**$74**	**$74**
"The Dreams in the Witch House"	$216	$216
WT, July 1933		
Total—1933	**$216**	**$216**
"Through the Gates of the Silver Key"	$102	$102
WT, July 1934		
Total—1934	**$102**	**$102**
Total—1935	**$00**	**$00**
At the Mountains of Madness (three parts)	—	—
Astounding Stories, February, March, and April 1936		
"The Shadow out of Time"	$595	$595
Astounding Stories, June 1936		
"The Haunter of the Dark"	$138	$138
WT, December 1936		
"The Shadow over Innsmouth"	$00	$00
Visionary Press, 1936		
Total—1936	**$733**	**$733**
"The Thing on the Doorstep"	$162	$162
WT, January 1937		
"Pickman's Model"	$56	$35
Not at Night Omnibus, Selwyn & Blount, 1937		
Total—1937	**$218**	**$197**
GRAND TOTAL FOR LOVECRAFT'S LIFETIME	**$3909**	**$3202**

Paid appearances of Lovecraft's poetry year-by-year

Estimates based upon 25¢ per line where it is known Lovecraft was paid; see Lovecraft to Morton, March 12, 1930 (*SL* 3.129; *JFM* 224).

symbols: ? = paid?   * = newspaper

1912

"Providence in 2000 A.D."   ?
    *Evening Bulletin**, March 4, 1912

1915

"An Elegy on Franklin Chase Clark, M.D."   ?
    *Evening News**, April 29, 1915

1916

"Quinsnicket Park"   ?
    *Evening News**, February 1916

"The Beauties of Peace"   ?
    *Evening News**, June 17, 1916

1917

"An Elegy on Phillips Gamwell, Esq."   ?
    *Evening News**, January 5, 1917

"The Marshes at Ipswich"   price(?)
    National Magazine (Boston), April 1917

"Ode for July Fourth, 1917"   ?
    *Evening News**, July 3, 1917

"Autumn"   ?
    *Evening News**, November 5, 1917

"Brumalia"   ?
    *Evening News**, December 7, 1917

1918

"A Winter Wish"   ?
    *Evening News**, January 2, 1918

"The Volunteer"   ?
    *Evening News**, February 1, 1918

"March"   ?
    *Evening News**, March 1, 1918

"Ver Rusticum"   ?
    *Evening News**, April 1, 1918

c. 1923   ?

"Waste Paper" (parody of "The Waste Land")   ?
    (newspaper)*, 1923?

1924

"Nemesis"		$16.50
	WT, April 1924	
"To a Dreamer"		$6.00
	WT, November 1924	

1926

"Yule Horror"		$3.75
	WT, December 1926	

1929

"The Messenger"		$3.50 ?
	Providence Journal* ("The Sideshow"), December 3, 1929	

1930

"East India Brick Row" (same as "Brick Row")		$12.00
	Providence Journal*, January 8, 1930	
"The Ancient Track"		$11.00
	WT, March 1930	
"Nostalgia" (XXIX)		$3.50
	Providence Journal*, March 12, 1930	
"Night-Gaunts" (XX)		$3.50
	Providence Journal*, March 26, 1930	
"Background" (XXX)		$3.50
	Providence Journal*, April 6, 1930	
"Recapture" (XXXIV)		$3.50
	WT, May 1930	
"The Dweller" (XXXI)		$3.50
	Providence Journal*, May 7, 1930	
"The Well" (XI)		$3.50
	Providence Journal*, May 14, 1930	
"The Familiars" (XXVI)		?
	Driftwind, July 1930	
"The Courtyard" (IX)		$3.50
	WT, September 1930	
"Star-Winds" (XIV)		$3.50
	WT, September 1930	
"Hesperia" (XIII)		$3.50
	WT, October 1930	
"Antarktos" (XV)		$3.50
	WT, November 1930	
"The Port" (VIII)		?
	Driftwind, November 1930	
"The Bells" (XIX)		$3.50
	WT, December 1930	
Total (1930)		**$61.50**

1931

"Azathoth" (XXII)		$3.50
	WT, January 1931	
"Nyarlathotep" (XXI)		$3.50
	WT, January 1931	
"The Elder Pharos" (XXVII)		$3.50
	WT, February–March 1931	
"Mirage" (XXIII)		$3.50
	WT, February–March 1931	
"The Lamp" (VI)		?
	Driftwind, March 1931	
"The Window" (XVI)		?
	Driftwind, April 1931	
"Alienation" (XXXII)		$3.50
	WT, April–May 1931	
Total (1931)		**$17.50**

1932

"The Canal" (XXIV)		?
	Driftwind, March 1932	
"The Gardens of Yin" (XVIII)		?
	Driftwind, March 1932	
"The Howler" (XII)		?
	Driftwind, November 1932	

1934

"Zaman's Hill" (VII)		?
	Driftwind, October 1934	

1936

"Recognition" (IV)		?
	Driftwind, December 1936	

GRAND TOTAL FOR LOVECRAFT'S LIFETIME   **$108.75**

No claim for completeness is made for the listing of Lovecraft poems which appeared in newspapers. There are undoubtedly many more. Poems embodied within astronomical articles are not included.

The following *Fungi* appeared in amateur and fan magazines during Lovecraft's lifetime:

    I. "The Book": *Fantasy Fan* 2, No. 2 (October 1934).

    II. "The Pursuit": *Fantasy Fan* 2, No. 2 (October 1934).

    III. "The Key": *Fantasy Fan* 2, No. 5 (January 1935).

    V. "Homecoming": *Fantasy Fan* 2, No. 5 (January 1935); *Science-Fantasy Correspondent* No. 1 (November–December 1936).

X. "The Pigeon-Flyers": *Ripples from Lake Champlain* 2, No. 4 (Spring 1932).
XX. "Night-Gaunts": *Interesting Items* 605 (November 1934); *Phantagraph* 4, No. 3 (June 1936); reprinted from *Providence Journal* (March 26, 1930).
XXIX. "Nostalgia": *Phantagraph* 4, No. 4 (July 1936); reprinted from *Providence Journal* (March 12, 1930).
XXX. "Background": *Interesting Items* 592 (September 1932); *Galleon* 1, No. 4 (May–June 1935).
XXXI. "The Dweller": *Phantagraph* 4, No. 2 (November–December 1935).
XXXIII. "Harbour Whistles": *Silver Fern* (May 1930); *L'Alouette* 3, No. 6 (September–October 1930); *Phantagraph*, November, 1936).
XXXV. "Evening Star": *Pioneer* 2, No. 4 (Autumn 1932).
XXXVI. "Continuity": *Pioneer* 2, No. [3] (Summer 1932); *Causerie* (February 1936).

Apparently unpublished during Lovecraft's lifetime were "A Memory" (XVII), "St. Toad's" (XXV), and "Expectancy" (XXVIII); they first appeared in the collected edition of the *Fungi* which Bill Evans mimeographed for FAPA in June 1943; this edition, however, contained only the first thirty-three of the thirty-six *Fungi*.

Shortly after Lovecraft's death, "The Book" (I) was republished in *Driftwind* (April 1937) and "The Well" (XI) in *The Phantagraph* (July 1937). *Weird Tales* began reprinting various ones of the *Fungi* in January 1938 but did not attain first publication of any of the remaining unpublished *Fungi*. All thirty-six *Fungi* were gathered together for the first time in *Beyond the Wall of Sleep* (published ca. November 1943).

* * *

Lovecraft's yearly income from his writing

The following estimates represent income from stories published in a given year (excluding revision); no claim is made that payment was actually made in the same year.

In the below chart the black bars represent the "high" estimates and the grey bars the "low" estimates. The right edge represents roughly the $15 per week income which Lovecraft considered minimally adequate.

226 APPENDIX: CALCULATIONS OF LOVECRAFT'S EARNINGS

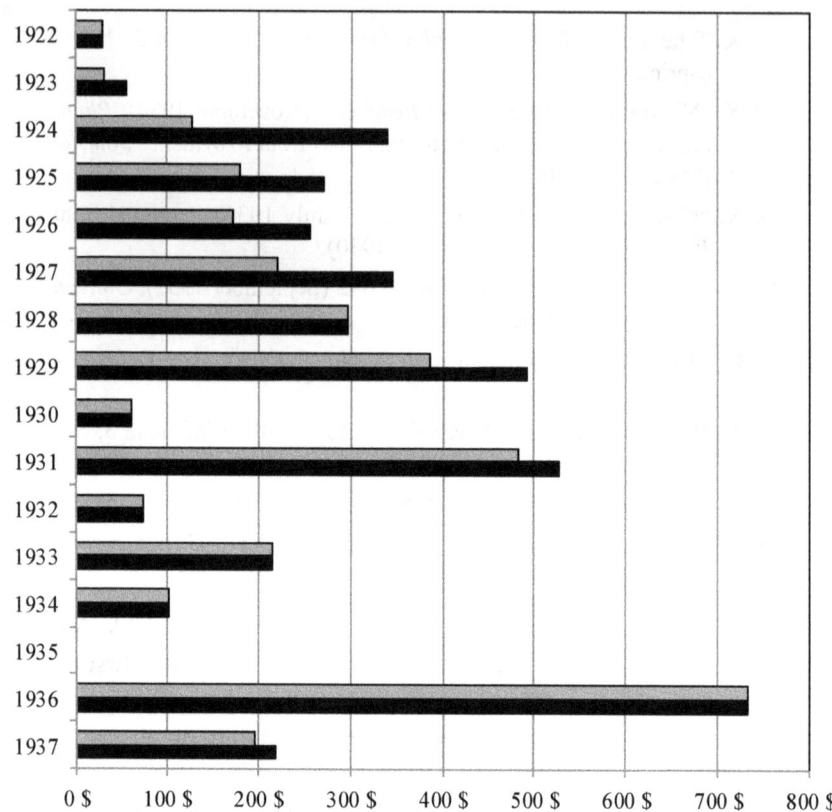

	High	Low
1922	$30.00	$30.00
1923	$56.00	$32.00
1924	$340.50	$128.50
1925	$270.00	$180.00
1926	$255.75	$171.75
1927	$345.00	$220.00
1928	$297.00	$297.00
1929	$491.50	$385.50
1930	$61.50	$61.50
1931	$527.50	$482.50
1932	$74.00	$74.00
1933	$216.00	$216.00
1934	$102.00	$102.00
1935	$0.00	$0.00
1936	$733.00	$733.00
1937	$218.00	$197.00
	$4017.75	**$3310.75**

Notes

CHAPTER 1:

1. The recent discovery by L. Sprague de Camp of letters of Louise Imogen Guiney referring to the Lovecrafts' stay with Miss Guiney and her mother in Auburndale, Massachusetts, obviates the necessity for most of the second part of our discussion in this note. Mr. de Camp will undoubtedly publish his discoveries in his biography *H. P. Lovecraft: Eldritch Yankee Gentleman*, forthcoming from Doubleday at the time of this writing.
[The book was published as *Lovecraft: A Biography* in 1975. See note 14.]

2. Although Scott does not reveal the source of this anecdote, I suspect that it may have been Albert Allison Baker (1862–1959), an attorney and friend of the family who served as Winfield's legal guardian from 1893 until his death in 1898 and as H. P. Lovecraft's own guardian (upon the application of his mother) from 1899 until Lovecraft attained the age of majority in 1911. He was named executor in Lovecraft's 1912 will and served in that capacity in 1937.

3. Curiously, although Scott found Sarah Susan Lovecraft's full medical record at Butler Hospital, where she was also confined at the end of her life (1919–1921), he could find no reference whatever to Winfield Lovecraft in the records of the hospital. Researcher R. Alain Everts was told by officials of the Hospital that all the relevant records were destroyed by fire in 1955, and has been trying to confirm this fact. When I myself consulted the Butler Hospital *Report* dated January 25, 1899, covering the year 1898, I found the following causes of death listed: "One case (a man), died of diabetes mellitus; one case (a man), of cerebral apoplexy; four cases (men), died of general paralysis; four cases (two women and two men), died of the debility of old age; one case (a man), of gangrene of the foot; one case (a woman), of sarcoma of the liver; one case (a man), of accidental asphyxia; one case (a man), of exhaustion from progressive muscular atrophy; one case (a man), from cerebral tumor." The next paragraph states that "most of the fatal cases had long suffered from incurable organic disease of the brain, and in none of those who died was there much reason to expect mental restoration." This listing of deaths at Butler Hospital in 1898 would seem to confirm Lovecraft's allegation that his father had been stricken by "complete paralysis" (*SL* 1.33; *RK* 66), or "general paralysis" as the *Report* puts it; but Mr. Everts told me that this was merely a euphemism of the day for paresis. In addition, Mr. Everts related that he was in possession of direct testimony from family friends that Winfield Lovecraft had died of paresis; so that the testimony of the City Hall death certificate is undoubtedly decisive. The absence of Winfield Lovecraft's records from Butler Hospital in 1943–1944, when Scott was doing his research, however, is very curious; perhaps, one might speculate, the family went to some pains to conceal the real nature of his illness and had the relevant records destroyed.

4. [Mrs. Lovecraft's commonplace book: call no. RARE PS3523.O82 Z778 (JHL).]

5. The witnesses to the marriage of Winfield and Sarah Susan are not given in the entry at the Registry of Marriages in Boston but rather in the entry in the recordbook of St. Paul's Cathedral Church. It is curious to note that Lovecraft himself chose *St. Paul's* Chapel at Broadway and Vesey Streets in Manhattan for the site of his own marriage to Sonia Greene on March 3, 1924—one cannot help thinking the site of his father's marriage was involved to at least some degree in his choice. The Episcopal service which the consummate Englishman Winfield undoubtedly had

at his marriage may also have influenced Lovecraft; note his assertion to James F. Morton (*SL* 1.327; *JFM* 74) that he had had a Church-of-England service. Sonia H. Davis also says in her memoir in *Something about Cats* (*LR* 257) that she agreed to a religious service. For the record, Lovecraft says in his letter of March 21, 1924 to Frank Belknap Long (*SL* 1.331) that he was married by the Reverend George Benson Cox, with Joseph Gorman and Joseph G. Armstrong as witnesses—the complementary information to that which we have given for Winfield's marriage. [For Lovecraft's marriage, see Faig in *EOD Letter* 14 (May Eve 2010).]

6. [The records of the Providence branch of Gorham & Co. are now in JHL, cf. *IAP* 1.536.]

7. [I.e., the school year 1907/08 ending on June 10, 1908. For details of Lovecraft's high school attendance, see *IAP* 1.100–102.]

8. In a letter to R. H. Barlow of April 20, 1935 (*OFF* 240), Lovecraft stated that Minster Hall, near Newton Abbott in south Devonshire, out of the Lovecraft family since 1823, had been demolished before 1850. In the same letter, Lovecraft recounted what he knew of the fate of the other residences of his great-great-grandparents. Great Fulford in Devonshire, home of the Fulfords, he did not know much of—he speculated that it was out of the family and destroyed. Nunwick (also spelled Nanwick), near Hexham in Northumberland, the home of the Allgoods, he said was in a remote branch of the family. The Asaph Phillips house, on Howard Hill in Foster, Rhode Island, he said had been destroyed by fire about 1910; the graves of his great-great-grandfather Asaph Phillips (1764–1829) and great-grandfather Jeremiah Phillips (1800–1840) were nearby. (Lovecraft gave an account of his visit to the site of the house and the nearby graves in his letter to Maurice W. Moe of Sept. 1, 1929 [*SL* 3.15–20].) The John Rathbone House, in Exeter, Rhode Island, he said was out of the family and probably demolished. (John Rathbone [1750–1810] was the father of Robie Rathbone, the wife of Lovecraft's great-grandfather Jeremiah Phillips.) The Stephen Place House, in Moosup Valley, Foster, Rhode Island, he said had been out of the family since 1869 but was still standing and in fairly good structural shape as of 1935. (Stephen Place [1736–1817] was the father of Stephen Place [1783–1849], the father of Robie Alzada Place [1827–1896], who became the wife of Whipple V. Phillips, Lovecraft's grandfather, in 1855.) In a later letter to Helen Sully, dated July 26, 1936 (ms., JHL), Lovecraft noted that this house, in which his mother and his grandmother Robie Place Phillips (the wife of Whipple Phillips) had been born, had recently been restored by an interior decorator; it probably still stands today. Lovecraft gave an account of his visit to the Stephen Place House and the nearby Place graveyard in his letter of October 26, 1926, to Frank Belknap Long (*SL* 2.85–86). (During the same trip to Moosup Valley, in Foster, Rhode Island, Lovecraft visited the homes of his relative Casey B. Tyler [where his aunt Mrs. Clark had been born]; of his great-uncle James Phillips, the brother of Whipple Phillips [where he had previously visited in 1896 and 1908]; and of Job Place, father-in-law of James Whipple Phillips. Lovecraft spoke of his intentions to search for Phillips family graves and residences of the fifth generation back and further in his letters of September 1, 1929, to Maurice W. Moe [*SL* 3.16] and of September 4, 1929, to August Derleth [*SL* 3.25; *ES* 1.210], but I do not know whether he ever actually undertook this search.)

Of later family residences, Whipple Phillips's house on Angell Street (corner of Angell and Elmgrove) passed out of the family in 1904 and was torn down about 1961; Whipple's house in Greene, Rhode Island, where he moved from Foster before 1860, described by local historian Squire G. Wood (*A History of Greene and Vicinity* 1845–1929, p. 12) as a "very comfortable home, with a large barn and carriage house," was according to Wood bought by Daniel Tillinghast following Whipple's removal from Greene; and after his death by Albert W. Cleveland, who was the occupant at the time of Wood's writing. (Wood dates Whipple's removal to Providence as ca. 1880—however, Whipple's own obituary in the *Providence Journal* for March 31, 1904, gives the date as 1873, and Lovecraft in his letter to Maurice W. Moe of

January 1, 1915 [*SL* 1.6] as 1873. Lovecraft himself met Squire Wood on his visit to western Rhode Island in 1926; cf. his letter to Long of October 26, 1926 [*SL* 2.88].) In his letter to Barlow of April 20, 1935 (*OFF* 241), he stated that all the Lovecraft residences in Rochester and Mount Vernon, New York—presumably he meant those of his direct line—had been demolished. He stated that he had once visited the site of the Mount Vernon residence, which was occupied by business establishments at the time of his visit. (However, according to Mr. R. Alain Everts, who has done extensive research on the Lovecraft family in England and America, several of the Lovecraft homes in Rochester are still standing.)

[For Lovecraft and Foster, see Faig's "Lovecraft's Travelogues of Foster, Rhode Island" (*Lovecraft Annual* No. 7) and "'The Silver Key' and Lovecraft's Childhood," *UL* 148–82. For the Lovecraft family homes in Rochester, see Richard D. Squires, *Stern Fathers 'neath the Mould* (1995).]

9. [For genealogical research on Lovecraft, see in general Faig, "Quae Amamus Tuemur: Ancestors in Lovecraft's Life and Fiction" (*UL* 14–49, containing ancestor tables). For his paternal line in Devonshire, see Docherty, Searles, and Faig, *Devonshire Ancestry of Howard Phillips Lovecraft* (2003); for the Lovecraft family in America, see Richard D. Squires, *Stern Fathers 'neath the Mould: The Lovecraft Family in Rochester* (1995), and R. Alain Everts, "The Lovecraft Family in America" (*Xenophile* 2, No. 6). For a brief summary of what has so far been unearthed concerning the ancestry, see *IAP* 1.3–6.]

10. [The listing of items in the Grill–Binkin collection (*A Catalog of Lovecraftiana*, 1975) verifies that Jack Grill had owned numerous photographs of Lovecraft and his family (thirteen are listed in the published catalogue): nos. 524–532, 534–536, and 539. Cf. George T. Wetzel's "Copyright Problems of the Lovecraft Estate" (*The Lovecraft Scholar*, p. 29): "The late Jack Grill, a great collector of Lovecraftiana, related to me in several letters descriptions of several unusual HPL items he had collected: [...] 'old original mounted' photographs of Winfield Lovecraft [cf. No. 539], the house in which HPL was born (relatives in the foreground) [no. 536], and a snapshot of the old school where HPL's grandfather had been a teacher."]

11. It may be somewhat unfair to completely dismiss Sarah Lovecraft as a "weak sister" (Albert Baker's phraseology) preoccupied by her own neuroses. Despite her mental deterioration at the end of her life, amply described by Winfield T. Scott in his essay in *Marginalia*, her early interest in literature and painting (cf. her commonplace book at the John Hay Library and Lovecraft to Moe, January 1, 1915, *SL* 1.6) bespeak an active intellect. In his introduction to the pieces by Clifford M. Eddy in *The Dark Brotherhood* (p. 97), August Derleth mentions that it was Sarah Susan's activity in the women's suffrage movement in the early years of the century which first brought her son and Clifford and Muriel Eddy into correspondence in 1918—certainly an uncharacteristic form of activity for a pitiable neurotic.

12. The evidence concerning the religious preferences of Lovecraft's family is not completely clear. The Lovecrafts were evidently Episcopalians, and both Lovecraft and his father evidently chose Episcopal ceremonies for their marriages.† According to Squire Wood's *History of Greene and Vicinity* (p. 24), Whipple and Robie Phillips at first attended the Rice City Christian Baptist Church (founded in 1815) after they came to Greene. However, in 1870 Whipple and his wife and several other couples withdrew from this church and began the foundation of the Grace Methodist Evangelical Church in Greene. When the permanent building of the Church was erected in 1873, Whipple and Robie became charter members. After coming to Providence in 1874, Whipple and Robie evidently attended the services at the First Baptist Meeting House; at least, according to Lovecraft's letters of March 7, 1920, to Rheinhart Kleiner (*SL* 1.110–111; *RK* 184) and of January 5, 1924, to Samuel Loveman (*SL* 1.277), Lovecraft himself attended services in the main auditorium there until 1895 and Sunday school until about 1902. Lovecraft had

last been in the building in 1907 to deliver a lecture upon astronomy to a boys' club when he, Morton, and Eddy visited the Meeting House on December 27, 1923.

† This assertion derives principally from Lovecraft's own statements that Episcopal clergymen were prominent in his ancestry and that he himself elected an Episcopal ceremony when he was married to Sonia Greene in New York in 1924. In addition, we have the marriage of Winfield Lovecraft and Sarah Susan Phillips at St. Paul's Church (Episcopal) on Tremont Street in Boston in 1889. However, the researches of R. Alain Everts have failed to turn up Episcopal clergymen in Lovecraft's ancestry and have in fact revealed that the Lovecraft family in America were not Episcopalians, but of several different religious sects. Mr. Everts has also expressed some skepticism regarding Lovecraft's assertion that he and Sonia were married in an Episcopalian ceremony; however, we should remember here Lovecraft's own assertion that he selected such a ceremony solely for its historical and cultural associations. If he and Sonia were able simply to present themselves and their marriage certificate at St. Paul's Chapel in Manhattan and be married, there was undoubtedly no time to confirm their backgrounds.

13. Query: Did Dr. Holmes keep a daybook or diary?

14. [Lovecraft biographer L. Sprague de Camp believed that letters from Guiney to F. H. Day (in the Library of Congress) dated May to July 1892 mentioning "two and a half" "confounded heathen" referred to the Lovecraft family and would therefore confirm their residency in the Guiney household (cf. *Lovecraft: A Biography*, p. 450n2), but on further examination Kenneth W. Faig, Jr. has now determined that these visitors were in fact some German boarders; the Lovecrafts' stay with her in Auburndale thus remains unverified. See further Faig, "The Friendship of Louise Imogen Guiney and Sarah Susan Phillips" (*UL* 70–86), and also *IAP* 1.18.]

15. [See also *RK* 66.]

16. In fact, there are further possible biographical interpretations of this entry. Winfield Lovecraft worked as a salesman for the Gorham Company of Providence, whose main offices were located at the corner of North Main and Steeple Streets in Providence. To the north, along North Main, were the remains of the most fashionable commercial district of the century before; a decaying area by Winfield's time. In view of Lovecraft's fascination with the history of his native city and the possible connection with his father, I think it is quite probable that his reference to "decaying business streets with gas lamps" is to this North Main area. The area between Canal and North Main is presently (1972) undergoing a major renovation.

CHAPTER 2:

17. The commonplace book of Sarah Susan Lovecraft (at the John Hay Library) lists the following children of Jeremiah Phillips (b. Jan. 29, 1800) and Robie Rathbone (spelled Rathbun in Sarah Susan's commonplace book; b. June 29, 1797), married Feb. 23, 1823: Wheaton Phillips (b.d. [an infant?]); Susan S. Phillips (b. January 1827 d. 1850); James Wheaton Phillips (b. Mar. 11, 1830 d. Feb. 11, 1901?), the uncle whose farm in Foster HPL visited in 1896, 1908, and 1926; Whipple V. Phillips (b. Nov, 22, 1833 d. Mar. 28, 1904); and Abbie E. Phillips (b. July 17, 1839 d. Nov. 7, 1873). Lovecraft's closest living relatives on the maternal side descend from the brothers and sisters of Whipple Phillips.

18. In Rhode Island, the counties are divided into incorporated cities and towns. Thus, Rhode Island towns are equivalent to "townships" elsewhere. Some towns include a village of the same name; some do not.

19. Perhaps the same as the Mrs. Nabby Tyler Kennedy whom Lovecraft and Mrs. Gamwell visited on their jaunt to Moosup Valley in 1926 (cf. Lovecraft to Long, October 26, 1926, *SL* 2.83–84). Lovecraft mentions seeing the Casey Tyler House in the same letter, and gives some details about Casey Tyler himself (*SL* 2.82–83).

[It does appear that Nabbie Emogene Tyler Kennedy (1854–1945) is one and the same as the wife of Alvero Arnold Kennedy (1854–1936).]

20. [This "Hugog" has recently been identified by researcher Chris Perridas as probably Caleb R. Hill of Warwick, R.I.; for an explanation of the word hugog (or hugag), see further <http://whipplevanburenphillips.blogspot.com/p/who-was-hugag.html>.]

21. [Dated June 19, 1894, and October 27, 1899; these two letters had been recovered by the Providence bookseller H. Douglas Dana, see note 45. A third letter from Whipple V. Phillips to Lovecraft describing "happenings on Snake River" and dated February 20, 1899, formerly part of the collection of Jack Grill (no. 477 in the published catalogue, misidentified as from "Winfield [sic] Phillips"), is now in JHL.]

22. [For more on this business venture, see Faig, "Whipple V. Phillips and the Owyhee Land and Irrigation Company" (*UL* 50–55).]

23. Although the commonplace book of Sarah Susan Lovecraft (John Hay Library) gives the date of the marriage of Edwin E. Phillips and Martha H. Mathews as July 30, 1894, Providence records show that they were not married until March 23, 1903. A possibility is that the 1894 date may refer to an earlier marriage. Edwin is generally reputed to have been the "black sheep" of the family; and his father Whipple may have opposed his second marriage. In any case, Whipple on July 2, 1903, wrote a new will (probated in Providence following his death in 1904) in which he virtually eliminated Edwin from consideration, apportioning $20,000 among his three surviving daughters (Sarah Susan, Lillian, and Annie) and two surviving grandchildren (Howard P. Lovecraft and Phillips Gamwell) before leaving a one quarter share of the remainder of the estate to Edwin. The 1911 Providence House Directory shows Mrs. Jennie E. Mathews (possibly the mother of Martha H. Mathews) living with Edwin and his wife at 63 East Manning Street; it also lists the offices of the Edwin E. Phillips Co., specializing in refrigeration, in the Banigan Building (where Whipple had his last offices) at 10 Weybosset Street.

[Edwin Phillips and Martha Mathews remarried after a divorce.]

24. For some of these outlooks upon Lovecraft's family background, I am indebted to Professor Henry L. P. Beckwith of the Rhode Island School of Design, who spoke on the subject at the Boston Science Fiction Convention in April 1972.

CHAPTER 3:

25. Annie Gamwell sent Barlow a telegram informing him of HPL's death on the evening of March 15—which may have arrived before the Brobst letter.

[Brobst's March 2, 1937 letter to Barlow has been printed in "The Last Days of H. P. Lovecraft: Four Documents." *Lovecraft Studies* No. 28 (Fall 1992): 36.]

26. Lovecraft's files were incorporated into the Library of Amateur Journalism—also called the Fossil Library and the Edwin Hadley Smith Collection—then at the Franklin Institute in Philadelphia but now at New York University.

[Presently at the University of Wisconsin-Madison; see note 122 and Faig's "Passion, Controversy and Vision: A History of The Library of Amateur Journalism," in *One Hundred Years of the Fossils 1904–2004* (2005).]

27. [Lovecraft and Cook had agreed that the one who lived longer would inherit the other's collection of *Old Farmer's Almanacs*, but unfortunately Cook had by 1937 lost his own collection (cf. *LR* 106).]

28. [For R. H. Barlow in this role, see Faig, "R. H. Barlow as H. P. Lovecraft's Literary Executor: An Appreciation" (*UL* 235–48), as well as George T. Wetzel, "Lovecraft's Literary Executor" (*The Lovecraft Scholar*, pp. 3–14).]

29. [It eventually transpired that Barlow had given the notebook containing the autograph manuscript of "The Shadow out of Time" to a student of his named Jane Ripley, after whose death it was discovered in Hawaii and donated to the John Hay Library in 1995. (For a more detailed account, see section E of the introduction to the textually corrected edition of the story based on this manuscript [Hippocampus Press, 2001].) Another Lovecraft manuscript in his possession which R. H. Barlow did not donate to the library is the so called "death diary" (in fact a pocket calendar for 1937 which apart from the brief diary entries that chronicled his terminal illness also contained addresses for Lovecraft's correspondents). Its current whereabouts remain unknown; the diary may have been destroyed by having been left behind by Barlow during one of his moves.]

30. [The correspondence between Derleth and Barlow makes clear the tremendous aid Barlow gave Derleth and Wandrei, particularly in the compilation of *The Outsider and Others* (1939).]

31. [The issues of *Le Vombiteur* which published these items were 1, No. 2. (February 4, 1939) and 2, No. 8 (April 1, 1939). The item printed in the former issue is reproduced below:]

WITH DISTINCT SORROW

We must say that the current feud between R. H. Barlow and Dereleth-Wandrei-Loveman, [*sic*] over the matter of rights on the effects of the late H. P. Lovecraft is still blazing. And most regrettable of all is the fact that Mr. Lovecraft's aunt, Mrs Gamwell, is, to use a turn of phrase, in the centre of the maelstrom. Whatever the outcome, there is this much to be said: Lovecraft did make Barlow his literary executor, giving him a free choice in the matter as to what he might take himself, (with the knowledge and consent of Mrs Gamwell) and Barlow and Lovecraft were on very intimate terms to the very end. Messers Dereleth, Wandrei, and Loveman, however, claim that Barlow made overt use of this, & had no rgt [*sic*] to take some things that B did[,] claiming that the sale of these articles would have brought in much-needed funds to Mrs Gamwell. The lady herself is more than a little dismayed at the proceedings now going on in this matter, and has expressed her trust in Barlow. Whether B will go through with the suit he has filed against the other side of the argument, is not yet definite. We can only express our deep regret at this instance and our feelings that, right or wrong, Barlow, or Dereleth and the Wandreis, this affair is the last thing that Lovecraft would have expected of his friends.

Incidentally, at the present moment, prospects for the Lovecraft Memorial Volume, the Omnibus edition, are not any-too bright.

32. [Barlow's incomplete typescript of *The Dream-Quest of Unknown Kadath* runs for 68 pages and that for *The Case of Charles Dexter Ward* 23 pages. (Lovecraft's autograph manuscripts of the novels consist of 110 and 147, respectively, together with 10 pages of inserts for the latter.)]

33. [Cf. a letter by Derleth and Wandrei to "The Eyrie" (*WT* May 1941, pp. 120–21; rpt. *WW* 99–100: "After Lovecraft's death, when we were collecting all the Lovecraft stories, published and unpublished, we located *Ward* in the possession of R. H. Barlow and secured its loan. When the package came [...] there was the original ms., but, to our greater consternation, less than half of it. After much correspondence, we decided that the rest of the ms. had been lost beyond any hope of recovery. [...] Recently, however, we received from the same source the remainder of the ms. which had somehow been separated and mislaid." Barlow noted in a letter to fanzine editor Larry B. Farsaci that he "gave Derleth whatever text he has" and continued that "it is airy babble to speak (as I [Barlow] think the publisher did) of their 'unearthing' it." (Barlow, "Three Letters on H. P. Lovecraft." *Golden Atom* 1, No. 10 [Winter 1943]: 31–32.)]

34. [The text of this letter (October 7, 1938) is given in George T. Wetzel's "Lovecraft's Literary Executor" (*The Lovecraft Scholar*, pp. 6–7), as is the October 19 letter in which Baker withdrew his demands (pp. 8–9).]

35. [Barlow is evidently referring to Loveman possessing "The Shunned House" and "Under the Pyramids," Rimel "The Thing on the Doorstep" (which was microfilmed by Barlow; the ms. in now in JHL), and Donald A. Wollheim "The Haunter of the Dark." See also note 52.]

36. [See note 34.]

37. [Walter Coslet (1922–1996). The New Orleans bookseller who handled the sale of collection was Cecil Davis of the Coronet Bookshop. Barlow's file of *Astounding* was sold to fan Charles Lee Riddle (1923–1968).]

38. The bulk of Lovecraft's library was sold to the Providence bookseller H. Douglass Dana following Mrs. Gamwell's death in January 1941; and most of the books were thereafter scattered, although Dana's Bookshop in Providence may yet have a few to offer the diehard Lovecraft collector. (Collectors ought to be wary of books with Lovecraft's signature or bookplate offered on the general market since there is a history of fraud concerning books with Lovecraft's signature, and reproductions of Lovecraft's bookplate—designed by his friend Wilfred B. Talman in 1929—were made available for the legitimate use of collectors by the bookseller Gerry de la Ree several years ago and might presumably have been misused by someone for the purposes of fraud.)†

† Query: Did Lovecraft have any earlier bookplate than the one designed by Talman?

[The contents of Lovecraft's personal library were eventually catalogued, based principally on the Spink listing, in *Lovecraft's Library*. Dana's Old Corner Bookshop was destroyed in January 1975 by a fire in The Wilcox Building (42 Weybosset Street, Providence). A scattered amount of genuine books from Lovecraft's library are in private hands, however; some of them were previously owned by Jack Grill (nos. 542–545 in the catalogue of his collection; according to it the first item does carry a hectographed bookplate).]

39. [*The National Amateur* 45, No. 5 (May 1923): 9.]

40. Actually, Fischer's contribution was a chalk drawing of Fritz Leiber's famous character Ningauble of the Seven Eyes. Lovecraft read Leiber's novel "Adept's Gambit" with great enthusiasm a few months before his death, but offered only a few technical suggestions for changes, which were presumably embodied in the text when "Adept's Gambit" was published in Leiber's Arkham House collection *Night's Black Agents* in 1947.

[An early, longer version of "Adept's Gambit" has now been published by Arcane Wisdom, ed. S. T. Joshi (2014). See also Lovecraft's letter to Leiber, December 19, 1936 (*Writers of the Dark*, pp. 38–44), reproduced in this edition.]

41. For those who read my listing of Lovecraft manuscripts in *Nyctalops* Nos. 5–6, the following seem to be the story manuscripts which Dana sold to Brown, all of them typescripts except for those marked with an asterisk (*): Section I: 2b, 3a, 4, 7, 11b, 19, 22, 30, 31b, 36b, 42, 47b, 48b/c (one of the two), 49, and 53. Section II: 3b/c (one of the two), 16*, 18, and 20*. Since the publication of the listing, Gerry de la Ree has written me that he now owns the important typescript (I.8) of "The Colour out of Space;" in addition, holograph manuscripts of "The Statement of Randolph Carter" and of "The Cats of Ulthar" not mentioned in my listing definitely survive. One final question regarding Lovecraft's manuscripts which still troubles me is the following: Derleth somewhere remarks† that Lovecraft's earliest juvenilia, as printed in *The Shuttered Room*, were discovered in the possession of a private collector; yet the original manuscripts of all the items which have been printed—and more—were present at the John Hay Library when I was doing work there in 1970–1972 and it was my impression from several

references to "Lovecraft's juvenilia" in Barlow's letters that he had had all this material and sent it to the John Hay Library early on. I wonder if anyone can resolve this apparent conflict.

† In fact, in his annotations for *H. P. Lovecraft: A Symposium* (Los Angeles, [Leland Sapiro], 1964), p. 14.

[The surviving holograph manuscripts of "The Statement of Randolph Carter (8 pp.)" and "The Cats of Ulthar" (4 pp., dated June 15, 1920) mentioned by Faig are not the original drafts but fair copies circulated by Lovecraft. The former has been published in facsimile (The Strange Co., 1976), while the latter was part of the Grill–Binkin collection (no. 554, shown in a photo plate in the published catalogue) and has been sold again recently, for $20,000—the manuscript had apparently been purchased by Jack Grill for $25 from August Derleth, who had obtained it from Rheinhart Kleiner.]

42. [*Fanciful Tales of Time and Space* No. 1 (Fall 1936): 5–18; ed. Donald A Wollheim. A facsimile edition of this magazine has been issued by Necronomicon Press (1977).]

43. [*CE* 4 finally collected together Lovecraft's various formal travelogues in 2005.]

44. [See the photograph issues of *The Arkham Sampler* (The Strange Co.): 1, No. 3 (1983) and 2, No. 4 (1985).]

45. Apparently Mr. Dana did recover from 66 College Street a group of "trivial" papers appertaining to Lovecraft along with the important material he sold to the John Hay Library. Mr. Dana's widow, Mrs. Mary V. Dana, so described these additional papers to me in 1971, saying that they had largely been mislaid but were probably still around her shop somewhere. They do occasionally, however, show up; for instance, the letters of Whipple V. Phillips which Mr. Robb Baker presented to the John Hay Library came from this source. I have no idea whether the "trivial" papers included any family photographs or not.

46. [In general, Lovecraft kept only the letters from Clark Ashton Smith, Donald Wandrei, Robert E. Howard, E. Hoffmann Price, Ernest A. Edkins, and C. L. Moore, although many isolated letters (or fragments thereof) survive on the versos of various manuscripts.]

47. [The reconstituted correspondence between Lovecraft and R. E. Howard has now been collected together as two volumes in *MF*.]

48. [A pencil and watercolor drawing of 598 Angell Street by Lovecraft himself survives (signed *HPL*), apparently once in the possession of H. C. Koenig.]

Chapter 4:

49. [Four decades later, a copy of *Home Brew* or an early issue of *Weird Tales* could well fetch a price in four figures.]

50. [Lovecraft's *WT* appearances have now been collected in a facsimile edition, *The Weird Writings of H. P. Lovecraft* (2010; 2 vols.), and replica editions also exist for certain complete *WT* issues, both having been issued by the Canadian imprint Girasol Collectables.]

51. [Morris, Harry O., Jr. "H. P. Lovecraft: A Story Listing." *Nyctalops* 1, Nos. 2, 3, and 4; see also Edward P. Berglund's "Addenda to HPL Story Listing" in the same magazine.]

52. Query: Does anyone know the provenance of this latter holograph manuscript?)

[The autograph manuscripts of "Under the Pyramids" and "The Shunned House" finally resurfaced in December 2006 when they were auctioned by Sotheby's (for $24,000 and $45,000, respectively) on behalf of the estate of Peter J. Maurer (1929–2005) who had purchased them from Samuel Loveman's collection, along with Lovecraft's letters to Frank Belknap Long (which Loveman had obtained; auctioned for $48,000 at the same time). The mss. for at least the following stories are also in private hands: "The Statement of Randolph Carter," "The Cats of

Ulthar" (see note 41), "The White Ship" (facsimile in *Whispers* 1, No. 4 [July 1974]), and "The Haunter of the Dark" (given to Donald A. Wollheim, who later sold it to Ronald E. Graham, after whose death in 1979 in Australia its whereabouts remain a mystery; see further Leigh D. Blackmore, "H. P. Lovecraft: The Mystery of the Missing Manuscript.").]

53. See Lovecraft's letter of March 28, 1915, to Rheinhart Kleiner, printed in part in "By Post from Providence," a collection of Lovecraft letters to Kleiner edited by Kleiner himself for the summer 1937 Lovecraft memorial issue of Hyman Bradofsky's *Californian*, one of the finest amateur magazines of its day and the one to which Lovecraft and his circle contributed the most prolifically in the 1930s. This Kleiner selection of letters contains many fascinating extracts appertaining to amateur journalism which are not reprinted in the *Selected Letters*.

[*Uncollected Letters* (1986) reprinted Kleiner's "By Post from Providence" selections; they have been combined with the partial Arkham House transcripts of the letters (and the text of otherwise unavailable facsimile pages included in *SL*) in *RK*.]

54. [Two facsimile editions of *The Californian* have been issued, one by The Strange Co. (for the Lammas 1976 mailing of the Esoteric Order of Dagon Amateur Press Association), and another by Necronomicon Press (1977).]

55. [W. Paul Cook printed the final four issues of *The Conservative*.]

56. [R. Alain Everts has attributed Cook's year of birth to 1880. (See "The Man Who Was W. Paul Cook.") For Cook and Coates, see Sean Donnelly's *W. Paul Cook: The Wandering Life of a Yankee Printer* (2007). Lovecraft's essay was also issued by Coates's Driftwind Press as a separate pamphlet, *The Materialist Today* (1926); see p. 70.]

57. His service on the *Driftwind* editorial board was not Lovecraft's only editorial experience within amateurdom. Of course, he was in charge of his own paper *The Conservative* for its thirteen issues from 1915 until 1923. In addition, George Wetzel found during his research with the Library of Amateur Journalism, then at the Franklin Institute in Philadelphia, a single issue of an amateur magazine entitled *The Providence Amateur*, dated February, 1916, with Lovecraft listed as official editor and his home at 598 Angell Street as the official place of publication. (This information is in the introduction to Wetzel's second published bibliography of Lovecraft's amateur press works, which appeared in two parts in the first and second issues of *Vagabond*. This was the mid-work between his first bibliography published in *Destiny* and the compilation [undertaken with Robert E. Briney] published in *The Lovecraft Collector's Library*.) Since Lovecraft remarked in some early letters to Edward H. Cole (at the John Hay Library) that most of his fellow Providence amateurs—some of whom were John T. Dunn, Victor Basinet, and Peter MacManus—were night high school students, there is little doubt that Lovecraft himself bore the principal responsibility for *The Providence Amateur*.[†] I don't have Truman Spencer's *History of Amateur Journalism* at hand to check, but I believe Lovecraft was also official editor of *The United Amateur* during his wife's terms as President of UAPA in the early 1920s, in addition to serving as President of UAPA himself in 1917–18. I do not know that he was ever official editor for *The National Amateur*, but he did serve as President in 1922–23, after the resignation of William J. Dowdell, and several times Warner relates in *All Our Yesterdays* that Lovecraft and Duane Rimel almost published a fanzine in collaboration but couldn't make arrangements for a press. (See Warner, pp. 11, 20. Many of the best fanzines of the thirties, like *The Fantasy Fan* and *Fantasy Magazine*, were printed by letterpress. Lovecraft and Rimel may have intended their magazine as a successor to Hornig's *Fantasy Fan*, which folded with the February 1935 issue.)

† Query: were there any more numbers of this magazine published?

[There was an earlier inaugural issue of *The Providence Amateur* for June 1915; both have been issued in facsimile by Necronomicon Press (1976, 1977). For the associated, short-lived Providence Amateur Press Club and its members, see Faig, *The Providence Amateur Press Club: 1914–1916* (Moshassuck Press, 2008).]

58. [Owings, Mark, with Jack L. Chalker. *The Revised H. P. Lovecraft Bibliography*. Baltimore, MD: Mirage Press, 1973.]

59. ["In Memoriam: Howard Phillips Lovecraft: Recollections, Appreciations, Estimates" (*LR* 106–156).]

60. [The bibliography of Lovecraft has now been exhaustively compiled by S. T. Joshi: *H. P. Lovecraft and Lovecraft Criticism: An Annotated Bibliography* (Kent State University Press, 1981), revised as *H. P. Lovecraft: A Comprehensive Bibliography* (University of Tampa Press, 2009).]

61. [In addition, the New York Public Library has a collection of amateur journalism, largely based on materials donated by Charles W. "Tryout" Smith (1852–1948).]

62. [The collection has been moved since the time of this writing; see note 26.]

63. [Hyman Bradofsky's collection of amateur journalism is now in The Bancroft Library, University of California, Berkeley (BANC MSS 2005/276 z). See also Faig's *Survey of Institutional Collections of Amateur Journals* (1999).]

64. [See Leigh Blackmore's "Leon Stone: Amateur Journalist and Pioneer Lovecraft Collector" and Faig's "The Fate of Two Ajay Collections."]

65. Of course, the listing of all of these contributions is the principal accomplishment of such research—and although Lovecraft's general essays and his amateur press criticism, along with his imitative eighteenth-century poetry—which surely together constitute the vast majority of his amateur press contributions—may have little interest to the general reader, they are surely invaluable for an understanding of the man and his work as they developed together from his advent to amateur journalism in April 1914 until his death in March 1937.

[The story of the Davison trunk was likely a hoax perpetrated by the disillusioned fan Francis T. Laney. See Laney's "Who was Howard Davison?" in *Spacewarp* No. 42 (September 1950): 54–57. (A World War I Draft Registration Card exists for a Howard Abe Davison, born 1898 and residing in Hannibal, Missouri; Laney's putative amateur journalist was, however, supposed to have hailed from, or at least died in Ohio. See also note 117.]

66. ["The Evil Clergyman" (retitled by Derleth for Arkham House collections) was written ca. Fall 1933 (see note 159) and published in *WT* (April 1939). "The Very Old Folk" is an excerpt from a November 3, 1927 letter to Donald Wandrei (*MTS* 177–84), who provided the text for its appearance in *Scienti-Snaps* 3, No. 3 (Summer 1940): 4–8.]

67. ["Some Causes of Self-Immolation" exists as a manuscript in JHL, dated December 13, 1931. The essay's *raison d'être* remains unclear; it may actually have been written to a specific correspondent as a separate enclosure, later returned to Lovecraft.]

68. ["Nyarlathotep": *The United Amateur* 20, No. 2 (November 1920): 19–21; *The National Amateur* 48, No. 6 (July 1926): 53–54. "Memory": *United Co-operative* 1, No 2 (June 1919): 8. "Ex Oblivione": *The United Amateur* 20, No. 4 (March 1921): 59–60.]

69. ["The Thing in the Moonlight." *Bizarre* 4, No. 1 (January 1941): 5, 20. The story as printed was indeed expanded from a letter excerpt (provided by Donald Wandrei) by Miske, who later confessed the fact to August Derleth.]

70. [The best of hope of recovering such fiction items probably lies in unearthing stories ghost-written or revised by Lovecraft, for which several tantalizing hints exist. See further J.-M.

Rajala, "Locked Dimensions out of Reach: The Lost Stories of H. P. Lovecraft," *passim*.]

71. [Kleiner was likely thinking of the collections of letters to himself, Samuel Loveman, Frank Belknap Long, James F. Morton, and Wilfred Blanch Talman.]

72. I note with trepidation, however, that in his Lovecraft bibliography in the L'Herne *Lovecraft* volume, Jacques Van Herp has assigned the appearance of "The Nameless City" in the *Transatlantic Circular* the specific date 1926. If this be a correct citation, perhaps the *Transatlantic Circular* was an amateur magazine unrelated to the earlier Transatlantic Circulator whose papers are in the Lovecraft collection in the John Hay Library.

[It does not appear that there was such a magazine.]

73. [The writings were first published unabridged as the chapbook *In Defence of Dagon* (Necronomicon Press, 1985); in *MW* 147–71, *CE* 5.47–65.]

74. [See note 150.]

Chapter 5:

75. [An holograph draft by Lovecraft of a proposed table of contents for Barlow's edition of *Fungi from Yuggoth and Other Verses* also exists: "Fungi from Yuggoth / I–XXXVI // Aletheia Phrikodes† // The Ancient Track / Oceanus† / Clouds† / Mother Earth† / The Eidolon† / The Nightmare Lake† / The Outpost / The Rutted Road† / The Wood / Hallowe'en in a Suburb† / The City / The House // Primavera / October // To a Dreamer / Despair†,‡ // Nemesis." ("Aletheia Phrikodes" being the central section of "The Poe-et's Nightmare.")

† "Probably not good enough."

‡ "Last moment. I think this is pretty bad. Better count it definitely out."]

76. I do not believe that the corrections indicated in pencil by Lovecraft in variant A were embodied in variant B—except for the elimination of "To a Dreamer." However, I am relying upon my memory here and may therefore be in error.

77. [See note 257.]

78. Barlow and Groo Beck did print a collection of George Sterling's verse for the bookseller John Howell in San Francisco in 1939; and the idea of the Howard collection *Echoes from an Iron Harp*—which was Howard's original title—persisted until this period. Barlow and Beck intended this for the "Druid Press" imprint and apparently succeeded in obtaining from Dr. Isaac Howard (1871–1944) permission for the collection, but they never did print it. In a letter of April 1, 1941, to Dr. Howard, Otis A. Kline—then agent for the Howard Estate—stated that he would try to reach the partners in the "Druid Press" to withdraw Dr. Howard's offer. (This letter was published in *OAK Leaves* No. 1.) Fortunately, Barlow made a microfilm copy of the poems which were intended for the collection; many of the originals were later lost when Dr. Howard moved, and the Barlow microfilm provided the text for many of the poems which Glenn Lord organized for the collection *Echoes from an Iron Harp*, ultimately published by Donald M. Grant in 1972. Of the other projects which he envisioned for the Dragon-Fly Press, Barlow does not seem to have mentioned to the Becks his intended collection of Whitehead letters—which was to be entitled *Caneviniana*—or his intended collection of Elizabeth Toldridge's poems. At least two proof pages of Barlow's intended edition of *Caneviniana* survive; later when it became evident that he would not be able to print the collection, he transferred some of the letters to stencils which were ultimately published as *The Letters of Henry S. Whitehead* by his friend Paul Freehafer in FAPA in December, 1942. The original letters which Barlow collected for *Caneviniana*—including at least one unpublished in Freehafer's edition—unfortunately seem to have dropped from sight.

Insofar as I know, there was never any work done on the Toldridge collection.

79. Derleth was not pleased by the appearance of the Futile Press edition of Lovecraft's *Commonplace Book* at about this time—he had asked Barlow to withhold Lovecraft material from publication in view of the hoped-for sale of an anthology (ultimately published by Arkham House itself) and the possibility of further sales to *Weird Tales*. Barlow, however, considered that he had the final word in such matters as Lovecraft's designated "literary executive," and saw in the Futile Press a means to carry out his frustrated plans for private press editions of Lovecraft and other fantasy authors. Indeed, Lovecraft himself had authorized Barlow's planned private press editions in his own lifetime. The bitter controversy over Lovecraft's books and magazines worsened the personal relations between Barlow and Derleth, but it is to the credit of both that they quickly acted to make clear their cooperation in the issuance of Lovecraft's work, to the considerable relief of Lovecraft's surviving aunt, Mrs. Gamwell, who had been badly distressed by the controversy. By the mid-forties full cordiality seems to have been restored between Barlow and Derleth; Barlow, for his part, wrote the introduction to the first Whitehead collection from Arkham House and also contributed a memoir of his relationship with Lovecraft to *Marginalia*.

80. [See note 89.]

81. Lovecraft sold some of the "Fungi" early on to *Weird Tales*—"Alienation" (April–May 1931), "Antarktos" (November 1930), "Azathoth" (January 1931), "The Bells" (December 1930), "The Courtyard" (September 1930), "The Elder Pharos" (February–March 1931), "Hesperia" (October 1930), "Mirage" (February–March 1931), "Nyarlathotep" (January 1931), "Recapture" (May 1930), and "Star-Winds" (September 1930)—and others appeared in those pages between 1938 and 1950. It has, however, not generally been recorded by Lovecraft bibliographers that Lovecraft in addition sold several of his "Fungi" to the *Providence Journal* for its Wednesday literary page edited by B. K. Hart: "Nostalgia" (March 12, 1930), "Night-Gaunts" (March 26, 1930), "Background" (April 16, 1930), "The Dweller" (May 7, 1930), and "The Well" (May 14, 1930).† This information was given by Winfield Townley Scott in a letter which appeared in Laney's *Acolyte* for fall 1944 (2, No. 4). (Scott mentions two additional Lovecraft poems which appeared in the *Providence Journal*: "The Messenger" [in B K. Hart's "Sideshow" column for December 3, 1929], wherein HPL recorded the results of Hart's threat to send a visitor to his door at three in the morning in retribution for Lovecraft's connection of his former residence at 7 Thomas Street in Providence with horrific happenings in the story "The Call of Cthulhu," and "The East India Brick Row" [same as "The Brick Row], which appeared on the Wednesday literary page for January 8, 1930. In general, however, the bulk of Lovecraft's newspaper verse—which began with "Providence in 2000 A.D." in the *Evening Bulletin* for March 4, 1912—is probably still undetected, although much of it may also have appeared in amateur magazines which have already been covered by Lovecraft bibliographers. Another seemingly unrecorded appearance of a "Fungus" was that of "The Canal" in Walter J. Coates's anthology *Harvest*, presumably published by the Driftwind Press sometime after 1930. [There is a full bibliography of Driftwind Press publications in one of the thirties issues—I believe—of the magazine *Driftwind* itself.]‡ Lovecraft stated in an unpublished letter that this appearance of "The Canal" was the first appearance of one of his poems between hard covers. I think, however, that he must have been forgetting, or choosing to ignore, the dedicatory poems which were published in *The Poetical Works of Jonathan E. Hoag*, which in fact he, Loveman, and Morton had edited for publication in 1923. Although I do not have the date of publication of *Harvest*—and anyone with access to the National Union Catalog or a file of *Driftwind* can rapidly find it—it must necessarily be later than 1930, since in fact the "Fungi" were composed from December 27, 1929 to January 4, 1930, according to Lovecraft's own typescript.) For *Harvest*, see Works Cited III.6.

† In addition, ten of the "Fungi" were published in Coates's magazine *Driftwind* between 1930 and 1937. [See the Appendix for details.]

‡ [*Driftwind* 6, No. 3 (November 1931).]

CHAPTER 6:

82. Indeed, 1930 seems to have been a very bad year for Lovecraft's friend Cook—his wife, who, like Lovecraft's wife, was years older than her partner, died, leaving Cook an emotional wreck, and his financial and physical collapse seem to have followed shortly thereafter. He even sold the majority of his fine collection of weird fiction to his friend H. Warner Munn—evidence enough of mental and fiscal strain in any bibliophile. (His financial failure took him to East Saint Louis, Illinois, where he participated for several years in a venture with fellow amateur Paul J. Campbell, afterwards returning cross country to North Montpelier, Vermont, to work as printer for Coates's Driftwind Press. Cook continued the work of the Driftwind Press for Coates's widow after Coates's own death in 1941, ending his work only with his own death in January 1948.

83. [This portion of the letter is omitted in *SL* 3.371–72.]

84. Cook's emotional and financial breakdown and removal to East Saint Louis following the death of his wife in 1930 undoubtedly accounted for Lovecraft's failure to learn of the fate of the edition of *The Shunned House* for such a long time. During his years in East Saint Louis (1930–1937), Cook was much troubled by alcoholism and largely dropped out of correspondence with Lovecraft and other amateur friends. After his return to New England to join Coates's Driftwind Press in 1937, he went on to publish many fine amateur items of unique interest.

85. [This portion of the letter is omitted in *SL* 5.209–13.]

86. Many thanks to Thomas G. L. Cockcroft and Larry Farsaci for bringing these letters to my attention and providing me with their text. [See note 33. The undated letter from Barlow to Farsaci is on the Smisor microfilm at the JHL. Others exist as photocopies in files deposited there by Faig.]

87. [The microfilm is in JHL. See n91]

88. The presumption that Cook shipped all the sheets in his possession to Barlow is further strengthened by Cook's own remarks in *H. P. Lovecraft: A Portrait* (p. 59; *LR* 151). [The set Barlow, not Cook, provided to Wandrei had a duplicate signature, which he ultimately replace.]

89. [Herman Moore Langworthy (1880–1956), married to Minnie Luella Leach (1878–1962), sister of Bernice (Leach) Barlow (1884–1962).]

90. [Dorcas Emlin Langworthy (1916–1992).]

91. [Cf. R. H. Barlow to August Derleth, May 24, 1949 (microfilm, JHL): "I know you wrote me that the Shunned House bundles turned out quite different, which I am sorry for. So many bundles of my books stored with different people have gone astray that the matter is irremediable, I fear. Later, I believe I found a few S. H. copies here & sent them to you, but it was during the dark ebb of this past terrible year & they probably went Pekin!" His mother did, however, later ship Derleth unbound copies of the book (cf. Bernice Barlow to Derleth, May 28, 1951, ms., Wisconsin Historical Society).]

92. [Possibly no. 388 in the catalogue: "bound in boards and green cloth. Barlow copyright with later cancel copyright notice pasted over it. Inscribed to Grill by Long." Long's inscription to the unbound copy (no. 386) reads "For Philip J. Grill / With the cordial regards of / Frank Belknap Long / Brooklyn, N.Y.—March 15, 1960."]

93. Glenn Lord, the agent for the Howard Estate, has however recovered the Howard letters to Lovecraft. In the presence of REH's library—or at least some of it—in the library of Howard Payne College even unto this day, it is remarkable to note, there is the possibility for an eager investigator to reconstruct the personal library of yet another of the Lovecraft Circle. (Recall

the Spink and Barlow Estate listings of Lovecraft's personal library.) This might be either an easy or a difficult task, depending upon whether or not the Howard Payne College Library kept a separate listing of the books from REH's library.

[A catalogue of Robert E. Howard's library has now been compiled (together with a listing of additional items) by Rusty Burke: *The Robert E. Howard Bookshelf* (1998; available at the website of The Robert E. Howard United Amateur Press Association).]

94. The dedicated collector who wants every state of this book is undoubtedly in for some tough work. First, there are the unbound sheets, with and without the Arkham copyright sticker, the latter being much rarer. (But extant—vide Squires's Loveman copy.) Then there are those copies which were "distributed" or given away as unbound sheets and later given private bindings by their owners; again, those copies without the Arkham sticker would presumably be by far the rarest. (Presumably, all the "slightly less than fifty" copies sold as unbound sheets by Arkham House fall into one or the other of these two categories. I cannot point to a copy in private binding without the Arkham House copyright sticker, but Wandrei's copy might have been one, had he bound it.) [Wandrei's set of *The Shunned House* was offered for sale for $2,750 in *Selections from the Donald Wandrei Archive: Manuscripts, Letters, Printed Ephemera and Original Art* (Pepper & Stern, Rulon-Miller, Steven A. Stilwell, 1994.)] Then, there is the Barlow-bound edition: at least five putative copies distributed and four additional copies found among Barlow's effects, three in Mexico, one in Cassia. These include at least three different bindings: the leather binding of Lovecraft's copy, the half-cloth binding of Squires's copy, and the "cloth back, paper sides" binding of at least two of the Mexico copies. These are probably about all equally rare, the best-bound of the "distributed" "half-dozen" copies presumably being the most desirable. The two "cloth back, paper sides" Mexico copies and the Cassia copy which were sold to August Derleth presumably have the Arkham sticker. (They may have been rebound for the one hundred-copy 1961 Arkham "edition." However, might the following copy, offered by P. M. Rainey in the December 1970 issue of *ERBdom–Fantasy Collector* be the Cassia Barlow-bound copy: "The Shunned House, Athol [*sic*], Mass., 1928. Stapled in faded green paper covers with copyright notice pasted in." One would hardly imagine that a private collector who bought an expensive set of sheets would give them such a cheap binding.) Then, there is the one hundred-copy Arkham "edition" of 1961. And Roy Squires (Catalog VI) relates that in fact there are two variants of the Arkham copyright sticker, one so far observed only in unbound sheets and the other so far observed only in the 1961 Arkham-bound "edition." If all that wasn't enough, Squires relates that there is an offset forgery in circulation, which is itself a collector's item; I leave it to others to compute precisely how many "states" the Lovecraft completist must search for.

Chapter 7:

95. [An at this point equally rare Lovecraft pamphlet—although perhaps not in its original print run—is *The Crime of Crimes* (1915); see the bibliography for more information on it as well as *The Cats of Ulthar*, *The Shunned House* and other items published (or printed) during Lovecraft's lifetime.]

96. Can anyone give the source of the bibliographic opinion that "it is probable that Lovecraft published this essay himself" (Chalker, "Howard Phillips Lovecraft: A Bibliography," *The Dark Brotherhood*, p. 215). According to Chalker, this essay appeared as a four-page mimeographed booklet (on two sheets), dated June 4, 1936. Yet, there is no indication in the Lovecraft letters at the John Hay Library that Lovecraft ever owned a mimeograph machine (as distinguished, of course, from the hectograph machine which he used to reproduce his juvenile astronomical publications). Had Lovecraft owned such a machine, it seems little likely that, as Harry Warner reports, he and Rimel would have found themselves frustrated in their plans to issue a joint

"fanzine," unless they wanted to issue only a printed publication. (What is the source of the story of the fanzine which Lovecraft and Rimel planned? I found no indication of such plans in Rimel's letters from Lovecraft at the John Hay Library, but I may well have missed something.) Perhaps Lovecraft had the essay commercially mimeographed or reproduced by a friend; however, I shall be more than glad to yield to evidence that he did mimeograph it himself (perhaps on a friend's machine or on some other accessible machine?). In general, these very rarest of Lovecraft's "separate" appearances are so obscure that future bibliographers would be well advised to provide census of extant copies to guide researchers in their work. Such a census might even extend to a coding of all of Lovecraft amateur press contributions to indicate the collections of amateur journals in which specific issues might be found. Such a bibliography would also presumably indicate the source of information on all items not examined by the bibliographer himself. The boon which would thereby be rendered to future Lovecraft researchers and collectors would be inestimable. Of the ante-mortem separates, I believe that *The Materialist Today*, *The Shunned House*, *The Cats of Ulthar* (Lovecraft's copy and a copy of the ordinary edition), and *Charleston* are all in the Lovecraft Collection at Brown University; I am unsure of the others.

[The pamphlet *Some Current Motives and Practices* was mimeographed R. H. Barlow on behalf of Lovecraft, who did not own the device (cf. letter to William Frederick Anger, June 20, 1935; *Letters to Robert Bloch and Others*, p. 239).]

97. [Cf. Lovecraft to Barlow, March 11, 1936 (*OFF* 326): "It seems that this folder was prepared by the Pres. of the Elec. Testing Laboratories [...] The president liked the rough sketches of Charleston architecture, & asked Koenig if he could use them. [...] only drawings of mine (aside from astronomical designs 30 years ago) ever typographically reproduced." This pamphlet, *Visit to Charleston of Edison Companies' Special Train Party* 25 January 1936, has been recently located. A copy resides in the Charleston County Library archives. (cf. Joshi, S. T. "March 15, 2016—A 'New' Lovecraft Manuscript?" S. T. Joshi's Blog. 15 March 2016. <http://stjoshi.org/news2016.html>)]

98. [*Nyctalops* 2, No. 4/5 (11/12, April 1976) did not print this bibliography, but see "Howard Phillips Lovecraft: The Early Years, 1890–1914: A Bibliography" in *Nyctalops* 2, No. 3 (January–February 1975).]

99. Barton St. Armand's article "Facts in the Case of H. P. Lovecraft" in the winter 1972 issue of *Rhode Island History* reproduced one of the drawings which HPL made of "Cthulhu" for his young friend Barlow in 1934, when Barlow was planning to sculpt a figure of Cthulhu. These drawings are now in the Lovecraft Collection at the John Hay Library; so also, for that matter, may be Barlow's sculpture of Cthulhu, since the list of material recovered from 66 College Street by H. Douglass Dana in 1941 and subsequently transferred to the John Hay Library—and I should acknowledge here that this list was provided me by George Wetzel—includes "2 heads of his [Lovecraft's] characters" as "literary ornaments." F. Lee Baldwin's short biographical sketch of Barlow in his column "Within the Circle" (p. 164) in *The Fantasy Fan* 1, No. 11 (July 1934) confirms that Barlow had completed "a clay bas-relief of Cthulhu and a statuette of Ganesa, the Hindoo Elephant God." Lovecraft's own letters confirm that the bas-relief (head?) of Cthulhu was presented to him and the sculpture of Ganesa to his friend William Lumley.

[See S. T. Joshi's *Index to the Selected Letters* for a listing of Lovecraft's drawings—including "the Blasted Heath"—within the five volumes of *SL*; his Charleston illustrations are reproduced in *CE* 4 and that of "Pickman's Model" in *MW* 96. In addition, published drawings by Lovecraft now include (but are not limited to): self-caricature, clothless in New York (Lovecraft to Lillian D. Clark, May 28, 1925, *NY* 130), tilted house in Coney Island (July 27, 1925, *NY* 152, 153); Denys Peter Myers in 1850 garb (Lovecraft to Wandrei, August 25, 1934, *MTS* 351); Quinsnicket Park (Lovecraft to Derleth, October 21, 1929, *ES* 1.224), birds in Dunedin, FL (May 29, 1931, *ES* 1.345), scales (November 12, 1932, *ES* 2.523), a Georgian door frame (May

17/23, 1933, *ES* 2.569), an astronomical chart (October 24, 1936 *ES* 2.753); 454 Angell Street (Lovecraft to Richard F. Searight, April 2, 1934, *RFS* 22), College Street (August 11, 1934, *RFS* 28), Clemence house, R.I. (August 27, 1936, *RFS* 79); John Teller house ("Notes on Hudson Valley History," *CE* 5.203); a Great Old One (notes for *At the Mountains of Madness*, *CE* 5.245); the Great Race of Yith (notes for "The Shadow out of Time," *CE* 5.257); the Great Race (notes for "The Challenge from Beyond," *CE* 5.258). See also note 48.]

CHAPTER 8:

100. [*The National Magazine* 45, No. 4 (January 1917): 588; Boston, MA: The Chapple Publishing Company, Limited (in *AT* 278). It has now been determined that the poems "Inspiration" and "Brotherhood" appeared in the preceding issues of this magazine: 45, No. 2 (November 1916): 287; 45, No. 3 (December 1916): 415 (*AT* 118, 119); while the following appeared later: "Respite," 45, No. 6 (March 1917): 826; "On Receiving a Picture of Swans," 45, No. 7 (April 1917): 25; "Ode for July Fourth, 1917," 45, No. 10 (July 1917): 121 (*AT* 118–19, 108, and 406–407).]

101. The letter, denouncing astrological predictions, is dated May 27, 1906. I wonder if it is the earliest Lovecraft letter of which the text survives. The earliest letter in *Selected Letters* is a "Thanksgiving note" (principally a poem) from Lovecraft to his mother. (This is in the Lovecraft Collection at the John Hay Library.) Lovecraft mentions in his letter to Maurice W. Moe of April 5, 1931 (*SL* 3.370) that he first blossomed as a "piquant letter-writer" in a correspondence on scientific and literary subjects which he conducted with his cousin Phillips Gamwell (1898–1916) from ca. 1910 until the latter's early death on December 31, 1916. When Lovecraft researcher Everts questioned surviving Gamwell relatives about this letter file, however, they assured him that it no longer existed. Mr. Everts does have knowledge of one file of letters dating as far back as 1909, however.

[An even earlier newspaper appearance has recently come to light: the *Amsterdam* [NY] *Daily Democrat and Recorder* for September 6, 1905 quotes remarks from a letter by Lovecraft under the heading "Long Distance Predictions: Weather Guessers Willing to Take Any Sort of Chances and Trust to Providence," an item dealing with a contest announced in *The New York Herald*, offering a $100 prize for the most accurate forecast for October 15–November 15.]

102. [*Golden Atom* 1, No. 9 (December 1940): 13–14. These letters—except the August 15, 1914 one to *All-Story Cavalier Weekly*, signed "H. P. Lovecraft" and also reprinted in *Golden Atom*—in fact originally appeared in *Argosy* 120, No. 1 (November 15, 1919) and 121, No. 2 (May 22, 1920), and were not written by Lovecraft (see note 245). An early letter to *Argosy*, partially quoted in the November 1911 issue (67, No. 4), has now been found.]

103. Although I no longer have my notes on Lovecraft's own hectographed juvenile scientific publications, my memory seems to tell me that one of them contained an indication that a Lovecraft letter had been printed in an issue of the *Scientific American*; this would presumably have appeared, if my memory is not deceiving me, between Lovecraft's first appearance in print on June 3, 1906, and the virtual cessation of his juvenile publications by the end of 1907.

[Lovecraft had two letters in *Scientific American*, in issues of July 16 and August 25, 1906).]

104. [Correspondence by and in response to him has been collected in *H. P. Lovecraft in The Argosy: Collected Correspondence from the Munsey Magazines* (1994).]

105. Lovecraft mentioned two additional fiction magazines which he had bought and read in his letters to Barlow—*Golden Book* (Lovecraft to Barlow, n.d. [October or November 1931], *OFF* 12) and the *Black Cat* (Lovecraft to Barlow, April 14, 1932, *OFF* 29). These might be ultimately searched for published letters by Lovecraft. [No such letters have been located.]

106. [The index was published: see T. G. L. Cockcroft's "An Index to 'The Eyrie' and Other Readers' Departments" in *Fantasy Commentator* 8, Nos. 3 & 4 (Fall 1995): 217–229. Lovecraft's

letters to *WT* have been reprinted in *H. P. Lovecraft in "The Eyrie"* (1979) and *Uncollected Letters* (1986); material by others on him is contained both in the former book and also in *WW*.]

107. If the subsequent essays on popular and little-known weird fiction by H. Warner Munn and Donald Wandrei (respectively) and the bibliography of weird fiction (also by Wandrei) which Lovecraft speaks of as being planned for future issues of the *Recluse* in his first letter to Starrett (December 6, 1927, *SL* 2.209–211) were ever written, they would undoubtedly even today make an exceedingly interesting and valuable volume if printed together with Lovecraft's own essay, as Lovecraft himself suggested to Starrett might be done when the series was concluded in Cook's *Recluse*. Unfortunately, of course, the first *Recluse* was the last. The second issue did proceed to the printing stage (as is evidenced in Lovecraft's letter of June 23, 1930, to Smith, cited in Squires's Catalog VI), but cf. Cook's own statement in his *H. P. Lovecraft: A Portrait* (pp. 58–59; *LR* 151): "There was no second issue of the *Recluse*. When in 1930 I took my release from that town [Athol], I had nearly a hundred pages in type and about forty printed on another number. It was to have been well over two hundred pages. I had the printed pages thoroughly destroyed. In type was Lovecraft's "The Strange High House in the Mist," which was destined to be first printed elsewhere. He had the proofs of it." Thus, it seems that the proof pages of Lovecraft's story are the only possible reliquiae—in printed form—of the second *Recluse*. (Does anyone know where they are today, if they exist?) Barlow as a collector wished to assemble in manuscript form all of the material which was intended for the second *Recluse*, but in this endeavor he was probably at most marginally successful. (He did obtain a manuscript of "The Strange High House in the Mist" which ultimately came to Brown University.) [Munn's piece was "A Strange Adventure"; Wandrei's were "The Monk, The Monk, and the Monk" (about Matthew Gregory "Monk" Lewis) and "The Woman at the Window." Barlow said he had obtained all but five pieces when he wrote Wandrei to borrow the proof of the Monk article.]

108. ["East and West Harvard Conservatism." *Mind Power Plus* (St. Louis: D. V. Bush, August 1922): 55–56; in *CE* 5.72–74. The issue in question is held at Harvard University.]

109. [See n108. Harvard's Widener Library has a partial file, including the issue cited.] An advertisement in Bush's book *The Silence* [1925] describes it as "the pace-making periodical in the field of mental science and advanced thought [...] a big 64-page monthly magazine that will help you 'Know Self'." By 1924 it had apparently changed its name to *Practical Psychology*.]

110. ["Some Dutch Footprints in New England." *De Halve Maen* 9, No. 1 (October 18, 1933): 2–4; rpt. *To Quebec and the Stars*, pp. 103–106; *MW* 407–10; *CE* 4.253–55]

111. R. Alain Everts recently resolved my doubts concerning the Miniter memorial chapbook listed by Wetzel and Chalker. Such a chapbook does exist and bears the following material on the cover: "In Memory of Edith May Miniter. A Coworker in Amateur Journalism 1884–1934. Issued by Laurie A. Sawyer, C. W. Smith." The booklet contains Lovecraft's poem "Edith Miniter," as both Wetzel and Chalker note (pp. 5–6); the title page has "In Memory of Edith Dowe Miniter," rather than "In Memory of Edith May Miniter," The more elaborate tribute envisioned by Cook was never published; its nearest realization being a selection of Miniter material in Hyman Bradofsky's *Californian*. (Regarding Mrs. Miniter, it is interesting to note that the Arkham transcriptions of Lovecraft's letters consistently gives the title of her published novel as *Our Nantucket Neighbours* [cf. Lovecraft to Mrs. Reed, July 28, 1928, *SL* 2.245, for instance]. In fact, the National Union Catalogue gives the title of her novel as *Our Natupski Neighbors*, published by H. Holt & Co., New York, 1916. It is the story of the struggles of an immigrant family in New England.)

[Neither the piece "Mrs. Miniter—Estimates and Recollections" nor the chapbook *In Memory Edith May Miniter* (Haverhill, MA: C. W. Smith, 1934; supplement to *The Tryout* 16, No. 8 [September 1934]) are listed in the Laney–Evans bibliography. *Our Natupski Neighbors* has been reprinted in Faig's edition of Miniter's *The Coast of Bohemia and Other Writings* (Glenview, IL: Moshassuck Press, 2000).]

112. [Academic holdings of *Weird Tales* are listed in Marshall B. Tymn and Mike Ashley's *Science Fiction, Fantasy, and Weird Fiction Magazines*, p. 735.]

113. [Faig is correct in his identification of "Abbie." For the Kleiner letters, see note 53.]

114. [In "Young Man Lovecraft" L. Sprague de Camp noted that Lovecraft was photographed by a Providence newspaper in Colonial garb (cf. *LR* 175); this photo has yet to be located.]

CHAPTER 9:

115. [See note 69.]

116. [See note 66.]

117. Mr. R. Alain Everts doubts the veracity of Laney's story of the discovery of the Davison letters from Lovecraft, related by him in his article "Who Was Howard Davison?" for *Spacewarp* in 1950. Laney purportedly discovered a trunk containing some of Davison's effects in the garage of a San Gabriel bookseller; and therein—among other things—was an unpublished story manuscript, "Xavier, the Werewolf," by H. P. Lovecraft; an early, and considerably extended version of the first section of "Herbert West—Reanimator;" several Lovecraft poems; and a file of Lovecraft letters dating from 1915 to 1917. Notwithstanding George W. M. Reynolds's *Wagner the Wehrwolf*, "Xavier, the Werewolf" seems a thoroughly unlikely Lovecraftian title; but even more suspect, in Mr. Everts's view, is Laney's assigning of a box number address to Davison in Columbus, Ohio and his assertion that "Herbert West—Reanimator" was at least partially written by 1917, whereas in fact it would appear to have been completely written for George Julian Houtain in 1921–1922. Perhaps the Laney letter files which Mr. Everts has recently uncovered will eventually yield a solution to the riddle. It should be remembered that by 1950 Laney had become completely disillusioned with Lovecraft, and might have enjoyed a joke at the expense of the rabid fans who likely wrote in the attempt to purchase the Davison material which he offered for sale. [See the editorial addition to note 65.]

118. This discussion of Lovecraft material lost—or at least unrecovered—in manuscript form has been lamentably devoid of concrete instances. However, a recent letter in the *Brown Alumni Monthly* for April, 1972, does contain an anecdote of one such instance, remarkably enough involving a story intended for professional sale. In his letter, Mr. Lew Shaw, a 1941 graduate of Brown, recounted how he had been introduced to Lovecraft on the corner of Benefit and College Streets in Providence one sunny afternoon when he and a mutual acquaintance were walking home from Classical High School. "My friend, who was interested in science-fiction," wrote Mr. Shaw, "had found where Lovecraft lived and had previously been there to meet him." (I wonder whether Mr. Shaw's friend was Kenneth Sterling, whose family lived in Providence for some time previous to and sometime after Lovecraft's death.) Here follows Mr. Shaw's essential narrative of the "lost" Lovecraft story:

> On that sunny noon, H. P. Lovecraft told us the strange story of what happened to a story he wrote about a hotel on Benefit Street, a building which stands there no longer.
> Lovecraft had written a story about a true incident. At one time there was a young woman, a chambermaid in the hotel on Benefit Street, who left and married into wealth. Sometime afterward, she returned to visit the hotel as a guest. When she found herself discourteously treated and snubbed, she departed but put a "curse" on the hotel, on all those who had humiliated her, and on everything concerned with the hotel. In short order, ill luck apparently befell all and the hotel itself burned down. Furthermore, if had never been possible, somehow, for anyone to rebuild on the site. Even on the day H. P. Lovecraft told us the story, the place where the hotel had stood was still a vacant lot.

Lovecraft had finished the story and, without making his usual carbon copy, made only one draft, which he then mailed to the publisher. His story never appeared in print. It was lost in the mails.

Lew Shaw '41
New York, N.Y.

Mr. Shaw's narrative certainly has the ring of truth; and perhaps some reference will ultimately be found in Lovecraft's letters to confirm it. A Providence antiquarian would probably be able to name the hotel involved with no trouble, and it might make an interesting pilgrimage to return to its site on Benefit Street to see whether, indeed, the curse still endures. It is interesting to ponder whether Lovecraft wrote this story with the female protagonist which Mr. Shaw's narrative seems to indicate; his only memorable female character at all seems to be Asenath Waite in "The Thing on the Doorstep," and she, of course, has actually been displaced by her father.

In connection with Mr. Shaw's anecdote, one might note the following 1919 entry in Lovecraft's Commonplace Book:

> (40) Warning that certain ground is sacred or accursed; that a house or city must not be built upon it—or must be or destroyed if built, under penalty of catastrophe.

[It seems that "Lew Shaw" can be identified with the Brown University graduate Lewis Shwartz (1920–2000), who may well have known Sterling in Providence and in acting and television work assumed the name Shaw. Rather than a hoax, as has also been suggested (cf. *IAP* 2.1001), it appears that his account is perhaps a garbled version of something that Lovecraft related, even if the actual details cannot now be recovered. One possibility is that the putative and seemingly atypical lost story was an early period work that had been mailed to an amateur publisher in a sole fair copy manuscript, as Faig suggests Lovecraft was in the habit of doing.]

119. August Derleth's remarks prefacing the section of "Early Tales"—"The Beast in the Cave," "The Alchemist," "Poetry and the Gods," "The Street," and "The Transition of Juan Romero"—published in *Dagon and other Macabre Tales* (1965)—indicate that "presumably all but 'The Transition of Juan Romero' were written when he [Lovecraft] was between fifteen and twenty." Manuscripts preserved in the Lovecraft Collection in the John Hay Library date the "The Beast in the Cave" as April 21, 1905, and "The Transition of Juan Romero" as September 16, 1919; and Lovecraft's own autobiography ("Some Notes on a Nonentity," *MW* 560; *CE* 5.209) dates "The Alchemist" as 1908. (When Lovecraft wrote in his autobiography that "The Beast in the Cave" [1905] and "The Alchemist" [1908] were the only tales which he had preserved from his earliest period of creative writing, abandoned in 1908 and not resumed again until "Dagon" and "The Tomb" were written in quick succession in July, 1917, he evidently meant to exclude the very early juvenile tales [dating 1896–1902] first published in *The Shuttered Room*. Another confirmation of the dating of "The Alchemist" occurs in Lovecraft's long autobiographical letter to Kleiner of November 16, 1916 [*SL* 1.40–41; *RK* 76]; curiously, Lovecraft had earlier written to Kleiner [January 20, 1916, *SL* 1.19] that "The Alchemist" "was written 11 years ago, yet is my latest attempt at fiction," but presumably he was here confusing the date of "The Alchemist" with that of "The Beast in the Cave," his earliest surviving "literate" tale. This latter letter to Kleiner also explains why "The Alchemist," although it was Lovecraft's amateur credential in the United Amateur Press Association [which he entered April 6, 1914], was not published until 1916, in the December issue of the *United Amateur* for that year—a matter which caused some confusion on my part in my listing for "The Alchemist" in my listing of Lovecraft manuscripts in *Nyctalops* Nos. 5–6.) No evidence for the dating of "Poetry and the Gods" and "The Street" appears to exist in the Lovecraft letters as yet published by Arkham House or in the manuscripts in the Lovecraft Collection in the John Hay Library (which do not include either of these

stories); yet, both of these stories would appear on the basis of textual evidence alone to be at least as mature as "The Alchemist" (1908), despite Lovecraft's dogmatic statement that he preserved only "The Beast in the Cave" and "The Alchemist" of his earliest stories and that he did no fiction writing whatsoever between 1908 and July, 1917. The final evidence against the dating of at least "Poetry and the Gods" as inter 1905–1910, however, occurs in Wetzel's "The Research of a Biblio" (p. 45), wherein he reveals that Lovecraft's presumptive collaborator in the writing of "Poetry and the Gods," Anna Helen Crofts—and I had long presumed this to be just another of Lovecraft's pseudonyms—had a story of her own, "Le Silent," in Charles W. Smith's *Tryout* for February, 1918. To clinch the matter, R. Alain Everts, who has been so successful in locating even the most obscure former correspondents and friends of Lovecraft's, recently wrote to me (December 1972) that he had located Anna Helen Crofts, now aged and unable immediately to remember her association with Lovecraft in the United Amateur Press Association, but nevertheless an actual individual. These facts almost certainly date "Poetry and the Gods" as 1917–1920, not *inter* 1905–1910. Even if Lovecraft's statement that he wrote no fiction between 1908 and 1917 is not dogmatic, "Poetry and the Gods" can be dated with near-absolute certainty as inter 1914–1920, since Lovecraft did not join the United until the former date. Because of Lovecraft's statements that "The Beast in the Cave" and "The Alchemist" were the only stories which survived from his prolific fiction-writing period which ended in 1908 and that he did not resume such writing again until July 1917, and also because of the textual evidence that "The Street" is at least as mature as "The Alchemist," I would propose that this tale, also, ought to be dated inter 1917 and its first appearance in print (*The Wolverine*, December 1920). Note that Lovecraft's "Some Notes on a Nonentity" (*MW* 561; *CE* 5.209) and his letter to Bernard Austin Dwyer of March 3, 1927 (*SL* 2.110) both say that he did not resume the writing of *weird* fiction again until July 1917; however, there is every indication that virtually all of Lovecraft's writing fell into the domain of weird fiction and its neighboring genres. Certainly, "Poetry and the Gods" and "The Street" qualify as "fantastic" or "weird" fiction. Moreover, there is Lovecraft's statement in his letter to Kleiner of January 20, 1916 (*SL* 1.19; *RK* 29) that "The Alchemist" was his "latest attempt at fiction."

[A letter to the Gallomo (*AG* 83) establishes a ca. late November 1919 date for "The Street." No references by Lovecraft to "Poetry and the Gods" have come to light, apart from a passing mention in a letter to Clark Ashton Smith (November 12, 1922; ms., JHL).]

120. [*CE* 5.263 (c. early 1932) and 270–71 (1937).]

121. The arrangement of Wetzel's first bibliography in *Destiny* (summer–fall 1951)—which I have not seen—is presumably alphabetical and not chronological. Nevertheless, as an even earlier compilation than the *Vagabond* listings, it ought to reflect, upon analysis, the same paucity of entries for 1920–1921. The results of his further research with the Library of Amateur Journalism in 1951–1953 and his correspondence with Leon Stone were first incorporated to a large degree in his bibliography of Lovecraft's amateur press works in volume VII of *The Lovecraft Collector's Library* (1955) and *HPL: Memoirs, Critiques, and Bibliographies* (1955)—which has remained his most complete published listing. It is a tribute to the thoroughness and originality of Wetzel's work that in the chronological rearrangement of the Chalker bibliography undertaken by Pierre Versins[†] for the L'Herne *Lovecraft* (1969), nearly all the listings of stories, poems, and essays for 1920–1921—greatly augmented from Wetzel's listings in *Vagabond*—can be found listed in his final 1955 bibliography.

† [French collector and genre historian Pierre Versins (born Jacques Chamson, 1923–2001). See Jaques Van Herp (et al.), "Bibliographie." *L'Herne* No. 12 (1969). The *Vagabond* listing contains the following entry for "Life and Death" by Wetzel:]

"Life and Death" (story)
(written 1920) where published)

122. During Wetzel's long struggles to publish his bibliographical data, he was treated shabbily by a number of fan editors who promised publication but simply used his listings to consult the Library of Amateur Journalism for the own private purposes and never thereafter even acknowledged his requests for return of manuscript. It is altogether possible that some such unprincipled individual barbarized the collection then at the Franklin Library and stole the amateur magazine including "Life and Death" and other items. The Library of Amateur Journalism was removed from the Franklin Institute in 1964 and finally relocated in the Special Collections of New York University in 1967; and when Lovecraft biographer Dr. James Merritt consulted this collection in 1971–1972, he wrote me that he had found the first issue of Lovecraft's *Conservative* cut from the bound file of that magazine. When one considers that that issue was by Lovecraft's own testimony commercially printed in an error-riddled small issue of 210 copies (see Lovecraft to Kleiner, March 28, 1915, published in part in "By Post from Providence," *The Californian* 5, No. 1 [Summer 1937]: 10; *RK* 15) and that the great majority of those copies have undoubtedly long vanished from this earth, one can appreciate the enormity of this deed. I am sure that we may happily (and securely) wish the perpetrator (who probably considers himself a "Lovecraft collector") several thousand long years in Purgatory copying out the contents of the first *Conservative* by hand (including the typographical errors!) again and again. It is indeed sad to think that a collection of materials philanthropically given to promote study and research could be so subject to such despicable depredation.

[See note 26. James D. Merritt's "literary-critical biography" of Lovecraft never appeared, despite being mentioned in Willis Conover's *Lovecraft at Last* (Arlington, VA: Carrollton Clark, 1975), p. 262 as "forthcoming" in 1975.]

123. It is fair to note here that Laney was by 1946 completely uninterested in Lovecraft and in fact even hostile to his work. Thomas G. L. Cockcroft quoted some of Laney's later views on Lovecraft from his autobiography *Ah! Sweet Idiocy!* in a letter of comment in *Nyctalops* No. 5.

124. The question of how "Life and Death" came to be listed in the Laney–Evans bibliography is a difficult one to answer. Laney's collaborator Bill Evans (William H. Evans) wrote me in the fall of 1972 that the source might have been any of the people who corresponded with both Lovecraft and Laney—for, presumably, the source of information on a presumably unpublished and repudiated story must have come from Lovecraft himself. Such correspondents included August Derleth, W. Paul Cook, R. H. Barlow, Duane W. Rimel, and F. Lee Baldwin at least. (I am inclined to rule out both Barlow and Rimel as sources for the listing, since I have read both of their files of letters from Lovecraft in the Lovecraft Collection in the John Hay Library and found no reference to "Life and Death." My own best supposition is that the listing was derived from a reference in a Lovecraft letter to F. Lee Baldwin—since it was Mr. Baldwin who in fact contributed a small section of—I might say some of the most precise—information which has yet appeared on Lovecraft's minor newspaper and amateur press association writing to that bibliography. It was also presumably his 1935 story listing which was used for this bibliography; indeed, this listing may very possibly have contained "Life and Death." If the story was marked in the listing or referred to in a letter as "repudiated," Mr. Baldwin or his editors may have taken the further step of assuming that it was unpublished; whereas, as we have seen, Lovecraft often "repudiated" published stories. When I wrote to him, Mr. Baldwin confirmed that he had had such a story listing but said his Lovecraft letters were in "absolute storage" pending hopeful publication some day. Of course, the source of last resort for information on how the "Life and Death" came to be listed in the 1943 Laney–Evans bibliography would be Laney's own correspondence files; Mr. R. Alain Everts has recently communicated to me news of the discovery of

these files, but it remains to see whether they will contain any enlightenment on "Life and Death." Mr. Wetzel has also offered the suggestion that the listing may have come from the recollection of a former amateur press association member who recalled the story. Indeed, the indefiniteness of the listing of "Life and Death" in the Laney–Evans bibliography would be indicative of such an indefinite recollection.)

[F. Lee Baldwin's letters from Lovecraft are now in JHL. It does not appear that Lovecraft mentions the putative story in any available correspondence. R. H. Barlow, however, had recalled to August Derleth in a letter that "'The Street' I saw once, I think and 'Life and Death'" (June 14, 1944; ms., Wisconsin Historical Society).]

125. Based upon his recollections, Mr. Wetzel related to me in a letter the story of yet another possible prose poem which remains unrecovered from its original appearance. In his 1955 bibliography and later bibliographies, one finds "A Singer of Ethereal Moods and Fancies" listed in the amateur press essays section as an essay "with poem" and in the amateur press poetry section as a poem "with article." Both sections list the piece as having appeared in the amateur magazine *Memoriam* for September, 1921. Mr. Wetzel now recalls "A Singer of Ethereal Moods and Fancies" as having been a prose poem and feels that his editors may have misinterpreted his listing of it as such to indicate an article with a poem embodied in the text. Evidence is not immediately available whether Mr. Wetzel actually found a copy of *Memoriam* for September 1921 in the Library of Amateur Journalism or whether his listing was derived from the review columns of the *United* or *National Amateur* or some other source—evidently, however, on the basis of Mr. Wetzel's recollection, the searching out of this particular amateur magazine would be a most worthwhile task for future Lovecraftian researchers.

[The essay is really a headnote to the poem "In Memoriam: J. E. T. D." (*AT* 350) for its appearance in the tribute to Edith Miniter's mother, *In Memoriam: Jennie E. T. Dowe*, ed. Michael White (Dorchester, MA: W. Paul Cook, 1921), p. 56. A Lovecraft poem recently unearthed from an amateur paper is "An American to the British Flag" (*AT* 407–408), which was located by Sean McLachlan in the file of *The Little Budget of Knowledge and Nonsense* (December 1917) in the British Library.]

CHAPTER 10:

126. [Some of Lovecraft's astronomical articles did appear in the *Morning* and *Sunday Tribune* editions.]

127. The research of R. Alain Everts has revealed that Lovecraft contributed to his uncle Edward Francis Gamwell's newspaper the *Cambridge Tribune* during this period.

128. It is curious to note that both of the surviving dailies have a distinct place in the bibliography of Lovecraft's work. The *Sunday Journal* of June 3, 1906 first put him into print with a letter on the editorial page, which commented upon the inaccuracies committed by an astrologer. The *Evening Bulletin* has the honor of first printing a Lovecraftian poem, "Providence in 2000 A.D.," in its issue of March 4, 1912. The *Journal*, as we have seen, later printed "The Messenger" and several of the "Fungi," in addition to a good deal of material relating to Lovecraft in Bertrand K. Hart's "Sideshow" column (1929–1941). (There was also Lovecraft's letter to the editor of the *Journal* of October 5, 1926, published there on October 10, 1926, commenting upon Providence's wealth of architectural heritage. This letter was published in *SL* II.) There may be in addition many Lovecraftian poems and letters which remain undetected in the pages of the *Journal* and the *Evening Bulletin*.

129. [The long-planned Arkham House collection *Miscellaneous Writings* finally appeared in 1995, edited by S. T. Joshi. Lovecraft's letters against Hartmann were first collected in *Science versus Charlatanry* (The Strange Co., 1979); they are now best found in *CE* 3.334–48.]

130. ["Astrology and the Future." [Providence] *Evening News* 45, No. 123 (October 13, 1914): 8. "Delavan's Comet and Astrology." 45, No. 134 (October 6, 1914): 8.]

131. It strikes me that "Does Vulcan Exist?" as published in *HPL: A Memoir* may well be an extract from Lovecraft's column "Are there Undiscovered Planets?" in the *Pawtuxet Valley Gleaner* for October 5, 1906. However, at this writing I do not have the text of the latter to compare the two.

[The column (*CE* 3.29–30) does seem to be possibly contemporary with "Does Vulcan Exist?" (*CE* 3.331) which, however, is a separate piece; S T. Joshi believes that it may be a juvenile ms. (see the editor's note *ad loc*).]

132. [This was the Skyscrapers, a society still existing. For further information on it, see <http://www.theskyscrapers.org>. The letter to Derleth is in *SL* 5.337–38 but the short extract there omits this portion; instead see *SL* 5.422 (*JFM* 392).]

133. There is at least one more known astronomical series written by Lovecraft, which appeared in the Asheville, North Carolina, *Gazette-News* in 1915. Ray Zorn announced the discovery of this series in the May 1949 issue of his small magazine the *Lovecraft Collector*, wherein he stated that the reference assistant of the Pack Memorial Public Library in Asheville had uncovered twelve of an announced series of fourteen articles published in the *Gazette-News* under the general title of "Mysteries of the Heavens Revealed by Astronomy" beginning February 16, 1915. George Wetzel found copies of the Asheville, N.C., *News-Gazette* in the Library of Congress and had uncovered thirteen of the announced fourteen articles by the time he wrote the preface to his second bibliography in *Vagabond*. He commented there upon the mystery of the missing article, stating that he had searched the newspaper through August 7, 1915. His 1955 bibliography, however, lists eighteen articles in the series, dating from February 16 to May 17, 1915, so that apparently the series actually exceeded the initially announced number of articles. Both the 1955 Wetzel–Briney bibliography and the Chalker bibliography have "Asherville" for "Asheville."

[Wetzel's 1955 listing counts articles published in two parts as separate items; the final fourteenth article (as well as the conclusion of the thirteenth) has not been found, but it may be that issues are missing and they were in fact published.]

134. Mr. R. Alain Everts has seen in addition a cutting of Lovecraft's poem "April," dated April 25, 1917, probably from the *Evening News*.

["April." [Providence] *Evening News* 50, No. 121 (April 24, 1917): 6. "Quinsnicket Park." (February 1916). "Brumalia." 51, No. 152 (December 7, 1917): sec. 2, 2. Lovecraft's astronomy articles for the magazine contain four untitled fragments (in the issues for June 30 and October 1, 1915, September 1 and October 2, 1916), in addition to "On Receiving a Picture of Swans" and a segment of "The Poe'et's Nightmare" (May 1, 1917) and two lines of "April" (April 1, 1918). The following poems were also published in the *Evening News*: "New England" (December 18, 1914); "April" (April 24, 1917); "Iterum Conjuctae" (June 12, 1917); "Lines on the 25th. Anniversary of the *Providence Evening News*, 1892–1917" (December 10, 1917); "The Power of Wine: A Satire" (January 12, 1918).]

135. [Hippocampus Press has now published editions of the correspondence to Rheinhart Kleiner and James F. Morton (based primarily on the abridged Arkham House transcripts of the letters). A similar collection of the correspondence to Maurice W. Moe is yet to be issued (some of the letters to him are in JHL); the letters to George W. Macauley have not been located, although they may survive, as one dated August 12, 1934 surfaced in 2010 in an online auction.]

136. Lovecraft seems to have read the *New York Times* while he was a resident of that city in 1924–1926; perhaps a search might sometime be made of appropriate reference volumes to see

whether he ever published any of his poems in those pages. (Unfortunately, there is no published index to any of the Providence newspapers, although the Providence Public Library has maintained a selective index in its Rhode Island Catalogue, a card catalogue in the reference department of the Library.) It would be a delight to find that something by Lovecraft like his marvelous "A Year Off"—dated July 24, 1925, in *Collected Poems*—had appeared in the *Times*. In the thirties, Lovecraft subscribed to the Sunday *New York Times* by mail.

[Evidently there were no letters by Lovecraft to *New York Times*.]

137. [The newspaper appearance is yet to be located, but the autograph manuscript of "Waste Paper: A Poem of Profound Insignificance" is in JHL (and has been published in facsimile in *Books at Brown* 26 [1978]: 48–52); text in *AT* 257–61.]

138. In an autobiographical essay—seemingly extracted from a 1929 letter just recently published by Gerry de la Ree under the title *E'ch-Pi-El Speaks*, Lovecraft makes clear that he meant to exclude his earliest productions like "The Mystery of the Grave-Yard" and "The Mysterious Ship" when he spoke in "Some Notes on a Nonentity" (1933) of destroying all his early fiction with the exception of "The Beast in the Cave" (1905) and "The Alchemist" (1908). This point earlier caused us some confusion.

[The letter in question was sent to an unidentified "Mr. Michael" (a young *WT* reader) and written July 8, 1929.]

139. [The article was "Can the Moon Be Reached by Man?" Cf. *MF* 2.583, *LVW* 34.]

140. Where can there be found a statement that "The Alchemist" as it appeared in the *United Amateur* for November 1916 was Lovecraft's first published fiction?

141. A thorough bibliographer could probably reasonably plan to cover all of the Rhode Island rural press for 1906–1908 in his quest for Lovecraft material. Aside from the *Gleaner*, which Lovecraft mentions, I do not think any one title suggests itself any more than the others, although the *Pawtuxet Valley Times* might be a likely starting point. Whatever rural paper had its principal circulation in the ancestral Phillips town of Foster might also be a likely choice to begin with. Certainly, however, even the opulent household of Whipple Phillips would not have received more than one or two of these local papers—and Lovecraft's presumptive appearance in them occurred after the family financial disaster of 1904 anyway.

CHAPTER 11:

142. [See note 29.]

143. ["The Dreams in the Witch House had been surreptitiously submitted by August Derleth while it was on loan; cf. *ES* 2.544–45. No evidence has come to light suggesting that Lovecraft destroyed any stories which had been typed for circulation, but there is, however, much evidence for stories being abandoned and discarded before completion or before they were shown to anyone. In at least one case Lovecraft did also substantially revise a story when he rewrote the ending of "The Whisperer in Darkness" after receiving criticism of it from Bernard Austin Dwyer (cf. *ES* 1.265). (For a reconstruction of the original version of this tale, see "The Vermont Horror" in *Crypt of Cthulhu* No. 101 (Eastertide 1999); also Steven J. Mariconda, "Tightening of the Coil: The Revision of 'The Whisperer in Darkness'.")]

144. [One such reference occurs in a February 29, 1928 letter to Donald Wandrei (*MTS* 210): "of my newer [i.e. post-"Alchemist"] stories I have repudiated & destroyed only two so far."]

145. [The photocopies were eventually acquired by JHL and the combined Lovecraft–Smith correspondence is currently pending publication. Unfortunately, Squires did not photocopy the postcards, which seem to have numbered more than 60 and are only partially available.]

146. All of the poems in Lovecraft's 1936 transcript, along with one other ("De Triumpho Naturae") dating to 1905, survive in the files of the John Hay Library. Of these poems, only "To Pan" from *Poemata Minora*, vol. II, has been published (in Derleth's *HPL: A Memoir*)—which is surprising, since Lovecraft's earliest poems, dating from 1897 ("The Poem of Ulysses") to 1902 (*Poemata Minora*, vol. II), are far more promising, and amusing, than his earliest stories. [This transcript was probably made by R. H. Barlow. The poems have now been collected in *AT* 30–32.]

147. Derleth observes in his annotations for the LASFS Lovecraft Symposium that Lovecraft's earliest juvenile stories, printed in *The Shuttered Room*, were originally found in the hands of a private collector; however, the fact that Barlow wrote to Larry Farsaci of having microfilm of Lovecraft's juvenilia and that all of the stories which were printed in *The Shuttered Room* are present today in the John Hay Library in the form of Lovecraft's original holograph manuscripts makes it seem likely that Barlow must have been this collector. According to Barlow's own letter to the John Hay Library of October, 1942, he had by that date transferred all of the Lovecraft manuscript material in his possession to the Library with the exception, as later noted in his *Marginalia* essay, of "The Shadow out of Time." In the introduction to his recent anthology *Beyond the Curtain of the Dark* Peter Haining indicates that the Lovecraft notes and fragments upon which the later Derleth–Lovecraft collaborations were based were found among Barlow's papers following his death; and while it is true that Barlow had made a typescript of these notes and fragments, the originals were all deposited with the John Hay Library in Providence before the time of his death, evidently by October 1942.

148. In his memoir of Jack Grill in Meade Frierson's *Huitloxopetl* No. 8, George Wetzel lists (p. 35) a previously unknown juvenile publication by Lovecraft, *The Illustrated Scripture History for the Young*, as among the items which Grill acquired for his collection. Perhaps Irving Binkin's catalogue of the Grill collection will contain a fuller description of this item. [The published catalogue (no. 542) reveals that this was merely a booklet rebound by Lovecraft.]

149. Interpretations of Lovecraft's semi-invalidism from his withdrawal from high school until the institutionalization of his mother (1919) differ. In an article published in *Nyctalops* No. 8, R. Alain Everts attributed many of Lovecraft's early ailments to a disastrous fall sustained as a teenager. All interpreters seem to be in agreement concerning the damaging influence of Lovecraft's overbearing mother. [For the fall, see also Harold W. Munro, "Lovecraft, My Childhood Friend" (*LR* 69–72).]

150. [It has recently been revealed (see note 135 for the letter), however, that Lovecraft apparently revised a story by the amateur George W. Macauley, "When Swords Were Bold," around February 1915. See further J.-M. Rajala, "Locked Dimensions out of Reach: The Lost Stories of H. P. Lovecraft," pp. 15–16.]

151. [Lovecraft admitted he did not read the Wells classic until its reprinting in *Amazing Stories* (August–September 1927); cf. HPL to Donald Wandrei, August 9, 1927 (*MTS* 146).]

152. [A letter to Robert Bloch (June 1, 1935; *Letters to Robert Bloch and Others*, p. 37) records the title of the 1907 story as "The Picture."]

153. Lovecraft's interest in the subject is also reflected in the following entry in his Commonplace Book, dating to 1934 or later:

> (210) An ancient house with blackened pictures on the walls—so obscured that their subjects cannot be deciphered. Cleaning—a revelation. cf. Hawthorne—Edw. Rand. Port.

154. The idea of horrific paintings is certainly a fascinating subject and would make an excellent topic for a thematic anthology of weird fiction. Too little has been done in this field, although Victor Ghidalia and Roger Elwood have made recent contributions in their paperback anthologies and Peter Haining in his hardcover collections.

155. [Several such anthologies have now appeared: *H. P. Lovecraft's Book of Horror*, ed. Stephen Jones and Dave Carson (Barnes & Noble, 1993). *H. P. Lovecraft's Favorite Weird Tales: The Roots of Modern Horror*, ed. Douglas A. Anderson (Cold Spring Harbor, NY: Cold Spring Press, 2005). *H. P. Lovecraft's Favorite Horror Stories*, ed. S. T. Joshi (vol. I: *The Ghost of Fear and Others*; vol. II: *The Dead Valley and Others*; Welches, OR: Arcane Wisdom, 2012).]

156. One of the most mysterious letter extracts in *Selected Letters*, the excerpted paragraph from Lovecraft's letter to Kleiner of June 27, 1918 (*SL* 1.66; *RK* 145), would seem to indicate that Lovecraft toyed with the writing of detective stories even after his resumption of fiction-writing in 1917. The letter extract was included for its listing of Lovecraft's pseudonyms, but seems to provide more bafflement than information:

> My *Hesperia* will be critical & educational in object, though I am "sugar-coating" the first number by "printing" a conclusion of the serial *The Mystery of Murdon Grange*. I will shew it to you when you call. It is outwardly done on the patchwork plan as before—each chapter bears one of my different aliases—Ward Phillips—Ames Dorrance Rowley—L. Theobald, &c. It was rather a good diversion to write it. Really, I think, I could have been a passable dime novelist if I had been trained in that noble calling! . . . .

Now "Hesperia" is the thirteenth of the *Fungi from Yuggoth*, but clearly Lovecraft cannot be discussing that work here since, first of all, the "Fungi" were not written until 1929–1930, and, secondly, Lovecraft is seemingly referring to some kind of "publication" rather than to a literary work. Nowhere, seemingly, does the title "The Mystery of Murdon Grange" appear in any bibliography or listing of Lovecraft's work; nor is any such title indexed in the Lovecraft Collection in the John Hay Library. The only guess which I can hazard is that Lovecraft may have intended to circulate a manuscript magazine entitled *Hesperia* among a circle of friends; just as he circulated stories and essays in the Transatlantic Circulator in 1920–1921. Of "The Mystery of Murdon Grange," however, I can say nothing. Surely, this entire mystery is a matter to be resolved by the Kleiner file or transcripts thereof, when and if either of these becomes available to researchers.
[Faig is correct in his guess of a manuscript magazine (cf. *AG* 33; *RK* 145, 149), but a copy of *Hesperia* has yet to come to light. "The Mystery of Murdon Grange" was evidently a round-robin serial begun by British amateurs in the magazine *Spindrift*. In a letter to Kleiner Lovecraft describes it as "a typical dime novel—with all the time-worn appurtenances of its type!" (September 22, 1918, *RK* 149).]

CHAPTER 12:

157. [For a corrected text of the Commonplace Book with annotations, see note 257.]

158. [All three appearances are distinct letters, with the version published as "The Very Old Folk" being addressed to Donald Wandrei (see note 66). They have been published together in *The H. P. Lovecraft Dream Book* (1994).]

159. "The Evil Clergyman" has usually been dated 1937, but as Thomas G. L. Cockcroft has pointed out, it seems quite dubious that the Lovecraft letter to Dwyer from which it was excerpted actually dated to 1937, in view of Lovecraft's letter to Smith of October 22, 1933, printed in part in *Dreams and Fancies*, pp. 36–37: "Some months ago I had a dream of an evil clergyman in a

garret full of forbidden books, and of how he changed his personality with a visitor. Fra Bernardus of West Shokan [Dwyer] is urging me to make a story of it."

160. [Dwyer, Bernard Austin. "The Snake God." *Fantasmagoria: The Literary Fan Magazine* 1, No. 5 (Perth Amboy, NJ: John J. Weir, Winter 1939–1940): 4–10.]

161. [See note 69.]

162. The abandoned line of which Lovecraft wrote used "grip cars" to pull ordinary trolley cars up the steep ascent of College Street, where Lovecraft himself lived from May 1933 until his death. This line was abandoned in 1914 when a grade-reducing tunnel, passing directly under Waterman Street (one block north of College Street) was completed. Although the last trolleys vanished from the streets of Providence in 1948, this tunnel is still used by Rhode Island Transit Authority buses. The 1972 *Rhode Island Yearbook* (The Rhode Island Yearbook Foundation, Inc., 1 Peck Avenue, Riverside, R.I. 02915; $2.00 per copy) has a fine article by Harold H. Young ("Clang! Clang! Clang! Went the Trolley"), illustrated by historical photographs including one of the College Hill grip car, which amply demonstrates the fascination of Providence's oldtime trolleys. (I am grateful to John Koblas for introducing me to the *Yearbook*, whose 1973 edition contains an article on Lovecraft by Charlene Szezsponik and on historical reminiscence of the Pawtuxet Valley among other fascinating articles. Recall that Lovecraft's first published articles appeared in the *Gleaner*, published in the town of Phenix in the Valley, and that he later placed the Charles Dexter Ward farm house on the banks of the Pawtuxet. I wonder if it may still be recognizable from his description.)

[Szezsponik, Charlene. "H. P. Lovecraft: The Man Who Could Not Die." *Rhode Island Yearbook* 10 (1973): 45–48.]

163. [I.e., "H. Lovecraft's Attempted Journey betwixt Providence & Fall River on the N.Y.N.H. & H.R.R." (*AT* 28–30). The longer variant title is given on the title page of the booklet in which the poem has been preserved.]

164. Lovecraft's letter to Derleth of November 18, 1936, published in part in *Some Notes on H. P. Lovecraft* (*ES* 2.756–57), describes this visit of October 28, 1936. Derleth's transcription of the letter gives the name of the hill as "Nentaconheunt," but a Providence map which I have shows it as "Neutaconkanut." There is still a park there, and one wonders whether any of the idyllic rustic scenes which Lovecraft saw to the south and west still exist. (According to Lovecraft's letter to Moe of September 1, 1929 [*SL* 3.16], the oldest Phillips homestead in Rhode Island, built by his great-great-great-great grandfather James Phillips, Sr., [d. 1746] lay out in this direction, "on the old abandon'd section of the Plainfield Pike," and was "falling to ruin" at the time of Lovecraft's writing. Asaph Phillips [1764–1829], the son of James Phillips, Jr., [d. 1807] settled in Foster [on Howard Hill] *inter* 1788–1790, according to the letter to Moe. [I do not know that Lovecraft ever visited this last ancestral site.] Genealogist Henry L. P. Beckwith, Jr., doubts the linkage between the Rhode Island Phillipses and the Reverend George Phillips [through his son Michael, who allegedly emigrated to Newport in 1668] which Lovecraft gave in his later letter to Moe of April 5, 1931 [*SL* 3.363]. Lovecraft never found the grave of Michael, which was allegedly in Newport, a city he knew well.) Of the parks near Providence, Lovecraft probably liked the best Quinsnicket woods, north of Providence, which is now Lincoln Woods. Of course, he delighted in the view of Providence from Prospect Terrace and often used the small park there to write his correspondence in warm weather; in addition, he liked the views and classical buildings in Roger Williams Park, in south Providence. In New York, he liked Prospect Park in Brooklyn, which was quite close to his first residence there, Sonia Greene's apartment at 259 Parkside Avenue. In fact, he called one section of Prospect Park "the vale of Pnath" in one of his letters to Mrs. Clark from New York—I imagine that some Lovecraft fans will be surprised to hear that that particular place lay in Brooklyn, of all places.

His steadiest favorite of all parklands, however, was probably Blackstone Park and the adjoining grounds of Butler Hospital and Swan Point Cemetery on the banks of the Seekonk in Providence. This area is still marvelously preserved.

[For Neutaconkanut hill, see also Lovecraft's final, uncompleted letter to James F. Morton (*SL* 5.423–24; *JFM* 393–94; *LVW* 341).]

165. [For Lovecraft's lost juvenile and planned Roman stories, see J.-M. Rajala, "Locked Dimensions out of Reach," pp. 12–14.]

166. [The booklet was in fact sent to Lovecraft by Harold Davis Emerson, "High Pontiff, Mayan Temple, Brooklyn, NY;" cf. Emerson to Lovecraft, May 11, 1929 (ms., JHL), enclosing this pamphlet. Boland's memoir is reprinted in *WW* 28–32; he and Lovecraft actually did not meet in person.]

167. [First collected in *The Fantastic Poetry*; in *AT* 95 (as parts of "Bouts Rimés").]

168. Perhaps some indication of Lovecraft's fascination with African themes is contained in his early story "Arthur Jermyn." It is curious to contrast Lovecraft's vision of man-descended-to-the-ape in this story with Kafka's vision of the-ape-risen-to-men in "A Report to an Academy." While both Lovecraft and Kafka were "outsiders," I think, Kafka's vision of life was clearly the more humane.

[Franz Kafka (1883–1924), "Ein Bericht für eine Akademie" (1917).]

169. [Lovecraft had read an early manuscript draft of the novel, titled *Dead Titans Waken!* This version has now been published by Centipede Press (2011).]

170. As Lin Carter remarked in his admirable chapter on "The Elder Gods" in *Lovecraft: A Look Behind the Cthulhu Mythos* (Ballantine, 1972), this story is one of the keynotes for Derleth's principal innovation in the Mythos: the introduction of a pantheon of benign "Elder Gods" opposing the "Ancient Ones." As T. G. L. Cockcroft has remarked in his addenda to the Carter glossary in *The Shuttered Room*, the phrase "elder gods" apparently occurs only once in Lovecraft's own writing, and that in a rather rhetorical and vague passage at the end of "The Call of Cthulhu." In general—and here Cockcroft cites Fritz Leiber—Lovecraft permitted no sure defense against his evil "Ancient Ones" as would surely have been provided by an opposing and coequal pantheon of "Elder Gods." Certainly, the timid earth gods of Lovecraft's stories like "The Other Gods," "The Strange High House in the Mist," and *The Dream-Quest of Unknown Kadath*—and these evidently include Nodens—cannot be construed as such an opposing and coequal pantheon. Indeed, Lovecraft seems to have intended the great cosmic races whose history he described in *At the Mountains of Madness* and "The Shadow out of Time" as the principal opponents of his "Ancient Ones"—whose minions, the shoggoths and the mysterious, primal whistling entities, they battle. May we not also reasonably assume that it was the "Great Race" which imprisoned Cthulhu in R'lyeh by means of the "Elder Sign"? Certainly, the concept of races and creatures controlled for their purposes by the evil "Ancient Ones"—which has been much expanded to include such bizarre groups as the Tcho-Tcho people and the Yeti—is a genuine Lovecraftian concept. Even in stories as early as "Polaris," "The Doom that Came to Sarnath," and "The Nameless City" we see the triumph of evil races over civilization; and, of course, in the central stories of the Mythos, we see families like the Whateleys, Marshes, and Waites in the service of the "Ancient Ones." Although of course it is natural to assume that some pantheon of "Elder Gods" provided the limited weapons which were available to oppose the "Ancient Ones," Lovecraft never seems to have crystallized this concept in his mind. Indeed, as Richard L. Tierney has remarked in an essay in *HPL* (Meade and Penny Frierson, 1972), the introduction of the "Elder Gods" into the Mythos as a coequal pantheon opposing the "Ancient Ones" introduces a good–evil duality similar to the struggle between those forces in Mithraism and other religions, a dual-

ity which the mechanistic and pessimistic Lovecraft would surely not have introduced. One imagines that any "Elder Gods" which he might have introduced would have been as inferior in comparison with the "Ancient Ones" as the Christian Devil is in comparison with the Christian God. (The weakness of his pantheon of earth gods is evidence for this contention.) Indeed, the world of Lovecraft's mythology is very nearly a distorted Christian world in which the devil and the forces of evil win the initial struggle in heaven.

[Tierney, Richard L. "The Derleth Mythos."]

171. [For Otaheité, see editorial addition to note 173 below.]

172. [Tierney, Richard L. "When the Stars Are Right." *Etchings & Odysseys* No. 1 (1973).]

173. The urbane Commander Rupert Gould discussed "The Auroras, and other Doubtful Islands" in his book *Oddities* (1928), but the nearest doubtful island to the site of R'lyeh which he discussed was Daugherty's Island, first sighted by *Nantucket whalers* in the 1830s, but (alas!) generally at S. Lat. 59°, W. Long. 116–120°. (The record of later searches convinced Commander Gould that Daugherty's Island could not exist in this range of longitude.) In his chapter "Vanishing Islands" in *Invisible Horizons* (1965), Vincent Gaddis instances several remarkable cases of volcanic islands, including one which rose above the surface 385 miles west of Hawaii in 1955, where the charts indicated a depth of 16,000 feet. "One of the most interesting facts about these volcanic islands, past and present, is that they do not spring out of any array of shallows, but push their way upward from the very bottom of the sea." In the same chapter, Gaddis relates the amazing story of a tourist ship which found Easter Island "missing" in 1928. He remarks further: "The report of the tourist ship was only the latest in a series of puzzling observations in an area where phantom islands have been reported for almost three centuries. Robert Casey, in his book *Easter Island* (1931), tells of the preceding incident, and discusses in detail the appearing and disappearing islands of the southeast Pacific." R'lyeh is not really in the southeast Pacific, but perhaps some nearby phenomena may come within the purview of Casey's book, which I have not seen. From Gaddis again: "Other phantom islands in the South Pacific never found include Sprague, Monks, Favorite, Duke of York, Dangerous, Grand Duke Alexander, Little Paternosters, Marqueen, Massacre, and Mortlock." Whether any of these islands reputedly lay anywhere near R'lyeh, I do not know; Gaddis also cites Karl Baarslag's *Islands of Adventure* (1940) as another principal source of information in addition to Gould.

Of course, hermetic and occult traditions would also have to be considered as source material for Lovecraft's envisioning of R'lyeh. He definitely read W. Scott-Elliot's *Atlantis and the Lost Lemuria*; I am less sure whether he was familiar the work of Lewis Spence and James Churchward. Scott-Elliot's map of Lemuria, which L. Sprague de Camp reproduces on p. 59 of the 1970 Dover edition of his book *Lost Continents*, does not include the site of R'lyeh, however. One last fascinating note from Gaddis: citing four works (Rev. William Gill, *Gems from the Coral Islands*, 1856; Rev. W. Wyatt Gill, *Rarotonga Records*, 1916; Lewis Spence, *The Problem of Lemuria*; and H. Macmillan Brown, *The Riddle of the Pacific*, 1924), he tells the story of the Tuanaki Islands of the Cook group, which apparently disappeared beneath the waves between 1842 and 1844. Now, the Cook Islands are among the closest island groups to the purported site of R'lyeh; and note the striking similarity of "Tuanaki" to HPL's "Kanaky." I wonder, can anyone point to "Otaheité or develop further information on Lovecraft's possible sources for his Pacific netherworld. Note that the ideas of volcanic upheavals of land in the South Pacific was occupying him as early as July, 1917, when he wrote "Dagon."

(The matter of phantom islands is by no means closed. A clipping which I have which looks like it came from the *Chicago Tribune* [probably ca. 1971] relates: "SYDNEY, Australia, Dec. 14 (AP)—A long lost tropical isle was reported by Capt. Peter Bennett of the inter-island steamer Tofua to have reappeared in the uninhabited Metis shoal north-northeast of Nukualofa, capital of the Tonga Kingdom in the Friendly Islands. At Nukualofa he told of sighting the unnamed isle after a volcanic eruption. It is half a mile long and 1,150 feet high, he said. The isle had disappeared after being recorded in 1886." Truly, "That is not dead which can eternal lie, And with strange eons even death may die.")

["Otaheité" is an obsolete form of Tahiti. The Associated Press item dates to December 1967.]

174. Strangely, one locale which seems to have eluded the attention of most Mythos writers is the Arctic: the realm of Poe's "boreal pole" and "ashen Yaanek," antipodal to Lovecraft's world of the Antarctic (Poe's also, in "Arthur Gordon Pym"). Lovecraft laid the basis for a development of the Mythos in the northern polar region with his "Polaris" (1918), apparently based at least in part on the dream related to Maurice Moe in his letter of May 15, 1918 (*SL* 1.62). I can think offhand of only one additional tale written in this locale—"The Pirrak" by Billy Keel, a rather good amateur story published in the first issue of *Ambrosia* (Alan D. Gullette, 1972).

CHAPTER 13:

175. [The "Dark Brotherhood Dream" is also in *SL* 4.325–27 and *The H. P. Lovecraft Dream Book*, pp. 35–36. The unedited Barlow journal has been reprinted, as "[Memories of Lovecraft (1934)]," in *On Lovecraft and Life* (1992), pp. 11–18, and *OFF* 401–407. The version edited by Derleth for Arkham House is in *LR* 351–55.]

176. [A posthumous collection of Derleth's Cthulhu Mythos stories containing the eponymous fragment appeared as *The Watchers Out of Time*. For Derleth's Mythos fiction, see also the volume *In Lovecraft's Shadow*.]

177. [Lovecraft's various notes and synopses for stories (both written and unwritten) have been collected in *CE* 5.243–59 (which, however, does not include the notes for "The Survivor," for which see note 211).]

178. [Nothing further about this projected novel has turned up as of yet.]

179. [The dream is related at more length in a letter to Barlow dated May 11?, 1935 (*OFF* 261).]

180. [For "The Survivor," see note 211.]

181. The following 1925 entries from Lovecraft's Commonplace Book outline yet another novel idea which he failed to develop:

> (130) N.E. region called 'Witches' Hollow"—along course of a river. Rumours of witches' sabbaths & Indian powwows on a broad mound rising out of the level where some old hemlocks & beeches formed a dark grove or daemon-temple. Legends hard to account for. Holmes—Guardian Angel.
>
> (134) Witches' Hollow novel? Man hired as teacher in private school misses road on first trip—encounters dark hollow with unnaturally swollen trees & small cottage (light in window?) Reaches school & hears that boys are forbidden to visit hollow. One boy is strange—teacher sees him visit hollow—odd doings—mysterious disappearance or hideous fate.

Of course, August Derleth later utilized these ideas for his story "Witches' Hollow" in *Dark Mind, Dark Heart*. Yet another idea—perhaps related to the project which Lovecraft outlined to Ernest Edkins near the end of his life—is found in a 1930 Commonplace Book entry:

> (180) A general house of horror—nameless crime—sounds—later tenants—(Flammarion) (novel length?)

CHAPTER 14:

182. [Much information could probably be found in Lovecraft's letters to Samuel Loveman, who directed some of the revision clients to Lovecraft, but unfortunately the majority of this correspondence remains unavailable; most of the letters that have surfaced have been printed in *Letters to Samuel Loveman & Vincent Starrett* (1994). Loveman apparently never made his letters from Lovecraft available to Derleth for transcribing, despite the latter's asking for them.]

183. [Richardson, Leon Burr. *History of Darthmouth College*. Hanover, NH: Dartmouth College Publications, 1932; 2 vols.]

184. [For instance the amateurs Agnes Richmond Arnold, James Laurence Crowley and James Larkin Pearson, and the fans Duane Rimel ("Dreams of Yith") and Wilson H. Shepherd ("Wanderer's Return"); for the text of such revision, see the Appendix in *AT* 467–76.]

185. When Elizabeth Toldridge enquired of Lovecraft about the Harris Collection of American Poetry and Plays at Brown University, he replied on October 28, 1932 (*SL* 4.99; *ET* 222): "About the Harris Collection of Poetry at Brown—it's really no honour to be in it. It includes everything indiscriminately—good & bad—for purposes of historic record. Among the contents are the pathetic brochures of some of my very 'dumbest' revision clients—including that immortal itinerant lecturer David V. Bush."

186. [This was Dr. Lee Alexander Stone, M.D. (1879–1955).]

187. I am grateful to Thomas G. L, Cockcroft for bringing this letter to my attention and for copying the text for me.

188. [Lovecraft denies the claim of being a Shakespearean authority in a November 1934 letter, feeling Ostrow had indeed confused him with Samuel Loveman (*Letters to Robert Bloch and Others*, p. 120). Ostrow was active in amateurdom and a member of the National Amateur Press Association (contributing an article called "Spare Time," *The Tryout* [December 1932].)]

189. [The letter was not printed in *SL* 5.]

190. [See Shea's "HPL and Films" (in *HPL* [1972] and *In Search of Lovecraft*), as well as Darrell Schweitzer's *Lovecraft in the Cinema* (1975). This subject has more recently been explored at length in *Lurker in the Lobby: A Guide to the Cinema of H. P. Lovecraft* by Andrew Migliore and John Strysik (Portland, OR: Night Shade Books, 2006) and Don G. Smith's *H. P. Lovecraft in Popular Culture: The Works and Their Adaptations in Film, Television, Comics, Music and Games* (Jefferson, NC: McFarland & Co., 2006).]

191. [See Darrell Schweitzer's "H. P. Lovecraft's Favorite Movie."]

192. [Resnais's *Providence* (1977) was partially filmed in the city.]

193. R. Alain Everts dates this photograph April 11, 1922. A photograph of Sam Loveman against the same background, taken at the same time by Lovecraft, confirms that he was along; however, the group photograph of Lovecraft, Long, and Morton was according to Mr. Everts taken by a fifth amateur journalist whom he does not name.

[The photograph was taken by Paul Livingston Keil (1900–1953); cf. his brief memoir "I Met Lovecraft" (*WW* 40–41).]

CHAPTER 15:

194. [It appears that Lovecraft used the services of the Old Colony Co-Operative Bank (Providence, R.I.), as a letter from to him from the bank survives on the verso of a page of the autograph ms. of *At the Mountains of Madness* (November 22, 1930, in JHL).]

195. Lovecraft did receive one larger literary check—for $595—from Street & Smith in 1936 for *At the Mountains of Madness* and "The Shadow out of Time." According to his letter to Barlow of January 29, 1932, he had tried to sell some of his early tales (like "From Beyond" and "Beyond the Wall of Sleep") to the Clayton *Astounding*—whose rate was 2¢ per word—but none had ever taken. (Lovecraft let Charles Hornig have both of these tales gratis for his *Fantasy Fan*—along with "The Other Gods" and "Polaris." "Celephaïs" and "The Doom that Came to Sarnath" he gave to William L. Crawford; "Ex Oblivione" and "The Nameless City" to Donald Wollheim; "The Quest of Iranon" to Lloyd A. Eshbach; and "Nyarlathotep" to Nils H. Frome. Of these stories contributed to thirties fan magazines only "From Beyond" and "The Nameless City" were truly unpublished (unless there was a magazine entitled *The Transatlantic Circular*); all the rest had appeared in amateur press association magazines a decade earlier. Needless to say, all were snapped up by *Weird Tales* following Lovecraft's death.) According to Thomas Cockcroft in a letter published in *Nyctalops* No. 6, Lovecraft received only $25.00 from Hugo Gernsback for "The Colour out of Space;" indeed, the meager rates which Gernsback paid only on or after publication—and often only under the threat of legal action—probably led Lovecraft to refuse to submit any further stories to *Amazing*.

Lovecraft's letter to Barlow of November 25, 1932 (*OFF* 43) further indicates that he sent only his "inferior items"—the early stories first printed in amateur press association magazines and later rejected by *Weird Tales*—to Clayton for consideration for *Strange Tales* and *Astounding*. In the same letter Lovecraft attributed his failure to sell any stories to Clayton to the fact that he had once told editor Harry Bates precisely what he thought of Clayton's policy of altering manuscripts—which had apparently affected some of his friends. Whether the lost story about the hotel on Benefit Street which Lew Shaw wrote about in his letter to the *Brown Alumni Monthly* (April, 1972) was submitted to Clayton or to some other publisher can only be speculated upon. However, I feel that if the story had been lost *en route* to *Weird Tales*, it would probably have become the subject of a famous anecdote many years ego. The only obvious possibilities besides *Strange Tales*, *Astounding*, and *Weird Tales* would be *Amazing* and *Wonder Stories*—and Lovecraft would hardly have wanted to offer his stories to the latter magazine since Gernsback controlled it. Neither magazine would have been a likely place to send a story such as Mr. Shaw described.

[Lovecraft's $25.00 fee for "The Colour out of Space" ("and that only after three dunning letters") is recorded by Barlow in "[Memories of Lovecraft (1934)]" (*OFF* 404). On Lew Shaw and the supposedly lost story, see note 118.]

196. Lovecraft's letter to Wilfred B. Talman of April, 1928, probably gives the price he received when "The Lurking Fear" was reprinted (from *Home Brew*, 1923) in the June, 1928, issue of *Weird Tales*: "What *is* of greater import is Wright's determination—despite my warning about technical consequences—to reprint *The Lurking Fear* from Houtain's defunct *Home Brew* and give me 78 iron men therefor! Thus at last I'm really cashing in on your Nieuw Nederland atmosphere—and the frightful House of Morteuse [*sic*]." Presumably, Lovecraft was worrying about the possibility of objections on Houtain's part.

197. ["Otis Adelbert Kline's Letters to Robert E. & Dr. I. M. Howard." *OAK Leaves* 1, No. 1 (Fall 1970): 4–11. The letter to the elder Howard, dated April 1, 1941, is on pp. 5–11.]

198. *Weird Tales* itself considered a collection of Lovecraft's but the failure of the earlier book *The Moon Terror* by A. G. Birch apparently dissuaded the magazine from further book-publishing plans.

[This portion of the letter to Helen Sully is omitted in *SL* 5.112–16. Simon & Schuster also asked Lovecraft to submit a novel to the publisher; cf. *IAP* 754–55.]

199. Neither Robert E. Briney nor Jack L. Chalker lists "The Music of Erich Zann" as among the Lovecraft stories which appeared in the eleven volumes of the "Not at Night" series and the *Not at Night* Omnibus; and perhaps editor Thomson ultimately decided not to use "The Music of Erich Zann." However, as T. G. L. Cockcroft remarked in his article "Some Notes on the Lovecraft Bibliography in *The Dark Brotherhood and Other Pieces*" in *Lore* No. 9 (published by Gerry Page, new editor of *Witchcraft and Sorcery*), both Briney and Chalker commit many errors in their treatment of the "Not at Night" series. Both Briney and Chalker list the third volume of the series as *You'll Need a Light*—whereas the actual title is *You'll Need a Night Light*, published by Selwyn & Blount in London in 1927. (That they are correct in listing the appearance of "The Horror at Red Hook" in this volume as Lovecraft's first anthological appearance, however, is verified by Lovecraft's letter to Donald Wandrei of December 19, 1927 [*SL* 2.211; *MTS* 195–96]. Herbert Asbury's anthology *Not at Night!* [Macy-Masius, 1928]—a selection from the first three "Not at Night" volumes [*Not at Night*, 1925; *More "Not at Night,"* 1926; *You'll Need a Night Light*, 1927] which included Lovecraft's "The Horror at Red Hook" from the third volume—was evidently the first American anthology to contain a Lovecraft story, although, as Cockcroft remarks, editor Asbury certainly does not deserve credit as the first American anthologist to discover Lovecraft. [Cockcroft: "This book [Asbury's anthology] has on the verso of the title page the curious statement: 'These stories were originally printed in England in *Weird Tales*.'"] Certainly, this honor belongs to T. Everett Harré, who selected Lovecraft's story "The Call of Cthulhu" for his anthology *Beware After Dark!* [1929]; see Lovecraft's letter to Farnsworth Wright of November 8, 1928 [*SL* 2.251–52], where Lovecraft evidently makes reference to the collection of work which *Weird Tales* for some time considered publishing in discussing the choice of stories to be offered to Harré. Harré later edited an anthology of famous love stories—a task for which he was apparently at least somewhat qualified by the titles of two earlier books of his listed in Bleiler: *Behold the Woman! A Tale of Redemption* and *The Eternal Maiden*.)

Furthermore, Briney and Chalker are in error with respect to the dates of two further volumes of the series containing Lovecraft stories—*By Daylight Only* should be 1929 rather than 1928 (Cockcroft: "Opposite the contents page in *By Daylight Only* we are told *First Printed October 1929*.") and *Switch on the Light* should be 1931 rather than 1928. Moreover, *The "Not at Night" Omnibus*, listed by Chalker as 1929, clearly cannot belong to that year, since as Cockcroft remarks, it contains material not published in *Weird Tales* until 1933; Bleiler gives the date of publication as 1937—after the publication of all of the eleven original volumes of the "Not at Night" series. It seems clear, therefore, that neither Briney nor Chalker saw all the volumes of this series in compiling their bibliographies; and it may well be that "The Music of Erich Zann" is in one of the post-1932 volumes.

[Curtis Brown Group Ltd is a still existing literary agency based in the United Kingdom. "The Music of Erich Zann" was included in *Modern Tales of Horror* but not in any of the volumes of the "Not at Night" series. It is worth noting that in his selection of stories for *Beware After Dark!* T[homas] Everett Harré (1884–1948) received aid from Donald Wandrei; cf. Lovecraft to Wandrei, September 12, 1929 (*MTS* 243).]

200. Asbury's Macy-Masius anthology *Not at Night* (1928) was apparently licensed by Selwyn & Blount or its receivers without the permission of *Weird Tales*; see Lovecraft to Wright, February 15, 1929, *SL* 2.260–61. Selwyn & Blount must not have vanished permanently from the scene in 1929, as Lovecraft indicates in his letter, however, for Cockcroft's research indicates that *Switch on the Light, Terror by Night,* and the *Not at Night Omnibus* were published no earlier than 1930, 1935, and 1933, respectively (cf. *Lore* No. 9). Bleiler—whose stated policy was not to list books not seen by himself or one of his collaborators—lists all eleven volumes of the "Not at Night" series and *The "Not at Night"*

Omnibus as published by Selwyn & Blount. Although he indicates that all three of the above-mentioned books bore no date of publication, he dates them 1931, 1934, and 1937, respectively. How he established these dates I do not know; notice, however, that he also indicates that *By Daylight Only* bore no date, whereas Cockcroft's copy contained at least the notice that it had been first printed in October 1929. (Cockcroft's copy of *Terror by Night*, however, bore no date. His copy of *You'll Need a Night Light*—containing Lovecraft's very first anthological appearance—was first printed in September 1927, according to the notice contained in it.) Perhaps the 1929 receivership of Selwyn & Blount was only temporary.

201. Actually, our estimate comes out just a little high for those *Weird Tales* stories for which we know the price Lovecraft was paid. "The Call of Cthulhu," estimated price $180 (30 Arkham pp.), actual $165; "The Dunwich Horror," estimated price $258 (43 Arkham pp.), actual $240; "The Whisperer in Darkness," estimated price $376 (66 Arkham pp.), actual $350; "The Strange High House in the Mist," estimated price $54 (9 Arkham pp.), actual $55; "The Lurking Fear," estimated price $120 (20 Arkham pp.), actual $78 (tentative). "The Lurking Fear" probably drew a lesser price since it was actually a reprint from *Home Brew*, January–February–March–April, 1923. Since we want to estimate Lovecraft's maximum earnings, we will let our estimate stand.

202. [See editorial addition to note 195.]

203. [*MTS* 365–66 and *ES* 2.717 record that Lovecraft was paid $315 for *At the Mountains of Madness* ($350 less Julius Schwartz' 10% agent fee) and $280 for "The Shadow out of Time."]

204. [Lovecraft did state that he and Price would "split the cash" (*OFF* 88).]

205. [Elsewhere Lovecraft noted that he "got $20.00 for the job, and Wright paid Mrs. Reed $45.00 for the completed MS" (HPL to Derleth, October 6, 1929, *ES* 1.222; *LVW* 205). *SL* 1.313 records a payment of $100.00 for "Imprisoned with the Pharaohs" (i.e., "Under the Pyramids").]

206. [A letter to Richard F. Searight (August 31, 1933) contains a table of Lovecraft's revision rates: see *RFS* 12, *LVW* 300–301.]

207. I have always considered it a tragedy that Lovecraft never came into correspondence with Machen, who became a warm friend and good correspondent of many American admirers of his work during the Machen "boom" in the 1920s. Lovecraft's few letters to Vincent Starrett in *Selected Letters* II are evidence of the richness such a correspondence could have developed. Although Lovecraft did not share Machen's Celtic mysticism, they would have had a world to talk about in their basic aesthetic motivations and purposes. While Machen was by no means as voluminous a correspondent as Lovecraft, his published letters are rich in wit and wisdom. Certainly, his volumes of autobiography ought to be basic reading for any students of Lovecraft.

[August Derleth and Donald Wandrei did correspond with the Welsh writer, but Lovecraft made no effort to secure his address from them. Selections of Machen's correspondence include *Selected Letters: The Private Writings of the Master of the Macabre*, ed. Roger Dobson, Godfrey Brangham and R. A. Gilbert (Wellingborough: Aquarian, 1988); *A Few Letters from Arthur Machen: Letters to Munson Havens*, ed. Munson Aldrich Havens; Roger Dobson (Upton, Wirral, Cheshire: Aylesford Press, 1993); *Arthur Machen & Montgomery Evans: Letters of a Literary Friendship, 1923–1947*, ed. Sue Strong Hassler and Donald M. Hassler (Kent, OH: Kent State University Press, 1994).]

CHAPTER 16:

208. The Harris Collection of American Poetry and Plays at Brown has a volume of cuttings of newspaper poems made by Lillian D. Clark; this includes a couple of poems by Muriel Eddy clipped from *Tryout* and a typescript of one of Arthur Goodenough's poems, but seemingly nothing by Lovecraft. Several newspaper cuttings of macabre poems by one

Thomas Haynes Bayley were certainly reminiscent of Lovecraft; but I learn from *Alibone*'s that Bayley was an actual early nineteenth century English poet and not a Lovecraft pseudonym.

CHAPTER 17:

209. [Lovecraft's *A Description of the Town of Quebeck* was first published in L. Sprague de Camp's compilation *To Quebec and the Stars* (1976).]

210. [Cf. essays by Will Murray ("In Search of Arkham Country") and Robert D. Marten ("In Rescue of the Lost Searchers").]

211. Along with his fine rendering of Lovecraft's map of Arkham published in the *Arkham Collector* for summer 1970 (No. 7, pp. 200–201), Gahan Wilson published (p. 216) a number of queries concerning unknown places marked on Lovecraft's original map (in the John Hay Library)—in particular the homes of "Repas Garrison" and of the "French Leach." I would suggest that these queries night best be answered by antiquarian research in Salem itself. Although many of the places name in Lovecraft's original map are clearly related to his fiction, they are also all genuinely New England names and many may actually figure as place names in Salem. Certainly, it would be worthwhile to investigate the history or the Garrison family in Salem; mayhap a "Repas Garrison" was among its scions. Regarding the "French Leach," Mr. Wilson stated at the Boston Science Fiction Convention in April, 1972, that it had already been suggested several times that Lovecraft meant thereby a French physician or surgeon. I would like to carry this suggestion one step further. Lovecraft's outline for the story which August Derleth ultimately wrote as "The Survivor" clearly concerns a French surgeon, Jean-François Charriére, who came to Arkham from Quebec in 1697 and built a house there in 1698–9. (This outline—the original version of which was penciled on the blank portion of a newspaper cartoon and is today in the John Hay Library—was published on pp. xviii–xix of *Some Notes on H. P. Lovecraft* and on p. 313 of *The Dark Brotherhood*. Moreover, Barlow wrote as follows regarding the inspiration for this never-written story (*Notes* xviii; *The Dark Brotherhood*, pp. 312–13):

> This syllabus, penciled on the blank portions of a newspaper cartoon, hints at plans for a last, never-written story. Lovecraft spoke of it with some fullness one afternoon in 1933, but since I expected to read it in a few months or a year, I retained only casual impressions of the shape it was to have had. Inspired by an actual 17th-century house in the Quebec style which interrupts a staid New England street, the tale would have dealt with a French wizard who sought to duplicate in himself the fabulous longevity of the crocodile, but who succeeded only in changing his form to a hideous extent. I remember there was to have been a scene where some one glimpsed the bent reptilian figure as it hurried across a miasmatic garden behind the strange house, to vanish in the well-mouth which its condition dictated as habitat; but I cannot establish other details.

What we must ask, of course, is whether there is indeed such a house in the 17th-century Quebec style interrupting a "staid New England" street in Salem—which Lovecraft obviously planned as the setting for the story. It is quite possible that a local antiquarian could give a prompt answer.

In developing Lovecraft's outline into "The Survivor," August Derleth transferred the setting of the story to Providence (on Benefit Street) and the denouement (which—from the outline—Lovecraft had evidently intended to occur in 1708) from colonial to modern times. I do not believe there is any building fitting Lovecraft's description of the Charriére house on Benefit Street in Providence (indeed the last genuine seventeenth-century building within the city limits of Providence was demolished in 1900); but failing the discovery of the house which we seek in Salem, I think there may yet be a possible Providence inspiration for the Charriére house. Witness Lovecraft's description of the residence of the painter Henry Anthony Wilcox in "The Call of Cthulhu" (*DH* 199):

> Wilcox still lived alone in the Fleur-de-Lys Building in Thomas Street, a hideous Victorian imitation of Seventeenth Century Breton architecture which flaunts its stuccoed front amidst the lovely Colonial houses on the ancient hill, and under the very shadow of the finest Georgian steeple in America.

Now—apart from Lovecraft's prejudice in favor of severe classical lines—this is all quite a voracious description of the Fleur-de-Lys Studio built at 7 Thomas Street in Providence by the prominent Rhode Island artist Sidney R. Burleigh in 1886—under the very shadow of the steeple of the First Baptist Meeting House—one of the finest Georgian buildings in Providence. The booklet *Seeing Providence* published by the Providence Journal Company states that the design of the building was "adapted from the 17th century Norman and Breton style" and that the decorations in stucco and wood were the work of Burleigh himself, who died in 1929. I ask: if the search for our Quebec-style house in Salem fails, might not this "hideous" 17th-century imitation have played some role in Lovecraft's envisioning of the Charriére story? (By the way, Lovecraft's use of the Fleur-de-Lys Building in "The Call of Cthulhu" resulted directly in his sonnet "The Messenger"—by a curious circumstance mentioned in my essay "Lovecraft's Providence" in *Tamlacht* No. 12.) Designed as an artist's studio, the building was in fact a wonderfully appropriate setting for Wilcox's lodgings; in fact, it is still used as a studio today.

Whatever the date of the newspaper cartoon upon which Lovecraft penciled the outline for the story which was to become "The Survivor," the following 1924 entry from his Commonplace Book would seem to show that the basic theme had been in his mind for quite some time:

> (123) Dried-up man living for centuries in cataleptic state in ancient tomb.

[For an examination of the planned story "The Survivor," see J.-M. Rajala, "Locked Dimensions out of Reach: The Lost Stories of H. P. Lovecraft," pp. 76–84. In short, correlating all of the currently available information (including references in letters), it would seem that Lovecraft had intended the denouement to take place in modern times, with someone (perhaps Repas Garrison) inheriting Charriére's house on what is then known as Arkham's French Hill. The person afterwards develops an urge to look intently across the town on a wooded graveyard on Hangman's Hill in the west and ultimately—somewhat as Robert Blake would in "The Haunter of the Dark," written later—the urge finally becomes so great that he disturbs a boulder blocking "an oddly hieroglyphed grave" of 1708, thus releasing the reptilian form into which Charriére has (unwittingly) devolved, apparently as the result of a failed quest of longevity. No actual synopsis survives, but the "syllabus" (a set of chronological notes) probably dates to Spring 1934 like Lovecraft's map of Arkham.]

212. [Charter Street is the correct form of the name, as printed in *FLB*.]

213. Winfield Townley Scott writes of a poem by Sarah Helen Whitman describing walks which she and Poe took in the wooded region along the bank of the Seekonk during their courtship; in view of Lovecraft's own love for this region, it would be interesting to see this poem reproduced in a Lovecraftian publication. Lovecraft undoubtedly knew the poem, since he owned a copy of Sarah Helen Whitman's *Poems* which later became the property of Scott himself.

214. [See note 111.]

215. Cook goes on the cite Mrs. Miniter's essay "Dead Houses"—published in the first issue of Barlow's *Leaves* in August 1937—as her definitive dissection of the lore and legendry of the Wilbraham region. Because of their importance for the understanding of the background for "The Dunwich Horror," surely this essay of Mrs. Miniter's and Lovecraft's own essay regarding

his visit to Wilbraham ought to be reprinted from the amateur publications in which they originally appeared.

[Faig himself has now done so in the Miniter collection *Dead Houses and Other Works*, co-edited with Sean Donnelly (New York: Hippocampus Press, 2008).]

216. An expert on New England dialects might be able to say something about the locale of the Dunwich region from the dialogue which Lovecraft used in "The Dunwich Horror"—that is, presuming that such a dialect as he presented therein ever existed. Lovecraft was a diligent student of varying dialects and word usages and one presumes that he was as careful in these matters as he was in his architectural and historical descriptions.

217. [Lovecraft did visit Cook in Athol, cf. e.g. *MTS* 151.]

218. Another of these motor trips with Cook and Munn in May 1929 took Lovecraft to Westminster, where he states in his letter to Elizabeth Toldridge (May 29, 1929, *SL* 2.348; *ET* 72) he and his mother had summered in 1899. This, however, was Westminster, Massachusetts, and not Westminster, Vermont, since by his own statement Lovecraft did not touch Vermont soil until 1927 (see Lovecraft to J. Vernon Shea, July 19, 1931, *SL* 3.383; *JVS* 28). Cook's memoir (pp. 38–39; *LR* 135) contains an amusing anecdote confirming this fact. Winfield Townley Scott says in his essay "His Own Most Fantastic Creation" (*LR* 12) that Lovecraft and his mother also summered in Dudley, Massachusetts.

219. I wonder whether the "cave" or "glen" near Athol in which King Phillip allegedly took refuge (Cook, pp. 30–31; *LR* 129) might have played any role in Lovecraft's conception of Lovecraft's "Cold Spring Glen" in "The Dunwich Horror"—after all, he did appropriate the name of Sentinel Hill for the Dunwich region and he may well have utilized an actual physical feature near Athol, too. Regarding the legendry of this "glen" near Athol, however, Cook says (p. 31): "These things must possess historical plausibility or possibility to be used in fiction, although local myths may be as wildly impossible as the stomachs of the citizens will stand." Lovecraft had convinced himself that the legend of King Phillip's seeking refuge in the cave could not be true.

The similarity of the actual inundation of the Quabbin Valley for the Quabbin Reservoir (completed in 1939) to Lovecraft's fictional inundation of a region "west of Arkham" (he was never more specific) for a reservoir for Arkham (Salem) his story "The Colour out of Space" is also too close to escape comment. Lovecraft's description of his setting "west of Arkham" (60–61) bears some similarity to his and Cook's description of the doomed Quabbin Valley; in fact, principally on the basis of Lovecraft's description of the Gardner farmstead and those surrounding in his story; Andrew Rothovius (*op. cit.*, p. 188) suggests that North Dana, in the submerged part of the valley, may have been Lovecraft's actual setting for "The Colour out of Space." It might be noted that Lovecraft also speaks in "The Dunwich Horror" (*DH* 163; *CF* 2.421) of the "Devil's Hop Yard—a bleak, blasted hillside where no tree, shrub, or grass-blade will grow;" of course, the "blasted heath" in "The Colour out of Space" is by contrast set in a valley. Lovecraft may well have had the same actual physical feature—if there was one—in mind when he wrote of the "Devil's Hop Yard" and the "blasted heath," however; perhaps his letter to Baldwin which contained a sketch of the "blasted heath" would reveal more details of its origin. Lovecraft's letter to Bernard Austin Dwyer of March 26, 1927 (*SL* 2.120) indicates that "The Colour out of Space" had been completed by that date; however, Lovecraft's motor tour through the Quabbin Valley might well have preceded his trip by rail through the valley in June, 1928, by several years. It is certainly possible that there are a number of visits of Lovecraft to Cook in Athol before March, 1927, which are unrecorded in the *Selected Letters*. Cook's remark that Lovecraft used the valley as the setting for "only one story" and his strong indication that that story was "The Dunwich Horror," however militate against the presumption that "The Colour out of Space" was also set in the valley.

[Regarding the "blasted heath," Lovecraft noted in the letter to F. Lee Baldwin (March 27, 1934; *FLB* 68) that his "idea was simply a region where all the vegetation had disintegrated to a grayish powder!"]

CHAPTER 18:

220. Actually, the background of "Pickman's Model" is far richer than the sinister site which originally inspired the story. In his brilliant essay "The Cthulhu Mythos: A Study" (*HPL*, pp. 35–41), George Wetzel pointed out the actual discovery of mysterious tunnels in Boston's North End. In a letter to me, Mr. Wetzel specified some of the sources of his data on these tunnels (he has himself done extensive research on old tunnels in Baltimore, his home city): *Old Landmarks and Historic Personages of Boston*, by Samuel Adams Drake (1900), pp. 199–200; *Rambles Around Old Boston*, by Edwin Bacon (1914), pp. 11–12; *Rambles in Old Boston*, by Reverend Edward Porter (1887), pp. 265–266, 348; *The Romance of Boston Bay*, by Edward Howe Snow (1944), pp, 42–45; and *The Crooked and Narrow Streets of Boston*, by Annie H. Thwing (1920). As Mr. Wetzel pointed out to me, Lovecraft himself owned at least the Thwing book (see Lovecraft to Clark, Nov. 4–5, 1924, *SL* 1.356); and even if he did not own the others (someone might check the Spink catalogue of his library in this regard), it is probable that he knew them. Lovecraft's fascination for underground tunnels and passages can be seen in many of his stories— "The Nameless City," *The Dream-Quest of Unknown Kadath*, "The Festival," "Pickman's Model," and "The Shadow out of Time" come immediately to mind; and in fact he once referred in conversation to Dorothy C. Walter and her mother to strange Providence structures resembling those found in Boston: "Did we know, he asked, his sombre eyes intent on our faces, that recently, when early buildings on Benefit Street and College Hill were razed to make way for new ones, deep, tunnel-like pits, seemingly bottomless and of undetermined usefulness, were discovered in the ancient cellars? Could we imagine for what purpose they might have been constructed?" (Dorothy C. Walter, "Three Hours with H. P. Lovecraft," *SR* 186; *LR* 45). Miss Walter states that her meeting with Lovecraft took place early in 1934. The buildings on the north side of College Street between North Main and Benefit were razed for the building of the Rhode Island School of Design administration building by 1936 (I believe Lovecraft refers to their already having been razed in his letter to Helen Sully of December 4, 1935, at the John Hay Library)— but I am not aware whether their demolition took place sufficiently early to figure in Lovecraft's conversation with Miss Walter in early 1934. (The south side of the same block was occupied by the old Providence County Courthouse until 1928, when the new, larger Courthouse was built.) Researchers intending to delve further into these matters should probably consult the Rhode Island Index in the Reference Department of the Providence Public Library for possible newspaper references to such discoveries. The College Street archway (leading to an inner courtyard) in the RISD administration building, however, is a genuine colonial survival—one of a very few such colonial archways surviving in America. Another is on Thomas Street—and here Lovecraft's longtime feline friend "Old Man" would lounge to greet him on his trips to and from downtown Providence at the base of the hill.

When I was in Providence myself in 1970–1972, I saw some queer-looking foundations of demolished and ruinous buildings in the general area of the juncture of Benefit and North Main Streets—where North Main climbs the hill to join Benefit and along the same hill above the Moshassuck. All of these will probably be gone soon though—the entire North Main area is being renovated and even before I left modern apartments were going up along the portion of North Main overlooking the Moshassuck. Mill Street branches from North Main when the latter begins to climb the hill, and I believe the bridge over the Moshassuck on Mill is the approximate site of the first mill in Providence. Northward, in the Randall Square area, were some of the most hideous slums—many of them clinging to precipitous slopes over the railroad—which Lovecraft ever discovered in Providence (see Lovecraft to Talman and Lovecraft to Long, April 23, 1926, *SL* 2.43–44; Lovecraft to Samuel Loveman, January 5, 1924, *SL* 1.278–79). Lovecraft writes to Loveman of passing the site of the original mill on the Moshassuck and of continuing past Olney Street:

> Then we turned into the maze of colonial alleys toward the river, and suddenly saw a sight of incredible picturesqueness. From one of these lanes an abrupt declivity fell, descending at steepness almost prohibitive to human feet, and provided with an iron hand-rail. Intersecting at intervals several hidden Georgian lanes on the hillside, it reach'd a group of early stone mill buildings—1815 or 1820—and slid betwixt two of them whose second stories were connected above it with a passage like the Bridge of Sighs, finally crossing the river by a wooden bridge and coming out near Randall-Square, a hideous polyglot slum district . . . .

Unfortunately, this entire area was leveled by the time I visited Providence in 1970–1972; what there is today is merely an embankment docking over the razed area through which the railroad tracks pass. From atop this embankment—to which I imagine Lovecraft's hideous riverward slums hung—on State Street (the first right after crossing the Smith Street bridge), however, one can still obtain a marvelous view of the great hill on which Providence's best residential district was built—perhaps the finest view in the city.[†] Just as Lovecraft remarks in *The Case of Charles Dexter Ward*, the dome of the Christian Scientist Church—which rises just across the street from the present site of Lovecraft's 66 College Street home—dominates the structures on the hill. (Perhaps the best vantage point to look west from the hill is Prospect Terrace, where Lovecraft often took his writing on warm days, although the new Albert and Vera List Art Building on College Street—on the original site of the 66 College Street house from whence it was moved in 1959—may offer a similarly fine view.) If "The Music of Erich Zann" were not dated 1921—three years before Lovecraft's discovery of this picturesque hillside street—I would be tempted to give it some role in the inspiration of that magnificent tale. Note these passages of description:

> The Rue d'Auseil lay across a dark river bordered by precipitous brick blear-windowed warehouses and spanned by a ponderous bridge of dark stone . . . . Beyond the bridge were narrow cobbled streets with rails; and then came the ascent, at first gradual, but incredibly steep as the Rue d'Auseil was reached . . . .
>
> I have never seen another street as narrow and steep as the Rue d'Auseil. It was almost a cliff, closed to all vehicles, consisting in several places of flights of steps, and ending at the top in a lofty ivied wall . . . . The houses were tall, peaked-roofed, incredibly old, and crazily leaning backward, forward, and sidewise . . . . There were a few overhead bridges from house to house across the street.

As it is, Lovecraft's inspiration for the Rue d'Auseil probably has to be placed somewhere among the many precipitous hillside streets which intersect Benefit, which he knew from his wanderings as a youth. In his "Biographic Notes on Lovecraft" (*HPL*, p. 25), George Wetzel attributes to Dorothy Walter the judgment that Thomas Street was the original Rue d'Auseil and that the Fleur-de-Lys Building the original boarding house of the "paralytic Blandot' where Erich Zann had his lodgings. In view of Lovecraft's description of the Fleur-de-Lys Building (which as we have seen he made the residence of the painter Henry Anthony Wilcox) in "The Call of Cthulhu" (*DH* 147; *CF* 2.24) and the fact that he describes the house of the paralytic Blandot as "tottering" and "the third . . . from the top of the street" (neither of which descriptions he could possibly have applied to the Fleur-de-Lys Building on Thomas Street), however, I must question Miss Walter's judgment in this matter. Actually, I believe the Rue d'Auseil was probably principally inspired by two other Providence streets which climb the hill from Benefit—Bowen and Meeting. Bowen, the northernmost, is cobbled from Benefit to the next parallel street, Pratt, and attains a truly precipitous grade in its ascent. On the northern side of this block is John Holden Greene's Sullivan Dorr House (1809), one of the most beautiful colonial mansions in Providence. On the southern side, however, is a row of leering, tottering tenements, each of which rises to three stories and more despite the precipitousness of the grade. (Can one doubt that the ninety-eighth entry in Lovecraft's Commonplace Book, which he dated "1922?" in 1934, refers to one of these hillside tenements: "Hideous old house on steep city hillside—Bowen St.—beckons in the night—black windows—horror unnam'd. Cold touch & voice—The welcome of the dead." Bowen from Congdon Street eastward is quite well-kept.) Moreover, from Pratt Street to Congdon Street, the next parallel street, Bowen becomes a mere dirt path; Prospect Terrace—built out from the hill by huge retaining walls—rises alone the southern side of the stretch. Note that Lovecraft says the Rue d'Auseil was "sometimes bare earth with struggling greenish-grey vegetation." (For all I know, there may once have been buildings along the southern side of this unpaved stretch of Bowen Street; there are ruinous foundations directly below Prospect Terrace on Pratt Street.)

So much for the case of Bowen Street. Meeting—a parallel street farther south—is today far less picturesque than Bowen Street, but it does have one advantage—the stretch from Benefit to Congdon ends in an "ivied wall," with a flight of steps leading to the continuation of the street beyond Congdon. (Cf. Lovecraft's description of the Rue d'Auseil, *DH* 89–90; *CF* 1.281–282.) Moreover, in his letter to Loveman of January 5, 1924 (*SL* 1.278), describing his tour of Providence with Morton and Eddy on December 27, 1923, Lovecraft speaks of "the *old-world* steps [my emphasis] that form a part of Gaol-Lane [the archaic name for Meeting Street]." (Actually, Meeting Street at one time connected with Congdon without the intervention of steps, according to Providence antiquarian and genealogist Henry L. P. Beckwith, Jr., but I doubt whether this was during Lovecraft's lifetime. Just how precipitous a grade this would have entailed can be seen from the juncture of Congdon and North Court Streets slightly northward—a juncture which I believe Lovecraft called "Tippy Corner"—with good reason—in the above-cited letter to Loveman. In "The Shunned House," Lovecraft placed the residence of Elihu Whipple on North Court Street, but I believe he probably envisaged it as one of the fine row of colonial houses along the stretch from North Main to Benefit, not as one of the houses along the steeper stretch from Benefit to Congdon.) Other than this flight of steps, Meeting has little character in common with Lovecraft's fictional Rue d'Auseil—the lower section from North Main to Benefit is full of well-preserved colonial buildings which Lovecraft describes in his letter to Elizabeth Toldridge of June 10, 1929 (*SL* 2.351–55; *ET* 74–77) but the upper section—leading up to the "ivied wall" with steps—is pretty much colorless, at least since the patch of countryside at Meeting and Benefit which Lovecraft described in his letter to Miss Toldridge vanished in 1929.‡

A final speculation concerning the Rue d'Auseil comes from Alfred Galpin's memoir "Memories of a Friendship" (*SR* 199–200; *LR* 171):

> After 1922 both Howard and I were drawn into a whirl of new activities and corresponded more rarely, but I continued to feel him my dearest friend, to whom I could always turn when I needed advice or sympathy. When we resumed a more steady stream of letters in 1925–26, I was studying music in Paris and was infatuated in particular with the old quarter, of sinister silences, back of the Pantheon, where Balzac places his pension Vauquer in *Le Pere Goriot*; I even visited a grimly squalid old house, about to be torn down, of which I had read in a journal that it had been occupied by Balzac in his quest for local color while writing the novel (a statement

which can scarcely have much truth to it). It was during this stage of our correspondence, unless my memory betrays me, that Howard had a dream which he expressed in the story (published in 1925), *The Music of Erich Zann*, set in the "rue d'Auseuil" [*sic*], a most grim and squalid street. I seem to recall that Howard wrote me, telling me how my letters had influenced his revision of the story prior to its publication in *Weird Tales*. After his death, I had the consolation of receiving from Mrs. Gamwell, his surviving aunt, the batch of annotated *Cartes Ivon* (mostly of Paris) which I had sent him in those years.

To return abruptly, from slum streets, to our original subject of mysterious tunnels, I know nothing of any in Providence other than those which Lovecraft himself described to Miss Walter and her mother in early 1934. Interestingly enough, there is a railroad tunnel which passes under most of the old East Side (entering around Gano and Amy Streets near the Seekonk and emerging once again just below the old Arsenal on Benefit Street). This tunnel was constructed in 1904 to give the Warren & Bristol line direct access to the Union Station.

† It is to be noted that Lovecraft's letter to Talman (cited above) speaks of discovering a slum area which he had not seen before, "the end of Chalkstone Ave. near Randall Sq. and the railway." Now, if one takes a look at a map of Providence, the easternmost end of Chalkstone Ave. is not especially close to Randall Sq. and the railway, but one imagines that Lovecraft intended to indicate the intervening valley through which the railroad still runs and the surrounding hills then filled with slum dwellings. I fancy his earlier explorations of December 27, 1923 were somewhat to the south of this area—perhaps even confined to the eastern bank of the Moshassuck. I can hardly claim to have an encyclopedic knowledge of this area, however, and I may well have missed something. The ultimate source for someone seeking to research these areas would of course be the old city maps.

‡ Since as Galpin reveals, Lovecraft did revise "The Music of Erich Zann" before its publication in 1925, I suppose that his discovery of an overhead bridge in his explorations of December 27, 1923 might have been written into the story after its original composition in 1921. Lovecraft also mentions handrails in connection with the streets leading to the Rue d'Auseil. I remember such rails on North Court, Meeting, and Hopkins Streets myself, and I am sure there are many more instances.

221. "Cool Air" would be a natural guess, but this story dates to 1926, the year before Lovecraft's letter to Dwyer announcing his intention to use 169 Clinton in fiction. Of course, Lovecraft might have used elements of his former residence in writing of the house in "Cool Air"—which was also a decaying "mansion of brownstone"—but Lovecraft's letter of February 2, 1934 to Duane W. Rimel, as-yet unpublished, makes the matter a little more specific by stating that the house in "Cool Air" was actually patterned on a house in which a friend of Lovecraft's had lived for a while in New York. (It might be noted here that Lovecraft's friend George Kirk for a time lived at 169 Clinton with Lovecraft.) If Lovecraft's setting of the house in his story on "West Fourteenth Street"—presumably in Manhattan—is correct, perhaps a stray envelope with a friend's address or the memory of one of Lovecraft's friends will eventually lead us to it. Lovecraft's description, unfortunately, is mostly of the interior of the building.

[The model for the "Cool Air" building was in summer and fall 1925 the location of George Kirk's Chelsea Bookshop and apartment at 317 West 14th Street.]

222. It might be noted here that the 149th entry in Lovecraft's Commonplace Book, dated by him as 1926, reads: "Fungi Evil alley or enclosed court in ancient city—Union or Milligan St."

[It seems that the Union Place intended by Lovecraft may have been located around 497 Union Street, between Bond Street and the Gowanus Canal. (There is also a Union Place—formerly Union Avenue—in Greenpoint.)]

223. [The Dutch Reformed Church is at 890 Flatbush Avenue, just off of the crossing of Church Avenue. The setting of "He" was inspired by a courtyard at 93 Perry Street in Greenwich Village (cf. *NY* 68, 77n9).]

224. In his fine memoir of Jack Grill published in Meade Frierson's amateur magazine *Huitloxopetl* No. 8 (1972), George Wetzel mentions (p. 34) that Grill knew well the neighborhood in which the Elizabeth avatar of the Shunned House was located, but related to Wetzel that the entire area had since been leveled for urban renewal.

225. Just how much veracity there may be in Lovecraft's fictional account of the house at 135 Benefit Street in Providence is a matter which is yet unsettled. According to an unpublished paper by Virginia L. Doris which resides in the Lovecraft Collection at the John Hay Library, the house at 135 Benefit Street was originally built by Stephen Harris in the eighteenth century; and Mrs. Doris discusses the same stories regarding transferred graves resulting from the straightening of Benefit (formerly Back) Street which Lovecraft tells in his story. When George Wetzel saw the same passage regarding the writing of "The Shunned House" which we have quoted above in manuscript during his March, 1958, visit to Providence, he traced the house to 135 Benefit through Lovecraft's reference to the Babbitt family. (According to Wetzel [see his "Biographic Notes on Lovecraft," *HPL*, p. 25], Babbitt was a civil war officer. The 1911 Providence House Directory which I have shows the house occupied by Mrs. Sophia C. Babbitt, George H. Babbitt [clerk; boarder], and Miss Sarah Babbitt [boarder].) At that time, Dorothy Walter told him that the house was known among local antiquarians as the Stephen Harris house and that the then-tenant, an aged widow named Mrs. Sarah Bullock, "had a lot of French books in the house." (Mrs. Bullock finally died in extreme old age around 1971, and since then the "Shunned House" has become slightly less sinister-looking as a result of a general repair of the house itself and a cleanup of the premises (which during Mrs. Bullock's tenure had been overgrown with weeds and other vegetation—just as Lovecraft described the house) by the new tenants. Now, clearly, Lovecraft altered the modern history of the house—since, according to his story, the house remained unoccupied between the deaths in 1860–61 and the destruction of the vampire on June 26, 1919. But the correspondence between the Harrises of his story and the Harrises whose name is in fact associated with the house in Benefit Street is enough to make one wonder just how much of his fictional history of the house may in fact be based upon actual legend or history. Did he merely appropriate the family name associated with the house and develop a completely fictional family history from there, utilizing in addition the stories of the graves transferred in the straightening of Benefit Street? Or is there in fact more of actual legend and history in his narrative than that? Clearly, what should some day be undertaken—if only for its value as an entertainment although it would in fact shed valuable light on Lovecraft's methods and sources—is the very kind of search of historical records regarding the house and the plot of land upon which it was built as Lovecraft had his protagonist undertake in the story. Certainly, it would be amazing to find that a Frenchman named Etienne Roulet had leased a portion of the original Throckmorton homelot—that portion embracing the modern site of the Shunned House—in 1697! Since Lovecraft wrote his story while he was living in New York, however, it is difficult to imagine that he could have consulted any such records in its writing—unless he had already done so before his departure from Providence. Indeed, Lovecraft's letter of March 16, 1934, to Duane W. Rimel contains a remarkable revelation about his own association with the house at 135 Benefit Street (*FLB* 148):

Glad the crude "Shunned House" sketch seemed to bear out the text. As for a peaked corner room—I'd say that the easternmost attic chamber of the wing ought to correspond to that description fairly well . . . . or the corresponding room of the main edifice might do so likewise. [The house at 135 Benefit Street had and still has a small addition or "wing" in the rear.] Here is a sketch of the approximate way the place looks from the rear—that is, from the higher part of the hill to the east. The rural grounds still run back to the next higher street [Pratt]—these bits of overtaken countryside forming one of the most fascinating features of Providence. I may call there before long; for after a long period of court litigation it has been bought back by members of the original family—friends of ours—whose claims were disputed by other heirs. In 1919 & 1920 my elder aunt Mrs. Franklin Chase Clark—now deceased—lived in the Shunned House; hence my familiarity with it. The other buildings near by are probably about 30 or 40 years later in date . . . . built around 1800. It was about 1800 that the solidly built part of the town approached the top of the hill—the house I now live in (near the top) [66 College Street] being of about that date. *[Ellipses are Lovecraft's.]*

Now, this passage is important for a number of reasons. First of all, Mrs. Clark's residence in the Shunned House in 1919 and 1920 reveals how Lovecraft came to be so intimately familiar with the interior as well as the exterior of the house. More importantly, however, this passage tells us that Lovecraft's family were friends of the family which had originally owned the house—presumably, the Harrises—who after a lengthy period of litigation recovered the house ca. 1934. (The court action alone would be a worthwhile matter for future researchers to investigate; in partial confirmation of Lovecraft's story, antiquarian and genealogist Henry L. P. Beckwith, Jr.—himself a distant relative of Lovecraft—told me that Mrs. Bullock was a Harris.) Here then is a direct source from which Lovecraft could have learned a great deal of the history and legendry of the house—probably far more than anyone could discover today. (Certainly, the library of the Rhode Island Historical Society would be a first recourse for researchers pursuing these questions. The library has among other items a complete file of Providence Directories, but unfortunately these only go back to the first half of the nineteenth century. Other records may supplement this lack, however. In addition, of course, there are the deeds and plat maps at the Providence City Hall—which could surely be turned to good use. Some of the earliest official records—including the alignment of the original homelots—have in fact been published. As far as the legendry of the house is concerned, researchers might well seek out local antiquarians and genealogists to see what they could contribute to the investigation. If the Harris family still survives—perhaps Mrs. Bullock was its last surviving member—they would of course also be a valuable source for information.) Lovecraft's strong interest in the house even before he left Providence in 1924 is made evident by his composition of the poem "The House" as early as 1920—when Mrs. Clark was still living there. (In fact, it is curious to note that Lovecraft has the denouement of his story occur in 1919, the same year that Mrs. Clark—whose husband Dr. Clark is clearly the prototype of Elihu Whipple in Lovecraft's story—took up residence there.) For Lovecraft's early interest in the house, there is also the testimony of the ninety-fifth entry in his Commonplace Book, deleted after its original writing and subsequently dated "1922?": "Shunned House. Horrible Colonial farmhouse & overgrown garden on city hillside—overtaken by growth. Verse "The House" as basis of story." Thus, if Lovecraft's 1934 dating of this entry is correct, he clearly had a story involving the Shunned House in mind even before he left Providence. (The entry in his Commonplace Book was probably deleted after he used it for his story.) There is even the possibility that his scholarly uncle Dr. Clark, who died in 1915, may have been interested in the house before him and have communicated to him before his death some of his own discoveries concerning the house—just as Elihu Whipple ultimately permitted the protagonist of Lovecraft's story to see his notes on the Shunned House. Dr. Clark did do a considerable amount of general historical and antiquarian writing—his three volumes of historical newspaper cuttings at the Rhode Island Historical Society are evidence of his interests in these directions—and a thorough researcher of the entire Shunned House mystery might ultimately do well to make a run through Dr. Clark's papers in the Brown University Archives—just in case. In his essay "The Cthulhu Mythos: A Study" (*HPL*, pp. 35–41), George Wetzel (p. 40) discusses several other likely sources for Lovecraft's story—notably, "The Green Picture" in Charles Skinner's *Myths and Legends of Our Own Land* (vol. 1, p. 76) and the account of the vampire Roulet in John Fiske's *Myths and Myth-Makers*.

CHAPTER 19:

226. I do not know where "The Book Notes" were published. The cutting of the column for March 15, 1890, which I found was laid into the front of the copy of Joel Dorman Steele's *A Fourteen Weeks' Course in Chemistry* which I found in the John Hay Library. The paragraphs which Mr. Rider quotes occur under the heading "Circulation of Matter" on pp. 259–60 of this edition.

[*Book Notes: Literary Gossip, Criticisms of Books and Local Historical Matters Connected with Rhode Island* 7, No. 6 (March 15, 1890): 46–47. Ed. Sidney H. Rider.]

227. Even Louise Imogen Guiney made her contribution to the literature of the subject, in her essay "On Graveyards" in her book *Goose-Quill Papers* (Boston, Roberts Brothers, 1885, pp. 135–36):

> Of Roger Williams, who was also granted solitary sepulture, a strange tale is told. There was question, some years back, of transplanting him from his sequestered resting-place to a stately mausoleum. The diggers dug, and the beholders beheld—what? Not any received version of that which was he, but the roots of an adjacent apple-tree formed into a netted oval, indented with punctures not wholly unlike human features; parallel branches lying perpendicularly on either side; fibres intertwined over a central area; and lastly, two long sprouts, knotted half-way down, and terminating in a pediform excrescence wonderful to see. It was plain, thought the *savants* of P., that the apple-tree had eaten of Roger; now who had eaten of the fruit of that apple-tree? Verily, "to what base uses we may return!"

228. Chapin, who was for some years a librarian of the Rhode Island Historical Society, may in fact have been a personal acquaintance of Lovecraft's. Writing to his friend Rheinhart Kleiner on December 4, 1918 (*SL* 1.77) about the accomplishments of his" childhood friends, Lovecraft stated that one had become "librarian" of the R. I. Historical Society." However, the transcription which Kleiner himself made of this letter for "By Post from Providence" in *The Californian* for summer, 1937 (p. 16) reads *"a librarian of the Rhode Island Historical Society"* [my italics]; in addition, my copy of the 1911 Providence House Directory shows a Clarence F. Allen, librarian, boarding in the home of Mrs. Lydia W. Allen at 625 Angell Street, just a few doors from the half-house at 598 Angell Street where Lovecraft lived with his mother and aunts from 1904 until 1924. So perhaps Lovecraft's childhood friend need not have been Howard M. Chapin. (He did later in life have an amateur friend Albert Chapin.) Of the others whom he mentions as among his childhood friends in his letter to Kleiner, Stuart Coleman was probably the army officer and Ronald Upham and perhaps Chester Munroe among the "rising young businessmen." (According to the statement of his father Addison Munroe in a letter to Winfield Townley Scott dated January 1, 1944, Chester Munroe (1889–1943) was Lovecraft's closest boyhood friend. His brother Harold Bateman Munroe (1891–1966) worked in law enforcement in Providence County before retiring to Florida. According to R. Alain Everts, none of the surviving Munroes know a thing of the early friendship of Chester and Harold with Lovecraft.)

[It would seem that Howard Miller Chapin (1887–1940) is perhaps not the person referred to by Lovecraft, as he was three years his senior and had graduated in 1904 from University School.]

229. Talman also stated in his letter that the note which Grill entitled "Who Ate Roger Williams?" had been given and not sold to him. Talman and Grill had a friendly and noncommercial relationship, and Grill presented Talman himself with a good deal of printed material by and about Lovecraft in return for the back numbers of *Weird Tales* and minor Lovecraft mementoes which Talman presented to him. I doubt that Talman saw the appearance of "Who Ate Roger Williams?" in Murdock's *Vagabond* but, of course, his description of the "Who Ate Roger Williams?" manuscript as a copy in Lovecraft's handwriting differs from Wetzel's description of it as a typescript with one correction by Lovecraft in pencil. Since Talman had apparently not seen the manuscript which he had given to Grill for several years when he wrote Wetzel in 1958, I would be inclined to accept Wetzel's statement in this regard. Wetzel had recently been in correspondence with Grill; and, moreover, a typescript with a correction in Lovecraft's hand is more feasible than a copy in his own handwriting if indeed the "Who Ate Roger Williams?" note was Talman's. However, I cannot give final judgment here; Talman's letter of January 19, 1958, to Wetzel does speak of "Mr. Grill's recent visit." Mr. Irving Binkin, the present owner of Jack Grill's collection of Lovecraftiana, did not answer my inquiry as to the nature of the "Who Ate Roger Williams?" manuscript.

[The ms. is not listed in the published catalogue of the Grill–Binkin collection.]

230. The discussion in "The Sideshow" to which Lovecraft referred took place on November 27, 1931. Bertrand K. Hart had found a strange old book by S. Grant Oliphant entitled *Queer Questions*; of the "queer questions," "Who Ate Roger Williams?" was the 145th. Hart printed Oliphant's "answer" and revealed that it had been cribbed word-for-word from Steele's book. (Steele from Allen, Oliphant from Steele . . . what a bunch of copycats.) BKH's final comments on the matter were:

> So THAT's what became of our great founder! . . . Apple sauce! I am endlessly indebted to the unknown Mr. Oliphant for this singular item . . . But what became in turn of the men who ate the apples? Did they return to earth and become cabbage-heads? . . . It is possible. But reverence dwindles under this too-material exposition and I share with you the wish to leave the theme where it stands . . . A rich little book, though. It has burned up a pleasant night.

231. [As Harry Brobst has noted (*LR* 387), Lovecraft was fond of showing the Roger Williams root to visitors.]

232. The only other article Talman wrote for *Casket and Sunnyside*, "Death Customs Among the Colonial Dutch," has also—along with "Who Ate Roger Williams?"—been attributed to Lovecraft. A ten-page typescript of this article written on the back of sheets with the *Texaco Star* letterhead was among the Lovecraft papers recovered by H. Douglass Dana following Mrs. Gamwell's death and is now in the Lovecraft Collection in the John Hay Library. George Wetzel first pointed out that this article was probably written by Talman and not by Lovecraft; Talman was himself at one time associated in an editorial capacity with the *Texaco Star*. Lovecraft did write for Talman an article entitled "Some Dutch Footprints in New England," which appeared in *De Halve Maen*, a small magazine Talman was then editing. [See note 110.]

233. [Most of the Lovecraft–Talman correspondence is now in JHL, with some scattered items in private hands (mainly originating from the Grill–Binkin collection). Nine postcards to Talman have been published in *Yr Obt Servt: Some Postcards of Howard Phillips Lovecraft Sent to Wilfred Blanch Talman* (1988).]

234. George Wetzel has seen in the "Who Ate Roger Williams?" notes an echo of the ghoulish nourishment which the trees around the Shunned House drew from the impregnated soil in "The Shunned House" and the poem "The House."

CHAPTER 20:

235. Lovecraft describes this journey in detail in his letter to Frank Belknap Long of November 8, 1923 (*SL* 1.264–67). Our discussion here will be much more understandable with the help of the official highway map of Rhode Island, available gratis from the Rhode Island Development Council, Roger Williams Building, Mayes Street, Providence, R.I. 02908. The following U.S. Army Map Service maps (series V815) show the area we discuss in much greater detail: Thompson (6667 IV NE); Chepachet (6667 I NW); East Killingly (6667 IV SE); and Clayville (6667 I SW). These maps were made during the 1940s, I believe.

236. Each Rhode Island county is divided into cities, shire towns, and towns. The town of Glocester includes Chepachet and its environs and has as its western border the western border of Rhode Island.

237. On Walling's 1863 map, Pine Hill is shown roughly one mile south west of the Dark Swamp, just north of the Snake Hill Road. (In 1863 the Snake Hill Road ran nearly due east just south of the Ponaganset Pond; today it is interrupted in its eastward course by the southern end of the Ponaganset Reservoir. The other hill involved in Lovecraft's account of the Dark Swamp may have been Durfee Hill itself, which is evidently not shown on Walling's 1863 map but which I find northeast of the present Ponaganset Reservoir on a modern map. Indeed, Lovecraft and Morton may have come far closer to the Dark Swamp—depending upon which fork in the road they took—in their September 1923 search for Durfee Hill, than did Lovecraft and Eddy on November 4, 1923.

238. The fragment of "Black Noon" left by Mr. Eddy has new been published in a collection of his supernatural stories, *Exit into Eternity* (Providence, RI: Oxford Press, 1973). Derleth was apparently unable to complete the fragment in time for *Dark Things*.

239. In his letter to the Gallomo concerning his expedition to the Great Meadow Hill Country Clubhouse, Lovecraft mentioned "Ron, Ken, and Stuart" as among the gang which met there until ca. 1913, in addition to Lovecraft himself and Chester and Harold Munroe. Ron and Stuart are surely Ronald K. Upham and Stuart Coleman. The ten miles bicycle ride to Rehoboth was certainly nothing for Lovecraft; recall that he would bicycle all the way from Providence to East Greenwich, Rhode Island during this period. Some additional information on Lovecraft's gang—composed mostly of neighborhood boys he knew from the Slater Avenue School—is given in Addison Munroe's letter in Winfield Townley Scott's "His Own Most Fantastic Creation" (*LR* 13).

["Ken" mentioned by Lovecraft is probably Kenneth Tanner (1890–1979).]

240. [The Great Meadow Country Clubhouse was still standing at the time of writing in 1973, but is now sadly demolished. For a photograph of the remains, see the picture insert to Faig's *Lovecraft: His Life, His Work* (1979).]

CHAPTER 21:

241. The pseudonym "Ames Dorrance Rowley" is given as "Ames Dorrance Rersley" in Lovecraft's letter to Rheinhart Kleiner of April 4, 1918 (*SL* 1.57–60; *RK* 133–35). However, "Laeta: A Lament," which Lovecraft listed as by "Rersley" in his letter to Kleiner, actually appeared under the byline of "Ames Dorrance Rowley" in *Tryout* for February, 1918. This poem seems to be the only use of the Rersley–Rowley pseudonym by Lovecraft yet noted by his bibliographers; however, it might be noted that in his letter to Rheinhart Kleiner of June 27,

1918 (*SL* 1.68; *RK* 145), Lovecraft attributes one of the parts of his serial "The Mystery of Murdon Grange" to "Ames Dorrance Rowley." Thus, the majority of evidence would seem to indicate that either Lovecraft or his transcribers at Arkham House erred in writing "Rersley" in the letter to Kleiner of April 4, 1918.

[The correct reading is Rowley (*RK* 135), parodying the amateur James Laurence Crowley.]

242. [The two cited poems as well as an additional piece of "Archibald Maynwaring" verse titled "Wisdom" from *The Silver Clarion* 3, No. 8 (November 1919) are listed in S. T. Joshi's comprehensive bibliography.]

243. In fact, Chalker's source for this reference was probably the article on Lovecraft's pseudonyms written by Mrs. Willametta Keffer, an authority on the amateur journalism of Lovecraft's day. This article appeared in *The Fossil* in the fifties (I lack the precise reference) and was followed by a rebuttal by August Derleth. (Files of *The Fossil* may be found in the New York University and Brown University libraries.) Mrs. Keffer was apparently the first to point out Lovecraft's articles under the pseudonym "Zoilus" in *The Wolverine*. Lovecraftian researcher R. Alain Everts claims the discovery of a number of Lovecraft pseudonyms in addition to those uncovered by Barlow, Derleth, Wetzel, and Keffer; and it is to be hoped that he will someday publish the results of his investigations in this area.

[Keffer, Willametta. "Howard P(seudonym) Lovecraft: The Many Names of HPL." *The Fossil* No. 158 (July 1958): 82–84. Derleth, August. "New HPL Pseudonyms Rejected by Derleth." *The Fossil* No. 159 (October 1958): 90.]

244. [It has been determined by S. T. Joshi that of the five Zoilus columns in Horace Lawson's amateur magazine *Wolverine* three were written by Lovecraft (Nos. 9, 10, and 12), with one each by James F. Morton (No. 14, previously thought to have been by Lovecraft as well) and Alfred Galpin (No. 11). See Joshi, "The Rationale of Lovecraft's Pseudonyms" (*Primal Sources*, p. 82), and *JFM* 44n2.]

245. [Further research has determined that the name was not a Lovecraft pseudonym, but belonged to a real person living in Providence, R.I., Augustus Taber Swift (1867–1939). The two letters earlier ascribed to Lovecraft are printed as an appendix to *H. P. Lovecraft in the Argosy* (1994).]

246. I have ignored minor variations of the "Theobald" and "Paget-Lowe" pseudonyms and have also counted only the original appearance of an item and not its reprints. (In some cases, pseudonyms were dropped in reprintings.) I have also counted groups of poems published together (and so listed by Wetzel–Briney and Chalker) as one appearance. Wetzel–Briney and Chalker give the same results using these methods—except for the inclusion of "Zoilus" by Chalker.

247. [The following items can now be attributed to these pseudonyms († = fiction; all poems in *AT*): *Lawrence Appleton*: "Hylas and Myrrha: A Tale," "Myrrha and Strephon." *Isaac Bickerstaffe, Jr.*: the two astrology spoofs cited. *John J. Jones*: "The Dead Bookworm." *Humphrey Littlewit*: "A Reminiscence of Dr. Samuel Johnson" (†); "The Waste Paper," "Perverted Poesie or Modern Metre." *Archibald Maynwaring*: "The Pensive Swain," "To the Eight of November," "Wisdom." *Henry Paget-Lowe*: "Poetry and the Gods" (†); "January," "October," "On a Grecian Colonnade in a Park," "On Religion." *Ward Phillips*: "Ex Oblivione" (†); ten poems. *Richard Raleigh*: "To a Youth." *Ames Dorrance Rowley*: "To the Old Pagan Religion" (in *Tryout* as "The Last Pagan Speaks"), "Laeta; a Lament," "To Maj.-Gen. Omar Bundy, U.S.A.," "The Volunteer." *Edward Softly*: "Ode to Selene or Diana" (in *Tryout* as "To Selene"), "Christmas," "Tryout's Lament for the Vanished Spider," "Chloris and Damon," "Damon and Delia, a Pastoral," "The Dream," "To Delia, Avoiding Damon." *Lewis Theobald, Jr.* (or variations

thereof): "Cats and Dogs," "The Convention," "The Trip of Theobald" (essays); some two dozen poems. *Albert Frederick Willie*: "Nathicana" (a collaboration with Galpin). *Zoilus*: 3 columns.

The following pseudonyms have also come to light: *Alexander Ferguson Blair*: "North and South Britons" (in *Tryout*, first identified by Tom Collins). *El Imparcial*: seven amateur press essays. *Jeremy Bishop*: "Medusa: A Portrait." *Michael Ormonde O'Reilly*: "To Pan" (in *Tryout* as "Pan"). The manuscript of the poem "Life's Mystery" is additionally signed "L. Phillips Howard," a transparent pseudonym, and "The Peace Advocate" and "The Unknown" were published under the byline of "Elizabeth Berkeley" only. See further S. T. Joshi, "The Rationale of Lovecraft's Pseudonyms" (*Primal Sources*, pp. 81–89).]

248. Thomas G. L. Cockcroft argues convincingly in the letters column of *Nyctalops* No. 5 (p. 48) that *The Case of Charles Dexter Ward* should be dated winter 1926–1927 rather than 1927–1928. In at least one holograph chronology in the Lovecraft Collection in the John Hay Library, I believe, Lovecraft dates both *The Case of Charles Dexter Ward* and *The Dream-Quest of Unknown Kadath* as 1926–1927 or 1927. My presumption is that both of these novels were omitted from the chronology upon which the *Dagon* chronology was based; and that *The Case of Charles Dexter Ward* was restored, inaccurately. *The Dream-Quest of Unknown Kadath* is not listed in the *Dagon* chronology.

[*The Dream-Quest of Unknown Kadath* was written between Fall 1926 and January 22, 1927, and *The Case of Charles Dexter Ward* between January and March 1, 1927, as Lovecraft's letters for the time reveal. The "complete chronology" given in the original Arkham House edition of *Dagon* was fabricated by August Derleth.]

249. ["The Picture in the House" was written December 14, 1920 (cf. *RK* 201).]

250. [Indeed, the letter is misdated in *SL*; *RK* 201 gives it in the correct chronological sequence.]

CHAPTER 22:

251. Her action was the result of a dispute which she had with August Derleth over her right to quote from her husband's letters in a book *The Private Life of H. P. Lovecraft*, which she intended to write.

[The original manuscript version of Sonia's memoir, first published in abridged form as "Howard Phillips Lovecraft as His Wife Remembers Him" in *The Providence Sunday Journal* of August 22, 1948 (*LR* 252–63), has been printed by Necronomicon Press (1985) as a chapbook under the above title. The surviving letter from HPL to Sonia was published as "Lovecraft on Love" in *The Arkham Collector* No. 8 (Winter 1971): 242–46.]

252. [In fact, Sonia does not quite put it in these terms. Her correspondence with Lovecraft is mentioned in *LR* 252–53, 257, 262–63.]

253. Sonia Lovecraft did, however, subsequently marry Dr. Nathaniel Davis in California—since she herself believed that she and Lovecraft had been divorced. Long widowed, she died in California on December 26, 1972, aged eighty-nine. She would have celebrated her ninetieth birthday on March 16, 1973.

254. [For more on Florence "Carol" Greene Weld (1902–1979), see R. Alain Everts, *Lovecraft's Daughter III* (1983).]

CHAPTER 23:

255. [*LR* 154 reads "Clutu," evidently revised by Cook for the Arkham House version.]

256. [See Lovecraft's letters to Duane Rimel (July 23, 1934, *SL* 5.10–11; *FLB* 194–195) and Willis Conover (August 20, 1936, *SL* 5.302; *RB* 388–389).]

CHAPTER 24:

257. [David E. Schultz' copiously annotated chapbook edition in two volumes fulfilled this wish in 1987, published by Necronomicon Press. (The weird fiction notes, omitted there as well as from *MW*, can now be found in *CE* 2.169–74, while the corrected text of the Commonplace Book itself is reproduced—however with only a few annotations—in *CE* 5.219–235; the remembrancer is given in 5.264).]

258. [David E. Schultz has deciphered the entry as "Man climbs mountain toward some horrible goal. Cloud passes over. Man seen no more." In the partially erased entry 63 he has deduced another name as "Nasht."]

259. We should really be more precise here. Holograph entries in manuscript (b) undoubtedly all predate May 7, 1934, when the manuscript was presented to Barlow. (With the possible exception of the last two entries, which may be in Barlow's hand.) Holograph entries in manuscript (c) undoubtedly all postdate May 7, 1934. Since entries 205–206 occur in manuscript (c) in holograph, their merger was a result of transcription by Arkham House, not by Barlow. The entries are separate in Barlow's 1937–1938 typescript (d), followed by the Futile Press for their edition. The annotations in the *SR* edition do not remark it, but I believe at least entry 206 is a definite precursor of themes found in "The Haunter of the Dark," i.e., Blake's intense concentration on the distant Starry Wisdom Church on Federal Hill in that story. It is evident that Lovecraft in real life loved to watch the city from his windows at 66 College Street (the obvious parallel to Blake's lodgings), too.

260. [The last Commonplace Book entry is the epigraph to John Buchan's book *Runagates Club*, taken from Stevenson's short story "Sing a Song of Sixpence." The epigraph to "The Call of Cthulhu" is from the tenth chapter of Blackwood's *The Centaur* (1911).]

261. [They are now included in *CE* 2.153–67.]

262. [The statement in *The Rim of the Unknown* is probably spurious, as there is no evidence to support the claim that Lovecraft authorized specific writers to use elements of what has come to be called the Cthulhu Mythos.]

263. [See Scott Connors, "The Commonplace Book: Its Use by Authors Other Than Lovecraft." *Kappa Alpha Tau*. Ed. Scott Connors. (Necronomicon Amateur Press Association, mailing 3, September 1976.)]

264. ["Orchid" is an error for "Druid" in *SL* 3.284; corrected in *MF* 1.144.]

265. [It seems that the deleted words in the Commonplace Book entry might instead read "Calef-kittie." If so, HPL's appellation presumably derives from the fact that at 79 North Main Street (at the foot of College Hill, the corner of Thomas Street and almost next to the Fleur-de-Lys building) in Providence there was a family market (grocery) operating under the name Calef Brothers (now demolished). Cf. HPL to Annie E. P. Gamwell, August 11, [1928] (ms., JHL).]

266. [See Smith's letter to Lovecraft of ca. October 24, 1930 (*Selected Letters of Clark Ashton Smith*, p. 128).]

267. My 1911 Providence House Directory shows the house of Mrs. John J. Banigan at 468 Angell Street, with Joseph Banigan and Richard E. Banigan (student) as boarders therein. Catherine G. Banigan (widow) has her house at 244 Angell Street and John B. Banigan boards at the same address. Persons further interested should check older directories at the Rhode Island Historical Society Library. I rather imagine that the Banigan brothers were Lovecraft's closest playmates during his very early boyhood; certainly, the Munroe boys (Chester and Harold) were his best friends from the beginning of the Slater Avenue era in 1898 until the end of the Great Meadow Country Clubhouse meetings in 1913 or so. However, according to the research of

R. Alain Everts, only Joseph of the three Banigans (Joseph, Richard E., and John B.) was the childhood friend of HPL.

CHAPTER 25:

268. [Olney Court extended from Olney Street to west of the North Main Street. (Note that Lovecraft utilized the name Olney for the protagonist of the story "The Strange High House in the Mist.") See Faig's *The Site of Joseph Curwen's Home in H. P. Lovecraft's The Case of Charles Dexter Ward* (2013).]

269. [The Col. Thomas Lloyd Halsey House at 140 Prospect Street (which Lovecraft moved to 100 Prospect Street for purposes of the story).]

270. [This church has now been determined to have been St. John's Catholic Church, which formerly stood on Atwells Avenue and was demolished in 1992.]

271. *Re* museums, whatever happened at the private museum of Col. George L. Shepley on Benefit Street which Lovecraft and his aunt Mrs. Clark visited on November 21, 1923 (see Lovecraft to Moe, November 24, 1923, *SL* 1.268)? According to George Wetzel's "Biographic Notes on Lovecraft" (*HPL*, p. 25), Lovecraft's other aunt, Mrs. Gamwell, was for some time librarian of the "Shapley [*sic*] Collection."

[The portrait resembling Lovecraft is evidently that of Commodore Abraham Whipple (1733–1819), his maternal ancestor.]

272. Lovecraft loved the grassy courts and other overtaken bits of countryside which once dotted College Hill far more numerously than they do today. I believe there is still an inner court off North Court Street; and there are bits of "countryside" below Prospect Terrace and adjoining the Weeds–Gerry Mansion.

[On the location of the "Garden House" at 66 College Street, see further Faig, "Can You Direct Me to Ely Court?: Some Notes on 66 College Street" in *Lovecraft Annual* No. 9 (2015): 54–69; and David E. Schultz, "66 College Street," *ibid.*, pp. 70–81.]

273. This is incorrect. The address of the movie theater is 270 Broadway. [*Author's note.*]

Bibliography

i. Kenneth W. Faig, Jr.

The following chronologically arranged bibliography should not be considered a complete register of works by and about Kenneth W. Faig, Jr., but merely a starting point toward a *catalogue raisonné*. A fair amount of items have probably escaped the attention of the editors; in particular, appearances of articles and essays on Arthur Machen seem to be lacking. Data on the issues of Faig's various amateur journals is also incomplete, and individual pieces printed in them have been noted only selectively. In other particulars, however, the bibliography is perhaps fairly comprehensive, containing a number of works giving further information on matters discussed in this book as well as many other topics that may be of interest to students of H. P. Lovecraft.

For works published by Faig's Moshassuck Press, details are primarily given in section II-B, cross-referenced from supplementary entries elsewhere. (The amount of copies printed [given in brackets] refer to initial printings, which may have included more than one state; in some cases, more copies may have been issued at a later date.) Note that no publication identified as No. 7 appears to have been issued in the Moshassuck Monograph Series. In compiling this listing, the kind assistance of John D. Haefele, Marcos Legaria, and the late Ned Brooks is gratefully acknowledged.

I. BOOKS AND PAMPHLETS WRITTEN

A. Fiction

1. *Tales of the Lovecraft Collectors*. Evanston, IL: Moshassuck Press, 1989 [II.B.5]. Rev. West Warwick, RI: Necronomicon Press, November 1995. 46 pp. [Contains four of the David Parkes Boynton stories (IV.C.2).]

2. *Life and Death: A Hoax and a Retraction*. Glenview, IL: Moshassuck Press, 1989 [II.B.6]. [Hoax story, reprinted in *Lovecraft's Pillow*.]

3. *Boy in Summer: Foster, Rhode Island, August 1896*. Glenview, IL: Moshassuck Press, 1996 [II.B.17]. [Commemorates Lovecraft's August 1896 visit to Foster.]

4. *From the Casebooks of Wilmott Watkyns, Psychic Investigator*. [EOD mailing 129 (Candlemas 2005): IV.C.11.]

5. *Lovecraft's Pillow and Other Strange Stories*. Glenview, IL: Moshassuck Press 2011 [II.B.35]. [Contains revised versions of the short stories "Life and Death," "A Bookseller's Romance," "Auto Traveller," "The Squirrel Pond," "A Pair of Old Shears," "Boy in Summer," "L. E.," "The Haunting of Huber's," "Lovecraft's Pillow," "Leng," "HDW," "Gothic Studies," "The Statement of Cornelius Felix," "The Man in the Window," "Rosenbluhme," together with an "Afterword" followed by "Sources."]

6. *Lovecraft's Pillow and Other Strange Stories*. New York: Hippocampus Press, August 2013. 234 pp. [A collection of Faig's best fiction, compiling an augmented version of the book *Tales of the Lovecraft Collectors*, selected stories from the Moshassuck Press edition of the same name, and the uncollected tale "Innsmouth 1984," omitted from the 2011 edition due to lack of copy text.]

B. Nonfiction

1. *Lovecraftian Voyages.* 1972/73. [Unpublished original monograph.]
2. *H. P. Lovecraft: His Life, His Work.* West Warwick, RI: Necronomicon Press, July 1979. 36 pp. [Contains "H. P. Lovecraft: A Biographical Sketch" and "Important Dates in the Life of H. P. Lovecraft" by Faig; also includes "A Chronology of Selected Works by Lovecraft" by S. T. Joshi and a picture insert. Faig's contributions translated in *Tutto Lovecraft 1: Azathoth* (ed. Gianni Pilo and Sebastiano Fusco; Rome: Fanucci, 1987), as "Lovecraft: la vita," "Lovecraft: le date;" *Tutti di Raconti 1: 1897–1922* (ed. Giuseppe Lippi; Milan: Arnoldo Mondadori, June 1989), as "Fortuna di Lovecraft," "Chronologia di Howard Phillips Lovecraft;" and *Lettere dall'Altrove: Epistolario 1915–1937* (ed. Giuseppe Lippi; Milan: Arnoldo Mondadori, October 1993), "Chronologia di Howard Phillips Lovecraft" only, as an appendix.]
3. *In Memoriam: Howard Phillips Lovecraft; Ethel M. Phillips Morrish.* Evanston IL: Moshassuck Press, 1987 [II.B.1]. (Commemorates the four mourners attending Lovecraft's funeral, especially Morrish [May 15, 1888–January 17, 1987], his last close relative.)
4. *The Parents of H. P. Lovecraft.* West Warwick, RI: Necronomicon Press, July 1990. 47 pp. Abridged version in *Der Einsiedler von Providence: Lovecrafts ungewöhnliches Leben* (ed. Frank Rottensteiner; Frankfurt am Main: Suhrkamp, 1992), pp. 37–38 (tr. by Jürgen Sander, as "Die Eltern Howard Phillips Lovecrafts"); *An Epicure in the Terrible: A Centennial Anthology of Essays in Honor of H. P. Lovecraft* (ed. David E. Schultz and S. T. Joshi; Rutherford, NJ: Fairleigh Dickinson University Press, 1991), pp. 45–77; rev. edition (New York: Hippocampus Press, 2011), pp. 43–76.
5. *Edward Francis Gamwell and His Family.* Glenview, IL: K. W. Faig, Lammas 1991. 50 pp. [50 copies. Also contains information on Lovecraft's aunt Annie E. P. Gamwell.]
6. *Some of the Descendants of Asaph Phillips and Esther Whipple of Foster, Rhode Island.* Glenview, IL: Moshassuck Press, 1993 [II.B.12].
7. *Corrections and Additions for Some of the Descendants of Asaph Phillips and Esther Whipple of Foster, Rhode Island.* Glenview, IL: Moshassuck Press, 1994 [II.B.14].
8. *When Grandma Went A-Courting: Ancestral Romance in the Poetry of Jennie E. T. Dowe and Edith Miniter.* Glenview, IL: Moshassuck Press, 1998 [II.B.21].
9. *A Centennial Remembrance: Samuel Joshua Steinberg, Born October 19, 1870, Indianapolis, Indiana; Died May 26, 1903, Alameda, California.* Glenview, IL: Kenneth W. Faig, Jr., 1998. 38 pp.
10. *Survey of Institutional Collections of Amateur Journals.* Glenview, IL: The Fossils, 1999. 46 pp. [Contains Faig's report on pp. 1–8. Libraries in the survey include: Milwaukee County Historical Society, New York Historical Society, Smith College Library, University of Tampa Library, University of Wisconsin-Madison Library, and Western Reserve Historical Society.]
11. *R. H. Barlow: An Account of the Life and Career of the Most Controversial Member of the Lovecraft Circle.* Columbia: SC: Dragonfly Press, 2000. In *The Unknown* Lovecraft, pp. 194–235.
12. *Big Heart: Remembering Robert Earl Hughes, 1926–1958.* Glenview, IL: Moshassuck Press, 2001 [II.B.27]. [On the person said to have been the heaviest man alive.]
13. *In Memoriam: Hyman Bradofsky, 1906–2002.* November 2002. 8 pp. [250 copies].

14. *Devonshire Ancestry of Howard Phillips Lovecraft*. With Chris J. Docherty and A. Langley Searles. Glenview, IL: Moshassuck Press, 2003 [II.B.28].

15. *The Dating of the Rebel Press Edition of a History of the Necronomicon*. Glenview, IL: Moshassuck Press, 2006 [II.B.30]. [Determines that the edition was issued in November 1937.]

16. *The Unknown Lovecraft: II: The Reluctant Laureate: Lovecraft and the Politics of NAPA's E. Dorothy Houtain Administration (1921–22)*. Glenview, IL: August 2006. 58 pp. In *The Unknown Lovecraft*, pp. 91–135.

17. *The Providence Amateur Press Club, 1914–1916*. Glenview, IL: Moshassuck Press, 2008 [II.B.31]; *The Providence Amateur Press Club, 1914–1916*. With David Haden. Moshassuck Press and Burslem Books, 2014. <http://www.jurn.org/providence_amateur_press_club_2nd_ed.pdf> [On the shortlived amateur press club of which Lovecraft was a member.]

18. *Qvae Amamvs Tvemvr: Ancestors in Lovecraft's Life and Fiction*. Glenview, IL: Moshassuck Press, 2008 [II.B.32]. In *The Unknown Lovecraft*, pp. 14–49. [Contains ancestor tables.]

19. *The Unknown Lovecraft*. New York: Hippocampus Press, 2009. 253 pp. [A collection of revised versions of Faig's essays; contains "Lovecraft: Artist or Poseur?," "Quae Amamus Teumur: Ancestors in Lovecraft's Life and Fiction," "Whipple V. Phillips and the Owyhee Land and Irrigation Company," "Lovecraft's Parental Heritage," "The Friendship of Louise Imogen Guiney and Sarah Susan Phillips," "The Unknown Lovecraft I: Political Operative," "The Unknown Lovecraft II: Reluctant Laureate," "Lovecraft's 'He'," "'The Silver Key' and Lovecraft's Childhood," "The Dream-Quest of Unknown Kadath," "Lovecraft's Unknown Friend: Dudley Charles Newton," "R. H. Barlow," "Robert H. Barlow as H. P. Lovecraft's Literary Executor: An Appreciation," as well as "Some Final Thoughts for Readers of This Collection."]

20. *George Elliott Lovecraft: Lost Scion of the House of Lovecraft*. Glenview, IL: Moshassuck Press, 2010 [II.B.34]. [On Lovecraft's second cousin.]

21. *The Site of Joseph Curwen's Home in H. P. Lovecraft's The Case of Charles Dexter Ward*. Glenview, IL: Moshassuck Press, 2013 [II.B.36].

II. BOOKS EDITED AND PUBLISHED

A. Editions of Works by Edith Miniter

1. *Going Home and Other Amateur Writings*. Glenview, IL: Moshassuck Press, 1995 [B.15]. 950 pp. [An extensive collection of Miniter's amateur press work.]

2. *The Coast of Bohemia and Other Writings*. Glenview, IL: Moshassuck Press, 2000 [B.26]. 972 pp. [Contains, among other work not included in the above volume, Miniter's professionally published novel *Our Natupski Neighbours* (Henry Holt and Company, 1916).]

3. *Two Poems*. (Epgephian Temple Press/The Hub, 2000). 5 pp. [Contains "Flanders Field Today" and "Dead Houses."]

4. *Dead Houses and Other Works*. Ed. with Sean Donnelly. New York: Hippocampus Press, 2008. 388 pp. [A selection of Miniter's best short fiction and amateur writings, including her Lovecraftian parody "Falco Ossifracus." Also contains material about Miniter by Lovecraft and others.]

5. *The Village Green and Other Pieces.* Ed. with Sean Donnelly. New York: Hippocampus Press, 2013. 363 pp. [Three novel fragments and selected short fiction and articles.]

B. Moshassuck Press Imprint

1. *In Memoriam: Howard Phillips Lovecraft; Ethel M. Phillips Morrish.* Evanston, IL: Moshassuck Press, March 15, 1987 [50 copies]. 12 pp. (Moshassuck Monograph Series No. 1.)
2. *Insidious Garden: A Look at Horror Fiction.* Edward W. O'Brien, Jr. Evanston, IL: Moshassuck Press, March 15, 1988 [75 copies]. 46 pp. Moshassuck Monograph Series No. 2. [Reprinted in facsimile from the August 6, 1987 issue of the Catholic newspaper *The Wanderer*; with a preface by Faig discussing unfavorable criticism of Lovecraft.]
3. *Within the Circle: In Memoriam Franklin Lee Baldwin, born March 26, 1913, Asotin, Washington, died August 30, 1987, Moscow, Idaho.* Franklin Lee Baldwin, Josephine Richardson, Kenneth W. Faig, Duane W. Rimel, and August W. Derleth. Evanston, IL: Moshassuck Press, September 30, 1988 [75 copies]. 100 pp. Moshassuck Monograph Series No. 3. [Compiles material by and about the Lovecraft associate F. Lee Baldwin; with a preface by Faig.]
4. *The Forbidden Room and How the Forbidden Room Happened.* Duane W. Rimel. Evanston, IL: Moshassuck Press, September 30, 1988 [75 copies]. 19 pp. Moshassuck Monograph Series No. 4. [Reprints Rimel's short story from *Fanciful Tales* (1934) together with Rimel's comments and a preface by Faig.]
5. *Tales of the Lovecraft Collectors.* Evanston, IL: Moshassuck Press, January 20, 1989 [25 copies]. 77 pp. [Collects fiction originally published in *Moshassuck Review* (EOD) between 1979 and 1988. Reissued by Necronomicon Press in 1995 (I.A.1).]
6. *Life and Death: A Hoax and a Retraction.* Glenview, IL: Moshassuck Press, April 1989 [19 copies]. 7 pp. ["Nineteen copies of *De Tenebris* #2 containing the hoax were uncovered during the relocation of the [Moshassuck] Press from Evanston to Glenview, Illinois and bound with a photocopy of the retraction for the patrons of the Press April 1989."]
7. *Howard Phillips Lovecraft and Nils Helmer Frome: A Recollection of One of Canada's Oldest Science Fiction Fans.* Sam Moskowitz. Glenview, IL: Moshassuck Press, May 1989 [110 copies]. 167 pp. Moshassuck Monograph Series No. 5. [On the Lovecraft associate; includes photos, Lovecraft's letters to Frome, and a publisher's preface by Faig. A 1p. "Added and Corrigenda" also issued.]
8. *To Yith and Beyond.* Duane W. Rimel. Glenview, IL: Moshassuck Press, February 1990 [125 copies]. 112 pp. [Collects Rimel's "best fantastic fiction and supernatural poetry": "The Disinterment," "The Metal Chamber," "The City Under the Sea," "Jungle Princess," "Norton and I," "The Tale of Rondo and Ilana," "The Small, Dark Thing," "The Sorcery of Aphlar" [fiction]; and "Contradiction," "Mood," "The Snake," "Across the River," "Estranged," "Fatality," "The Little Ones," "The Whisperer," "Wind from the River," "Reverie," "Dreams of Yith," "Late Revenge" [poems]. Contains an introduction by Faig.]
9. *The Recluse, 1927.* Ed. W. Paul Cook. Glenview, IL: Moshassuck Press, 1990 [125 copies]. 79 pp. [A facsimile edition of the only issue of Cook's magazine.]
10. *Young Ronan: A Lovecraftian Tale.* Edward W. O'Brien. Glenview, IL: Moshassuck Press, May 1991 [60 copies]. 18 pp. [Reproduces handwritten ms. of a story published in *Crypt of Cthulhu* 9, No. 6 (73, St. John's Eve 1990).]

11. *The Miskatonic: Lovecraft Centenary Edition.* Glenview, IL: Moshassuck Press, May 1991 [97 copies]. 652 pp. [Reprints in facsimile the entire run of Dirk W. Mosig's EOD fanzine [1973–79] together with an introduction and indices by Faig; 2 vols.]

12. *Some of the Descendants of Asaph Phillips and Esther Whipple of Foster, Rhode Island.* Glenview, IL: Moshassuck Press, 1993 [125 copies]. 332 pp. [Contains preface, ancestor table, photos, bibliography, and an index.]

13. *Early Historical Accounts of Foster, Rhode Island.* Charles C. Beaman and Casey B. Tyler. Glenview, IL: Moshassuck Press, 1993 [100 copies]. 125 pp. [Contains Beaman's *Sketches of Foster* (from the *Providence Journal,* 1858–1859, seventeen installments) and Tyler's *Historical Reminiscences of Foster* (from the *Pawtuxet Valley Gleaner* 1892–1893, twenty-one installments) together with a preface and indices by Faig.]

14. *Corrections and Additions for Some of the Descendants of Asaph Phillips and Esther Whipple of Foster, Rhode Island.* Glenview, IL: Moshassuck Press, 1994 [100? copies]. 13 pp. [Includes an introduction.]

15. *Going Home and Other Amateur Writings.* Edith Miniter. Glenview, IL: Moshassuck Press, June 1995 [100 copies, printed by Anundsen Publishing Co.]. 950 pp. [Contains an introduction and a bibliography by Faig; hardbound.]

16. *Susan's Obituary: Sketches of New England Life I.* Franklin Chase Clark. Glenview, IL: Moshassuck Press, 1996 [100 copies, printed by Anundsen Publishing Co]. 196 pp. [A previously unpublished short novel, illustrated by Robert H. Knox; contains a sketch of the author and a bibliography by Faig; hardbound.]

17. *Boy in Summer: Foster, Rhode Island, August 1896.* Glenview, IL: Moshassuck Press, 1996 [100 copies]. 4 pp.

18. *Three Poems of the Supernatural.* Ray Hchkavik Zorn. September 1997 [200 copies]. 4 pp. [By the publisher of *The Lovecraft Collector.*]

19. *Criticism of Amateur Verse: A Selection from the Critical Department of the National Amateur.* H. P. Lovecraft. Glenview, IL: Moshassuck Press, 1998 [100 copies]. 48 pp. [Reprints amateur press material, some in facsimile; contains an introduction by Faig.]

20. *The Ideal Amateur Paper: A Symposium.* Ralph W. Babcock, Ernest A. Edkins, H. P. Lovecraft, Robie M. Macauley. Glenview, IL: Moshassuck Press, 1998 [100 copies]. 12 pp. [A reprint of "Defining the 'Ideal' Paper." *The National Amateur* 62, No. 3 (June 1940). Contains an introduction by Faig.]

21. *When Grandma Went A-Courting: Ancestral Romance in the Poetry of Jennie E. T. Dowe and Edith Miniter.* Glenview, IL: Moshassuck Press, March 1998 [25 copies]. 14 pp. Moshassuck Monograph Series No. 6.

22. *Observations on Amateur Verse.* H. P. Lovecraft. Glenview, IL: Moshassuck Press, Christmas 1998 [300 copies]. 4 pp. [Excerpt of a letter by Lovecraft to Edwin Hadley Smith (10 March 1933). Reprinted from "Lovecraft on Poetry Writing." *Boys Herald* 71, No. 1 (Point Pleasant, NJ: October 1941): 7–8.]

23. *The United's Policy 1920–1921.* Alfred Galpin and H. P. Lovecraft. Glenview, IL: Moshassuck Press, St. Valentine's Day 1999 [300 copies]. 4 pp. [Reprinted from *Zenith* (ed. George Julian Houtain; January 1921); with "Commentary" by Faig.]

24. *Two Views of Lovecraft.* W. Paul Cook and William J. Clemence. Glenview, IL: Moshassuck Press, 1999 [300 copies]. 4 pp. [excerpt from Cook's *In Memorium: Howard Phillips Lovecraft—Recollections, Appreciations, Estimates* concerning William J. Clemence (*LR*

140–141); comments by Clemence reprinted from his *After Hours*. No. 4. Providence, RI: November 1937.]

25. *Memories of an Old Girl*. Louise Imogen Guiney. Glenview, IL: Moshassuck Press, June 1999 [25 copies]. 9 pp. [Reprints a piece originally written for the reunion of the Elmhurst Alumnae Association in April 1907; contains photos.]

26. *The Coast of Bohemia and Other Writings*. Edith Miniter. Glenview, IL: Moshassuck Press, November 2000 [100 copies, printed by Anundsen Publishing Co]. 972 pp. [Includes photographs, an introduction and other ancillary material by Faig.]

27. *Big Heart: Remembering Robert Earl Hughes, 1926–1958*. Glenview, IL: Moshassuck Press, June 2001 [25 copies]. 48pp. (Moshassuck Monograph Series No. 8.)

28. Chris J. Docherty, A. Langley Searles, and Kenneth W. Faig, Jr. *Devonshire Ancestry of Howard Phillips Lovecraft*. Glenview, IL: Moshassuck Press, 2003 [110 copies]. 46 pp. Moshassuck Monograph Series No. 9.

29. *A Cornish Legend*. S. Baring-Gould. Glenview, IL: Moshassuck Press, May 2005 [200 copies]. 3 pp. [One folio, with dialogue excerpt from Baring-Gould's *Mrs. Curgenven of Curgenven* (1893) on the inner pages, and Faig's publisher's note on the last page.]

30. *The Dating of the Rebel Press Edition of a History of the Necronomicon*. Glenview, IL: Moshassuck Press, 2006 [? copies]. 38 pp. Moshassuck Monograph Series No. 10.

31. *The Providence Amateur Press Club, 1914–1916*. Glenview, IL: Moshassuck Press, 2008 [25 copies]. 38 pp. Moshassuck Monograph Series No. 11.

32. *Qvae Amamvs Tvemvr: Ancestors in Lovecraft's Life and Fiction*. Glenview, IL: Moshassuck Press 2008 [75 copies]. 30 pp. Moshassuck Monograph Series No. 12.

33. *Leviathan: Some Notes on Martin Blimp Levy 1905–1961*. Glenview, IL: Moshassuck Press, 2009 [30 copies]. 30 pp. Moshassuck Monograph Series No. 13. [On the professional fat man and wrestler; contains facsimile pages.]

34. *George Elliott Lovecraft: Lost Scion of the House of Lovecraft*. Glenview, IL: Moshassuck Press, May 31, 2010 [25 copies]. 22 pp. Moshassuck Monograph Series No. 14. [Contains an appendix of facsimile plates. In memory of A. Langley Searles and Christopher J. Docherty.]

35. *Lovecraft's Pillow and Other Strange Stories*. Glenview, IL: Moshassuck Press 2011 [30 copies and a second corrected printing (2013) of 15 copies]. 120 pp. [Reissued with other material by Hippocampus Press in 2013 (I.A.6).]

36. *The Site of Joseph Curwen's Home in H. P. Lovecraft's The Case of Charles Dexter Ward*. Jason C. Eckhardt and Kenneth W. Faig, Jr. Glenview, IL: Moshassuck Press, 2013 [25 copies]. 57 pp. Moshassuck Monograph series No. 15. [Erratum for p. 12 also issued. Announced as "likely … the last of the Moshassuck Monograph Series."]

37. *Miss Edna Winsor Lewis Born January 31, 1868, Providence, Rhode Island Died April 17, 1955, Westborough, Massachusetts*. Glenview, IL: Moshassuck Press, 2015 [e-book]. Moshassuck Monograph Series No. 16.

III. JOURNALS EDITED

A. Amateur Press

EOD = The Esoteric Order of Dagon (founded 1973); FAPA = The Fantasy Amateur Press Association (founded 1937); NAPA = The National Amateur Press Association (founded 1876); NECRONOMICON = The H. P. Lovecraft Amateur Press Association (1976–1982).

1. *The Moshassuck Review.* No. 1 (Candlemas 1973); No. 2 (Roodmas 1973); No. 3 (Lammas 1973); No. 4 (1974); No. 5 (Lammas 1974); No. 6 (Roodmas 1975); No. 7 (Hallowmas 1975); No. 8 (Candlemas 1976); No. 9 (Lammas 1976); No. 10 (December 6, 1975); No. 11 (July 1977); No. 12 (February 1978); No. 13 (Summer 1978); No. 14 (December 1978); No. 15 (1979); No. 16 (1979)]; No. 17 (December 1979); No. 18 (February 1980); No. 19 (February 1981); No. 20 (August 1981); No. 21 (October 1981); No. 22 (February 1982); No. 23 (August 1982); No. 24 (February 1983); No. 25 (August 1983); No. 26 (February 1984); No. 27 (August 1984); No. 28 (February 1985); No. 29 (August 1985); No. 30 (February 1986; combined with the final issue of *De Tenebris* [q.v.] and a joint "Special Correction of Past Errors and Omissions Issue" dated November 1985); No. 31 (August 1986). The following issues unnumbered: Candlemas, Summer 1987; February, May Eve 1988; March, Summer, Hallowmas 1989; February, August, October 1990; Candlemas, April, August, Hallowmas 1991; Candlemas, May Eve, Hallowmas 1992; Candlemas, May Eve 1993; June 23, 1993; October 2, 1993; November 27, 1993 (Candlemas 1994); May Eve, Lammas, Hallowmas 1994; Candlemas, May, August, October 1995; February, August, May, November 1996; May, August, November 1997; February 1998. [EOD; replaced by *The Snake Den*.]

2. *The United Co-operative.* No. 1 (October 1973); No. 2 (December 1973)]. No. 3 (February 1974). [EOD; co-edited with R. Alain Everts and David E. Schultz.]

3. *The Ghoul's Court Advertiser.* No. 1 (March 1975).

4. *De Tenebris.* No. 1 (August 30, 1976); No. 2 (December 5, 1976); No. 3 (March 11, 1977); No. 4 (1977); No. 5 (1977); No. 6 (December 14, 1979); No. 7 (September 1981); No. 8 (1982); No. 9 (?); No. 10 (March 10, 1985). [Necronomicon; Nos. 3, 4, and additional issues dated September 1, 1985 (combined with *Moshassuck Review* No. 30) also in EOD mailings (Lammas 1977, Candlemas 1978, and 1986, respectively).]

5. *Tekeli-li.* No. 1 (November 1976); No. 2 (August 1977); No. 3 (1978); No. 4 (1979); No. 5 (1980?); No. 6 (1981); No. 7 (1982?); No. 8 (1983); No. 9 (1984?); No. 10 (1985?); No. 11 (1986?); No. 12 (1987?); No. 13 (1988?); No. 14 (1990?). [FAPA.]

6. *Dunwich.* Lammas 1977.

7. *More Than Meets the Ear: An Occasional Journal.* No. 1 (February 1996); No. 2 (July 1996); No. 3 (August 1996); [...]; No. 8 (January 2001) [Fossilbed (an amateur press association bundle circulated by Guy Miller, supporting The Fossils); "largely devoted to Edith Miniter."]

8. *Leather or Prunella: A Journal of Indifferent Stuff.* No. 1 (May 1996); No. 2 (December 1996); No. 3 (May 1997); No. 4 (September 1997); No. 5 (March 1998); No. 6 (June 1998); No. 7 (December 1998); No. 8 (May 1999); No. 9 (October 1999); No. 10 (February 2000). [NAPA; title derived from Pope's *An Essay on Man* (1734), IV.203.]

9. *The Pear Tree.* No. 1 (December 1996); No. 2 (April 1997); No. 3 (November 1997); No. 4 (March 1998); No. 5 (September 1998); No. 6 (May 1999); No. 7 (December 1999); No.

8 (November 2000); No. 9 (February 2001). ["An occasional journal devoted to the descendants of Asaph and Esther (Whipple) Phillips of Foster, Rhode Island and related families."]

10. *The Snake Den.* No. 1 (May 1998); No. 2 (1998); No. 3 (November 1998); No. 4 (1999); No. 5 (May 1999); No. 6 (1999); No. 7 (1999); No. 8 (2000?); No. 9 (May 2000); No. 11 (2000); No. 12 (Candlemas 2001); No. 13 (May 2001); No. 14 (November 2001); No. 15 (Candlemas 2002); No. 16 (May Eve 2002); No. 17. August 2002.; No. 18. October 2002.; No. 19. May 2003.; No. 20. August 2003.; No. 21 (November 2003); No. 22. May 2004.; No. 23. August 2004. No. 24 (May Eve 2005). [EOD; replaced *The Moshassuck Review*, and itself replaced by *EOD Letter*.]

11. *Moshassuck Chat.* 1999. [EOD mailing 106.]

12. *The Hub Club: One Hundredth Tenth Anniversary. March 10, 1890–March 10, 2000.* March 2000 (Epgephian Temple Press/The Hub). [NAPA.]

13. *Aftermath* No. 1 (September 2001); No. 2 (August 2002); *Aftermath Supplement* (September 2002). [NAPA; No. 2 and Supplement also in EOD mailings 119 and 120, respectively.]

14. *The Fossil: Official Publication of The Fossils, Inc., Historians of Amateur Journalism.* Official editor from 101, No. 1 (322, October 2004) to 108, No. 4 (353, July 2012) [32 issues].

15. *A Bicentenary Commemoration.* Hallowmas 2005. [EOD mailing 132.]

16. *EOD Letter.* No. 1 (Hallowmas 2005); No. 2 (Candlemas 2006); No. 3 (Candlemas 2007); No. 4 (May Eve 2007); No. 5 (Lammas 2007); No. 6 (Hallowmas 2007); No. 7 (Candlemas 2008); No. 8 (Hallowmas 2008); No. 9 (Candlemas 2009); No. 10 (May Eve 2009); No. 11 (Lammas 2009); No. 12 (Hallowmas 2009); No. 13 (Candlemas 2010); No. 14 (May Eve 2010); No. 15 (Lammas 2010); No. 16 (Hallowmas 2010); No. 17 (Candlemas 2011); No. 18 (May Eve 2011); No. 19 (Lammas 2011); No. 20 (Hallowmas 2011); No. 21 (Candlemas 2012); No. 22 (May Eve 2012); No. 23 (Lammas 2012); No. 24 (Hallowmas 2012); No. 25 (Candlemas 2013); No. 26 (May Eve 2013); No. 27 (Lammas 2013); No. 28 (Hallowmas 2013); No. 29 (May Eve 2014). [EOD; replaced *The Snake Den*.]

17. *Occasional Essays.* No.1 (March 2007); No. 2 (January 2009); No. 3 (December 2011). [NAPA; also circulated in EOD.]

18. *Celebrating the One Hundredth Anniversary of the Birth of Harry Kern Brobst February 11, 1909, Wilmington, Delaware.* Candlemas, 2009. [EOD mailing 145.]

19. *Analecta Genealogica Lovecraftiana.* No. 1 (March 2015). ["An occasional electronic journal devoted to the history of the Lovecraft and Lovecroft families."]

In addition to miscellaneous notices, an "Editor's Notebook" appeared in the following issues of *The Fossil* edited by Faig (titled "Official Editor's Report" and "Editor's Notes" in the first and second instance, respectively):

101, No. 1 (322, October 2004): 3–4; No. 2 (323, January 2005): 13; No. 4 (325, July 2005): 15–16.

102, No. 1 (326, October 2005): 18–19; No. 2 (327, January 2006): 14–15.

103, No. 1 (330, October 2006): 23–24.

104, No. 2 (335, January 2008): 28; No. 3 (336, April 2008): 35–36.

105, No. 2 (339, January 2009): 22–23; No. 3 (340, April 2009): 12–13; No. 4 (341, July 2009): 50–52.

106, No. 1 (342, October 2009): 15–16; No. 3 (344, April 2010): 16–17; No. 4 (345, July 2010): 24–25.

107, No. 1 (346, October 2010): 12; No. 2 (347, January 2011): 31–32; No. 3 (348, April 2011): 19–20; No. 4 (349, July 2011): 15–16.

108, No. 1 (350, October 2011): 18–19; No. 2 (351, January 2012): 20–21; No. 3 (352, April 2012): 18; No. 3 (352, April 2012): 18; No. 4 (353, July 2012): 29–30.

IV. CONTRIBUTIONS TO BOOKS AND PERIODICALS

A. Essays and Introductions

1. "A Lovecraftian Note." *Dark Brotherhood Journal* 1, No. 1 (June 1971): 10–12. (Ed. George H. Record. Albuquerque, NM.) [On the mentions of Lovecraft in school yearbooks.]
2. "A Note Regarding the Harold Farnese Musical Pieces." *Dark Brotherhood Journal* 1, No. 1 (June 1971): 12–14.
3. "The Lovecraft Circle: A Glossary." *Mirage* No. 10 (1971): 27–40. (Ed. Jack L. Chalker. [Baltimore?], MD.) [A listing of brief biographical entries for many of Lovecraft's acquaintances.]
4. "The Lovecraft Fiction Manuscripts: A Listing [Part 1]." *Nyctalops* 1, No. 5 (October 1971): 28–36. (Ed. Harry O. Morris, Jr. Albuquerque, NM: Silver Scarab Press.)
5. "Lovecraft's Providence." *Tamlacht* 2, No. 2 (12, n. d. [December 1971?]): 4–9. (Ed. Victor Boruta & Alfred A. Attanasio. Linden, NJ: Victor Boruta and Alfred A. Attanasio.)
6. "The Lovecraft Fiction Manuscripts: A Listing [Part 2]." *Nyctalops* 1, No. 6 (February 1972): 35–39.
7. "Howard Phillips Lovecraft: The Early Years, 1890–1914 [Part 1]." *Nyctalops* 2, No. 1 (8, April 1973): 3–9, 13–15. Tr. by Franz Rottensteiner as "Howard Phillips Lovecrafts frühe Jahre 1890–1914." In *Die dunkle Seite der Wirklichkeit: Aufsätze zur Phantastik [The Dark Side of Reality: Essays on Fantasy]* (Frankfurt-am-Main: Suhrkamp, 1987), pp. 228–74.
8. "A Quaff of Arthur Machen." *Moebius Trip Library: Science Fiction Echo* No. 17 (May 1973.): 82–92. (Ed. Edward C. Connor. Peoria, IL.)
9. "Lovecraft's Own Book of Weird Fiction." *The HPL Supplement* No. 2 (July 1973): 4–14. (Ed. Meade and Penny Frierson. Birmingham, AL.) [On Lovecraft's letters to the "Sideshow" column in the *Providence Journal*.]
10. "Readings." *Ambrosia* No. 2 (August 1973): 10. (Ed. Alan Gullette. Gullette Publishing.) [A column installment.]
11. "Whipple van Buren Phillips: A Portrait." *United Co-Operative* 1, No. 1 (Dec. 1918 [*sic*; 1973]; ed. R. Alain Everts.) [An excerpt from I.B.1.]
12. [Untitled.] *Moshassuck Review* (May 19, 1974): 2–12. [On *The Shunned House* book.]
13. "Howard Phillips Lovecraft: The Early Years, 1890–1914 [Part 2]." *Nyctalops* 2, No. 2 (9, July 1974): 34–44.
14. [Untitled.] *Moshassuck Review* (September 15, 1974): 1–11. [On Lovecraft's lost fiction.]

15. [Untitled.] *Moshassuck Review* (January 5, 1975): 1–12. [On Lovecraft's appearances in Providence newspapers.]
16. "Howard Phillips Lovecraft: The Early Years, 1890–1914: A Bibliography." *Nyctalops* 2, No. 3 (10, January–February 1975): 46–49, 54.
17. "HPL: The Book That Nearly Was." *Xenophile* No. 11 (March 1975):118–123. (Ed. Nils Hardin. St. Louis, MO.) [Also distributed in the Pulp Era Amateur Press Society mailing No. 12 (1990). On R. H. Barlow's intended edition of Lovecraft's *Fungi from Yuggoth*.]
18. [Untitled.] *Moshassuck Review* (December 6, 1975): 1–15. [On Lovecraft's destroyed fiction.]
19. "A Note and an Anecdote." *Myrddin* No. 3 (1976): 24–27. (Northbrook, IL: Lawson W. Hill.) [On the Driftwind Press edition of Lovecraft's *The Materialist Today*.]
20. [Untitled.] *De Tenebris* No. 3 (March 11, 1977): 15–24. [On Lovecraft's Dunwich.]
21. "Lovecraft: A Biographical Sketch." *Cynick* 1, No. 3 (September 1977; ed. S. T. Joshi.)
22. "[Foreword:] Robert H. Barlow and H. P. Lovecraft: A Reflection." In R. H. Barlow's *Annals of the Jinns* (West Warwick, RI: Necronomicon Press, 1978), pp. 1–6.
23. "R. H. Barlow." *Journal of the H. P. Lovecraft Society* No. 2 (1979): 7–34. (Ed. Scott Connors. South Heights, PA: H. P. Lovecraft Society.) [Part 1 only; whole text published as I.B.11; in *The Unknown Lovecraft* (I.B.19), pp. 194–234.]
24. [Untitled.] *De Tenebris* No. 6 (December 14, 1979). [On Edith Miniter and her relations with H. P. Lovecraft.]
25. "H. P. Lovecraft: His Life and Work." (With S. T. Joshi.) In *H. P. Lovecraft: Four Decades of Criticism* (ed. S. T. Joshi; Athens, OH: Ohio University Press, 1980), pp. 1–19. [Japanese translation of the book issued by Kokusho-Kankokai in 1983–84 (Tokyo, 2 vols.).]
26. "About Bram." *Romantist* No. 4/5 (1980–1981): 39–40. [On Bram Stoker.]
27. "In Memoriam: J. Vernon Shea." *Moshassuck Review* No. 20 (August 1981).
28. "A Note on the Religious Affiliations of the Phillips Family." *Moshassuck Review* No. 24 (February 1983).
29. "The Editor Visits the Sacred City." *Moshassuck Review* No. 27 (August 1984).
30. "The Revision of Dracula." *Count Dracula Fan Club Annual* 5, No. 1 (1985). (Ed. Tom Peck. Flushing, NY: Amity Hallmark.)
31. "A Lovecraft Reference Shelf AD 2001." *Moshassuck Review* No. 29 (August 1985).
32. "A Letter of Comment for the Necronomicon APA." *De Tenebris* (September 1, 1985).
33. "The Editor Revisits The Sacred City." *Moshassuck Review* No.30 (February 1986).
34. "A Relative of Howard P. Lovecraft passes: Roy A Morrish, Jr." *Moshassuck Review* No. 31 (August 1986).
35. "The Howard Family; Or, The Pawtuxet Valley Gleaner Redivivus." *Moshassuck Review* No. 31 (August 1986).
36. "Ethel M. Phillips Morrish: May 15, 1888–January 17, 1987." *Crypt of Cthulhu* 6, No. 5 (47, Roodmas 1987): 51–53. [Obituary of Lovecraft's second cousin.]
37. "Biographische Schriften zu H. P. Lovecraft: Ein Literaturüberblick." *Quarber Merkur* 25, No. 1 (67, July 1987): 28–36. As "Biographical Writing on H. P. Lovecraft: A Review of the Literature." *Lovecraft Studies* No. 19/20 (Fall 1989): 42–48.
38. [Obituary of Donald Wandrei.] *Moshassuck Review* (February 1988).

39. "F. Lee Baldwin." *Locus* 21, No. 5 (328, May 1988): 68. (Ed. Charles N. Brown. Oakland, CA: Locus Publications.) [Obituary.]
40. "Whipple V. Phillips and the Owyhee Land and Irrigation Company." *Owyhee Outpost* No. 19 (May 1988): 21–30. (Murphy, ID: Owyhee County Historical Society). In *The Unknown Lovecraft* [I.B.19], pp. 50–55.
41. "Lovecraft's Ancestors." *Crypt of Cthulhu* 7, No. 7 (57, St. John's Eve 1988): 19–25.
42. "Publisher's Preface." *Insidious Garden: A Look at Horror Fiction* [II.B.2].
43. "Publisher's Preface." *Within the Circle: In Memoriam Franklin Lee Baldwin* [II.B.3].
44. "Publisher's Preface." *The Forbidden Room and How the Forbidden Room Happened* [II.B.4].
45. "Robert H. Barlow as H. P. Lovecraft's Literary Executor: An Appreciation." *Crypt of Cthulhu* 8, No. 1 (60, Hallowmas 1988): 52–62. In *The Unknown Lovecraft* [I.B.19], pp. 235–48.
46. "Whipple V. Phillips and Masonry." *Moshassuck Review* (Candlemas 1989).
47. "Back To Wilbraham." *Moshassuck Review* (Candlemas 1989).
48. "Whipple V. Phillips at the Paris Universal Exposition of 1878." *Moshassuck Review* (Summer 1989).
49. "Introduction." *To Yith and Beyond* [II.B.8], p. 1.
50. "To Whom Does HPL Belong?" *Moshassuck Review* (August 1990).
51. "HPL and Commodore Abraham Whipple." *Moshassuck Review* (August 1990).
52. "Lovecraft: Artist or Poseur?" *Providence Sunday Journal Magazine* (ed. Elliot Krieger; August 5, 1990): 11–12 (abridged, as "His Loneliness"). *Lovecraft Studies* No. 22/23 (Fall 1990): 46–49. (As part of "Six Views of Lovecraft"). *Etudes Lovecraftiennes* No. 9 (Christmas 1990): 5–10. (Ed. Joseph Altaraic; tr. by "Etienne Roulet" as "Lovecraft, artiste ou poseur?") In *The Unknown Lovecraft* [I.B.19], pp. 9–13.
53. "The H. P. Lovecraft Centennial Conference." *Moshassuck Review* (Hallowmas 1990).
54. "Heaven and Hell: Abnormal Mental States in 'N' and 'The Exalted Omega'." *Machenalia* 1, No. 1 (October 1990): 31–67. (Ed. R. B. Russell. Lewes, UK: Tartarus Press. Newsletter of the Friends of Arthur Machen.)
55. "The Centennial Year Draws To A Close." *Moshassuck Review* (Candlemas 1991).
56. "Lovecraft's Parents." *The H. P. Lovecraft Centennial Conference: Proceedings* (West Warwick, RI: Necronomicon, March 1991), pp. 24–25. [Transcript of a panel discussion.]
57. "Some Further Thoughts Concerning Winfield Scott Lovecraft." *Moshassuck Review* (May Eve 1991).
58. "Some Errata for The Parents Of Howard Phillips Lovecraft." *Moshassuck Review* (May Eve 1991).
59. "Edward F. Gamwell: Preface." *Moshassuck Review* (August 1991).
60. "Lovecraft Sexual Orientation." *Moshassuck Review* (Hallowmas 1991).
61. "H. P. Lovecraft and Mowbra Castle." *Moshassuck Review* (Hallowmas 1991).
62. "Some Addenda and Corrigenda for Edward Francis Gamwell and his Family." *Moshassuck Review* (Candlemas 1992).
63. "The Phillips Family of Kingstown, Rhode Island." *Moshassuck Review* (Candlemas 1992).

64. "Observations on the Luminous Appearance of the River Water at Providence on the Night Following the 16 of Sept. A.D. 1784." *Moshassuck Review* (Candlemas 1992). Tr. by Joseph Altaraic as "Observations sur un phénomène lumineux apparu à Providence dans l'eau de la rivière, au cours de la nuit du 16 September 1784." *Etudes Lovecraftiennes* No. 11 ("Epiphanie 1992"): 16–23.
65. "Lovecraft's Last Yeoman Farmer Ancestor." *Moshassuck Review* (Candlemas 1992).
66. "The Ancestors of Howard Phillips Lovecraft: Working Towards Ahnentafel." *Moshassuck Review* (May 1992): 7–71.
67. "'The Silver Key' and Lovecraft's Childhood." *Crypt of Cthulhu* 11, No. 3 (81, St. John's Eve 1992.): 11–47. In *A Century Less a Dream: Selected Criticism on H. P. Lovecraft* (ed. Scott Connors; Holicong, PA: Wildside Press, 2002), pp. 10–44; *The Unknown Lovecraft* [I.B.19], pp. 148–82. [Extensive discussion of Lovecraft's visits to Foster, R.I., and their influence on the story.]
68. "Lovecraft's Ancestry Revisited." *Moshassuck Review* (Candlemas 1993).
69. "Howard Phillips Lovecraft: Some Royal Lines of Descent." *Moshassuck Review* (May Eve 1993): 7–23.
70. "A Source For 'The Drinking Song' From 'The Tomb'?" *Moshassuck Review* (Hallowmas 1993).
71. "A Necronomicon Convention Report." *Moshassuck Review* (Hallowmas 1993).
72. "Silver Key Sidelights." (Candlemas 1994).
73. "Some Thoughts about the Origins of the Phillips Family." (Candlemas 1994).
74. "A Day I'd Like to Have Spent at Brown University." (Candlemas 1994).
75. "Thanksgiving with Belknap Long." (Candlemas 1994).
76. "Some Thoughts on Louise Imogen Guiney." *Moshassuck Review* (May Eve 1994): 1–15.
77. "Whipple V. Phillips and Greene, Rhode Island." *Moshassuck Review* (May Eve 1994).
78. "The Aunts, Uncles and Cousins of Asaph Phillips." *Moshassuck Review* (Hallowmas 1994).
79. "Lovecraft's Parental Heritage." *Books at Brown* No 28/29 (1991/1992 [*sic*; 1995]): 43–65. (Ed. John H. Stanley. Providence, RI: Friends of the Library of Brown University.) In *The Unknown Lovecraft* [I.B.19], pp. 56–69. [Revision of A.56.]
80. "Introduction." *Tales of the Lovecraft Collectors* [I.A.1], pp. 5–8.
81. "Good-Bye, Frank and Lyda." *Moshassuck Review* (Candlemas 1995).
82. "The Impact of the Fulford Will on Lovecraft's Claims of Fulford Ancestry." *Moshassuck Review* (August 1996): 1–3.
83. "The Lovecrafts and the Guineys." *Moshassuck Review* (November 1996): 1–5.
84. "Lovecraft's 'He'." *Lovecraft Studies* No. 37 (Fall 1997): 17–25. (Ed. S. T. Joshi. West Warwick, RI: Necronomicon Press.). In *The Unknown Lovecraft* [I.B.19], pp. 136–47.
85. "In Memoriam: Victor E. Bacon 1905–1997." *Moshassuck Review* (November 1997): 8–9.
86. "In Memoriam: Duane Weldon Rimel." *Moshassuck Review* (November 1997): 10–11.
87. "Necronomicon Third Edition: A Convention Report." *Moshassuck Review* (November 1997): 13–15.
88. "The Friendship of Louise Imogen Guiney and Sarah Susan Phillips." *Crypt of Cthulhu* 18, No. 1 (100, Hallowmas 1998): 19–32, 15. In *The Unknown Lovecraft* [I.B.19], pp. 70–86.

89. "The Unknown Lovecraft I: Political Operative." *Crypt of Cthulhu* 19, No. 1. (103, 1999): 13–15. In *The Unknown Lovecraft* [I.B.19], pp. 87–90. [On DeMarest Lloyd and Lovecraft.]

90. "Lovecraft's Sonnet Cycle: *Fungi from Yuggoth*." *Saat von den Sternen* / *Fungi from Yuggoth*. Tr. by Michael Siefener (as "Lovecrafts Sonett-Zyklus: *Fungi from Yuggoth*"). Bellheim: Edition Phantasia, 1999. [A bilingual illustrated edition; 200 copies.]

91. "An Amateur Journalist Sighting?" *Leather or Prunella* No. 9 (October 1999): 1–4.

92. "An Early Amateur Clerihew?—Not!" *Leather or Prunella* No. 10 (February 2000): 1–2.

93. "R. H. Barlow: A Selected Bibliography." *Continuity* (New Series) No. 5 (February 2000; Columbia, SC): 16–23. Rev. (with Scott Connors) as "Selected Bibliography" in *R. H. Barlow: An Account of the Life and Career of the Most Controversial Member of the Lovecraft Circle* [I.B.11], pp. 30–37.

94. "Edward Francis Gamwell: Lovecraft's Precursor in Amateur Journalism." *Snake Den* No. 20 (August 2003): 1–4.

95. [Interview with Ralph Babcock] *Fossil.* No. 313. (June 2001).

96. "Lovecraft in Service to the National: 1931–1936." *Snake Den* No. 21 (November 2003): 1–5.

97. "Passion, Controversy and Vision: A History of the Library of Amateur Journalism." (2003; 96 pp.) In *One Hundred Years of the Fossils 1904–2004* (ed. Guy Miller and Kenneth W. Faig, Jr. Springfield, OH: Potpourri Private Press, March 2005). [50 copies].

98. "Finding a New Home for the Library of Amateur Journalism." *Fossil* 101, No. 2 (323, January 2005): 6–13.

99. "Dining with The Fossils." *Fossil* 101, No. 3 (324, April 2005): 14–26.

100. "The 54th Annual Reunion and Dinner" *Fossil* 102, No. 1, (326, October 2005): 10–13.

101. "They Met in Ajay." *Fossil* 102, No. 2 (327, January 2006): 11–13. [On Paul J. Campbell and his wives Ada Parkhurst and Eleanor Barnhart.]

102. "About Ernest A. Edkins." *Fossil* 102, No. 3 (328, April 2006): 16–17.

103. "About C. Hamilton Bloomer, Jr." *Fossil* 102, No. 3 (328, April 2006): 18–19.

104. "Lavender Ajays of the Red-Scare Period: 1917–1920." *Fossil* 102, No. 4 (329, July 2006): 5–17.

105. "AAPA Conventioneers Visit Warren J. Brodie Amateur Journalism Collection at Western Reserve Historical Society in Cleveland, Ohio." *Fossil* 103, No. 1 (330, October 2006): 19–20.

106. "Edwin B. Hill: The Story of a Great Amateur Printer." *Fossil* 103, No. 2 (331, January 2007): 5–8.

107. "Sean McLachlan Discovers Unrecorded Lovecraft Publications in the British Library." *Fossil* 103, No. 2 (331, January 2007): 23–24. [On the discovery of the text of "An American to the British Flag."]

108. "Sotheby's, New York City, December 11, 2006." *EOD Letter* No. 3 (Candlemas 2007): 1–7.

109. "Lovecraft Takes a Knock or Two." *EOD Letter* No. 4 (May Eve 2007): 1. [On a parody cartoon of Lovecraft in the amateur magazine *Cleveland Sun*.]

110. "Some Documents from Wikisource." *EOD Letter* No. 5 (Lammas 2007): 1–2. [On the will of Annie Gamwell (January 10, 1940) and a letter from Ethel P. Morrish and Edna Lewis to August Derleth and Donald Wandrei, May 2, 1941 (the "Morrish–Lewis gift").]

111. "Sotheby's, December 11, 2006 Revisited." *EOD Letter* No. 5 (Lammas 2007): 2–4. [Remarks on the paper catalogue of the auction (Design Books) and corrections to *EOD Letter* No. 3]

112. "Another Document from Wikisource." *EOD Letter* No. 6 (Hallowmas 2007): 1–4. [On Lovecraft's last will of 1912; speculates how his estate might have been probated had he lived past 1937.]

113. "Amateur Journalism: Cradle of Illustrious Authors." *Fossil* 104, No. 1 (334, October 2007): 10–13.

114. "Jesse Root Grant: Amateur Journalist." *Fossil* 104, No. 2 (335, January 2008): 12–14.

115. "Sexual Themes in Amateur Journals 1935–1955." *Fossil* 104, No. 2 (335, January 2008): 16–20.

116. "Does a Hobby Have a History? A Reflection." *Fossil* 104, No. 2 (335, January 2008): 21–24.

117. "The Fate of Two Ajay Collections." *Fossil* 104, No. 3 (336; Glenview, IL: April 2008): 38–42.

118. "Robert E. Howard, The Lone Scouts, and *The Junto*: A Neglected Chapter in Ajay History." *Fossil* 104, No. 4 (337, July 2008): 13–16.

119. "Who Was Arthur Fredlund?" *EOD Letter* No. 8 (Hallowmas 2008): 1–6. [On Lovecraft's boyhood friend.]

120. "Thomas Gray Condie, Jr." *Fossil* 105, No. 1 (338, October 2008): 20–22.

121. [*Song for Remembered Earth: The Oregon Observer* (2008) by Kent Clair Chamberlain.] *The Fossil* 105, No. 1, (338, October 2008): 24–26.

122. "Some Final Thoughts for Readers of This Collection." *The Unknown Lovecraft* [I.B.19], pp. 249–53.

123. "Two Illustrious Bicentenaries: Abraham Lincoln and Edgar Allan Poe." *Occasional Essays* No. 2 (January 2009): 1.

124. "A Colleague Departs," *EOD Letter* No. 9 (Candlemas 2009): 1–2. [On the late Christopher J. Docherty, co-author of *The Devonshire Ancestry of Howard Phillips Lovecraft* (II.B.28).]

125. "Was Sonia Lovecraft Davis HPL's Widow." *EOD Letter* No. 9 (Candlemas 2009): 5–8.

126. "August and I." *EOD Letter* No. 9 (Candlemas 2009): 8. [On Faig's contact with Derleth.]

127. "Two Illustrious Bicentenaries: Abraham Lincoln and Edgar Allan Poe." *Occasional Essays* No. 2 (January 2009): 1.

128. "Tad Lincoln and the Brown School Holiday Budget: Reflecting upon a President's Son and a School Paper on the Occasion of the Bicentenary Birth of President Abraham Lincoln." *Fossil* 105, No. 2 (339, January 2009): 12–21.

129. "Another Friend Departs." *EOD Letter* No. 10 (May Eve 2009): 2. [On the late William A. Spicer III.]

130. "The Passing of Janet Pollock." *EOD Letter* No. 10 (May Eve 2009): 5. [On the daughter of Arthur Machen]

131. "Ethnic Names in Lovecraft's 'The Dreams in the Witch House'." *EOD Letter* No. 10 (May Eve 2009): 5–9.
132. "Sonia Greene and Her Brother in the 1930 Census." *EOD Letter* No. 10 (May Eve 2009): 9–10.
133. "Some Additions for Lovecraft's Ancestor Table." *EOD Letter* No. 10 (May Eve 2009): 12–13.
134. "The Strange Story of 'Poetry and the Gods' by Anna Helen Crofts and Henry Paget-Lowe." *The Fossil* 105, No. 4 (341, July 2009): 6–17.
135. "An Arkham Oddity." *EOD Letter* No. 11 (Lammas 2009): 1. [On Derleth's Sac Prairie novel *Restless is the River* (Scribner's, 1939).]
136. "Ethnic Names in Lovecraft's 'The Dreams in the Witch House': Chapter II." *EOD Letter* No. 11 (Lammas 2009): 1–5.
137. "City of Providence Probate Court Docket 37854: Estate of Howard P. Lovecraft." *EOD Letter* No. 11 (Lammas 2009): 5–8.
138. "Sonia in the 1900 Census." *EOD Letter* No. 11 (Lammas 2009): 8.
139. "*EOD Letter* Gets a Review: Some Mea Culpas." *EOD Letter* No. 11 (Lammas 2009): 8–9. [Comments on a review of *EOD Letter* No. 9 in *Media Junky* No. 10 (March 2009) by Jason Rodgers (Nashua, NH), and on that issue of *EOD Letter* itself.]
140. "Another Arkham Oddity." *EOD Letter* No. 12 (Hallowmas 2009): 1–2. [On "Stephen G. Grendon's" [August Derleth's] *Through Wisconsin on a Bicycle* (Arkham House, 1940).]
141. "From Me to You." *EOD Letter* No. 12 (Hallowmas 2009): 5–6. [On the late Ben P. Indick; recent publications by Faig.]
142. "Lovecraft in the 1930 Census." *EOD Letter* No. 12 (Hallowmas 2009): 6–7.
143. "The Juvenile Writer and the Urge to Publish: The 'Family Magazine' and the Amateur Journalism Impulse." *Fossil* 106, No. 2 (343, January 2010): 4–11.
144. "Institutional Collections of Amateur Journals." *Fossil* 106, No. 2 (343, January 2010): 15–16.
145. "Amy [Amelia] (Hogg) Machen, 1850–1899." *Faunus* No. 21 (Spring 2010): 6–18. (Ed. Mark Valentine & Ray Russell. Usk, UK: The Friends of Arthur Machen.) [Discusses Machen's first wife.]
146. "The Fossils and New York City: A Twentieth-Century Love Affair." *Fossil* 106, No. 3 (344, April 2010): 7–14.
147. [Untitled.] *EOD Letter* No. 14 (May Eve 2010): 1–2. [On the 150th EOD mailing and Rev. George Benson Cox (minister at the marriage of Lovecraft and Sonia Greene).]
148. "The Providence Amateur Press Club—An Addendum Plus a Miscellany on Hats, Lovers, Excuses and Ghosts." *EOD Letter* No. 14 (May Eve 2010): 2. [Addendum for II.B.31; on Sonia Greene's hat shop and other matters.]
149. "Zine-O-Scope." *Fossil* 106, No. 4 (345, July 2010): 5–18. [On Ray H. Zorn's *Nix Nem*.]
150. "Were Il Duce's Sons Amateur Journalists?" *Fossil* 106, No. 4 (345, July 2010): 18–20.
151. "A Visit to Québec City." *EOD Letter* No. 15 (Lammas 2010): 4–6.
152. "A Poem by Thyril Ladd." *EOD Letter* No. 16 (Hallowmas 2010): 1–2. [On Ladd's poem to Helen Vivarttas Wesson (1919–2006) and Wesson herself.]
153. "Odds and Ends." *EOD Letter* No. 16 (Hallowmas 2010): 6. [On *The Mystery of Murdon Grange*.]

154. "Charles A. A. Parker (1878–1965): The Story of a Boston Ajay Pioneer." *Fossil* 107, No. 2 (347, January 2011): 6–12.
155. "A Lovecraft Reference in August Derleth's Novel *The Hills Stand Watch*." *EOD Letter* No. 17 (Candlemas 2011): 1–3.
156. "Afterword." *Lovecraft's Pillow* [I.A.5], pp. 118–19.
157. "Finding New Homes for Amateur Journalism Collections." *Fossil* 107, No. 4 (349, July 2011): 16–18.
158. "Lovecraft and Sex—Some Testimony from Robert H. Barlow." *EOD Letter* No. 20 (Hallowmas 2011): 11.
159. "The Best of H. P. Lovecraft—Selections of Five Editors." *EOD Letter* No. 21 (Candlemas 2012): 1–3. [Compares *Tales* (ed. Peter Straub; Library of America, 2005), *Best Supernatural Stories of H. P. Lovecraft* (ed. August Derleth; World Publishing Co., 1945); *Tales of H. P. Lovecraft* (ed. Joyce Carol Oates; Ecco, 1997); *The Best of H. P. Lovecraft: Bloodcurdling Tales of Horror and the Macabre* (ed. anon.; Create Space, n. d.); *The Best of H. P. Lovecraft* (ed. anon.; Allen & Unwin, 2010).]
160. "Some Family Notes." *Fossil* 108, No. 4 (353, July 2012): 16–19. [On Charles W. "Tryout" Smith.]
161. "James F. Duhamel (1858–1947): The Last Survivor of the Boys of '76." *Fossil* 108, No. 4 (353, July 2012): 26–27.
162. "Lovecraft's 1937 Diary." *Lovecraft Annual* No. 6 (2012): 153–78.
163. "In Lieu of White Space." *EOD Letter* No. 24 (Hallowmas 2012): 6. [Edwin E. Phillips a director of the Rotary Club of Providence.]
164. "Gidlow versus Lovecraft." *Cyäegha* No. 7 (Autumn 2012): 22–33. (Ed. Graeme Phillips. Renfrew: Scotland.) [On Elsa Gidlow.]
165. "My Friend and Mentor: Guy G. Miller 1926–2012." *Fossil* 109, No. 1 (354, October 2012): 2–5.
166. "Susanna Paine (1792–1862): The First Wife of James Phillips (1794–1878)." *EOD Letter* No. 25 (Candlemas 2013): 1–5.
167. "The Best of Lovecraft." *EOD Letter* No. 26 (May Eve 2013): 2–3. [Addendum to the above comparison (item 159).]
168. "Looking for the Lovecraft Surname on Ancestry." *EOD Letter* No. 26 (May Eve 2013): 6–7.
169. "Moshassuck Press." *EOD Letter* No. 26 (May Eve 2013): 7. [Announces that Moshassuck Press is "essentially dead."]
170. "An Amateur's Amateur." *Fossil* 109, No. 3 (356, June 2013): 22–23. [On Leland M. Hawes, Jr.]
171. "Foreword." *H. P. Lovecraft in the Merrimack Valley*. David Goudsward. New York: Hippocampus Press, 2013.
172. "Lovecraft's Travelogues of Foster, Rhode Island." *Lovecraft Annual* No. 7 (2013): 75–135.
173. "Preface." *Lovecraft's Pillow* [I.A.6], pp. 9–14.
174. "NecronomiCon Report." *EOD Letter* No. 28 (Hallowmas 2013): 20–22.
175. "Envoi." *EOD Letter* No. 29 (May Eve 2014): 2.
176. "Lovecraft's Third Meeting with David V. Bush." *Lovecraft Annual* No. 8 (2014): 162–77.

177. "Centenaries of 2014 and Fossil Centenarians of 2015." *Fossil* 111, No. 1 (361, October 2014): 7–10.
178. "The Future of the Library of Amateur Journalism: Challenges and Opportunities." *Fossil* 111, No. 2 (362, January 2015): 7–9.
179. "The Wonderful Diversity of Institutional Collections of Amateur Journals: What Does It Betoken for the Future?" *Fossil* 111, No. 3 (363, April 2015): 4–8.
180. "Visiting LAJ and Considering a July 2016 AJ Conference in Madison." *Fossil* 111, No. 4 (364, July 2015): 2–4.
181. "Can You Direct Me to Ely Court?: Some Notes on 66 College Street." *Lovecraft Annual* No. 9 (2015): 54–69.
182. "Clergymen among Lovecraft's Paternal Ancestors." *Lovecraft Annual* No. 9 (2015): 136–81.
183. "LAJ Fundraising, Madison 2016, and Early African American Amateur Journalists." *Fossil* 112, No. 1 (365, October 2015): 3–6.
184. "Amateurs of a Certain Age: 1870 and 2016." *Fossil* 112, No. 2 (366, January 2016): 11–13.
185. "Conferences, Elections, Oliver Optic, and Mottos." *Fossil* 112, No. 3 (367, April 2016): 7–9.
186. "A Brief History of the LAJ." *Fossil* 112, No. 4 (368, July 2016): 1–4. [On the Library of Amateur Journalism.]
187. "Vision and Passion." *Fossil* 112, No. 4 (368, July 2016): 8–9.
188. "Lovecraft Quoted in Support of David V. Bush." *Lovecraft Annual* No. 10 (2016): 178–90.
189. "Two Milestones." *Fossil* 113, No. 1 (369, October 2016): 6–8.
190. "Timely Updates." *Fossil* 113, No. 2 (370, January 2017): 7–10.

B. Reviews

1. [*Selected Letters III* (1971) by H. P. Lovecraft.] *Nyctalops* 1, No. 6 (February 1972): 21–22. (Ed. Harry O. Morris, Jr. Albuquerque, NM: Silver Scarab Press.)
2. [*Selected Letters III* (1971) by H. P. Lovecraft.] *Shadow: Fantasy Literature Review* No. 16 (May 1972): 28–32. (Ed. David A. Sutton. Birmingham, UK: David A. Sutton, May 1972. With James Wade.)
3. [*The Late Great Creature* (1972) by Brock Brower.] *WSFA Journal* No. 80 (May 1972). (Ed. Donald L. Miller. Wheaton, MD: Washington Science Fiction Association.)
4. [Book Review.] *Ambrosia* No. 1 (June 1972; ed. Alan Gullette. Gullette Publishing.)
5. "Of Peter Haining and *Beyond the Curtain of Dark*." *Moebius Trip Library: Science Fiction Echo* No. 17 (May 1973): 65–71. (Ed. Edward C. Connor. Peoria, IL.)
6. [*Ratman's Notebooks* (1969) by Stephen Gilbert.] *Etchings & Odysseys* No. 1 (1973): 27. (Ed. Eric Carlson & John J. Koblas. Duluth, MN: MinnCon Publications.)
7. [Book Review.] *Moebius Trip Library: Science Fiction Echo* No. 23/24 (August–December 1975): 119–21. [Review of *The Transition of Titus Crow* (1975) by Brian Lumley; *Lovecraft: The Fiction: An Index to Dagon and Other Macabre Tales, The Dunwich Horror and Others, At the Mountains of Madness and Other Novels* (1974) by Donald Cochran; *The Chaos Spawn* (1975) by F. C. Adams; *The Devil Ground* (1975) by Ted Pons.]

8. [*Men of Dunwich: The Story of a Vanished Town* (1979) by Rowland Parker.] *Lovecraft Studies* 2, No. 1 (6, Spring 1982): 33–35.
9. [*The Arkham Sampler II, No. 4: Special Photograph Issue II* (The Strange Company, 1985).] *De Tenebris* (September 1, 1985).
10. [*Abolitionist, Actuary, Atheist: Elizur Wright and the Reform Impulse* (1990) by Lawrence B. Goodheart.] *Transactions of the Society of Actuaries* 43 (October 1991): 486–88.
11. "Actuarial Pioneer and Reformer Subject of New Book." *Actuary* 26, No. 2 (February 1992): 15. [A variant of the above review.]
12. "A Peek at the Future." [Review of *Federalism and Insurance Regulation: Basic Source Materials* (1995) by Spencer L. Kimball and Barbara P. Heaney.] *Contingencies* 8, No. 3 (May/June 1996): 20.
13. "Lovecraft's Involvement with NAPA." [Review of *H. P. Lovecraft: A Life* (1996) by S. T. Joshi.] *National Amateur* 119, No. 3 (March 1997): 11–14.
14. [*HCK: Herman Charles Koenig* (2004) by Eugene J. Biancheri.] *Fossil* 101, No. 1 (322, October 2004): 8.
15. [*H. P. Lovecraft, Collected Essays: Volume 1: Amateur Journalism* (2004) ed. S. T. Joshi.] *Fossil* 101, No. 1 (322, October 2004): 8–9.
16. [*Willis T. Crossman's Vermont* (2005) by W. Paul Cook.] *Fossil* 101, No. 3 (324, April 2005): 12–14.
17. [*Letters to Rheinhart Kleiner* (2005), *Letters from New York* (2005) by H. P. Lovecraft.] *Fossil* 101, No. 4 (325, July 2005): 11–14.
18. [*The Printer: Monthly for Letterpress.* Ed. Mike Phillips.] *Fossil* 103, No. 2 (331, January 2007): 26.
19. [*Ah! Sweet Laney!: The Writings of a Great Big Man* (2007) by Francis T. Laney.] *Fossil* 103, No. 3 (332, April 2007): 30–31.
20. [*The Library Window* (2006) by Margaret Oliphant; *A Study of Destiny* (2006) by Elizabeth Winston Cheiro] *Fossil* 103, No. 3 (332, April 2007): 31–32.
21. [*Marblehead: A Novel of H. P. Lovecraft* (2006) by Richard A. Lupoff.] *EOD Letter* No. 4 (May Eve 2007): 5–6.
22. [*The Structures Minds Erect* (2007) by Thomas Whitbread.] *Fossil* 103, No. 4 (333, July 2007): 39–40.
23. [*O Fortunate Floridian: H. P. Lovecraft's Letters to R. H. Barlow* (2007) ed. S. T. Joshi and David E. Schultz.] *Fossil* 104, No. 2 (335, January 2008): 24–28.
24. [*The CCC Chronicles: Camp Newspapers of the Civilian Conservation Corps* (2004) by Alfred Emile Cornebise.] *Fossil* 105, No. 1 (338, October 2008): 22–24.
25. [*Song for Remembered Earth: The Oregon Observer* (2008) by Kent Clair Chamberlain.] *Fossil* 105, No. 1, (338, October 2008): 24–26.
26. "The Lovecraft Fiction in One Volume." [*H. P. Lovecraft: The Fiction* (2008) ed. S. T. Joshi; *Necronomicon: The Best Weird Tales of H. P. Lovecraft* (2008) ed. Stephen Jones; *H. P. Lovecraft: Masters of the Weird Tales* (2008).] *EOD Letter* No. 9 (Candlemas 2009): 2–4.
27. "'The Dreams in the Witch House' Comes to the Stage in Chicago." *EOD Letter* No. 10 (May Eve 2009): 2–5. [A theatrical adaption of the story staged in the Athenaeum Theater by Chicago's Wild Claw Theater company; directed by Charley Sherman.]

28. [*Tour de Lovecraft: The Tales* (2006) by Kenneth Hite.] *EOD Letter* No. 10 (May Eve 2009): 10–11.

29. [*Just after Sunset: Stories* (2008) by Stephen King.] *EOD Letter* No. 10 (May Eve 2009): 11–12.

30. [*Dead Names: The Dark History of the Necronomicon* (2006) by "Simon."] *EOD Letter* No. 10 (May Eve 2009): 12.

31. "Abbey Kerins on Lovecraft's Youth and Juvenile Writings." *EOD Letter* No. 11 (Lammas 2009): 9–10. [A Brown University course paper "Walking Upon Hollow Earth: The Juvenilia of H. P. Lovecraft" (2008).]

32. [*The Buckross Ring and Other Stories of the Strange and Supernatural* (2009) by L. A. G. Strong.] *EOD Letter* No. 11 (Lammas 2009): 12.

33. [*The Horrifying Presence and Other Tales* (2009) by Jean Ray.] *EOD Letter* No. 12 (Hallowmas 2009): 2–3.

34. [*Irish Titan, Irish Toilers: Joseph Banigan and Nineteenth-Century New England Labor* (2008) by Scott Molloy.] *EOD Letter* No. 12 (Hallowmas 2009): 3–4.

35. [*H. P. Lovecraft's Nyarlathotep* (Boom! Studios, 2008), illustrated by "Chuck BB."] *EOD Letter* No. 12 (Hallowmas 2009): 4.

36. [*The Alchemist, Dagon, and Ex Oblivione* (Dodo Press, n. d.) by H. P. Lovecraft; *Collected Tales 1: Publications Before 1923* (Wildhern Press, 2008) by H. P. Lovecraft.] *EOD Letter* No. 12 (Hallowmas 2009): 4–5.

37. [*The Double Eye* (2009) by William Fryer Harvey; *Time Grows Thin* (2009) by Lilith Lorraine.] *EOD Letter* No. 12 (Hallowmas 2009): 7.

38. [*H. P. Lovecraft: A Comprehensive Bibliography* (2009) by S. T. Joshi.] *EOD Letter* No. 13 (Candlemas 2010): 8–9.

39. [*The Caves of Death and Other Stories* (2008) by Gertrude Anderson; *The Dead Hand & The Bride's Chamber* (2009) by Charles Dickens and Wilkie Collins.] *EOD Letter* No. 13 (Candlemas 2010): 9–10.

40. [*The Lost Villages of Scituate* (2009) by Raymond A. Wolf.] *EOD Letter* No. 13 (Candlemas 2010): 10–11.

41. [Dogtown: Death and Enchantment in a New England Ghost Town (2009) by Elyssa East.] *EOD Letter* No. 13 (Candlemas 2010): 11.

42. [*A Means to Freedom: The Letters of H. P. Lovecraft and Robert E. Howard* (2009) ed. S. T. Joshi, David E. Schultz, and Rusty Burke.] *EOD Letter* No. 13 (Candlemas 2010): 12.

43. [*Baker Street Irregular* (2010) by Jon Lellenberg.] *EOD Letter* No. 16 (Hallowmas 2010): 2–4.

44. [*The Hound Hunters* (2009) by Adam Niswander.] *EOD Letter* No. 16 (Hallowmas 2010): 4–6.

45. [*I Am Providence* (2010) by S. T. Joshi; *The Case of Charles Dexter Ward* (University of Tampa Press, 2010) by H. P. Lovecraft.] *EOD Letter* No. 17 (Candlemas 2011): 3–6.

46. [*Commodore Abraham Whipple of the Continental Navy: Privateer, Patriot, Pioneer* (2010) by Sheldon F. Cohen.] *EOD Letter* No. 17 (Candlemas 2011): 6–7.

47. [*Codex Dagon* (2010) by Cardinal Cox.] *EOD Letter* No. 17 (Candlemas 2011): 7–8.

48. [*The Dream World of H. P. Lovecraft: His Life, His Demons, His Universe* (2010) by Donald Tyson.] *EOD Letter* No. 18 (May Eve 2011): 2–5.

49. [*Against Religion* (2010) by H. P. Lovecraft.] *EOD Letter* No. 18 (May Eve 2011): 5–6.
50. "More Collected Lovecraft." [*H. P. Lovecraft: The Fiction: Complete and Unabridged* (2008) ed. S. T. Joshi; *H. P. Lovecraft: The Complete Fiction* (deluxe version of the preceding); *The Weird Writings of H. P. Lovecraft* (2010) ed. Neil & Leigh Mechem.] *EOD Letter* No. 19 (Lammas 2011): 1–4.
51. [*The Early Works of H. P. Lovecraft* (2009).] *EOD Letter* No. 19 (Lammas 2011): 5–6.
52. [*Supernatural Horror in Literature & Other Literary Essays* (2008) by H. P. Lovecraft.] *EOD Letter* No. 19 (Lammas 2011): 6.
53. [*Writings in the United Amateur, 1915–1922* (Filiquarian Publishing) by H. P. Lovecraft.] *EOD Letter* No. 19 (Lammas 2011): 6–7.
54. [*Eldritch Evolutions* (2001) by Louis Gresh.] *EOD Letter* No. 19 (Lammas 2011): 7.
55. [*Conspiracy of Silence / Tragedy at Sarsfield Manor* (2011) by S. T. Joshi.] *EOD Letter* No. 19 (Lammas 2011): 7.
56. "More Lovecraft." [*The Dream-Quest of Unknown Kadath and Other Oneiric Works* (2011), *Herbert West: Reanimator* (Dodo Press), *The Shunned House* (Ægypan Press), *The Shunned House* (Arkham House, 2008), *The Crawling Chaos and Others: The Annotated Revisions and Collaborations of H. P. Lovecraft Vol. 1* (2011) by H. P. Lovecraft.] *EOD Letter* No. 20 (Hallowmas 2011): 1–4.
57. "Poetry by Cardinal Cox." [*Codex Ulthar* (2011) by Cardinal Cox.] *EOD Letter* No. 20 (Hallowmas 2011): 4–5.
58. "Derleth on the Comics." [*Comics in America* (2011) by August Derleth.] *EOD Letter* No. 20 (Hallowmas 2011): 5–7.
59. "Donald Sidney-Fryer: A Summation." [*The Golden State Phantastciks* (2011), *The Atlantis Fragments* (2011) by Donald Sidney-Fryer.] *EOD Letter* No. 20 (Hallowmas 2011): 7–9.
60. "More Lovecraft." [*H. P. Lovecraft: Eldritch Tales: A Miscellany of the Macabre* (2011) ed. Stephen Jones; *The Best of H. P. Lovecraft* (Gollancz, 2010); *The Best of H. P. Lovecraft* (Prion, 2010); *The Best of H. P. Lovecraft: Bloodcurdling Tales of Horror and the Macabre* (Create Space, n. d.); The Shadow over Innsmouth (IAP, 2010); The Colour out of Space (no pub., n. d.).] *EOD Letter* No. 21 (Candlemas 2012): 3–4.
61. "The Lovecraft Fiction in Three Volumes: Yet Another Contender." [*The Call of Cthulhu and Other Dark Tales*; *At the Mountains of Madness and Other Weird Tales*; *The Other Gods and More Unearthly Tales* (Barnes & Noble, 2009–2010).] *EOD Letter* No. 21 (Candlemas 2012): 5–6.
62. "A Feast of Barloviana." [*Dim-Remembered Stories: A Critical Study of R. H. Barlow* (2011) by Massimo Berruti (Hippocampus Press, 2011); *Eyes of the God: The Weird Fiction and Poetry of R. H. Barlow* (2002) ed. S. T. Joshi, Douglas A. Anderson and David E. Schultz.] *EOD Letter* No. 21 (Candlemas 2012): 6–8.
63. "A First Poetry Collection." [*The Land of Bad Dreams* (2011) by Kyla Lee Ward.] *EOD Letter* No. 21 (Candlemas 2012): 8–9.
64. "From Bad Dreams May Come Beauty." [Review of *The Land of Bad Dreams* (2011) by Kyle Lee Ward.] *Dead Reckonings* No. 11 (Spring 2012): 86–87. (Ed. June M. Pulliam and Tony Fonseca. New York: Hippocampus Press.)
65. "Editions of Lovecraft." [*The Call of Cthulhu and Other Weird Stories* (2011) ed. S. T. Joshi; *H. P. Lovecraft Goes to the Movies: The Classic Stories That Inspired the Classic Horror Films* (2012) by "Michael Kelahan;" H. *P. Lovecraft: Great Tales of Horror* (Fall

River Press, 2012); *Horror Out of Arkham: Tales by H. P. Lovecraft* (IDW, 2011).] *EOD Letter* No. 22 (May Eve 2012): 1–3.

66. "David Haden on Lovecraft." [*Walking with Cthulhu: H. P. Lovecraft as Psychogeographer, New York City, 1924–26* (2011); *Lovecraft in Historical Context: Essays* (2010); *Lovecraft in Historical Context: Further Essays and Notes* (2011); *Ice Cores: Essays on Lovecraft's Novella At the Mountains of Madness* (2010); *Tales of Lovecraftian Cats* (2010); *The Cats of H. P. Lovecraft* (n.d.) by David Haden.] *EOD Letter* No. 22 (May Eve 2012): 3–6.

67. "Sean Elliot Martin, Ph.D. on Lovecraft." [*H. P. Lovecraft and the Modernist Grotesque* (Duquesne University Ph.D. thesis, 2008).] *EOD Letter* No. 22 (May Eve 2012): 6–7.

68. "The Return of Cardinal Cox." [*Codex Nodens* (2012) by Cardinal Cox.] *EOD Letter* No. 22 (May Eve 2012): 7–8.

69. [*The Complete Adventures of Judith Lee* (2012) by Richard Marsh.] *EOD Letter* No. 23 (Lammas 2012): 1–2.

70. [*Above Ker-Is and Other Stories* (2012) by Evangeline Walton.] *EOD Letter* No. 23 (Lammas 2012): 2.

71. [*Dissecting Cthulhu: Essays on the Cthulhu Mythos* (2011) ed. S. T. Joshi.] *EOD Letter* No. 23 (Lammas 2012): 2–3.

72. [*The Fantasy Fan: Fan's Own Magazine* (2010), facsimile edition by Lance Thingmaker.] *EOD Letter* No. 23 (Lammas 2012): 3.

73. [*Codex L'ng* (2012) by Cardinal Cox.] *EOD Letter* No. 23 (Lammas 2012): 3–4.

74. [*Gaslit Romance* (2012) by Cardinal Cox.] *EOD Letter* No. 23 (Lammas 2012): 4–5.

75. [*Strange Epiphanies* (2012) by Peter Bell.] *EOD Letter* No. 24 (Hallowmas 2012): 1.

76. [*Great Horror Stories: Tales by Stoker, Poe, Lovecraft and Others* (Dover, 2008).] *EOD Letter* No. 24 (Hallowmas 2012): 1–2.

77. [*The Color Over Occam* (2012) by Jonathan Thomas.] *EOD Letter* No. 24 (Hallowmas 2012): 2–3.

78. [*Confessions of a Five-Chambered Heart: 25 Tales of Weird Romance* (2012) by Caitlin R. Kiernan.] *EOD Letter* No. 24 (Hallowmas 2012): 3–4.

79. [*Black Wings II: New Tales of Lovecraftian Horror* (2012) ed. S. T. Joshi.] *EOD Letter* No. 24 (Hallowmas 2012): 4.

80. [*Devil's Drums* (2011) by Vivian Meik.] *EOD Letter* No. 24 (Hallowmas 2012): 4–5.

81. [*On the Hills of Roses* (2012) by Stefan Grabinski.] *EOD Letter* No. 24 (Hallowmas 2012): 5–6.

82. [*Ghost Stories and Other Dark Tales* (2012), *The Lovecraft Circle and Others as I Remember Them* (2012) by Jack Koblas.] *EOD Letter* No. 25 (Candlemas 2013): 5–7.

83. [*Avatars of Wizardry* (2012) ed. Charles Lovecraft.] *EOD Letter* No. 25 (Candlemas 2013): 7.

84. [*Tenebrae* (2012) by Ernest G. Henham.] *EOD Letter* No. 25 (Candlemas 2013): 7–8.

85. [*Yellow Leaves #3* (n. d.) by Cardinal Cox.] *EOD Letter* No. 25 (Candlemas 2013): 8.

86. "Two Models of Specialty Publishing." [*Worlds of Cthulhu* (2012) ed. Robert M. Price; *Urban Cthulhu: Nightmare Cities* (2012) ed. Henrik Harksen.] *EOD Letter* No. 26 (May Eve 2013): 1–2.

87. "Poetry of Cardinal Cox." [*Codex Ponape* (2013) by Cardinal Cox.] *EOD Letter* No. 26 (May Eve 2013): 3.
88. "Writing and Artwork by Joe West." [*Aim High: Collected Poetry, Prose and Artwork* (2012) by Joseph A. West.] *EOD Letter* No. 26 (May Eve 2013): 3–4.
89. [*Unutterable Horror: A History of Supernatural Fiction* (2012) by S. T. Joshi.] *EOD Letter* No. 27 (Lammas 2013): 1–3.
90. [*A Look Behind the Derleth Mythos* (2012) by John D. Haefele.] *EOD Letter* No. 27 (Lammas 2013): 3–5.
91. [*Night & Demons* (2012) by David Drake.] *EOD Letter* No. 27 (Lammas 2013): 5.
92. [*From the Cauldron* (2012) by Fred Phillips.] *EOD Letter* No. 27 (Lammas 2013): 6.
93. [*Lovecraft in Historical Context: A Third Collection of Essays* (2012) by David Haden.] *EOD Letter* No. 27 (Lammas 2013): 6–7.
94. [*Risk: No Eulogy for Tin Soldiers* (2012) by Johnny Meah.] *EOD Letter* No. 27 (Lammas 2013): 7–8.
95. [*The Complete Adventures of Sam Briggs* (2013) by Richard Marsh.] *EOD Letter* No. 27 (Lammas 2013): 8–9.
96. [*The Strange Dark One: Tales of Nyarlathotep* (2012) by Wilum Pugmire.] *EOD Letter* No. 27 (Lammas 2013): 10.
97. "Book Reviews." [*The House of Oracles and Other Stories* (2013) by Thomas Owen; *Not to be Taken at Bed-Time & Other Strange Stories* (2013) by Rose Mulholland; *Lovecraft and Influence: His Predecessors and Successors* (2013) ed. Robert H. Waugh; *The Legacy of Erich Zann and Other Tales of the Cthulhu Mythos* (2013) by Brian Stableford; *Codex Hastur* (2013) by Cardinal Cox; *The Man from Mars: Ray Palmer's Amazing Pulp Journey* (2013) by Fred Nadis; *War over Lemuria: Richard Shaver, Ray Palmer and the Strangest Chapter of 1940s Science Fiction* (2013) by Richard Toronto; *H. P. Lovecraft's Dark Arcadia: The Satire, Symbology and Contradiction* (2013) by Gavin Callaghan; *Lovecraft in Historical Context: The Fourth Collection of Essays and Notes* (2013) by David Haden; *Intimations of Unreality: Weird Fiction and Poetry* (2012) by Alan Gullette; *Spores from Sharnoth and Other Madnesses* (2013) by Leigh Blackmore; *A Certain Slant of Light* (2012) by Peter Bell; *The Sea-Change & Other Stories* (2013) by Helen Grant; *New Critical Essays on H. P. Lovecraft* (2013) ed. David Simmons; *H. P. Lovecraft: The Classic Horror Stories* (2013) ed. Roger Luckhurst; *The Whispering Horror* (2013) by Eddy C. Bertin; *Good Old Mac: Henry Everett McNeil, 1862–1929* (2013) by David Haden; *The Kind Folk* (2012) by Ramsey Campbell; *The Dark Lord: H. P. Lovecraft, Kenneth Grand and the Typhonian Tradition in Magic* (2013) by Peter Levenda; *Dark Muse* (2012) by David C. Smith.] *EOD Letter* No. 28 (Hallowmas 2013): 1–19.
98. [*The Other Mr. Lovecraft: A True Story of Tragedy and the Supernatural from H. P. Lovecraft's Family Tree* (2013) by David Acord.] <http://www.amazon.com/review/R2XU941HB8JDOC/ref=cm_cr_rdp_perm>
99. "Book Reviews." [*Thirteen Conjurations* (2913) by Jonathan Thomas; *Written by Daylight* (2013) by John Howard.] *EOD Letter* No. 29 (May Eve 2014): 1–2.
100. "Two Books Reviewed." [*The Juvenile Rebellion* (2009) by William Taylor Adams; *The Collected Works of Martha Elizabeth Sherwood Shivvers: Volume Two: Poetry and Verse* (2014).] *Fossil* 111, No. 4 (364, July 2015): 5–6.

C. Fiction

1. "Life and Death." *De Tenebris* No. 2 (as by H. P. Lovecraft): 2–4. Also issued as part of the pamphlet *Life and Death: A Hoax and a Retraction*. Glenview, IL: Moshassuck Press, 1990 [II.B.6]. In *Lovecraft's Pillow* [I.A.5], pp. 1–2; [I.A.6], pp. 129–32. [A hoax version of the purportedly lost Lovecraft story.]

2. "Tales of the Lovecraft Collectors." *Moshassuck Review* (1979–1983, EOD) [*MR*]. Rpt. in *Tales of the Lovecraft Collectors* [I.A.1] and *Lovecraft's Pillow* (2013 ed. only) [I.A.6].
   a. "Introduction." *MR* 16 (July 1979; EOD mailing 27): 1–5. [I.A.1] pp. 5–8; [I.A.6] pp. 15–19.
   b. "Collector the First: Major Geoffrey Hopkinton-Smith (1857–1943)." *MR* 16 (July 1979): 5–8; *MR* 17 (February 1980; EOD mailing 29): 1–10; *MR* 18 (February 1980; EOD mailing 31): 1–7. [I.A.1] pp. 9–18; [I.A.6] pp. 20–42.
   c. "Collector the Second: Dean Alan Edgerton-Noble (1876–1959)." *MR* 19 (February 1981; EOD mailing 33): 1–6; *MR* 20 (May 1981; EOD mailing 35): 1–6; *MR* 21 (September 7, 1981; EOD mailing 36): 1–8. [I.A.1] pp. 19–30; [I.A.6] pp. 43–69.
   d. "Collector the Third: Charles Wilson Hodap (1842–1944)." *MR* 22 (December 30, 1981; EOD mailing 37): 1–15. [I.A.1] pp. 31–38; [I.A.6] pp. 70–89.
   e. "Collectors the Fourth and Fifth: David Parkes Boynton (1897–1956) and Another Gentleman of the Hope Club." *MR* (September 10, 1988; EOD mailing 64): 1–14. [I.A.1] pp. 39–46; [I.A.6] pp. 90–106.

3. "George A. Lederer Addresses the Association of Pennsylvania Bookmen Upon the Occasion of His Retirement." *Moshassuck Review* No. 25 (Lammas 1983). In *Lovecraft's Pillow* (2011 ed. only) [I.A.5], pp. 3–12 (as "A Bookseller's Romance").

4. "Road Traveller." *Moshassuck Review* No. 26 [EOD mailing 45, Candlemas 1984.] In *Lovecraft's Pillow* (2011 ed. only) [I.A.5], pp. 13–19 (as "Auto Traveller").

5. "The Squirrel Pond." *Moshassuck Review* No. 28 [EOD mailing 49, Candlemas 1985.] In *Lovecraft's Pillow* [I.A.5], pp. 20–24; [I.A.6], pp. 133–40.

6. "Innsmouth 1984." *De Tenebris* No. 10 [Necronomicon mailing 25, March 1985]: 1–6. In *Lovecraft's Pillow* (2013 ed. only) [I.A.6], pp. 141–50.

7. "Writings on Theodore Winthrop Phillips (1836–1904)." *Tekeli-li* (December 1986).

8. "Lovecraftiana from the Collection of the Late Harry E. Macalmont." *Moshassuck Review* (February 1987). [A hoax "compilation."]

9. "A Pair of Old Shears." *Moshassuck Review* [EOD mailing 76, Hallowmas 1991]: 20–37; rpt. *Black Book* No. 3 (2003): 44–61. In *Lovecraft's Pillow* [I.A.5], pp. 25–36; [I.A.6], pp. 107–28 (as "Collectors the Sixth and Seventh: Miss Susan M. Rounds (1780–1878) and James N. Arnold (1844–1927)"). [A David Parkes Boynton story, omitted from I.A.1.]

10. "Boy in Summer." Issued as a pamphlet [II.B.17]. [EOD mailing 96, Hallowmas 1996.] In *Lovecraft's Pillow* [I.A.5], pp. 37–39; [I.A.6], pp. 151–56.

11. "L. E." [EOD mailing 125, Candlemas 2005.] In *Lovecraft's Pillow* (2011 ed. only) [I.A.5], pp. 40–49. [A Wilmott Watkyns story.]

12. "The Haunting of Huber's." In *Lovecraft's Pillow* [I.A.5], pp. 50–63; [I.A.6], pp. 157–80. [A Wilmott Watkyns story.]

13. "Lovecraft's Pillow." [EOD mailing 136, Hallowmas 2006.] In *Lovecraft's Pillow* [I.A.5], pp. 64–81; [I.A.6], pp. 181–208. [Based on an idea by Stephen King.]

14. "Leng." In *Lovecraft's Pillow* [I.A.5], pp. 82–90; [I.A.6], pp. 209–224.
15. "HDW." In *Lovecraft's Pillow* (2011 ed. only) [I.A.5], pp. 91–97.
16. "Gothic Studies." In *Lovecraft's Pillow* [I.A.5], pp. 98–102; [I.A.6], pp. 225–32.
17. "The Statement of Cornelius Felix." In *Lovecraft's Pillow* (2011 ed. only) [I.A.5], pp. 103–106.
18. "The Man in the Window." In *Lovecraft's Pillow* (2011 ed. only) [I.A.5], pp. 107–112.
19. "Rosenbluhme." In *Lovecraft's Pillow* (2011 ed. only) [I.A.5], pp. 113–17.

D. Poetry

1. "A.W.D." *Weirdbook* No. 5 (1972): 26. (Ed. W. Paul Ganley. Chambersburg, PA: W. Paul Ganley.)
2. "The Lost Man." *Etchings & Odysseys* No. 1 (1973): 72. (Ed. Eric Carlson & John J. Koblas. Duluth, MN: MinnCon Publications.)

E. Published Letters

1. *WSFA Journal* No. 76 (April–May 1971): 121–22. (Ed. Donald L. Miller. Wheaton, MD: Washington Science Fiction Association.)
2. *Nyctalops* 1, No. 5 (October 1971): 49–51. (Ed. Harry O. Morris, Jr. Albuquerque, NM: Silver Scarab Press.)
3. *WSFA Journal* No. 79 (November 1971–January 1972): 39–42.
4. *The HPL Supplement* No. 1 (April–October 1972): [n.p.]. (Ed. Meade and Penny Frierson. Birmingham, AL.)
5. *OAK Leaves* 1, No. 10 (Winter 1972–73): 15. (St. Michael, ND: Modern Limited Publications.) Rpt. David Anthony Kraft, ed. *The Compleat OAK Leaves: Volume One of the Official Journal of Otis Adelbert Kline and His Works* (Clayton, GA: Fictioneer Books/San Bernardino, CA: Borgo Press, 1980), p. 15.
6. *Moebius Trip Library: Science Fiction Echo* No. 17 (May 1973): 191. (Ed. Edward C. Connor. Peoria, IL.)
7. *The HPL Supplement* No. 2 (July 1973).
8. *From Beyond the Dark Gateway* 1, No. 3 (April 1974): 38. (Ed. Edward P. Berglund. [Albuquerque, NM?]: Silver Scarab.)
9. *Nyctalops* 2, No. 4/5 (11/12, April 1976): 44.
10. *Fantasy Commentator* 5, No. 1 (33, Winter 1983): 73. [Rpt. from *Tekeli-Li* No. 6 (1981).]
11. *Crypt of Cthulhu* 2, No. 5 (13, Roodmas 1983): 44.
12. *Crypt of Cthulhu* 4, No. 6 (31, Roodmas 1985): 47.
13. *Crypt of Cthulhu* 6, No. 6. (48, St. John's Eve 1987): 45–46.
14. *Crypt of Cthulhu* 7, No. 9 (57, St. John's Eve 1988): 50.
15. *Crypt of Cthulhu* 7, No. 9 (59, Michaelmas 1988): 69.
16. *Crypt of Cthulhu* 8, No. 3 (61½, Yuletide 1988): 33.
17. *Crypt of Cthulhu* 9, No. 1 (68, Hallowmas 1989): 63.
18. *Crypt of Cthulhu* 10, No. 1 (76, Hallowmas 1990): 18.
19. *Crypt of Cthulhu* 11, No. 2 (80, Eastertide 1992): 14.

20. *Crypt of Cthulhu* 12, No. 1 (82, Hallowmas 1992): 46.
21. *Avallaunius* No. 11 (Autumn 1993): 31. (Ed. Michael Butterworth. Caerleon, UK: The Arthur Machen Society.)
22. *Crypt of Cthulhu* 13, No. 2 (86, Eastertide 1994): 63.
23. *Lovecraft Studies* No. 30 (Spring 1994): 35–36.
24. *Crypt of Cthulhu* 14, No. 1 (88, Hallowmas 1994): 56.
25. *August Derleth Society Newsletter* 15, No. 1 (1994): 7. (Ed. Kay Price. Sauk City, WI: August Derleth Society.)
26. *August Derleth Society Newsletter* 15, No. 4 (1994): 11.
27. *Crypt of Cthulhu* 19, No. 1 (103, Hallowmas 1999): 37–38. (Ed. Robert M. Price. Poplar Bluff, MO: Mythos Books.)
28. "Remembering Sam (Part III)." *Fantasy Commentator* 9, No. 4 (52, Spring 2000): 284. [Obituary of Sam Moskowitz.]
29. *August Derleth Society Newsletter* 29, No. 4 (2008): 4.
30. *August Derleth Society Newsletter* 30, No. 2 (2009): 2.

F. Miscellany

1. "Photographs and Drawings of Lovecraft: A Provisional Listing." [Unpublished paper.]
2. "Questions Regarding the Literary Estate of Howard P. Lovecraft." [Unpublished paper.]
3. "Some Thoughts on Lovecraft as a Revisionist." [Unpublished paper.]
4. "Some Lovecraft Places in Providence." Providence, R.I.: Kenneth W. Faig, Jr., August 31, 1971. [Unpublished paper.]
5. [Lovecraft genealogy chart]. *Crypt of Cthulhu* 11, No. 3 (81, St. John's Eve 1992): 47.
6. Michael Siefener. "Cuthubutt." In *Mythos Tales & Others* (ed. David Wynn; Poplar Bluff, MO: Mythos Books, 1996), pp. 41–45. [Translated by Faig.]
7. *The Investigator's Companion: A Core Game Book for Players*. Chaosium. [*Call of Cthulhu* roleplaying game supplement; multiple editions. Faig as a contributor.]
8. *The 1920s Investigator's Companion: A Core Game Book for Players*. Chaosium. [*Call of Cthulhu* roleplaying game supplement; multiple editions. Faig as a contributor.]
9. "Professional Writings of Kenneth W. Faig, Jr." *Occasional Essays* No. 3 (December 2011): 3–4. [A bibliography of works in the below sub-section.]

G. Actuarial and Other Professional Writings

1. "Deregulation of Life Insurance." *Record of the Society of Actuaries* 9, No. 4 (1983): 1779–1800. [Panel discussion between Michael Davlin, R. Fred Richardson, Frank W. Speed and William W. White; moderated by Richard A. Burrows. Contains a comment by Faig on p. 1796.]
2. "Reversionary Annuities." *Product Development News* (July 1988).
3. "Joint and Survivor Annuity Reserves." *Financial Reporter* No. 3 (March 1992): 21. [Letter.]
4. "Mortality Rates by Marital Status." *Transactions of the Society of Actuaries* 46 (1994): 363. [Contribution by Faig to a discussion following Charles L. Trowbridge's paper.]

5. "Life after Omega." *Financial Reporter* (March 1995): 7–8, 15.
6. "What We Say in the NAIC Annual Statement Blank Actuarial Opinion." *Journal of Actuarial Practice* 4, No. 2 (1996): 275–86.
7. "Diversity of State Valuation Laws and Regulations: Opportunity or Curse?" *Journal of Insurance Regulation* 15, No. 2 (Winter 1996): 212. [Co-recipient of the Spencer L. Kimball Award, 1997.]
8. "Thaddeus Q. Actuary Writes Verse and Makes Merry." *Contingencies* 9, No. 2 (March/April 1997): 14.
9. "Mortal Danger." *Best's Review* 97, No. 12 (April 1997): 66.
10. "Indemnity Contracts, Investments Contracts and Contracts in Between." *Product Development News* (May 1997).
11. "Codifying Actuarial Practice." *Contingencies* 10, No. 4 (July/August 1998): 10.
12. "Current Reserving Issues for Disability Insurance." *Record of the Society of Actuaries* 25, No. 3 (1999): [Panel discussion between Vincent H. Demarco, Kenneth W. Faig, Jr., and Charles A. Meinteil; October 17–20, 1999; moderated by Vincent H. Demarco.]
13. "Difficulties Could Arise Where Triple-X is Adopted 'By Default'." *National Underwriter* (Life & Health/Financial Services Edition, January 24, 2000). [Letter.]
14. "Readers React to 'Big Tent' Speech in January Issue." *Actuary* 34, No. 4 (April 2000): 14–15. [Letter.]
15. "Predictions for Electronically-Effected Ins." *National Underwriter* (Life & Health / Financial Services Edition, August 21, 2000). [Letter.]
16. "To Admit or Not to Admit: Is That the Question?" *Financial Reporter* No. 45 (March 2001): 18–21.
17. "Crystal Gazing: Thinking about Life Insurance in 2050." *Contingencies* 13, No. 2 (March/April 2001): 40–44.
18. *Reported Deaths of Centenarians and Near-Centenarians in the U.S. Social Security Administration's Death Master File.* [Paper for the Society of Actuaries *Living to Age 100 Symposium*, January 2002; 37 pp.]
19. "Examining Mortality and Life Expectancy." *Best's Review* (November 1, 2002). [Letter.]
20. "The Murder of the Insured by the Beneficiary: Attempting to Quantify One of the Moral Hazards Relating to Life Insurance Contracts." *Journal of Insurance Regulation* 21, No. 3 (Spring 2003): 3.
21. "Moving from Accumulation to Income." *Record of the Society of Actuaries* 29, No. 1 (2003): 1–22. [A panel discussion with Novian E. Junus, Frank P. Sabatini and Matthew P. Sharpe on May 29–30, 2003; moderated by Novian E. Junus. Contains a comment by Faig on p. 18.]
22. "The Mirror World of Negative Interest Rates in a Sustained Deflationary Environment." [Paper for the *Enterprise Risk Management Symposium*, July 27–30, 2003; winner of the Extreme Value Model Group essay contest (2003).]
23. "2001 CSO Valuation Mortality Table: A New Era for Escheat of Life Insurance Proceeds." *Journal of Insurance Regulation* 21, No. 4 (Summer 2003): 41.
24. "Author Reply." [Faig's reply to Ward Kingkade's discussions of G.18 at the *Living to 100 and Beyond: Survival at Advanced Ages Symposium*, January 2008; 4pp.]

25. "Communication Columns: A Brief and Sentimental History." *Contingencies* 22, No. 4 (July/August 2010): 28–33.
26. "Health Care in the United States: Preserving the Rights of Stakeholder Professionals." *Occasional Essays* No. 3 (December 2011): 1–2.
27. "Pillars of the Profession: Charles Trenerry, William Sutton Gover and Frederick Hendriks." *Contingencies* 24, No. 1 (January/February 2012): 18–22.

V. WORKS ABOUT

A. Bibliographies and Histories

1. Joshi, S. T. "The Development of Lovecraftian Studies 1971–1982 [Part II]." *Lovecraft Studies* 4, No. 1 (10, Spring 1985). (Ed. S. T. Joshi. West Warwick, RI: Necronomicon Press.) [Faig is discussed on p. 25.]
2. Chalker, Jack L., and Mark Owings. *The Science-Fantasy Publishers: A Critical and Bibliographical History*. 3rd Edition. Westminster, MD: Mirage Press, 1991. [Moshassuck Press discussed on pp. 550–51. Updated in four published supplements.]
3. Haefele, John D. *Opera Omnia: The Moshassuck Press Bibliography*. New Berlin, WI: Hesperia Press, 2000 (13 pp.); rev. 2002 (19 pp.).
4. Phillips, Graeme. *A Speculative Listing of EOD Titles by Member*. [Distributed in EOD mailing 163 (Lammas 2013); material by Faig listed on p. 6.]

B. Reviews of Works by Faig

1. Shea, J. Vernon. *H. P. Lovecraft: His Life, His Work* [I.B.2]. *Lovecraft Studies* 1, No. 1 (Fall 1979): 30–33.
2. [Unsigned.] *H. P. Lovecraft: His Life, His Work* [I.B.2]. *SFRA Newsletter* 27 (December 1979–January 1980): 2. (Ed. Roald Tweet. Eugene, OR: Science Fiction Research Association.)
3. Carter, Paul A. *H. P. Lovecraft: His Life, His Work* [I.B.2]. *Science Fiction & Fantasy Book Review* 2, No 13 (February 1980): 29. (Ed. Neil Barron. San Bernardino, CA: The Borgo Press.)
4. Price, Robert M. *In Memoriam: Howard Phillips Lovecraft; Ethel M. Phillips Morrish* [I.B.3]. *Crypt of Cthulhu* 6, No. 6 (48, St. John's Eve 1987): 39.
5. Joshi, S. T. *Tales of the Lovecraft Collectors* [I.A.1]. *Lovecraft Studies* No. 19/20 (Fall 1989): 70–71.
6. Dziemianowicz, Stefan. *Tales of the Lovecraft Collectors* [I.A.1]. *Crypt of Cthulhu* 9, No. 2 (69, Yuletide 1989): 42.
7. ———. *Life and Death: A Hoax and a Retraction* [I.A.2]. *Crypt of Cthulhu* 9, No. 2 (69, Yuletide 1989): 42–43.
8. ———. *The Parents of Howard Phillips Lovecraft* [I.B.4]. *Crypt of Cthulhu* 10, No. 1 (76, Hallowmas 1990): 28–30.
9. Joshi, S. T. *The Parents of Howard Phillips Lovecraft* [I.B.4]. *Lovecraft Studies* No. 22/23 (Fall 1990): 60–63.

10. Searles, A. Langley. *The Parents of Howard Phillips Lovecraft* [I.B.4]. *Fantasy Commentator* 7, No. 1 (41, Fall 1990): 39–41.
11. Collins, Bob. *The Parents of Howard Phillips Lovecraft* [I.B.4]. *Science Fiction and Fantasy Book Review Annual 1991*: 732–733 (Ed. Robert A. Collins and Robert Latham. Westport, CT: Greenwood Press)
12. Dziemianowicz, Stefan. *Some of the Descendants of Asaph Phillips and Esther Whipple* [I.B.6]. *Crypt of Cthulhu* 12, No. 3 (84, Lammas 1993): 43–44.
13. Joshi, S. T. *Some of the Descendants of Asaph Phillips and Esther Whipple of Foster, Rhode Island* [I.B.6]. *Lovecraft Studies* No. 29 (Fall 1993): 33–35.
14. Fiske, Jane Fletcher. *Some of the Descendants of Asaph Phillips and Esther Whipple of Foster, Rhode Island* [I.B.6]. *American Genealogist* 69, No. 1 (273, January 1994): 57–58.
15. [Unsigned.] *Some of the Descendants of Asaph Phillips and Esther Whipple of Foster, Rhode Island* [I.B.6]. *Thorny Trail* 23, No. 2 (Spring 1995): 88. (Midland, TX: Midland Genealogical Society.)
16. Rodgers, Jason. [Review of *EOD Letter* No. 9.] *Media Junky* No. 10 (March 2009).
17. Everett, Justin. *The Unknown Lovecraft* [I.B.19]. *SFRA Review* No. 292 (Spring 2010): 10–11. (Ed. Karen Hellekson and Craig Jacobsen. [n.p.]: Science Fiction Research Association.)
18. Lovecraft, Charles. *George Lovecraft: Lost Scion of the House of Lovecraft* [I.B.20]. *Different Feathers of Weird Wings* (August 2010): 8. (Ed. Danny & Margaret Lovecraft. EOD mailing 151, Lammas 2010.)

C. Reviews of Moshassuck Press Publications

1. Price, Robert M. *Insidious Garden: A Look at Horror Fiction* by Edward J. O'Brien, Jr. [II.B.2]. *Crypt of Cthulhu* 7, No. 9 (59, Michaelmas 1988): 66.
2. Joshi, S. T. *Insidious Garden: A Look at Horror Fiction* by Edward J. O'Brien, Jr. [II.B.2]. *Lovecraft Studies* 7, No. 2 (17, Fall 1988): 36.
3. Price, Robert M. *Within the Circle: In Memoriam: Franklin Lee Baldwin 1913–1987* by Josephine Richardson, et al. [II.B.3]. *Crypt of Cthulhu* 8, No. 3 (61½, Yuletide 1988): 11.
4. ———. *The Forbidden Room* by Duane W. Rimel [II.B.4]. *Crypt of Cthulhu* 8, No. 3 (61½, Yuletide 1988): 11.
5. Mariconda, Steven J. *The Forbidden Room* by Duane W. Rimel [II.B.4]. *Lovecraft Studies* 8, No. 1 (18, Spring 1989): 28.
6. ———. *Within the Circle: In Memoriam: Franklin Lee Baldwin 1913–1937* by Josephine Richardson, et al. [II.B.3]. *Lovecraft Studies* 8, No. 1 (18, Spring 1989): 28–29.
7. Price, Robert M. *Howard Phillips Lovecraft and Nils Helmer Frome: A Recollection of One of Canada's Oldest Science Fiction Fans* by Sam Moskowitz [II.B.7]. *Crypt of Cthulhu* 8, No. 8 (67, Michaelmas 1989): 64–65.
8. Price, Robert M. *To Yith and Beyond* by Duane Rimel [II.B.8]. *Crypt of Cthulhu* 9, No. 5 (72, Roodmas 1990): 41.
9. Dziemianowicz, Stefan. *The Recluse, 1927* by W. Paul Cook [II.B.9]. *Crypt of Cthulhu* 9, No. 6 (73, St. John's Eve 1990): 38.
10. Indick, Ben P. *The Miskatonic: Lovecraft Centenary Edition* by Dirk W. Mosig [II.B.11]. *Lovecraft Studies* No. 25 (Fall 1991): 32–34.

11. Dziemianowicz, Stefan. *Early Historical Accounts of Foster, Rhode Island* by Charles C. Beaman & Casey B. Tyler [II.B.13]. *Crypt of Cthulhu* 12, No. 3 (84, Lammas 1993): 44.

12. Joshi, S. T. *Early Historical Accounts of Foster, Rhode Island* by Charles C. Beaman & Casey B. Tyler [II.B.13]. *Lovecraft Studies* No. 29 (Fall 1993): 33.

13. Warner, Harry. *Susan's Obituary* [II.B.16]. *Horizons* 58, No. 2 (229, May 1997); rpt. *Moshassuck Review* (November 1997): 12.

14. Indick, Ben P. *Susan's Obituary* by Franklin Chase Clark [II.B.16]. *Lovecraft Studies* No. 37 (Fall 1997): 34–35.

ii. Works Cited

I. BOOKS AND PAMPHLETS BY H. P. LOVECRAFT

A. Fiction and Poetry

1. *The Ancient Track: Complete Poetical Works.* Ed. S. T. Joshi. San Francisco, CA: Night Shade Books, 2001; rev. Hippocampus Press, 2013. [The revised edition adds a number of poems newly discovered, along with ancillary matter.]

2. *At the Mountains of Madness and Other Novels.* Selected by August Derleth. Sauk City, WI: Arkham House, 1964; rev. 1985 (with texts ed. S. T. Joshi).

3. *Beyond the Wall of Sleep.* Ed. August Derleth and Donald Wandrei. Sauk City, WI: Arkham House, 1943. [The second Lovecraft omnibus; contains selected fiction (including revisions) and poetry, the Commonplace Book, and "Some Notes on a Nonentity"]

4. *Collected Fiction: A Variorum Edition.* New York: Hippocampus Press, 2015–17; 4 vols. [The fourth volume contains Lovecraft's revisions and collaborations.]

5. *Collected Poems.* Ed. August Derleth. Sauk City, WI: Arkham House, 1963. [Actually only a limited selection of Lovecraft's poetry.]

6. *Dagon and Other Macabre Tales.* Selected by August Derleth. Sauk City, WI: Arkham House, 1965; rev. 1986 (texts ed. S. T. Joshi). [The revised edition omits the spurious story "The Thing in the Moonlight" (a hoax by J. Chapman Miske).]

7. *The Dunwich Horror and Others.* Selected by August Derleth. Sauk City, WI: Arkham House, 1963; rev. 1984 (texts ed. S. T. Joshi).

8. *The Fantastic Poetry.* Ed. S. T. Joshi. West Warwick, RI: Necronomicon Press, 1990; rev. 1993. [The second edition adds the poem "The Unknown."]

9. *Four Acrostic Sonnets on Edgar Allan Poe.* Milwaukee, WI: Maurice W. Moe, 1936. [A small hectographed edition of the versions by Lovecraft, R. H. Barlow, Adolphe de Castro, and Moe.]

10. *The Fungi from Yuggoth.* [Washington, DC?]: Bill Evans, 1943. [Mimeographed in probably less than 100 copies; omits sonnets XXXIV–VI.]

11. *The Horror in the Museum and Other Revisions.* Ed. August Derleth. Sauk City, WI: Arkham House, 1970; rev. 1989 (ed. S. T. Joshi). [The textually corrected revised edition adds a number of stories (and omits one in the 1970 edition).]

12. *HPL.* Bellville, NJ: Corwin F. Stickney, 1937. [25 copies. Contains the poems "The Wood," "Homecoming," "Nostalgia," "Night-Gaunts," "The Dweller," "Harbour Whistles," "In a Sequestered Churchyard Where Once Poe Walked," "Astrophobos."]

13. *In Memoriam: Jennie E. T. Dowe*. Ed. Michael White. Dorchester, MA: [W. Paul Cook], 1921. [Contains Lovecraft's note "A Singer of Ethereal Moods and Fancies" and the poem "In Memoriam: Jennie E. T. D."]
14. *In Memory of Edith May Miniter. A Coworker in Amateur Journalism 1884–1934*. Issued by Laurie A. Sawyer and C. W. Smith. Haverhill, MA: C. W. Smith, [1934]; supplement to *The Tryout* 16, No. 8 (September 1934). [Contains Lovecraft's poem "Edith Miniter." The title echoes an earlier publication: *In Memory of Susan Brown Robbins: A Co-worker in Amateur Journalism 1891–1898*. Issued by Edith Miniter and C. W. Smith. Haverhill, MA: C. W. Smith, 1910.]
15. *The Outsider and Others*. Ed. August Derleth and Donald Wandrei. Sauk City, WI: Arkham House, 1939. [The first Lovecraft omnibus; contains selected fiction and *Supernatural Horror in Literature*.]
16. *The Shadow out of Time: The Corrected Text*. Ed. S. T. Joshi and David E. Schultz. New York: Hippocampus Press, 2001. [Based on the autograph manuscript that surfaced in 1995.]
17. *The Shadow over Innsmouth*. Everett, PA: Visionary Publishing Co., 1936. [The only book by Lovecraft issued in his lifetime, in 200 copies.]
18. *The Shunned House*. Athol, MA: The Recluse Press, 1928. [150 copies of the surviving unissued edition were eventually bound by Arkham House in 1959 and 1961; a handful (probably less than 10) copies had been handbound by R. H. Barlow ca. 1934–36. Reissued by Arkham House in facsimile in 2008 (50 numbered and 17 lettered copies, the latter containing an original signature of the 1928 printing.). A forgery (ca. 1965) of the Arkham House edition also exists.]
19. *The Statement of Randolph Carter*. Ed. R. Alain Everts. Madison, WI: The Strange Co., 1976. [Contains facsimile of an autograph manuscript of the text.]
20. *The Weird Writings of HP Lovecraft*. Mississauga, ON: Girasol Collectables, 2010; 2 vols. [Lovecraft's *WT* appearances in two facsimile volumes, the first of which contains material from the oversized early issued (up to July 1924).]

B. Letters

1. *Dreams and Fancies*. Ed. August Derleth. Sauk City, WI: Arkham House, 1962. [Compiles letter excerpts of dream descriptions as well as stories inspired by dreams.]
2. *Essential Solitude: The Letters of H. P. Lovecraft and August Derleth*. Ed. S. T. Joshi and David E. Schultz. New York: Hippocampus Press, 2008; 2 vols.
3. *Fritz Leiber and H. P. Lovecraft: Writers of the Dark* (with Fritz Leiber). Ed. Ben J. S. Szumskyj and S. T. Joshi. Holicong, PA: Wildside Press, 2003.
4. *The H. P. Lovecraft Dream Book*. Ed. S. T. Joshi, Will Murray and David E. Schultz. West Warwick, RI: Necronomicon Press, 1994. [A compilation of letter excerpts.]
5. *H. P. Lovecraft in the Argosy: Collected Correspondence from the Munsey Magazines*. Ed. S. T. Joshi. West Warwick, RI: Necronomicon Press, 1994. [Also contains letters by others responding to Lovecraft and an appendix of the two apocryphal Swift letters.]
6. *H. P. Lovecraft in "The Eyrie."* Ed. S. T. Joshi and Marc A. Michaud. West Warwick, RI: Necronomicon Press, 1979. [Letters by and about Lovecraft in the correspondence column of *WT*. The former have been reprinted in *Uncollected Letters*, while the latter can be found in *A Weird Writer in Our Midst* (II.B.13).]

7. *Letters from New York*. Ed. S. T. Joshi and David E. Schultz. San Francisco, CA: Night Shade Books, 2005. [An abridged selection of letters written in 1922–26.]
8. *Letters to Alfred Galpin*. Ed. S. T. Joshi and David E. Schultz. New York: Hippocampus Press, 2003.
9. *Letters to F. Lee Baldwin, Duane W. Rimel, and Nils Frome*. New York: Hippocampus Press, 2016.
10. *Letters to Elizabeth Toldridge and Anne Tillery Renshaw*. Ed. David E. Schultz and S. T. Joshi. New York: Hippocampus Press, 2014.
11. *Letters to James F. Morton*. Ed. David E. Schultz and S. T. Joshi. New York: Hippocampus Press, 2011.
12. *Letters to J. Vernon Shea, Carl F. Strauch, and Lee McBride White*. Ed. S. T. Joshi and David E. Schultz. New York: Hippocampus Press, 2016.
13. *Letters to Rheinhart Kleiner*. Ed. S. T. Joshi and David E. Schultz. New York: Hippocampus Press, 2005.
14. *Letters to Robert Bloch and Others*. Ed. David E. Schultz and S. T. Joshi. New York: Hippocampus Press, 2015.
15. *Letters to Richard F. Searight*. Ed. David E. Schultz and S. T. Joshi with Franklyn Searight. West Warwick, RI: Necronomicon Press, 1992.
16. *Letters to Robert Bloch and Others*. Ed. David E. Schultz and S. T. Joshi. New York: Hippocampus Press, 2015
17. *Letters to Samuel Loveman and Vincent Starrett*. Ed. S. T. Joshi and David E. Schultz. West Warwick, RI: Necronomicon Press, 1994.
18. *Lord of a Visible World: An Autobiography in Letters*. Ed. S. T. Joshi and David E. Schultz. Athens, OH: Ohio University Press, 2000.
19. "Lovecraft on Love" (to Sonia H. Greene, ca. 1922). *The Arkham Collector* No. 8 (Winter 1971): 242–46. (Ed. August Derleth. Sauk City. WI: Arkham House.)
20. *A Means to Freedom: The Letters of H. P. Lovecraft and Robert E. Howard*. Ed. S. T. Joshi, David E. Schultz, and Rusty Burke. New York: Hippocampus Press, 2009; 2 vols.
21. *Mysteries of Time and Spirit: The Letters of H. P. Lovecraft and Donald Wandrei*. Ed. S. T. Joshi and David E. Schultz. San Francisco, CA: Night Shade Books, 2003.
22. *O Fortunate Floridian: H. P. Lovecraft's Letters to R. H. Barlow*. Ed. S. T. Joshi and David E. Schultz. Tampa, FL: University of Tampa Press, 2007.
23. *Selected Letters*. Ed. August Derleth, Donald Wandrei, and James Turner. Sauk City, WI: Arkham House, 1965–76; 5 vols.
24. *Uncollected Letters*. Ed. S. T. Joshi. West Warwick, RI: Necronomicon Press, 1986. [Compiles most (but not all) of the letters published in various magazines during Lovecraft's lifetime and shortly thereafter.]
25. *Yr Obt Servt: Some Postcards of Howard Phillips Lovecraft Sent to Wilfred Blanch Talman*. Ed. R. Alain Everts. Madison, WI: The Strange Co., 1988. [Nine postcards.]

C. Essays and Miscellany

1. *Autobiography: Some Notes on a Nonentity*. Sauk City, WI: Arkham House, Arkham House, 1963. [Annotated by August Derleth.]

2. *The Californian: 1934–1938.* Ed. Marc A. Michaud. West Warwick, RI: Necronomicon Press, 1977. [Lovecraft's appearances in the amateur magazine in facsimile.]
3. *The Cats of Ulthar.* Cassia, FL: The Dragon-Fly Press, 1935. [Issued by R. H. Barlow as a Christmas Present to Lovecraft and associates in 40 copies.]
4. *Charleston.* New York: H. C. Koenig, 1936. [First edition mimeographed in probably no more than 25 copies, with a second edition (revised by Lovecraft) in 30 to 50 copies (both have variant states that may or may not contain photostats of Lovecraft's illustrations). Issued in facsimile by The Strange Co. in 1975 (150 copies).]
5. *Collected Essays.* Ed. S. T. Joshi. New York: Hippocampus Press, 2004–2006; 5 vols. [Collects nearly all of Lovecraft's surviving essays and miscellany, exclusive of certain juvenile material.]
6. *Commonplace Book.* Ed. David E. Schultz. West Warwick, RI: Necronomicon Press, 1987; 2 vols. [A critical edition with exhaustive commentary.]
7. *The Crime of Crimes.* Llandudno, Wales: A. Harris, 1915. [Only few copies survive; one previously owned by the publisher Arthur Harris was sold in 2012 for roughly £2000.]
8. *The Dark Brotherhood and Other Pieces.* Ed. August Derleth. Sauk City, WI: Arkham House, 1966. [Compiles material mostly about (rather than by) Lovecraft, together with Derleth's eponymous posthumous "collaboration."]
9. *In Defence of Dagon.* Ed. S. T. Joshi. West Warwick, RI: Necronomicon Press, 1985. [First publication of the surviving Transatlantic Circulator essays.]
10. *E'ch-Pi-El Speaks: An Autobiographical Sketch.* Saddle River, NJ: Gerry de la Ree, 1972. [Excerpt from a July 8, 1929 letter to a "Mr. Michael."]
11. *Further Criticism of Poetry.* Louisville, KY: George G. Fetter, 1932. Rpt. in facsimile: Duluth, MN: Eric Carlson, 1976. [A separate pamphlet of Lovecraft's essay that could not be accommodated by *The National Amateur*.]
12. *Looking Backward.* Haverhill, MA: C. W. Smith, [1920]. [40 copies. Reprints Lovecraft's history of the halcyon days of amateur journalism from Smith's *Tryout* 6, Nos. 2–6 (February–June 1920).]
13. *The Lovecraft Collector's Library.* Ed. George T. Wetzel. North Tonawanda, NY: SSR Publications, 1952–55; 7 vols. Rpt. Madison, WI: The Strange Co., 1979 (single volume). [Vols. 1–2: *Selected Essays*; vols. 3–4: *Selected Poetry*; vol. 5: *The Amateur Journalist*; vol. 6: *Commentaries* (memoirs and criticism); vol. 7: *Bibliographies*. Vols. 6 and 7 rpt. in *Howard Phillips Lovecraft: Memoirs, Critiques and Bibliographies* (II.A.27).]
14. *Marginalia.* Ed. August Derleth. Sauk City, WI: Arkham House, 1944. [The first Arkham House compilation of diverse material by and about Lovecraft; contains photographs and facsimiles.]
15. *The Materialist Today.* North Montpelier, VT: Driftwind Press, 1926. [15 copies; three are known to survive.]
16. *Miscellaneous Writings.* Ed. S. T. Joshi. Sauk City, WI: Arkham House, 1995. [Collects together essays (and fiction) both from earlier Arkham House editions and elsewhere (including previously unpublished items). A compilation with this title had been planned and announced by Arkham House as early as the 1970s.]
17. *The Notes and Commonplace Book.* Lakeport, CA: The Futile Press, 1938. [R. H. Barlow's edition; 75 copies.]

18. *Science versus Charlatanry: Essays on Astrology* (with J. F. Hartmann). Ed. Scott Connors and S. T. Joshi. Madison, WI: The Strange Co., 1979.

19. *The Shuttered Room and Other Pieces*. Ed. August Derleth. Sauk City, WI: Arkham House, 1959. [See *Marginalia*.]

20. *Some Current Motives and Practices*. De Land, FL: R. H. Barlow, 1936. [Probably less than 100 copies of two mimeographed sheets, apparently prepared by Barlow from Lovecraft's manuscript for circulation in the National Amateur Press Association.]

21. *Something about Cats and Other Pieces*. Ed. August Derleth. Sauk City, WI: Arkham House, 1949. [See *Marginalia*.]

22. *To Quebec and the Stars*. Ed. L. Sprague de Camp. West Kingston, RI: Donald M. Grant, 1976. [Collects together various essays by Lovecraft, most notably the previously unpublished long travelogue *A Description of the Town of Quebeck*.]

II. ABOUT H. P. LOVECRAFT

A. Bibliographies, Catalogues and Indices

1. *A Catalog of Lovecraftiana: The Grill/Binkin Collection*. Catalogued and annotated by Mark Owings and Irving Binkin. Baltimore, MD: Mirage Press, 1975.

2. Berglund, Edward P. "Addenda to HPL Story Listing." *Nyctalops* 1, No. 3 (February 1971): 8; 1, No. 4 (June 1971): 21–25; 1, No. 5 (October 1971): 13, 47. [Corrections to A.13.]

3. Bleiler, Everett F. *The Checklist of Fantastic Literature: A Bibliography of Fantasy, Weird and Science Fiction Books Published in the English Language*. Chicago: Shasta Publishers, 1948.

4. Brennan, Joseph Payne. *H. P. Lovecraft: A Bibliography*. Washington, DC: Biblio Press, 1952.

5. Briney, Robert E. "Professional Works and Miscellany." In *The Lovecraft Collector's Library: Bibliographies* (I.C.13), vol. 7, pp. 18–42; rpt. In *Howard Phillips Lovecraft: Memoirs, Critiques and Bibliographies* (A.27), pp. 59–83.

6. Chalker, Jack L. *The New H. P. Lovecraft Bibliography*. Baltimore, MD: The Anthem Press, 1962. Rev. "Howard Phillips Lovecraft: A Bibliography" in *The Dark Brotherhood* [I.C.8], pp. 198–241.

7. Cockcroft, T. G. L. "An Index to 'The Eyrie' and Other Readers' Departments." *Fantasy Commentator* 8, Nos. 3 & 4 (47/48, Fall 1995): 217–29.

8. ———. "Some Notes on the Lovecraft Bibliography in *The Dark Brotherhood and Other Pieces*." *Lore* No. 9 [Autumn 1967]: pp. 137–38. (Ed. Gerald W. Page. Atlanta, GA: Gerald W. Page and Jerry L. Burge.)

9. Joshi, S. T. *H. P. Lovecraft and Lovecraft Criticism: An Annotated Bibliography*. Kent, OH: Kent State University Press, 1981; rpt. Holicong, PA: Wildside Press, 2003. Rev. as *H. P. Lovecraft: A Comprehensive Bibliography*. Tampa, FL: University of Tampa Press, 2009.

10. ———. *An Index to the Selected Letters of H. P. Lovecraft*. West Warwick, RI: Necronomicon Press, 1980; rev. 1991.

11. Joshi, S. T, and Marc A. Michaud. *Lovecraft's Library: A Catalogue*. West Warwick, RI: Necronomicon Press, 1980. Rev. New York: Hippocampus Press, 2002; further rev. 2012.

12. Laney, Francis T., and William H. Evans. *Howard Phillips Lovecraft (1890–1937): A Tentative Bibliography.* Los Angeles, CA: Acolyte-FAPA Publications, 1943; rpt. Madison, WI: The Strange Co., Roodmas 1977.
13. Morris, Harry O., Jr. "H. P. Lovecraft: A Story Listing." *Nyctalops* 1, No. 2 (October 1970): 7–10; 1, No. 3 (February 1971): 9–12; 1, No. 4 (June 1971): 25–27. [See also A.2.]
14. Owings, Mark, with Jack L. Chalker. *The Revised H. P. Lovecraft Bibliography.* Baltimore, MD: Mirage Press, 1973.
15. Person, Carl. *Howard Phillips (H. P.) Lovecraft (1890–1937): A Catalog of 187 Items.* Tacoma, WA: Carl's Bookstore, Spring 1970.
16. Squires, Roy A. *A Bibliographic Catalog of the Largest Collection Ever Offered for Sale of the Works of Clark Ashton Smith and H. P. Lovecraft.* [Catalog 1] Glendale, CA: Roy A. Squires, June 1968; *Supplement,* January 1969.
17. ———. *Clark Ashton Smith—H. P. Lovecraft—Robert H. Barlow: Catalog II.* Glendale, CA: Roy A. Squires, [1969].
18. ———. *H. P. Lovecraft: A Basic Collection of 100 Items.* [Catalog 3] Glendale, CA: Roy A. Squires, [1970/71].
19. ———. *Modern Literature: Catalog 6.* Glendale, CA: Roy A. Squires, [1972].
20. ———. "The Mystery of *The Shunned House.*" In *Modern Literature,* pp. 11–13.
21. Stone, Leon. "Lovecraftiana." *Koolinda* No. 5 (April, 1948): 11–13; No. 6 (December 1949): 14–15; No. 7/8 (1950–51): 15–16; No. 9 (December 1952): 11–14. [Bibliographical data for Lovecraft's amateur press works.]
22. Van Herp, Jaques (et al.). "Bibliographie." *L'Herne* No. 12 (1969): 359–79; rpt. 1984. Special H. P. Lovecraft issue. (Ed. François Truchaud. Paris: Editions de l'Herne.) [Rearranges Chalker's bibliography (A.6) in chronological order.]
23. Wetzel, George T. "Amateur Press Works." In *The Lovecraft Collector's Library: Bibliographies* (I.C.13), vol. 7, pp. v–17; rpt. In *Howard Phillips Lovecraft: Memoirs, Critiques and Bibliographies* (A.27), pp. 47–57.
24. ———. "Biblio Notes." [In part 2 of A.26.]
25. ———. "Lovecraft's Amateur Press Works." *Destiny* 1, No. 4/5 (Summer/Fall 1951): 23–25. (Ed. Malcolm Willits and Jim Bradley. Portland, OR.) *Operation Fantast* 2, No. 1/2 (13/14, Winter 1952): 39–40. (Ed. Kenneth F. Slater. Sutton Coldfield, England.)
26. ———. "Howard Phillips Lovecraft in the Amateur Magazines." *Vagabond* No. 1 (Spring 1955): 41–46; No 2 (Summer 1955). (Ed. John W. Murdock. [Kansas City, MO?].)
27. ———, ed. *Howard Phillips Lovecraft: Memoirs, Critiques and Bibliographies.* North Tonawanda, NY: SSR Publications, 1955. [Originally appeared as volume seven of *The Lovecraft Collector's Library* (I.C.13).]
28. ———. "The Research of a Biblio." In *Memoirs, Critiques and Bibliographies* (A.27), pp. 41–46.
29. [Unsigned.] "A Listing of Some Lovecraft Manuscripts." *Nyctalops* 1, No. 3 (February 1971): 13–14.

B. Biographies and Memoirs

1. *The Arkham Sampler* 1, No. 3 (1983). Special Photograph Issue: Howard Phillips Lovecraft. Ed. R. Alain Everts. Madison, WI: The Strange Company. *The Arkham Sampler* 2,

No. 4 (1985). Special Photograph Issue—II: Howard Phillips Lovecraft and His Friends & Relatives Ed. Eric A. Carlson, John J. Koblas and R. Alain Everts. Madison, WI: The Strange Company.

2. Barlow, R. H. *On Lovecraft and Life*. West Warwick, RI: Necronomicon Press, 1992.
3. Cannon, Peter, ed. *Lovecraft Remembered*. Sauk City, WI: Arkham House, 1998. [Compiles most of the memoirs of Lovecraft, with the majority taken from previous Arkham House collections; with introductory matter by Cannon.]
4. Cook, W. Paul. *In Memoriam: Howard Phillips Lovecraft: Recollections, Appreciations, Estimates*. North Montpelier, VT: Driftwind Press, 1941. Rpt. as *H. P. Lovecraft: A Portrait*. Baltimore, MD: Mirage, 1968. [In *Lovecraft Remembered*, pp. 106–156.]
5. Davis, Sonia. *The Private Life of H. P. Lovecraft*. Ed. S. T. Joshi. West Warwick, RI: Necronomicon Press, 1985 (rev. 1992). [Based on the original manuscript in JHL; abridged version in *Lovecraft Remembered*, pp. 252–63.]
6. de Camp, L. Sprague. *Lovecraft: A Biography*. Garden City, NY: Doubleday, 1975; rpt. London: New English Library, 1976 (revised); New York: Ballantine Books, 1976 (abridged); New York: Barnes and Noble, 1996 (as *H. P. Lovecraft: A Biography*).
7. de Camp, L. Sprague. "Young Man Lovecraft." *Xenophile* 2, No. 6 (October 1975): 8. In *Lovecraft Remembered*, pp. 173–75. [Based on an interview with John T. Dunn.]
8. Derleth, August. *HPL: A Memoir*. New York: Ben Abramson, 1945.
9. ———. "Lovecraft's Sensitivity." In *Lovecraft Remembered*, pp. 32–37.
10. ———. *Some Notes on H. P. Lovecraft*. Sauk City, WI: Arkham House, 1959; rpt. West Warwick, RI: Necronomicon Press, 1982. [Contains Lovecraft's notes for "The Survivor" (an unwritten or destroyed story), otherwise uncollected. Reprinted as "Final Notes" in *The Dark Brotherhood* (I.C.8), pp. 302–321.]
11. *H. P. Lovecraft: A Symposium*. Los Angeles, CA: Los Angeles Science Fantasy Society, 1964. [A panel with Fritz Leiber, Robert Bloch, Sam Russell, Arthur Jean Cox, and Leland Sapiro; annotated by Derleth.]
12. Joshi, S. T. *I Am Providence: The Life and Times of H. P. Lovecraft*. New York: Hippocampus Press, 2010; 2 vols. [Unabridged and revised edition of the biography originally published as *H. P. Lovecraft: A Life* (Necronomicon Press, 1996).]
13. ———, ed. *A Weird Writer in Our Midst: Early Criticism of H. P. Lovecraft*. New York: Hippocampus Press, 2010. [A miscellany compendium of otherwise uncollected memoirs of Lovecraft, reader letters to magazines, as well as contemporary and early criticism and book reviews.]
14. Munro, Harold W. "Lovecraft, My Childhood Friend." In *Lovecraft Remembered*, pp. 69–72.
15. Scott, Winfield Townley. "His Own Most Fantastic Creation: Howard Phillips Lovecraft." In *Marginalia* (I.C.14); rev. *Exiles and Fabrications* (Garden City, NY: Doubleday, 1961), pp. 50–72; rpt. in *Lovecraft Remembered*, pp. 7–27.
16. Shaw, Lew. [Lewis Shwartz?] "The Day He Met Lovecraft." *Brown Alumni Monthly* 49, No. 4 (April, 1972): 3.
17. Wetzel, George T. "Biographic Notes on Lovecraft." In *HPL* (F.5), p. 25–27.

C. Lovecraft's Family and Associates

1. Baldwin, F. Lee. "Within the Circle." *The Fantasy Fan* 1, No. 11 (July 1934): 164. [A very short sketch of R. H. Barlow.]
2. Donnelly, Sean, ed. *W. Paul Cook: The Wandering Life of a Yankee Printer*. New York: Hippocampus Press, 2007.
3. Everts, R. Alain. "The Lovecraft Family in America." *Xenophile* 2, No. 6 (18, October 1975): 6–7. (Ed. Nils Hardin. St. Louis, MO.)
4. ———. *Lovecraft's Daughter III*. Ed. R. Alain Everts. Madison, WI: Candlemas 1983.
5. ———. "The Man Who Was W. Paul Cook." *Nyctalops* 3, No. 2 (16, March 1981): 10. (Ed. Harry O. Morris. Albuquerque, NM: Silver Scarab Press.)
6. Squires, Richard D. *Stern Fathers 'neath the Mould: The Lovecraft Family in Rochester*. West Warwick, RI: Necronomicon Press, 1995.
7. Wetzel, George T. "Lovecraft's Literary Executor." *Fantasy Commentator* 4, No. 1 (29, Winter 1978–79): 34–43. Rpt. *The Lovecraft Scholar* (F.16), pp. 3–14.

D. Stories and Other Works

1. Barlow, R. H. "Pseudonyms of H. P. Lovecraft." *Acolyte* 1, No. 4 (Summer 1943): 18. (Ed. Francis T. Laney. Clarkston, WA.)
2. Blackmore, Leigh D. "H. P. Lovecraft: The Mystery of the Missing Manuscript," *Arkham Horror and Fantasy Magazine* No. 3 [Winter 1984]: 21–27.
3. Connors, Scott. "The Commonplace Book: Its Use by Authors Other Than Lovecraft." *Kappa Alpha Tau*. (Washington, PA: September 1976. Ed. Scott Connors. Necronomicon Amateur Press Association, mailing 3.) Rpt. *Continuity* 3, No. 1 (Madison, WI: The Strange Co./Washington, PA: October 1976): 3–12. (Ed. Scott Connors and George T. Wetzel. Esoteric Order of Dagon Amateur Press Association, mailing 16.)
4. Derleth, August. "New HPL Pseudonyms Rejected by Derleth." *The Fossil* No. 159 (October 1958): 90.
5. Joshi, S. T. "The Rationale of Lovecraft's Pseudonyms" In Joshi, *Primal Sources: Essays on H. P. Lovecraft* (New York: Hippocampus Press, 2003), pp. 81–89.
6. Keffer, Willametta. "Howard P(seudonym) Lovecraft: The Many Names of HPL." *The Fossil* No. 158 (July 1958): 82–84.
7. Mariconda, Steven J. "Tightening of the Coil: The Revision of 'The Whisperer in Darkness'," *Lovecraft Studies* 32 (Spring 1995): 12–17; rpt. Connors, Scott, ed. *A Century Less a Dream: Selected Criticism on H. P. Lovecraft*. Holicong, PA: Wildside Press, 2002 (pp. 243–52).
8. Rajala, J.-M. "Locked Dimensions out of Reach: The Lost Stories of H. P. Lovecraft." *Lovecraft Annual* No. 5 (August 2011): 3–90. (Ed. S. T. Joshi. NY: Hippocampus Press.) [An exhaustive study of Lovecraft's various planned, abandoned, or lost stories and novels]
9. St. Armand, Barton Levi. "Facts in the Case of H. P. Lovecraft" *Rhode Island History* 31, No. 1 (February 1972): 3–19. [On *The Case of Charles Dexter Ward*. Illustrated; contains Lovecraft's drawing of Cthulhu.]

10. Scott, Winfield Townley. "A Parenthesis on Lovecraft as a Poet." In *Exiles and Fabrications* (Garden City, NY: Doubleday, 1961), pp. 73–77; rpt. *Lovecraft Remembered* (B.3), pp. 431–35.

E. The Cthulhu Mythos

1. Carter, Lin. *Lovecraft: A Look Behind the Cthulhu Mythos* New York: Ballantine Books, 1972.
2. Tierney, Richard L. "The Derleth Mythos." In *HPL* (F.5), pp. 53; rpt. *Essays Lovecraftian* (F.11F.10), pp. 57–59; *Crypt of Cthulhu* No. 24 (Lammas 1984): 52–53.
3. ———. "When the Stars Are Right." *Etchings & Odysseys* No. 1 (ed. Eric Carlson & John J. Koblas; Duluth, MN: MinnCon Publications, 1973): 56–57; rpt. *Essays Lovecraftian* (F.11), pp. 84–89.
4. Wetzel, George T. "The Cthulhu Mythos: A Study." In *Howard Phillips Lovecraft: Memoirs, Critiques and Bibliographies* (A.27), pp. 18–27; rev. *HPL* (F.5), pp. 35–41.

F. Books and Miscellaneous Items

1. Barlow, R. H. "Three Letters on H. P. Lovecraft." *Golden Atom* 1, No. 10 (Winter 1943): 31–32. (Ed. Larry B. Farsaci. Rochester, NY: Kodak City Publications.)
2. Blackmore, Leigh D. "Leon Stone: Amateur Journalist and Pioneer Lovecraft Collector." *Red Viscous Madness* 1, No. 1 (August 1984); rpt. *Fossil* 105, No. 3 (340, April 2009): 7–12.
3. Brobst, Harry. [Letter to R. H. Barlow, March 2, 1937]. As part of "The Last Days of H. P. Lovecraft: Four Documents." *Lovecraft Studies* No. 28 (Fall 1992): 36. (Ed. S. T. Joshi. West Warwick, RI: Necronomicon Press.)
4. de Camp, L. Sprague. "Literary Swordsmen & Sorcerers: Eldritch Yankee Gentleman." *Fantastic* 20, No. 6 (August): 98–106; 21, No. 1 (October 1971): 100–108, 114; rpt. in de Camp's *Literary Swordsmen and Sorcerers: The Makers of Heroic Fantasy* (Sauk City: WI: Arkham, House, 1976), pp. 64–113.
5. Frierson, Meade, and Penny Frierson, ed. *HPL*. Birmingham, AL: Meade and Penny Frierson, 1972. [A one-off tribute issue to Lovecraft.]
6. Laney, Francis T. "Who was Howard Davison?" *Spacewarp* No. 42 (September 1950; ed. Art Rapp): 54–57.
7. Marten, Robert D. "Arkham Country: In Rescue of the Lost Searchers." *Lovecraft Studies* No. 39 (Summer 1998): 1–20.
8. Moskowitz, Sam. "H. P. Lovecraft and the Munsey Magazines." In *Under the Moons of Mars* (III.A.32ii.III.A.32).
9. Murray, Will. "In Search of Arkham Country." *Lovecraft Studies* 5, No. 2 (13, Fall 1986): 54–67. "In Search of Arkham Country Revisited." *Lovecraft Studies* No. 19/20 (Fall 1989): 65–69.
10. Schiff, Stuart David. "Notes on Collecting Lovecraftiana." In *HPL* (F.5), pp. 44–45.
11. Schweitzer, Darrell, ed. *Essays Lovecraftian*. Baltimore: T-K Graphics, 1976; rpt. San Bernardino: Borgo Press, 1980. Rev. as *Discovering H. P. Lovecraft*. Mercer Island, WA: Starmont House, 1987; rev. Holicong, PA: Wildside Press, 2001. [A collection of

12. ———. "H. P. Lovecraft's Favorite Movie." *Lovecraft Studies* No. 19/20 (Fall 1989): 23–25, 27. Rpt. *Windows of the Imagination: Essays on Fantastic Literature*. San Bernardino, CA: Borgo Press, 1998; Wildside Press, 1999.
13. ———. *Lovecraft in the Cinema*. Baltimore, MD: T-K Graphics, 1975.
14. Shea, J. Vernon. "HPL and Films." In *HPL* (F.5), pp. 28–30; rpt. in Shea's *In Search of Lovecraft* (West Warwick, RI: Necronomicon Press, 1991), pp. 15–17.
15. Wetzel, George T. "Copyright Problems of the Lovecraft Estate." In *The Lovecraft Scholar*, pp. 23–39.
16. ———. *The Lovecraft Scholar*. Darien, CT: Hobgoblin Press, 1983.
17. ———. "A Memoir of Jack Grill." *Huitloxopetl* 8 (1972; ed. Meade Frierson): 27–36; rpt. *The HPL Supplement* No. 3 (March 1974): 46–54.

III. OTHER SOURCES

A. Prose and Poetry

1. Asbury, Herbert, ed. *Not at Night!* New York: Macy-Masius, 1928. [Contains "The Horror at Red Hook."]
2. Beckford, William. *The History of Caliph Vathek*. London: J. Johnson, 1786.
3. Birch, A. G. *The Moon Terror. And Stories by Anthony M. Rud, Vincent Starrett, and Farnsworth Wright*. Indianapolis: Popular Fiction Publishing Co., [1927].
4. Blackwood, Algernon. *The Centaur*. London: Macmillan, 1911.
5. Blunck, Hans-Friedrich. *Die Urvätersaga*. Jena: Eugen Diederichs, 1934.
6. Coates, Walter J., ed. *Harvest: A Sheaf of Poems from Driftwind*. North Montpelier, VT: The Driftwind Press, 1933. [Contains "The Canal" (*Fungi* XXIV).]
7. Derleth, August, ed. *Dark Mind, Dark Heart*. Sauk City, WI: Arkham House, 1962.
8. ———. *In Lovecraft's Shadow*. Sauk City, WI: Mycroft & Moran, 1998.
9. ———. *The Lurker at the Threshold*. Sauk City, WI: Arkham House, 1945.
10. ———, ed. *Tales of the Cthulhu Mythos*. Sauk City, WI: Arkham House, 1969; rev. 1989.
11. ———. *The Watchers Out of Time and Others*. Sauk City, WI: Arkham House, 1974.
12. Guiney, Louise Imogen. *Goose Quill Papers*. Boston: Roberts Brothers, 1885.
13. ———. *Happy Ending*. Boston: Houghton Mifflin Co. 1909; rev. 1927.
14. ———. *Songs at the Start*. Boston: Cupples, Upham and Co., 1884.
15. Haining, Peter, ed. *Beyond the Curtain of the Dark*. New York, Pinnacle Books, 1972.
16. Hammett, Dashiell, ed. *Creeps by Night: Chills and Thrills*. New York: John H. Day Co., 1931. [Contains "The Music of Erich Zann."]
17. ———. *Modern Tales of Horror*. London: Victor Gollancz, 1932.
18. Harré, T. Everett. *Behold the Woman! A Tale of Redemption*. Philadelphia: Lippincott, 1916.
19. ———, ed. *Beware After Dark!* New York: Macaulay, 1929. [Contains "The Call of Cthulhu."]
20. ———. *The Eternal Maiden*. New York: M. Kennerley, 1913.

21. Hoag, Jonathan E. *The Poetical Works of Jonathan E. Hoag.* New York: [privately printed], 1923; Rockville, MD: Wildside Press, 2009. [Contains a preface by Lovecraft.]
22. Howard, Robert E. *Echoes from an Iron Harp.* West Kingston, RI: Donald M. Grant, 1972.
23. Kafka, Franz. *Amerika.* New York: New Directions, 1946.
24. ———. *The Castle.* New York: Knopf, 1930.
25. ———. *The Trial.* New York: Knopf, 1937.
26. Leiber, Fritz, Jr. *Night's Black Agents.* Sauk City, WI: Arkham House, 1947.
27. Long, Frank Belknap, Jr. *The Goblin Tower.* Cassia, FL: Dragon-Fly Press, 1935. [40 copies, issued by R. H. Barlow. Lovecraft helped to set the type.]
28. ———. *The Horror from the Hills.* Sauk City, WI: Arkham House, 1963.
29. Mann, Thomas. *Death in Venice.* New York: Knopf, 1925.
30. Moskowitz, Sam, with Alden H. Norton, eds. *Ghostly by Gaslight: Fearful Tales of a Lost Era.* New York: Pyramid Books, 1971.
31. ———, ed. *Science Fiction by Gaslight: A History and Anthology of Science Fiction in the Popular Magazines, 1891–1911.* Cleveland, OH: World, 1968; rpt. Westport, CT: Hyperion, 1974.
32. ———, ed. *Under the Moons of Mars: A History and Anthology of "The Scientific Romance" in the Munsey Magazine, 1912–1920.* New York: Holt, Rinehart and Winston, 1970.
33. Serviss, Garrett P. *A Columbus of Space.* New York: D. Appleton & Co., 1911.
34. ———. *The Second Deluge.* New York: McBride, Nast & Co., 1912.
35. Shelley, Mary. *Frankenstein; or, The Modern Prometheus.* New York: H. G. Daggers, 1845.
36. Stoker, Bram. *Dracula.* London: Constable, 1897.
37. ———. *The Garden of Evil.* New York: Paperback Library, 1966.
38. ———. *The Lair of the White Worm.* London: William Rider, 1911.
39. Smith, Clark Ashton. *Nero and Other Poems.* Lakeport, CA: Futile Press, 1937.
40. ———. *Sandalwood.* [Auburn, CA: The Auburn Journal, 1925.]
41. ———. *Selected Poems.* Sauk City, WI: Arkham House, 1971.
42. Thomson, Christine Campbell, ed. *By Daylight Only.* London: Selwyn & Blount, 1929. [Contains "Pickman's Model."]
43. ———. *More "Not at Night."* London: Selwyn & Blount, 1926.
44. ———. *Not at Night.* London: Selwyn & Blount, 1925.
45. ———. *The "Not At Night" Omnibus.* London: Selwyn & Blount, [1937]. [Contains "Pickman's Model," "The Curse of Yig," and "The Horror in the Museum."]
46. ———. *Switch on the Light.* London: Selwyn & Blount, 1931. [Contains "The Rats in the Walls" and "The Curse of Yig."]
47. ———. *Terror by Night.* London: Selwyn & Blount, [1934]. [Contains "The Horror in the Museum."]
48. ———. *You'll Need a Night Light.* London: Selwyn & Blount, 1927. [Contains "The Horror at Red Hook."]
49. Verne, Jules. *An Antarctic Mystery; or, the Sphinx of the Ice Fields.* Philadelphia, PA: Lippincott Co., 1899.
50. Verne, Jules. *The Works of Jules Verne.* New York: V. Parke & Co., 1911.

51. Wandrei, Donald. *Dead Titans Waken! and Invisible Sun: Two Complete Novels.* Lakewood, CO: Centipede Press, 2011.
52. Wandrei, Donald. *The Web of Easter Island.* Sauk City, WI: Arkham House, 1948.
53. Whitman, Sarah Helen. *Poems.* Providence: Preston & Rounds, 1894 (2nd ed.).
54. Wilson, Colin. *The Mind Parasites.* Sauk City, WI: Arkham House, 1967.
55. ———. *The Philosopher's Stone.* New York: Crown Publishers, 1971.

B. General Works

1. Baarslag, Karl. *Islands of Adventure.* New York: Farrar & Rinehart, 1940.
2. Bacon, Edwin. *Rambles around Old Boston.* Boston: Little, Brown & Co., 1914.
3. Brown, H. Macmillan. *The Riddle of the Pacific: Account of the Burial Platforms, Sculptures, and People of Easter Island.* London: T. Fisher Unwin, 1924.
4. Cady, John Hutchins. *Civic and Architectural Development of Providence, 1636–1950.* Providence, RI: The Book Shop, 1957.
5. Carter, Lin: "The Real Hyborian Age." *Amra* 2, No. 56 (June 1972): 4–10. (Ed. George H. Scithers. Philadelphia, PA: Terminus, Owlswick, and Ft. Mudge Electrick Street Railway Gazette.)
6. Casey, Robert J. *Easter Island: Home of the Scornful Gods.* Indianapolis: Bobbs-Merrill, 1931.
7. Chapin, Howard Miller. *Gazetteer of Rhode Island.* [Unpublished typescript, 1927.]
8. ———. *Report on the Burial Place of Roger Williams.* Providence, RI: Rhode Island historical society, 1918.
9. Cockcroft, Thomas G.L. *Index to the Weird Fiction Magazines.* Lower Hutt, NZ: T. G. L. Cockcroft, 1962, 1964; 2 vols.
10. Day, Donald B. *Index to the Science-Fiction Magazines (1926–1950).* Portland, OR: Perri Press, 1952; rev. Boston: G. K. Hall & Co., 1982.
11. de Camp, L. Sprague. *Lost Continents: The Atlantis Theme in History, Science, and Literature.* New York: Dover Publications, 1970.
12. Drake, Samuel Adams. *Old Landmarks and Historic Personages of Boston.* Boston: Roberts Bros, 1872; rev. Boston: Little, Brown, & Co., 1900.
13. Evans, William H. "Thumbing the Munsey Files." *Fantasy Commentator* 2, No. 8 (Fall 1948): 292–93.
14. Fiske, John. *Myths and Myths-Makers: Old Tales and Superstitions Interpreted by Comparative Mythology.* Boston, New York: Houghton, Mifflin and Co., 1872; 1900.
15. Gaddis, Vincent. *Invisible Horizons: Strange Mysteries of the Sea-True Stories That Defy Logic.* Philadelphia, PA: Chilton Book, 1965.
16. Gill, William. *Gems from the Coral Islands; or, Incidents of contrast between savage and Christian life of the South sea islanders.* Vol 2: Eastern Polynesia. London: Ward and Co., 1856.
17. Gill, William Wyatt. *Rarotonga Records: Being Extracts from the Papers of the Late Rev. W. Wyatt Gill.* New Plymouth, NZ: The Polynesian Society of Honolulu, 1916.
18. Gould, Rupert Thomas. *Oddities: A Book of Unexplained Facts.* London: Philip Allan & Co., 1928; 2nd ed., London: Geoffrey Bles, 1944; 3rd ed., New York: University Books, 1965.

19. Guiney, Louise Imogen. *The Letters of Louise Imogen Guiney.* New York: Harper & Brothers, 1926; 2 vols.
20. Haley, John Williams. *The "Old Stone Bank" History of Rhode Island.* Providence, R.I.: Published by Providence Institution for Savings, 1929–44.
21. Howard, John. *The Illustrated Scripture History for the Young.* Philadelphia: J. D. Carson & Co., [1859?].
22. Iokimidis, Demètre, and Pierre Strinati. "Tekeli-Li. La Posterité littéraire d'Arthur Gordon Pym." *Cahiers d'Etudes d'Ailleurs* No. 3 (January 1959); rpt. *Fiction* No. 74 (January 1960): 123–29.
23. Kline, Otis Adelbert. "Otis Adelbert Kline's Letters to Robert E. & Dr. I. M. Howard." *OAK Leaves: The Official Journal of Otis Adelbert Kline and His Works* 1, No. 1 (Fall 1970): 4–11. (Ed. David Anthony Kraft. St. Michael, ND: Modern Limited Publications.)
24. Laney, Francis T. *Ah! Sweet Idiocy!* Los Angeles: F. T. Laney and C. Burbee, 1948.
25. Mather, Cotton. *Magnalia Christi Americana; or, The Ecclesiastical History of New-England, from Its First Planting in the Year 1620, unto the Year of Our Lord, 1698.* London: T. Parkhurst, 1702.
26. Moskowitz, Sam. *The Immortal Storm: A History of Science Fiction Fandom.* Atlanta, GA: Atlanta Science Fiction Organization Press, 1954; rpt. Westport, CT: Hyperion Press, 1974, 1988.
27. Oliphant, S. Grant. *Queer Questions and Ready Replies.* Boston: New England Pub. Co., 1886.
28. Porter, Reverend Edward. *Rambles in Old Boston, New England.* Boston: Cupples, Upham & Co., 1887.
29. Renshaw, Anne Tillery. *Well Bred Speech.* Washington, DC: Renshaw School of Speech, 1936. [Revised by Lovecraft.]
30. Reynolds, Aidan, and William Charlton. *Arthur Machen: A Short Account of His Life and Work.* The Richards Press, London, 1963.
31. Richardson, Leon Burr. *History of Dartmouth College.* Hanover, NH: Dartmouth College Publications, 1932; 2 vols. [Revised by Lovecraft.]
32. St. Armand, Barton Levi. "H. P. Lovecraft: The Outsider in Legend and Myth." Brown University M.A. thesis, 1966.
33. Scott-Elliot, W. *The Story of Atlantis and the Lost Lemuria.* London: Theosophical Publishing House, 1925.
34. *Seeing Providence.* Providence, RI: Providence Journal Co., 1948.
35. Skinner, Charles. *Myths and Legends of Our Own Land.* Philadelphia: J. B. Lippincott Co., 1896; 2 vols.
36. Snow, Edward Howe. *The Romance of Boston Bay.* Boston: Yankee Pub. Co., 1944.
37. Spence, Lewis. *The Problem of Lemuria: The Sunken Continent of the Pacific.* London: Rider and Co., 1933.
38. Spencer, Truman. *The History of Amateur Journalism.* New York: The Fossils, Inc., 1957.
39. Steele, Joel Dorman. *A Fourteen Weeks' Course in Chemistry.* New York: A. S. Barnes & Co., 1867.

40. Talman, Wilfred Blanch. "Who Ate Roger Williams?" *Vagabond* No. 3 (Winter 1955–56): 20. [A note previously thought to have been written by Lovecraft.]
41. Tenison, E. M. *Louise Imogen Guiney: Her Life and Works, 1861–1920.* London, Macmillan and Co., 1923.
42. Thwing, Annie H. *The Crooked and Narrow Streets of the Town of Boston 1630–1822.* Boston: Marshall Jones Company, 1920.
43. Tymn, Marshall B., and Mike Ashley. *Science Fiction, Fantasy, and Weird Fiction Magazines.* Westport, CT: Greenwood Press, 1985.
44. Warner, Harry Jr. *All Our Yesterdays: An Informal History of Science Fiction Fandom in the Forties.* Chicago: Advent Publishers, 1969.
45. Wood, Squire G. *A History of Greene and Vicinity 1845–1929.* Providence, RI: [n.p.], 1936.

Index

Poems and stories mentioned in the appendix tables (pp. 219ff.) and the corresponding listing in chapter 15 (pp. 136–139) are not indexed. For entries marked with an asterisk (publications during Lovecraft's lifetime or immediately thereafter), additional information can be found in the bibliography of works cited. The endnotes are indexed by their number only (nX).

"?" (Lemon) 113

"Account in Verse of The Marvelous Adventures of H. Lovecraft, Esq., ..." See "H. Lovecraft's Attempted Journey ..."
Acolyte 40, 44, 72, 89, 101, 118, 169, 171, n81
Adams, A. M. 175
Adams, Ernest 175
"Addenda to HPL Story Listing" (Berglund) n51
"Adept's Gambit" (Leiber) n40
Aegean Sea 183
Aeneid (Virgil) 145
Africa 118, 120, 121, n168
Ah! Sweet Idiocy! (Laney) n123
Alabama 4,
Albert and Vera List Art Building (Providence) 207, n220
"Alchemist, The" 39, 44, 84, 85, 87, 102, 107, 109, 111, 112, n119, n138, n140, n144
Alciphron 203
"Aletheia Phrikodes."
See "The Poe-et's Nightmare"
algebra 143
Alibone n208
"Alienation" (*Fungi* XXXII) n81
Allen, Clarence F. n228
Allen, Lydia W. n228
Allen, Zachariah 158–61, n230
'Allen, Zadok' 119
Allen's Avenue (Providence) 212
Allgood, Sarah 8, n8
All Our Yesterdays (Warner) 31, 43, 86, n57
All-Story (Cavalier) 74–75, 111–13, n102
Alouette, L' 225
Amazing Stories 36, 126, n151, n195
Ambrosia n174
"American to the British Flag, An" n125
Amerika (Kafka) 88
Ames, Samuel 158
Amra 120
Amsterdam Daily Democrat and Recorder n101

'Ancient Ones' n170
"Ancient Track, The" n75
Ancient Track, The (Barlow edition) 50
Ancient Track, The n100, n125, n137, n146, n163, n167
Anderson, Douglas A. n155
Andre, Major John 161
Andrews, Roy Chapman 120
Angell Street 3, 6, 8–9, 13, 17, 20–22, 35, 108, 110, 117, 144, 211, n8, n48, n57, n228, n267
Anger, William Frederick n96
Antarctic 110, 195, n174
"Antarktos" (*Fungi* XV) n81
"April" n134
Arctic n174
"Are There Undiscovered Planets?" 102, 112, n131
Argosy 74–75, 111, 171, n102
arithmetic 143
Arkham, MA 146–47, 148, n211, n219
Arkham Collector 167, 176, n211, n251
Arkham House: Publishers 10, 27, 28–29, 31–32, 37, 44–45, 48–50, 54–55, 60–61, 63–67, 86, 95, 101, 113, 123, 179–82, 190, n79, n94, n119, n175, n241, n255, n259; transcripts 4, 28–29, 35, n53, n111, n135, n156, n259
Arkham Sampler n44
Armstrong, Joseph G. n5
Arnold, Agnes Richmond n184
Arnold, Benedict 161
Arnold–Palmer house 216
"Arthur Jermyn" 16, 90, 127, n168
Arthur Machen: A Short Account of His Life and Work (Reynolds & Charlton) 142
Arthur Machen & Montgomery Evans: Letters of a Literary Friendship, 1923–1947 n207
Asbury, Herbert n199, n200
Asheville, N.C. n133
Asheville Gazette-News n133
Asotin, WA 57
Asquino, Mark 178

Associated Press n173
Astounding Stories 25, 36, 105, n37, n195
"Astrology and the Future" 94–95, 172, n130
Athol, MA 150–51, n107, n217, n219
Atlantis and the Lost Lemuria (Scott-Elliot) n173
At the Mountains of Madness 25, 84, 105, 110, 123, 132, 139, n170, n194, n195, n203
Attica 183
Atwells Avenue (Providence) 39, 205, 207, n270
Auburndale, MA 3, 5–8, 10–14, n1, n14
"August Skies" 99
Australia 40, 87, n52, n173
"Autumn" 99
'Azathoth' (entity) 183
"Azathoth" (fragment) 84, 123–25
"Azathoth" (*Fungi* XXII) n81
Aztecs 117

Baarslag, Karl n173
Babbitt house (Providence) 156, n225
Babbitt, George H. n225
Babbitt, Miss Sarah n225
Babbitt, Mrs. Sophia C. n225
"Background" (*Fungi* XXX) n81, 225
Back Street (Providence) n225
Baird, Edwin 36, 76, 124, 126, 142
Baker, Albert A. 9, 29, 31, 33, n2, n34
Baker, Robb 20, 155, n45
Baldwin, F. Lee 46, 57, 59, 63, 69, 72, 87, 96, 103, 131, n99, n124, n219
Bancroft Library n63
Banigan Building (Providence) 19, n23
Banigan family 193–94, n267
"Barge of Haunted Lives, The" (Terhune) 112
Barlow, Bernice n89, n91
Barlow, Everett Darius Jr. 58
Barlow, Robert H. (RHB) 35, 36, 40, 46–47, 52, 54, 62, 65, 66, 70, 71, 75, 88, 105, 111–12, 119–120, 126–27, 134–36, 139, 148, 169–71, 211, n8, n25, n28, nn30–33, n35, n37, n41, n79, nn92–94, nn96–97, n99, n105, n107, n124, n146, n179, n195, n211, n215, n243; diary of, 13, 123, 178, n175; and HPL's commonplace book, 91, 113, 115–16, 179–85, 187, 188–190, n259; as HPL's literary executor 26–34, 37, 39, 43–44, 78–79, 80–81, 84, 123, n29, n31, n79, n147; as publisher 49–55, 56–69, 70, n75, n78, n88, n91, n94
Barnes, Fred 164, 167
Barnes Street (Providence) 34, 108, 161, 199, 210
Barrett, Dr. C. L. 31
Barrett, Edward G. 5
Barrington River (R.I.) 22

Basinet, Victor n57
Bayley, Thomas Haynes n208
"Beast in the Cave, The" 39, 87, 102, 107, 109, 111, 112, 114, n119, n138
"Beauties of Peace, The" 99
Beck, Claire P. 29–31, 51–53, 65, 179, 181
Beck, Clyde F. 51–52, 65, 181
Beck, Groo 51–53, 65, 181, n78
Beckwith, Henry L. P. 8, n24, n164, n220, n225
Beebe, Evanore 148–52
Behold the Woman! (Harré) n199
"Bells, The" (*Fungi* XIX) n81
Benefit Street (Providence) n118, n195, n211, n220, n225
Bennett, Capt. Peter n173
Benton, Thomas Hart 62
Berglund, E. Paul 191, n51
Berkeley, CA 54, 65
'Berkeley, Elizabeth Neville' (pseud.) 172, n247
Berkeley Square (1933) 133
Bertin, Eddy C. 73
Beware After Dark! (Harré) n199
Beyond the Curtain of the Dark (Haining) n147
"Beyond the Wall of Sleep" 33, n195
Beyond the Wall of Sleep 48, 179–80, 225
"Beyond Zimbabwe" 118
Binkin, Irving 161, n148, n229
"Biographic Notes on Lovecraft" (Wetzel) n220, n225, n271
Birch, A. G. n198
Bishop, Zealia 56, 129, 140–41, 148, 153–54, 171, n205
Bizarre 44–45, 84, 116, n69
Black Cat 111, 192, n105
"Black Druid" (Long) 190–92, n264
"Black Island, The" (Derleth) 119
"Black Noon" (Eddy) 167, n238
"Black Orchid." *See* "The Black Druid"
"Black Vortex, The" (Long) 191
Blackmore, Leigh D. n52, n64
Blackstone Park (Providence) 155, 212, n164
Blackwood, Algernon 190, n260
Blake, Mrs. 83, 103
Blake, Robert 206–208, 210, n259
'Blasted Heath' (imaginary) 72, n99, n219
Bleiler, E. F. 132, n199, n200
Blish, James 69
Bloch, Robert 32, n152
Blue Pencil Club 175
Blunck, Hans Friedrich 121
Boland, Stuart Morton 118, n166
Bond Street (Brooklyn) n222
Bonaparte, Marie 16
Bonner, Margaret 193

"Book, The" 224, 225
Book Notes (Rider) 158, n226
Books at Brown n137
Boonsboro [MD] *Odd Fellow* 158
Bordley, Thomas Kemp 131–32
Boston, MA 3, 5–7 11, 24, 56, 73, 92, 144, 146, 150–54, 197, n220; city directories, 6
Boston Public Library 6, 14
Boston Science Fiction Convention ("Boskone") 133, n24, n211
Boston Store 198
"Bouts Rimés" n167
Bowdish Reservoir (R.I.) 165
Bowen Street (Providence) 157, 160, n220
Bradofsky, Hyman 38, 42, 79, n53, n63, n111
Brangham, Godfrey n207
Brennan, Joseph Payne 41, 66, 73
"Brick Row" 99, n81
Bridge Street (Elizabeth, N.J.) 156
Briney, Robert E. 40–41, 78–79, 97, 100, 169–73, n57, n133, n199, n246
Bristol, R.I. 117, n220
Bristol Dining Room (Brooklyn) 155
British Museum/Library 81, n125
Broadway (Manhattan) n5
Broadway (Providence) 20, 211, 216, n273
Brobst, Harry K. 26, 231, n25, n231
Brod, Max 88
Brook Street (Providence) 205
Brooklyn, N.Y. 133, 155–56, 175–76, n164, n166, n225
"Brotherhood" n100
Brown Alumni Monthly n118, n195
Brown, H. Macmillan n173
Brown, Stephen H. 18
Brown University 27, 56, 68, 80–81, 84, 93, 97–98, 110, 133, 164–65, 167, 203–204, 207–208, n96, n107, n118, n185; Archives, 144–45, 271, n225; Library, 132, 165, n243
Brownwood, TX 68
"Brumalia" 100, n134
Buchan, John 190, n260
Bullen, John Ravenor 46, 129
Bullock, Mrs. Sarah n225
Burke, Rusty n93
Burleigh, Sidney R. n211
Burroughs, Edgar Rice 112, 121
Bush, David Van 77, 129–30, 141, n109, n185
Butler Avenue (Providence) 117
Butler Hospital 3–5, 15, 93, 155 n3, n164
Butler, Samuel 192
By Daylight Only (Thomson) n199, n200
"By Post from Providence" 38, n53, n122

Cady, John Hutchins 199
Cady's Tavern 164–65
Cahiers d'Etudes d'Ailleurs 132
California 29, 47, 51, 54, 65–66, 79, 180, n253
Californian 38, 42, 45, 107, 148, n53, n54, n111, n122, n228
"Call of Cthulhu, The" 119–20, 134, 141–42, 178, 190, 203, n81, n170, n199, n200, n211, n220, n260
Cambodia 119
Cambridge, MA 23–24, 144,
Cambridge Tribune n127
Campbell, Paul J. n82
"Can the Moon be Reached by Man?" 102–103, 112, n139
Canal Street (Providence) n16
"Canal, The" (*Fungi* XXIV) n81
Caneviniana (Whitehead) 59, n78
Carlson, Eric 97, 153
Carolines 118–19
Carson, Dave n155
Carter, Lin 27–28, 120, n170
Carter, Randolph 124, 197
CAS: Nyctalops 76
Case of Charles Dexter Ward, The 22, 28, 65, 84, 113, 133, 154, 173, 197, 201, 212, n32, n33, n220, n248, n268
Casey, Robert n173
Casket and Sunnyside 161, n232
Cassia, FL 49, 57–59, 62–63, 65, 67, n94
"Cassius" (Whitehead) 191
Castle, The (Kafka) 88
Catalog of Copyright Deposits 69
Catalog of Lovecraftiana, A (Owings & Binkin) n10
"Catechism of Mayan Doctrine, A" 118
"Cats of Ulthar, The" 90, 186, 193, n41, n52
Cats of Ulthar, The * 49, 59, 61, 70–71, n95, n96
Causerie 224
Cavalier. *See All-Story (Cavalier)*
"Celephaïs" 90, 140, 173, 187, n195
Centaur, The (Blackwood) n260
Chalker, Jack L. 37, 41, 70–71, 73, 75, 78–79, 89, 99, 136, 140, 170–73, n58, n96, n111, n121, n133, n199, n243, n246
Chalkstone Avenue (Providence) n220
Champlin Memorial Library 96
Chapin, Albert n228
Chapin, Howard Miller 159–60, 166–67, n228
Charles St. Burying Ground (Salem) 147
Charleston (book) * 71–72, 146, n96
Charleston, S.C. 72, 146, n97, n99
Charlton, William 142
Charriére house (imaginary) n211

Charter Street (Salem) 147, n212
Chelsea Bookshop n221
Chepachet, R.I. 164, 167, n235, n236
Chestertown, MD 131
Chestnut Street (Providence) 213, 215
Chicago Tribune 130, n173
Chile 120
Chipping Campden, U.K. 14
Christian Scientist Church (Providence) n220
Church Avenue (Brooklyn) 156, n223
Churchward, James n173
"City, The" n75
Civic and Architectural Development of Providence, The (Cady) 199
Civil War (U.S.) 11
"Clang! Clang! Clang! Went the Trolley" (Young) n162
Clark, Dr. Franklin C. 9, 110, 144, n225
Clark, Lillian Delora 9–10, 24–25, 35, 108, 117, 133, 143–44, 146, 154–56, 176, 217, n8, n23, n98, n164, n208, n220, n225, n271
Classical High School (Providence) n118
Claverick Street (Providence) 215
Clayton Magazines, Inc. n195
Clayville, R.I. 19, n235
Cleveland, Albert W. n8
Cleveland Public Library 42
Clinton, Sir Henry 161
Clinton Street (Brooklyn) 155, 176–77, n221
"Clouds" n75
Club of the Seven Dreamers, The 124
Coast of Bohemia and Other Writings, The (Miniter) n111
Coates, Walter J.
  38, 56–57, 63–64, 70, n56, n81, n82, n84
Cockcroft, Thomas G. L. 22, 76, 114, 126, 139, 191, n86, 106, n123, n159, n170, n187, n195, n199, n200, n248
Coffin's Corners, R.I. 18
Cohasset, R.I. 153
Col. Thomas Lloyd Halsey House (Providence) n269
'Cold Spring Glen' (imaginary) n219
Cold Spring Press n154
Cole, Edward H. 78–79, n57
Coleman, Stuart n228, n239
Collected Essays
  44, 73, 105, 122, 125, 153, n43, n73, n99, n108, n110, n120, n129, n179, n257, n261
Collected Poems 50, n136
College Hill (Providence) n162, n220, n272
College of the Holy Cross (Worcester) 12
College of Physicians and Surgeons of Columbia University 145

College Street (Providence) 22, 32, 34, 71, 108, 118, 130, 144, 176, 193, 202, 206–210, n45, n99, n118, n162, n220, n239
Collins, Tom 273n247
"Colour out of Space, The"
  37, 72, 139, n41, n195, n219
Columbia University 145
Columbus, OH n117
Columbus of Space, A (Serviss) 112
commonplace book (HPL) 16, 30, 51, 84, 90–91, 112–113, 115, 116, 121, 124, 126, 160, 179–93, 214, n79, n118, n153, n157, n181, n211, n220, n222, n225, n257, n258, n259, n260
commonplace book (Sarah Susan Lovecraft)
  5, 11, n4, n11, n17, n23
"Commonplace Book: Its Use by Authors Other Than Lovecraft, The." (Connors) n263
Commonwealth Labour College 52
Concord (frigate) 204
Coney Island n99
Congdon Street (Providence) n220
Connors, Scott n263
Conover, Willis 69, 132, n122, n256
"Conqueror Worm, The" (Poe) 125
Conservative 38, 70, 99, n55, n57, n122
"Continuity" (*Fungi* XXXVI) 225
Cook, W. Paul 26, 32, 38–39, 41–42, 46–47, 49, 52, 56–60, 62–66, 67–69, 77–79, 109, 111, 125, 129–130, 147–53, 162, 173–74, 178, n27, n55, n56, n82, n84, n88, n107, n111, n124, n125, n215, n217, n218, n219, n255
Cook Islands n173
"Cool Air" n221
Copp's Hill Burying Ground (Salem) 154
"Copyright Problems of the Lovecraft Estate" (Wetzel) n10
Coronet Bookshop (New Orleans) 67, n37
Coslet, Walter A. 31, 54, n37
Cour des Miracles 213
"Courtyard, The" (*Fungi* IX) n81
Coventry, R.I. 18
Cox, Rev. George Benson n5
Crawford, William L. 140, n195
Creeps by Night (Hammett) 135
Crime of Crimes, The * n95
Crofts, Anna Helen 87, 172, n119
Crooked and Narrow Streets of Boston, The (Thwing) n220
Crowley, James Laurence n184, n241
'Cthulhu' 113, 116, 120, 178, 186, 208, n170; drawings of, 72, n99; sculpture of, n99
Cthulhu Mythos
  80, 119, 126, 146, 153, 190–91, n170, n262

Index 323

"The Cthulhu Mythos: A Study" (Wetzel) n220, n225, n262
Cuba 146
Cummings, Ray 121
Currier, C. H. 98
"Curse of Yig, The" 140
Curtis Brown, Ltd. 135, n199
Curwen, Joseph 197–200, 212, n268
Custom House Street (Providence) 19

Daas, Edward Francis 111
"Dagon" 36, 39, 46–47, 73, 76, 105, 111, n119, n173
Dagon and Other Macabre Tales 125, 136, 173, n119, n248
Damon, Samuel Foster 27–28, 36
Dana, H. Douglass 32–33, 43–44, 71, 73, 118, 130, n21, n38, n45, n99, n232
Dana, Mary V. n45
Dana, MA 149
Dana's Bookshop (Providence) n38
"Dark Brotherhood, The" (Derleth) 123, 206
Dark Brotherhood and Other Pieces, The 41, 123, 149, 153, 171, 178, 212, n11, n96, n199, n211
"Dark Brotherhood Dream" (Lovecraft) n175
Dark Brotherhood Journal 8, 83, n11
Dark Mind, Dark Heart (Derleth) n181
Dark Swamp (R.I.) 164–67, 212, n237
Dark Things (Derleth) 167, n238
Dartmouth College 129
Daugherty's Island n173
Davis, Cecil 67, n37
Davis, Dr. Nathaniel n253
Davis Park (Providence) 207
Davis, Robert H. 74
Davis, Sonia H. (Greene) 24, 37, 176–77, n5, n12, n251, n252, n253
Davison, Howard 86, n65, n117
Day, Frederick Holland 12, n14
de Camp, L. Sprague 130, 140, n1, n14, n114, n173, n209
de Castro, Adolphe 62, 70, 140, 148,
De Halve Maen n110, n232
De Land, FL 59, 63
de la Ree, Gerry 105, n41, n138
"De Triumpho Naturae" n146
"Dead Houses" (Miniter) 78–79, n215
Dead Houses and other Works n215
Dead Titans Waken! (Wandrei) n169.
See also *The Web of Easter Island*
"Death Customs Among the Colonial Dutch" (Talman) n232
Death in Venice (Mann) 90

"Defence Reopens, The" 46, 73
"Delavan's Comet and Astrology" 95, 172, n130
Dench, Ernest 175
Derleth, August 4, 15, 27–31, 35, 44, 46, 49–50, 52–55, 60–61, 64–67, 68, 84, 97, 99, 102, 111, 115–17, 119, 123, 127, 148–49, 152–53, 167, 169–70, 175, 179–80, 182, 185, 191, 193, 206, 212, 216, n8, n11, n30–31, n33, n41, n66, n69, n79, n91, n94, n99, n119, n124, n132, n143, n146, n147, n164, n170, n175, n176, n181, n182, n205, n207, n211, n238, n243, n248, n251; estate of, 190; papers, 61
"Derleth Mythos, The" (Tierney) n170
"Descendant, The" 84, 123
Description of the Town of Quebeck, A 32–33, 146, n209
"Despair" 40, 89–90, n75
Destiny 89, n57, n121
'Devil's Hop Yard' (imaginary) n219
Devonshire, U.K. 9, n8
Devonshire Ancestry of Howard Phillips Lovecraft (Faig, et al.) n9
Dexter, Mrs. Arthur 18–19
Dial, The 101
Dictionary of American Biography 10
Dobson, Roger n207
Docherty, Chris J. n9
"Does Vulcan Exist?" 97, 99, 102, n131
Donnelly, Sean n56, n215
"Doom that Came to Sarnath, The" 47, 140, n170, n195
Doris, Virginia L. n225
Dorchester, MA 3, 5–6
Dorr, Sullivan 158
Doubloon Street (Providence) 200
Dove Street (Providence) 204
Dowdell, William J. n57
Dowe, Jennie E. T. n125
Doyle, Mayor Thomas A. 216
Doyle, Sir Arthur Conan 114
Dracula (Stoker) 125
Dragon-Fly Press 49–50, 56, 58–59, 61–62, n78
Drake, Samuel Adams n220
Dream-Quest of Unknown Kadath, The 28, 65, 84, 124, 173, n32, n170, n220, n248
Dreams and Fancies 44, 115–16, 123, 205, n159
"Dreams in the Witch House, The" 106, 147, n143
"Dreams of Yith" (Rimel) n184
Driftwind 38, 70, 77, 80, 225, n57, n81
Driftwind Press 38, 70, 80, n56, n81, n82, n84
Druid Press n78
druids 191–92

Ducie 120
Dudley, MA n218
Dudley Street (Providence) 214
Dumas, Theodere J. 216
Dunedin, FL 217, n99
Dunn, John T. n57
Dunsford, U.K. 9
Dunwich, MA (imaginary) 149–50, n216
"Dunwich Horror, The" 127, 134, 148–53, n200, n215, n216, n219
Dunwich Horror, The (1970) 133
Dunwich Horror and Others, The 4, 136, 175, n219
Durfee Hill 164, n237
Durfee Hill Road 164–66
Dutch Reformed Church 155–56, n223
"Dweller, The" (*Fungi* XXXI) 225, n80
Dwyer, Bernard Austin 3, 6, 8, 44, 107, 109–11, 116, 147, 155, 192, n119, n143, n159, n160, n219, n221

"East and West Harvard Conservatism" n108
East Greenwich, R.I. 17, 22, n239
East Greenwich Academy 17
"East India Brick Row." *See* "Brick Row"
East Killingly, CT n235
East Manning Street 23, n23
East Saint Louis, IL 38, n82, n84
Easter Island 118–120, n174
Easter Island (Casey) n174
Eastern New Mexico University 81
Eblis 124
E'ch-Pi-El Speaks n138
Echoes from an Iron Harp (Howard) 52, n78
Eddy, Clifford M. Jr. 164–67, 205, 212–14, 216, n11, n12, n220, n237
Eddy, Muriel 144, n11, n208
"Edith Miniter" 78–79, n111
Edkins, Ernest A. 59, 78, 126–27, n46, n181
Edwin E. Phillips Co. n23
Edwin Hadley Smith Collection n26
"Eidolon, The" n75
'Elder Gods' n170
"Elder Pharos, The" (*Fungi* XXVII) n81
"Elegy on Franklin Chase Clark, M.D., An" 99
"Elegy on Phillips Gamwell, Esq., An" 99
"Elements of a Weird Story & Types" 180
Eliot, T. S. 101
Elizabeth, N.J. 156, n224
Elizabeth Avenue (Elizabeth, N.J.) 156
Ellwood, Roger n154
Elmgrove Avenue (Providence) 8, 17, 20, 211, n8
Elmhurst 11
Emerson, Harold Davis n166
Endless Caverns (VA) 146

Enfield, MA 149
England, George Allan 112
ERBdom–Fantasy Collector n94
Eshbach, Lloyd A. n195
Esoteric Order of Dagon Amateur Press Association n54
Etchings and Odysseys 120, 208, n172
Eternal Maiden, The (Harré) n199
Evans, William H. 40–41, 46, 54, 73, 79, 87, 89–91, 96, 103–104, 113, 131, 225, n111, n124
Evanston, IL 142
"Evening Star" (*Fungi* XXXV) 225
Everts, R. Alain 8–9, 22–23, 34, 39, 41, 43, 54, 63–64, 66, 68, 82–83, 93, 110, 132, 144, 168, 177, n3, n8, n12, n56, n101, n111, n117, n119, n124, n127, n134, n149, n193, n228, n243, n254, n267
"Evil Clergyman, The" 43, 85, 116, n66, n159
"Ex Oblivione" 44, 84, 87, n68, n195
Exeter, R.I. n8
Exiles and Fabrications (Scott) 21
Exit into Eternity (Eddy) n238
"Expectancy" (*Fungi* XXVIII) 225
"Eyrie, The" (*Weird Tales*) 36, 76, 130–31, n33

"Facts in the Case of H. P. Lovecraft" (St. Armand) n99
Faig, Kenneth W., Jr. n5, n8, n9, n14, n22, n26, n28, n41, n57, n63, n64, n111, n215, n240, n268
"Falsity of Astrology, The" 94
Fanciful Tales of Time and Space n42
Fantasmagoria: The Literary Fan Magazine n160
Fantastic Poetry, The n167
Fantasy Commentator 34, 113, n106
Fantasy Fan 57, 190, 224–25, n57, n99, n195
Fantasy Magazine n57
FAPA (Fantasy Amateur Press Association) 40, 54, 225, n78
Farsaci, Larry B. 59–60, 63–64, 75, 123, n33, n86, n147
"The Fate of Two Ajay Collections" (Faig) n64
Federal Hill (Providence) 39, 205–208, 211, 216, n259
"Festival, The" 146, 183, 186, n220
Few Letters from Arthur Machen: Letters to Munson Havens, A n207
Field of Ice, The (Verne) 132
Finlay, Virgil 71
First Baptist Church (Providence) 200
First Baptist Meeting House (Greene) n12, n211
Fischer, Harry O. 32, n40
Fiske, John n225
Fitzroy (publisher) 132

Index

Flatbush Avenue (Brooklyn) n223
Fletcher, Mrs. Ruth A. 143
Fleur-de-Lys Studio (Prov.) n211, n220, n265
Florida 29, 31, 49, 54, 57, 60, 62–66, 70, 119, 127, 146, 218, n228
Fossil Library 40, n26
Fossil 42, n243
Fossils, The 42, n57
Foster, R.I. 17–19, 27, 135, 144, n8, n17, n141
Four Acrostic Sonnets on Edgar Allan Poe* 70–71
Fourteen Weeks in Chemistry (Steele) 159, n226
Fox Point (Providence) 203–205
Fox Point Hurricane Barrier 200, 202
Frankenstein (Shelley) 187
Franklin Institute 39–40, 88, 169, n26, n57, n122
Fraternal and Ancient Order of Masons 18
Freehafer, Paul n78
'French Leach' n211
Fresco 175
Friendly Islands n173
"The Friendship of Louise Imogen Guiney and Sarah Susan Phillips" (Faig) n14
Frierson, Meade 25, n148, n70, n224
Frierson, Penny 25, n170
"From Beyond" 87, n195
Frome, Nils H. n195
"Fruit of the Vine, The" (Talman) 161–62
"Fungi from Yuggoth" (sonnet cycle) 38, 49, 54, 59, 70, 155, n75, n156
Fungi from Yuggoth and Other Verses (Barlow edition) 49, 54–55, 60–62, n75
Further Criticism of Poetry * 71
Futile Press, The 30, 49, 51, 53, 55, 59, 65, 84, 115–16, 179–80, 185, 187, n79, n259

Gaddis, Vincent n173
Galaxy 135
Galleon 225
'Gallomo' 167, 186–87, n119, n239
Galpin, Alfred 131, n220, n244
Gammell, George 203
Gamwell, Annie E. Phillips 10, 13, 23, 25–28, 35, 58, 65, 67, 82, 108, 127, 144, 167–68, 176, 190, 197, 203–204, 208, 211, n19, n23, n25, n31, n38, n79, n220, n232, n271
Gamwell, Edward F. 9–10, 23–24, 144, n127
Gamwell, Marion Rhoby 10
Gamwell, Phillips 24, 99, n23, n101
Gano Street (Providence) 204–205, n220
Gaol-Lane (Providence) n220
Garden of Evil, The (Stoker) 125
'Garrison, Repas' n211
HMS *Gaspée* 197–98
Gaynor, Leonard 133
Gazetteer of Rhode Island (Chapin) 166

Gems from the Coral Islands (Gill) n173
Germany 121
Gernsback, Hugo n195
Ghidalia, Victor n154
Ghost 32, 38
Ghostly by Gaslight (Moskowitz & Norton) 111
'Ghoul's Court.' *See* Gould's Court
Gilbert, R. A. n207
Gill, Rev. William n173
Gill, Rev. W. Wyatt n173
Glocester, R.I. 165–66, n236
Gloucester, MA 152
Gloucestershire, U.K. 14
Gobi 120
Goblin Tower, The (Long) 58–59, 61
Golden Atom 59–60, 66–67, 75, 84, 123, n33, n102
Golden Book 111, n105
Goodenough, Arthur 129, 150, n208
Goose Quill Papers (Guiney) 11, n227
"Gorge Beyond Salapunco, The" (Derleth) 119
Gorham Company 4, 6, n6, n16
"Gorilla, The" (Lemon) 111–13
Gorman, Joseph n5
Gould, Commander Rupert n173
Gould's Court (Providence) 213–16
Gould's Place (Providence) 215–16
Gould's Street 215–16
Gowanus Canal (Brooklyn) n222
Goya, Francisco 213
Grace Methodist Evangelical Church (Greene) n12
Graham, Ronald E. n52
Grayson, Allan Brownell 217
Great Fulford, U.K. n8
Great Meadow Hill (Rehoboth, R.I.) 167–68
Great Meadow Hill Country Clubhouse 168, n239, n240, n267
'Great Race' 195, n99, n170
"Green Picture, The" (Skinner) n225
Greene, Florence 177, n254
Greene, John Holden 216, n220
Greene, R.I. 10, 18–20, 95, 143, 211, n8, n12
Greene, Sonia. *See* Sonia H. Davis
Greenpoint (Brooklyn) n222
Greenwich Village n223
Grill, Philip Jack 10, 32–34, 41, 48, 68, 82, 144, 156–58, 160, 161, n10, n21, n38, n41, n92, n148, n224, n229
Grill–Binkin collection n10, n41, n148, n233
"Guide to Charleston, South Carolina, A" 71
Guiney, Janet Margaret (Doyle) 11
Guiney, Louise Imogen 3, 6–8, 10–15, n1, n14, n227

Guiney, Patrick Robert 22
Gullette, Alan D. n174

"H. Lovecraft's Attempted Journey betwixt Providence & Fall River on the N.Y.N.H. & H.R.R." n163
H. P. Lovecraft: A Basic Collection of 100 items ... (Squires) 71
H. P. Lovecraft: A Comprehensive Bibliography (Joshi) n60, n242
H. P. Lovecraft: A Portrait (Cook) 129, 148, 153, 173, n88, n107
"H. P. Lovecraft: A Story Listing." (Morris) n51
H. P. Lovecraft: A Symposium n41
H. P. Lovecraft and Lovecraft Criticism: An Annotated Bibliography (Joshi) n60, n242
"H. P. Lovecraft and the Munsey Magazines" (Moskowitz) 74
H. P. Lovecraft Dream Book, The n158, n175
"H. P. Lovecraft: Eldritch Yankee Gentleman" (de Camp) n1
H. P. Lovecraft in The Argosy: Collected Correspondence from the Munsey Magazines n104, n245
H. P. Lovecraft in "The Eyrie" n106
H. P. Lovecraft in Popular Culture (Smith) n190
"H. P. Lovecraft: The Man Who Could Not Die." (Szezsponik) n162
"H. P. Lovecraft: The Mystery of the Missing Manuscript." (Blackmore) n52
"H. P. Lovecraft: The Outsider in Legend and Myth" (St. Armand) 80
H. P. Lovecraft's Book of Horror (Jones and Carson) n155
H. P. Lovecraft's Favorite Horror Stories (Joshi) n155
"H. P. Lovecraft's Favorite Movie" (Schweitzer) n191
H. P. Lovecraft's Favorite Weird Tales: The Roots of Modern Horror (Anderson) n155
Hagerstown, MD 158
Haining, Peter n147, n154
"Hallowe'en in a Suburb" n75
Halsey Mansion (Providence) 199, n269
Hamilton, Edmond 121
Hamlet (Shakespeare) 131
Hammett, Dashiell 135
Hampden, MA 149–152
Hannibal, MO n65
Hansen, Peter Andreas 112
Happy Ending (Guiney) 10
"Harbour Whistles" (*Fungi* XXXIII) 225
Harré, T. Everett n199
Harrington, Rev. Eugene J. 12

Harris Collection of American Poetry and Plays (Brown University) 27, n185, n208
Harris, Rev. William J. 5
Hart, Bertrand K. 101, 160, n81, n128, n230
Hartford, CT 19, 117
Hartford Press 158
Hartford, Providence, and Fishkill Railroad 19
Hartmann, J. F. 94–95, 172, n128
Harvest (Coates) n81
"The Hashish-Eater" (Smith) 51–52
Hassler, Donald M. n207
Hassler, Sue Strong n207
Hathaway, Abbie A. 82, n113
"Haunted House, The" 109
Haunted Palace, The (1963) 133
"Haunter of the Dark, The" 106, 127–28, 154, 206–208, 210, n35, n52, n211, n259
Havens, Munson Aldrich n207
Hawaii n29, n173
Hazlitt, William 202
"He" 156, n223
Hearn, Lafcadio 214
Helen Street (Providence) 213
Henderson 120
Henneberger, J. C. 125, 142
"Herbert West—Reanimator" 36, 76, 134, 136, n117
Hesperia n156
"Hesperia" (*Fungi* XIII) n81, n156
Hess, Clara L. 15, 93
Hexham, U.K. n8
Hill, Caleb R. n20
Hill, Isaac 9, 23
Hippocampus Press n29, n135, n215
"His Ancestor's Head" (Sheehan) 112, 114
"His Own Most Fantastic Creation" (Scott) 4, 93, 101, 202, n218, n239
Historical Reminiscences of Foster, R.I. (Tyler) 19
History of Amateur Journalism (Spencer) 42, n57
History of Caliph Vathek, The (Beckford) 124
History of Dartmouth College (Richardson) n183
History of Greene and Vicinity (Wood) 18, n8, n12
Hoag, Jonathan E. 129
Hoffmann, E. T. A. 124
Hogarth, William 203, 213
Holmes, Dr. Oliver Wendell 7, 13, 144, n13, n181
Home Brew 125, 134, n49, n196, n201
Hope Street High School (Providence) 8, 81–82
Hopkins Street (Providence) 202, n220
Hornig, Charles D. 52, 58, n195
"Horror at Red Hook, The" 37, 155, n199
Horror from the Hills, The (Long) 116
Houdini, Harry 141, 170–71

"Hound, The" 155
"House, The" 156, n75, n225, n234
House of the Worm, The 125–26
Houtain, George Julian 36, 76, 134, n117, n196
Howard Hill (R.I.) 17, n8, n164
Howard Payne College 34, 68, n93
"Howard P(seudonym) Lovecraft: The Many Names of HPL." (Keffer) n243
Howard Phillips Lovecraft (1890–1937): A Tentative Bibliography (Laney and Evans) 40–41, 46, 79, 87, 89–91, 96, 103, 131, n111, n124
"Howard Phillips Lovecraft: A Bibliography" (Chalker) 37, 41, 70–71, 75, 78, 89, 99, 136, 139, 170–73, n96, n121, n133, n199, n246
"Howard Phillips Lovecraft as His Wife Remembers Him" (Davis) n251
"Howard Phillips Lovecraft: The Early Years, 1890–1914: A Bibliography" n98
Howard, Dr. Isaac M. 34, 68, 134, n78, n197
Howard, Leslie 133
Howard, Robert E. (REH) 3, 13, 100, 126, 190, 193, n46, n47, n197; estate of, n78, n93
HPL (1972) n170, n190, n220, n225
HPL: A Memoir (Derleth) 97, n131, n146
HPL: Memoirs, Critiques, and Bibliographies (Wetzel) 40–41, 43, 87, 169, n121, n132, n246
"HPL and Films" (Shea) n190
Hugo, Victor 213
'Hugog' 19, n20
Huitloxopetl n148, n224

I Am Providence: The Life and Times of H. P. Lovecraft (Joshi) n6, n7, n9, n14
"I Met Lovecraft" (Keil) n193
"Idiosyncrasies of H.P.L." (Edkins) 126
"Idle Days on the Yann" (Dunsany) 183
Iles Gambier 120
Illustrated Scripture History for the Young, The n148
Immortal Storm, The (Moskowitz) 116
"Imprisoned with the Pharaohs" 37, 140–41, 171, n35, n52, n205.
"In Defence of Dagon" 46–47, n73
In Lovecraft's Shadow (Derleth) n176
"In Memoriam: Howard Phillips Lovecraft: Recollections, Appreciations, Estimates" (Cook) n59
"In Memoriam: J. E. T. D." n125
In Memory of Edith Miniter * 78–79, n110
"In Rescue of the Lost Searchers" (Marten) n210
"In Search of Arkham Country" (Murray) n210
In Search of Lovecraft (Shea) n190

"In the Walls of Eryx" 121
Incantations (Smith) 51–53, 61–62
Independent Order of Good Templars 18
"An Index to 'The Eyrie' and Other Readers' Departments" (Cockcroft) n106
Index to the Science Fiction Magazines 1926–1950 (Day) 191
Index to the Selected Letters (Joshi) n99
Index to the Weird Fiction Magazines (Cockcroft) 191
India Street (Providence) 203
Innsmouth, MA (imaginary) 153
"Inspiration." n100
"Instructions in Case of Decease" (Lovecraft) 26–27, 30, 120, 190
Interesting Items 225
"Interlude with Lovecraft" (Boland) 118
Invisible Horizons (Gaddis) n173
Iokimidis, Demètre 132
Ipswich, MA 153
Ireland 194
"Is Mars an Inhabited World?" 102–103, 112
"Is there Life on the Moon?" 103, 112
Islands of Adventure (Baarslag) n173
"Iterum Conjunctae" n134
Ivens, Roy M. 129

Jackson, Fred 75–76
Jackson, Winifred Virginia 172
John Brown House (Providence) 160, 200, 209
John Day Co. 135
John Hay Library 5, 7, 11, 20, 27–29, 31–36, 39, 42–47, 49, 51, 54–56, 59, 62–63, 65, 68, 71, 73–74, 75–80, 85, 87, 90–91, 94, 97, 99, 100–101, 105–106, 108, 117–118, 123–24, 132, 139, 141, 144, 147, 154–55, 162, 175–76, 182, 187, 193, 203, 208–210, n8, n11, n17, n23, n29, n41, n45, n57, n72, n96, n99, n101, n119, n124, n146, n147, n156, n211, n220, n225, n226, n232, n248; LOVECRAFT COLLECTION, 20, 35, 37, 44, 51, 62, 76–80, 87, 91, 94, 97, 99–100, 105, 123, 147, 155, 175–76, 181, 187, 19, 203, n72, n96, n99, n101, n119, n124, n225, n232, n248
John Rathbone House n8
"John, the Detective" 109
Jones, Stephen n155
Joseph Nightingale House (Providence) 200
Joshi, S. T. n40, n60, n99, n129, n131, n155, n242, n244

Kafka, Franz 88, n168
Kalem Club 175
Kamin, Martin 175
Kanaky 119, n173

Kansas City, MO
    26–27, 29, 49, 52–55, 59–60, 62, 64–66
Kansas City Art Institute 62, 64–65
'Kappa Alpha Tau' 193, 209–210
Kappa Alpha Tau (Connors) n263
Kay, James 168
Keel, Billy n174
Keffer, Mrs. Willametta n243
Keil, Paul Livingston n193
Keller, Dr. David H. 110, 126
Kennedy, Nabby Tyler 19, n19
"Key, The" (*Fungi* III) 224
Key West, FL 146
Khmer ruins 119
King Phillip n219
'Kingsport,' MA 122–23, 146, 148, 152–53
Kirk, George 175, n221
Kleiner, Rheinhart
    3–5, 7, 9, 11, 13, 21, 26, 38–39, 45, 47, 73–
    74, 81–85, 92, 95–97, 100–101, 103–104,
    107–109, 111–14, 116, 124, 126, 133, 154,
    167, 171, 173–75, 186, n12, n41, n53, n71,
    n113, n119, n122, n135, n156, n228, n241
Kline, Otis Adelbert 134, n78, n197
Knack, Otto 175
Knopf, Alfred A. 135
Koblas, John J. n162
Koenig, Herman C. 71–72, 146, 175, n48, n97
Kraft, David A. 134
Kuntz, Eugene B. 129

Ladd Observatory (Providence) 97–98
"Laeta: A Lament" n241
"Lair of the Star–Spawn, The"
    (Derleth and Schorer) 119
Lair of the White Worm, The (Stoker) 125
Lakeport, CA 29, 47, 51, 53–54, 59, 180
"Lamp of Alhazred, The" (Derleth) 117
Laney, Francis T. 40–41, 44, 46, 73, 79, 87, 89–
    91, 96, 103–104, 131, n65, n81, n111, n117,
    n123–24
Langworthy, Dorcas Emlin 66, n90
Langworthy, Herman Moore 65, n89
Lapham Seminary (Scituate) 98
Law, E. F. 165–66
Law, Ernest 165–67
Law, H. 166
Law, N. 166
Lawson, Horace 171, 213, n244
Last Year at Marienbad (1961) 133
Le Pere Goriot (Balzac) n220
Leavenworth, KS 50–52, 54, 59, 65
Leakey, Mary 120
Leaves 47, 53, 59, 62, 65, 78, 84, n215

Leeds, Arthur 175
Lehigh Street (Providence) 212
Leiber, Fritz, Jr. n40, n170
Lemon, Don Mark 111–14
"Leon Stone: Amateur Journalist and Pioneer
    Lovecraft Collector" (Blackmore) n64
"Le Silent" (Crofts) n119
Letters of Henry S. Whitehead, The n78
Letters of Louise Imogen Guiney, The 11
Leverett, MA 149
Lewis, Edna W. 25
Library of Amateur Journalism
    88, n26, n57, n121, n122, 125
Library of Congress 12, 42, 69, 80, 81, n14, n133
"Life and Death" 45, 88–91, n121, n122, n124
"Life's Mystery" n247
Lincoln Woods (R.I.) n164
"Lines on the 25th. Anniversary of the Providence
    Evening News, 1892–1917" n134
"List of Certain Basic Underlying Horrors ... "
    180, 190
"List of Primary Ideas ... " 180
Little Budget of Knowledge and Nonsense 125
"Little Glass Bottle, The" 107–108
Livebook 130
Liverpool, U.K. 20
"Locked Dimensions out of Reach: The Lost
    Stories of H. P. Lovecraft" (Rajala)
    n70, n150, n165, n211
London, U.K. 20, 75
London Evening Standard 136
"Long Distance Predictions: ... " n101
Long, Frank Belknap
    8, 58, 68, 72, 76, 101, 116, 124–25, 129, 133,
    144, 150, 152, 164, 175, 190–91, n5, n8, n52,
    n71, n92, n193, n220, n235, n262
Looking Backward * 71
Lord, Glenn 35, 54, 60, 68, n78, n93
Lore n200
Loring & Mussey (publisher) 135
Lost Continents (de Camp) n173
Louise Imogen Guiney: Her Life and Works
    (Tenison) 11
Louisiana 4
Lovecraft (*L'Herne*) 170, n72, n121
Lovecraft: A Biography (de Camp) n1, n14
Lovecraft: A Look Behind the Cthulhu Mythos
    (Carter) 27, n170
Lovecraft at Last (Conover) n122
Lovecraft Circle 28, n93
Lovecraft Collector 110
Lovecraft Collectors' Library (Wetzel)
    40, 44, 126, 169, n57, n121

"Lovecraft and the New England Megaliths" (Rothovius) 149
"Lovecraft as a Conversationalist" (Loveman) 175
"Lovecraft as I Knew Him" (Davis) 176
"Lovecraft Comes Back Ad Criticos" 74
Lovecraft, Emma 9, 23
"Lovecraft Family in America, The" (Everts) n9
Lovecraft, George 4, 8–9, 11
Lovecraft, Helen (Allgood) 4, 8, 211
Lovecraft, H. P.:
  LIFE: amateur journalism, n57; ancestry, 8–9; birth, 3–4; childhood and adolescence, 22, 81–82, n149 ; death, 26; divorce, 177, n253; earnings, 25, 134–142, 219–25, n206; education, 8, 81–83, 110–11 n7; last will, 26–27, 30; marriage 37, 177, n5, n12; parents, 4–5, 9–10, 15–16; photographs of, 33–34, 82, n193; travels and outings, n164, n218, n235
  PSEUDONYMS: 'Appleton, Lawrence' 169, 170, 172, n247, 'Bickerstaffe, Isaac, Jr.' 94–95, 172, n247, 'Blair, Alexander Ferguson' n247, 'Howard, L. Phillips' n247, 'El Imparcial' n247, 'Jones, John' J.' 169, 170, 172, n247, 'Littlewit, Humphrey' 169, 171–72, n247, 'Maynwaring, Archibald' 169, 171–72, n242, n247, 'O'Reilly, Michael Ormonde' n247, 'Paget-Lowe, Henry' 87, 169, 170, 172, n246, n247, 'Phillips, Ward' n156, n247, 'Raleigh, Richard' 169, 170–72, n247, '"Rersley," Ames Dorrance' 169, n241, 'Rowley, Ames Dorrance' 169, 170, 172, n156, n241, n247, 'Softly, Edward' 169, 170, 172, n247, 'Swift, Augustus T.' (apocryphal), 169, 171–72, n245, 'Theobald, Grandpa' 76, 117, 197, 'Theobald, Lewis' 169, 170, 172, n156, n246, n247, 'Willie, Albert Frederick' 169, 170, 172, n247, 'Zoilus' 170–72, n243, n244, n246, n247;
  RESIDENCES: Auburndale and Dorchester, 3, 5–7, 12–13; 10 Barnes St. 34, 108, 161, 199, 210; 66 College St. 22, 32, 34, 71, 108, 118, 130, 144, 176, 193, 206, 208–210, n45, n220, n225, n259; 169 Clinton St. 155, 161, 176–77, n221; 259 Parkside Ave. 133, 155, n164; 454 (194) Angell St. 3, 6, 22, 108, 110, 117, 144, 211; 598 Angell St. 21, 108, 211, n48, n57, n228;
  THOUGHT: atheism , 109; dreams, 44, 113, 115–18, 123, 126, 173, 178, 186–88, 206, n158, n159, n174, n175, n179, n220;
  WORK: amateur journalism, 37–39, 41–43, n65; artwork, n48; correspondence, 34–35, 43–45, 74–77, n46, n207; "death diary," n29; lost works, 45–46, 85–91, n70, n143, n156, n211; manuscripts, 27–28, 30, 32–33, 47, n41, n229; in newspapers, 92–104; revisory works, 25, 77, 127, 129–130, 136, 140–41, 182, nn205–206; travelogues, 32–33, 146, 154, n8, n43, n45; of Charleston, S.C., 71–72, 146, n97, n99; verse, 32, 45, 50–51, 73–74, 76, 99–101, 117, 129–30, 141, 222–25, n75, n81; *see also* commonplace book
Lovecraft in the Cinema (Schweitzer) n190
"Lovecraft in Providence" (Wandrei) 105, 178
Lovecraft, Joseph 9
"Lovecraft, My Childhood Friend" (Munro) n149
"Lovecraft on Love" n251
Lovecraft, Sarah Susan (Phillips) 3, 5–13, 15, 17, 21–24, 35, 93, 95, 108, 143–44, 155, 211, 217, n3, n5, n11, n12, n17, n23, n149, n218. *See also* commonplace book of
Lovecraft Scholar, The (Wetzel) n10, n28, n34
Lovecraft, Tom 9
Lovecraft, Winfield Scott 4–7, 9–10, 12–13, 15–16, 24, 34, 211, n2, n3, n5, n10, n12, n16, n28; death certificate of, 5, n3
Lovecraft's Library (Joshi) n38
Lovecraft's Daughter III (Everts) n254
"Lovecraft's Literary Executor" (Wetzel) n34
"Lovecraft's Providence" (Faig) n211
"Lovecraft's Sensitivity" (Derleth) 15, 93
"Lovecraftian Note, A" 8
Loveman, Samuel 8, 30, 37, 60–63, 131, 133, 154–56, 175, 177, 203, n12, n31, n35, n52, n71, n81, n94, n182, n188, n193, n220
Lowell, Percival 97
Lower Hutt, New Zealand 76
Lowndes, Robert A. W. 28, 69
Lumley, Brian 119
Lumley, William n99
Lurker at the Threshold, The (Derleth) 84
Lurker in the Lobby: A Guide to the Cinema of H. P. Lovecraft (Migliore and Strysik) n190
"Lurking Fear, The" 16, 127, 134, 182, n196, n201
lycanthropy 127

Macauley, George W. 100, n134, n150
Macbeth (Shakespeare) 131
Machen, Arthur 142, n207
Machu Pichu 119
MacManus, Peter n57
Macy-Masius (publisher) 141, n199, n200
Magistris, Mariano de 25

Magnalia Christi Americana (Mather) 26, 147
Magnolia, MA 153, 176
Maine 146, 152, 164
Mann, Thomas 90
maps: Arkham (HPL) 147, n211, (Wilson) n211; Dark Swamp (R.I.) 164; Durfee Hill (R.I.) 164; Innsmouth (Carlson), 153; Lemuria (Scott-Elliot) n173; Pacific (Rand McNally) 120; Providence County Atlas 165; Providence plat maps 215, n220, n225; Rhode Island (Walling) 166, n237; Rhode Island highway map 165–66, n235; U.S. Army Map Service maps 166, 168, n235
Marblehead, MA 146–49,152–53, 184, 186
"March" 99
Marginalia 4, 20–21, 37, 44, 71, 81, 88, 105, 116, 122, 147, n11, n79, n147
Mariconda, Steven J. n143
Market Square (Providence) 201, 202
"Marshes at Ipswich, The" 73–74, 92
Marten, Robert D. 260n210
Marvel Tales 140
Massachusetts 3–4, 7, 13, 22, 146, 148, 149, 152–53, 154, 168
Materialist Today, The * 70–71, n56, n96
"Materialist Today, The" (essay) 38, 70
Mather, Cotton 26, 147
Mathews, Martha. *See* Martha Phillips
Mathews, Mrs. Jennie E. n23
Maurer, Peter J. n52
Maya 117
'Mayan Temple' n166
McFarland & Co. n190
McGrath, Patrick 155, 175
McNeil, Everett 175
Meeting Street (Providence) n220
"Memories of a Friendship" (Galpin) n220
"Memories of Lovecraft (1934)" (Barlow) n175, n195
"Memory" (story) 44, n68
"Memory, A" (*Fungi* XVII) 225
Merritt, A. 37, 119
Merritt, Dr. James D. n122
Merritt, Pearl K. 175
Merry Minutes 73–74
"Messenger, The" 99, n81, n128, n211
Metis shoal n173
Mexico 28–29, 31, 50, 53–54, 58–60, 66, 67, 70, 105, 118, n94
Michael, Mr. n138
Migliore, Andrew n190
Mill Street (Providence) n220
Miller, Charles 159
Mind Parasites, The (Wilson) 126

Mind Power Plus 77, n108–109
Mineral Mountain (MA) 151
Miniter, Edith 78–79, 148–50, 152, n110, n215
'Minster Hall' 8–9, n8
"Mirage" (*Fungi* XXIII) n80
Miscellaneous Writings 47, 95, n129
Miske, J. Chapman 44, n69
Mississippi 4
Modern Tales of Horror (Hammett) 135, n199
Moe, Maurice W. 4, 6, 8–9, 11, 15, 17–25, 70–71, 76, 94–96, 100–101, 143–44, 150, 154, 172, 177, 205, 213, 215, n8, n11, n101, n135, n164, n174, n271
Monson, MA 149–52
"Moon: A Brief Description of Our Satellite" 103
"Moon Pool, The" (Merritt) 119
Moon Terror, The (Birch) n198
Moore, C. L. 62, 69, n46
Moosup, CT 17–18, n8
Moosup River 17
Moosup Valley (R.I.) 18, n8, n19
Morris, Harry O., Jr. 37, n51
Mount Pleasant (Providence) 207
More "Not at Night" (Thomson) n199
More, Sir Thomas 14
Morrish, Ethel Phillips 25
Morse, Richard Ely 132
Morton, James Ferdinand, Jr. 26, 100, 129–30, 133, 164, 175, 203–204, 222, n5, n12, n71, n81, n135, n164, n193, n237, n244
Moshassuck Press (Faig) n57, n111
Moshassuck river 199, 202, n220
Moskowitz, Sam 74–76, 95, 100, 111, 116, 171,
Mother Ann (Gloucester, MA) 152
"Mother Earth" n75
Moulton, Louise Chandler 12
Mount Vernon, N.Y. 9, n8
"Mrs. Miniter—Estimates and Recollections" 78–79, 148–49, n111
Mumford, Captain Samuel 209
Munn, H. Warner 47, 150, n82, n107, n218
Munro, Harold W. n149
Munroe, Addison n228, n239
Munroe, Chester n228, n239, n267
Munroe, Harold Bateman 167–68, 197, n228, n239, n267
Munsey Magazines 74–76, 100, 113, 171
Murdock, John 88, 157, n229
Murray, Will n210
"Music of Erich Zann, The" 135–36, 141, n199, n220
Mycroft & Moran n176
Myers, Denys Peter n99
Mynydd Maen 142

"Mysteries of the Heavens Revealed by
    Astronomy" n133
"Mysterious Ship, The" 107–108, n138
"Mystery of the Grave-Yard, The"
    107–109, n138
"Mystery of Murdon Grange, The" n156, n241
Myths and Legends of Our Own Land
    (Skinner) n225
Myths and Myth-Makers (Fiske) n225

"Nameless City, The"
    33, 46, n72, n170, n195, n220
Narragansett Bay (R.I.) 202
*Narrative of Arthur Gordon Pym of Nantucket,
    The* (Poe) 132, n174
National Amateur
    32, 44, 73, 87, 173, n39, n57, n68, n125
National Amateur Press Association (NAPA)
    73, 131, n188
National Magazine 73–74, 92, n100
National Union Catalog n81, n111
natural history 143
Nazis 121
Necronomicon Amateur Press Association n263
Necronomicon Press
    n42, n54, n57, n73, n251, n257
"Nemesis" n75
Nero and Other Poems (Smith) 51
Neutaconkanut Hill (R.I.) 117, 212, n164
New England 77, 121–22, 127, 147–48, 152,
    195, 217, n84, n111, n211, n216
"New England" n134
New Haven, CT 117
"New HPL Pseudonyms Rejected by Derleth"
    (Derleth) n243
New Orleans., LA 31, 67, 146,
New York Herald n101
New York Public Library 37, 132, 161, n61
New York Times n136
New York University 39, n26, n122, n243
New Zealand 76, 120
Newburyport, MA 153
Newport, R.I. 32, 203, 208
Newton Abbott n8
"Night-Gaunts" (*Fungi* XX) 225, n81
"Nightmare Lake, The" n75
Night's Black Agents (Leiber) n40
Ninth Massachusetts Infantry 11
Niswonger, Mrs. Deborah 76
"Noble Eavesdropper, The" 107–109
North Court Street (Providence) n220, n272
North Dana, MA n219
North Main Street (Providence)
    199, 202, 205, n16, n220, n265, n268

North Montpelier, VT 38, n82
North Scituate, R.I. 98
North Wilbraham, MA 148–50
Northumberland, U.K. n8
Norton, Alden H. 112
Norton, MA 11, 143, 168
"Nostalgia" (*Fungi* XXIX) 224, n81
Not at Night (Thomson) n199, n200
Not At Night Omnibus (Thomson) n199, n200
"Not at Night" series 136, n199, n200
Notes and Commonplace Book, The * 49
Nostradamus 94
Notre Dame 214
Nukualofa n173
"Nyarlathotep" (story) 44, 84, 87, 173, n68, n195
"Nyarlathotep" (*Fungi* XXI) n81
Nyctalops 22, 37, 41, 47, 72–73, 76, 92, 114,
    139, 153, n41, n51, n98, n119, n123, n149,
    n195, n248

OAK Leaves 134, n78, n197
"Oceanus" n75
"October" n75
Oddities (Gould) n173
"Ode for July Fourth, 1917" 99, n100
"Of Evil Sorceries" 123
Old Colony Co-Operative Bank n194
Old Farmer's Almanac 26, n27
*Old Landmarks and Historic Personages of
    Boston* (Drake) n220
'Old Man' (cat) n220, n265
Old North Burial Ground (Providence)
    160, 199–200, 213
"Old Stone Bank" History of Rhode Island
    (Haley) 160
Olduvai Gorge (Africa) 120
Oliphant, S. Grant n230
Olney Court (Providence) 198–99, n268
Olney, Epenetus 198–99
Olney Street (Providence) 198–99, n220, n268
"On Graveyards" (Guiney) n227
On Lovecraft and Life (Barlow) n175
"On Receiving a Picture of the Marshes at
    Ipswich." *See* "The Marshes at Ipswich"
"On Receiving a Picture of Swans" n99, n133
One Hundred Years of the Fossils 1904–2004
    n26
Orton, Vrest 175
Ostrow, Alexander 131, n188
Otaheité. *See* Tahiti
"Other Gods, The" 173, n170, n195
"Other Notes" 84, 123,
Our Natupski Neighbors (Miniter) n111
"Outpost, The" 118, n75

Outsider and Others, The 28, 48, 59, 64, n30
Owings, Mark S. 41, 68, 73, n58
Owyhee Land & Irrigation Company 20–22
Oxford, U. K. 14

Pacific–Antarctic Ridge 120
Pack Memorial Public Library (Asheville) n133
Page, Gerry n199
Pantheon (Paris) n220
Papeete (Tahiti) 120
"Parenthesis on Lovecraft as a Poet, A" (Scott) 88
Paris 177, 214, n220
Paris Exposition 20
Partridge, John 94
"Passion, Controversy and Vision: A History of The Library of Amateur Journalism" (Faig) n26
Pawtuxet River (R.I.) n162, 197, 212
Pawtuxet Valley (R.I.) 198, n162
Pawtuxet Valley Gleaner 92, 95–96, 101–102, n131, n141, n162
Pawtuxet Valley Times 96–97, n141
"Peace Advocate, The" n247
Pearson, James Larkin n184
Pelham, MA 149
Pelham, NY 9
"Pensive Swain, The" n247
Perry Street (Manhattan) n223
Person, Carl 47
Perth Amboy, N.J. 116, n160
Phantagraph 224, 225
Phi Beta Kappa 144
Philadelphia, PA 39–40, 88–89, n26, n57
Phillips, Abbie E. n17
Phillips, Asaph 17, n8, n164
Phillips, Edwin E. 23–24, 93, n23
Phillips, Emeline 10
Phillips, George n164
Phillips, James, Sr. n8, n164
Phillips, James Whipple n8, n17
Phillips, Jeremiah 17–18, n8, n17
Phillips, Martha H. Mathews 23, n23
Phillips, Michael n164
Phillips, Robie Alzada Place 9–10, 18–19, 23, 211, n8, n12
Phillips, Susan S. n17
'Phillips, Ward' (pseud) 72, 169–70, 172, 218, n156, n248
Phillips, Wheaton n17
Phillips, Whipple V. 3, 6, 8–10, 15, 17–21, 23–25, 95, 108, 211, n8, n12, n17, n21, n23, n45, n141
Philosopher's Stone, The (Wilson) 119

physiology 143
Pickman, Richard Upton 154, 214
"Pickman's Model" 72, 154, 178, 214, n99, n220, n249
"Picture, The" n152
"Picture in the House, The" 90, 127, 173, n249
"Pigeon-Flyers, The" (*Fungi* X) 225
Pine Hill (R.I.) n237
Pine Street (Providence) 215
Pioneer 225
"Pirrak, The" (Keel) n174
Pinnacle Books n147
Pitcairn 120
Place, Job n8
Place, Stephen 144, n8
Plainfield Pike (R.I.) 117, n164
Planet Street (Providence) 197
"Planets and Stars for May" (Currier) 98
'Plateau of Leng' (imaginary) 120
Poe Cottage (Manhattan) 133
Poe, Edgar Allan 62, 147, n213
Poe Street (Providence) 212–13
"The Poe-et's Nightmare" n75, n134
"Poem of Ulysses, The" n146
Poemata Minora 109, n146
Poems (Whitman) n213
Poetical Works of Jonathan E. Hoag, The n81
"Poetry and the Gods" (Lovecraft–Crofts) 44, 84, 87, n119
"Polaris" n170, n174, n195
Polynesian folklore 120
Ponaganset Pond and Reservoir (R.I.) 166–67, n237
Ponape 118–19
Pope, Alexander 14
Pouliot, Judge J. 177
Pound, Ezra 101
"Power of Wine: A Satire, The" n134
Practical Psychology. See Mind Power Plus
Pratt Street (Providence) n220, n225
Prescott, MA 149
Price, E. Hoffmann 57–58, 69, 94, 98, 124, 134–36, 139, 146, n46, n204
Primal Sources: Essays on H. P. Lovecraft (Joshi) n244, n247
"Primavera" n75
Private Life of H. P. Lovecraft, The (Davis) n251
Problem of Lemuria, The (Spence) n173
Prospect Park (Brooklyn) 155, n164
Prospect Street (Providence) 22, 199, 207–210, n269
Prospect Terrace (Providence) 160, n164, n220, n272

Providence (1977) n192
Providence, R.I. 146, 154, 176, 195–217, n6, n12, n16, n23, n162, n164, n211, n220, n225; City Hall, n3, n225; Conference Seminary, 17; County, 9, 23, 165–66, 202, n228; County Courthouse, 202, n220; Harbor, 212; House Directory, n225, n228, n267; Public Library, 75, 96, 100, 159–60, n136, n220
Providence Amateur n57
'Providence Detective Agency' 114
Providence Evening Bulletin 39, 74, 94, 99, 111, n81, n128
Providence Evening News 92–95, 97–100, 102–103, 172 n130, n134
"Providence in 2000 A.D." 39, 74, 94, 99, n81, n128
Providence Journal 16, 18–19, 23, 32, 97–100, 160, 202, 208, 224–25, n8, n81; *Providence Sunday Journal* 74, n128, n251
Providence Journal Company n211
Providence Preservation Society 199, 202
Providence River 200, 202, 205
Providence Tribune 72, 82, 92–96, n126
"Pseudonyms of H. P. Lovecraft" (Barlow) 40, 169
Psi Delta house (Providence) 210
"Psychopompos" 47
"Pursuit" (*Fungi* II) 224
Putnam Pike (R.I.) 164–65, 167
Putnam's Sons, G. P. (publisher) 135

Quabbin, MA 149
Quabbin Reservoir (MA) 149, n219
Quabbin Valley (MA) 150–52, n219
Quebec 32, 33, 146, n209
Queen Anne 94
Queer Questions (Oliphant) n230
"Quest of Iranon, The" 173, n195
Quinn, Seabury 158, 160–61
"Quinsnicket Park" 100, n134
Quinsnicket Woods (R.I.) 100, 212, n164
Quonochontaug, R.I. 153

"R. H. Barlow as H. P. Lovecraft's Literary Executor: An Appreciation" (Faig) n28
Railroad Review: Published by the Little Fourke 117
Rainey, P. M. n94
Rajala, J.-M. n70, n150, n165, n211
Rambles Around Old Boston (Bacon) 220
Rambles in Old Boston (Porter) n220
Randall Square (Providence) n220
Randall tomb (Providence) 160, 200

Random Amateur 79
Rarotonga Records (Gill) n173
Rathbone, Robie 17, n8, n17
"Rationale of Lovecraft's Pseudonyms, The" (Joshi) n244, n247
"Rats in the Walls, The" 16, 37, 127, 142
"The Real Hyborian Age" (Carter) 120
"Recapture" (*Fungi* XXXIV) n81
Recluse 38, 41, 49, 52, 77, 90, 141, n107
Recluse Press (Cook) 49
"Red Brain, The" (Wandrei) 154
Red Hook (Brooklyn) 155
Reed, Zealia Brown. *See* Zealia Bishop
Rehoboth, MA 167–68, n239
Renshaw, Anne Tillery 77, 127, 129, 133–34, 140,
"Report on the Burial Place of Roger Williams" (Chapin) 159
"Report to an Academy, A" (Kafka) n168
"Research of a Biblio, The" (Wetzel) 40, 43, 87–88, 91,169–70, 179, n119
Resnais, Alain 133, n192
"Respite" n100
Revised H. P. Lovecraft Bibliography, The (Chalker & Owings) n58
Reynolds, Aidan 142
Reynolds, George W. M. n117
Reynolds, O. 166
Reynolds Road (R.I.) 165–66
Reynolds, Squire James 164
Rhode Island 4–5, 7, 11, 94, 96, 98, 153, 158, 164–67, 177, 193, n18; Development Council, n235; Hospital, 145; House of Representatives, 19; Transit Authority, n162
Rhode Island Fish Company 202
Rhode Island Historical Society: Library, 19, 96, 145, 165–66, 198, n225, n228, n267; Museum, 209
Rhode Island History 197, n99
Rhode Island Index, The 159–60, 208, n220
Rhode Island Journal Astronomy 109, 112
Rhode Island School of Design 8, n24, n220; Museum, 209
Rhode Island State Normal School 144
Rhode Island Yearbook n162
Rhodesia 118
Rice City Christian Baptist Church n12
Richardson, Leon Burr n183
Richmond Street (Providence) 213, 215
Riddle, Charles Lee n37
Riddle of the Pacific, The (Brown) n173
Rider, Sidney H. 158, n226
Rim of the Unknown, The (Long) 190, n262

Rimel, Duane W. 30, 33, 37, 46, 57–60, 63, 68–69, 147, 154, 155, 192, 205, 207, n35, n57, n96, n124, n184, n221, n225, n256
Ripples from Lake Champlain 225
Ripley, Jane n29
'R'lyeh' 119–20, 178, 208, n170, n173,
Robert E. Howard United Amateur Press Association, The n93
Robert E. Howard Bookshelf, The (Burke) n93
Robert Ervin Howard Memorial Collection 34, 68
Robinet, Lee 112
Rochester, N.Y. 4, 9, n8
Rockefeller Library (Brown University) 202
Roger Williams Building (Providence) n235
Roger Williams Park 157, 212, n164
Roger Williams root 157–58, n231
Roman architecture 117
Romance of Boston Bay, The (Snow) n220
Rome 117
Rothovius, Andrew E. 149–53, n219
Roulet, Etienne 198, n225
Round Top Beneficent Congregational Church 216
Roxbury, MA 6, 11
"Round Tower, The" 84, 123
Runagates Club (Buchan) n260
Russell, John 95
"Rutted Road, The" n75

Sabin's Tavern (Providence) 197
St. Armand, Prof. Barton L.
  80. 133, 190, 197, n99
St. Augustine, FL 146
St. John's Cathedral (Providence) 6
St. John's Catholic Church (Providence) n270
St. John's Churchyard (Providence) 70, 147
St. Paul's (Cathedral) Church (Boston) 5, n5, n12
"St. Toad's" (*Fungi* XXV) 225
Salem, MA 146–49, 198, 213, n211, n219
San Francisco, CA 54, 66, 140, n78
San Gabriel, CA n117
Sandalwood (Smith) 51
Sapiro, Leland n41
Sawyer, Laurie A. n111
Sayles Hall (Brown University) 97
Schilling, George 85
Schorer, Mark 119
Schultz, David E. n257, n258
Schwartz, Julius 105, n203
Schweitzer, Darrell 133, n190, n191
Science-Fantasy Correspondent 225
Science Fiction by Gaslight (Moskowitz) 111
Science Fiction, Fantasy, and Weird Fiction Magazines (Tymn and Ashley) n112
Science versus Charlatanry 94, n129

Scientific American n103
Scientific Gazette 109
Scienti-Snaps 45, 116, n66
Scott, Winfield Townley 4–5, 14, 20–22, 88, 93, 100–101, 144, 155, 195, 202, n2, n3, n11, n81, n213, n218, n228, n239
Scott-Elliot, W. n173
Seagrave, Frank 98
Searight, Richard F. n99, n206
Searles, A. Langley n9
Sechrist, Edward Lloyd 120
Second Deluge, The (Serviss) 112
"Second Man, The" (Robinet) 112, 114
"Secret Cave or John Lees Adventure, The" 107–109
"Secret of the Grave, The" 109
Seeing Providence n211
Seekonk River (R.I.) 22, 186, 200, 204, 212, n164, n213
Sela-y-Gomez 120
Selected Letters 3, 28, 35, 69, 72, 76, 81, 86, 94, 101, 106, 108, 115, 123, 129–33, 139, 146, 150, 153, 165, 167, 173, 209–11, n53, n99, n101, n156, n207, n219
Selected Letters: The Private Writings of the Master of the Macabre n207
Selected Poems (Smith) 51
Selwyn & Blount (publisher) 136, 141, n199, n200
"Semblance" (Smith) 52
Sentinel Hill 151, n219
Serviss, Garrett P. 112
"Settlement of Rhode Island, The" (Miller) 159
Seven Sleepers of Ephesus, legend of, 124
"Seven Turns in a Hangman's Rope" (Whitehead) 113
"Shadow out of Time, The" 25, 28, 37, 84, 105, 121, 139, 193, n29, n147, n170, n195, n203, n220
Shadow Over Innsmouth, The (book) * 48
"Shadow over Innsmouth, The" 84, 119–20, 127, 153
Shakespeare, William 130–31, n188
Shaw, Larry 207
Shaw, Lew n118, n195
Shea, J. Vernon 4, 7, 15, 22, 59, 101, 107, 133–34, n190, n218
Sheehan, Perley Poore 112
Sheldon Hill Road (R.I.) 165–66
Shelley, Mary 87
Shepherd, Wilson H. 33, n184
Shepley, Col. George L. n271
Shepley Museum (Providence) 25, n271
Sherman, French, & Co. 73

Shiel, M. P. 125
Shunned House, The (book) *
    48–49, 55–70, n84, n91, n94, n95, n96
"Shunned House, The" 22, 37, 57, 64–65, 69, 84,
    154, 156, 158, 198, 202, n35, n52, n220,
    n224, n225, n234
Shutesbury, MA 149, 151
Shuttered Room and Other Pieces, The 10, 34,
    84, 107–109, 115–16, 147, 179, 180, 185,
    193, n41, n119, n147, n170, n259
Shwartz, Lewis. *See* Shaw, Lew
"Side Glance" (Baldwin) 59
"The Sideshow" (Hart)
    101, 160–61, n81, n128, n230
Silence, The (Bush) n109
Silver Clarion n242
Silver Fern 224
"Silver Key, The" n8
Simaetha (cat) 193
Simon & Schuster (publisher) n198
"Sing a Song of Sixpence" (Stevenson) n260
"Singer of Ethereal Moods and Fancies, A"
    45, n125
Site of Joseph Curwen's Home ... (Faig) n268
Skinner, Charles n226
Skyscrapers (society) n132
Slater Avenue School 81–82, 114, n239, n267
Smith, Charles W. ("Tryout") n61, n111, n119
Smith, Clark Ashton (CAS)
    26, 28, 32, 34, 50–52, 56, 61–62, 68–69, 76,
    106–107, 121, 123–124, 129, 131, 134, 139,
    193, 205, n46, n107, n145, n159, n266
Smith, Don G. n190
Smith, Edwin Hadley 26, 39–40, 42–43, n26;
    See also Edwin Hadley Smith Collection
Smith, Dr. Frank B. 18
Smisor, George T. 50, 54, 60–61, 67,
"Snake God, The" (Dwyer) n160
Snake Hill Road (R.I.) n237
Snake River Valley, ID 20, n21
Snow, Edward Howe n220
"Some Causes of Self-Immolation" 44, n67
Some Current Motives and Practices * 72, n96
"Some Dutch Footprints in New England"
    n110, n232
Some Notes on H. P. Lovecraft 13, 27, 29, 123,
    n164, n211
"Some Notes on Interplanetary Fiction" 122
"Some Notes on a Nonentity"
    101–104, 105, 109–110, n119, n138
"Some Notes on the Lovecraft Bibliography in
    The Dark Brotherhood ..." (Cockcroft) n199
Something about Cats and Other Pieces 153, n5
Songs at the Start (Guiney) 11

Sotheby's n52
South Main (Town) Street (Providence)
    197, 200–203
South Pacific 119–20, n173
South Water Street (Providence) 200, 203
Southwestern Pacific Basin 120
Spacewarp n65, n117
"Spare Time" (Ostrow) n188
Spence, Lewis n173
'Spencer, Dr. Eben' (imaginary) 183, 186–87
Spencer, Truman J. 42, n57
Sphinx of the Ice Fields, The (Verne) 132
Spink, Miss Mary 32, n38, n93, n220
Spindrift n156
Sprague, Mr. 164
Springfield, MA 149–50
Squires, Richard D. n8, n9
Squires, Roy A. 51, 54–56, 58, 60, 63, 67–72,
    106, n94, n107, n145
Stampers' Hill (Providence) 198–99
"Star-Winds" (*Fungi* XIV) n81
Starrett, Vincent 36, 76–77, 130, 141, n107, n207
Starry Wisdom Church 206–207, n259
State Board of Valuation (Rhode Island) 19
State Historical Society of Wisconsin 61, 66, 99
"Statement of Randolph Carter, The" n41, n52
State Street (Providence) n220
Steele, Joel Dorman n226
Steeple Street (Providence) n16
Stephen Harris house n225
Stephen Place House 144, n8
Sterling, George 76, n78
Sterling, Kenneth 36, 58, 69, 121, n118
*Stern Fathers 'neath the Mould: The Lovecraft
    Family in Rochester* (Squires) n8, n9
Stevens, Frances 112
Stevenson, Robert Louis 189, n260
Stickney, Corwin 49
Stoker, Bram 125–26
Stone, Dr. Lee Alexander M.D. n186
Stone, Leon 40–41, 43, 73, 87, n121
Stonehenge 119
Strange Co., The n41, n44, n54, n129
"Strange High House in the Mist, The"
    134, 152–53, n107, n170, n201, n268
Strange Tales 191, n195
"Street, The" 44, 84, 87, n119, n124
Street & Smith (publisher) 25, 139, n195
Strength to Dream, The (Wilson) 195
Strinati, Pierre 132
Strysik, John n190
Sue, Eugène 214
"Suggestions for Writing Story" 180
Sullivan Dorr Mansion 202, n220

Sully, Helen 34, 82, 135, n8, n198, n220
Sunapee, NH 56, 59–60
Supernatural Horror in Literature 52, 76, 125, 190
Survey of Institutional Collections of Amateur Journals (Faig) n63
"Survivor, The" (Derleth) 84, 123, 127, n177, n211
Swan Point Cemetery (Providence) 4, 200, 217, n164
Swanson, Carl 135
Swift, Augustus T. 169, 171–72, n245
Swift, Jonathan 94
Switch on the Light n199, n200
Sydney, Australia n173
Szezsponik, Charlene n162

Tahiti 119, n173
Tales of the Cthulhu Mythos 119, 153
Talman, Wilfred B. 44, 77, 157–58, 160–62, 175, n38, n71, n196, n220, n229, n232
Tamlacht n211
Tanner, Kenneth n239
Taunton, MA 167–68
Taunton Pike 167–68
Taylor, John L. 5
'Tcho-Tcho people' (imaginary) n170
"Tekeli-Li. Le posterité littéraire d'Arthur Gordon Pym" 132
"Temple, The" 91
Tenison, E. M. 11
Tennessee 4
Terhune, Albert Payson 112
"Terrible Old Man, The" 90
Terror by Night (Thomson) n200
Texaco Star n232
Textron, Incorporated 4
"Thanksgiving note" (Lovecraft) n101
"Thing in the Moonlight, The" (hoax) 44–45, 84, 116, n69
"Thing on the Doorstep, The" 126, 146, n35, n118
Thomas Street (Providence) 192, n81, n211, n220, n265
Thomson, Christine Campbell 136, n199
Thompson, CT n235
"Three Hours with H. P. Lovecraft" (Walter) n220
"Three Letters on H. P. Lovecraft" (Barlow) n33
Thrilling Wonder Stories 191
"Through the Gates of the Silver Key" 139
Thurston's Tavern (Providence) 197–98
Thwing, Annie H. n220
Tierney, Richard L. 120, 208, n170, n172

"Tightening of the Coil: The Revision of 'The Whisperer in Darkness'" (Mariconda) n143
Tillinghast, Daniel n8
Tillinghast, Leonard 18
Titus, Charles E. 216
"To A Dreamer" n75
"To a Young Poet in Dunedin" 218
To Quebec and the Stars n209
Toldridge, Elizabeth 34, 44, 50, 56, 61–64, 68, 117–19, 129, 150, 211, n78, n185
"Tomb, The" 39, 105, 111, n119
Tonga Kingdom n173
"To the Eighth of November" 169
"To Pan" n146, n247
Transatlantic Circulator 46, 73, n72, n156, n195
"Transition of Juan Romero, The" 87–88, n119
"Tree, The" 33, 87, 90
Tremont Street (Boston) 5, n12
Trial, The (Kafka) 88
Tryout 48, n111, n119, n188, n208, n241, n247
Tuamoto Archipelago 120
Tuanaki Islands n173
Twyn Barlwm, Wales 142
Tyler, Casey B. 18–19, n8

U.S. Army Map Service 166, 168, n235
Under the Moons of Mars (Moskowitz) 74, 111–12, 171
Uncollected Letters n53, n106, n219
"Under the Pyramids." *See* "Imprisoned with the Pharaohs"
"Unfinished Manuscripts, The" (Derleth) 123
Union Catalog of Manuscripts 12
Union Station (Providence) 37, n220
Union Street (Brooklyn) n222
United Amateur, The 39, 72, 85, 87, 173–74, n57, n68, n119, n125, n140
United Amateur Press Association (UAPA) 38, 111, n57, n119
United States history 143
University of California, Berkeley n63
University of Kansas 81
University of Minnesota Libraries n96
University of Wisconsin-Madison n26
"Unknown, The" n247
Unknown Lovecraft, The (Faig) n8, n9, n14, n22, n28
"Unnamable, The" 147
Upham, Ronald n228, n239
Upton, Prof. Winslow 97–98
Urvätersaga (Blunck) 121

Vagabond 40, 42, 72, 88, 157, 161–62, n57, n121, n133, n229
"Valley of the Worm, The" (Howard) 126

Van Herp, Jacques 170–72, n72, n121
Vagrant, The 39, 47, 162
Vanguard (publisher) 135
Vathek. See The History of Caliph Vathek
Venus 95,
"Ver Rusticum" 99
Vermont 38, 59–60, 64, 146, 151, n82, n218
"Vermont Horror, The" n143.
  See also "The Whisperer in Darkness"
Verne, Jules 112, 132
Verrazzano, Giovanni da 202
Versins, Pierre n121
"Very Old Folk, The" 44–45, 85, 116, n66, n158
Vesey Street (Manhattan) n5
Victor Gollancz, Ltd. 135–36
Virgil 145
Visionary Press (Crawford).
  See *The Shadow Over Innsmouth*
"Vivisector, The" 171
Voelchert, Miss 175
"Volunteer, The" 99, n247
Vombiteur, Le 28, n31

W. Paul Cook: The Wandering Life of a Yankee Printer (Donnelly) n56
Wagner the Wehrwolf (Reynolds) n117
Waite, Asenath n118
Wallace, Bill 207
Walling, Henry Francis 166, n237
Walpole, Horace 171, 213
Walter, Dorothy C. 32, n220
"Wanderer's Return" (Shepherd) n184
Wandrei, Donald 27, 29, 31, 35, 44, 62, 63, 65, 68, 105, 115–16, 119, 150, 154, 178–80, 185, 190, 193, n30–31, n33, n46, n66, n69, n94, n107, n144, n151, n158, n199, n207
Wandrei, Howard 28
War of the Worlds, The (Wells) 112, n151
Warner, Harry 31, 43, 86, n57, n96
Warren, RI 117, n220
Warwick, RI n20
Washington, D.C. 58, 68, 132, 157
"Waste Land, The" (Eliot) 101
"Waste Paper" n137, n247
Watchers Out of Time, The (Derleth) 123, n176
Waterman Street (Providence) 108, 209–210, n162
Web of Easter Island, The (Wandrei) 119
Weeden, Ezra 200
Weeds–Gerry Mansion n272
Weekapaug, R.I. 153
Weinberg, Robert 73
Weir, John J. 116, n160

Weird Tales 28, 30–31, 36–38, 54, 64–66, 69–70, 76, 80–81, 84, 100, 114, 116, 119, 125, 126, 130, 134–36, 140–42, 148, 154, 180, 190–91, 225, n49, n50, n79, n81, n112, n195, n196, n198, n199, n200, n201, n229
Weird Writer in Our Midst, A (Joshi) 131, n33, n105, 166, n193
Weird Writings of H. P. Lovecraft, The n50
Well Bred Speech (Renshaw) 127, 129, 140
Wellesley College 12
"Well, The" (*Fungi* XI) 225, n81
Wells, H. G. 112, n151
Wendell, MA 149
"Werewoman" (Moore) 62
West Clifford Street (Providence) 215
West Point 161
West Shokan, N.Y. n159
West Warwick, .RI. 95–96
Westminster, MA n218
Westminster Street (Providence) 216
Wetzel, George T.
  25, 40–46, 71–73, 75, 78–79, 87–91, 97, 100, 147, 156–57, 160–61, 169–73, 179, 182, n10, n28, n34, n57, n99, n111, n119, n121, n122, n124, n125, n133, n148, n220, n224, n225, n229, n232, n234, n243, n246, n271
Weybosset Neck (Providence) 197, 199
Weybosset Point 197
Weybosset Street 213–14, 216, n23, n38
"What the Moon Brings" 32–33, 44, 87
Whateley, Wilbur 133, 151, 195, n170
Wheaton College (Norton, MA)
  11, 143–44; Library, 143
Wheaton (Female) Seminary.
  See Wheaton College
"When Swords Were Bold" (Macauley) n150
Whipple, Commodore Abraham n271
Whipple, Elihu n220, n225
Whipple V. Phillips & Company 19–20, 23
"Whipple V. Phillips and the Owyhee Land and Irrigation Company" (Faig) 21, 23, n22
whippoorwills 148
"Whisperer in Darkness, The"
  121, 134, 146, 193, n143, n201
Whispers n52
"White Ape, The." *See* "Arthur Jermyn"
"White Elephant, The" 118
White, Michael Oscar n125
"White Ship, The" 173, n52
Whitehead, Henry S. 113, 190–91, 217, n78, n79
Whitman, Sarah Helen 148, 213, n213
Whitney, Anne 12
"Who Ate Roger Williams?" (Talman) 157–62, 202, n229, n230, n 232, n234

"Who Was Howard Davison?" (Laney) n65, n117
"Wicked Clergyman, The."
    See "The Evil Clergyman"
Wilbraham, MA 148–52, n215
Wilcox Building (Providence) 19, n38
Wilcox, Henry Anthony n211, n220
Wilderness 11
Williams, Betsey 157, 160, 162
Williams, Roger 157–61, 166, 205, n226
Williams Street (Providence) 203, 205
Willie Woodhead Road 165–66
Willoughby Street (Brooklyn) 155
Wilson, Colin 15, 119, 126, 153, 195
Wilson, Edmund 195
Wilson, Gahan n211
"Wind that is in the Grass, The"
    (Barlow) 37, 81, 120
"Winter Wish, A" 99
"Wisdom" n242, n247
'Witch House' (Salem, MA) 147
Witchcraft and Sorcery n199
"Witches' Hollow" (Derleth) n181
"Within the Circle" (Baldwin) 57, n99
Wollheim, Donald A. 69, n35, n42, n52, n195
Wolvercote Cemetery (Oxford) 14

Wolverine 171, n119, n243, n244
Woman's Home Companion 129
Wonder Stories n195
Wood, Squire 18–20, n8, n12
"Wood, The" n74
Woonasquatucket River 202, 205, 207
Worcester, MA 12
Works of Jules Verne, The 132
"Worm, The" (Keller) 126
Wright, Farnsworth
    28, 65, 130, 134–35, 141, n196, n199, n205

"Xavier, the Werewolf" (hoax) n117
Xenophile n9

Yaanek n174
"Year Off, A" n136
Yeti n170
YMCA 26
You'll Need a Night Light (Thomson) n199, n200
Young, Harold H. n162
"Young Man Lovecraft" (de Camp) n114
Yr Obt Servt: Some Postcards of Howard Phillips Lovecraft Sent to Wilfred Blanch Talman
    n233

www.ingramcontent.com/pod-product-compliance
Lightning Source LLC
Chambersburg PA
CBHW060108170426
43198CB00010B/808